THE AUTHOR

ROBERT M. MacIVER has taught political science, economics, and sociology at Aberdeen University, the University of Toronto, Barnard College, and Columbia University. In addition to his undergraduate and graduate degrees from Oxford and Edinburgh, he has been awarded honorary degrees by Harvard, Yale, Princeton, Columbia, Toronto, the Jewish Theological Seminary, the New School, and Edinburgh. Alongside his work as a teacher, he has served as vice chairman of the Canadian War Labor Board, and president, later chancellor, of the New School for Social Research. Active in many learned societies, Professor MacIver is a Fellow of the Royal Society of Canada, the American Academy of Arts and Science, the American Philosophical Society, and the World Academy of Arts and Science and a member of the American Sociological Association, the Institut International de Sociologie, and the British Academy. For the past fifty years, Professor MacIver has consistently brought insight and clarity to the problems of the social sciences and society generally in his numerous articles and books.

THE EDITOR

DAVID SPITZ is Professor of Political Science at Ohio State University, where he has been a member of the faculty since 1947. He received his B.S.S. from the City College of New York and was awarded his A.M. and Ph.D. by Columbia University. He has held fellowships from the Fund for the Advancement of Education, the Fund for the Republic, and the Rockefeller Foundation, and has been Visiting Professor at, among others, Hunter College, Cornell University, Kenyon College, the University of California at Berkeley, and the Johns Hopkins University Bologna Center, Italy. Professor Spitz is the author of *Patterns of Anti-Democratic Thought*, *Democracy and the Challenge of Power*, and *The Liberal Idea of Freedom*, and the editor of *Political Theory and Social Change*. In addition he has contributed widely to scholarly and popular journals.

POLITICS AND SOCIETY

Robert M. MacIver

POLITICS & SOCIETY

EDITED BY DAVID SPITZ

ATHERTON PRESS • NEW YORK • 1969

Preface

The essays printed here constitute a selected rather than a collected edition of Robert M. MacIver's occasional writings. Omitted are a number of articles on sociology and social theory that are expected to go into a companion volume, essays that have been incorporated into one or another of MacIver's books, and some still unpublished papers that do not strictly fit into the scope and organization of this volume. Happily, too, though he is already eighty-six years of age, MacIver is still at work; so in addition to an essay now in press we can anticipate future publications.

All but seven of the forty-seven essays included here have previously been published—many in journals printed in other countries, some in books, a good number going back in time not merely to the first half but to the first quarter of the century. Some consequently are likely to have escaped the attention even of the diligent reader. Six previously unpublished papers, together with a small collection of letters, appear here as Chapters 8, 10, 17, 22, 24, 37, and 38.

In general I have printed each essay as it initially appeared. Spelling and punctuation have been altered where necessary to conform to American usage. A few phrases have been eliminated that referred to the immediate occasion of delivery.

In one case, the essay on "The Art of Contemplation," I have reincorporated passages from the original typescript that were omitted from the printed version. In the essay on *Mein Kampf*, I have deleted nearly all the lengthy quotations from Hitler's book that MacIver had attached at the head of each section; his own exposition and analysis seemed to me to render these unnecessary. In a very few instances I have provided an explanatory word or note; these are clearly marked in brackets. The reader will understand, I trust, that in thus keeping my own interventions at a minimum, I have exposed him in one or two places to a slight repetition of argument. This was unavoidable if I were also to retain the coherence and integrity of the individual essays; and since many of them have been referred to in the literature, I felt this to be the compelling consideration.

Save for book reviews, both by MacIver and on his writings, which were so numerous as to run to an inordinate length, the bibliography at the end of this volume contains the first complete listing of MacIver's work and includes too a fair number of references to the critical literature. Those who wish to trace particular ideas or concepts across the several essays may find the detailed index of value.

I have to thank two of my graduate students, Mr. Charles Wilhelm and Mr. Stephen LaBash, for assisting me in the compilation of the bibliography and index, respectively, and Mrs. Karen L. Huffer for her cheerful and devoted service as typist. Robert M. MacIver provided translations of Greek passages in the essay on "The Ethical Significance of the Idea Theory" and approved the selection and organization of the essays. I did not trouble him, however, with my editorial changes or with this preface and introduction.

D.S.

Introduction

A collection of another man's essays is in some sense an act of piety, a tender of affection to a revered teacher and friend. If, as in the present instance, it incorporates essays written over a span of some sixty years, it is also the record of an intellectual journey. If, further, it makes readily accessible the otherwise fugitive papers of a major social and political theorist, even some that are no more than occasional reflections on minor and incidental themes, it serves to round out the central corpus of his work. These are, I suppose, the customary reasons for publishing a volume of essays; and I should not wish to deny their partial applicability here.

But other and more significant reasons attend this particular effort. To select but a portion of the nearly one hundred essays that MacIver has written in addition to his many books is to be concerned less with the record of his intellectual journey than with the contribution these papers may make to the understanding and resolution of certain key issues. And here MacIver has but rarely addressed himself to the minor or seemingly trivial; almost always he has focused on some of the central concepts and problems of the age. And because they have been interrelated problems, what emerges is not a collection of fragments but a unified work, one that also, albeit incidentally, attests to the astonishing scope and versatility of MacIver's mind and adds an essential dimension to the understanding of his thought.

More than anything else this unity derives from the fact that MacIver is a multidimensional rather than a monistic thinker. It is a commonplace that we live today in a time of increasing disciplinary specialization and fragmentation. Problems are no longer seen whole; they are surgically dismembered and treated as discrete parts. As a result, the historian, the political scientist, the economist, even the sociologist and the moral philosopher—each sees and discusses but a portion of the entity. MacIver is that rare scholar who by training and concern focuses instead on the many-sidedness, the interrelatedness of things. He looks not simply for facts but for the connections between facts. He seeks not the mere existence of things but the ways in which things are different, alike, and above all related to each other. For it is here, in the connections and interrelationships of things, that meaning alone resides.

The enlarged understanding of MacIver's work is yielded in two somewhat different ways. On the one hand, a number of his earlier essays, like those on Plato's Idea Theory and on the passions, reveal his interest and striking competence in the classics and moral philosophy, areas not normally associated with his primary work in sociology and political theory. At the same time, a number of previously unpublished papers, like those on Bertrand Russell and Hitler's *Mein Kampf*, and even more intriguingly on the art of contemplation, manifest the play of his mind on subjects not covered, or but passingly dealt with, in his books. On the other hand, the essay form is itself a more sharply delineated and at times even a more revelatory display of MacIver's long-recognized scholarly qualities: a vast yet controlled erudition, a rigorous logic, a marked sensitivity to language, above all an insightful imagination. A book normally stands to an essay as a symphony to a quartet, or a giant and multicolored canvas to an etching. But to those aware of the greater delicacy and sureness of touch, the clearer sound and the more sharply drawn line, that are required in the smaller work, the essay often carries rewards as rich as those garnered from the larger achievement.

I do not propose to dwell here on the several characteristics and achievements of MacIver's work. For one thing, I have essayed this task, though only in outline, elsewhere.[1] For another, they are adequately revealed by a reading of the essays themselves, and even more by the

---

1. David Spitz, *The Liberal Idea of Freedom* (Tucson: University of Arizona Press, 1964), Chap. 6.

books that have established MacIver's reputation. I shall venture instead simply to remark, and quite briefly, first, on two or three methodological considerations that have been insufficiently noted, and at times even ignored, in critical evaluations of MacIver's work; and second, to suggest the primary theme that pervades and unifies the seeming disparity of topics included in this book.

II

It is easiest, perhaps, to begin by emphasizing a point already made: that MacIver is a multidimensional thinker. It is a fiction, though one that curiously lingers and is sometimes mistaken for truth, that there is somehow a greater charm, even a greater power, in being a one-eyed man. We do not believe this when we chance to meet such a disfigured person on the street. On the contrary, our instinctive reaction is one of pity. We feel a sense of dismay at the limitation of his vision. We recognize as a hindrance his inability to share the full perspective afforded the more fortunate among us. But in the world of social and political thought the reverse of this sensible attitude is often accounted a virtue. The one-eyed man, the person who sees but one thing and because he can see but that one thing seizes upon it and proclaims it the whole, to the neglect of all manner of qualifying and inhibiting considerations clearly visible to the more careful and able viewer, is hailed as the more significant thinker. Thus Freud and Wittgenstein and other flamboyant if lesser figures become for a time the intellectual mileposts of the day.

No doubt there is something to be said for this veneration of the one-eyed man. The very narrowness of his vision may light up the firmament as does the piercing light of a shooting star. He may help us see more sharply what we did not fully perceive before. But when the flame has settled, it is the deeper and more searching analyst who is called for. He now corrects the partial and one-sided explanation of the single-factor theorist by relating it to the totality that gave it birth and meaning. The religion of a group, for example, is understood only when related to its economic conditions, and these in turn to its mores. The government of a country is understood only when one knows too how its citizens live and think, and its laws can be understood only when one knows also its customs. Recognition of the essential interdependence not merely of the social sciences but of the elements that constitute a social situation is the indispensable first step toward an adequate grasp of reality.[2]

2. As MacIver expressed it: "You cannot deal with human situations unless you comprehend the humanity in the situations, and you cannot get to grips with social

Thus it is that in the course of human history the one-eyed man is displaced or superseded time and again by the less dramatic but more sober and more profound multidimensional mind. I said less dramatic, but it is not really so; for there is no more exciting an intellectual experience than to witness the way in which a first-rate mind executes this most intricate and demanding of tasks. Here MacIver is at his strongest and best; and without a masterful exploitation of this capacity no man can hope to build a monument of abiding importance.

It is fashionable today to equate philosophy with linguistic analysis or the elucidation of concepts. This restrictive view of what was once the commanding discipline is associated above all with the name of Ludwig Wittgenstein who, if we are to heed his disciples, was at once the founder and leader of the most momentous revolution in the history of philosophy. But it is surely strange to have put forward as a novel and revolutionary approach that which has been the traditional hallmark of Talmudic and Jesuit scholarship. And what are we to do with Socrates who in the Platonic Dialogues dealt carefully and at length— even if by modern standards inadequately—with such concepts as power and justice and beauty and good? Or with Aristotle and Hobbes and Hume? Or with John Stuart Mill, whose superb elucidation of economic concepts in his *Principles of Political Economy* and other works still merits attention? Or now with MacIver?

Those who think linguistic analysis began with the Vienna Circle or with the Oxford philosophers may find it instructive to consult MacIver's essay on the Idea Theory of Plato, written long before Wittgenstein appeared on the scene, or his papers on "Society and State" or on "Interests and Social Pressures." There as in his other writings they will find an attentiveness to words and meanings that amply justifies what one commentator has said of MacIver: that if we are to seek an explanation for his many contributions we will find it in the first instance in his careful and persistent drawing of distinctions—between the like and the common, community and association, interest and attitude, culture and civilization, and so on through a long catalogue of social and political concepts. Indeed, this same writer went on to say, it is precisely here that MacIver has given us the most precious of all contributions —"understanding, and the example of clear thinking and expression." [3]

---

problems unless you realize the whole social background out of which they arise. No partial or one-sided expertness will suffice. Aside from certain purely technical issues there is no important aspect of human life that can be separated from the rest and studied exclusively by itself. That is why any narrow specialism in the social sciences is self-defeating." Introduction to Frank Tannenbaum, *Crime and the Community* (Boston: Ginn & Co., 1938), p. xi.

3.   Harry Alpert, "Robert M. MacIver's Contributions to Sociological Theory," in M. Berger, T. Abel, and C. H. Page (eds.), *Freedom and Control in Modern Society* (New York: D. Van Nostrand Co., 1954), Chap. 13.

But where, for Wittgenstein and his followers, the elucidation of concepts is the end of the philosophic enterprise, for MacIver it is but the necessary beginning of inquiry. We draw distinctions, we rigorously define and use our terms, not in order to revise the Oxford English Dictionary, not even merely to avoid ambiguities and the raising of unanswerable questions, but to gain understanding. Understanding of what? Of the social and political system, of order and the processes of change, of the individual in relation to the group, the group in relation to other groups, groups in relation to society, the society in relation to other societies. We seek, in a word, to understand the One and the Many, the Many in the One, and the One again in the Many.

This brings me to the third and last of my remarks on MacIver's methodological concerns. The political and social sciences are today, and have been for some time past, in a dismal state. Despite the vaunted claims put forward by the self-styled vanguard of their practitioners, political science and sociology remain for the most part chaotic, confused, and backward disciplines. This is primarily because they—the behavioralists, the model-builders, the functionalists, and the like—mistake a science with mere description or schematic classification and fail to focus on the structure of relationships; because they fuss over methods and techniques rather than over substantive results; because they have neglected the historical aspects of the phenomena with which they deal and take photographs of relatively static situations, localized in space and time. They do not understand what is required for a meaningful and viable political or social theory, and so they play with theories of political science, or of sociology, when what is needed are theories of political life, or of society.[4]

To these absurdities MacIver has never fallen prey. He has understood always that while political science is analytical and descriptive rather than normative, the ideals that move men and that serve also to guide their way are an essential part of the knowledge of human behavior. He has grasped too the larger principle that for this knowledge to be intelligible, the theorist must go beyond the multitude of facts that are but the raw material of science and establish their connections, incorporate them into a system of knowledge. Such a system must do more than account for institutional mechanisms; it must do more than merely record a succession of events; it must deal with order and process and above all with the causal relations between events and conditions. It must offer a perspective on the nature and significance of the structure of social and political relationships. As MacIver put it:

---

4. Cf. MacIver's essay, "The Backwardness of Social Theory," *Mémoire du XIX Congrès International de Sociologie*, III (1961), 241–248.

Every science is a construct of relationship, built on the foundation of social data and bringing order into the multiplicity of particular evidences, the evidences derived from research and reflection on research. All the calculations and computations of our researches end nowhere unless they lead to the discovery or establishment or verification of relationships. The theory of a science is the major frame of relationships it has so far established, along with hypotheses concerning further relationships that have a reasonable probability in the light of definitive evidences. In social science these relationships connect individuals in groups, groups in larger unities; they reveal the tie-up of institutions and customs, motivations and institutions, habits and interests, and so on, in an extraordinary complex and ever-changing scheme. There are major forces and multitudes of lesser pulls playing over and into the social fabric. To explore the operation of these forces, to follow the resulting trends of social change, to relate the constants or near constants of human nature to the variables in the historical configuration of social order and disorder—there lies the task of social theory. It is a field that calls for endless enterprise, and the frequent reformulation and refinement of theoretical systems.[5]

Now what is crucial in the understanding of political and social systems is that they are always in process. We cannot know them except in the light of the past, and we cannot bid them stay still while we take a portrait for they are already changing—becoming, unfolding, developing, mutating, regressing, branching, in every kind of direction. We must probe then for the principles of social dynamics; we must seek to understand the social and political forces that make and remake the institutions and create the order in disorder of the ongoing life of society. We must study not merely specific lines of change but a whole changing order. And since there are systems within systems, orders within orders, we must seek to interpret not simply the motion of the whole but the changing relationships of the several systems and orders— the political, the economic, the technological, the cultural, and the like— within the changing larger system or order. For the political order is not coequal with the social and cultural orders, or with the technological order: the technological order embraces, or is gradually embracing, the entire world; the cultural order cuts across national lines; but the political order is cohesive only within the boundaries of a state and is lacking between states. Nor are the principles animating these orders the same: the technological order is governed by the drives to efficiency

5. *Ibid.*, p. 242.

and profits (which are not always compatible); the religious order is associated with authority and stability; the political order, at least the democratic political order, seeks freedom and responsibility. Nor, again, do all these different orders proceed in the same direction or at the same pace. How, then, are we to comprehend the system—the political system in relation to the other systems? How are we to formulate a political theory—a theory of the political life in relation to the larger social life of which it is but a part?

Only, it is clear, by scientifically and imaginatively dealing with the whole—with process and structure and not merely with one or the other alone, with the multiplicity of systems and not merely with something called the political system, above all with the ever-changing, ever-evolving relationships that pervade and characterize these structures and processes. This is, admittedly, an ambitious task, perhaps the most ambitious task that can be undertaken by a man. But the failure to attempt it is what distinguishes the journeyman from the social and political theorist; and the degree of success that attends one's effort is what delineates the run-of-the-mill scholar from the significant thinker.

That MacIver has both essayed and executed this task with eminent skill is not the least of his distinctive achievements.

III

I turn now to the theme that unifies these essays and that also, I venture to think, runs as a persistent thread through MacIver's many books. This is the relationship between the One and the Many, the Many in the One, and the One again in the Many.

It is no accident or mere coincidence that this theme was the subject of the very first of his publications, again the subject of the first few volumes edited by MacIver for the Institute for Religious and Social Studies and also for the Conference on Science, Philosophy, and Religion in Their Relation to the Democratic Way of Life, and yet again the recurring subject of his own books, *Community*, *The Modern State*, *Society*, and *The More Perfect Union*, as well as of a good number of his other writings. [6] For this is the theme that embraces, in one way or another, nearly the totality of individual and social relationships. It is thus at the core of any meaningful social and political theory.

It is of course a very old as well as continuing problem; for at least from the time that the Greek philosopher Heraclitus noted that we cannot

6. See, for example, the essays grouped together in *Politics and Society*, Chap. 13 below.

step twice in the same river, no serious thinker has been able to avoid coming to grips with the nature of permanence in a world of flux. The concept of the One and the Many is an attempt to resolve this problem. It does so by locating the permanence in the frame or structure of the relationship between the One and the Many, and the change in the ever-evolving character or process of that relationship. How MacIver works this out, how he pursues this theme in a variety of contexts and with an extraordinary attentiveness to nuance and detail, constitutes, I believe, his major contribution to political and social theory. It is clearly impossible to spell out the content of this teaching in the few pages allotted me here. I will try, however, to indicate its main outlines and leading consequences.

The problem of the One and the Many is at the outset the problem of the individual in relation to his group, and of the group in relation to other groups. No man emerges into the world alone; nor does he remain alone; indeed, it is the very meaning of a man that he becomes an individual only through a socializing process. But the process of socialization does not denude him of his individuality. It does not make him exactly like any other man. He is a social animal, a member of a group, but he is also a person.

In the intense and exclusive communal spirit of the clan or tribe, to be sure, this person is hardly distinguishable from others. He is bound together with the others in a common locality, a common kinship, a common religion, a common tradition, a common customary law. He has the same friends and foes, the same interests, the same thoughts, as all the tribe. He dwells in a circle wherein universal uniformity is the absolute condition of exclusive devotion. But as that circle widens, as the clan and the tribe give way to the city and national state and begin the long and difficult march toward the international community, he finds new interests and new associations. He differentiates himself from some of his fellows. He is more influenced by some groups than by others. He discovers new and sometimes confused and crossing allegiances. And in the process his personality is liberated from a primitive uniformity. Thus emerge the foundations of diversity and conflict and the need to harmonize or contain these differences within a larger unity.

Now the problem is not simply one of the individual and the group, the claims of difference and the claims of conformity. It is also the problem of the group in relation to other groups, and even more of the individual and the group in relation to the larger unity that now needs to be formed out of the multiplicity of groups. Each group has its own ways, its own values and creeds, its own consciousness of kind. When isolated from others, the group breeds a sense of exclusiveness that makes for hostility and then for conflict. Ignorance and fear keep groups apart. But the processes of change—of technological innovation and economic growth, of social and political evolution, of the penetration of cultures, and the like—inextricably bring them together. We have then both inner and outer pressures and strains—the individual seeking both solitude and the liberation of his personality, on the one hand, and a sense of identity with and belongingness to the group, on the other; the group striving for both separateness and an inner cohesiveness, on the one hand, and union or at least peaceful coexistence with other groups in a larger community, on the other. The need for unity seems to call for a consciousness of community based on common and exclusive factors. But the need for individuality and separateness calls for the recognition of differences, for diversity rather than uniformity. To secure both claims —to establish order and at the same time to respect personality, to strengthen the sense of common interest and at the same time allow for the free play and development of separate interests—this is the task of the Many now seeking to become One.

No longer is government, or the state, the representative of a single group, a single creed, a single way of life. No longer is law the expression of a single tradition, a single ethic, a single set of customs. Now government and law must reflect the interests and will of a multigroup society, and in so far as individuals and groups within that society seek different or opposing ends, hold different or opposing moralities, government and law must be limited to those things essential to the maintenance of the common; they must respect, by leaving alone, those things that promote differences without simultaneously endangering the welfare of others and the order necessary to the preservation of the whole. The Many are in the One, but that One cannot, without also destroying itself, do away with the Many.

This One, this unity that has been formed out of the multigroup society, is not, however, the ultimate entity, the final end of the evolutionary process. There are other unities, other societies, outside of itself and to which it stands in a multitude of relationships. Nation may be marked off from nation, but the interests of one nation, much less the interests of groups within the nation, are not similarly marked off from those of others. Religious and cultural interests transcend the boundaries of nations. Technological inventions and economic practices make their way without regard to the differences of national states. The principle of isolation and exclusiveness, once associated with groups and now sought by some to be identified with nations, runs into the hard fact of the interdependence of interests both of nations and of groups across nations. This interdependence compels coordination and intercommunity, for where interests are nonexclusive, what injures the interests of one injures also the interests of others.

So we are brought back again, though now at a different level, to the problem of the One and the Many. The One, the national state, seeks exclusiveness and the development of its own identity, but it also seeks membership in, because it cannot deny its interdependence on, the greater community of which it is a part. Thus there is need not only of a state but of an international organization as permanent and as extensive as the common interests of the nations now in individual states. The One in the Many must yield in its turn to the Many in the One. The deeper and wider common interests must prevail over the narrower differences. Only in this way can we realize the truth, and the abiding satisfactions that come from the fulfillment of this truth, that men— their problems, their needs, their destinies—are like each other far more than they are different. Yet the differences too are real, and no international organization should obliterate those differences among nations and men any more than should a national organization obliterate the differences among groups and individuals. So we end as we began, with the One and the Many, the Many in the One, the One again in the Many, and hopefully, perhaps inevitably, the Many ultimately in the One.

IV

Some consequences of this analysis may now briefly be noted. And here I shall be brief to the point of enumeration rather than exposition, for the details are fully provided in the ensuing essays.

A distinction must be drawn and carefully maintained between the state and the community, both internally within the national state and externally across states. Only in this way can the notion of a limited state, and consequently the principle of diversity, be secured within a multi-group society. Similarly, only in this way can we recognize and build upon the sense of community that transcends states.

The primitive ideal of uniformity as a basis of unity must be abandoned. Modern society is a multigroup society, with all that this implies in the way of multiple and sometimes competing loyalties. If unity is to be achieved, it must indeed rest on that which is common to men, but what is common is not merely their interests but also the desire, even need, to be different in some respects. Unity and diversity, unity through diversity, unity based upon and in furtherance of diversity—this is the indispensable principle of order in modern society.

Democracy then becomes the only proper and legitimate principle of political order, for only democracy explicitly recognizes and rests upon the distinction between the state and community, and only democracy institutionalizes the free play of differences, above all of opinion and culture. The central conception of democracy is that it is the person as person who counts, and the final argument for democracy is that it not only accepts differences, and thus respects personality, but that by accepting differences it does not deny or seek to obliterate other and sometimes conflicting loyalties. Indeed, by not requiring its citizens to abandon their loyalties to family, to group, to cause, it more easily binds them together in an attachment that transcends their partial interests.

Some kind of permanent international organization, with appropriate organs for the resolution of disputes among national states and for the formulation and enforcement of a true international law, is a necessary device to safeguard the peace and secure the common interests of men. The idea of national sovereignty is no longer relevant to the needs of the international community and must be abandoned. Men, not states, are the ultimate reality; and the interdependence of men, not the exclusiveness of national states, dictates international coordination and intercommunity and hence international government.

The failure to observe these principles will condemn men to a continuing misery. Group isolation and exclusiveness will continue to breed attitudes of superiority and inferiority, will separate racial and religious and ethnic groups into hostile factions, and will produce that discrimination of group against group that divides men from one another and degrades some in the narrow and self-seeking interests of others. The economic, social, and political costs of such divisiveness and discrimination are already only too well known; they are monumental and tragic. And what is true of group pitted against group is even more true of nation pitted against nation; for here the inevitable and more terrible consequence is war, with all that this means in the destruction and dehumanization of the race.

The failure to observe these principles carries at least one other penalty that needs to be noted here. This is the alienation of individuals and groups from the larger society to which they want to belong but from which, by virtue of the impossible demands put upon them, they are rejected and estranged. How can a Negro be loyal to a social and political order that dehumanizes him? How can a cultural minority be expected to give its allegiance to a social and political system that threatens its very existence? If we are to minimize civil disobedience, if we are to avoid riots and rebellion, we can do so not by suppressing the discontented but only by removing the grounds of their discontent. To effect such changes it is of course insufficient merely to appeal to good will; such an appeal can scarcely make headway against the conditions that everywhere foster prejudice and stimulate unfavorable attitudes. But it is also true that without a change in attitudes—without the overcoming of the passions and prejudices, the stupidity and ignorance, the misconceived self-interests and the denial of what is common and abiding—we are not likely to achieve a change in conditions. For, as MacIver observed in another connection: "There is harm in nature but evil only in man, because he alone can deny the universal he must seek." [7]

V

I have said enough perhaps to indicate the rewards that await the reader of these essays. I hope I have said enough, too, to support my conviction that MacIver's eminent achievements, in both method and vision, stamp him as the most distinguished of our social and political theorists. Whether history will share this judgment it is not now of course possible to say. But that MacIver has resolutely stood in the mainstream of social and political theory, that he has remained true to the noblest traditions of his calling, that he has significantly extended the frontiers of our knowledge—these are beyond contestation.

DAVID SPITZ

---

7. See his essay "My Religion," *American Weekly* (March 9, 1947), p. 21.

Contents

III STATE AND SOCIETY

IV GOVERNMENT AND SOCIAL CHANGE

THE QUEST *for* MEANING I

The Freedom to Search
for Knowledge

I   There has never been so much commotion over the freedom of the scholar or the educator as there is in this country today. In the past there has indeed been less, much less, academic freedom—for in the ages of authority it was at best a very limited affair. But never in modern times has there been so massive and many-sided an assault upon it. Many of these assaults have been repelled, but more than a few have succeeded. All across the country there are groups that, under one banner or another, are seeking to limit it. Dozens of organizations are "investigating" it, including at present three Congressional bodies. There is not a single important institution of learning that has not been the object of some accusation concerning it. There is scarcely a college or university president who has not run into some troubles over it.

Why is there so much concern over it? These things need to be explained, for the people are being misled about these questions, and even some educators are by no means sufficiently alert to the situation.

Academic freedom means the freedom of the educator to do his proper work, to fulfill his function, to render to his society the special service that he has to offer. His work is to learn and to teach, and this is what every genuine scholar wants above all to do. That is what he is appointed to do. That is what the institution of learning is for. Here lies its unique function, its primary mission in society.

Every major type of social organization has its own unique function which requires an appropriate range of freedom to fulfill. The church aspires to one. The family another. So also the academy, the college or the university. Academic freedom then is the freedom of the men of the academy, the faculty members, within their various areas of competence, in the field of learning and teaching.

Observe that this freedom is not the freedom to express opinions on any matter under the sun. In a democratic country that is the freedom of the citizen. What we're talking about is a special form of freedom derived from a special function—the freedom proper to the member of a particular profession, without which the calling is perverted and falsified and the service it renders is betrayed. Just as the medical man needs a particular area of freedom for his work, or the man of law, so does the man of the academy.

The effort to seek and impart knowledge means a limit to the control of any external authority over the institution of learning. Where this freedom exists, no authority can say: "This is the truth, this is what you must teach." Or: "This is the truth; if your investigations lead you to doubt it or to deny it, you must refrain from doing so."

It is the freedom to reach conclusions through scholarly investigation. It does not imply the freedom to *act* according to your conclusions, if such action is against the law. It is emphatically not a freedom to conspire to overthrow government or to incite others to do so. But it embraces the freedom of the serious student of government to reach and express conclusions regarding its nature and regarding the good or evil results of this or that form of government.

Academic freedom is at the same time a high responsibility. It is not a privilege possessed by an academic guild. It is not a concession granted by a government or by a community to an enclave of scholars. It is claimed as a necessity, not a luxury; as a condition of service, not as a social award. As we shall presently see, it is a fundamental condition of a free society.

Some enemies of this freedom say: "We are perfectly willing to let the teacher do his job. His job is to impart information—we don't in the least want to interfere with that. What we object to is when the teacher throws his weight around and starts indoctrinating his students. That's not his business. By all means let him give the students any knowledge he has, but let him keep to the facts and keep his valuations out of it. We don't pay him to teach values, especially values contrary to our own."

This sounds plausible—perhaps even reasonable. But let us see how it works out. Suppose, for example, you are a teacher of English literature. What would confining yourself to "the facts" mean? What sort of understanding would you convey of a play of Shakespeare or, say, Walt Whitman's poems if you confined yourself to "the facts"? Would it not deaden any incipient interest the student might have, or at the least deaden his interest in you, unless you did a bit of interpretation? And if you do that, you are no longer giving "the facts."

Or suppose you are an economist and you're talking about inflation. Would you reel off changing index numbers and stop there, or would you analyze inflation as a problem? If the latter, are you confining yourself to "the facts"? Are you even steering clear of "values"?

Or you are a sociologist, and you're discussing, say, a housing shortage in some part of the country. But why call it a shortage? A shortage is not a "fact" but a conclusion you believe to be borne out by the evidence. And why deal with it at all if you're eschewing values altogether? The facts are of interest because they have meaning for us. If you exclude the meaning your teaching is dead. If you include it you cannot altogether exclude values.

He who seeks knowledge is seeking the connections between things. He is not interested in mere detached items of information. He wants to find out how things are related. His mere opinions do not count and he should not foist them on his students. But he should be free to express any conclusions he reaches as a result of his study in his own field, explaining how he reaches them. His conclusions may be faulty, but there is no other road to knowledge. Nor is there any other way to education since the teacher is out to train the student's mind, not to load his memory with undigestible "facts."

This, then, is the freedom the scholar needs, the freedom that is now on the defensive. Why is it important? Why does it matter much to anyone but the scholar? Why should the people, too, be concerned if this freedom is threatened or abridged?

Academic freedom is important to us all because knowledge is important, because the search for knowledge is important, and because the spirit of the search for knowledge is most important of all.

That knowledge is important needs no telling. Knowledge is power and knowledge is opportunity. Knowledge alone enables the "frail reed," man, to make nature serve his purposes. On knowledge alone can intelligent policy be based and successful action be carried through.

The search for knowledge has again a value outside of the direct rewards it brings. Anything we know, we know only in part, and many things we think we know are not knowledge.

At one time men knew the earth was flat and that the heavenly bodies revolved around the earth. Until recently Newtonian physics, itself a tremendous advance, was the last word in knowledge. But there is never a last word. To the seeker after truth all horizons are eternally open. He is the enemy of all the hard, proud dogmatisms that fasten on the minds of men and breed intolerance and sharp division between group and group, between people and people, between nation and nation.

The business of the university is not so much the guardianship of knowledge as the search for knowledge, the keeping open of the intellectual horizon. This service is invaluable. The one institution supremely dedicated to the spread of enlightenment is the institution of learning. Its individual members have interests and prejudices and passions like other men. They go wrong like other men. But together, each in his own field, they seek for knowledge, and thus the institution is redeemed. It is the belief in the supreme importance of the freedom to seek knowledge which unites them.

Without that belief and its triumphant vindication in our colleges and universities the right of a man to think for himself, to inquire, to have his own opinions, would lack any sure foundation. Democracy, in a world of incessantly whirling propaganda, would have no strong defense. And civilization, what remained of it, would become no more than a mesh of techniques designed for the enslavement of body and mind, as it was in Hitler's Germany, as it is in Soviet Russia.

Only the spirit that animates the endless search for knowledge can save us from these things. This spirit must continue to flourish outside our universities as well as within their walls. It is the same spirit that keeps the press free. It is back of the democratic willingness to let the views of every group be decently heard. It is the spirit that repudiates the right of the state or the church or any other bodies to establish a censorship over the expression of opinion or the freedom of inquiry.

It is now endangered. In every society there are always those who, fearful for their interests or secure in their dogmatisms, are ready to suppress or to control the search for knowledge. In ours today they have found a formidable new weapon.

Under the guise of protecting us from communism they employ a Communist technique to further their own interest to acquire political capital or economic advantage. They brand as "red" or "pink" or "subversive" or at the least "un-American" everything they happen to dislike, whether it be progressive education or state hospitals or anti-

certainly do not, or emphatically should not, fall into any such category. The genuine scholar is of the breed of Chaucer's clerk of Oxenford,

Gladly would he learn and gladly teach.

The major obligations of the scholar merely spell out the ways in which he exercises the full freedom of the spirit of learning.

We shall accordingly signify his rights by reference to the restraints to which he should not be subjected and his obligations by pointing to the positive implications of the rights he must claim.

The rights of the scholar are invaded when within the institution of learning, policies and programs that call for his professional competence are decided for him by non-scholars—when, for example, faculty nominations for new appointments are overruled, when a faculty member is dismissed without faculty consultation or against the consensus of his faculty colleagues, when curriculum changes or admission standards are made from above without faculty approval, when books are stricken from college reading lists because a Board member or an outside organization protests against them. It is elementary that the medical profession has the responsibility for making decisions on essentially medical problems, and similarly for the legal profession or, say, for the church. But the scholarly profession is in this country not infrequently ignored or at least overridden concerning matters that clearly fall within its field. While the boards of the most distinguished universities observe a due respect for the scholar's rights in this crucial respect, a large number of others are in varying degrees less scrupulous, and some, including a few large state universities, have been flagrantly disregardful of them.

Such violations of the rights of the scholar are committed not only by certain governing boards, as well as, in a more disguised form, by political bodies but also, it may happen, by administrators within the academy itself. They may be committed by a dean or other official, or by the president of the institution. The presidency of an American college or university is a most interesting and rather peculiar phenomenon. He may be a distinguished scholar, he may be a faculty member who is selected not for his scholarly distinction or even his executive capacities, but because he is regarded by higher authority as eminently safe and sound, or he may have no pretensions to scholarship whatsoever, being appointed for services rendered in some other field. He is the intermediary between faculty and board, sometimes the only nexus between them. Much depends on whether he identifies himself with the world of scholarship or with the world of affairs. In the latter event he may not only cease to represent his faculty, he may even, in times of trouble, take the lead in the gross violation of their rights. How else can we describe, for example, the action of the president of an Eastern state university who dismissed a faculty member, in line with the ideas of his board, against the strong opposition of a practically unanimous faculty, or that of a Midwestern university president who promoted a board ukase that every questionnaire issued by any staff member must be approved by himself, or that of another university president from farther West, who secured the dismissal of a professor of botany because the latter led a protest against a board policy that lowered the admission standards of the institution?

The dismissal of a professor for his defense of educational standards against administrative policies represents a particularly flagrant violation of the scholar's rights. There are, however, many less obvious violations arising out of the conditions of the scholar's employment.

The occupation of the professor has many advantages, but no one would list the monetary return as one of them. As some offset he enjoys, when he makes the grade, a certain security of tenure, and in most institutions he has a strong expectation of passing in due course through the stage of assistant professor and associate professor to full professor. But tenure in the first instance and promotion in the second depend on the recommendation of superiors. No one can say how often candidates are by-passed not because their ability or their achievement or their teaching capacity is inferior but because someone in a higher echelon dislikes their points of view or their conclusions or objects to them on some other academically irrelevant ground. Here the violation of the scholar's rights hardly ever comes into the open, since it is practically impossible to prove it. But anyone who has had a lengthy experience of academic life must have known or heard of cases where a superior candidate has been rejected because his department head wants yea-men or because someone in the line of hierarchy dislikes his economics or his politics.

No one has an intrinsic right to be selected for any position. It is for the qualified faculty members to assess the relevant factors in making their selection. But it is surely a violation of right when scholarly superiority is made secondary to considerations that have little or nothing to do with the demands of the service to be rendered. Someone has failed to meet his obligation, and someone, or perhaps the institution as a whole, is thereby wronged. In the same context it is necessary nowadays to point out that the scholar's right is violated when any body of non-scholars arrogates to itself the function of determining the fitness of a particular scholar to occupy a faculty position. The perfervid hunt for "subversives" has led boards, state legislatures, and other bodies to take on themselves this function. To the present writer such action is an invasion of faculty rights. It may be granted that any responsible party is entitled to raise the question of a scholar's fitness, but the decision properly lies with his faculty colleagues. To presume otherwise is to cast doubts on the integrity of the faculty itself. And it takes the power of decision away from the body that alone has the intimate knowledge of the case and at the same time is more likely to use its discretion without being affected by public clamors or political opportunism.

Finally, let us observe that these functional or professional rights of the scholar do not diminish his general rights as a citizen. He has certainly no prerogative to use his classroom as a sounding board for deliverances on all and sundry subjects, but he should be in no way precluded, outside the classroom, from making public statements on controversial subjects. In some quarters the idea prevails that a scholar somehow implicates his university when he expresses his own opinion in public—a most quaint notion of what a university means. Even more quaint is the notion, trumpeted in a book that damned a great university, that the scholar, in his intramural discourses, should confine himself to the "facts" and not draw any conclusions not absolutely "verified" by the facts. This doctrine would turn the scholar into a kind of intellectual eunuch. As every scholar knows, or should know, the great scientific advances have never come from a simple reading of the facts but from the imaginative play upon them of the trained mind, expressed in hypotheses, inferences, suggestions, and hunches.

As for the obligations of the scholar, are they not easy enough to sum up? Do they not amount simply to the requirement that he be faithful to his trust as a seeker after knowledge, knowledge in its amplest sense, which at the further margin widens into wisdom, and that he impart his knowledge with the same faithfulness with which it must be sought?

More specifically, he is called on to be thoroughly scrupulous in his respect for evidence, and most of all for such evidence as may appear to be out of accord with his point of view or his doctrine or his interest. At the same time he must give fair and open-minded consideration to the arguments of those who reach different conclusions from his own. He must not yield to the temptation to magnify his conclusions, to overstate his evidences, to announce certainty where he has only some degree of probability, or, say, to claim credit for discoveries that belong as much to his co-workers as to himself. In a world where the fine art of propagandism is supreme, he must set a somewhat lone example, if he propagandizes at all, by avoiding all distortion of either side of the case.

Furthermore, his obligation as a teacher requires that he be more concerned to have his students think for themselves than to enroll them as his disciples, nor must he in his recommendations show any partiality for less qualified scholars because they belong to his own school of thought. And he must be on his guard lest he temper or modify or soft-pedal his findings, in order to placate some authority, nor should he take refuge in the pious conclusion that there is much to be said on both sides, when he is convinced that there is more to be said on one side than on the other. Let us not forget that the scholar, if he is not to become an industrious nonentity or a mere peddler of others' wares, must interpret as well as seek for evidences, and that, whether his field be physics or history or economics or literature or anything else, he must deal with probabilities and leads and indications and inferences, a long way short of the certainty we often think of as the scholar's goal.

At the outset it was suggested that the obligations of the scholar are in effect the conditions requisite for the all-round advancement of scholarship itself. The obligations of scholarship and its objectives coincide. At the same time the scholar, being as human as other men, is subject to the particular ambitions, rivalries, vanities, foibles, and oversights that tempt him to relax, here or there, consciously or unconsciously, the constant integrity the pursuit of knowledge demands. Finally, there remains one obligation of the scholar of which, as considerable evidence shows, he seriously needs to be reminded. It is that he rally to the defense of academic freedom when it is endangered by attacks on his fellow scholars, whether in other institutions or in his own. With a public that is still so uneducated to the essential worth of learning, with certain political figures still making capital on this score, in a world where propaganda has myriad voices and the spirit of truth how few, there is needed a greater solidarity of scholarship, not contented to make a few defensive gestures, but ready to combat every encroachment on its proper freedom.

[1957]

The Social Sciences

3   If I were compelled to run a college and were left free to
plan it as I pleased, I would institute one fundamental rule.
There would be two broad divisions of the curriculum.
Division One would contain all the subjects that explore
or reveal the permanent relations and systems of reality,
the universal verities that are neither made nor changed by
man. Here would come mathematics, which deals with the
dateless abstract, and physics and chemistry and biochemistry,
which deal with the dateless laws and processes of the material
universe, and cosmology and geology and biology, which
trace the operation of these laws and processes in the dated
record. There would be various other candidates for entry
into this division, such as anthropology and psychology, and
in so far as they proved their claims under the rule they too
would be admitted. The condition is that a subject must
essentially be concerned with what permanently is or with
what inexorably has become. Division One is the area of the
calculable, the ungainsayable, the absolute. It is the whole
world that science seeks to envisage *sub specie aeternitatis*.
It would include the history of all that is external to man,
but it would not include human history. And if the historian
should protest against this limitation we would say to him:
"It is true that Caesar crossed the Rubicon, but that mere

act of locomotion is not history. What you are interested in is Caesar's imperial ambition and the tangle of conditions that gave it play and its impact on the further course of human life. These things are not in the objective record. You cannot photograph Caesar's ambition on a sensitive plate. You cannot see it or interpret it except in the light of your own discernment. So you must come over to Division Two, where others also are seeking indubitable facts but recognize that the interpretation of them, or in other words the more inclusive and meaningful fact, is always relative and never finally attained."

Our Second Division would embrace all the humanities. Under it would come the study of literature, of the fine arts, and of the social sciences. Here too we would place philosophy and religion. Division Two would deal with all the changing systems of human values, all the institutions, and all the creative works of man. A corollary of our fundamental rule would be that no one shall teach any subject in Division Two as though it belonged to Division One. No one shall teach as though he had the whole truth or the final formula about anything. No one shall offer precise formulae for human equations, capable of being worked out to the nth decimal point. No teacher shall divest the "facts" of meaning or treat meanings in detachment from situations. For this is the negative condition on which alone he can attain the proximate, the relative truth, and save himself and his students from the dogma that blinds understanding. It is in the social sciences that our rule would be most necessary and most important. Most necessary because, as sciences, they must strive forever toward the goal of final certitude that is forever denied to them. Most important because, as we shall endeavor to show, the particular educative virtues that they possess would be lost or frustrated without this condition.

Since for the ends of education the two divisions are complementary and neither can provide the training that is the proper function of the other, my Utopian college would enact one further rule. Every student would be obliged to choose a focus of study in each of the two divisions. He would be taught the quest for truth alike in the realm of humanity and in the infinitely encompassing realm of nature. Thus, in so far as instruction can avail, he would acquire an intellectual orientation to both his worlds, the world of human values and the world of external certitudes, and would avoid that confusion of the two whence spring a multitude of human errors alike in practice and in thought.

We have here hinted at the impressive reason for including the social sciences in any scheme of liberal education. How we learn at college is more important than what we learn. What we learn is mostly forgotten when the time of examination is ended or else it is learned anew and better because we apply the knowledge in our daily life or to our daily tasks.

Unutilized or merely memorized knowledge is a cerebral load of which a kindly nature soon relieves us. In the spiritual realm we possess only what we use. Let it be granted that by specializing within the social sciences a student may become an expert in monetary problems or in public finance or in civic affairs or in relief administration or in the psychology of advertising. That is not our present concern. What we are interested in is not the end-product but the process. What difference does it make, or can it make, to the student as a human being that he has devoted himself at college to studies in economics or in political science or in cultural anthropology or in social psychology or in sociology? What methods, attitudes, or approaches may thus become habitual to him that will give him new perceptions or new insights of the world in which he lives?

The answer to this question rests on the distinction we have already drawn between the sciences of nature and the sciences of man. The latter, striving with the rest toward the common goal of truth, have one remarkable compensation for the lack of finality that is their lot. Social facts are all in the last resort *intelligible* facts. When we know why a government falls or how a price is determined or why a strike takes place or how a primitive tribe worships or why the birth-rate declines, our knowledge is different in one vital respect from the knowledge of why a meteor falls or how the moon keeps its distance from the earth or why liquids freeze or how plants utilize nitrogen. Facts of the second kind we know only from the outside; facts of the first kind we know, in some degree at least, from the inside. Why did the citizens turn against the government? Why did the union call a strike? To answer these questions we must project ourselves into the situations we are investigating. We must learn the values and the aims and the hopes of human beings as they operate within a particular situation. There is no inside story of why a meteor falls or why a liquid freezes. We comprehend it as a datum, as the expression of a law, and nothing more. It is because on the other hand there is always an inside story, or in other words a meaning, in human affairs that we never attain more than partial or relative truth. Here is the paradox of knowledge. The only things we know as immutable truths are the things we do not understand. The only things we understand are mutable and never fully known.

After much travail and many false beginnings the social sciences have in effect learned this lesson. In this respect they have passed through two stages. At first they were so engrossed in moral or religious considerations that they concerned themselves lightly with the social reality. They were more interested in how men ought to be governed than in how they actually were. They were more minded to prescribe the proper system of familial relationships than to study what actually happened in family life. They gave far more thought to the determination of the fair or just price than to the conditions that actually determined prices. From all that Confucius and his followers wrote about the family we learn very little about family situations in China. From all that Plato wrote in *The Republic* and *The Statesman* and *The Laws* we gain scarcely a glimpse of the political institutions of Athens or Sparta. It is true that Aristotle catalogued the constitutions of a great many city-states and that Xenophon wrote in detail of the constitution of Athens. Though these accounts were largely static and formal they marked a stage in the advance of the social sciences. But the advance again turned into a retreat. Under the Roman Empire the nearest thing to an exploration of social reality was the obverse moralizing of the satirists, and even a clear-eyed writer like Tacitus wrote an anthropology of the German tribes only to bring out the robust virtues they displayed by contrast to the decadence of Rome. Then came the enthronement of orthodoxy in the Middle Ages and the practical disappearance of the social sciences altogether. So slowly did the social sciences re-emerge that at the beginning of the nineteenth century the Professor of Political Economy (and various other subjects) at Columbia University could characteristically say that what religion revealed to be right political economy proved to be expedient.

The second stage arose as the attitude of factual exploration developed in the increasingly complex and changeful societies of modern times, without yet freeing itself from moralistic or religious preconceptions. The result was a series of inadequate and oversimple generalizations about social reality. This stage appeared first and most clearly in the nascent subject of economics. It is illustrated by the principles of the mercantilists, the cameralists, and the physiocrats, but it has its most famous exposition in Adam Smith. His doctrines concerning the relation of government to industry, the equalizing role of competition, and the harmony between self-interest and social well-being, were all rooted in his perception of social-economic realities, but he gave them an absolute, unconditional, and timeless character that obscured the relative truths contained in them. Throughout the nineteenth century the history of the social sciences was still a record of the overconfident formulation of simple laws, such as the diffusionist law in anthropology, Marx's theory of social classes, and the law of organic growth and decay in sociology. But the continuing process of historical change refused to fit into the patterns prescribed for it, and the ever more intensive investigation of social facts revealed its vast complexity and the consequent need for a more patient, more cautious, and more devoted scholarship.

The social sciences have on the whole passed beyond these two stages and in consequence they have acquired a richness of interest and a potentiality of advance they never possessed before. Because what seemed simple has become complex the boundaries of social discovery are constantly enlarged. Great fields of exploration still remain in the pioneering state. Governments and other agencies present us with a formidable array of social statistics and other data. Multitudes of individual investigators garner their own harvests of facts. But all these are only the raw material of science. In a thousand directions the social scientist is challenged to make use of them, to discover their connections, to incorporate them into a system of knowledge. How are the multifarious phenomena of social change related to one another? What is the meaning, the hidden causation, of the ups and downs of business activity, with their tremendous repercussions on all social life? Why is there here a trend toward democracy and here a revulsion from it? What is happening to the family as it sheds so many of its former functions? What changes are taking place in social stratification as life becomes more urbanized and functionally specialized and why do such changes take place? What can be done to control unemployment, economic insecurity, exploitation, social maladjustment, crime? These are a few of the numerous questions, theoretical or practical, that call for exploration, and each of them has a multitude of aspects. Here there is a demand for all the discernment and all the ingenuity and all the vision of the student. And while he sincerely pursues such questions he gains wisdom as well as knowledge, for he is learning about the thing that comes closest to himself, human nature in its infinite variety.

In making this claim I am not pretending to exalt the social scientist over his brother, the natural scientist. That would be mere foolishness. But I think he often becomes too modest in face of the superior certitude attained by his brother, and I therefore wish to insist on the compensation which he can receive for the peculiar scientific problems that beset him. In facing these problems the student of the social sciences gains his own social education. It is worthy of note that to be socially educated we have all, as individuals, to pass through the two stages that the social sciences themselves have historically exhibited. We begin with moral absolutes of approval and disapproval in terms of our own egocentric values, with no attempt to understand what people are really like or why they differ from us. Then we become incorporated into our own social groups and so we arrive at over-simple and usually over-moralistic explanations of the social order. If any reader has doubts on this head let him read, for example, the admirably discerning studies by Jean Piaget of the social life of the child. Or let him even look around him and observe how the mass of men everywhere cherish the idols of the tribe and pay the heavy costs of delusion and vain conflict. In our present world of distraught and perilous interdependence such a survey inevitably recalls a reflection made by Plato, who at the dawn of social science lived in a smaller world that was no less perilously disunited. He said in effect that so far as the other arts and sciences were concerned it sufficed that some should learn one and some another but that it would not suffice to limit social education to a particular group. Unless it were common to all, the wellbeing of the whole could not be attained.

If we review more particularly the tasks to which the social sciences are now setting themselves—save in countries where the mass-sustained dogmatism of governments prohibits them—we shall see what sort of intellectual adventures await the student. Incidentally, we may point out that no one of the social sciences can intelligently be studied in separation from the others. Economics cannot be detached from political science or political science from sociology. All these subjects are foci for the study of human relationships and the institutions they create. If any one of them endeavors to become self-contained, as economics at times has sought to be, it grows schematic, arid, and lifeless. The multitudinous facts of society have no exclusive labels on them. They are all manifestations of the social behavior of men.

The social sciences have to deal, for their different purposes, with these multitudinous facts. On the surface there is the constant succession of events. No science has any use for isolated "facts." It cannot believe in them. It seeks to find the order of things within which events belong or from which they spring. The simpler part of the search is that for the time-sequence of phenomena of the same type, for the processes and trends of change. Some of these series can be statistically traced, such as the expansion and contraction of industries, of money and credit, of governmental activity, of population, and so forth. Others are less completely recorded, such as changes in customs, fashions, manners, opinions, social attitudes. Some trends move in the same direction for indefinitely long periods, such as those toward urbanization and specialization. Others are more variable. Some series seem to move in an irregularly wave-like or cyclical mode. In recent times these trends of change have excited particular interest among social scientists. In following them we are feeling the pulse of social life. Many studies have been made of them, such as the cooperative researches undertaken under the auspices of committees appointed by ex-President Hoover and published with the titles of *Recent Economic Changes* and *Recent Social Trends*.

Once he has obtained his charts and graphs and tables of social changes the more intriguing and the more difficult task of the social scientist begins. Why do some series move in the same direction and some contrariwise? Why does an agricultural depression manifest itself while industry is moving upwards? Why do the industries devoted to consumption goods maintain a fairly steady level at a time when the capital goods industries are slumping? Why does the percentage of unemployed increase over a period in which the per capita output of goods is increasing? Why does the census of church members show an increase when the circulation of religious periodicals is exhibiting a marked decline? Why is it that while the divorce rate is higher in the urban than in the rural areas it is higher also as we pass from the more urbanized East to the less urbanized West? These are a few samples of the innumerable questions that challenge the social scientist in the study of social change. Some are relatively easy to answer, some are very baffling. We may discover that different series follow similar curves without being able to learn what, if any, is the connection between them. In every situation, and behind every trend, there is a multitude of factors. How human nature responds to their ever varying conjunctures is not expressed in any chart.

We cannot go far in this enterprise before discovering that all these specific currents are components of one great moving stream, the changing order of society itself. We learn that we are enmeshed in an invisible system which we have inherited but which we are forever recreating. It has various aspects which we distinguish as economic, political, religious, familial, educational, and so forth, but they are all interdependent. There are systems within systems. There are contradictions and conflicts, stresses and strains. Nevertheless the whole order moves and changes forever, and the record of its movement is human history. The social scientist is studying not merely specific lines of change but a whole changing order. He must conceive society as a system and then seek to interpret its motion. This is his most ambitious task, for the moving system, with all its harmonies and disharmonies, is sustained by group attitudes and valuations. Corresponding to the institutional system is a system of human values. The social scientist cannot comprehend the one without understanding the other. But he must not assume that the values in the name of which men maintain or remodel the system are identical either with the values they are seeking or with those that the system, as compared with alternative systems, particularly fosters. Karl Marx flung into the social sciences the disturbing concept of *ideology*, meaning thereby the scheme of ideas with which men defended outworn or obsolete systems. Ideologies were value-systems that did not reflect the underlying realities. But Karl Marx still hugged his own absolute, where valuations corresponded with the basic facts. The social scientist no longer has this refuge. As scientist he must be content with his world of relative values. Whatever his own convictions may be, he must be constantly alert not to impose them on the changeful scheme of things.

Having thus returned to our starting-point we can now more readily answer the question: What do the social sciences offer to the student? Aside from technical training or professional equipment, what do they offer him that may be of service in the business of living? What interests do they stimulate? What insights do they make more accessible? What intellectual habits do they inculcate? Our answer of course presumes that the student himself is seeking more than technical training or professional equipment, and that he approaches his subject with some openness of mind, willing to follow where it leads. We do not ask him to sacrifice any of his loyalties—that would not make him a better social scientist—but only that he suffer intellectual honesty to keep them company.

In the first place the social sciences enlarge the range not merely of our knowledge but also of our experience. The range of our experience is the range of the effective relationships we make with the world about us. Its limit is the limit of our understanding, in a sense of our sympathies. The child's experience is narrow and enclosed because it cannot yet establish a meaningful reciprocity beyond the range of its primary needs. Outside of that circle it sees other human beings in the manner of the hitherto blind man who has just recovered his sight—like trees walking. Grown-ups still see the vastly greater part of the human scene after the same manner. They are bound within a circle by their private interests, their group-interests, their imperfect sympathies, and their prejudices. They are class-bound, party-bound, race-bound, nation-bound. But the social scientist cannot be true to his claims unless he takes to himself the motto from the Roman poet: "I am a human being; I count as alien to me nothing that is human." His loyalties must set no bar to his intelligent exploration of what other people are like and of how and why they cherish different beliefs and different institutions. If he is a believer in democracy, he will with no less patience seek to understand the conditions that have created fascism. If he is a socialist, he will not minimize the credit entries in the capitalist ledger. If he is a Catholic, he will still dispassionately seek the reasons for the widespread growth of birth-control in modern civilization. In general he will avoid what a distinguished sociologist of the recent past, F. H. Giddings, was wont to term "wishful thinking." This mode of thinking is very congenial to us all, and nowhere so much as in the social sciences is it necessary to guard against it. So besetting is this sin that even the most faithful scholars are sometimes guilty of it. Nevertheless the avoidance of it is the primary discipline imposed by the social sciences.

In all his social studies the student is occupied in translating fact-indices into meanings and thus, even without being aware of it, in extending his social horizon. He is always learning how people live, how they respond to their different situations. As economist, he goes into the marketplace and sees not only the fluctuations of business but also the complex of material conditions and human calculations on which they depend. He studies the distribution of wealth, not merely in the analytic sense in which it is divided into profits and wages and interest and rent but also in its concrete significance for income levels and standards of living. He studies the growth of the vast organizations which concentrate economic power and engage with one another, or even with the state, in far-reaching struggles for domination. He studies the profound changes in the place and power of labor which have developed within the industrial system. As sociologist, the student goes into the home and into all the meeting places of men. He learns how family life is adjusting itself to the conditions of a changing civilization. He learns the differences between the ways men think and act according as they live in the country, in "middletown," and in the great city. He learns of changing mores and changing social classes. He studies the behavior of crowds and masses. He studies the movements of population and the ways in which men accommodate themselves to ever-changing situations. He studies the ways in which men enter into cooperation and into conflict, and the manifold forms of adjustment and maladjustment that arise among them. As political scientist the student enters into the assembly-hall, the caucus, and the council chamber. He brings the processes of government down to the factual earth where they belong. He learns not merely the mechanism of the great engine of state but also the strange mixture of devotion and self-seeking, of high enterprise and petty ambition, of foresight and of folly, by which it is directed. He studies the tides of public opinion. He studies not only the art of governing but also, in some measure, the principles that men have proposed and fought over, with words and with swords, as the right and proper ends of government. He studies the making of the state, and the vexed momentous problem of the making of a larger order transcending the frontiers of the state.

Thus the events of the day take on a broader interest for the student of the social sciences. The newspaper ceases to be a record of detached happenings, a new batch coming every day. Facts are no longer isolated facts but glimpses and indications of the tides in the affairs of men. Many seemingly minor occurrences assume a new significance, while the more spectacular phenomena, such as great strikes, political landslides, economic crises, revolutions, wars, cease to be spasmodic disturbances of a *status quo* and become revelations of forces that work long and darkly beneath the surface. The student learns that things seemingly remote have strong links with the things that are near. He comes to appreciate the kernel of truth in the extreme saying of Carlyle, that an Indian cannot quarrel with his squaw on the shores of Lake Athabasca without impinging on the rest of the world—"will not the price of furs rise?" He has thus a chance of salvation from the mentality of the "practical man," the man who has a keen sense of what is here and now beneath his nose but is dulled to everything that lies beyond, the man who lives on the edge of the moment and thinks that longer considerations are "academic," the man who wants "facts" and has no use for "theories." The channeling of habit in the routine of earning a living tends to turn us all into "practical men." The discipline of the social sciences helps us to resist this intellectual myopia.

What in short the student gains, as he advances in social exploration, is a particular kind of perspective. All science gives perspective, the proportioned vision that looks beyond the immediate and near phenomenon to the limitless system from which it emerges. But the perspective the social scientist attains is a perspective on the human scene. Nor is it the perspective of the historian as such, who sees things in their datedness, as the moving finger writes. It is not events as they occur in time but systems as they change through time to which the social scientist directs his attention. The difference is one of conceptual framework, of approach and emphasis. Since the time order is primary for the historian he is more engrossed with the succession of events; since the existential order of relationships is primary for the social scientist he is more concerned with the continuity of processes.

A few illustrations will serve to bring out this difference, and also throw light on an essential activity of the social sciences that we have so far left unconsidered. At all times the social sciences are dominated by certain operative concepts without which they would be unable to construe into any order the complex and changeful data with which they deal. The history of the social sciences is in large part a history of the evolution, refinement, and restatement of these concepts, and the issue between different schools is always the question as to which concepts or variations of concepts are most valid, most applicable, or most relevant. An instance is the concept of equilibrium in economics. The simple idea of a balance of forces, such that, for example, prices and costs maintain a constant relationship, goes back to the beginnings of economic thought. It was greatly developed by Adam Smith and the classical school. It was restated again and again, to supplement deficiencies in earlier statements or to make it applicable to changing conditions. It has taken a new significance in the elaborate half-competitive, half-controlled economies of modern times. It has been extended and refined by a whole series of modern exponents, from Marshall to such present-day economists as Keynes, Hayek, Schumpeter, Hansen, and many others. It has been applied in many directions, for example to the relation of savings and capital expenditures. It has become the concept of a moving instead of a static balance, and of a complex balance of various factors instead of a simple balance of two or perhaps three. It has been modified to meet the problems caused by the "interferences" or the "rigidities," such as monopoly, government control, price agreements, tariffs, monetary policies, and so forth, that block the free action of the automatic regulants. Many battles are being fought and will long continue to be fought around the interpretation of the concept, but no economist, whether socialist or capitalist, can do without it. Whatever its qualifications and limitations, it remains an indispensable instrument for the understanding of the economic order.

An example of a quite different kind may be cited from the region of sociology. The problem of defining a social order as a whole is still greater than that of defining the economic or the political nexus within it. Here we have to get at the essential or distinctive character of a society within the flux that has shaped it out of some older order and is reshaping it into some newer one. Even if every age is "a dream that is dying or one that is coming to birth"—or both together—it still has its typical "feel," its own manner and quality of being. It has its particular mores, thought-forms, institutions. Some thinkers have believed that a given society could be adequately characterized by reference to one aspect conceived as mainly determinant or expressive of its other aspects. For Marx that aspect was the economic one, for Spengler the cultural style, for others the technological stage, for others again the political form. The most distinguished of German sociologists, Max Weber, not content with these partial identifications, developed the concept of the "ideal type," the unity of aspects inter-active and congenial to one another that together comprise the significance and the historical mode of a social system. The "ideal type" is not the totality of social conditions but the discriminative and many-faceted principle that runs through them. It is a specific life-form that can be discerned by the disciplined understanding as it plays upon the multiplicity of historical phenomena. It is an instrumental principle, a guide to the discovery of order and an incentive to fuller investigation, subject to revision as it proceeds. In the light of it Max Weber made a famous study of the early stage of modern capitalist society in Western Europe and America, in which he showed in particular the kinship between the rise of capitalistic enterprise and the "worldly-ascetic" protestant modes of life and thought.

As a last example we shall briefly cite the prevalent use in modern anthropology of the concept of the "culture area," a concept developed by Graebner, Wissler, Boas, and many others. For their particular purposes the anthropologists extended the term "culture" to cover practically all human activities and products, but they regard these as tending to form an inclusive and fairly consistent "pattern." Any area within which such a "pattern" appears to prevail is then a "culture area." They find a coherence, though one perhaps difficult to express, in its rituals, its beliefs, its lores, its customs, its recreations, its particular arts, its resources, and its material products. For the comparative study of human societies, especially of primitive societies, this concept has proved a very useful instrument of investigation.

The examples we have given have all been of large view-finding concepts, but the same method is followed for every scale of social enquiry. Many formulations are tried out and rejected; some achieve a limited usefulness; others gain an ever richer content and significance as they are applied the more. Though in no sense like the "laws" of the physical sciences, they fulfill for the social sciences a similar function. In their own way and in their own place they serve to establish order, meaningful order, in the multifarious phenomena of social change. Thus they are useful not only because they enable us to carry on more fruitful investigations but also because they enable us to view with broader and more understanding vision the whole social scene. None of them is final. They are all subject to change with the growth of our knowledge. But many of them are illuminating, and it is through them that we both gain and advance that particular kind of perspective, that outlook on the social world, which enables us to transcend the indoctrinated thought-forms of class and station and economic group and race and nation, and to see with clearer eyes the social reality.

That candid and delightful Greek historian, Herodotus, remarked nearly twenty-five hundred years ago that if all peoples were to have placed before them the customs of one another and were then asked to examine them all and select the best, each would infallibly choose its own. An orientation in the social sciences does not discountenance these inbred loyalties. On the contrary, it shows by many an example the danger and the futility of the attempt of one people or one group to impose its own mores or institutions upon others. The social ways of every people are not only the basis of its solidarity, they are also its particular solution of the problem of living under the geographical and historical conditions to which it is subject. But the student of the social sciences learns no less how new conditions and new occasions make new adjustments necessary. Especially is he made aware how in times of accelerated change and of the expansion of boundaries, themselves responding to man's inventive thought, the fixations of usage and of traditional belief impede these necessary adjustments, and strain, sometimes to the breaking-point, the fabric of social organization. He learns how true are the words of the Roman sage who exclaimed: "Do you not know how tiny a spark of wisdom regulates the world of men?"

He learns how susceptible groups and nations are to blind mass reactions, to popular hysterias, to irrational hates, to fanatical devotions, to all sorts of crazes, to the emotions of the herd. He discovers how the primitive always lurks perilously in the civilized.

Moreover, he cannot gain an insight into these things without achieving for himself some degree of intellectual liberty. He learns to weigh opinions and policies in the scales of his own judgment. He acquires some measure of social initiative. He becomes less merely imitative and more autonomous. When an idea is congenial to them the mass of men take suggestion as a cat laps milk. They do things merely because others do them, they think things only because others think them. They see things through a socially darkened glass. From this half-aliveness the social sciences offer a discipline of liberation. They provide the intellectual conditions for a wider and fuller experience. This individually acquired gain, if it should extend far enough, to the leaders of men and perhaps through them to the peoples, might have also a profound significance for the future of society itself. For social experience discovers the greater community of man, since nothing that is human is alien to it. Consequently it sees the futility, or worse, of that shutter of enforcement which segregates peoples from one another and sunders the growing web of social relationships. The social scientist who retains the open-mindedness that is the prerequisite of his trade is learning to live as well as to investigate. When he goes forth to gather facts he brings home more than facts, he brings a modicum of social wisdom as well. Are we merely pleading a case when we surmise that widespread participation in what he learns and in what he experiences would be a good thing for the world at large?

[1938]

Signs and Symbols

4 My object in this introductory statement is to point out a theme, not to develop one; to plead for the recognition of a distinction, not to apply it.

There is a form of communication of the highest social importance that we have to describe as symbolic. The symbol, in the particular sense I seek to distinguish, is the essential and peculiar means through which this form of communication is rendered possible. All communication depends on signs, whether in the form of words, figures, marks, gestures, and so forth. This form of communication requires, in addition, the symbol that is more than a sign.

The primary function of the sign is to denote; it stands for something, by convention refers to, represents, recalls that something. So does the symbol that is more than and irreducible to the sign. The two functions are so distinct, and the respective roles they play in intercommunication are so different, that the whole analysis of the processes of expression might be greatly advanced if we had a separate word—that is, a separate verbal sign, for the sign itself and for the symbol that is more than, other than, simply a sign.

We shall here use the word "symbol" in this special sense. Symbols and signs are alike tokens, forms, images, objects of vision, sounds, all kinds of things that are made also to indicate or stand for something other than themselves. But the way in which the symbol, in the special sense, *indicates* its kind of meaningfulness, the kind of communication it conveys, depends on a special psychological process.

Let us begin with an example. The written characters "m–a–n," in that order, denote a human being. So does the sound they conventionally make. By usage, by social acceptance, the written word or its sound means "man." Now take the word "f–l–a–g." It also denotes something, according to its content. Sometimes the word is itself the sign of a sign. Flags are used in signaling, and then the flag itself "stands for" a letter or a word or a whole message. But sometimes it is the sign of a symbol. That happens when the piece of colored and patterned cloth "stands for" a country.

What is the difference? The flag of a country "stands for" it in a peculiar sense. It is not needed as a primarily denotative sign. The letters "USA," the words "United States of America," are sufficient for that purpose. The flag, the Stars and Stripes, is designed to represent the spirit, the quality, the sense of a nation. It is not merely a substitute or an alternative for the letters "USA." The flag is never used for the mere purpose of designating the country. You never say that the flag made a treaty or elected a President.

A flag is one of a great array of symbols, of the most varied character. They include emblems like the cross, the crescent, the swastika; totems like the snake, the emu, the bull, the fish, and so on; ritual objects like the altar, the candlestick, the cup of wine, the throne; vestments like the robe, the chasuble, the judge's wig; gestures like the bended knee and the bowed head; representations of motion like the flying arrow and the burning bush; sounds like the tolling of the bell; carved figures like the kind we sometimes call idols. Anything in or on or above the earth may be made symbolic in this sense. Anything conceived by the fancy or imagination of man, whether written or spoken or pictured or gesticulated, can also serve.

These symbols have a considerable number of diverse social functions but they have a common quality that brings them all under our one category. They are devices for a special kind of communication. Unlike primarily denotative signs, such as ordinary words, they are not intended in the first instance to enable different people to have the same objects of reference. An intrinsic symbol is intended to convey in the first instance an attitude, a sense of relationship, toward a value-laden concept. It assumes the acceptance of a common value and seeks to give it more expressive and more vivid consciousness. Unlike the mere sign, the word, or the pictograph, the symbol fails wholly the purposes of communication unless the value-concept is accepted by the communicating parties. Its use is therefore limited to particular occasions or situations, appropriate to the evocation of the value sense. The flag is flown on national celebrations; it is carried on parades. The symbol, to serve the function of communication, must be employed in a particular way. The flag is flown at the masthead; it is carried in front in the parade. The throne is set up on the dais, the cynosure of men's eyes.

In short, the intrinsic symbol serves a very particular kind of communication. It has a profound significance in human society that has never been really explored. Here I shall confine myself to suggesting some aspects.

The intrinsic symbol conveys the suggestion of a meaning beyond the recognition of the communicating agents. It may be the symbol of a faith, of a tradition, of a social value, of the unity of a tribe or a nation. What any of these things means is not grasped by the participant in the communication—it is not envisaged or articulated. He senses that it is there, but he does not attain what he thus senses. He cannot express it; he can only, by his attitude, recognize its feeling. Here, then, is a function that no mere sign fulfills.

From this follows a second great property of the symbol. It does not merely recall the appropriate concept; it vivifies and reinforces it. The symbol is dynamic. It breathes the very presence of that which it signifies. In a sense or in a degree it embodies it. The way in which in the Christian communion the bread and wine are declared to be metamorphosed is, from this point of view, simply a more complete incarnation than is implied in many a symbolic presence. The flag does not merely represent the country; it conveys the spiritual attributes of the country. A peculiarly literal belief in this kind of incarnation is involved in the primitive attitude toward the totem.

From these two attributes there follows a third one that has tremendous social significance. The intrinsic symbol is a powerful stimulant of group or social solidarity. The members of a nation do not possess a common intellectual perception of the nature of national unity. The notions they may have of it may be dim or clear. They will certainly be variant. What does the U.S.A. stand for? What are the grounds of its unity? Its diverse citizens would answer differently where they would answer at all. But the flag is to them all the symbol of their unity. It is one focus to which they can all look without any sense whatever that their respective interpretations differ. It calls for a common feeling or attitude, not for a common system of ideas. In a sense it is all things to all men, but the many is merged in the one.

The symbol is often serviceable in another way. Being employed to adumbrate something that is hard to conceive, something that at best is seen through a glass darkly, something often that the symbol-user feels toward but does not grasp, or again something that the listener or the reader is not mature enough to understand in a more intellectual form, it serves to stimulate the imagination and lead it on. In this way it is the stuff of much of the finest poetry, and a great asset of the dramatist and the novelist. It helps open the horizons of fancy. Often it is susceptible of different interpretations, so that men of different training or background give it a quite different significance. Take, for example, the quest of the white whale in *Moby Dick*. Possibly it is not used symbolically by Melville, but again very possibly it is. Consequently, various writers have found in it some to them congenial meaning. "Mr. D. H. Lawrence sees in the conflict a battle between the blood-consciousness of the white race and its own abstract intellect, which attempts to hunt and slay it. Mr. Percy Boynton sees in the whale all property and vested privilege, laming the spirit of man. Mr. Van Wyck Brooks has found in the white whale an image like that of Grendel in *Beowulf*, expressing the Northern consciousness of the hard fight against the elements; while for the disciples of Jung the white whale is the symbol of the Unconscious, which torments man and yet is the source of all his proudest efforts."[1] Others again have seen in the white whale the spirit of evil itself.

For the creative work of the artistic imagination, through all its media of expression, this great latitude of potential interpretation, this liberation of all horizons, may be much more an advantage than a disadvantage. But the peril as well as the service of the resort to symbols, or of the interpretation of presumptive symbols, is amply illustrated when they are employed under the auspices of science. For then the elusive symbol, the presumptive symbol, or the entirely dubious symbol is likely to be taken out of its proper realm of liberty and made the hard-working slave of a doctrine—a charge that can be brought against no small amount of psychoanalytic interpretation of social phenomena.

Possessing the remarkable attributes we have here merely touched upon, the symbol plays a very important part in almost every area of human behavior. It has its special functions according to the area, whether it be religion or government or the arts or the ways of the family or the phenomena of life and death, seedtime and harvest, peace and storm. It is the suggestion of this paper that here, in the study of the intrinsic symbol, is a neglected subject that richly deserves an exploration.

[1953]

---

1.   Lewis Mumford, *Herman Melville*.

The Historical Pattern
of Social Change

5 The search for principles of order in history is beset by
peculiar difficulties. When the historian traces the concate-
nation of events he generally treats them as falling into
parallel or marginally connected sequences and tends to
view these as together establishing an epoch or historical
stage or as revealing the life-course of a nation or a civilization. But two assumptions are therein implicit: first,
that the epoch or the nation or the civilization is itself a distinctive unity, not merely a convenient name or label under
which to range the myriad activities that are taken as its
manifestations; and second, that the unity is continuous
through change, not merely from event to event but throughout the whole sequence. These assumptions are rarely
examined and still more rarely justified. Yet they supply
the two dimensions, the space dimension and the time
dimension, of the historian's universe. Without them history-
writing on any scale becomes no more than an assemblage
of accidentally associated tales. On the other hand, those
writers who, not content with the more academic mode,
essay the task of discovering large-scale patterns or recurrences
in the web of history generally postulate as the substratum
of change an organic totality that reveals afresh, age upon
age, the persistent character of its fundamental being.

As recent instances of this more ambitious style one may cite the interpretations of Spengler, Pareto, and Arnold Toynbee.[1] The eclectic use which such synoptic writers make of the historical data and the persuasive manner in which they richly illustrate and plausibly reinforce their very divergent conclusions suggest the need for a re-examination and clarification of the initial postulate. What is the nature of the unity that at any given moment characterizes an area of human society? What is the nature of the continuity that any such area maintains throughout its changes? Is it an integral unity of the organic sort that responds as a whole and changes as a whole? Or is it a unity more loosely woven of diverse strands that have different motions and principles of change? If the latter, then we may be led to approach history by another road and to find in the time-sequence some other order than that of recurrent rhythms, of like responses to like situations, or of the successive waxing and waning of like organic forms.

It is an inveterate human tendency to conceive of unities too simply and too absolutely, whether the unity be nation or state or culture or religion or race or generation or anything else which we include within the bracket of a social name. The practical consequences of this simplification are rife in the world today. The theoretical consequences alone concern us here. Falsely conceived entities cloud the thoughts of the common man and invade the speculations of the philosopher. The one philosophically-minded statesman of the First World War, General J. C. Smuts, said at its close: "There is no doubt that Mankind is once more on the move. The very foundations have been shaken and loosened, and things are again fluid. The tents have been struck, and the great caravan of Mankind is once more on the march." Some tents have been struck and some stand pegged. Some parts of the "great caravan" move in one direction and some in another, forward or backward. What is the whole that marches whither?

Let us admit with the synoptic historian that there is history only of that which in each of its moments is a unity and in all its sequences persists through change. Where this condition is lacking we have no history, but manifold histories. If the condition does not hold for human aggregates, then we still have histories of industry and agriculture, of housing and of standards of living, histories of mathematics and magic and medicine and engineering and warfare and government, of all the conditions and arts and contrivances of man—but not of his peoples and tribes, countries and nations. Without this concept of unity historical

1. Oswald Spengler, *Der Untergang des Abendlandes*, translated by C. F. Atkinson as *The Decline of the West* (New York, 1926–28); Vilfredo Pareto, *Trattato di Sociologia Generale*, edited by Arthur Livingston as *The Mind and Society*, see especially Vol. IV (New York, 1935); A. J. Toynbee, *A Study of History* (London, 1934).

research is only cutting separate trails through the jungle of events. If a hundred million agriculturists over the face of the earth suffered simultaneously from drought or famine, this would no more constitute a single historical event than if they enjoyed simultaneously the most diverse fortunes. Even were every one of the hundred million linked at some point with his neighbors so that a nexus of relationship threaded them all together, we should still be far from the necessary condition of a common history. All we could attain would be a multitude of cross-referenced biographies, lacking historical focus or significance. And even were the whole multitude subject to some single human organization, such as a tax-gathering and soldier-recruiting empire, that touched their lives sporadically from afar, we should still have to exclude from the content of a common history the vast extent of all they did and suffered. The incidents of their lives might have much human interest and in that sense they might attract the attention of the historian, who is—sometimes to the confusion of his art—a human being no less than an historian.

For there is history only of that which in itself, as a unity, undergoes processes of change. This proposition, being self-evident, everyone admits in principle. No one, for example, would set out to write a history of Patagonia-plus-Ethiopia. In the demarcation of an historical subject, whether it be the village of Blind Man's Gap or mankind itself, there is always, as we have stated, the assumption that here is a distinctive entity which grew and achieved and suffered as a whole. But the proposition may be accepted in principle and evaded in application. We may assume unities into whose reality and into whose nature we do not enquire. We may take a geographical area, a territory, as the equivalent of a social unity. We may regard a mere power-system, an empire, as the incorporation of a culture-system. Or we may use the term "culture" as an anthropological blanket to cover all the characteristics of human life within an area territorially defined. Or we may use the term "state" as if it connoted a common way of life, although frequently a system of government extends over many schemes of life and many creeds, and frequently a scheme of life or a creed extends over many systems of government.

Unless we define our unity, what criterion have we to distinguish the relevant from the irrelevant? In the multitude of affairs and changes, what matters for the record, in what degree and why? These are the embarrassing questions that the historian of commonwealths and peoples must answer—or fail to answer. These questions have little sting for the specialist of military or political history or economic history or the history of science. But the general historian evades them at his peril. How much weight should he give to "the drums and tramplings of a thousand conquests" and how much to the changing tides of opinion that are revealed in the songs and gossipings of common men? Should Alexander, who wept that he had no more worlds to conquer, have more space in the record than his tutor Aristotle, who took all knowledge to be his province? What prominence shall Savonarola have beside Galileo, or Cesare Borgia beside Machiavelli? What significance shall the historian attach to the squabbles of politicians for spoils as compared with the quiet toil of scientists and inventors, to the money-makers as compared with the wealth-creators, to the leaders of men as compared with the dreamers of dreams? For what, *to what*, are they severally significant?

The historian cannot evade these questions, unless he is content to make the historical record an arbitrary reflection of his own selective interest in events or unless, in a vain objectivity, he is ready to assess events by the amount of clamor or commotion which they aroused. But no scientific observer could accept the latter criterion. A flaming meteorite is vastly less significant to the astronomer than a faint nebula. And so may the spectacular figures and events of history mean far less to the scheme of things entire than the dim processes of change that are unheralded by the fame of men.

The essential difficulty is that the historical data nowhere fall within a single closed system with determinate frontiers of space or of time. Systems, of course, abound: political systems, economic systems, class systems, community systems, technological systems, religious systems, language systems, thought systems, mode-of-living systems. These systems are interwoven and interdependent, but their interdeterminate and changing frontiers are bewilderingly non-coincident except perhaps in some rare fastnesses where small tribes still live remote from contacts —and from history. There alone, if anywhere, is the dream of totalitarianism realized in our present world. Elsewhere the various systems refuse the measure of any Procrustean bed devised by race fanatics or culture purists, who would make the world conform to the simplicity of their own thoughts. It has been so ever since what we name civilization began. In this fact, which could be amply demonstrated did space permit but which may be sufficiently obvious without demonstration, we find one main reason for rejecting the notion that societies or civilizations, on any scale whatever, are organic wholes, all of whose elements and systems are bound together in indissoluble unity, grow together, flourish together, and at length die together.

From this negative fact we start on the quest for another conception of social unity. But, if we do not accept the organismic hypothesis, are we not abandoning altogether the unity that historians desiderate? If we think of society as an array of diversely ordered systems overlapping and merging into one another, how can we find any coherence, any focus, any pattern even, in this flux? We can, of course, take any one system, say the economic, as our main interest, and seek to show its dynamic relation to all the others, but unless we assume, as in the Marxist position, that this particular system is primary and in effect determinant of all the rest, we come no nearer to a synthetic principle. For that we look beyond the systems to the mentality that creates and sustains them. An economic system, a political system, a religious system, all systems of human relationship, exist only in and through the conscious experience of them. Take away that experience and they leave not a wrack behind. Likewise a technological system, apart from the contriving consciousness, is neither technology nor system. The engines and the guns become merely curious shapes of metal and the houses and gardens are houses and gardens no more. Territory is no longer country and the frontiers of men's allegiance fall into oblivion. These very obvious facts lead us through to a less obvious conclusion. In the realms that the historian of society explores the sole purely objective reality is the experiencing subject, the sole inclusive unity is the coherence of a scheme of life, over the range within which it determines the activities and the thoughts of men, and the sole available synthesis is that which interprets the character, the derivation, the conditions, the trends and the transformations of these socially established modes of being. All the systems we have referred to, economic, military, religious, and so forth, are but the articulations or instruments of some embodied vision wherein or whereby man lives. Egyptian priestly dynasties, familially-minded China, caste-bound India, Minoan and Mycenean societies, the Greek city states, the Roman imperium, the intestate civilization of Maya, Christian feudalism, Japanese feudalism, nineteenth-century capitalism, and the newborn orders of a shaken world are all to be understood, in the last resort, as nuclei of such relatively coherent schemes of life.

Whatever may be the relation of race or geography or economic nexus or control-institutions to such a scheme of life, the unity itself is clearly none of these things. It manifests itself dynamically as a system of incorporated values, and the scale of the unity is the range over which these distinctive human valuations are incorporated. We have thus three main elements in every historical situation and in every historical process. First and focal are the incorporated values themselves, which, using the term in the older, non-anthropological sense, we shall call the culture; in the second place come the utilitarian or instrumental systems that sustain the culture, though, of course, they serve to mold it as well —the economic, political, and technological systems with all their organizations, contrivances, authorities, controls, and educational devices. Finally, there is the third element, the material factors which, as such, exist apart from the scheme of life and its sustaining systems but which are essential determinants of them—the eternally interactive biological and environmental factors. When we bring these factors, the population as a biological entity and the geographical conditions, into relation to the scheme of life and the utilitarian systems, we discover various types and degrees of interdependence between them all. Thus we conceive of the totalities we name peoples, nations, societies, and civilizations.

The incessant change of these variously named totalities is the theme of history, and what I wish here to suggest is that in an analysis of the contingent and unstable adjustment of these three elements we shall find the main key to the interpretation of historical change. Further, I hope to show that, in the larger historical perspective, the changes in the mode of adjustment between these elements follow a particular pattern. This is what I mean by the historical pattern of social change. It is not a changing pattern with which I propose to deal, but a pattern of change itself. But before I proceed to elucidate it I shall endeavor to justify the selection of our three primary categories. Why mark off into these three groupings the myriad diverse phenomena of social life? Why assume that they are more adequate and more relevant than any other categories? Why assume a certain order to relationship between them that gives logical priority to subjective group values, regards the nexus of institutions mainly as their instruments, and lumps together the concrete realities of human stock and physical environment as though they were merely the oil and the lamp for the flickering flame of these insubstantial values?

If we are to answer these questions, a fuller definition of our first two categories is necessary. We are distinguishing here between the activities, personal relationships, products, and finally states of being, which are in normal human experience immediate values, and those which are by contrast conditional or indirect values. We are distinguishing between the things men pursue because they want them and those they pursue because they are the conditions of their attaining what they want. Taken from a psychological standpoint this distinction does not help us. One man reads because it helps him to sleep and another because he enjoys reading. One man plays golf because it is good for his health and another because he likes golf. One man preaches because he finds it a comfortable profession and another because he believes in his message and calling. From the psychological standpoint values-as-ends and values-as-means are inextricably and hopelessly intermingled. But from the sociological standpoint, as I have elsewhere shown, the distinction is tenable and serviceable.[2] For values-as-means cohere into charac-

---

2.   In my book, *Society: Its Structure and Changes* (New York, 1931), Chap. XII.

teristic systems which differ in important respects from the systems that express values-as-ends. The economic, the technological, and the political systems are *typically* embodiments of values-as-means; while the family, the church, the club, the discussion group, the gossip party, the sport organization, the associations of the fine arts and of the sciences, the alumni association, and certain forms of educational institution, are *typically* embodiments of values-as-ends.

The importance of the distinction lies in the fact that we can envisage the utilitarian systems, the economic, the technological, and the political, as constituting one great nexus of means, and find in the relation of this nexus to the cultural life, to the colorful confusion of the realm of ends, the clue to a major problem of human history. It is a commonplace observation of our times that the nations of the world, in spite of their manifold cultural apartnesses, are meshed in the same expansive machine-technology, and it is scarcely less obvious that their economic systems are interdependent in spite of strong attempts on the part of many to assert independence, and that their political systems laggardly follow, in uneasy compromises with their sense of sovereign isolation, the inevitable demands of economic-technological expansion. This current situation is a phase of the larger pattern with which I wish to deal. I refer to it here since it may serve to illustrate one of a number of reasons why for the discovery of this pattern of change we draw a line between the utilitarian order and the cultural life.

For this nexus of means has a mode and tempo of expansion other than those of the creeds and the philosophies, the *Weltanschauungen* and the mores, which dominate cultural expression. Technology and scientific application move always forward. They march to ever new conquests. The economic system is caught up in the advance, being the area which first and always receives the impact of technology. The political system follows in the rear, slowest to respond to that impact, but follows, nevertheless, with strange twistings and tergiversations, as it is forced to abandon the trenches of ancient authority. The economic and the political cannot for long go separate ways, still less so the economic and the technological. For together these constitute an interwrought scheme of means and powers, and there is chaos where they are not conjoined. Every economy is, and always has been, even in the extreme moments of laissez-faire, essentially a political economy. And since means can be added to means and powers added to powers, the utilitarian nexus is inevitably expansive and tends to embrace within one homogeneous organization ever larger areas of society. Here it stands in contrast to the characteristic organizations of the cultural life. The latter, with their deeper bite into human personality, with their appeal to final values and goals of living, as variable as the minds that respond to them, have more limited, precarious, and temporary conditions of expansion. Culture tends to be a subjective possession, enjoyed and cultivated in congenial person-to-person relationships, and even the one culture-aspect which makes universalist claims, religion in certain of its forms, arouses in the minds of those who accept its claims a thousand competing interpretations of that universality. But traders will deal with one another across any culture barrier and machines will work as well for pagans as for Christians, for Soviet collectives as for American capitalists. Hence a phenomenon that emerges in various degrees from the dawn of history to the present. The South Sea Islander embarks on a bartering expedition to alien tribes; the ancient empire incorporates in its political system the outer barbarian; and modern nations gladly enter into alliance with others whose ways of life and thought they abhor.

But the utilitarian order has an inner as well as an outer principle of expansion that differentiates it from the cultural order. The steady, seemingly irresistible advance of technology has no counterpart in the realm of cultural values. In technology the highest attainments of yesterday are surpassed today, and those of today will be surpassed tomorrow. These attainments are not merely outmoded, like the popular songs and plays of yesteryear. They are replaced by more effective devices, by finer instruments, by more powerful engines, by more ingenious mechanisms. For in this sphere, once it grows distinct, the appeal is no longer to authority or to phantasy or to tradition. Here only the pragmatic appeal, the demonstrable test of competitive efficiency, is determinant, and here alone, in spite of the yearnings of certain philosophers, is that test available. If one machine will, at less cost, do more work than another, that machine will send the other to the scrap heap, and no odor of sanctity or cherished sentiment will save it. Cultural variations can be subjected to no analogous test. There is no clear or accepted criterion whereby to compare them. The values by which men live also conform to processes of change but, as we shall see, the processes are very different, though interrelated, and the results are far less predictable. Here there is ebb and flow, oscillation, recurrence, and neither triumphant march nor yet any clear signposts to point the way of indubitable advance.

It is scarcely possible that an older technology should overpower its later developments, but it is nothing remarkable in the history of values that an older culture type should reassert itself over a newer one, either in its original home or in some other cultural focus. The vitality of culture is of an entirely different order from that of technology. Frequently, in designs of living and in the fine arts, there is a return to earlier styles, but the technological arts reject the cyclical mode. On the grander scale of world history, as Rome and Byzantium and

Islam and Renaissance Europe can testify, there is offered again and
again the spectacle of an older culture successfully invading the newer.
"Conquered Greece has taken us captive," admitted a Roman poet.
But the language of victory and defeat is not fully applicable to the
relation of culture to culture. Cultures do not normally replace one
another. They blend and permeate and fuse, forming new coherences
of elements, new and old. And the elements that reassert themselves
from out the past are not only those that represent what we may regard
as the higher values. The more primitive aspects lie quiescent in the dominant higher culture, and may at any time, and particularly as war
or crisis or disaster or panic beats on the spirit of a people, emerge
triumphant, to defeat our fond notions of progress. We may have less
reason than past civilizations had to fear the invasion of primitivism
from without, but we have still good reasons to fear its eruption from within. The study of the recurrence of cultural primitivism is full of interest,
and it is perhaps not without present significance that an historical
investigation of this theme has recently been inaugurated.[3] But in technology primitivism is a rare and evanescent dream. When modern
states seek to return to the good old ways they still develop modern
diplomacies, modern police methods, and the most modern instruments
of war.

Many other contrasts could be drawn between the utilitarian
process and the cultural process, but what has been said may suffice to
validate our distinction and to permit us to proceed to the last of our
preliminary questions. We have tentatively taken the position that what
enables us to conceive of a people as a unity in space and time is something
other than the biological stock and the geographical environment,
and something other than the economic-political organization. We
are not denying that these things are essential conditions, even determinants, of that unity, but we are suggesting that the unity itself, however
begotten and however conditioned, must be understood in other terms.
We are suggesting that in the configuration of cultural values is to be
found the inner bond, the factor of cohesion that alone entitles us to
claim that what we call a people, a nation, or a civilization has any unity
through space and time, that alone entitles us to speak of Egypt and Greece
and Palestine and China and England and the United States of America
as historical entities. Think away the sense of common values, and
what cohesion remains? Remove the participation in common values,
and what gaunt framework of power can hold a people together?
In so far as there are common or inclusive cultural attachments—not

---

3. H. O. Lovejoy and associates, *Primitivism and Related Ideas in Antiquity*
(Baltimore, 1935).

merely *like* attitudes, but *common* ends—there is social unity as well.

It is not the culture in its entirety that sustains this collective being, but the cementing efficacy in it which we may roughly identify with the sense of *common* values. There may be great divergences in culture, and yet the sense of common values may be triumphant, a situation that tends to be characteristic of modern nations. On the other hand, there may be great uniformity of culture, and yet no transcendent sense of community. Nor is mere distinctiveness of culture enough. Ancient Greece possessed this to an unusually high degree, but ancient Greece was never a coherent unity. And modern China possesses it to a high degree, but is at present socially disrupted. Repeatedly in the course of sociocultural change the awakened sense of a larger community has been lost or dissipated, sometimes to be restored, sometimes to disappear altogether. Thus, for example, the vision of community that grew clear at certain times in medieval Europe broke into a multicolored series of separate visions, and the mechanism of international organization that in recent days has attempted to create a new unity has been powerless against the ideals of national separatism. The sense of grave common peril is too negative to overcome the aggressive sense of cultural difference.

The unity, then, that we find in human societies is in the last resort a quite subjective bond, the operative sense of community, institutionally incorporated, sustained by and responsive to a utilitarian order, and ultimately dependent on the biological adjustments of man to his total environment. Being itself subjective, it has been generally identified, though at the risk of serious misconceptions of its nature, either with the systems of our second order, such as dynasty, state, and empire, or with the biological or the environmental factors of our third order, such as kin, tribe, race, and country. It was an historical advance over these conceptions when culturally united groups began to think of themselves as nations, for the term "nation" does not connote a biological or a territorial or even a political datum, but only that degree of cultural cohesion in a people which makes them desire to have or to maintain a politically unified life. It does not imply uniformity of culture, such as established religion, but only the cementing quality of a culture that permits differences to live together in relative peace and freedom. Unfortunately the drive of separatism, seeking for its own ends to dissever the larger unities of culture, attempts to recapture the concept of the nation and to give it the meaning of the older terms which it was replacing.

But that issue belongs to another theme. What we are here maintaining is the logical priority, in the quest for historical unities, of collective valuations, collectively sustained quests and designs of living, with their attendant thought-forms, myths, creeds, and dreams. This conclusion will seem very unsatisfactory to those who regard such things as mere ideologies, mere epiphenomena, compared with the economic facts, the possession of material resources, the strength, size, and vigor of populations, and so forth. But again we are not disputing the dependence of cultural values on the concrete realities. We cannot conceive the former apart from the latter, any more than we can conceive a painting apart from its pigment and canvas; but we are unable to resolve either the unity of a picture or the unity of a people into material elements that in themselves present no such unity. The unity in both instances belongs to the realm of idea-values. Therein lies their essence, meaning, reality. And it is no difficult task to show that those who reject such interpretations, in the name, it may be, of blood or of iron or of property or of economic necessity, and are therefore scornful of ideologies as ineffective phantasms, are themselves actuated to this scorn by other ideologies, other value-impregnated thought-forms, which can come to terms with the former only in the eternal arena of ideas. Our age, like every other, is in the grip of its own changing and conflicting thought-forms, and in our age, as in every other, the historian, the philosopher, and the sociologist essay the understanding alike of the present and of the past in the light of their own cultural loyalties. Thus history is never written but always rewritten. The energy with which we attack ideologies is ideologically derived, and even the armies of objective scholarship, when they advance to battle, have idea-symbols inscribed on their banners. Frequently their leaders do not read the symbols, and then they are like generals who plan a war in great detail and with much calculation but without asking what they are fighting for.

The scholar who deals with the value-facts of society cannot achieve objectivity by denuding these facts of value, for if he treats them as non-values he does not treat them at all. The best he can aspire to is the catholic comprehension and the tolerance that find nothing alien in anything human. Even so, he cannot escape from the relativity of values. For every culture-system persistently attempts, as scholars like Dilthey have shown, to interpret in its own terms the total given reality, persistently evaluates it all, means and ends in one, together with the sustaining earth and the indifferent cosmos itself. The culture-system turns fact not only into value-fact but also into symbol. That is its necessity, its life, as well as its peril. And that is why, in our search for historical unities, we give logical priority to what we have, for lack of another term, called the culture-element.

In the typical sequences of the modes of interaction of these three orders we shall look for our pattern of social change. In passing we may remark that the history of cultural values has received much less attention than the history of the sustaining economic, political, and technological systems. In particular, the history of the ideas that permeate a people in their everyday behavior, in their love-making, in their family life, in their relations to authority and power, in their strivings and their fears, is rarely traced with the devotion that is bestowed on the history of scientific or philosophic ideas. Consequently, we know far more of the rise and fall of monarchies than of the changing conceptions of authority that sustained or undermined them, of the establishment and disestablishment of churches than of the breathing faith and doubt that made these institutional changes possible, of the heyday and decline of patriarchal systems than of the sentiments that clustered about them and gave them or bereft them of strength.

Within the limits of this paper, all we can hope to do is to suggest in briefest outline the manner in which the changing interrelation of the three orders follows a distinctive pattern. We shall first consider it in the broadest evolutionary sense. As society evolves from primitive types to developed civilizations, the three orders undergo a process of demarcation from one another, a process which also marks the expansion of each particular civilization. We cannot deal with the curious context of tensions, liberations, fusions, and again separations that complicate the process; we can but point out the main result. In primitive life the utilitarian system is utterly undetachable from the cultural life. No device, no lore, no art, is solely utilitarian. The cultural is deeply interfused with the utilitarian, and *vice versa*. Ritual is as important as craftsmanship in the making of a canoe or in the cultivation of the soil. Prayers are as important as arms in the conduct of war. Religion is compounded with magic and cannot be divorced from the business of living. The dance is as much a means of warding off evil spirits or of inducing fertility as it is a mode of social recreation. The success of a fishing expedition is as much endangered by a woman's touching the fishing tackle as by unfavorable weather. Sickness comes from spells and the breaking of taboos. The people are bound in spirit to the soil, the home of their ancestors and their gods. Everything in nature is instinct with social meaning and enshrined in social ceremony. Culture, technique, authority, people, and land are subjectively unified.

It is obvious that in this primitive scheme of things ends and means are fused. Everything has simultaneously a cultural and a utilitarian aspect. In this fusion, primitive society lies poles apart from our present civilization, which has carried further than any previous one the demarcation of utility from cultural significance. In the process that brought our modern civilization into being, the land, the focus of feudal values, gradually lost most of its cultural associations and has become a marketable commodity, overpowered by the impersonal category of capital. Capital itself has grown so detached from specific ends, so purely utilitarian that it embodies itself in ageless and anonymous corporations, served by transient myriads of workers bound to them by the ephemeral nexus of cash. Finance, the most intangible and the most protean form of capital, inherently neutral and free to enlist on the side of any cultural alternatives, to serve war or peace, tyranny or freedom, has in turn detached itself from industry, thus becoming impersonal control raised to the second power. Technology, inspired by experimental science, has loosed itself from tradition and become a closed system of means, closed in the sense that it need no longer placate an established culture but develops almost entirely in response to its own particular incentive, utilitarian efficiency. And in doing so it devises modes of relationship between man and man that stand as remote as its own instruments and engines from any considerations other than those of sheer utility. No ceremonies salute the time clock and the steam whistle, no hierophants unveil the mysteries of the counting house, no myths attend the tractor and the reaper-binder, no dragons breathe in the open-hearth furnace. For multitudes the art of living is detached from the business of living and must find what refuge it can in the now lengthened interval between today's work and tomorrow's.

In making this contrast we are not at all implying the reversionary attitude that accents the cultural loss as against the cultural gain of the process of detachment. The terms of the comparison cannot be drawn in so naive a way. The enormously more complex potentialities of cultural development that emerge in the process are beset by problems unknown to the primitive world, unknown precisely because they are concerned with the controllable relationship of the now detached systems, economic, technological, and political, to the primary desires and the final wants of men. But here we are interested in the fact of social evolution, not in the hypothesis of progress. And within that fact we are minded particularly to show how the all-inclusive unity of primitive society breaks up into a number of partial semi-independent systems of diverse social range—economic systems such as capitalism in its various forms and with its necessary but insecure relation to political systems such as democracy; technological systems representing various stages of the one all-conquering system of industrial mechanization; cultural systems infinitely variable in many respects though cohering around certain foci of devotion and certain symbols of loyalty; with ancillary systems, such as the educational, which perplexedly move in response to the divergent currents of change. In such a world the corporate unity of the primitive is unattainable, and the subjective absorption of the individual life into one all-inclusive solidarity is attained only by those who in their atavistic need blind themselves to large areas of the presented reality. In this multifarious world other concepts of integral unity are discovered that were unrealized before, the concept of the organism as a whole, of nature as a whole, of the cosmos as a whole. But the primitive concept of a society as a corporate whole is obsolete, though there may be many who set out along strange paths in quest of its restoration.

The process of demarcation which our own civilization so markedly exhibits has occurred in various modes and degrees in the civilization of the past. One or two glimpses must here suffice, even though they can suggest but little of the rich variety of historical experience in which the pattern of change unfolds itself. Of all the examples that history offers none surpassed in its cultural adventurousness that which ran through the Greek world from the Homeric age to the fourth century B.C., with its amazing intensification in the Athenian sector between the Persian invasion and the Peloponnesian War. Pareto somewhere remarks that to the Greek sailor prayers to Poseidon were just as much a part of the art of navigation as rowing with oars. But from this fusion of culture and utility the Greek went further in emancipating himself than probably any human being on the earth before. There is a Greek epigram which, reflecting on the votive tablets to Poseidon of sailors who had escaped shipwreck, quietly asks: Where are the votive tablets of those who have been drowned? Even before the city-state was attained, while the Greeks were still a congeries of tribal bands under chieftains, they had attained a degree of cultural liberation that was fatal to the primitive fusion. Their receptive culture was not straitened in the bonds of tradition, of caste, and of religious taboo. In a manner beyond precedent they made technique the servant of their art. They exhibited more than any other people the attitude that Lucretius ascribes to one of their great thinkers, the attitude that dares to lift the eyes to heaven and without dreading the thunderbolt of Zeus seeks boldly for the causes of things. The heroes of Homer, in their less sophisticated way, revealed this same attitude in their free encounters with the gods, even on the battlefield. Thus was set the stage for the extraordinary development that culminated in the fifth century B.C., during which Prometheus, the daring inventor, removes one by one the shackles in which Zeus, the Father-God of the static order, would have held bound the race of men. The gradual untrammeling of Greek culture is witnessed in the history of its philosophy, of its drama, of its art, of its festivals and sports; and the unique fact is that in all these directions the Greek élite was as freely responsive to creative need as it was to the utilitarian urge of economic enterprise and political adventure. More so, in truth, for after achieving a characteristic form of political union, the city-state, the Greek genius was unable to advance beyond it when the combined perils of inter-Hellenic warfare and external invasion threatened its very existence. In the culminating period the analytic spirit that detaches the cultural from the utilitarian at length attacked the social bond. "Custom is the king of men," Herodotus had said, viewing with dispassionate curiosity the opposing mores of different peoples, and the sophists were quick to draw the conclusion that the union of men in society has no warrant but convention. But the sorely needed constructive principle that transcends the differences of culture in a larger loyalty was never available. At this point, the Greek adhered to the primitive concept of unity. Nor was this due solely to the prejudice of the masses, for when the need was most instant the intellectual leaders too found no remedy but primitivism. Euripides in the *Bacchae* recants his flouting of the old traditions, Plato dreams of a rigid totalitarian Utopia, and both he and Aristotle advocate a caste-system on the Spartan model within the confines of a narrowed city-state; and this at the time when the Spartan system was collapsing with the Athenian into common ruin for lack of a larger concept of political unity.

The case of Greece illustrates one aspect of an eternal problem that presents itself wherever the pattern of change, from the fusion to the demarcation of the three orders, witnesses to the growth of a civilization. We have suggested that the tempo, pulse, and style of change are inherently different for the three orders; that, for example, technological change, once the primitive fusion is broken, is not subject to the same authoritarian controls or to the same reversals of direction as religious change, and that, to take another example, the expansion of population is not subject to the same principle as the growth of economic wealth. Moreover, within each order, the mode of change varies for the different factors in accordance with their closer or remoter attachment to factors of the other orders. Thus the fundamental institutions of the political system, being more deeply embedded in the older culture-complexes, adapt themselves with more difficulty to changing conditions than do the institutions of the technological system. Hellenic civilization, in the face of obvious perils, proved incapable of devising a political order more inclusive than the city-state, a situation not dissimilar to that which, on a greater scale, is menacing our own civilization. This problem of the readaptation of the political system to the needs of a changing world is but one aspect of the more inclusive problem that attends the growth of every civilization, the problem of the rediscovery and reinterpretation of the social unity that man, the preeminently social animal, is bound to seek when the former narrow home of his spirit transforms itself into a seeming maze of many changeful mansions.

The endlessly variant situations in which the general pattern of social change is forever presenting itself anew are well revealed in the growth of our own civilization. Its matrix was a social system that, concreted out of heterogeneous elements in an age-long turmoil and mingling of populations within the broken frame of an older civilization, at length took definite shape in Western Europe. This medieval system was formally dominated by a universalist religious culture, hierarchically organized and rigidly doctrinal, in such wise that it did not so much respond to the cultural impulses of the populations it embraced as impose itself upon them in the name of a higher and unequivocally supra-social rule of life. Both its strength and its weakness lay in this authoritarian superimposition. Beneath it lay indigenous cultures that spoke with indigenous tongues instead of the universal Latin and that through persistent strife with one another pursued their respective ambitions and cherished their respective myths. But the formidable authoritarianism of religion cloaked with its mystic orthodoxy the contradictions and tensions inherent in the situation. While the ecclesiastical authority could achieve only an uneasy compromise with the political powers of feudalism it impressed itself more effectively on the underlying social system and in particular it determined the thought-form of the patriarchal family. Thus the everyday life of man revolved again within a circle as closed as that of Ptolemaic astronomy. The scheme of things was subjectively unified, the cultural and the utilitarian were fused, and whatever failed to conform to the established principle of relationship was conveniently dismissed as heresy in thought and sin in deed. A caste system prescribed for men their lot on earth, and the Most Holy Inquisition safeguarded their souls.

The manner in which this closed system broke up and the ever-new energies of ever-new generations resumed the quest for sociocultural unities, amid endless confusion and trampling back and forth, reveals with peculiar significance the different roles of our three great orders in the processes of historical change. But we must limit ourselves to a very few observations. Medieval civilization, unlike the Hellenic, made authority the palladium of unity. This authority underwent assaults initiating in each in turn of the three changing orders.

First, within the culture itself, there came the challenge of new valuations, the inevitable diversities of school and sect that arise from the variety of human nature and human experience no matter what indoctrinations they are subject to or what sanctions they must confront. Next there came the new formations of land and people, turning the universalist culture into a patchwork under the formula of *cuius regio eius religio* and at length splitting with the keen wedge of nationalism the inclusive loyalties that remained. But a third mode of assault was also maturing, unheralded, impalpable, cumulative, and irresistible, the indirect assault that came from the changing utilitarian order.

Technology, once set on the road of change, follows the principle of efficiency, a principle that has no clear application in the realm of culture. It has thus a continuity of direction that cultural movements do not exhibit. While faiths veer and fashions oscillate, techniques advance. Advancing, they not only transform the economic system and the social relationships entangled in it, they subtly and profoundly change the scheme of values. Authority may resist the frontal attack of heresy or repair the schisms that it causes, but neither the secular nor the spiritual sword is potent against the habituations and attitudes that respond to new ways of earning a livelihood, to the manipulation of new mechanical powers, to the new resources, new luxury, new leisure, new freedom, and new servitude that their exploitation brings with it, and to the new relations between men and groups of men that they engender. We need not pursue this theme, since it has been effectively presented by Veblen and his followers. It is not unreasonable to hold that in the course of Western civilization the line of technological innovators, from Roger Bacon to—shall we say?—Henry Ford, have done more, unwittingly more, than any other men to dissolve the sanctity of tradition and to transform the nature of authority.

New schools and sects usually attack the established order from premises that belong within it. But new technology, by changing the basis of life, prepares for a change in the very basis of thought. It is thus of particular potency in undermining the established notions of authority held by the masses of men. For these masses, subjected to continuous discipline and immersed in the struggle for livelihood, do not freely conceive new loyalties or new goals. If they have advanced from primitivism it is not because they have thought their way, or fought their way, out of it, but only because they have responded to ideas congenial to the new conditions of life that technological change has gradually substituted for the old.

The epochal example of Soviet Russia might at first sight seem an exception to this rule. In reality, it illustrates remarkably well both the fact that new technology prepares the way for revolutionary cultural change and the fact that cultural and not merely utilitarian ideas determine the unity and character of a society. The Marxist idea, bred in the transition from a feudal to an industrial economy, seized the minds of powerful leaders brought up in a similar stage of transition and through them was conveyed to a people shattered and disillusioned, thus breaking the resistance of their bankrupt traditions and becoming for them a gospel of liberation from chaos and despair, the vision of a new scheme of life.

Though technology, unlike culture, marches continually in the same direction, it does not advance at an even pace. When it conquers certain strategic points, its march is vastly accelerated. Such conquests occurred especially in the history of our own civilization and have given it its most distinctive character. In consequence of this acceleration the utilitarian, as we have already pointed out, has become more completely detached from the cultural life than ever before. This fact has had very important repercussions on the nature of authority and on the problem of social unity. With a brief reference to each of these closely related aspects we must bring our argument to a close.

The detachment of utility, involving among other things the vast growth of organizations specifically and exclusively economic, has been a powerful solvent of class distinctions, of political dynasties, and of all vested powers that claim an intrinsic right to rule the lives of men. This new condition does not spell the greater liberty of the individual, but it does mean that authority must, as never before, specify its objectives and justify them in the eyes of the masses, a corollary being that the arts of propaganda have been enormously developed. Authority must constantly readapt itself to technological change, a principle of which Bismarck provided a remarkable illustration. But Bismarck applied the principle to maintain a traditional class dominance that was nevertheless fundamentally out of accord with the process of technological change. The groups that control the levers of power may represent, according to the conditions, any cultural level of the population. In England, for example, the control of municipal politics is in the hands of a very different type of leadership from that which is generally dominant in the cities of the United States. Recent transformations of authority in various European countries witness on the national scale to the new contingency of power.

Power and cultural leadership are thus apt to be divorced—a situation that stands in marked contrast to the union of the two in medieval civilization. It is this change that most of all spurs the modern quest for sociocultural unity. If we seek for unity of the old type we can find it only by a resort to a totalitarianism that suppresses the varieties of culture and does violence to the principle of cultural growth. The alternative is to accept alike the contingency of power and the diversity of culture, and to be content with partial unities of different range, with a series of loyalties none of which is absolute or all-inclusive, so that the focus of unity must in the last resort be the integrating personality itself. The direction in which the pattern of change moves is toward a greater variety of divergent and interpenetrating cultural coherences within an ever more inclusive and uniform utilitarian order. This solution makes greater demands on human nature and is possible only in a society that is not subject to severe exploitations from within or from without. But, given these conditions, it becomes a hopeful alternative. For there are two great types of common interest that have always aroused the loyalties of men. One is the social group, the kin, the tribe, the community, the nation. The other is the cultural value in itself, the things conceived of as good and beautiful and true, as desirable in any degree or on any level. These things, no less than their social groups, unite men in social bonds, because they must be pursued in cooperation, even in communion. The unity they create is the unity of the like-minded seeking common goals, and it cannot be identified with the unity of the social group. But from their dwelling-place in the social group men may pursue it through a thousand vistas of challenge and adventure. This is the alternative we set up against the organic theory of society, which requires that the cultural system and the social system be one and indivisible and which, on mystical grounds, assumes that the differentiation of the primitive totality, as the pattern of change unfolds, is also the dissolution of society.

[1936]

Intellectual Cooperation in the Social Sciences

6 UNESCO, more than any previous organization within our knowledge, summons the intellectual world to assume a *political* task that is wholly consonant with the ideals of scholarship and with the integrity of the liberal arts. The task demands that UNESCO be a dynamic, not merely a cooperative organization. It has a much larger opportunity in this respect than its immediate predecessor, the Committee on Intellectual Cooperation. It should not limit itself to the interchange of knowledge, to the business of making more accessible to the intellectuals of each country the contributions of every other, important though that business is. UNESCO must be creative in the realm of human culture. Otherwise it will not fulfill the mission expressly assigned to it, that of aiding "to construct the defences of peace in the minds of men." It is challenged to dispel not only ignorance but also prejudice. While it is properly called upon to enlighten each people concerning the ways and lives of the others it must go considerably further if it is to "educate humanity for a peace founded upon the intellectual and moral solidarity of mankind."

The goal of science everywhere is the discovery and exploration of the more inclusive order in which every unit, constituent, or field finds its relation to all the rest, is given its due place and proportion, and is seen in its perspective within the total scheme of things. There is entire accord between this goal and the function of UNESCO, to explore the bases of mutual understanding, to discover the common firmament that is deeper and more enduring than the differences between groups and races and peoples, and to propagate the knowledge of it in order to build and to sustain the larger scheme of human values. The strength of the United Nations, as of any other organization, depends on the community of purpose and interest on which it rests, not on the consensus of its policy makers at the top. There are always sharp disagreements over policy, and on that level the alternatives are merely compromise and conflict. Continuous compromise, unless the purpose is strong and deep, breeds first irritation and finally cleavage. Unless the constituents of an organization are bound to it by a deeper allegiance than considerations of policy it will not withstand the tides of change. The foundations must be strengthened by the creative forces of cultural identification, by the cultural commitments that are more abiding than the calculations of immediate advantage. The peoples must be enlisted or the governments will fail. A world organization must conspire with the forces that make and move the world, and these are the forces of which scholars, scientists, artists, thinkers, educationalists are the interpreters and even the custodians. The humanities, the sciences, the philosophies, and the arts must assume on a larger scale their role of intercommunication, of community-making. As they did in the Middle Ages, but now with wider vision and with greater power they must create the spirit of the more universal community, without which there will not arise the spirit of the more universal law.

It is this conception of the function of UNESCO that inspires the remarks that follow. Their object is to make some broad suggestions regarding a program in the area of the social sciences. The social sciences have a particular mission in the furtherance of the cause of the United Nations. Not only can they join with the other sciences and arts in the cooperative enterprise of strengthening the bases of mutual understanding but they are specially qualified to explore the conditions of understanding, to discover the obstacles to it, and to suggest ways in which these can be overcome. For example, one obstacle to the establishment of a world community is the prejudicial concepts that peoples entertain of one another. The division of nation from nation, like the division of group from group, foments sociopsychological distortions of the social reality. The actual differences of people from people, particularly their cultural differences, constitute a very enticing field for scientific investigation. In the workaday world these differences are continually misconstrued. Our interests, our allegiances, our relative positions in the competitive world are emotionally projected into the images that represent for us these other peoples, and in the eternally changing conjunctures of our relation to them these images often undergo rapid transformations. But as they do we merely exchange one distorted picture for another. The pragmatic determination of our concepts falsifies our world and makes it harder to discover the true foundations of social understanding.

The scientist must believe that the best foundation is truth and that, therefore, the pragmatic is often the enemy of the practical. In the long run and often even in the short run men fight a losing battle against the truth. We are scientific enough in studying the cultures of primitive peoples but we have not yet the impartiality to study scientifically the ways of the great nations. I suggest that here too the truth if it were sought would make us free, free first from certain prejudices, and next, if we could spread the truth enough, from the wasteful and confused conflicts that are directed by false conception of the relation of our well-being to that of other peoples. No one can read the history of peoples or their governments without a sense of the endless futility and ruinous folly, ending always in universal loss, that have characterized this aspect of human affairs.

I should therefore place as a long-range goal for UNESCO the laying of the scientific foundations for the interpretation of people to people, through the comparative study of their ways, their achievements, their problems, and of the historical and environmental derivation of such differentiations of a common humanity as they may exhibit. I am not pretending that this better knowledge will obviate the conflicts between peoples, will reconcile clashes of interests, and turn the sessions of the United Nations into meetings of the Society of Friends. Between nations, as between all groups, relative interests and relative position will always engender differences of policy and conflicts of aims. The danger is that relative interests will become absolute, outweighing the far greater common interest and destroying the basis of unity. Mutual understanding can prevent that catastrophe. Conflict will never cease but with mutual understanding it will take place on another level, with far less waste and friction. The relations of the peoples will far less than before be jangled into hopeless blind enmities, in which policy is confounded by passion and the well-being of them all becomes the plaything of the men of power.

Before UNESCO can advance very far toward this goal it must undertake various immediate tasks. For example, it is of little avail to seek to build mutual understanding between the nations unless the results of its labors are made accessible to them. I conceive that the educational efforts of UNESCO will be directed not solely or even mainly to the community of scholars, but to the peoples themselves. Its contributions must be translated into the language of the workaday man. And first of all there must be no barrier to access. There must be no sanctity and no censorship against its truth. Which means that the peoples must have the right to listen and to learn. The primary barrier against understanding must be assaulted everywhere. UNESCO must use all its persuasive powers to aid in the opening of communication, so that the written word shall not be unwinged, so that the voice of the radio shall be as free as the air through which it travels.

The radio opens up various interesting possibilities of international communication that have still to be explored. For example, might it not be feasible for UNESCO to sponsor and organize world-wide international programs? At first these might have to be limited to the only cultural medium that is not restricted by the frontiers of language—music. The United Nations needs some symbols of its unity. One of these might be a great festival, on a special Day of the United Nations, for which day UNESCO might plan a world-wide program of this kind. Furthermore, in order that in due course the living word shall carry over the earth, UNESCO might set itself to considering the difficult question of a common medium of speech, as a second tongue of all the peoples. When the ends of the earth are brought together by the advance of technology, when the physical means of communication and transportation are revolutionized, the education of the children of the future, and even of the present, clearly calls for some such development.

Before I pass from these major objectives, which to some may appear overambitious or grandiose but which I regard as the simple and logical commitments of our culture to our needs, I shall touch on one other problem of education for the world of tomorrow. It is clear that some mitigation of the ethnocentricity of our education is greatly needed if we are to attain such a degree of understanding and cooperation against universal ruin. No one should seek to diminish the allegiance of men to their fatherlands but every scholar should work and protest against the falsifications of truth by which that allegiance is falsely promoted. This falsification is stimulated, for example, by the way in which history is taught to the young, in our own land and in all other lands. Is it not possible to attach due importance to the interest and pride that every nation cherishes in its own history and yet to set that history in its proper perspective against the history of mankind? Is it not possible to extol the contributions of one's own nation and yet show fairly how without the contributions of other nations they would never have come into being? Is it not desirable to acknowledge that many achievements attributed to nations as such are not in any proper sense national at all but the work of the selected and gifted minds who appear, like the wind blowing where it lists, now in this land and now in that? Would it not be wise as well as scientific to deal objectively, in teaching the young, with the errors and gross shortcomings of our historical figures, as well as with their virtues and their glories?

These are elementary issues, but there lies beyond them a more searching question. Why is it so difficult to attain objectivity in historiography? The question concerns not the narrative of place and circumstance, the record of what men have done and suffered, but the exposition of the sequence of cause and effect, the assessment of the relation of policy to performance, the attribution of significance to events and to trends, and the selective presentation and due proportionment of the historical scheme and the environmental setting. In this field the judgment of scholars will always vary with their fundamental philosophies, but cannot the historians of many lands, and of the East as well as of the West, combine in a great enterprise to trace the major currents in human affairs so as to reveal in some measure the history of mankind itself? Why should this task be mainly relegated to amateurs? Historians of many minds have not infrequently got together to write the story of a people or of an age. Could they not also build a history of mankind that would be not a compendium of the histories of different countries differently told but a genuine attempt, not lost in the multiplicity of its details, to exhibit the ever changing roles of the peoples in the making of the world we now inherit? And might not UNESCO organize and foster this monumental task?

I have taken the vast field of history as an outstanding case of a social science that has been confined and cramped by ethnocentricity. But it is not alone in that respect. Sociology, for example, has suffered from the same limitation, and here there is perhaps less excuse. For sociologists have been pre-eminently concerned with social relations as such. Their studies have not been directed, for the most part, to the particular sociologies of nations in the sense in which historians have written the histories of particular nations. Yet they have exhibited a too parochial point of view and have too little profited by the approaches, the methods, the insights, and the theories developed in other lands. American sociology is too American, not because it is concerned about American conditions but because it is too unconcerned about non-American contributions to the common field. In the same way French sociology has been too French and German sociology too exclusively German.

UNESCO can do much to remedy this condition over the whole area of the social sciences. On the whole, international conferences have in the past done relatively little, at least in the area of the social sciences, to bring into effective and stimulating contact the members of the various scholarly organizations. They have been infrequent, inadequately financed, and insufficiently representative. I submit two suggestions for the consideration of UNESCO. One is that some of these conferences should be planned around programs specifically dedicated to the current problems of the United Nations. Such conferences could sound out the potentialities of effective cooperation on matters of international economic, social and educational policy, could discover the limits of consensus and at the same time clarify the nature of the differences that lie beyond these limits, which itself may be a way of enlarging the common ground. The Social and Economic Council and other organs of the United Nations might find it advantageous to formulate projects for UNESCO that could be made the themes, after due preparation, of such conferences.

Another suggestion is that the members attending the conferences should not be selected for honorific reasons, that seniority or eminence should be secondary considerations, and that opportunity, and the necessary financial aid, should be available for the younger men who show promise of becoming the intellectual leaders of the future. International conferences should play a more resounding role than they have done in the past The National Committees of UNESCO can do much to prepare the way for their success and among other things can see to it that the men specially qualified in the studies most relevant to conference themes are brought to the attention of the proper authorities.

The more consideration we give to it the more are we impressed by the rich variety of important projects to which the social science division of UNESCO can devote itself. Within my limits I must confine myself to the mere mention of a few types of scholarly inquiry serviceable to the cause of the United Nations. In the first place UNESCO can do much to promote a common frame of reference for international studies. For example, it could deal with the problem of devising a workable basis for comparative cost-of-living and standard-of-living investigations and more generally it could work out plans for uniform or at least readily comparable systems of statistical indices. UNESCO has here certain advantages just because it is not a policy-making body or an official organ of the United Nations. It can discuss matters without the sense of political commitment that weighs on the members of the international organization proper. It could examine the more freely such questions as the relative advantages of different national systems, say in the field of social security. If it held, for example, a conference to explore a monetary problem it would not be a case of Mr. A presenting the position of England and Mr. B that of the United States. It would have the same advantage if it undertook to examine, say, the variant conceptions of human rights in the political realm that are dominant in different countries and to seek for some common measure of these that might perhaps one day be incorporated in an international charter of human rights.

In making these suggestions I am going on the assumption that the members of UNESCO, though they may be appointed by the several governments, will not be appointed as spokesmen of these governments but as the free representatives of the cultural life of their respective countries. Were it otherwise the creative opportunity of UNESCO would be shackled from the start.

The activities of UNESCO, in fulfillment of its broad commission to advance the cause of mutual understanding and to lead the nations to a "truer and more perfect knowledge" of one another, fall into two main categories. One is to contribute to this knowledge, to explore the grounds of mutual understanding, the other is to propagate this knowledge. We have dealt mainly on the former of these activities and before turning briefly to the latter we would call particular attention to a task of the social sciences that closely binds the two together. We referred at the outset to the prejudices, the false images, the so-called stereotypes, that groups and peoples entertain concerning one another. Now while it is exceedingly easy for the members of every group to see other groups in the form of grotesquely simple generic images that are always distorted in one direction or another, it is an extraordinary, difficult thing, even for a social scientist, to apprehend the true character of a social group. The difficulty is particularly great when we contemplate so complex a community as a modern nation. We may indeed question whether it is possible to apprehend the being or the character of a people. It holds within it endless diversities and yet it seems to retain throughout its changes some elusive but distinctive quality. But when we think we have grasped this quality it surprises us by new and unexpected manifestations. Our traditional manner of conceiving and portraying collectivities of all kinds, not merely nations, is unscientific. And just as we forever entertain erroneous conceptions of nations, so do we concerning those aspects of national existence that most dangerously lead us into strife. What, for example, do we mean by "national interest"? How do we assess it? How do we segregate it? On what do our calculations rest when we claim that it is injured, say, by the economic advance of some other country? These are only a few of many questions on which we need clearer thinking, and in the clarification of which UNESCO could do signal service.

Finally, to return to our starting point, the more we contribute to the advancement of knowledge in this field the more we add to the intellectual foundations of our one world. In his *Protagoras* Plato recounts the famous tale of Prometheus and Epimetheus. When the gods fashioned the creatures of the earth Epimetheus distributed among them the means of self-preservation, and to some he gave strength and to some swiftness, to some he gave sharp tooth and claw, to some he gave the power of concealment, to some he gave great fertility. But he overlooked man who alone of all creatures remained naked and protectionless. So to save man from destruction Prometheus stole fire from heaven and the arts that can utilize it and gave them to men. But they lacked still the art of government and so they set to destroying one another and were again in danger of extermination. But Zeus took pity on them and bade Hermes carry to them the gifts of reverence and justice to be the bond of union between them. When Hermes asked whether these arts should be distributed like all the other arts, to special practitioners, to the experts, the Lord of Heaven answered, "No. They must *all* share these arts, for otherwise states cannot endure." The moral has a wider range today. It is not enough for the students of society and government to explore the grounds of mutual understanding. The peoples must learn what these can teach. UNESCO is commissioned to foster among all the peoples the knowledge that makes for understanding. It is bidden to use all its powers and all its endeavors to promote this end. In doing so it faces two series of obstacles. One is the networks of prejudice that block the road of social knowledge. The other is the bars of many kinds that prevent intercommunication between group and group, between nation and nation, shutting off the opportunity to learn and sometimes forbidding even the right to listen or to read. The preamble of the Constitution of UNESCO proclaims that education of humanity is a sacred duty of all the nations. For UNESCO the fulfillment of that sacred duty becomes the permanent agendum.

[1946]

ETHICS *and* POLITICS II

Ethics and Politics

7   "It is not, perhaps, the same thing in every case to be a good man and to be a good citizen."[1] In this tentative form Aristotle gave expression to a doubt which has often been echoed since his day, alike in philosophic thought and popular representation. Thinkers and statesmen alike have declared that the laws of ethics not only do not coincide, but sometimes must actually conflict with the principles of politics.[2] And yet to accept this position would be not simply to limit the sphere of ethics, it would be to undermine the foundations of ethics. If the ethical claim is not necessarily and always valid, it is meaningless and contradictory. It is not enough to mark off two distinct spheres, each with its own laws, as if there were two sciences of conduct, one determining the action of man as man, the other of man as citizen. All such attempts involve the same faulty analysis which is responsible for the original problem. To meet the difficulty, no less than to see how it arose, it is necessary to understand the relation that exists between the individual man and the various societies of which he is a member and in which his

1. Aristotle, *Ethica Nichomachea*, V, 2, 11.
2. Lord Acton, in his introduction to Mr. Burd's edition of *The Prince*, collected a remarkable number of representative opinions bearing out the above statement.

life is fulfilled. It is a problem in the interpretation of individuality.

Historically, the recognition of individuality has taken the following form. It is assumed at first that some one relationship —generally the tribal, though sometimes a religious association takes the place of the tribe proper—provides an adequate controlling principle for the whole of life and conduct. One society sums up the whole value of human life, until slow experience proves its inadequacy to meet all the demands made upon it. It appears then that man is a member of more than one society, since no one by itself can fulfill his sphere of activity. The individuality of man refuses to be summed up in a single relationship. The family, the church, the industrial society are seen in their distinctness from the state, and the idea of citizen becomes gradually clarified and limited. Now, strictly speaking, the attribution of individuality implies that no number of "memberships" is a full account of the being to whom it is attributed, but it is only a very developed society that can understand that the man is more than the citizen because he is a man, not merely because he is also a kinsman or churchman. The way of freedom lies through the recognition not of individuality as such, but of a widened sociality, which is after all the greater part of the truth.

The following analogy seems to the writer to suggest the truth of this matter. What we perceive as an individual object we know only, or at least can describe only, as a complex of general attributes. Similarly we recognize the individuality of man in the various relationships into which he enters. What we are recognizing are various aspects of his nature, all of them social, i.e., all capable of general expression. But just as in fact no number of common attributes is ever the adequate description of the individual object, so no number of associations is ever the full measure of the individuality of man. All the sides of his nature admit of, or rather demand, a common, that is, a social expression, but the expression because common is never exhaustive. The more the forms of recognized relationship increase, the less becomes the unexpressed residue, but it is never a vanishing quantity. The average man can be largely and for all practical purposes, but never wholly, summed up in his memberships. As his life grows complexer, these increase, and besides the formal and recognized institutions of society there spring up, answering to new needs, various unconstituted informal groupings, unions, cliques, and so forth, the essence of society being recognition and intercommunication of some common interest.

I have labored this point, obvious as it is, because the failure to recognize it accounts for much confused thought concerning the relations of politics and ethics. There has generally been a tendency to make one form of society not merely superior but all-comprehensive, and with authority proportional to its comprehensiveness. In the early stages of society it was the patriarchal or more generally the tribal relation that determined human activity; in certain Eastern countries and in the Europe of the Middle Ages it was, theoretically at least, the ecclesiastical relation; but as a rule the claim to comprehensive control has been based on the political relation, the relation of the man to the state. It was so in the days of Aristotle. Aristotle called man a "political animal" where we would have said "social,"[3] but the Greek language made no distinction. The Greeks did not distinguish society from the state—or the political organization of society; the state accordingly was supposed to determine conduct in every instance,[4] so that ethics was strictly a political and therefore a relative study. The individual had no wider standpoint than that of citizenship. In our own day socialism[5] seems to be desirous of establishing in practice the same identification that held for the Greeks in theory, of making society one with the state, summing up the family[6] and the individual in their relation to the state. Further it may be fairly held that even Hegel, for all his distinction of the family and "civic" society from the state, never really freed himself from the Hellenic conception from which he started. If we remember the association of the term "state" with the organization of a community in respect of government and law, is it not at least misleading to call the State "objective mind," "the realized ethical idea or ethical spirit," "the ethical whole and the actualization of freedom," and so forth?[7]

This doctrine would seem to lead us back, under vastly altered circumstances, to that Hellenic view which found indeed a unity in all

3. So we speak of "political economy" where "social" would be the more appropriate adjective.

4. This is not to say that the state was supposed to dictate in every instance; it means that all conduct was supposed to be determinable by consideration of the welfare of the state.

5. This was written before the distinction between socialism and totalitarianism was demarcated—Ed.

6. Even moderate socialists (bearing in mind the distinction noted immediately above) speak of children being "born to the state" as if that were an adequate expression of the fact.

7. See Hegel, *Grundlinien der Philosophie des Rechts*, §§ 257, 258. *Die Wirklichkeit der sittlichen Idee — der sittliche Geist. Der Staat an und für sich ist das sittliche Ganze, usw.*

Mr. Bosanquet, following Hegel in his *Philosophical Theory of the State*, seems rather confused in this matter. He, too, speaks of the state as the "incarnation of the general or real will . . . *understood as the will that wills itself*" [italics are mine], but yet admits that state action is necessarily external action, limited to the "removal of hindrances." What other will is left, on this view, from the way of whose fulfillment the will that wills itself removes hindrances? Mr. Bosanquet is fond of saying "society or the state," as if the two terms were almost interchangeable, and it is difficult to understand alike his definition of the term "state" (pp. 150 *ff.*) and the distinction he actually draws between state and society (p. 184).

the relations of human life, but found it by the entire subordination of all other relations to the one. This was to make ethics coincide with politics, whereas ethics should itself be the science which seeks the unity of the various relations of men to one another, of which one is the political. Ethics, recognizing the various claims made by the various societies upon men, should seek to determine, in the light of the single and chief end of man which these in different ways fulfill, the place of each in the life of conduct. There would thus be but one science of conduct, and whatever problems might arise would at least be recognized as within the limits of that science, as purely ethical problems. It is in fact as absurd for politics to set up absolute rules to decide what the citizen ought to do, as it is for economics to make absolute rules for "economic man." The citizen and the economic man so considered are abstractions. It is only the science of ethics which, considering the whole nature of man, can or should determine how far the claims, valid *in abstracto*, on the citizen or economic unit, hold for the man who is an individual, a political, and a social being at once.

The political claim is not in danger thereby, nor its importance and necessity diminished. A clear recognition of the claims of the state is only possible when its nature and its limits also are realized. When it is realized that political is only one form of social activity, then only is the true value of the state manifest. Its very definite limits constitute the reverse side of its very definite claims. If it can work only through institution and visible external organization and so far as such means are effective, yet that organization constitutes the basis, the essential basis which upholds and preserves the common life and common interest of society, and is consequently itself established in the common will to maintain that end. And thus is justified its claim or "right," first of all in all matters where the preservation or welfare of the community as a whole is involved. Because whatever is detrimental to the state-organization, endangers that very life of society in which alone the individual can realize himself, therefore its claim has, ethically (and its force must ultimately have an ethical basis) a high pre-eminence. But, on the other hand, when this authority is made absolute and all-comprehensive, there arises that tyranny of the political society which most competent observers have found in the Hellenic states, and which is so marked a characteristic of the Platonic "Republic." There the organization absorbs private and family life, comprehends within itself all the social relations, aesthetic, religious, ethical, thus contradicting the factor of freedom and spontaneity which is essential in these. In the Platonic state there was indeed a twofold externality thrust upon the inner life. For not only was a rule imposed upon that life so that its development was no longer free, but that rule came *ab extra*, from an original constitution autocratically determined, and could not, at least in the long run, be regarded as self-imposed. This was the direct consequence of a view which made the political relation, in which externality is necessarily involved, all-comprehensive.

The political relation, then, for the solution of our problem, must be clearly recognized as one particular type of social relation. We may then regard political science as a branch of sociology.[8] Just as economic science investigates one form of social activity, political science investigates and abstracts another. These various sciences give the basis of ethics, which must regard man in the total humanity into which the different social relationships enter. But since conduct is an expression of the whole character of a man, the sciences just mentioned can never be truly normative. Ethics alone stands out as the science of conduct, because it alone can look beyond the various particular spheres, and, regarding man as in his complete self-consciousness he presents the world of his activity to himself, can thus alone lay stress on motive, the inward and vital principle of action. The other sciences but analyze certain of the relations which that consciousness finds in the world of its activity. Again, so far as they are simply analytic or descriptive, there is no possibility of antagonism between these sciences and ethics. The facts of existence can never enter into conflict with the ethical claim, since every such claim is relative to the conditions under which action must take place. It concerns what I ought to do under the given circumstances, not what the circumstances ought to be or to have been. To the ethical mind certain of these conditions, certain of the facts of existence, may seem undesirable as hindering the ethical development of those who are subject to them, but since only action and the conscious principle prompting to action, the choice of an alternative, is morally good or evil, it follows that the necessary conditions of a particular act, however they may have arisen, cannot, in relation to that act, be called morally good or evil. The scientific fact is simply the given condition. Because every ethical act is determined by the recognition of conditions, every change of circumstance must modify its external character (if its inner quality of ethical is to remain the same), and so every extension of our knowledge must affect the direction or manifestation of ethical decisions.

It is a fact not always recognized by scientists that while the different sciences, at least those which bear on the facts of human life, furnish a basis for ethical theory, they can never become themselves normative, if only because, being limited each to one particular sphere or relation

8. The science of sociology is necessarily indefinite: if it comprehends the various social relations, it breaks up into a group of sciences, of which economic science and political science are the best defined, whereas if it studies simply the common character of all social mind, it becomes a social psychology too abstract to be very fruitful.

of life, they can never lead us to the comprehensive viewpoint at which all those relations appear focused in the central consciousness of the one subject of all relations, to the viewpoint from which action is understood in the light of motive.

This conclusion appears to solve the much-vexed question from which we started, the question of the relation of political and ethical claims. The answer offered is that there can be no theoretical conflict here, because politics regards man simply as a member of political society, i.e., in a particular *abstract* relation, whereas ethics regards man in his concreteness as a human being, one of whose characteristics is to be a "political animal."

The subject, however, is of such importance, historically at least, that it may be permissible to work out this solution in detail.

Political science looks upon the state as a unity; and even when it avoids the dangerous biological analogy of the organism, must at least talk of the general or common will of the community. But it will simplify our discussion if we remember that however much meaning we put into such expressions as "collective mind" or "common consciousness," so far as laws of action are prescribed, the actions must be those of individuals who feel or recognize this community. When we talk of the state acting as a whole, we can only intelligibly mean the action of individuals realizing their common membership and pursuing an organized course sustained by the idea of a common good. Hence we may conveniently consider the question under two aspects. The organized state must contain two classes, ruler and subject, governor and governed. The ideal of self-government can never be so realized as to break down this division, and even if it could, even if ruler and ruled were actually identical, the two aspects would still remain.

This division gives us the two great historical problems concerning the relation of politics and ethics, one of which, touching the duty of the citizen, might be called Aristotle's problem, while the other, the duty of the prince or governor, might be called the problem of Machiavelli. The latter may be first disposed of, being more obviously due to a confusion of thought.

1. Machiavelli sought for the principle by which in an age of corruption a ruler could maintain a united state, and his observation told him it was not by following the recognized principles of ethics but rather by violating these. Hence his famous advice to the prince: "You have to understand this, that a prince, especially a new one, cannot observe all these things for which men are esteemed, being often forced, in order to maintain the state, to act contrary to fidelity, friendship, humanity, and religion." So he boldly declared that right and wrong have nothing to do with government.

The faultiness of this analysis is obvious. Machiavelli, not content with isolating ruler from ruled, actually isolates the citizen from the man. The ethics, the right and wrong upon which he turns his back, prescribes laws for an abstract being who is a man and yet not a citizen; his politics dictates to a citizen who is nothing more. Thus his politics by its own false abstractness has given an abstractness to his ethics also. Hence a wrong use of absolute terms, and a wrong dilemma. He says, for instance: "Inasmuch as it needs a good man to recognize the political life of a city, and a bad man to become by violence lord of a republic, it is therefore very rarely found that a good man will desire to acquire rule by bad means, even for a good end,[9] or that a bad one, having acquired rule, will act justly or think of using for good the authority he has won by evil." Strictly speaking, this distinction of good "end" and bad "means" is impossible and meaningless. If goodness and badness is an attribute of will alone, a means cannot in itself, in abstraction, be judged either good or bad. In so far as it is merely means, in so far as the sole reason why it is entertained is its causal relation to the end, in so far, in more technical language, as it enters into the intention of the agent without forming part of his motive, so far it cannot be judged as if it stood as end in itself, but must be regarded in the light of *the* end. So the question comes to be: Is a certain end such as to justify—not a *moral* wrong, for if justified it cannot be such: there is neither here nor elsewhere question of the greater right set over against the lesser wrong, but —a certain loss of those "goods" which in one way or another (according to our conception of the moral end) morality secures? It is a question not between ethics and politics, but within ethics, a problem of values, a question to be answered only in the light of the ethical end, of such a final standard of value as we are able to set up. Similar questions arise everywhere in the interweaving relationship involved in the different social activities, and these are all ethical questions.

2. If we turn next to the side of the subject in the state, another and more real difficulty presents itself. This difficulty arises ultimately from the fact that political self-government is at best only a partially realized ideal, and that therefore there must be occasions when the law will come as an external command, alien or even antagonistic to the inner principle. So long as the subject feels that it is his representative who is acting, that the voice of law is the voice of the general will, he is virtually, as regards the principle of conduct, in the position of the governing authority, and thus can always obey in accord with the ethical maxim. But what of the citizen to whom the command comes as the mandate

9.   *Cf.* the words of Walpole: "No great country was ever saved by good men, because good men will not go the lengths that may be necessary."

of an external authority? What of the citizen whose ethical sentiment is offended by the command?

(It might be said that since the law, even when enacting in favor of universally accepted ends, demands their fulfillment from a maxim other than the ethical, viz., by attaching a penalty to disobedience, it is always antagonistic to free moral action—and this is the position of the anarchist—but the reply is that law, regarding its own violation as exceptional, does not regard its observance as the consequence of the penal sanction, that in fact the political suasion is intended to apply only in the exceptional cases where the ethical sentiment, in virtue of which alone its enactment was possible, does not exist.)

It is first to be noted that, even when the law does come as an external command, i.e., where it is felt by the subject to be alien or antagonistic to his ethical sentiment, it may still be fulfilled in accordance with the ethical principles. Under the Hellenic conception this would, of course, invariably happen, for if "the goodness of the citizen is relative to the state,"[10] it must be expressed in obedience to the state. This theory is perfectly brought out in Plato's *Crito*, where Socrates, regarding himself as unjustly condemned, yet refuses to avail himself of the means of escape put within his reach, because so to thwart the law would be to deny the *ethical* principle. It is of no use, he says, to put forward as a ground for disobedience the plea that the sentence is unjust.

> "And was that our agreement with you?" the law would answer, "or were you to abide by the sentence of the state? . . . Tell us, What complaint have you to make against us which justifies you in attempting to destroy us and the state? In the first place, did we not bring you into existence? Your father married your mother by our aid and begat you. Say whether you have any objection to urge against those of us who regulate marriage?" None, I should reply. "Or against those of us who after birth regulate the nurture and education of children, in which you also were trained? Were not the laws, which have charge of education, right in commanding your father to train you in music and gymnastic?" Right, I should reply. "Well then, since you were brought into the world and nurtured and educated by us, can you deny in the first place that you are our child and slave, as your fathers were before you? And if this is true, you are not on equal terms with us: nor can you think that you have a right to do to us what we are doing to you."[11]

---

10.   Aristotle's *Politics*, III, 4, 3.
11.   *Crito*, p. 50.

Whether Socrates "did well to die" or not, he died true to the Hellenic doctrine of the state.

To us also, though we may discard that doctrine, the principle of obedience to law once laid down has a strong if not the same absolute claim, but our argument must be a different one. The general case is, of course, where the end secured by "loyalty" outweighs in importance the end the law seems to contradict, primarily where disobedience would strike at the security of the state or tend seriously to weaken the habit of law-abidingness so essential to an ordered community. In that case, since the security of the state is indeed the basis of all moral life, since at the least it protects the "life" without which the "good life" is impossible, its claim is paramount. An instance here, I think, would be the case of a country's going to war in what seemed to a minority an unjust cause. While the citizen whose ethical sentiment is offended by that action must protest against it, and before the final decision do what he can to prevent it; yet, once the decision is taken and the issue becomes the very security of the state, it is his first duty to make that end his own. In such a case the political end may become simply and solely the ethical end, not being of itself coextensive, but rather in that conflict of ends which is the heart of every moral issue becoming established as the "ought." In a word, it is always "conscience"—or whatever the inner principle of action be called—that is the ultimate court of appeal, even though it err. Because conscience is essentially individual, always, however clarified, a particular *perspective* of the universal, we must always, in the analysis of conduct, remain at the point of view of the individual with *his* recognition of a common good.

It is possible to misapprehend this point. It is in no sense an argument for "individualism." The individualism which followed Aristotle did not really solve Aristotle's problem, for while the Aristotelian view seemed to regard man simply as a member of a state, the post-Aristotelian philosophy regarded man simply as abstract individual, and as the latter being was the greater abstraction of the two, the reaction, as may sometimes happen, represented less the true account. It had not yet become clear that the individuality asserted is a question more of freedom, of spontaneity of action, than of difference in action, that in fact the principle of freedom, instead of narrowing, really widens the area of the common will (so that political philosophy may find a certain satisfaction in regarding free and common action as ultimately identical). It may be admitted that none of the ancient thinkers had attained to what must be the center of any political theory, a clear doctrine of the general will, its character and its limitations. Aristotle, identifying the state with society, identified the general or common will of the state with the infinite complex of willing which is the life of society. Further, he at least did not use the term "state" loosely, but clearly declared that a state was identified by its constitution.[12] Hence the problem. Aristotle saw the difficulty of reconciling the theory of the Hellenic state with the claim of individuality. The two were in fact incompatible. The more adequate conception of individuality, the realization that man is a member of the state and also something more, disposes of the Aristotelian problem by modifying the Aristotelian theory of the state. For either the "goodness" of a citizen is not to be regarded solely in the light of state-claims, or else such goodness is to be distinguished from the true ethical goodness, and the good citizen, like the good economist and the good churchman, ceases to be identified with the good man. But in the latter case, if we talk of "good economist" or "good citizen," we are really using the term "good" in a specialized sense, and no true opposition is logically possible. There is therefore no possible conflict between ethics and politics; they cannot be regarded as opposing or even distinct normative sciences. Even such a question as that of "priority" between the two, elaborately discussed, e.g., by Sidgwick,[13] is essentially meaningless.

In conclusion we may indicate in a word what real problem underlies the false distinction made between ethics and politics. The inward character of ethical action obviously renders possible an opposition between the public or authoritative and an individual conception of some end of action. I have tried to show how obedience, even to an alien political end, such obedience being calculated to further the ethical end, may often remain free or ethical. On the other hand, it is obvious that cases must arise where the motives inspiring such obedience cease to bear, where the individual conception of the public good refuses to coincide with the state-conception. This is the real problem—a problem that does occur, though perhaps rarely. Nor, after what has just been said regarding the nature of ethical action, can we agree with those thinkers (e.g., Plato and Spinoza) who held that it is in every case the individual's duty to suppress his own conviction in favor of that held by the community in general. It is noteworthy that these philosophers held a purely static view of political society, whereas perhaps the strongest argument in support of the individual's claim to obey his conscience is based on the developing, progressive character of society. As a community advances on its way, it must therefore move from one conception of the end to another. But the recognition of the broader, or the altered, end does not come as a revelation to a whole people or state at once. The way of change is from the smaller to the greater; the recognition moves from the individual to the society. It operates first at an individual point.

12. *Politics*, III, 3, 9.
13. *Methods of Ethics*, Chap. I, 2.

It would seem that there are cases where both the antagonistic views are right, where the state is justified in supressing what seems a destructive doctrine, and where the individual, believing it to mean not destruction but a better reconstruction, cannot choose but maintain it. Was not the Athenian state as much justified in banishing Anaxagoras and in putting Socrates to death as the Roman state in seeking to drive out foreign cults?[14] All new gospels are not true. What is there in the end but experience to test their truth? The fact of progress, or of change, involves a certain relativity in ethics, and out of the heart of relativity springs the true ethical problem.

The state must at least maintain its law, however "conscientious" the objection of the individual. The individual must seek to be loyal to the ethical end, even when, in rare cases, such loyalty is incompatible with obedience. Considering the function of the state and its importance, the cases where disobedience would be the greater loyalty must indeed be rare, but, considering the difficulty of realizing self-government, the cases where obedience finds its ethical justification only in a consideration of the greater as opposed to the lesser good, may not be inconsiderable.

[1909]

14.   On political, i.e., not on religious grounds.

Ethics and History

8   The doctrine of evolution, it has been said, has given a new importance to the study of history. The more intimate relation of present and past which it reveals involves new problems and indicates new standpoints, brings history into closer contact in particular with the sciences of conduct —ethics and politics. In especial, it has given new vigor and new support to that view of good and bad which is founded on the judgment of history. It is the tendency of evolutionary historians to justify consequences as such, i.e., to justify success, not perhaps in detail, but in the broad resultant. "By plausible and dangerous paths," says Lord Acton, "men are drawn to the doctrine of the justice of history, of judgment by results, the nursling of the nineteenth century, from which a sharp incline leads to *The Prince*," a statement he supports by a large number of quotations from historians and philosophers alike.[1] Here then history, regarded as evolutionary, seems to set an important problem to ethics, and it may be worth while to analyze an opinion so widespread, to consider those tendencies of present-day

Subtitled "An Analysis of Certain Ethical Problems Suggested by the Evolutionary View of History."

    1.   Introduction to Mr. Burd's edition of *Il Principe*.

thought which give it support, and to estimate how far they justify this conclusion. In the following pages it is proposed (I) to show that, logically considered, such a conclusion involves a false identification of the *is* and the *ought*, and (II) to deduce some more positive results from this demonstration, in particular to indicate the relation of politics to ethics and the true bearing of history on ethics.

I

We are concerned here not with the ethical attitude which justifies an act because the consequences are good, but with the attitude which justifies consequences simply because they have resulted. In its crudest form such an attitude would justify every act—"whatever is, is right," because it *is*—but generally it takes the more plausible form—whatever *endures*, is right.[2] Ethical value is here regarded as, if not dependent on, at least tested by duration—an attitude which in its combination of caution and optimism makes a readier appeal to us and which when preached by a Carlyle threatens to become a religion.

This is really an attempt to identify the *is* and the *ought*. We start from a universal distinction, found universally in language and thought, of *ought* and *is*. This *ought* has in it elements contradictory to the *is*, for it implies:

1. a contrast between a present state and a state set in conception over against it, involving an adverse judgment on the former in the light of the latter.

2. an injunction to realize this latter state, its realization from the very nature of the claim it makes, from the character of ought as an imperative, being regarded as within the scope of the will.

An *ought* therefore involves a present disharmony and a potential harmony, and the present disharmony exists because the *is* contains also the *ought not*. In the recognition of this disharmony the conception of *ought* arises, and in the realization of the potential harmony the *ought* disappears, it becomes something other than, something more than *ought*.

(It is of course essential to remember that *ought* relates to the whole set of circumstances within which it is predicated, that the *ought* is not the ideal, an absolute *ought* being merely a contradiction or a confusion with an absolute best. Practical knowledge being necessary in order to know the *ought*, it follows, as Aristotle insisted, that ethics must be thoroughly based on experience.)

---

2. The theological form of this view is the doctrine, so strongly asserted by Aeschylus, e.g., that divine providence and divine retribution, though they linger, always overrule.

Before considering the possibility and the claims of such an identification of the *ought* and the *is*, the modern influences tending to promote it may be indicated.

These come mainly from the side of scientific experience. Science has demonstrated the march of order and necessity from one type and stage of life to another, from nature to man, till it conceives all existence as conforming to these principles; and the fact of an established order and necessity seems itself the proclamation of an existent *ought*, for order is at least one predicate of the *ought* and necessity seems to dismiss the possibility of any other. Further, as the relation of part to part becomes more evident, and as the role played by things which (we say) "ought not to be" in fostering the things which (we say) "ought to be" becomes manifest in history, then the firmness of conviction is lost.[3] Further, the greater scale of everything becoming more and more revealed, rendering futile the measuring rods men were wont to use so confidently, suggests that it is presumptuous on the part of the human intellect to set up an *ought* against the *is*—since an *ought* is itself a judgment of condemnation against the *is*. And so the attitude has changed: we may contrast for instance the old idea of the "restoration" of a past, an age of gold from which everything has grown worse, with the modern view which for the restoration of a past substitutes fulfillment in a future.

In general, we may say that the two principles which support the attitude under consideration are (1) the principle of evolution, and (2) the principle of necessity. Do these principles bring legitimate or illegitimate support? Let us consider the place of *ought* in a world conceived as ruled by these principles.

The Idea of Evolution. a. If we regard merely the evolution of the physical world, this cannot possibly have an ethical significance. As physical evolution it cannot even be called progress, which of course implies the idea of an end, i.e., relation to an intelligence. In respect to the purely physical, there is no *ought*.

b. But of course physical evolution has a further relation, i.e., to those intelligent beings who because of their physical nature must adapt themselves to a physical environment, and the suggestion is that the *ought* here lies in the adjustment of the various processes, or perhaps in the adaptation on the part of the intelligence of its physical nature to that of its environment; in so far as this adaptation is attained, there is an identity of *is* and *ought*.

But, to express it very summarily, it has to be noted that merely physical adaptation to secure merely physical ends (i.e., permanence, stability, growth of the physical nature) becomes less and less important

---

3.   So science finally exhibits the uses of death itself in furthering life (Weismann).

as intelligence advances, ceasing to be one of the primary factors, that intelligences form environment as much as conform to it—nay more that, regarded as physical phenomena, everything always is adapted to its environment or it could not form part of it, and that therefore it is a spiritual (which will presently appear to be a moral) need which directs the process of conscious adaptation.

c. This leads to a consideration of evolution as a spiritual development, of that evolution of which history rather than science furnishes the record. Here is the center of our problem. Given a certain *milieu*, a certain spiritual environment, does the *ought* essentially mean the command to conformity which each individual who helps to compose that *milieu*, who is sensible of his environment, must feel? Is the *ought*, in fact, the justification of the *is*? This is a view to which so great an ethical thinker as Aristotle inclines, but it can hardly be maintained. There are many spiritual environments of which the individual is sensible. Which provides the *ought?* It is possible that a man should feel in complete conformity to a certain environment and yet recognize that another is "better," that his *ought* lies elsewhere. Roughly we may say that the surest test of adaptation is "happiness," and it is by no means agreed that the desire of happiness actually provides the *ought*. Most hedonists would only say that it "ought to."

And of course the idea of *ought* arises just because the mind does not "justify" the whole. It is the expression of a disharmony within the spiritual development. If the mind justified the whole, the ethical attitude would be lost. The identification of the *is* and the *ought* therefore remains a contradiction.

The Idea of Necessity. Suppose we add to the conception of evolution that of necessity, and regard the world of history as governed by both those principles. Here at the first glance we do seem to have found a means of eliminating from the *is* the *ought not* and so of identifying what is with what ought to be (understanding *ought* as above explained, i.e., as relative to the whole particular situation). For if the process of evolution is necessary, there is no alternative realizable *better* such as *ought* implies; and, again, if we can discern even the smallest progress at the end of a necessary process, then each step is justified as the necessary means by which the purpose of an absolute good, i.e., the better, is realized. This in fact is a point of view which historians often, consciously or unconsciously, adopt.[4] Of course the principle, logically carried out, would forbid both justification and condemnation, since in the inevitable sequence of events the good follows the bad even as the bad the good, and under the aspect of necessity we must therefore condemn the better

4. As, for example, when they call Attila the "scourge of God."

because the worse succeeds and extol the worse because it precedes the better—necessarily!

A little analysis shows wherein the unsoundness of the position lies. We must distinguish two aspects of necessity:

1. In our application of the term "necessity" to nonrational nature, i.e., in science properly so-called we have no disharmony of *ought* and *is*, because we are out of the sphere of *ought*. Scientific law knows no *ought*, but only a *must*, and *ought* is a contradiction of *must*.[5] We are concerned here with the scientific "law," not the moral, and are in danger of confusing the two only because the term "law" is used in two so dissimilar senses. But, to take an immediate distinction, it is an essential characteristic of a scientific law that it is inviolable, a "necessary connection," while a moral is violable.

2. Therefore it would seem as if the scientist, in seeking to extend the sphere of scientific law, is *ipso facto* seeking to narrow that of moral law—and often he is himself under this impression. It is only when we remember the second aspect of necessity that the confusion here involved is revealed. For necessity as a relation within the spiritual world is conceived of quite differently from an outside necessity, of which we are merely cognizant as a relation among phenomena. The former is a necessity for us, but it is also *of* us, *our* necessity.

Which difference is here implied? It means that here we have *formally* the determination of the rest of the universe, *actually*, because the self is a purposive self-conscious self whose acts are attempts to attain an end so related to the self that it conceives their fulfillment as a self-realization, *actually*, they possess the quality of freedom. Freedom may be regarded in this sense as nothing more than spiritual necessity unembarrassed or at least unthwarted by necessity of another kind, i.e., able to control those physical means which somehow are requisite to its fulfillment. The nature of the self forbids the extension to it of inferences drawn from the world of physical or phenomenal necessity. The application of such inferences would be on a par with the conduct of a physicist who would object to the biologist that by the laws of matter, because gravitation pulls to a horizontal position, a man cannot stand upright! Further, the attempts which are made to identify the characteristic principles of these two necessities, to identify will power and physical force, have not succeeded. The materialist attempt to reduce will to energy or force obliterates the distinction just emphasized, while the oppo-

---

5. It is of course only subjectively that the *must* and the *ought* are contradictory. It remains true that being constituted as I am, I must conceive the *ought* in a certain way and must respond to its claim in a certain way. For the bearing of this fact, see the next paragraph.

site tendency which would reduce force or energy to will, simply assumes, without being able to establish any links of connection, that the unknown, the external or phenomenal, possesses the same nature as the known, the conscious principle of action.[6]

This realized, we see how the distinction of *ought* and *is* must remain for us at the very heart of self-conscious action. Consciousness is purposive and selective; outside the question of determination altogether (which is mainly an empty question) it remains true that to this selective consciousness before a decision is made there are *alternatives*, alternative ends, and that to consciousness after decision, there *were* alternatives.[7] Our world of action and thought rests on this consciousness of alternatives, without which purposive action is impossible; and in this consciousness there is rooted the distinction of *ought* and *is*, with the ultimate attributes of "good" and "bad." Because our intellect, even in its most speculative working, is still a "practical" intellect, it must always move within this sphere of alternatives; it can never blot out the distinction of *ought* and *is*. We may call it a subjective distinction if we please, but it is a necessary condition of our thought; it is "transcendental." The ethical distinction is thus grounded in the very nature of consciousness, and this is the limit of the ethical question. We have found that the doctrine of evolution and necessity, which might at first be supposed to remove the distinction, only posits a process itself resting upon it, upon that self-conscious action which starts from a recognition of alternatives, not indifferent to the self, but related as better and worse.

II

From the conclusion that under no categories of evolution and necessity can the *is* and the *ought* be identified, it follows at once that these principles can give no support to the doctrine of success or the "judgment of history." In a word, we can still retain our estimate of values, which such a doctrine, by making them all equal, would destroy. Success, the exis-

---

6. Cf., for example, Martineau, *Essays and Reviews*, pp. 156 ff., especially the argument by which he concludes, "It follows that will is the true type of the conception" (p. 158).

7. It might be said again—history looking backward sees the alternatives which were present to the consciousness of the actors, but does not regard them as alternatives. Of course there was no alternative in the sense that the actors could have chosen the opposite course, but the reason is that they were just what they were when the alternative motives presented themselves. An historian may retain the faith that above and beyond the imperfection of choice due to the nature and capacity of the choosing self there is an end of perfection working itself out. So a recent editor says of Ranke, "Er sucht Gott in der Geschichte."

tence, permanence, growth, which some historians (cf. Carlyle and Mommsen) think justifies itself, is therefore only justified when an attribute of a moral value; it is as a vessel or vehicle of good or bad, neutral in itself. But of these values a purely physical science cannot speak, for a purely physical science is a science of existence, not of value.

This may throw light on a question of more practical importance, viz., the relation of politics and ethics. These subjects are supposed to differ not only in range but also in point of view. In ethics, the stress is laid on the law of *ought*, in politics on the conditions of existence, on the actual forms realized in communities and the methods by which they are maintained. But in the former case, as already emphasized, the knowledge of the conditions and relations of the individual's existence is necessary for the application, even for the determination of this law, and in the latter case, while politics is concerned with the conditions of the existence, permanence, and growth of states, it really regards these, since it necessarily makes judgments and criticisms, as presuppositions of values; ultimately it is interested in them as the conditions of the existence, permanence, and growth of values.

Let us try to apply this conclusion more precisely, by looking at the history of the breach between these two studies, politics and ethics. We may say, that, in the history of political thought, the first important sign of severance is to be found in Aristotle's *Politics*,[8] and that as a fully developed separation it stands to view in the *Discourses* and *Prince* of Machiavelli, who left it as a legacy to the modern world. Aristotle in the *Politics* is led to the view that only in the best state is the good man identical with the good citizen. He did not, however, draw the logical conclusion that since every state is necessarily imperfect, the good man and the good citizen are never identical. It is to Machiavelli we must look for the clear enunciation of this principle, and because Machiavelli from the very imperfection of the state in which he lived[9] was forced to proclaim in the most emphatic manner the divorce of ethics and politics, it is to his writings we must turn to understand its full significance. Machiavelli wished to show the means by which a united state

---

8. διόπερ τὴν ἀρετὴν ἀναγκᾶιον εἶναι τοῦ πολίτου πρὸς τὴν πολιτείαν (*Politics*, III, 4. 3), an opinion previously but more tentatively expressed in the *Ethics*. Aristotle gradually abandoned the position of Plato in this regard.

9. Machiavelli was a practical man of an age fuller of imperfections than most, and of a political world more disordered than most. We have but to recall the names of its famous men, the popes Alexander VI and Julius II, the princes Cesare Borgia and the Medici, the emperor Maximilian, the king Louis XII, to see its character. Machiavelli fully understood his age—as secretary and envoy to the Ten of Florence he had met most of these ruling forces and understood the methods by which they gained and maintained their power.

could be maintained, and his observation told him that it was not by following the recognized principles of ethics,[10] but rather by violating these. Hence his famous advice to the prince—"You have to understand this, that a prince, especially a new one, cannot observe all these things for which men are esteemed, being often forced, in order to maintain the state to act contrary to fidelity, friendship, humanity and religion."

Clearly to Machiavelli the opposition seemed one between the *is* and the *ought*. He identifies the ethics which the prince must sometimes reject with the *ought*, not seeming to realize that the very unity of the state which he seeks so to maintain constitutes also for himself an *ought*, that he is really raising an opposition not between *is* and *ought*, but between two seemingly conflicting *oughts*. Once this is realized the question takes an altogether different form.

Before looking at the question in this form it is necessary to make it clear that this is the real opposition, as certain forms of statement obscure it. For instance, Lord Morley declares that Machiavelli "represents certain living forces in our actual world . . . because energy, force, will, violence still keep alive in the world their resistance to the control of justice and conscience, humanity and right. . . . He represents one side in that eternal struggle."[11] But such a statement obscures the true antithesis. In a state do we not actually enlist "force, energy, will, violence" on the side of justice and right? Further, do not moral forces actually evoke physical forces, as in the overthrow of Napoleon? It is not properly a question of force versus right. The conflict lies in the contradictory ends, moral and immoral, which these forces may serve.

Machiavelli thought he was raising a clear distinction between politics and morality. "Inasmuch," he says, "as it needs a good man to reorganize the political life of a city, and a bad man to become by violence lord of a republic, it is therefore very rarely found that a good man will desire to acquire rule by bad means, even for a good end, or that a bad one, having acquired rule, will act justly or think of using for good the authority he has won by evil." He is really raising a question within morality, a problem of *ought*. He implies in this passage that the end involved in the endeavor to preserve and unify the state is a moral end, but regards it as a moral end of which morality itself forbids the fulfillment. Can this paradox remain? Can a means be bad which is purely devoted to the attainment of a good end, when the whole purpose is the realization of the imperative good? The distinction of end and means

10. Machiavelli's contemporaries Guicciardini and Bernardo del Nero are equally emphatic. Cf. the words of the latter: "Whoever in these days wishes to maintain states and dominions should when possible act with mercy and goodness, but whenever this is not possible, with cruelty and remorselessness."

11. Romanes Lecture on Machiavelli.

is misleading. Strictly speaking, a means as means can be neither good nor bad, for since goodness or badness is an attribute of will alone, the means must be regarded as in some sense purposes or ends to deserve this attribution. But in so far as they are merely means, in so far as the sole reason why they are entertained is their relation to the end, in so far, in more technical language, as they enter into the intention of the agent without forming part of his motive, so far they cannot be judged as if they stood as ends in themselves but must be regarded in the light of *the* end. So the question comes to be: Is a certain end such as to justify —not a *moral* wrong, for, if justified, it cannot be such: there is neither here nor elsewhere question of the greater right set over against the lesser wrong, but—a certain loss of those "goods" which in one way or another (according to our conception of the moral end) morality secures? Does it justify the infliction of a certain amount of pain, unhappiness, death? Does it, in Kant's language, though Kant would not have admitted the problem, justify a certain interference with the "autonomy" of beings who are ends to themselves? And the general opinion[12] of history is with the statesman who has the strength and insight to save and unify the state even at a great price.

But the security, the stability of the state, is itself a moral end. The enlistment of force to secure this end is therefore a purely moral action. This Machiavelli did not see. He made the mistake of saying that right and wrong have nothing to do with government, forgetting that the very basis of moral life is the existence of organized society, and that therefore the first question of morality is the securing of that existence. Just as to live is regarded as a moral action (hence the condemnation of suicide) so that the state should live is a moral end.

Not only therefore can we never reduce the *ought* to the *is;* we can never get out of the sphere of *ought*, and the only problems that can arise are problems between conflicting ideals.

Once this is realized, the opposition between ethics and politics breaks down. In the history of ethics itself we have a record of various conflicting ideas which set theory in opposition to theory. *But there cannot be this kind of opposition between ethics and politics,* for whichever of these conflicting ideals a man or body of men adopts, that ideal, unless it is self-contradictory, will hold equally for the state and the individual. The ideal is self-contradictory if its adoption by one individual is a hindrance to its adoption by another, for it is so far disintegrative of that state, that society, in which and through which alone can the

12. This average opinion is, I think, largely hedonistic and justifies those inflictions because they are necessary to the avoidance of greater unhappiness or have ensured greater happiness afterwards.

individual realize that very ideal he proposes. Any true ideal must therefore hold for the whole society to which the individual belongs—all ideals, that is, are capable of becoming common.

Politics, we saw, is a practical science like ethics, it seeks the means by which a certain ideal can be realized. But it follows from what has been said that the common good which it seeks to realize must be just the ethical good looked at in its relation not to the individual alone but to the society which individuals compose. If we analyze the possible relations of individual and common good, they are: (1) Common and individual good may be opposed or may be identical in nature. (2) If they are identical, there may yet be opposition between the public and an individual *conception* of the good. (3) If they are identical, still the means by which the good is realizable respectively by a society acting as a whole and by the individual may be different and even contradictory.

It only remains to consider (2) and (3), for in the case of (1) it has been shown that the relation is one of identity. When it is seen that in the case of (1) there can be no opposition, the ground may be shifted to the maintenance of (3).[13] But, in the light of what has been already said regarding means and end, this position would mean a divorce of ethics and politics only if there were two, and not one, moral orders, or if there were a sphere of state-action outside the moral order. The former position is not put forward; the latter has frequently appeared in political theory, e.g., in Spinoza, who held that while within the state the civil condition and consequently the ethical order prevailed, without the state there existed the so-called condition of nature, a condition of hostility. In other words, the action of a state in relation to other states is not subject to ethical claims.

Ethical action is action in relation to ethical beings. If one state were wholly isolated from another state, we could call neither, in any sense, an ethical being, for to ethical action is primarily necessary a recognition of common interest, a common world. The early view regarded states as outside this common interest, and so drew the conclusion that their action in relation to one another was free from the claims of an ethical order. But in international relations the conception of common interest has grown steadily, and an identity of end—not perhaps an absolute identity, any more than we can postulate an absolute identity of end for two individuals, but an identity so far that all recognize themselves as bound in one common order in the maintenance of which their mutual welfare consists—is recognized almost universally. In fact

---

13. Cf., for example, Kirchmann (quoted in Acton's Introduction to *Il Principe*): "Es spricht nur für seine (i.e., Machiavelli's) tiefe Erkenntniss des Staatwesens dass er die Staatgewalt nicht den Regeln der Privatmoral unterwirft."

it seems impossible to escape the conclusion that if this order holds at all, i.e., if it conduces to the welfare of any plurality whatever of ethical beings, it is an order which holds universally for ethical beings—and for "ethical" here we may substitute "rational" (see conclusion to part I). In one aspect the history of civilization is the record of the progress of this recognition, at first narrowed to family or tribe, gradually extended after the seemingly "accidental" way in which history moves, to cities and to states and so inevitably—simply because it is an ethical relation —embracing the civilized world. In one sense this order is established by the recognition of it; in another, it is involved in the very constitution of men as thinking "practical" beings whose ends (we need not here assume more than a formal identity of end) are interdependent and realizable only under ethical conditions. It is curious that while the ethical end is (theoretically at least) involved in much dispute, the character of the ethical order is fundamentally agreed upon.

The remaining point (2) involves a lesser distinction. A discrepancy between the end to which a state commits itself and that which some individuals in the state may conceive to be the true end involves no breach between ethics and politics. At the same time, a discussion of this difficulty will perhaps throw light on the wider topic.

Let us turn once more to the conception of evolution. We have spoken hitherto as if ends were fixed or static, but now it must be remarked that an end is always a realization in a definite environment, that therefore even if it remain formally the same, even if we can express it in some concept such as "happiness" or "self-realization," it will nevertheless assume quite a different aspect and necessitate quite different means. Ends are therefore not fixed but relative.

As a society advances on its way, it must therefore move from one conception of the end to another. But the recognition of the broader, or the altered, end does not necessarily come as a revelation to a whole people or state at once. The way of change is from the smaller to the larger; the recognition moves from the individual to the society. It operates first at an individual point.

Hence the problem of the public as against the private conception may sometimes be a problem of transition. The problem does arise, and the above consideration disposes of the view (held, for instance, by Spinoza, with his static view of the state) that the individual's duty is to suppress his own conviction in favor of that held by the community in general. It would seem that there are cases where both the antagonistic views are right, where the state is justified in suppressing what seems a destructive doctrine, and where the individual, believing it to mean not destruction but a better reconstruction, cannot choose but maintain it. Was not the Athenian state as much justified in banishing Anaxagoras and in putting Socrates to death as the Roman in seeking to drive out foreign cults? All new gospels are not true. What is there in the end but experience to test their truth? So both the old and the new conception, the individual no less than the state-conception, must seek to maintain themselves. The old conception has always a justification, inasmuch as experience has already proved it; the new conception has always a claim, since experience cannot rest at any point. Progress—or change —in history means relativity in ethics.

But, further, we have still not fully expressed the character of relativity which underlies experience. Man, as we have insisted upon, works by the recognition of ends, i.e., of alternatives not equally desirable. But not only does the development of man's nature, and his unceasing activity, modify the character of those ends which he seeks to fulfill himself; apart from the modifications due to his conscious activity there is a ceaseless movement beyond it. Man recognizes ends, and seeks to fulfill them. But what is realized is not the fulfillment of these ends. It is something more, something other. Man neither creates those ends, those alternatives in which he thinks, nor yet fully realizes, in the infinite complexity of action and life, the value and the effect of his striving and his realization. He is no independent workman, with tools and materials by his side; he too is part of the work. He can dream no longer of attaining a fixed ποῦ στῆ whence he may survey a changeless world of essential Ideas, for whatever his ultimate faith may be, life and thought manifest themselves in action only as process, and process means relativity.

[Previously unpublished; written in 1908]

The Ethical Significance
of the Idea Theory

9

I

The Idea theory of Plato when it has not been reduced to a mere logical doctrine faultily expressed has generally been regarded as the strange aberration of a mind dominated by abstract notions. The value and the meaning of the theory has been greatly obscured in consequence. We generally approach the theory from the logical side, and forget that Plato was from first to last, from the *Laches* to the *Laws*, primarily an ethical thinker. To ethical thought a fact finds its explanation not in its relation to a system of efficient causes but in its relation to a culminating purpose. Plato's thought is fundamentally teleological: and if we approach it from the ethical point of view most of the difficulties vanish which are thought to beset it, and in particular the Idea theory reveals itself as the first really masterly attempt to solve the ultimate problem of philosophy. In this paper I shall attempt to show how a perception of the fundamentally ethical quality of Plato's thought explains the rise, the development, and the modification of his Idea theory.

Everyone must grant that a teleological explanation, when and if possible, is the fullest and ultimate explanation. The only causes we can really be said to know are the final causes of our own conscious activity. As soon as we pass from final to efficient causes our difficulties begin, for we have to ask—and cannot answer—how the final cause is itself the efficient cause of the first member in the chain of efficient causes to which it is prior. Because we thus fail to relate the two principles we can never outside the experience of our own activity deduce the presence of the final from the presence of the efficient cause. No "argument from design" can ever be more than probable, because design itself can never be demonstrated. Hence science whose nature it is to seek certitude will have nothing to do with teleology. It is right for science to reject it, but not to deny the ultimate value of such an explanation were it possible. Where it is possible, i.e., in the experience of our own activity, it is at once manifestly the fullest explanation. In fact, science to secure her partial explanation has to forego forever the full understanding of what she seeks to explain. A fact, and more particularly a process, is only truly known when its relation to a purpose is known, and even a denial of purpose, which equally with its affirmation is beyond science, becomes a form of explanation inasmuch as it is an answer to this necessary question.

It is just the necessary questions beyond the scope of science that philosophy considers, and certainly Plato believed that for knowledge the teleological explanation is ultimate. It is quite mistaken to regard him as a philosopher to whom the ethical is a secondary consideration, to whom, "ethics, politics, logic, physics are so many forms of applied metaphysics."[1] On the contrary, the metaphysical theories of his predecessors and the logical concepts he himself helped to develop are rather his instruments or means for the solution of the problem of speculative ethics, poor enough instruments at first for so gifted a mind, but becoming finer and finer in his hands, themselves gradually shaped in the progress of the work they are meant to accomplish.[2] Consider, e.g., how in the *Meno* the important logical distinction of knowledge and opinion arises out of the ethical question, and is introduced in order to solve it. There seems no reason to regard the ethical starting point in this and so many other dialogues as merely a literary introduction. If we take it for what it purports to be, many difficulties are avoided.

One further presupposition must be made. It is no longer possible to deny a development in Platonic theory from period to period, and therefore to understand it we must presume a certain order of the dialogues. The following chronological facts, which seem sufficiently established, will

---

1. R. D. Archer-Hind's *Introduction to the Phaedo*.
2. *Cf. Philebus*, 23 C, where in a dialogue that is essentially one of reconstruction Plato talks of "requiring weapons of another make from those he has used before, tho' some of the old ones will do."

be here assumed: (1) that the small "Socratic" dialogues are earliest; (2) that the *Symposium* is earlier than the *Phaedo* and that both are earlier than the *Republic;* (3) that the "dialectical" dialogues, *Theaetetus, Parmenides, Philebus, Sophist,* are later than the *Republic;* (4) that the *Timaeus* and *Laws* fall in the last period.

Two seemingly inconsistent tendencies are characteristic of deeply ethical natures. (1) They insist on a certain direction of one's being, toward the good and away from the evil that is in the world, an insistence on the goodness of the good which derives half its strength of appeal from the implied acknowledgment that evil too is a real thing. (2) Yet they tend ultimately to deny the very existence of evil, and to make the good not only the supreme *ought* but also the absolute *is*. Such a type of mind will at the end of an essentially teleological system come to deny teleology altogether. For purpose, the differentia of the ethical idea, in the necessity for its realization implies a present imperfection, and, more than imperfection, it implies duality. In religion similarly it would almost seem as if a man can hardly be in earnest about God unless he believe also in the devil. So the ethical system moving, as all systems strive to do, toward monism moves toward self-destruction.

Plato began by making the good *one*, this is the work of the early dialogues—and then he made it *all*. As a disciple of Socrates he followed the method of concepts, but as a fundamentally ethical thinker he transformed—where too he may simply have followed Socrates—a logical into an ethical ideal. In doing so he took into account only one side of that logical doctrine. It was a method of saving reality in a world where else it would seem that "all things leak like a pot" (*Crat.*, 440 C), and its importance to Plato was that it saved those things which mattered. Plato's first thought was to save the reality of the good, and for the present he was heedless that his method of concepts must preserve equally that of evil also. The ethical claim is primarily for the security of the good: while it must admit the present existence of evil, it denies its right to existence and postulates the possibility of its final annihilation. But the good must be eternal. "The good," said Epicharmus, "is a thing-in-itself."[3]

Plato therefore asked: "Tell me whether there is or is not any absolute beauty or good, or any other absolute existence?" (*Crat.*, 439 C). In putting the question in this form Plato is not thinking merely of the reality and stability assured by a system of concepts. The ethical universal is clearly to him something more than any other. It has an attractiveness

---

3. τό γα
ἀγαθόν τι πρᾶγμ' εἶμεν καθ' αὑθ': ὅστις δέ κα
εἰδῇ μαθὼν τῆν', ἀγαθὸς ἤδη γίνεται.

for and a claim[4] on the knower of it, making the relation between knower and known seem almost reciprocal, implying that they are indeed objects of knowledge, permanent realities answering to the permanence of mind, as distinct from the ever-changing and therefore unknowable objects of sense.

This is the starting point of the Idea theory of the *Symposium*. Here the good appears under its form of beauty, under the form, i.e., which reveals most clearly its quality of attractiveness, and to it there answers love, the generic name for all attraction. " 'There is nothing men love except the good, is there?' 'No, certainly,' I should say, 'there is nothing.' 'Then,' she said, 'it is the simple truth that men love the good' " (*Sym.*, 206 A). The important fact is that the good is loved for itself. We desire some things because they fall inside other purposes or schemes —they are rendered attractive because they fit in, a new item of knowledge, for example, that gives completeness to knowledge already possessed— but in contradistinction to these the beautiful or good has an immediate, even abrupt, attraction which gives it a sense of greater objectivity, and it is just this quality which made the Idea theory psychologically possible. No concepts can be simply "creations" of the mind, but ethical concepts least of all.

Once this foothole in reality has been found, logic comes to the aid of the ethical claim. There are logical grounds for regarding these concepts of beauty and goodness as fundamental. It might be said:

1. Other universals only cover a part of the nature of that thing to which they are applied. What is white is much else besides that bears no relation to whiteness. But "beautiful" and "good" (taking "beauty" [κάλλος] in that extended meaning it has in the *Symposium*, as applying to the internal as well as the external nature, so that we can speak of the beauty of holiness or of goodness itself) are concepts which determine the whole nature. So far as they do not it is because there is contradiction in that nature, i.e., because it has in it that opposite which is the only limitation of the good. An object may hold not-white attributes without any diminution of its whiteness, but can it hold not-good attributes without having its goodness thereby limited or modified? Just as beauty in its ordinary acceptation comprehends all the external character of an object, so the beauty that is called goodness, if the term is applicable to anything without limitation, must comprehend its whole nature.

And we can go further. Suppose we take any beautiful material thing, a statue or a picture, it might be held that a single particular of

---

4. The Greeks, more loyal to life than we, preferred to see in the good the attractive rather than the imperative, but both aspects of the ethical idea, its attractiveness and its bindingness, the good as eternal law and the good as eternal source of satisfaction, presuppose this quality of, so to speak, *felt* independence.

that thing, a single feature of the statue, a ray of light and shade in the picture, is potentially determinant of the whole, so far as that whole is adequate to the conception of beauty. (True, we cannot deduce the whole from the part, but then we have always in these matters to accept approximation and we recognize that our idea of beauty is imperfect no less than the object; as the artistic sense grows, more and more determinations would be ruled out as incongruous, thus suggesting the possibility of one unique perfection.) Given a starting point of sense, the single conception of beauty may determine what the unity of the whole should be, so that any beautiful object, in so far as that unity is realized in it, is simply a particular embodiment of the one beauty. Its beauty is individual, true, but this individuality can be regarded as simply the limit set on the universal beauty when it is forced to submit to empiric laws; it may be the necessary particular way in which beauty appears under certain conditions of sense. And just as the beauty in all parts of any object is one, so is the beauty of all objects one.

This conception underlies the account in the *Symposium* of the soul's progress toward Beauty, as it moves up from particulars to the Idea. It is really a progress in knowledge, in the knowing of what we are all the time seeking. We desire the thing, the phenomenon, because it is an embodiment of beauty; if we only knew, therefore, it is the beauty manifested through it, the Idea of beauty, that we really desire. We seek without knowledge, not knowing even what it is we seek. This knowledge is the revelation of the Idea, and the nature therein revealed is "beauty absolute, separate, simple, and everlasting, without diminution and without increase, or any change, in which participate the ever-growing and perishing beauties of all other things."[5] Such a nature is not "in the likeness of a face or hands or any other part of the bodily frame, or in any form of speech or knowledge, or existing in any other being, as for example, in an animal, or in heaven or in earth or in any other place." This assertion of the ὑπερουσιότης ("transcendent," to use a scholastic expression) of the good is very important. The essential, primary, Idea is to Plato ὑπερούσιον, above substance, the maker of realities, the disposer of substance. This is no mere hyperbole. Plato's Idea in the *Symposium* is beyond what we mean by substance, and the difficulties of the Idea only begin when Ideas cease to be ὑπερούσια.[6]

2. We know things partly under concepts which cover—or mean— part of their nature, wholly under those which cover the whole. In fact

5. Here for the sake of accuracy I modify Jowett's translation, which I use for the various quotations from Plato.

6. Lutoslawski and Shorey maintain that the superiority of the good to substance, i.e., material substance, cannot be taken literally, whereas in fact this superiority is not only quite intelligible but is necessary for the Platonic scheme; the concept of good

we can only be said to know a thing in so far as it is comprehended under one concept. But the good appears as the all-comprehensive concept, and therefore the knowledge of the good is the completest knowledge of reality.

In the *Phaedo* this point of view has considerably developed. The question raised by Socrates, "Must not true existence be revealed to the soul in thought, if at all?" (*Phaedo*, 65 C) is immediately particularized in the form, "Is there or is there not an absolute justice . . . and an absolute beauty and absolute good?" This identification of the good with the true was to carry Plato very far. The ethical motive which at first merely guided in the *direction* of the good, other ways being possible for the soul, now leads step by step to the denial of any reality but that object of study.

At the close of the *Symposium* two ways of development remained open. (1) Plato might have retained the one all-comprehensive Idea. Just as he had found the unity of the virtues in knowledge, so he might have found the unity of knowledge in the good. He might have limited the doctrine to the single Idea of the good, including thereunder whatever can be regarded as giving an absolute value to things, their beauty or desirableness. (2) He might extend the doctrine to include other Ideas than that of the good. Such an extension would weaken the original teleological character of the system, but on the other hand the logical argument for the Idea of good, the argument from universals, held equally for other Ideas. One further type of concepts in particular fascinated Plato, those of mathematical science. Not only did these illustrate excellently the higher perfection of thought-object over sense-object (as Plato had already shown in the *Meno*), a doctrine essential to the Idea theory, but there was also a very important precedent in the number philosophy of the Pythagoreans.

Plato therefore was led to extend the sphere of Ideas, and in the *Phaedo* another class of Ideas besides the ethical, viz., the mathematical, make their appearance. It is true that the Ideas of beauty and goodness are still those most insisted upon; when the question is one as to the nature of reality they remain in the foreground (*cf.* 77 A: "For there is nothing which to my mind is so patent as that beauty, goodness, and the other notions of which you were just now speaking, have a most real and absolute existence"), but those other Ideas begin to claim a place in reality also (*cf.* 78 D), though the difficulties they bring with them

---

is prior to every other, including that of substance; logically substance is prior to attribute, but ethically the comprehensive attribute of good is prior to substance. (We must remember also that Ideas of attributes are no less self-existent than Ideas of substances.) The great source of confusion in the Idea theory is that it does not distinguish logical from ethical presuppositions.

have not yet appeared. The Idea of the good is still the principle of explanation, and thus though no longer alone is exalted above all other Ideas.

This is clearly expressed in the famous autobiographical passage of the *Phaedo* (97 C *sqq.*), a passage of very great importance for the interpretation of Plato. Unfortunately, this passage itself requires interpretation, more than one view of its meaning being possible. The interpretations generally offered seem to me either logically inconsistent or linguistically unsound, and this must be my excuse for dwelling on this section at some length.

Socrates has been relating his ineffectual attempts to master natural science, the problems of physics and physiology. He declares the subject fascinated and yet bewildered him. All this talk of hot and cold principles controlling growth and decay drove out of his head other and self-evident facts, e.g., that growth is in man the result of certain (consciously performed) actions, viz., eating and drinking. His bewilderment led him to conclude that he had no natural capacity for this study, and indeed leaving natural science out of the question he found in the most ordinary facts of perception much to perplex him.

"Then I heard some one reading, as he said, from a book of Anaxagoras, that mind was the disposer and cause of all, and I was delighted at this notion, which appeared quite admirable, and I said to myself: If mind is the disposer, mind will dispose all for the best, and put each particular in the best place; and I argued that if any one desired to find out the cause of the generation or destruction or existence of anything, he must find what state of being or doing or suffering was best for that thing, and therefore a man had only to consider the best for himself and others, and then he would also know the worse, since the same science comprehended both. And I rejoiced to think that I had found in Anaxagoras a teacher of the causes of existence such as I desired, and I imagined that he would tell me first whether the earth is flat or round; and whichever was true, he would proceed to explain the cause and the necessity of this being so, and then he would teach me the nature of the best, and show that this was best; and if he said that the earth was in the center, he would further explain that this position was for the best, and I should be satisfied with the explanation given, and not want any other sort of cause" (97 C-E).

Of this hope he was sadly disappointed on examining the system of Anaxagoras. That philosopher forsook mind altogether, and instead of explaining the reason that is in things if mind has ordered and disposed them, he had "recourse to air, and ether, and water, and other eccentricities." Anaxagoras like the rest failed to distinguish cause (τὸ αἴτιον τῷ ὄντι) from condition (ἐκεῖνο ἄνευ οὗ τὸ αἴτιον οὐκ ἄν ποτ' εἴη αἴτιον). "And thus one man makes a vortex all round, and steadies the earth by the heaven; another gives the air as a support to the earth, which is a sort of broad trough. Any power which in arranging them as they are arranges them for the best never enters into their minds; and instead of finding any superior strength in it, they rather expect to discover another Atlas of the world who is stronger and more everlasting and more containing than the good; of the obligatory and containing power of the good they think nothing; and yet this is the principle which I would fain learn if any one would teach me" (99 B).

Socrates himself has also failed in this pursuit, and has had to follow a second-best method (τὸν δεύτερον πλοῦν). This is explained in the following passage: ἔδοξε τοίνυν μοι μετὰ ταῦτα, ἐπειδὴ ἀπείρηκα τὰ ὄντα σκοπῶν, δεῖν εὐλαβηθῆναι, μὴ πάθοιμι, ὅπερ οἱ τὸν ἥλιον ἐκλείποντα θεωροῦντες καὶ σκοπούμενοι διαφθείρονται γάρ που ἔνιοι τὰ ὄμματα, ἐὰν μὴ ἐν ὕδατι ἢ τινι τοιούτῳ σκοπῶνται τὴν εἰκόνα αὐτοῦ. τοιοῦτόν τι καὶ ἐγὼ διενοήθην, καὶ. ἔδεισα, μὴ παντάπασι τὴν ψυχὴν τυφλωθείην βλέπων πρὸς τὰ πράγματα τοῖς ὄμμασι καὶ ἑκάστῃ τῶν αἰσθήσεων ἐπιχειρῶν ἅπτεσθαι αὐτῶν. ἔδοξε δή μοι χρῆναι εἰς τοὺς λόγους καταφυγόντα ἐν ἐκείνοις σκοπεῖν τῶν ὄντων τὴν ἀλήθειαν. ἴσως μὲν οὖν ᾧ εἰκάζω τρόπον τινὰ οὐκ ἔοικεν. οὐ γὰρ πάνυ συγχωρῶ τὸν ἐν τοῖς λόγοις σκοπούμενον τὰ ὄντα ἐν εἰκόσι μᾶλλον σκοπεῖν ἢ τὸν ἐν τοῖς ἔργοις. ἀλλ' οὖν δὴ ταύτῃ γε ὥρμησα, καὶ ὑποθέμενος ἑκάστοτε λόγον, ὃν ἂν κρίνω ἐρρωμενέστατον εἶναι, ἃ μὲν ἂν μοι δοκῇ τούτῳ. συμφωνεῖν, τίθημι ὡς ἀληθῆ ὄντα, καὶ περὶ αἰτίας καὶ περὶ τῶν ἄλλων ἁπάντων τῶν ὄντων, ἃ δ' ἂν μή, ὡς οὐκ ἀληθῆ. [7] He goes on to explain that the method is the familiar way of Ideas, postulating the existence of an essential beauty and goodness and greatness and so on (ὑποθέμενος εἶναί τι καλὸν αὐτὸ καθ' αὑτό). These are the only causes he pretends to understand. "I know nothing and can understand nothing of any other of those wise causes which are alleged; and if a person says to me that the bloom of colour, or form, or any such thing is a source of beauty, I leave all that, which is only confusing to me, and simply and singly, and perhaps foolishly, hold and am assured in my own mind that nothing

---

7. "It seemed to me that having failed to behold the realities I ought to watch out lest I suffer what happens to those who look at the sun in the process of an eclipse unless they look only at its image in the water or otherwise reflected. So it was with me, I feared I would lose the soul's vision if I looked to the reality with my eyes or sought it with any of the senses. It seemed to me necessary to resort to the concepts, the mental images, in order to seek the truth of the realities. The simile may not be perfect—I by no means agree that he who sees the realities in their thought-forms sees them more indirectly than he who sees them in their workings. Well, this was the way I set about it—I postulated the concept or principle that seemed to be most fitting, and concluded that whatever agreed with this was true and what disagreed was untrue."

makes a thing beautiful but the presence and participation of beauty in whatever way or manner obtained; for as to the manner I am uncertain, but I stoutly contend that by beauty all beautiful things become beautiful" (100 D).

Of this very interesting account the following interpretations have been offered:

1. The knowledge Socrates abandons as too hard for him is the knowledge of natural science, the investigation of physical causes, from looking at which Socrates turned to study the "inner world of thought," making thought a sort of mirror of reality.

But it is totally unlike Plato to give the objects of physical science any reality at all, much more to make them superior in reality to the objects apprehended by thought (concepts as distinguished from percepts), to λόγοι (concepts). Would Plato for a moment have regarded the knowledge of final causes (revealed by the method of Ideas) as "second-best"? Would he have thought the modifying clause (οὐ γὰρ πάνυ συγχωρῶ, κ.τ.λ. —"I by no means agree") a sufficient criticism of a view that was a denial of his whole philosophy? Besides, Socrates has been explaining that the principle he has failed to attain to was the principle of the sustaining power of the good (99 C), and that both the first and the second methods lead to the knowledge of this the final cause (τὸν δεύτερον πλοῦν ἐπὶ τὴν τῆς αἰτίας ζήτησιν —"the second voyage in the quest of cause"). But natural science with its "airs and ethers and waters," recks nothing of final causes.

These objections have led to another interpretation which has at least the merit of not attributing to Plato a doctrine subversive of all his principles.

2. The method Socrates abandons as beyond his reach is the direct study of the eternal Ideas. He is driven to investigate the ultimate reality not in itself but in thought-images, in universals or concepts "which shall represent the Ideas to him."

This view has the support of Mr. Archer-Hind and Professor H. Jackson, the former of whom argues as follows—"The passage, as I read it, has the following significance. I attempted, says Socrates, to discover τὸ ἀγαθὸν (the good) as the ultimate cause working in nature. But when, after long endeavour, I failed in the struggle I began to fear that by fixing my gaze too intently on realities I might be blinded in soul, as men are bereft of their bodily vision by gazing on the sun. So I bethought me of framing in my own mind images or concepts of those realities which I desired to study, and in them safely to examine the nature of their types. But though I admit these concepts are but images of the realities, mind I don't allow they are so in any greater degree than material phenomena: both in fact are images; but whereas phenomena are the images presented to us by our senses, concepts are the images deliberately formed by our understanding; concepts therefore are more real than phenomena in proportion as understanding is more sure than sense" (*Phaedo*, App. ii., p. 189).

This interpretation has no support in either the language or the logic of the passage.

A. (1) There is nothing in the Greek to suggest the distinction of "universal" (λόγος) and Idea, and there are several expressions which imply their identity; *cf.* particularly 100 A, ὑποθέμενος ἑκαστότε λόγον ("postulating everywhere the universal form"), with 100 B, ὑποθέμενος εἶναί τι καλὸν αὐτὸ καθ' αὑτό ("postulating beauty itself as such"),[8] where λόγος (concept) and εἶδος (form, or "idea") seem equivalent, just as we have οὐσίαν τε καὶ λόγον in *Phaedrus* 245 E.

(2) The interpretation gives a very forced sense to straightforward expressions. Surely ἐπειδὴ ἀπείρηκα τὰ ὄντα σκοπῶν ("when I failed to see the realities") must refer to what has just preceded, the history of Socrates' experiment in the study of nature, and the words μὴ παντάπασι τὴν ψυχὴν τυφλωθείην βλέπων πρὸς τὰ πράγματα τοῖς ὄμμασι καὶ ἑκάστῃ τῶν αἰσθήσεων ἐπιχειρῶν ἅπτεσθαι αὐτῶν ("lest I should wholly blind my soul looking at the realities directly with my eyes or seeking to apprehend them with my senses"—99 E) lose all their meaning unless they refer to sense-objects grasped in sense-perception. The argument that τυφλωθείην here cannot apply to the obscurer objects of sense is absurd. The word was used in just the same meaning a few pages back (96 C). The rapid and ceaseless process of phenomena as they appear to the philosopher's eye might be compared with the effect of a dazzling light, though Socrates himself is unwilling to press the analogy. Further, it is so difficult to fit into the view under consideration the words that follow, that both Mr. Archer-Hind and Professor Jackson are inclined to resort to the desperate theory of interpolation. But their case demands a far more rigorous excision.

B. The logical difficulties are no less serious. (1) If Plato had made this distinction of "universal" and Idea he would have cut himself off from all knowledge of reality, though he has in this same dialogue already expressed confidence in his power to grasp it. The theory of ἀνάμνησις (recollection) might indeed suggest the distinction of concepts or the "reminiscences" of Ideas from the Ideas themselves, but such a distinction would have been self-destructive, for being forever cut off from knowledge of the Ideas we are forever incapable of knowing that the concepts are like or "represent" the Ideas. The tentative and tem-

---

8. Since writing the above, I notice that this argument has been employed already by Mr. R. P. Hardie in *Mind*, N.S., V, 171.

porary theory of ἀνάμνησις must not be pressed to this conclusion, for Plato here in the dialogue which introduces that theory states very clearly his belief in the soul's direct knowledge of reality, her "communion with the unchanging" (79 D), her "pure apprehension of pure existence" (83 A).

(2) The interpretation fails entirely to account for the discussion of physical or efficient causes and to relate that investigation to the course Socrates represents himself as now pursuing, and it fails to show how one or the other method of study is connected with the ultimate principle, "the necessary and containing power of the good."

The whole difficulty arises from a failure to recognize that in fact the teleological explanation was for Plato the ultimate principle of *all* knowledge. Why did the philosophy of Anaxagoras cause so profound a sense of disappointment in the mind of Socrates? "And I thought that I would then go on and ask him about the sun and moon and stars, and that he would explain to me their comparative swiftness, and their returnings and various states, active and passive, and how all of them were for the best" (98 A). Natural science is no knowledge at all unless it seeks to answer this last question. *His* natural science, the study he perforce abandoned, sought to answer this question. It was to be something more than the science of the physicists who mistake the presuppositions of knowledge for knowledge itself. The science that constituted his first method was not physical science at all, as ordinarily understood. Physical science investigates physical law, but law reveals reason and reason seeks an end. Therefore we postulate an end behind the law, and because science or the knowledge of law is not necessarily the knowledge of the end which it implies, it can never by itself satisfy such an inquirer as Socrates or be regarded by him as knowledge at all. He himself tried to find the knowledge which consists in the relation of the facts of science to the principle of the good, but found the task too hard. He could not rest content with the efficient causes, but when he tried to go beyond them, the multiplicity of the phenomenal world bewildered him. It was as if one should attempt, say, from the movements of the chisel to explain the beauty of a statue or, to take his own instance, from the various coordinations of muscle and bone to explain the presence of Socrates in the State prison of Athens. Or perhaps we may compare it to the attempt to read the design of a tapestry from the crossing and interweaving of the threads, a method more difficult and more minute and conceivably impossible. It may happen we are looking on the wrong side of the cloth, that which does not reveal the design. In rational conduct this design, the only possible design, is the good. "When we walk we walk for the sake of the good and under the idea that it is better to walk, and when we stand we stand equally for the sake of the good" (*Gorg.*, 468 A). In the phenomena of experience this design is too hard to unravel. We give up the attempt, in this world of constant becoming, to understand how behind it there lies the "binding power of the good." Yet since the world is essentially rational (this view is fundamental for Plato's earlier thought, that the forces of the world without us are actuated by the same power that lives and moves in us) such a connection must remain a "hypothesis."[9]

This then is the method that Socrates abandons for his alternative way. Instead of seeking the goodness of the phenomenal and changing,[10] we may turn our attention to the permanent revealed in and through this constant process, the universal that abides, which is in truth all that is known or knowable in the world of becoming. If we can relate these permanent elements to the principle of the good, can see these to be reasonable, we shall have explained everything in the phenomenal as well—except the fact of its phenomenality. The abiding is the real; if we can explain the abiding, or the universal, we shall have accomplished even more than was possible by the first method, we shall have shown the goodness or the reason of the permanent in its permanence, instead of in its transient manifestation—we shall have understood reality.

(It was only at a later stage that Plato saw how little it availed to call some obstructing element "unreal," and indeed the later realization of this truth had much to do, as will appear presently, with the modification of the theory.)

So far as the ultimate principle is concerned, Plato might have left the universals outside the rank of the Idea, but this the logical method rendered impossible. That method gave the same kind of reality to all universals. What Plato therefore has to do is to show the relation of these inferior Ideas to the archetypal Idea, and this begins to appear, though obscurely, in the *Phaedo*. Everything is what it is by participation in some λόγος; the great, the small, the equal share in greatness, smallness, equality—they are what they are in virtue of the form or proportion they exhibit. So far then they are explained by reference to what is more real than themselves. But these reals are not reals in their own

---

9. We may note that in the *Timaeus* Plato does make the attempt, though only on "probable" grounds, to construct the natural science here abandoned as too hard, a science, *i.e.*, which relates laws to ends.

10. Note that Plato says τὸν ἐν τοῖς ἔργοις (σκοπούμενον τὰ ὄντα) — "he who looks at the realities in their operations") (100A), not τὸν τὰ ἔργα σκοπούμενον ("he who looks at the realities themselves"). The ὄντα are the phenomena known in their reality, *i.e.*, in their relation to the good (for Plato holds with Parmenides, ταὐτὸν δ' ἐστι νοεῖν καὶ οὕνεκεν ἐστι νόημα—"the concept is the same as that of which it is the conception"), the ἔργα the inadequately known objects of physical science. How else can the opposition be accounted for?

right, and therefore not a sufficient explanation (*cf.* ἄλλην αὖ ὑπόθεσιν ὑποθέμενος, ἥτις τῶν ἄνωθεν βελτίστη φαίνοιτο, ἕως ἐπί τι ἱκανὸν ἔλθοις —laying down another principle that whatever appears most beautiful only partakes of beauty itself—*Phaedo*, 101 D). A thing is great because it shares in greatness, we must say, but only when we know that it is good to share in greatness, i.e., that greatness shares in goodness, have we the true explanation. Just as phenomena reflect the Ideas, so do the lower Ideas reflect the good. The system begins to appear as a hierarchy. The only way up from these lower Ideas is by the recognition of their participation in the good, just as the only way from the world of sense is by the recognition of its participation in the Ideas. The two methods of the *Phaedo* are now clear; the one would go straight from phenomena to the archetypal Idea, the other uses the lower Ideas as media. This is the explanation of the ascent by hypotheses suggested in the *Phaedo* (101 D) and more explicitly described in the *Republic* (511 C).

Already in the *Republic* the difficulty caused by the introduction of the second class of Ideas has forced itself on Plato's attention. In the *Republic* he virtually says that these both are and are not Ideas; he admits in fact that only the self-explanatory is Idea, only that in which the light of its own purpose is manifest. Hence the division of the world of νοητά into two sections, of which the higher consists simply of the true or ethical Ideas. (Plato distinguishes these latter Ideas as the good, the beautiful, and the true, but it is obvious that the lower members of that hierarchy are there at all because of their ethical significance, their immediate attractiveness or "value".) The lower section is only potentially or "hypothetically" Ideal, the "hypothesis" being not the existence of these objects, but their goodness,[11] that they are best and for the best. When

---

11. Professor Jackson, in an otherwise instructive article in the *Journal of Philology* X, 144, misses this important point. He says: "His meaning must be that the geometer starts from such propositions as, 'There may be such a thing as length without breadth, henceforward called a line,' but does not show, or even attempt to show, that there is such a thing. If he could prove that there is such a thing, this which is now a ὑπόθεσις (an assumption), *i.e.*, an ἀρχή ἀναπόδεικτος (a principle of interpretation), would become an ἀρχή proper (a principle in itself)." But in the first place the geometer never does make such a proposition—he is not concerned with any other existence of lines and circles than that existence which they have for his thought, and his study is not in the least affected by the denial of straight lines "in nature." In the second place, no philosophy proves or tries to prove these "hypotheses," and Plato least of all would suggest that the mathematician may be making a mistake by investigating thought-realities for whose objective existence he has no warrant. How can they be placed in the region of νοητά (concepts) at all unless already they are recognized as belonging to the real? What is yet unconfirmed is their relation to the supreme reality. Because the world is rational—this being the fundamental hypothesis—they *must* be related to the good, but so far this is taken on trust. The hypothesis is simply the act of faith which the full vision of goodness will render needless.

they are seen in the light of the good, when they reflect the good, they become objects for the pure intelligence (καίτοι νοητῶν ὄντων μετὰ ἀρχῆς, 511 D). We destroy their hypothetical character.[12]

Within the world of Ideas there is now an essential cleavage manifest, in fact there is a certain inconsistency in making these mathematical concepts Ideas at all, for if the objects of sense "reflect" the various Ideas and yet are not, when seen in this light, made objects of pure intelligence, why should τὰ μαθηματικά become such intelligibles when they reflect the good? If these are to be Ideas we want a new name altogether for the highest class of existences. It may have been a perception of this difficulty that led Plato at some time to give the mathematical concepts a place midway between Ideas and phenomena.

But in the *Republic* this inconsistency has not yet broken up the Ideal system. In Books vi and vii Plato definitely attempts to read the universe in the light of the Idea, and the scattered hints of the *Cratylus*, *Symposium*, *Phaedo* and perhaps *Phaedrus*[13] are now developed into a coherent system. It may be well to look at this unification before considering how the unreconciled elements rendered the unity only apparent, and led Plato, who showed here an energy of self-criticism unparalleled in the history of philosophy, to a deep and progressive process of modification and reconstruction.

The world is fundamentally rational. The real is the abiding, and the abiding is the knowable, therefore the real is the knowable. The reason that is in us is the reason that is in the world. Reality has two aspects, the known and the knower, and these correspond in every relation—as is the kind of object so is the kind of knowing. "All nature is akin and the soul has learnt all things," Plato had already said in the *Meno* (81 C), and now he shows how truth and understanding are begotten of the contact of the pure intelligence with the pure Idea (*Rep.*, 490 B). So again to the desire of mind there corresponds the desirableness of the object of mind. The philosopher is not simply the knower of knowledge, but also the lover of it because knowledge is lovable; and the universe is representable as a scale of existences corresponding to the various faculties of knowing. There is no attempt so far to give priority

12.   *Cf.* 533 C, οὐκοῦν ἡ διαλεκτικὴ μέθοδος μόνη ταύτῃ πορεύεται, τὰς ὑποθέσεις ("This dialectic alone proceeds directly to the first principle, doing away with hypotheses"), when their goodness is manifested or their relation to the good. The mathematician does not ask the value of the square and circle, he keeps within the bounds of his spatial systems; but if "God always geometrises," it is not for the sake of geometry. As the phenomenon is an image of the Idea, so is the lower Idea, the mathematical object, an image of the highest—when seen in its goodness (*cf. Rep.*, 517 B *sqq.*).

13.   Certainly the argument of the *Phaedrus* suggests a fairly early date, though stylometric evidence seems to place it not earlier than the *Republic*.

to either aspect, mind or existence. The Ideas are eternal, and so is mind
that knows the Ideas.[14]

It is noteworthy that the description Plato here gives of the Ideas
is truest—and indeed profoundly true—of the ethical Ideas. The pe-
culiarity of these has already been dwelt upon; being able to serve as
ends or purposes they are something more than mere concepts, and all
the characteristics which Plato ascribes to his Ideas are *in some sense*
applicable to these. They are powers, being final causes. In a rational
world—the world as now conceived by Plato—there can finally be no
distinction between *ought* and *is*, the possible of realization and the
realized, and so also whatever *becomes* possible is *ipso facto* made actual.[15]
We may compare how even Aristotle who so constantly attacked the
dynamical deficiency of Plato's theory made the conclusion of his practical syllogism not the recognition of some particular end as to be done,
but the doing itself.[16] Further they are exemplars to be realized in action,

14.   Zeller and other critics argue in favor of making the Idea of the good identical with Deity. This view does not fit into the construction outlined above. The Ideas
are powers but not intelligences; they are even akin to intelligence inasmuch as mind
can only know what is of its own nature, but they are essentially the correlates of mind
in an eternal correspondence. The difficulties of the position we may well believe led
Plato to postulate an original creative mind (of which there are hints already in the
Republic), just as a further difficulty to be considered later led him at last to postulate
two world-spirits—but by that time the Idea theory had undergone much modification.
The Idea theory demands this correspondence throughout, so that at the summit of
the scale of existences there would be the good as perfectly known (*i.e.*, the good as it
fully is) and the perfectly pure intelligence that knows it, *i.e.*, God. This is the logical
relation of the Deity and the Idea of the good, as is implied in *Parm.*, 134 D, "and if
there be such a thing as participation in absolute knowledge, no one is more likely than
God to have this most exact knowledge." The development of the view that creative
intelligence is prior to created existence is part of the process of reconstruction (*cf.*
Philebus, 22 C). In the present view mind is not regarded as originally creative nor yet
are the Ideas powers in themselves. It is out of the correspondence of mind and Idea
that creation is created. If so, Zeller's question (*Plato and the Older Academy*, Eng. ed.,
p. 267n.), "Is the Divinity actually a second cause together with the Idea, or merely
another expression for the causality of the Idea?" presents no dilemma at all. Plato,
who had to face as had never been done before the question of the relation of knower
and known, of the subject and object of thought, did not begin with but only ended
in dualism.

15.   *Cf.* Kant, *Kritik der Urtheilskraft*, "Eine intelligibele Welt in welcher alles
darum wirklich sein würde, bloss nur weil es (als etwas Gutes) möglich ist" (A world
of intelligibility, in which everything would be actual simply because it is possible,
as something good).

16.   *Cf. De Motu Animalium*, 701 *a* 9 *sqq.* "Whereas in the theoretical syllogism
the end is inference, the apprehension of the two premises being the apprehension and
putting together of the conclusion, in the practical syllogism the conclusion that arises
from the two premises is action. Thus when a man apprehends that every man should
walk and that he himself is a man, an act of walking immediately follows." Of course

"fore-pictures" of something to be produced (as Fichte said), thought-schemes to which a phenomenal counterpart, a concrete action, can somehow correspond. They are prior and "above substance," in so far as in a rational world the goodness of a thing is the very ground of its existence. They are purer, more perfect than their realizations in action, for "what act is all its thought had been"? What exemplar is not better than its copy? In all conscious production it might be held that the idea or form being manifested is better than the manifestation, that the expression is never adequate to the thought that is expressed.[17] Finally they all lead up logically to one supreme end presupposed in every mediate end and making them all coherent, an end which so far as the world is rational is the ultimate explanation of all things. So much perhaps we may say without entering on the controversial ground of metaphysic at all, though the elements of controversy are not far off.

But the further we pass from the ethical Ideas the greater do the difficulties grow, the more alien are the elements introduced into the system. This becomes manifest in the last book of the *Republic* itself, where now the logical principle is openly asserted—"whenever a number of individuals have a common name, we assume them to have also a corresponding Idea" (*Rep.*, 596 A), and accordingly the instance of a bed is chosen, and the analogy drawn, picture of a bed: a bed:: a bed: Idea bed—an analogy not possible in the case of the ethical or even of the mathematical notions. We seem to have now introduced a third class of Ideas, with which our difficulties grow exceedingly. In fact in such a case the Idea can be nothing except the form or shape of the object given by analogy, a kind of self-subsistence, and the famous "third man" argument (attributed to the sophist Polyxenus but really only a development of an objection suggested by Plato here [597 C]) depends entirely on the conception of Ideas as shapes or forms. This objection, like many another, is quite inapplicable to the earlier conception, to the "colourless and *shapeless* and intangible essence" that originally the term Idea signified (ἡ ἀχρώματός τε καὶ ἀσχημάτιστος καὶ ἀναφὴς οὐσία ὄντως οὖσα, *Phaedr.*, 247 C).

In fact to understand the Idea system as a coherent whole, to understand the scheme of *Rep.*, vi and vii, we must remember that it is based

the ethical concept cannot unless particularized, cannot as a pure Idea of the good, become an end, and does not necessarily become one even then, and if it does become an end, its realization does not necessarily follow. What is said above of ethical Ideas must be understood with this reservation.

17.   It is true that Goethe speaks of his work as containing more than he knew, and Kant declares that we can sometimes better understand an author in his words or writings than he understood himself, but that does not touch the question of the relation of the end as conceived to the end as realized. It is, to say the least, logically impossible that the realization (or expression) should be *more* than adequate.

on and leads up to the primary Idea of the good. This Idea is ultimate, ultimate for knowledge and for reality. If so, it must be admitted as a fundamental "hypothesis" that whatever we know is what it is because that is for the best and that whatever becomes becomes for the best, in short, that every efficient cause is for the sake of a fully rational final cause. But here the inconsistency of a metaphysic at once absolute and teleological reveals itself (though it is perhaps less obvious in a system which makes the ideal a good to be attained rather than a law to be observed). Plato realized the difficulty, and after various attempts to save the situation by calling "unreal" whatever was neither absolute nor "for the best," by making the objects of opinion, the world of multiplicity and error, a strange union of "real" and "unreal," "tossing about in some region which is halfway between pure being and pure not-being," chose to be greater than his system, to reveal rather than obscure its difficulties. The main difficulty was the obvious problem of all ethical or religious monism; if the world is rational, whence the "unreal," and whence error: if good, whence evil? If the real is the abiding, is not becoming itself an abiding principle? Thus the two problems, the problem of change, in general of movement, the problem of evil, in general of imperfection, are unsolved, nay insoluble, on the Idea system as now conceived. It was to the fuller consideration of these that Plato now turned.

Hitherto he had somewhat neglected one side of reality. His characterization had been of the known rather than of the knower, of the Idea rather than of the soul for which it is. But now that the difficulties just mentioned became prominent, he was led to consider more especially this other side.

For the real evil is the evil in the soul (*Rep.*, 353 E *sqq.*), and as for movement, surely it must be explained by the self-moving, the soul which is the beginning of motion (*Phaedr.*, 245 D). What if after all the τόπος νοητός be νοῦς itself?

II

We have seen how Plato, taking his stand on the principle that philosophy —being explanation, an answer to the question "Why?"—is the search for final cause, ultimately for *the* final cause, was led to his Idea of the Good. For the Good is the objective existence of the final cause, and Plato must therefore find all reality within it. We have seen further how the method he adopted was in itself logical or scientific, the search for the One in the Many, involving the faith that the question "Why?" is ultimately answerable, and that to know the real is also to know the Good.

His earlier thought was thus dominated by the attempt to coordinate the results of the logical method with the intuitions of an ethical mind.

The result is the Platonic system as developed in the *Phaedo* and the *Republic*. Here a seemingly complete system (only seemingly, for the two constituents of the Idea world, mathematical objects and ethical universals, remain distinctly heterogeneous) is attained by means of such a coordination, whose ultimate expression is the Idea of Good. This system, in a word, identifying the real and the abiding and the rational, identifies therefore the real and the Good. It follows that the phenomenal, the sensible, and the evil are classed together as unreal. By this short method the universal supremacy of the final cause, the all-comprehending reality of the Idea or nature of Good, is established.

It seems pretty clear that we can call the system so constructed "Megarian," for it is essentially based on the doctrine that Oneness and Goodness, the world regarded as scientific system and the world as the manifestation of purpose, are identical, this in turn being a consistent development of the original Socratic doctrine that virtue was knowledge. Plato, as we have insisted, was interested not so much in inventing a metaphysical system as in "explaining" the world by means of such a system. To this end he adopted freely all the conceptions of his predecessors and contemporaries which seemed to him fruitful, all that he could find suitable for his purpose in the Pythagoreans, Heraclitus, Parmenides, Socrates, and even Euclides. And he certainly did not invent his "way of Ideas." It is necessary to recognize this fact in order to understand the unity of Platonic thought under the changes of its development. The thought of Plato is both relative to his time—we can no more understand it apart from the thought of his age than we can, say, understand Mr. Schiller (so far as we do understand him) without knowing the position of Mr. Bradley—and also transcends it. The conceptions he is working with are those of his time, but throughout there is the Platonic spirit, in its richness and earnestness, informing and translating those conceptions.

We may go on therefore to divide for our purpose the later dialogues into two classes, (1) dialogues of criticism, the *Theaetetus* and the *Parmenides*, (2) dialogues of reconstruction, the *Sophist*, *Statesman*, *Philebus*, *Timaeus*, and possibly the *Laws*. The criticism is esentially criticism of the Megarian position. Both the *Theaetetus* and the *Parmenides* are definitely associated with Megarian thought. The conversation reported in the *Theaetetus* is supposed to be a record made by Euclides himself and is read at Megara in the house of Euclides. The *Parmenides* again, one of the most remarkable works of criticism ever written, is clearly an examination of the Megarian or Neo-Eleatic "One"—though in calling the doctrine criticized in that dialogue "Megarian" we must

not forget that it is also the doctrine which made the construction of
the *Republic* possible.

1. Again, it must be maintained that the primary end of these
dialogues, as of the earlier, is ethical. Schaarschmidt was essentially
right in making the presence of ethical purpose a test of authenticity for
the Platonic writings, but instead therefore of doubting the more "dialectical" dialogues he should have found under the dialectic the living
thought of Plato. Even in so "dialectical" a piece of work as the *Parmenides*
there is present, not obscurely nor as a doubtful inference, but clearly
expressed, the acknowledgment of an ethical end. The exercise is undertaken because without it we cannot "define the beautiful, the just,
the good, and the Ideas generally" (135 C). The *Theaetetus* also, seemingly
the most sceptical of all the dialogues, can be understood only in the
light of its ethical purpose. What, we must ask, is the common bond
of the three theories that Socrates masses together in such a seemingly
arbitrary way, the theories of the Flux, of Man as Measure, and of Knowledge as Sensation? Simply their common ethical consequence. And
the "turning-point of the whole dialogue," as Campbell[18] saw, depends
on the conception of the good. Because Protagoras must not count
goodness at least in the number of merely relative things, he is driven
to divorce goodness and truth. "Those thoughts which the inexperienced
call true, I maintain to be only better, and not truer than others" (*Theaet.*,
167 B). Therein consists his true antagonism to Plato and to Plato's
ideal. Behind all Plato's thought there is an unassailable belief in the
relation between knowledge and good, and in the *Theaetetus* the good
is sought for under its aspect of the true. But that dialogue only reveals
a difficulty in the account hitherto given of that relationship. If
Protagoras is wrong, is the contrary of Protagorean doctrines right?
Is sense-perception nothing? Does it offer *no* reality? Must we not say
"we know what we see and hear" (163 C), the letters we see as much
as the meaning we understand, must we not admit that perceptual
knowledge is not knowledge only because it is not all knowledge (*cf.* 206)?
It is not adequately realized that what endangers the absolute distinction
between knowledge and opinion and the system resting thereon is the
new importance which Plato is here forced to give to the world of sense.
The *Theaetetus*, analyzing the subjective as the *Parmenides* analyzes the
objective side of the correspondence, makes a searching and unsuccessful
attempt to find a mark of distinction between the faculties of opinion
and knowledge, to find a difference of kind that will distinguish right
opinion from the knowledge it was supposed merely to imitate. Does

18.   Introduction to his edition of the *Theaetetus*, p. xxxvi.

not the very phrase "right opinion" involve the inference that here too in opinion there is knowledge itself? "Right opinion implies the perception of differences" (209 D). And would not the Socrates of the *Republic* have shared the disappointment of the Socrates of the *Theaetetus* at the breakdown of the attempted distinction between the two, and the consequent breakdown of "the most promising of all the definitions of knowledge" (209 E)? Just as perception itself is now seen (186 D) to involve a thought-element (not recognized, *Rep.*, 523), so must opinion itself involve knowledge. The absolute identifications and distinctions of the *Republic*, the consequences of that first daring identification of the Good and the One, are in process of modification.[19]

As a result, the problem of error and above all the problem of evil take a new form and offer a new difficulty. Their reality, which was cancelled with the reality of the sense world, can no longer be denied. The problem of falsehood becomes insistent, and the solution is no longer ready to hand—the only positive suggestion is that the responsibility lies with the mind, no longer with the object (*cf.* 188 *sqq.*). The problem of evil is also affected. If evil is real, evil too is object of knowledge. The roads of Science and Ethics no longer coincide. To know is no longer simply to know the good, but rather to know good and evil as they are, for what they are. Philosophy becomes the "investigation of very Justice *and* Injustice,[20] in their own nature, and in their difference from one another and from all other things" (175 C). For "two patterns stand in the world, the divine pattern that is most blessed, and the godless that is most wretched" (παραδειγμάτων ἐν τῷ ὄντι ἑστώτων, τοῦ μὲν θείου εὐδαιμονεστάτου, τοῦ δὲ ἀθέου ἀθλιωτάτου, 176 E). The evil pattern is no longer appearance; the terms employed imply both fixity (ἑστώτων) and reality (ἐν τῷ ὄντι), and Socrates expressly declares that this evil can never pass away from our "mortal nature." It is no longer simply "phenomenal" and accidental, but real with the reality of the rest of the universe. Because there is a real nature of evil in the world, there is a real nature of evil in the soul, if the correspondence of object and subject is to hold. For desire requires affinity, and the desire of evil is the desire of an evil soul. So the unity of the world is breaking into dualism at its very heart.

The *Parmenides*[21] analyzes the objective side of the primary identi-

---

19. Thus τὸ δοξαστόν can no longer be identified with τὸ αἰσθητόν. The doctrine of relativity, as applied to δόξα (matters of opinion), is subversive; as applied to αἴσθησις (matters of perception), it may even be true.

20. We do hear of an Idea of injustice in the *Republic* (*cf.*, *e.g.*, 476 A), but the admission has no effect upon the system.

21. I must here acknowledge my indebtedness to Professor A. E. Taylor's penetrating analysis of the *Parmenides* in *Mind*, N.S., Nos. 19-21, though my interpretation, as summarized above, differs in some respects from his.

fication of the Good and the One and the Real and the Knowable. Plato had seemed with his fellow-disciple Euclides to make Unity the extensive and Good the intensive aspects of the same single reality. There was thus a gulf fixed between the multiplicity that must belong to the sense-world and the unity that belongs to the world of thought, and phenomena were a shaky bridge between the two, a bridge of which one end was securely fixed in the abiding reality while the other passed over to nothingness. It is this aspect of the Idea doctrine that Parmenides attacks. He insists that, so understood, the multiplicity of the sense-world can never be related to the unity of the thought-world. There is no way of connection between the two, no bridge at all. Yet the sense-world exists, for we perceive it, and the Idea-world exists, for "whither will you turn if the Ideas are unknown"? Parmenides' own method of criticism, no less than the failure of Socrates to answer him, shows the need for the succeeding analysis. For if Socrates has overlooked one side of the relation, Parmenides has overlooked the other. Parmenides' own historical theory involves the same confusion. "All is One" might mean simply that the universe is a unity, but the arguments of Parmenides and more particularly of Zeno are not relevant to such a unity but just to what Plato would call the Idea of One, the nature Oneness. This Idea or thought-nature Parmenides nevertheless treats as if it were a sense-nature, and he proceeds to refute multiplicity on that assumption. In the present dialogue he is represented as attacking the theory of Ideas on the same assumption. Because the Idea, in its relation to particulars, is like neither a sail that covers a number of men at once nor a day that is one and the same at once in many places, the Idea stands condemned. But the reason why this attack is not regarded by Plato (though it seemed to satisfy his opponents) as fatal is that he sees the weakness of Parmenides' own position. His own argument can be turned round against himself. It implies the existence in some wise of those very Ideas he is assailing. "The dualism of the Ideal and the Sensible" tells against Parmenides as much as against Socrates, against the opponents of Plato as much as against Plato himself.

The way out is therefore not to be found in giving up Ideas, but in showing how these thought-natures interpenetrate to the uttermost recesses of sense, to "things like hair and mud and dirt and anything else that is most paltry and of no account" (*Parm.*, 130). Plato must show that the despised sense-world is through and through ideal. This is the logical conclusion of the whole argument, hitherto unrealized, hitherto obscured by the predominant interest of the ethical Ideas. Plato must now face all the problems of the new situation, with its essential difficulty that it seems to make evil no less than good a constituent of reality. So he undertakes that "roundabout progress through all things" (ταύτης τῆς διὰ πάντων διεξόδου τε καὶ πλάνης, 136 E), of which the *Parmenides* is an essential part.

The immediate problem is just the question of the nature of unity and its relation to the nature of multiplicity. That the One is found in the Many is no doubt the basis of the whole system and indeed of every system, but we have by no means disposed of the Many when we have found its One. For the Many are not isolated particulars, or otherwise they could never guide us to the One. Their diversity no less than their unity must be real for thought. Multiplicity cannot belong to the sense-world alone, nor unity to the thought-world alone. We may see ultimately that instead of being divided off into two alien worlds they are so closely interrelated as to be only two sides of the same thought-nature, and Oneness itself just one characteristic, one element or fact in the constitution of that universe which there is for thought to apprehend.

Consider, says Plato, the consequences that must follow if we admit or deny the existence *in the Idea-world*,[22] i.e., as objects for thought, of the One and the Many. Let us try to admit one without the other, and consider the consequences for both. Let us consider if it is logically possible to break up existence into two opposed worlds, if it is not logically necessary to remove that opposition. The whole of the intricate analysis which follows (137-166) is devoted to this problem, and the solution, though not expressly stated, is, I think, clear. As however I cannot enter here into details of analysis, I must state my account of that solution rather dogmatically.

When Plato and Euclides[23] identified the One with the Good and

22.   I take τἆλλα (other things) to be the other Ideas — the whole discussion is relative to the Idea-world (*cf.* 135 E) — and not the particulars of sense. We may, if we like, speak of τἆλλα as the Idea of diversity, having in view the relativity presently to be discovered in the Idea-world. Plato is facing the problem of Unity and Multiplicity at the only place where it really presents a problem. So again I take the One here to be not directly *the* Idea, but a particularly significant Idea for the present purpose; the Idea or nature of Oneness. The real problem is no longer, I believe, "how the one Idea could spread itself out, so to speak, over a plurality of particulars" (Professor Taylor in *Mind*, VI, 38). Once a plurality of Ideas has been admitted, is not that question subordinate to and dependent on the question how the idea of Oneness is related to the other Ideas? Once plurality of Ideas is admitted, the particular is no longer the particular of one Idea, related simply as the many instances are to the one type, or the many species to the one genus. Rather the particular *in so far as it is understood* is known as a manifestation of a certain union of Ideas or essential natures. And the only problem here arising, the problem discussed in the *Philebus* and the *Timaeus*, must concern the medium or process of manifestation.

23.   It may be objected that Plato never expresses the extreme doctrine of Euclides, that in the *Republic*, e.g. he admits degrees of reality. But the degrees are due to the mixing of the real with the μὴ ὄν (not-being) which in the *Republic* is simply nothingness. The *Republic* and the *Timaeus* form an interesting contrast in this respect.

with the All, they necessarily left all multiplicity outside of the world as it is truly apprehended in thought. The difficulties of so extreme a cleavage were beginning to appear in the *Republic;* we are now to see that it leads to the very annihilation of thought. Suppose, runs the first hypothesis of the *Parmenides*, that the nature of Oneness is all, suppose that, as Parmenides seemed to hold, there is nothing in the universe but the form or nature of Oneness, then even that nature cannot exist. To apply any possible attribute to it would be to attribute the multiplicity which *ex hypothesi* is absent, so that finally we must deny its own existence. "If the One is, it is nothing." Suppose, on the other hand, you assert —this is the second hypothesis—not that the whole is identical with the nature Oneness, but, what was really meant in that false assertion, that it partakes in Oneness, or that the One is real. From this starting-point we can arrive at the positive principle that multiplicity is involved essentially in unity, and that the nature of Oneness, if it exists, cannot exist alone. The barrenness as well as the richness of each single Idea is here revealed. That Idea alone tells us nothing of the reality of the world: we can deduce from it only its proper scheme of relations, the system of numbers (144), and that whole scheme at once implies and is meaningless apart from the other Ideas (τἆλλα τοῦ ἑνός). Not only is unity restored on this hypothesis, but so is the whole world of the other essential natures. And the conclusion is that Oneness—and likewise any other Idea that may in any aspect claim to be the unity of the world—both must exist and cannot exist alone, but only in diversity. So "it has both name and expression, and it is named and expressed, and everything of this kind that appertains to the other appertains also to the One" (155 E). The same conclusion is confirmed by the remaining hypotheses, which look either to the presence of the Many or to the absence of the One. It may seem a thin and abstract result, the fit conclusion of a rarefied dialectic. In reality, it is Plato's way of asserting, in the infancy of logic, a growing conviction of deep importance. Presently we find him asserting the reality of "not-being" (162 A). This is no sophism, but a discovery which shook the whole system of ethics he had built. If the One dethroned from its place of unique reality, what of the Good that is identified with the One?

It is very important for the understanding of Plato to recognize his growing insistence of the "being of not-being," in other words, on the relativity and therefore interdependence of the Ideas. A recognition of this fact must in especial remove a false conception of the "substantiality" of the Ideas. Down to the present day, critics have, like his own *dramatis persona* Parmenides and like his disciple Aristotle, looked upon Plato's Ideas as if they were some kind of *material* substances, or rather have imported into them just that part of the conception of material substance which our knowledge of matter itself least justifies.[24] In reality the argument can be turned against these critics just as it is turned here against the Eleatic. Plato, unlike Aristotle, is far from regarding arguments like that of the "third man" as fatal, and rightly so, because such arguments only apply to the metaphors, necessarily physical and therefore misleading, by means of which he had described the Ideas. The question is not whether, but how, the objects of our thought exist. If we do not admit their reality, then "what shall we do about philosophy?" But if mind and being are so related that being is what mind knows and mind is what knows being—a position Plato never gave up and which perhaps no philosophy can without contradiction give up—then the "what" of concepts,[25] being essential knowledge, must constitute essential being. In knowing them we know that they are more than a state of knowing, that either knowledge itself is vain and illusive, or these Ideas are the constituents of reality. It was no alternative to urge, as Aristotle[26] did, "immanence" against "transcendence." It is no solution to say that the Idea is immanent, for it is ultimately a question of what we are to understand by immanence. Thus to call sense-attributes, white, hot, etc., immanent might seem an explanation of the common attribution, because here the metaphor, *for it is nothing more*, being physical is more easily applicable to the physical object; but what of the common attributes of nonphysical objects; still more, what of attributes common to physical and nonphysical, such as unity itself, where the metaphor of immanence ceases even to look like an explanation? Yet the attribute is not "in our heads." How shall we understand it as applying to, as forming part of, the constitution of the world? This was the deeply metaphysical question which Plato raised and which so few of his critics have understood.

---

24.   Even so sympathetic a writer as Gomperz speaks of Plato's "peculiar proneness to objectifying concepts." Unless objectifying means materializing, why should that constitute a difficulty?

25.   *Cf.* Bonitz, *Plat. Stud.*, 194: "Unter Ideenlehre verstehe ich die für die Platonische Philosophie charakteristische Lehre, dass das Was des logischen Begriffes als solches selbständige Realität hat" (Under the doctrine of ideas I understand the doctrine characteristic of the Platonic philosophy, that the "what" [content] of the logical concept as such has substantive reality).

26.   Aristotle is really engaged on a subordinate question. Plato's problem is not simply the problem of predication, Aristotle's is. When, for instance, Aristotle in the *Categories* distinguishes ἐν ὑποκειμένῳ from καθ᾽ ὑποκειμένου he does not touch the question at issue here. Plato discusses the logical question in the *Sophist*, and in the main solves it, by a system of categories, but he does not rest there.

It may not be going too far to agree with critics like Zeller and Natorp that the great disciple did not understand the great master, even in matters where his discipleship is to us most plain.

By his insistence in the *Parmenides* and later dialogues on the relativity or interdependence of the Ideas, Plato has already taken the first step toward an explanation of how the Ideas exist.[27] The ideas must now extend themselves into an infinite system, and the shores of the unknowable recede to the ἄπειρον (unlimited) itself. In the process, since it appears that their interrelationship is itself a part of their reality, and they tend to become simply aspects or lines of a universal nature or constitution of things, the Ideas lose something of their rigidity and definiteness in the unity of that scheme. But the interrelation and interpenetration of the Ideas in no sense, unless we think in crude metaphors, takes away from their real nature as constituents of the universe. They are no less real than they were, but their reality is understood in a new way. They are not independent, but interdependent.

A new unity has thus been found for the Idea-world—and this is the significant point for our argument. In seeking the unity that would satisfy the philosopher Plato has found only the unity that would satisfy the scientist. It is becoming more and more clear that only one part of the initial philosophic faith can be fulfilled. If the One is good yet Goodness is no longer the reverse side of Unity, and the binding power of the Ideas must be found in their coherence as system, not as purpose. There exists no longer the clear confidence that everything can be "explained," or seen in the light of the good, for the light of the good no longer penetrates all reality. To the necessary extension of reality which the *Parmenides* has revealed, of the two aspects of the primary Idea, its oneness and its goodness, only the former continues adequate. Hence there begins the divorce of those two natures. A third mysterious nature thrusts itself between them. The *Parmenides* thus reveals a breaking Idealism, but assuredly not because Plato is losing his belief in Ideas.

2. In the *Theaetetus* and the *Parmenides* the argument is ostensibly critical, and we now turn to the dialogues which render explicit the result of that criticism in a series of attempts to reconstruct the system whose insufficiency stood revealed. "Not being," that phantom whose phantom-nature was so convenient for the philosopher of the *Republic*, has turned out to be only too substantial. Its true character as now revealed fits but ill into an absolute teleology. It brings with it endless perplexities (*cf. Soph.*, 245 E). If "not-being" is real, sense and multiplicity and error

---

27.   They exist as a system or constitution of reality. It at once appears that the opposition of immanence and transcendence must be false. For instance, if the nature of whiteness only exists in white objects, yet it is neither distributed among nor summed up in that aggregate. Though all the particular white objects should pass away there is left a universe in which the nature of whiteness is or was possible, having been actual. That this relation entered into the scheme of relations in which we know the objective world remains an essential fact in regard to that world.

and evil demand their place in reality. "We shall find as the result of all, that the nature of being is quite as difficult to apprehend as that of not-being" (*Soph.*, 246 A). Plato like his philosophers of the *Republic* must descend from the contemplation of the sunlit universals, from his constant "converse with the Idea of being" (*cf. Soph.*, 254 A), down to the darkness of the underworld, for there too among the shadows being is, though more difficult to discern. He must try to read "the long and far from easy syllables of facts" (*Stat.*, 278 D). Plato in fact is now coming to grapple with the essential difficulties of a teleological system, and abandoning the all-comprehensive and therefore self-contradictory teleology of the *Republic* is led to the view that there is in the world something not fully subordinated or obedient to the designing thought. Reality is both more and less than it had formerly appeared. The essential natures are still essential, but they cannot exist apart from motion and change and sense "in awful unmeaningness an everlasting fixture" (*Soph.*, 249 A). The universe has become more complex for Plato than either the materialist or the idealist admits it to be. The philosopher, with all his reverence for the Ideas, cannot possibly accept them as sole reality, apart from the changing world. "As children say entreatingly 'give us both,' so he will include both the movable and immovable in his definition of being and all" (*Soph.*, 249 D). For it is manifest that our life itself is steeped in this anomalous phenomenal nature, which is no longer an alien element out of which it can be lifted entire and so made pure. Therefore our knowledge defeats itself in its search for purity. The passage in the *Philebus* where Socrates—forgetting the principles of the *Phaedo*—admits, "like a doorkeeper who is pushed and overborne by the mob," the claims of every kind of knowledge, might well stand as a prelude to the reconstituted system.

"*Soc.* Let us suppose a man who understands justice, and has reason as well as understanding about the true nature of this and of all other things.

"*Pro.* We will suppose such a man.

"*Soc.* Will he have enough of knowledge if he is acquainted only with the divine circle and sphere, and knows nothing of our human spheres and circles, but uses only divine circles and measures in the building of a house?

"*Pro.* The knowledge which is only superhuman, Socrates, is ridiculous in man.

"*Soc.* What do you mean? Do you mean that you are to throw into the cup and mingle the impure and uncertain art which uses the false measure and the false circle?

"*Pro.* Yes, we must, if any of us is ever to find his way home" (*Phil.*, 62 A).

In the companion dialogues of the *Sophist* and the *Statesman* the master Socrates significantly becomes the disciple. It is now the "Eleatic stranger," himself by no means a bigoted Eleatic, who enters into the fray "between Giants and Gods," between the out-and-out materialists and the "pure" Idealists, the "friends of Ideas," and proposes a ground of reconciliation. Let us admit, he says in effect, the existence of both the material and the immaterial reality, and let me suggest that the nature which the two must hold in common is indicated by the term "power." "My notion would be that anything which possesses any sort of power to affect another, or to be affected by another, if only for a single moment, however trifling the cause and however slight the effect, has real existence; and I hold that the definition of being is simply power" (*Soph.*, 247 E). And the notion is tentatively accepted.

This does not at all mean, as I understand it, that the Ideas now become powers of "living forces," as Bonitz and Zeller interpret this passage. The Idea was never perhaps in Plato's thought meant to include the whole of being (we saw there was no Idea of soul) but rather to explain it. Now the center of explanation is moving, as was inevitable in an ethical thinker, from object to subject, from νοητόν (mental) to νοῦς (mind). "Under being we must include both motion and that which is moved" (*Soph.*, 249 B), in other words, both the Idea and that living force, that designing thought which cannot suffer the Idea to be a passive motionless existence. There are now therefore two kinds of power recognized, one clearly and one darkly, corresponding respectively to final and efficient cause, one consisting in the relation of mind and Idea, design and the designing thought, which form a single reality; the other in a reality which seems to lie outside the correspondence of mind and object, and is accordingly mysterious. Yet this outside mysterious nature affects both sides of that correspondence. (1) The final cause operates only in the world of efficient causes. Being is no longer static nor motionless, but in process. Being has "mind and life and soul," and so "becoming must be attributed to being"[28] (249 A). The activity of mind, therefore, in relation to the Idea cannot consist in "the pure contemplation of pure existence." From the very beginning the purpose that first appeared illuminating the Idea but now is revealed as being only reflected there implied a heavier task. The ordering power of reason implied a world to be ordered. Plato has therefore to insist on the formative power of thought, the moving cause that corresponds to the process of the world. The stress shifts from

---

28. Plato does not say that either mind or the forms come to be: "the most divine things of all remain unchanged" (*Stat.*, 269 C). What then becoming is, *which involves both*, is a question that he has presently to face.

the form to the forming mind, from good as object or form of creation to good as will or creative power. The importance of the thought-subject, at first obscured in the discovery—for to Plato it was nothing less—of the thought-object, is now insisted on. In the *Sophist* it is stated that the belief that God is the Creator of things must *in course of time* come to be held by every philosophical mind (265 D), and in all the later dialogues the superior if not supreme mind-power is insisted upon.[29] This conclusion was implicit all along in the teleological scheme. (2) The thought-object also is involved in a new complexity. Were there only mind and the Ideas, all might be well, for the Ideas essentially correspond to the designing mind. If they cease to be by themselves powers or purposes, they remain the counterpart of purpose as designs. But the correspondence, owing to this pervading third nature, is unhappily imperfect. The ordering power of reason implies imperfection in the world to be ordered. Reason works through means that are far from being its obedient instruments, through efficient causes that only imperfectly minister to design, and yet are somehow necessary to its existence. So the conception of necessity appears as the complement of the conception of power —an inevitable concession made to the claim of the "Giants." For the admission of necessity is a denial of the Idealist position, inasmuch as it gives some degree of independence to "efficient causes," and therefore to some nature that is neither the designing mind nor the character of design. Where there is necessity the efficient cause is incompletely controlled by the final cause—perplexing conclusion which Plato is now driven to express in the form of myth. In the *Statesman* God is represented as for a time rolling the world on its course, but "there is a time, on the completion of a certain cycle, when he lets go, and the world being a living creature, and having originally received intelligence from its author and creator, turns about and by an inherent necessity revolves in the opposite direction" (269). The efficient cause is not for ever subservient to the final, and Plato's intensely ethical mind finds here a mystery opaque to thought. The whole problem now centers round the relation of efficient and final causes, and the question the *Phaedo* had professed to solve is reopened in the *Philebus* and *Timaeus*.

In the *Philebus* and the *Timaeus* Plato faces the essential difficulties, now revealed, of a teleological system. Plato finds the road of explanation no easy one: rather "the storm gathers over us and we are at our wits' end" (*Phil.*, 29 B). The increasing activity of differentiation and the in-

---

29. *Cf.*, besides the passage referred to, *Stat.*, 269 C, 270 A; *Phil.*, 27 B; *Tim.*, 29 E and *passim; Laws*, 892 *sqq.*, 962. With these passages we may contrast *Rep.*, 516 C; *Phaedo*, 99 C.

creasing catholicity which we have been tracing in his thought set
great difficulties in the way. When the tools are finer the task is the more
hard. Plato cannot now, like the "wise people of the day," his Megarian
friends, pass immediately and casually from the One to the Unlimited.
He has realized the infinite stages that intervene. (*Phil.*, 16 A-17 A.)
And therefore again he cannot like the same wise men abstract reason
and knowledge from the world they illumine and find the good in a light
that shines only in the void. "The life of mind" in turn proves insufficient. "I want to know," asks Socrates, "whether any one of us would
consent to live, having wisdom and mind and knowledge and memory
of all things, but having no sense of pleasure or pain, and wholly unaffected by these and the like feelings?" (*Phil.*, 21 E.) The good must
be sought somewhere and somehow in the "mixed life." The nature
of the universe, like the nature of man, is a mixture. The good for man
is still found in the good of the universe. The harmony of the universe,
"the seasons and all the delights of life," and "ten thousand other things
such as beauty and health and strength, and the many beauties and high
perfections of the soul" (26 A), arise from the union of the Unlimited
with the principle of law and order. And because this harmony is good,
above it all there must exist as cause the creative power of mind, which
is king of heaven and earth, and ordains laws and appoints measures
for the nameless fluidity of the ἄπειρον.

In the *Philebus* the two determinant elements of the Idea of the
Republic are at last clearly distinguished. The form becomes the πέρας
(limit), but the power is transferred outside the form to the αἰτία (cause).
(If so the laborious attempts of German scholars to identify the earlier
Idea with one or other of the classes of the *Philebus* are beside the point.
One would think, to read the various solutions offered, that Plato had
here set a "Puzzle—Find the Ideas" to his commentators.) We may
note also that this distinction enables us to relate the Idea doctrine of the
Philebus to the Idea as criticized by Aristotle, in which the formal aspect
alone remains. The Ideas stripped of their character as powers are becoming
more and more just abstract principles of proportion or numbers. In
a sense this transference of value removes the principles of the good
from the Idea world while it explains the relation of good and proportion.
For even if the good is always realized in proportion, it is not identical
therewith, because the goodness of mathematical ratios does not rest
on considerations falling within the mathematical sphere, on mere
considerations of simplicity and numerical perfection. (Plato had seemed
to say originally that God "geometrised" for the sake of geometry.)
The proportion that is good is the good proportion. As proportion its
goodness is mediate or reflected, and mind finds the "why" not in the
ratio or number as such, but in the reason beyond the ratio—a reason

which we can simply call goodness[30]—which brought the proportion into being; not in the equation which gives the curve but in the beauty or service which is the goodness of the curve. (It follows, though Plato does not insist on the fact, that for the fulfillment of the world not only proportion and number but also the anomalous third nature is necessary, and thus good and evil, in the world, we know appear as curiously related as Socrates pronounced pleasure and pain to be.) The εἶδος (idea, form) is therefore only secondary for the ethical mind;[31] it is the moving principle that is the object of search. Hence the comparative neglect of the Idea in the later dialogues. If Plato's interest had been, as generally represented, logical or metaphysical, the later works, after the demarcation of the formal principle in the *Philebus*, would have constituted a neo-Pythagorean metaphysic such as his one-sided disciples pursued, instead of works on ethics and politics. To find the Good still in the Form is to misunderstand the development. The center of ethical struggle must be the soul, and ethical explanation must be sought there. It begins to appear that it is the mind which is the seat at least of some desires (*Phil.*, 47 E), that it is the mind round which ethical struggle centers, and that it is from the mind, not from "forms of ignorance," that there arises error, which all along has been baffling our construction. It may seem an objection that in the list of goods mind has only third place, but (1) it is obviously (*cf.* 28 and 22 E) the human intelligence in so far as it only apprehends and does not create measure which Plato classes as third; (2) the standard of all measure is mind, though not human mind: ὁ δὴ θεὸς ἡμῖν πάντων χρημάτων μέτρον ἂν εἴη μάλιστα (God above all would be for us the measure of all things).

Hence the starting-point of the *Timaeus*. In the *Timaeus* Plato seeks once more to "explain" the universe as it is in the broadened and differentiated conception to which he has now attained. His object now as ever being to find first the good in the universe, that then he may bring it down to man (so the doctrine of the *Critias* was to have completed that of the *Timaeus*), he must start no longer with the Idea, but with mind, and explain the object-world as it answers to the creative purpose, the fulfillment, so far as there can be explanation, of the design of God. But the form of the *Timaeus* is significant, for Plato can no longer pretend to justify the world in reasoned discourse, after the short and easy method of the *Republic*. Parts of the explanation must necessarily be dark.

---

30. The underlying thought is here quite consistent with the doctrine of the *Republic*, but has to find a different form of expression.

31. *Cf. Laws*, 875, where law and order are represented as second-best; also *Stat.*, 294, where the idea is applied to the government of the State.

Mind, the designing rational thought, is according to the *Timaeus* not supreme nor alone. Apart from the "patterns" — whose relation to mind is no difficulty for Plato, nor indeed does there seem to be here any problem that could profitably be discussed[32]—there exists the third nature that is outside the *Republic*. In the *Phaedo* Socrates had denied that efficient causes are causes at all; they are simply "conditions" that seem to offer no resistance to the final cause for which they are conditions. In the *Timaeus* efficient causes are still not fully causes (αἴτια) but they are contributory (ξυναίτια). Efficient or secondary causes are ἐξ ἀνάγκης πεφυκότα (begotten of necessity) to God as well as to men (68 E), the necessary means and sometimes the obstacle, in that sphere in which man must live and which God has tried to make most fair, to the realization of the divine. Having reality they have therefore power, and having power they must share too in life, in "soul," though not in mind. Thus the world-soul, as Zeller points out, "represents primarily the efficient forces in the universe," and is perhaps the last expression Plato gave to his refusal to accept as an ultimate explanation of anything the formula of mechanical causation. So, strangely enough, all the elements of the Platonic universe, body and soul of the created world, the lesser Gods and the God himself, are now endowed with life—except the forms. These are still maintained, are still necessary. If indeed the final cause is prior to the efficient the form must exist before realization in the world. But the self-sufficiency of the Idea is no more.

Lastly, in the *Laws* the same conclusion is borne out, though the reasoning is looser. In the *Laws* Plato again definitely states the problem of materialism and idealism in terms of efficient and final causes, identifying with materialism (891 C) the doctrine of the self-sufficiency of efficient causes. But his position is not really idealistic, but dualistic, and that in a rather confused way. Although the argument ψυχὴ ἀρχὴ κινήσεως (soul is the source of motion) is brought forward, and all motion is referred to soul, the self-moving, and with motion all that was hitherto associated with becoming, even evil (896 *sqq.*), yet that is not properly the earlier contention that the final is always prior to the efficient cause. Soul in Plato is not mind (*cf.* 892 and 962), nor should the movement of "soul" be necessarily the working of intelligence. Because in the *Laws* the

---

32.   The contention of certain ancient Platonists and modern critics that the forms in the *Timaeus* are "only" "the thoughts of God," while meant to reduce one side of the eternal correspondence, seems to involve an essential misunderstanding of Platonism. It seems to regard "thoughts" as somehow only subjective, a perfectly meaningless hypothesis from the Platonic point of view. The forms are doubtless the thoughts of God, but they are also the forms which God thinks. So for Plato "the pattern exists from eternity" (38 C).

place of intelligence is contracted (*cf.* 728 A) and "soul" and "mind" hardly distinguished, the original problem whose steady movement we have hitherto traced is in no wise advanced there. The analysis is throughout incomplete—in fact the work does not intend to be analytic, but only "popular" and dogmatic. The ethical dilemma is nowhere more apparent—wherever the mind of Plato can trace unity of system it seeks, but without success, to find unity of design. So at one time Plato speaks of God as the measure of the direct correspondence of mind and object. We know it only by "a kind of bastard reason," though we have long ago, in the perplexities of ethical explanation, been compelled to infer its existence. The identification of the good and the rational, the living thought that essentially only the good in existence is intelligible, can be held now only on the supposition that the designing mind is not all-powerful. "God desired that all things should be good and nothing bad, so far as this was attainable" (κατὰ δύναμιν, 30 A). The material even of the cosmos can never fully answer the sculptor's design. Plato was perplexed by the combination of wonderful adjustment in the physical world with instability and perishableness. Given the initial "impurity" of sense material, physical law, the taking on of form, is the realization of the best through that material.

So in the *Timaeus* Plato constantly and in a great variety of ways suggests that the limitation imposed by mind on its world is the source of the evil that exists. The divine mind though always desiring the good perhaps looked sometimes on the pattern of the created instead of on the unchangeable (28 A). Or he delivered the creation of mortal body into the hands of the children of God, who can only imitate the divine originator (41 D). Or, less mythically, the creative mind has to persuade necessity in order that its creation may be perfect, which is only in those things wherein intelligence "gets the better of" necessity (48 A). So God in the creation of the mortal and visible must work in the material of mortality, must bring time into being and accept the necessities of space,[33] and with the "necessary contributory causes" as his ministers accomplish his work (68 E). Thus in the *Timaeus* Plato admits at last, though with no less of faith in Ideas, the facts on which any materialism must be based, and expends all his ingenuity of thought to suggest a way of reconciliation. The whole problem turns on the relation of final and efficient causes, and the dilemma is that while Plato must admit the reality and indeed the necessity of the latter he must equally insist on the superiority

---

33. The conception of time in especial and its relation to plurality was a great difficulty for Plato. In the *Parmenides* the very important notion of the "moment" breaks in upon but does not further the argument (155 E *sqq.*). In the *Timaeus* the difficulty of time is postponed for future discussion (38 A).

and priority of the former. How can the mysterious efficient cause be at once dependent and necessary?

It is significant to compare the account of the relation of efficient and final causes given in the *Timaeus* with that of all things (716 D) and of the universe as the organism of the good (*cf.* 903 B), and at another he declares that there is more of evil than of good (906 A). But in the main, in spite of its "popular" representations, we must regard the argument of the *Laws* as that of a divine mind shaping through conflict a world that resists the impress of intelligence and the good. We must note that Plato speaks of an evil world-soul, but not of an evil God. Intelligence and good are still essentially related, though the relationship is more complex and harder to understand than it was before.

III

To sum up the argument of this paper. The Idea theory of Plato was the expression of an ethical need. Plato saved the good in a world of Heraclitean change by adopting the way of Ideas. The Idea had thus for Plato a double character, due to the divergence between the means of finding the Idea, the method of concepts, and the end the Idea served. The method was, under the fundamentally ethical activity of Plato's thought, reduced, indeed wrested, to the service of the ethical end. Hence the system of the *Phaedo* and the *Republic*, which finding the real in the Idea and identifying therefore the real with the Good, solves the ethical problem by dismissing to unreality all that is phenomenal and transient and false and evil. Where it cannot find value, it denies existence, and thus we may call reality both One and Good. For a moment the ethical and metaphysical claims seem in accord, but the reconciliation is only apparent. The ethical attitude implies the reality of evil, being as essentially an aversion from evil as a contemplation of Good. Further, the double nature of the Idea involves a contradiction which becomes clear as the method is applied more widely. In fact it becomes evident that the way of Ideas gives reality to evil no less than to good. Plato had thought to find everywhere the λόγος (word, i.e., reason), the designing mind; if the Idea is everything, then everything is explicable, for the Idea is the revelation of the λόγος. But a thousand things resisted explanation, resisted inclusion in the Idea —change and all becoming, time and space, the contradictions and inconstancies of sense.

The Form is manifested only in the world of becoming; and the Good we are seeking must be sought for in this "composite" world, and so must be regarded not as simply form but as that form which mind impresses—mind always fulfilling so far as possible the good—upon the inchoate. So the ethical interest moves from the form to the forming mind. The essential process of the theory is due to this necessary shifting of the ethical center of gravity, the centering of "value" no longer in the object of ethical contemplation but in the subject who contemplates —and does more than contemplate. Through this transference the Idea loses its original and composite character, and becomes simply form, the good proportion impressed by the forming mind, διεσχη ματίσατο εἴδεσί τε καὶ ἀριθμοῖς (designed in forms not numbers— *Tim.*, 53 B). So in the later doctrine the One, or the scheme of relations in which the world exists for thought, and the Good, or the purpose revealed in that scheme, are partially divorced. The difficulty of this divorce is never overcome, perhaps never can be for ethical thought. All we can say is that Plato moved nearer and nearer to the heart of the difficulty. But because he was not building a metaphysical system but seeking an "explanation," his work neither was nor could be completed. The work stopped not because the building was complete but because the builder was old. We can however trace the aim of the builder, and we can understand how the dominating ethical motive determined the work. From the ethical standpoint the development is consistent throughout. Only it is important to see that this very development was itself conditioned by the ethical postulate that metaphysical truth in its turn is the revelation of the system of being in and through which the good is realized. Hence the dilemma from which Plato has after all been unable to escape, the essential problem of reconciling teleology with any metaphysical construction, ultimately the issue between the ethical attitude with its insistence on a necessary antagonism and the metaphysical with its demand for unity.

[1909, 1912]

The Passions and Their Importance in Morals

10 THE NATURE OF THE PASSIONS

The difficulty which all psychical phenomena present to the scientist is supposed to be peculiarly emphasized in the case of "feelings." Of them in especial it is true that—to modify a Stoic formula—when we analyze them they are no longer present, and when they are present we no longer analyze them. The difficulty is essential, and yet it is very possible to misunderstand and to exaggerate it, and to deny the possibility of knowledge because we have started with a misleading definition of its object. Thus it is maintained by some writers on ethics, e.g., Dewey, that "feelings can only be felt"—a statement immediately self-contradictory. True, the feelings of each age and condition are almost impossible to recall when we have passed beyond it, and we distinguish the "thought" which can be expressed and recorded from the "feeling," the more intimate and subjective element, that is incommunicable and known only by its presence. Yet because we can name the feeling, even seek to define it, that very presence is itself a fact of knowledge. Our emotions do not escape our self-knowledge or pass utterly from memory. A critic can define poetry with some assurance as "emotion recollected in tranquility," and the poet can indeed remember how the sounding cataract haunted him like a passion.

Such statements as that criticized above imply a strange isolation of the aspects or modes of our conscious life. Shall we similarly say that desires "can only be desired" and that volitions "can only be willed"? The very absurdity of the question reveals the fact that whatever distinctions we may find within our psychical experience, these fall within a unity of self-consciousness and they have at least the identity involved in the condition of knowability. They are distinguishable aspects, not separable functions, aspects which the self-conscious being knows in his self-consciousness and by reason of it. In our very consciousness of these aspects is involved their unity within consciousness. This is the condition of self-revelation and its limit. If the nature of self-revelation, to which we with such difficulty give meaning, precludes the possibility of complete self-revelation, if the very conditions that render self-knowledge possible also render it necessarily incomplete, that very limitation, the condition of knowability, ensures both the unity and the essential coherence of the aspects known. One can thus know the interrelation of feeling and thought, reason and passion; we need not so far postulate the *Unbewusstsein*.

In order to explain how the passion element enters into the moral life, it is first necessary, owing to the incoherent state of psychological science, to put forward some definite view of the part the passions play in the economy of the mind.

In present-day usage, the term "passion" seems to mean simply an intensified emotion, and so it is more especially applied to emotions which normally involve a high degree of intensity. Here the term will be used in the older sense, as simply equivalent to emotion, except where it is desirable to emphasize the degree of intensity involved. Our first object must now be to analyze the relations of emotion to these psychical factors with which it is most intimately bound in the complex organization of the mind. The failure to distinguish these relations has led to, and still causes, much confusion. We must in particular consider the relation of emotion to instinct, pleasure-pain, and motive.

The Relation of Emotion to Instinct. Emotion has been defined as a concomitant or aspect of instinct. This view has been expressed by Mr. H. R. Marshall and more recently by Mr. William McDougall.[1] Emotion has undeniably a most intimate relation to instinct, but Mr. McDougall's account does not seem to me to be adequate or entirely satisfactory. In his statement, emotion is defined as the "affective aspect of instinctive processes" or the "affective quality of each instinctive process, and the

---

1. *Social Psychology*, Chap. II, and *Physiological Psychology*, Chap. VI.

sum of visceral and bodily changes in which it expresses itself."[2] To these "modes of affective experience" language provides the names of "anger," "fear," "curiosity," and so forth. The principal or primary instincts determine therefore the primary emotions, the secondary emotions being "the result of the compounding of a relatively small number of primary or simple emotions." Thus gratitude, for example, is a "binary compound composed of tender emotion and negative self-feeling."[3]

It will be one object of the ensuing discussion to show that emotion is itself a psychical state and cannot be understood as merely an aspect or quality of psychical states. To begin with, the "feeling-tone" involved in emotion does not seem to be what we are naming as the emotion. "Feeling-tones" are essentially difficult to isolate. Even the more definite and less difficult sensational feelings have no names as such beyond "pleasure" and "pain," and are only distinguished by terms which relate to their concomitants or effects or location. Similarly I believe the subtle quality distinctions involved in the emotions are not named by such terms as "fear" and "anger" and "love." In the case of the emotions, there is beyond the inherent difficulty of distinguishing the quality of tone a further reason why that quality should not be isolated and named. It is that, as we shall see, the emotional consciousness is directed not toward its own feeling state but away from it toward an object which evokes the emotion. When we feel pain or pleasure, it is the fact of feeling that is prominent. That above all is the central and too obvious truth in the case of suffering. When we hope and fear, the direction of consciousness is no longer toward the "feeling" of hope and fear, but to the object hoped and feared. Hence it is unlikely *a priori* that the quality of feeling involved should be specially named, and presently we shall have definite proof of this fact.

If, then, emotions are not simply "affective qualities" at all, they cannot be so defined in relation to instinct. "Instinct," according to James, "is usually defined as the faculty of acting in such a way as to produce certain ends without foresight of the ends, and without previous education in the performance."[4] Mr. McDougall thinks this type of definition lays too much stress on the absence of experience, since instinct persists after foresight of the ends.[5] At the same time it is admitted that instincts do not necessarily involve the experience of the individual, being inherited or innate tendencies, and so do not necessarily involve a foresight of the end. They are, then, at the least "functional correlates

2. *Social Psychology*, p. 46.
3. *Ibid.*
4. James, *Psychology*, II, p. 383.
5. McDougall, *Social Psychology*, p. 29n.

of activity"[6] or primary *dispositions* to action. But an emotion is not a disposition to act; it is a specific mental activity or reaction. It is neither a primitive disposition such as instinct nor an acquired diposition such as a habit or a virtue. We act in accordance with instinct or habit, but our hopes and regrets and fears are themselves acts, psychical activities, not the possiblities of such activity.

This determines the relation of emotion to instinct. The primary emotions are those correlate to primary dispositions. They are the reactions that arise when the disposition or function is aroused, when the tendency is made active in the presence of its object. They are the first ways of response of the conscious being, and so lie at the roots of consciousness. In all that lives and develops there is the distinguishing principle of response. The stone is moved and lies. The dead tree is a log. The living alone resists or responds in virtue of its own nature. Emotion is the response of the conscious life, in virtue of its nature, and involves whatever elements of knowing and feeling and striving are characteristic of conscious life. The first emotions are the fulfillments of instinct, not aspects of instinct.[7]

The case of sex-love illustrates the difference between emotion and instinct. It is in the fruition of the instinct that passion arises, and the passion has in every form an object toward which it is directed, apart from which it cannot exist, and in its highest form the object is uniquely determined. The instinct, the mere instinct, is objectless, indeterminate, blind.

One further criticism of Mr. McDougall's account must be made. Following the evolutionary method, and assuming that to each instinct there corresponds a specific emotion, he gives a list of primary emotions and assumes that the others are compounded of these. "Envy is a binary compound of negative self-feeling and of anger." "Admiration is a binary compound, awe a teritiary compound." Although such defini-

---

6. James, *loc. cit.*

7. A concrete instance may show the difficulty of Mr. McDougall's view. He regards fear as the affective aspect of the instinct of flight. One might say fear was rather the motive or cause of flight, not an aspect of it, and itself arose from the instinct of self-preservation. But apart from this difficulty, what shall we make of hope? Is it an aspect of the same instinct or not? Mr. McDougall says nothing of hope. Again, just as surely as the fact of danger excites fear, the fact of loss excites regret. But Mr. McDougall does not mention regret, although it is surely a simple emotion. Mr. McDougall, working from the side of instincts and seeking to find a specific emotion forming an element of each, fails to explain these emotions. The instinct leads us toward appropriate objects and actions, but the emotions are the variable responses or reactions determined by the degrees and ways in which instincts and all the tendencies of the conscious being are or are not realized. In the early pages of this essay I venture to disagree with Mr. McDougall, though in what follows I am much indebted to his important work.

tions may throw some light on the more complex emotions, they do not provide a satisfactory account. They are essentially inadequate, because the explanation is simplistic. The explanation of the more developed and the more complex as the mere compounding of simple elements has been the discrediting of much philosophy, and of still more psychology. Evolution does not seem to work in that way, nor do we truly understand the later phases of development when we know the earlier stages. In the knowledge of evolution we can reason neither backwards nor forwards. Has purpose evolved out of instinct and self-consciousness out of sentiency? It seems probable, but we cannot understand it so, simply because for us it *is* an evolution, an unfolding of what before lay unrevealed. In evolution, there is necessarily something new. Accordingly, on first principles, it seems possible that new instincts and new emotions should develop. The higher animals have instincts not found in the lower; why should man not have instincts lacking in the former? We do not learn all the instincts of the higher animals from a study of the lower; why all those of man from a study of the former?[8] New human instincts may conceivably have arisen,[9] and in many cases it would not follow that in the course of evolution the later instincts are developed *out of* the earlier, still less that they have developed by any compounding of these.

The Relation of Emotion to Pleasure-Pain. The theory we have been criticizing falls into the large class of theories which identify emotion with some kind of feeling-tone or affective quality, and we must determine the relation of emotion to feeling and especially to pleasure-pain feeling. The view that emotions are simply species of feelings has been elaborated in every conceivable form, the extremest being of course the James-Lange theory which makes emotion simply the feeling of organic sensation. One remove from this is the view of Kulpe that emotion is the fusion or connection of pleasure-pain feeling with organic sensation; and finally we come to the doctrines which explain emotion —feelings as distinct from others not by reason of their subjective quality but by the form of their occurrence, by their association with objects. This last view is the most popular. It was the doctrine of Spinoza and is more or less the doctrine of most modern psychologists.

A simple argument is enough to show the falseness of all these views. In ordinary language we speak of "love *for*," "fear *of*," "affection *toward*," "wonder *at*," "indignation *against*," the prepositional difference being due to the character of the active attitude involved. If emotions were merely "feeling-tones" we could similarly speak of feeling-tone "of,"

---

8. Cf. *Social Psychology*, p. 49.
9. Cf. H. R. Marshall, "The Religious Instinct," *Mind*, N. S. VI (1897), 40-58.

"for," "toward," "at," or "against" objects or persons. Language does not permit us to do so, and the reason is that, as already stated, emotion is not simply feeling, but at the least a feeling-activity, a reaction or response directly borne to its object.

Nor is it sufficient to say that together with the feeling-tone the idea of an object is present. Love is *not* "pleasure accompanied by the idea of an external cause."[10] All pleasure-pain, all feeling, involves the consciousness of an object, if only of the part affected. It is not on that account an emotion. It is when the object makes a successful appeal that the emotion is excited, not when it is merely recognized. Its significance is expressed not merely in a change of feeling-tone in the subject; with that feeling-tone, and indissolubly united with it, there is a new direction of the self, the immediate "practical judgment" of the self.

a. The significance of the object may be a pleasure-pain significance, prospective or actual, but the emotion is none the less distinct from its basis of pleasure or pain. An instance will make the relation clear. The news of the death of a friend may at first cause simply pain, an aching sense of loss, whence the only emotion to arise may be a self-directed emotion, a dim grief for the suffering self in its privation; then as the idea of the object becomes clear again, the emotion of yearning, *desiderium*, arises. To both these emotions there is the same basis or concomitant of pain. Similarly, where the recognition of another's suffering causes sympathetic pain, that same pain basis in the self may arouse one of two almost contradictory emotions, repulsion or pity. The mere presence of pleasure or pain, however closely associated with the idea of an object, will not itself determine the emotional reaction it may occasion. The emotional reaction, with its judgment of significance, depends on the structure of the self. Our emotions are ourselves in action. In emotion the consciousness is spontaneously self-directed to some object—in fact, to some realization of itself. It is a *moving out* to an object or end the value of which is taken for granted, while the recognition of the significance of the object is the essential cognitive element involved. An emotion is thus a psychical state while pleasure-pain is only a psychical aspect. Our emotions we attribute to ourselves, approve or disapprove, pass moral judgment upon; pleasure and pain, though we may be morally ashamed that certain objects cause us pleasure or even morally gratified that certain objects cause us pain, are essentially not ourselves in action, are essentially in the literal sense *passions*—what we suffer, not what we are or do.

b. Emotions then are not simply pleasures and pains; neither are they, to take a further step, simply reactions toward pleasure and away

10. Spinoza, *Ethica*, Pt. III. Def. VI.

from pain. "Pleasure and pain," says Locke, "are the hinges on which passions turn." There is a truth underlying the remark, but it requires more careful statement. For even if we suppose that our emotions are reactions toward an object *because* it brings pain, we can no longer say that the emotion is a seeking of pleasure or an aversion from pain. It is directed primarily to its object; it is that which in the first instance is loved or hated, hoped or feared, and in the sequel it will also appear that it is not always because the object of the emotion is for us the source of pleasure or pain, that we love or hate, hope or fear, despise or admire.

c. Meantime we must consider the relation of emotion not to pleasure as such, but to the pleasure of satisfaction. When any desire, any instinct, any striving, is fulfilled, there is the pleasure of realization, of satisfaction; before it is fulfilled there is the prospect of satisfaction. It is undoubtedly the fact of this invariable law that, misinterpreted, has led to the fallacies of hedonism; and nothing reveals more clearly the defect of hedonism than a study of the nature of passion. Passion is concerned with nothing but its object; if it be concerned with anything else—the *pleasure* of its own fulfillment, say—it is so far distracted and broken. It is not primarily the memory of previous feelings of satisfaction and the prospect of attaining a like satisfaction that determine our present actions, but rather present needs themselves demanding fulfillment.

Ultimate needs are too deeply rooted to exist merely for the sense of satisfaction their fulfillment may bring. Here is revealed the superiority of the mind to the considerations of pleasure and pain. Pleasure may lead to love, pain to hatred and anger, but these emotions can in their turn trample upon pleasures and scorn pains greater than those whence they have sprung. Their goal is not pleasure nor the avoidance of pain, but directly their own fulfillment, and a strong passion will fulfill itself, will maintain itself, in spite of all the pains it may entail and all the seduction of alien pleasure. It is just this resistance of emotion to the claims of pleasure and pain that makes possible the moral emotions with their essential disinterestedness.

Already we can draw ethical inferences. It is a false view of the relation of the pleasures of satisfaction to emotion and desire that has led to two opposing and extreme ethical theories, to hedonism and to asceticism. Both make these pleasures "entities" in some sense independent, for they regard pleasures as in the one case things to be shunned, in the other to be sought after. They value pleasures by themselves in the one case as absolutely valuable, in the other as absolutely valueless, not realizing that in the cases we are considering, the value of pleasure is integrally bound up with the end or object whose satisfaction it is, and therefore cannot be absolute in either direction. It is noteworthy that Kant, no less than such a writer as Mill, regards pleasure as the object of desire.

Some hedonistic writers realize the difficulty the nature of emotion presents to their theory, though hardly in its full gravity. Their attempts to meet it are instructive. Bain, for instance, admits that "an emotion persists in the mind and dominates the course of the thoughts, not because it is pleasureable or painful, but because it is strong."[11] The difficulty thus presented to his theory, but only partially stated in his admission, he meets by the characteristic phrase "emotional perversion." "In such a state the mind is no longer in its calm centre; the judgments and convictions are liable to perversion and bias." The recognition of the great role of the emotions in the formation of all primary ends of action is here totally lacking, and the true refutation of such views as Bain's must be found in the account of that role. Meantime it might suffice to remark that all primary satisfaction is that attained in the attainment of an end, and that the end is first presented emotionally. The only possible question for the hedonist is: Whether as beings, conscious of our ends, we should invest the order prescribed by our nature, and instead of finding satisfaction because we have attained our end, seek ends because of the feeling of satisfaction. No arguments have been put forward to show the desirability of the latter course as a universal principle, and many doubts must arise as to its possibility. Such a principle would involve in fact the elimination of the emotions or of all except one inglorious emotion—the secondary reaction toward the feeling of satisfaction.[12] It would make valueless many elements in our nature, those we value most. It would weaken the unity of personality and make our spirits like to poor workmen who work for hire and the reward bestowed at the end of labor.

The Relation of Emotion to Motive. If the preceding criticism is correct, it follows that an essential element in emotion, in this way distinguished from mere "feeling," from pleasure-pain "tones," is active direction; the emotion is not merely directed as it were by some other principle of the mind, by some "will-power," but direction is part of its meaning, its very nature. If we must use the ambiguous term "feeling," it is feeling *toward*, not feeling of, its object—such language however is still external and regards the emotion as still separable from its object, which is the idea underlying the identification of emotion with feeling qualities. If we put out of count the direction of emotion, we are left with a mere array of neuropsychical concomitants or effects. The emotion itself has vanished, but with surprise we parade what "introspection" has revealed and say: "See what anger and love and despair amount to!" "Common sense says we lose our fortune, are sorry, and

11. *Emotions and Will*, p. 381.
12. It is noteworthy that the "man of pleasure" is essentially unemotional.

weep; we meet a bear, are frightened and run; we are insulted by a rival, are angry and strike. The hypothesis here to be defended says that this order of sequence is incorrect, that the one mental state is not immediately induced by the other, that the bodily manifestations must first be interposed between, and that the more rational statement is that we feel sorry because we cry, angry because we strike, afraid because we tremble, and not that we cry, strike, or tremble because we are sorry, angry, or fearful, as the case may be."[13] Common sense and James do not *mean* the same thing by regret, anger, and fear.

Emotion no less than feeling is direction and activity, and to explain its relation to motive and conduct we must now consider the kind of activity involved. If we reflect on, say, the emotion of gratitude or of pity, we can distinguish two forms of activity. The grateful man *desires* to benefit in turn his benefactor, the pitiful to remove the miseries of the wretched, but apart from the fulfillment of these desires they *feel* gratitude or pity toward their respective objects. The emotion-activity is not the activity, the striving, that reaches out to some end as yet unrealized; it is an energizing complete in itself and not necessarily demanding any greater future fulfillment. A passion if very strong is wholly engrossed in the present, looking neither before nor after, making no question of ends or search for means. We must distinguish the activity from the activities to which it prompts. The practical distinction involved is best explained by calling emotion motive and not desire. Passion leads us to desire, but is not itself desire; according to the situation the same passion may serve as the motive to contrary actions, may awake contrary desires. "Fear may be associated with the tendency to run away, the impulse to dissimulate, the desire to receive aid from others, the impulse to 'give up,' according to the nature of the occasion and the individual."[14] The fear remains the same attitude throughout. It is a way of regarding an object, not of turning from it. While we fly from danger, fear still looks toward the dangerous object. It is because the mind regards the object that the face is averted from it and the legs prompted to flight. The object threatens danger, it has a hostile significance for us. Because it is significant for us, we react *toward* it; but because it is hostile, we desire to escape *from* it. This distinction of reactive attitude and the engendered desire explains how fear can become fascination, where the active direction toward the object becomes so strong as to lead the victim itself toward and not from the object of terror. Settled despair works in like

13. James, *Psychology*, II, p. 450.
14. Irons, *Psychology of Ethics*, p. 34. The nature of emotion seems to me to be nowhere better analyzed than in the first chapter of this book, though the author fails to develop systematically the conclusions at which he there arrives.

manner. It is the existence of an emotional attitude which in its less intense form stimulates to effort and struggle for the removal of the hostile conditions, but becoming strong, tends to exclude even the desire of deliverance. Again, the victim is wholly given over to the engrossment of the passion, which, contrasted with the previous or normal consciousness, comes to be felt as something stronger than he, overpowering his normal self-direction, so that he feels subject to passion and thinks of it as a force outside himself, again literally a *passion*, a power from which he suffers and cannot escape. But it is himself he cannot escape.

Why this should be, why a strong passion should seem to overpower the self, whose self-direction it is, why in general the same emotion is motive to contrary activities and desires, can only be understood when we realize how the emotions become organized in sentiments and character. Thus, to anticipate a later part of the discussion, the emotion of fear has its source in the positive sentiment of self-regard.[15] It is thus fear *for* the self, as well as fear *of* the object; and in the form of "apprehension" it is the former side of the relation that is prominent. According to the quality and type of the fear-reaction will be the further activity motived by the fear.

Emotions then are activities which, in so far as they produce further activites, are called motives. We usually speak of them as motives *of* and *to* the will, but this is a misleading form of speech. An emotional reaction is itself a form of willing, a fact often overlooked through our habit of thinking of the will as only concerned with yet unattained ends. To love and hate is to will though the emotions may involve no further endeavor, as when the loved object needs nothing for its happiness, or the hated object be past our power of harm. To respect or admire is to will, though the emotions may involve only a distant attitude toward their object, no stretching out of hands, no emulation, no further desire. To regret is to will, though it only means the wistful backward direction of the spirit aware that here desire is vain. In these cases, in all emotion, what is willed is the present direction of the self to an object apprehended as actual. Emotion is possible only because the object is in some sense actual, and emotion is sometimes careless of the kind of reality possessed. A man may love a character in fiction as if he were a fellow human being, and feel no concern because the object lives only in the imagination. But desire looks not on the actuality of its object, but on its lack of actuality, and the will that is based on desire is the endeavor to achieve actuality for what is yet ideal.

15. A further complication is introduced when the fear is not *for* the self, but for some object positively significant to the self.

We can understand this latter will only by relating it to the former. In the will that sustains the present self-direction lies the possibility of the will that in some way seeks to make that present activity more complete. Emotion is realization, but present realization is rarely complete and further realization may be in itself undesirable. So within the realization desires and emotions arise. The positive desires are primary, and the aversions are necessarily determined by the possibility of greater positive realization. Thus the desires for the removal of the realization and activity of fear arise from the presence and for the sake of the realization we call self-regard. In every case, therefore, desires are desires of further realization and are continuous with a present realization. Will cannot be regarded as some independent power which the emotions move or "motive." Emotions are activities, and so are "motives" to that further activity that going beyond the present realization finds ways of making it more perfect. Emotion is active self-direction, and what we call will is simply the most permanent and determined self-direction regarded as fulfilling itself. How this self-fulfillment is possible, we could determine if we saw how it were possible that an end can be furthered by "means." But in any case the end to be realized is only a further stage of a present realization. The justification for Kant's view that the good will is the only good without qualification, is found in the fact that the will is the character in activity, the character so far as unified and effective, so far as realized in the active and incessant relating of itself to its world. But "mere" or "pure" will is a phrase without meaning. This we shall see more clearly when we come to distinguish the will as determined by "duty" from the will as spontaneously or emotionally determined. In every case we shall see that some emotional determination is primary, differing in degree according to the unity or integration of the character determined.

THE DEFINITION OF EMOTION OR PASSION

We can by the aid of these distinctions give a tentative definition of emotion. *An emotion or passion is the spontaneous reaction of the self toward an object realized as significant.* It is a psychical state, not merely an element of such a state, and it contains all the conditions of knowing and feeling and willing—if we so distinguish mental functions—which constitute a state of consciousness.

Before proceeding to show the place of emotion as so defined in the moral life, we may consider two possible objections to the definition. First, it may be objected that all emotion does not necessarily imply an object. The definition given may serve for such passions as anger, love, despair, resentment, hope. No doubt these involve activity directed toward an object, and so are not merely "feeling-tones." But what, it may be asked, of the emotion of joy, serenity, melancholy, sorrow? Where is the object here, and the response to its significance? May not these be simple states of feeling, and feeling alone? It is, I think, undoubtedly true that the terms "joy" and "sorrow" mean something more than emotions, and have a peculiar reference to feeling qualities. But in this matter I think Mr. McDougall is essentially right to point out how complex may be what seem the simple states of joy and sorrow.

> The joy of a loving mother as she tends her beautiful and healthy child may involve these many elements: (1) There is the aesthetic pleasure in the contemplation of the beauty of the object, a pleasure that any onlooker may share; (2) sympathetic pleasure reflected by, or induced in, the mother from her smiling child; (3) tender emotion in itself pleasantly toned and progressively attaining satisfaction; (4) positive self-feeling also intrinsically pleasant, and also attaining an ideal satisfaction; for the mother is proud of her child as an evidence of her own worth; (5) each of these two primary emotions of the mother is developed within the system of a strong sentiment, the one within the system of her love for her child, the other within the system of her regard for herself, the two strongest sentiments of her nature which in so far as the child is identified with herself, becomes welded together to constitute a master sentiment or passion; this renders the emotion more intense and more enduring; (6) the fact that the emotions are not aroused as merely isolated experiences by some casually presented object, but are developed within strongly organized and enduring sentiments gives them a prospective reference; they project themselves into an indefinitely prolonged future, and so hope or pleasant anticipation is added to the complex.[16]

Numerous as are the elements presented by this analysis, they are probably fewer rather than more than those involved in the actual experience of joy, which then turns out to be neither simply a sense of pleasure nor simply an emotion. We may of course say that joy is the feeling-tone of all the activities involved, being (a) the pleasure accompanying the energizing of inherently pleasant emotions, and (b) the satisfaction resulting from all fulfilled or progressively fulfilled activity, whether the activity is itself pleasant or not; but (a) it is doubtful if we could mean by joy simply a pleasure we cannot, except for the purposes of

16. *Social Psychology*, p. 151.

psychology, conceive apart from the activity, and (b) the satisfaction, it has to be remembered, is itself emotional, being active direction toward that type of object which is an end achieved.[17] It is of the first importance, from the point of view of morals, to understand that such complexes as joy involve emotion as well as pleasure. For in its most comprehensive form, when it arises out of the harmonious functioning of the whole united self, the joyous state becomes *happiness*, which "both the many and the superior sort alike call the highest of all realizable good."[18]

One further objection to our definition may also be mentioned. Emotion was defined as a reaction determined by the significance objects have for the self. It might be objected that such an emotion as contempt depends on the insignificance of the object toward which it is directed, but of course the answer is that the consciousness of significance may be realized in an emotion which condemns the object as insignificant. So it is when we condemn or despise; were the object utterly indifferent, there would be no reaction, no sense of contempt. The mere perception of a fact cannot account for any emotional reaction with its degrees and varieties. It is the fact realized as significant.

This fact of significance may give us a clue to the classification of emotions. Emotion is the way our whole consciousness on any given occasion realizes the significance in some particular of its being or of its world, the significance an object has for it, or itself as an object of significance. In terms of significance we can thus distinguish two types of object *toward* which we react: (1) the self as known, as object, the self whose significance is ultimately realized as that which makes all objects significant; and (2) the objects which are significant not in themselves, but in their relation to that self. These are the inner and the outer objects of the emotional attitude. Further, there are two kinds of significance, two main ways of reacting, which are perhaps best distinguished according to the type of *desire* the emotion produces. We may desire the conservation, the furtherance, the presence of the object, or we may desire its destruction, its hurt, its absence. Ultimately, wherever there is the recognition of significance, there is a judgment, however dim or however complex, of good and bad.

It is the relation of the inner and outer object that makes a classification of emotions so difficult. In primitive types of emotion there may seem to be a simple reaction toward the outer object, with no

---

17. The object toward which we react in emotion is not necessarily an "external" object. The end unachieved evokes one emotion, the end achieved, another. From the latter desire is absent, hence its intrinsic and complete pleasantness.

18. Aristotle, *Ethics*, I, 4–2. Perhaps no definition of happiness was ever truer than the ἐνέργεια ψυχῆς definition of Aristotle.

objectification of the reacting self. In the primitive realization of significance there may not be any intellectual judgment which is distinguished from the whole reactive attitude; what element of cognition it involves it may be impossible to determine, though we must, to explain the emotion at all, at any rate suppose that the animal or human being is conscious somehow and to some degree of the significance of the object. As intelligence advances, however, the subject becomes aware of his self as determining the significance of outer objects. His self has thus become in turn an object, and the emotional attitude becomes complex. Further, in distinguishing his own self as inherently significant from the objects to which it lends significance, the self-conscious being distinguishes it from other selves; these are objects intrinsically significant to other subjects, and to him also that intrinsic significance becomes itself an object. Thus in regard to other selves, the emotional attitude with its apprehension of significance may be very complex indeed. They appear as both outer and inner objects, both inherently and secondarily significant in a variety of conflicting relations. So arise the great moral problems, the conflict of egoism and altruism, all the questions of social unity and relationship. In seeking to solve these, the emotional consciousness becomes reflective; but the problems arise first out of the emotional nature with its judgments of significance. They are problems of values, and while emotion is determined by the apprehension of value, it is our emotional nature that itself determines value.[19]

THE ORGANIZATION OF
THE PASSIONS IN SENTIMENTS

We must go on to consider the organization of the passions. It is obvious that all passions are not equally central, are not directed toward objects equally significant or permanent. Some are in their nature transient, some enduring. Ethical reflection, however, has on the whole been so concerned to point out the transient nature of some passions that it has seldom perceived the significance of the permanence of others, has scarcely observed how passions in becoming permanent organize themselves into psychical systems. We can distinguish the passions according to their degree of organization, according as they arise fitfully and incidentally or are the expression of a definite passion–disposition, involving a direction of the self toward the object more permanent than that determined by the passing mood. Various psychologists have distinguished the mere passion-mood from the stable passion-disposi-

19. Cf. Westermarck, *Origin and Development of the Moral Ideas,* Chap. I.

tion,[20] and the distinction is absolutely necessary if we are to understand how the multitude of conflicting emotions of our experience can consist with a stable character and an ordered society.

We must therefore find some term to signify an organized emotion, an emotion which involves a definite pre-existing disposition or has created such a disposition for itself, and in what follows I shall use the term "sentiment" in this sense, to mean either such an emotional disposition toward an object or the emotion itself that involves such a disposition—in Aristotelian language to signify either the emotional ἕξις or its actual ἐνέργεια. Thus by the sentiment of patriotism would be meant that disposition of mind which renders one's country an object of permanent emotional significance or else the actual emotional excitement of that disposition.

Mr. A. F. Shand has given currency to the distinction of emotion or passion and sentiment.[21] As, however, he uses the term sentiment in a somewhat different sense, and even criticizes such an application of it as that just made,[22] it is advisable before going further to justify the distinction we have drawn. Mr. Shand means by sentiment a kind of "feeling" which is to be distinguished from emotion. Thus love is for him a sentiment, and *never* an emotion.[23] He draws a distinction of kind, and refuses to admit that emotions can become sentiments. In our view the proper distinction is one of degree, and the integration of character is to be understood by a consideration of how emotions becoming central form themselves into sentiments, and some sentiment, becoming central, determines the unity of the whole nature. A brief criticism of Mr. Shand's doctrine is therefore necessary.

> The sentiment, as interpreted from the outside is the thought of an object, as a permanent thing or quality. While the emotion, when it has a thought, refers to some change or event, not to a permanent quality. As the relatively stable thought of the sentiment is modified and becomes, for instance, the thought of this man whom I like as injured or insulted, or this thing which I like as broken

20. Cf., e.g., Eduard von Hartmann's distinction between sympathy and love: "Das Mitgefühl ist eine vorübergehende flüchtige *Gefühls-Reaction*, die Liebe ist eine dauernde Gesinnung, eine beständige decidirte *Willensrichtung*: ersteres ein wankelmüthiger unzuverlässiger *Affect*, letzere ein *Ethos*." *Phänomenologie des sittlichen Bewusstseins* (Berlin, 1886), p. 271.

21. "Character and the Emotions," *Mind*, N.S. V (1896), 203-226.

22. "M. Ribot's Theory of the Passions," *Mind*, N.S. XVI (1907), 477-505. M. Ribot uses the term "passion" in much the same sense as "sentiment" above (cf. Ribot, *Psychology of the Emotions*, pp. 19ff.).

23. *Mind*, N.S. V, 223.

or lost, so an emotion is excited and merged in the sentiment, and the emotion is to the sentiment as this change of thought is to the identity of thought on which it rests. And this identity of thought which refers to the same object with its feeling-tone and conative tendency, which persists through the emotional phases excited in it, is the sentiment.[24]

That statement at least does not involve any hard-and-fast line between sentiment and emotion, for the "change of thought" is stated to be a modification of the "identity of thought." It may be doubted however if such an analogy meets the case. For we must note that the secondary emotions within the sentiment may or may not be directed to the object of the primary emotion. If the man I like is insulted, my anger is directed toward the cause of the insult, and the emotion of affection is not necessarily modified thereby; if, however, he is injured, my sorrow is concerned with the man himself in a particular aspect, the man whom I like and who is suffering. My affection is for the whole man, my sorrow for the man as suffering. The central significance of the man, the man as object of affection, remains the same throughout. Corresponding to that significance is the stable emotion.

But, Mr. Shand would ask, what is the stable emotion? "What," he asks in criticism of M. Ribot, "is the fixed emotion of avarice? Is it the joy of the avaricious man in the possession of his wealth, present in the thought of it, expressed in his handling of it, and gloating over the sight of it? This at least seems to be the centre of his passion in favourable circumstances to which his activities converge. But suppose that he loses his wealth or a part of it, or even that he fears to lose it. What becomes of his joy? It is replaced by sorrow or fear. But if his passion is identical with joy, then it ceases to exist when his joy ceases."[25]

The answer is that the miser's passion does not consist in his joy in the possession of wealth, but is simply the love of wealth, a love that may only be intensified by its loss and his consequent sorrow. Further, it must be noted that any emotion may be a secondary reaction involved in a sentiment. The love of wealth, for example, may be secondary within the sentiment of ambition, or *vice versa*. On the other hand, any emotion may be organized in a disposition and form a center round which secondary emotions group themselves. In the case of the miser one of the secondary emotions is fear, but fear, negative as it is, may itself be a sentiment, as in the case of the timorous man, for whom love and hate may be determined by the way objects affect his security. Certainly the central

24. *Ibid.*, p. 224.
25. *Mind*, N.S. XVI, 482.

emotion may be modified by being organized, but it still retains its character as an emotion. The love that in the course of years has involved joys and fears, triumphs and sorrows, is different from first love, even as the object itself is different now, but it is the same even as the object is the same.

The "gamut of the emotions" may indeed center round one emotional disposition, but it is important to observe how and why. The secondary emotions cannot be regarded as modifications of the primary emotion. In many instances they are not directed toward the object of that emotion at all, as when we are angry at whatever wrongs the object of our love, or fear whatever endangers it. In other instances they are directed to the object in some particular situation, not to the object as such, as when we regret the absence of the object, feel disappointed at the conduct of the loved one, gladness in its present welfare, hope for its future welfare. The main significance of the object remains undisturbed so long as the primary passion for the object as such remains. The primary passion, the direction of the self which determines the sentiment, may be likened to a wave borne steadily onward, in spite of its ups and downs and breakings-back. The joy of the lover may turn to sorrow without affecting his love, but his love in turning to hate annihilates itself. Conflict and disintegration arise when an emotion is the central emotion of the sentiment, involving toward its object a contrary direction of the self, enters in. Then the being is bewildered and distracted.

> Odi et amo; quare id faciam fortasse requiris.
> Nescio, sed fieri sentio et excrucior.[26]

We must then regard the difference of emotion and sentiment as one of degree. Every emotion arises out of some disposition of the self, though not necessarily a unified disposition. And any emotion may become a sentiment, though not in the highest degree, while according to the type of sentiment that predominates will be the type and degree of the unity of the formed character. If we apply our system of classification this becomes manifest. (a) Emotions implying the negative or hostile significance of objects cannot form so true an integration of character as those implying positive or friendly significance. Thus timorousness, a sentiment of fear, and maliciousness, a sentiment of hate, really imply a sentiment of self-regard working itself out in a negative rather than a positive direction and have all the weakness of

---

26.   I hate and I love; you perhaps ask why I do so.
       I do not know, but I feel it happens so and it tortures me.

merely defensive or purely offensive attitudes. Sentiments of aversion can only be secondary to sentiments of attraction. The latter essentially extend the range of the self; the former contract it, and have therefore less capacity of emotional inclusiveness. Malevolent feeling separates the self from its object; benevolent feeling unites it to its object. (b) Emotions directed toward objects of secondary significance cannot in their nature be so true centers of disposition as those directed toward objects inherently significant. Thus passions for mere objective goods can have their place in a full development of character only in being limited by a due estimate of the self for which they are significant, and passions directed to beings themselves inherently significant only develop truly when that intrinsic value is recognized and related to the intrinsic value of the self. So Mr. McDougall says "that there is only one sentiment which by becoming the master-sentiment can generate strong character in the fullest sense, and that is the self-regarding sentiment,"[27] or perhaps we should say the sentiment which regards the self in its relation to, and unity with, other selves.

In the ensuing discussion, in accordance with the double classification already made, we shall consider sentiments in their subjective and in their objective aspects. It is especially important to keep the *object* of emotion in view in such a discussion since the emotion is itself determined as a direction toward an object. Terms which denote merely the subjective side, terms such as love or aversion, are extremely vague determinants. Love may be love of any one of a thousand objects, objects of any degree of significance, secondary or intrinsic, and the nature of the sentiment varies accordingly.

All that will be attempted will be to show in outline how with the development of the sentiments the moral ideas also develop. It is obvious that society rests on certain primary sentiments arising out of the primary instincts. A primitive society may be organized simply in respect of the most necessary sentiments, those that make family life possible; its moral ideas, being essentially ideas of social relationship, would correspond. As societies advance, we can conceive them organized in respect of more and more sentiments until finally a man's place in his society is determined in respect of his whole character. So the moral ideas would develop also. From the subjective and from the objective side we may briefly consider the essential stages—not necessarily the historic stages—of the development.

Sentiments Considered from the More Subjective Side. More subjectively, we distinguished emotions according as the object had a positive or a negative significance for the self, according as in conse-

27. *Social Psychology*, p. 261.

quence the subject desired its presence or absence, furtherance or harm, preservation or destruction. From this point of view sentiments would fall into two classes:[28] sentiments of attraction and sentiments of aversion, the former being necessarily prior. The first emotions are the fulfillment of the first instincts. Whatever interferes with that fulfillment arouses the first aversion. It must have been out of such interference with instinctive ends that the mind awoke to conscious ends and so to morality. Did active impulses always fulfill themselves without let or contradition, probably the idea of end would never have arisen. It is when the instinct fails to reach its end that in the very failure to realize it, it becomes recognized. It is thereby defined in the consciousness and conceived as an end. So the mechanical nature of instinct becomes broken down, its direction is made conscious, and the being is led to the fulfillment of the end not altogether ignorant of what his action involves.

The stages in this recognition are obvious if we consider any case of baffled instinct. In the endeavor to fulfill it first the means to its fulfillment occupy the attention, while the end is not necessarily brought into clear consciousness at all, for there is no need to reflect on that. Deliberation, as Aristotle said, is always of the means to the end, and the hungry man does not deliberate what he shall eat, but how he shall get food. The instinct or formed disposition determines the end; when present to consciousness it is present emotionally as that toward which we react, but it is the means that the reflective consciousness is concerned about. Here arises the first distinction of the emotional from the reflective consciousness. Always, however far we advance, reflection concerns the means to an end emotionally presented. Only, the more comprehensive the end the longer becomes the chain of means to its realization, and in the preoccupation with the means, the end may disappear from the foreground, and the emotional impulse, with its peculiar *felt* direction of the being, grow faint. Ends to which the self, in the hour of emotional insight, has been set thus come to be fulfilled when the strong reaction has passed away, or comes to be fulfilled as tasks. The self has been set in a certain direction, and remains set, but the driving impulse has grown weak. So there arises the idea of *ought*, to sustain the activity first realized as *good*.

Let us consider how such ideas of moral approval and disapproval might arise out of the sentiments by which a primitive society is organized. Whatever furthers any sentiment meets approval, approval

---

28. Mr. McDougall has three types: love, hate, and respect; but so far as respect is an emotional attitude and not simply an intellectual judgment of worth, it belongs, I think, to the class of sentiments of attraction. In respect, the gaze at least is attracted toward the object, though perhaps we neither approach it, as in the sentiment of admiration, nor draw it to us, as in the sentiment of love.

being a secondary emotion within the sentiment; what conserves or furthers the social sentiments of the community meets social approval, or more definitely, what offends the social sentiments, the tribe feelings, excites disapproval. Customs and institutions are simply hardened social sentiments, and at an early stage the society is wholly determined in respect of these. Hence the rigidity of early society, which recognizes only a certain number of social sentiments in its members. The social code becomes hard-and-fast. The individual's approval, directed to a permanent unchanging end, becomes a kind of reverence or submissiveness, while breach of the code excites in him intense resentment. He can hardly be said to choose to obey the code. His emotion in obeying is expressed by the term *must*, and we may compare the attitude of a child in its early moral development. There are certain precepts to disobey which never enters its mind as possible. This is a *must* recognized as *right*, not the *must* of external reluctant obedience which is involved in the attitude of the child toward some other precepts. The latter *must* could not maintain a society; the spirit here is submissive, the self-emotion is in accord with submission, but the positive significance of the self is not yet realized.

It is noteworthy how religious emotion in early societies furthers this type of social approval, promoting a spirit of submissiveness, stereotyping the emotions of approval and disapproval and so conserving under a strong emotional sanction the existing customs and institutions.[29] The religious emotions of the savage seem to resemble his social emotions in that both involve a predominant sense of *must*, a kind of submission, though not necessarily a reluctant submission.[30] So in the sphere of law it was only when custom was violated that the possibility of violation was recognized.[31]

The feeling of *must* becomes that of *ought* when the subjective possibility of breaking custom or law is understood. The *must* forbids the very thought of the contrary, the *ought* implies choice. So far this is an advance, because the agent is thrown back upon himself in choosing. It is the beginning of the knowledge of good and evil. It is the first recognition of the intrinsic worth of the self. But it is still under authority. "Choose ye," comes the command, but it is "choose ye whom ye will serve." Again we may compare the case of the child. When he partly emerges out of the sphere of the first parental authority and feels the influence of contradictory social authorities, to him also is given a choice of service. And again we may compare the corresponding religious

29. Cf. Bagehot, *Physics and Politics*, pp. 55ff.
30. Cf. Westermarck, *Origin and Development of the Moral Ideas*, II, p. 659.
31. Cf. Maine, *Ancient Law*, Chap. I.

attitude. The central fact for the religious consciousness may become this possibility of disobedience, arousing the ideas of sin and transgression and punishment. The greater stress is laid on the side of disobedience, because the authority is still external. "It is the law" is the final word.[32]

Men advance from negative to positive morality, from the old commandment, "Thou shalt not," to the "new commandment," "that ye *love*." It is important to observe the emotional significance of the change. We pass from the recognition of *ought* as a social standard to the recognition of *good*. On such a recognition the self-reaction is at last made wholly harmonious with the social end. We saw that approval is a secondary emotion that arises within every sentiment of attraction, and in a unified self there will accordingly be present, with the consciousness of the unity of its activity, approval of the essential direction of that activity. This is the comprehensive idea of good, since in general good is simply what we approve.[33] But early society recognizes only sentiments, not character, as of social importance. It cannot therefore rest on that recognition of good which arises from the unity of character. So it must look not to acts as they express the nature of the individual but to acts as they conform to principles. The social emotion attaches to principles, and the idea of *good* is therefore secondary to the idea of *ought*. The act is good because it accords with the principle. On the other hand, when an act is looked upon directly in relation to a character of which it is the expression, the idea of good becomes primary. So as more and more sentiments become socially recognized until finally a man's whole character determines his place in society, the positive idea of good assumes an increasing prominence.

In such a process the conception of the intrinsic significance of the self is gradually developed. This is the true moralization of the passions. Each passion insists on the significance of some object; when that significance is interpreted in the light of the intrinsic significance of the self, and limited thereby, the passion has become moralized. From the objective side, to which we now turn, we can show with greater clearness how the growth of morality is simply this process of the moralization of the passions.

Sentiments Considered from the More Objective Side. We distinguished the object of emotion according as it was either significant for a self or inherently significant, i.e., a self-made objective. In the full develop-

---

32.   The same attitude, of course, survives in modern social conventions, when we accept or adopt anything because it is the fashion, "the thing." It is as much "respect for the Law" as Kant himself could desire.

33.   Cf. Westermarck, *op. cit.*, I, p. 146.

ment of self-consciousness, the relation of the former type of object to the latter is realized, so that emotion is not directed simply toward the outer object, but toward the other object viewed in its relation to the inner. The two are present in a kind of unity and the emotion is now directed not to the object as such but to the object in the light of an *end*. It is in this sense that T. H. Green conceives that the moral consciousness in presenting ends to itself realizes them as having intrinsic worth.[34] The end has worth, however, or is good, simply for the self or for other selves whose intrinsic significance is furthered in its fulfillment; and this intrinsic significance at any rate must ultimately be immediately recognized, that is, it must be realized in the emotional consciousness of value. We must later consider more widely the relation of the emotional to the reflective consciousness, but meantime we may note that (1) in our ordinary consciousness a large part of our activity cannot be called deliberate or purposed at all—it is almost as unconscious as the work of bees, almost as much the driving of some necessity we seek neither to understand nor to refer beyond itself: our "works are ushered into being with the same blindness to ends, with the same unintentionality, which marks the processes of organic nature"[35]; and (2) in the most developed self-consciousness the relationship of outer to inner object, though recognized, is not in every case an object of reflection and should not be—such reflection would be a weakness of character. For where the reaction is that of the whole nature, reflection might cast doubts on the whole nature, might involve distrust of the realized self such as would seriously interfere with further realization and would imply an absence of the strong central emotion which is itself the realization of an ultimate and unquestionable end. The end is indeed presented to the self, but not as something it may choose or reject.

When a being realizes an object actual or ideal in its relation to a self or selves of intrinsic values, his passion for that object or end becomes moralized. We may now consider the process of moralization.

In its primitive form a passion for an object of secondary significance may involve scarcely any conception of the self that determines this significance. This is true also of our own uncontrolled passions. A wrong or insult fills us with anger and the desire for revenge; danger rouses immediate fear. We may not realize the relation of the passion to the object—self. Yet, it is this self as object, as an object wronged or threatened, that gives meaning to the passion, gives it a kind of reason, and ultimately justifies it to our self-consciousness. If our anger and resentment are misguided it is because the intrinsic significance of the

34. *Prolegomena to Ethics*, Bk. II, Chap. 1.
35. Wallace, *Inaugural Lecture at Oxford*, 1882.

self is not really affected by the supposed wrong. If our fears are foolish it is not in that no action of ours can avoid the danger but in that the danger is unreal—the *self* was not endangered. So all the passions toward mere objects find their true proportions in their relation to the intrinsic self. Hope looks to the self in its prospect of attaining a desired good. Shame, disgust, repentance, despair, look to the self as humiliated, as having failed to attain, as turning to better satisfactions, as baffled or defeated. And these emotions are justified in so far as the sentiment of self-regard they imply is a regard for the intrinsic self in its true relation to objects and ends. How the self-regard is itself moralized we must presently consider.

The case is obvious in regard to objects whose significance for the self is a hostile one. True self-regard determines their proper proportions, but objection may be raised to this solution in the cases where the object has no such significance. Take the emotions of contempt and respect. How are they determined by the intrinsic self? Or take the emotion of love. *Should* it be determined or justified by a self-centered sentiment, the sentiment of self-regard? Is not such a determination repugnant to its very nature? The consideration of such cases will advance the argument a step further, for we are now led to recognize other intrinsically significant objects than the primary self. The former emotions related the self to an outer world of objects; these relate the self to other selves.

The passion of love well illustrates this further extension of the self. Love resists the self-regarding attitude, is directed away from the self, "seeketh not its own." But in its first form it takes the self away from itself, only that it may find its own happiness realized in another, in nearness to or possession of another; hence it demands first exclusive possession and then reciprocity. When it has become organized, while its center is this outward attitude of the self, the hopes and fears, joys and sorrows, triumphs and despairs in which it is so liberal and which fulfill the sentiment, are still self-regarding; they regard the self in its changing relations to the loved object, in the degree of fulfillment or disappointment of its central passion. This is all that the passion-attitude in itself implies, a reaction toward an object significant for the self. In self-consciousness that significance is realized.

But in this case the relation of the self to its object may become profoundly changed when it recognizes that the object, being also intrinsically significant to itself, counterclaims a relation to the object. So love may take a new form. For while the pebble of the brook declares that:

> Love seeketh only Self to please,
> To bind another to its delight.

the trodden clod of clay can sing:

> Love seeketh not itself to please,
>   Nor for itself hath any care,
> But for another gives its ease.[36]

In the first outward direction toward the object of love there was latent the possibility of this spirit also, which comes into being when the object reveals its intrinsic significance to the self first attached to it by its great secondary importance. The recognition of this new significance must have been the moral awakening of the world, the beginning of moral struggles (so essentially related to the passion of love), of egoism and altruism, of moral good and evil.

It is when other selves are recognized as ends to themselves that such emotions as respect or contempt can arise, for in those emotions we view those other selves as failing or attaining even as we fail or attain. In the unity of men in a society, that success or failure is of significance in a double way: significant because other selves have intrinsic value, and significant because their intrinsic value affects our own.

So there arises the conflict of egoism and altruism. That an emotion centers round an object which may be an end to itself does not make the emotion altruistic until that further end itself becomes a determinant of activity. The emotion in itself is neither egoistic nor altruistic, though it holds the seed of both principles. Emotional life at its source as perhaps also at its goal, though not in the intermediate stages, knows nothing of the antagonism of altruism and egoism. In every emotional state the self, careless of all prior "whys," is self-moved toward its object because of the mere appeal of the object. It is never in its origin altruistic, however much it regards another. Spencer is, I think, wrong in attributing altruism to animal conduct where the animal merely centers its affection round others, as the mother about her young.[37] Altruism arises when in the fulfillment of such an instinct as the maternal it comes to be recognized that the end of other beings is subserved in that fulfillment; and the object related to the self in the emotional attitude is recognized as also an end to itself. Then the meaning of the instinct is revealed, and the emotion is developed and transformed by the revelation. It may involve moral struggle, for the maternal sentiment by no means necessarily recognizes this instrinsic significance of its object and may even be antagonistic to it, seeking unduly to make its object merely an object of its devotion. But by this recognition the sentiment

36. Blake, *Songs of Experience.*
37. *Data of Ethics,* Chap. XII.

is moralized, and may well be strengthened, not weakened, in the process.

Without such moralization of the emotions society in the proper sense is impossible. The only society we understand depends on some recognition by its members of the intrinsic significance of one another. Such a recognition *in itself* could neither originate nor maintain a society; there must also exist the secondary significance of each member for the others, the recognition of the individual advantage of mutual service. But, as in the case we considered, where the object subserving our ends is an end also to itself, that intrinsic significance becomes gradually realized and establishes new relations. Essentially it is the moralization of the sentiments, as the self which all along has realized some significance in other selves awakens to the fact that these beings, significant for him, are indeed *selves*. Just as men originally think their own world the center round which all other worlds revolve, so they think their own selves the centers which give significance to all others. The discovery that other selves are equally intrinsic or indeed that the center of significance is outside the individual self altogether—this is the "Copernican revolution" of morality. The growth of this realization is the social process, and the germ of it is present in the most primitive society. "Such society" as we know

> is founded on the recognition by persons of each other and their interest in each other *as persons*, i.e., as beings who are ends to themselves, who are consciously determined to action by the conception of themselves, as that for the sake of which they act. They are interested in each other *as persons* in so far as each, being aware that another presents his own self-satisfaction to himself as an object, finds satisfaction for himself in procuring or witnessing the self-satisfaction of the other. Society is founded on such mutual interest, in the sense that unless it were operative, however incapable of expressing itself in abstract formulae, there would be nothing to lead to that treatment by one human being of another as an end, not merely a means, on which society even in its narrowest and most primitive forms must rest. There would be nothing to countervail the tendency, inherent to the self-asserting and self-seeking object, to make every object he deals with, even an object of natural affection, a means to his own gratification.[38]

The social process, here revealed in its full character, is however a slow one, and we may now trace in outline the more objective stages of moralization, corresponding to the types of moral concept already

38.   Green, *op. cit.*, Bk. II, Chap. 2.

considered. Again the process is revealed as a progress from the more negative to the more positive realization of the self.

All society implies at least social sentiments, but only in its full development is it based on social or moral character. In its early stages, when it recognizes only certain sentiments as of social value, when it is determined by the sentiments based on the instincts of gregariousness or sociability and the instincts which underlie some form of family life, society appears not as a union of selves but as a solidarity of sentiments. That solidarity ensures the preservation of the society, and so far the individual knows his own significance to be bound up with that of others. But the social significance both of himself and of others is very limited. Each is important as a member of a tribe or large family bound together in a system ensuring self-preservation. The further significance of each self is neglected—hence the rigid communistic character of early societies. Each counts as a member of the tribe or family and as that alone. Whoever is outside the tribe remains outside of the society. Here the most comprehensive social sentiment is simply race-feeling, a fact witnessed to by the system of fictitious adoption[39] and the practice of the blood covenant.[40] It is in relation to the conservation of the whole that the individual self has its value.

But here the social emotions are already in being; under the form of race-feeling the individual is learning to realize the intrinsic significance of the other selves thereby bound up with him, and his sentiments are acquiring though within narrow limits a certain disinterestedness; in a word, they are becoming moralized.

More and more sentiments of the individual come to acquire social value, and the end of society and the meaning of morality widen correspondingly. But sentiments are unified only in character, and it is when the whole character of the individual enters into the social fabric, when his social value is no longer exclusively determined by his kinship or religious brotherhood or even citizenship, that he becomes fully autonomous in his social relations. It is only then that the final object of emotional significance is revealed, the intrinsic self in its relation to a society of intrinsic selves. It is only then that the widest social emotions are possible, reaching out beyond the narrow sentiment of race-pride, with its meagerness of content. It is only then that the negative ideals expressed by *must* and *ought* are fully comprehended in the positive ideal of *good*.

39. Cf. Maine, *Ancient Law*, Chap. II.
40. Cf. Westermarck, *op. cit.*, II, p. 208.

CHARACTER AS THE ORGANIZATION
OF SENTIMENTS

Character can be regarded as the organization of sentiments just as sentiments are the organization of emotions. Further, just as sentiments are organized around one predominant emotion, so character is organized around one predominant sentiment. A true character possesses unity, comprehensiveness of interests, and stability, and we have already indicated that there is only sentiment comprehensive enough and deep enough to give character its full development—i.e., the sentiment for the self as an object of intrinsic significance. Books of "characters" such as those of Theophrastus and La Bruyère are in the main attempts to depict the anomalies that result when a partial sentiment determines the whole nature, a regard for extrinsic objects or even a regard for the self determined by a false conception of its intrinsic value.[41] Thus a character determined by pride, vanity, self-seeking, is indeed based on a sentiment of self-regard, but the significance of the self is wrongly conceived. The true or at any rate the moral significance of the self is only understood when it is regarded in its relation to a world of intrinsically significant selves. Just as the child comes to know its physical body in the series of its relations to external physical objects, so he comes to know his psychical self in a series of relations to a world of selves. But there is the important difference that the significance of these selves for us is bound up in the most intimate way with their significance for themselves. As they are significant alike for us and for themselves, so we are significant alike for ourselves and for them. When our reactions are determined by recognition of this double and reciprocal significance, then emotion is moralized and the highest and completest object of emotional significance is revealed. Then character is not only comprehensive but also moral. For the self, the nearest and most effective object of emotional significance, is thereby to the fullest possible extent realized.

It follows, if the above account is correct, that a moral character does not mean simply a specific moral sentiment or sentiments but a

---

41.   It is possible also to describe "characters" from the point of view of *temperament*, i.e., in respect of certain formal qualities of reaction ("slow," "quick," "intermittent," and the like) considered apart from the direction and the type of object involved. French psychologists (Perez, Fouillée, and to some extent Paulhan and Ribot) tend to classify character in terms of temperament (as "lively," "slow," "ardent," "sensitive," "active," etc.), but character is a development not explicable in terms of the formal and abstract aspects of reactions. These on the whole remain unchanged throughout the development, though it would be important, in any treatise on the subject, to consider how far they form the basis to, as distinct from the content of, character.

moralization of the whole nature. Every sentiment can be moralized, however narrow or however extended its range. So we cannot, for instance, derive morality simply from the sentiment of sympathy, as Adam Smith and Schopenhauer both tend to do. Sympathy implies the previous development of the moral nature of the individual, and is only moral when based on that nature. For a man can be as sympathetic to evil as to good, and sympathy unguided by the strong central direction of a unified character may prove a weakness rather than a strength. Nor can we isolate certain emotions and say these and these alone are the moral emotions. This doctrine, that there are specific moral emotions —the modern equivalent of the doctrine of the moral sense—has recently been put forward by Professor Westermarck. The moral emotions he regards as moral approval and disapproval, the former being a species of "retributive kindly emotion" and akin to though distinct from the emotion of gratitude, the latter a species of resentment, and akin to anger and revenge.[42] It is difficult at the outset to see why all moral emotion should be retributive emotion, and why within these limits anger and gratitude should not be, in their due place, of moral value. We must note that Professor Westermarck is only seeking to trace the emotions that give rise to judgments of morality, but moral conduct is more than moral judgment on conduct, whether that of others or our own. Accordingly, the emotions of moral approval and disapproval —if indeed these are specific emotions at all—are not the only moral *motives*, and do not by themselves create moral character. Within every sentiment the emotion of approval may arise, and that approval is moral if it fulfills the condition already set forth.

RELATION OF THE EMOTIONAL TO THE REFLECTIVE CONSCIOUSNESS

We have seen that the moralization of sentiments is possible only when the emotional consciousness becomes reflective. It would follow that the difference between the emotional and the reflective attitude is in no sense absolute and that not even here can we draw any dividing line. This is the truth of Hume's remark that "what is commonly, in a popular sense, called reason, and is so much recommended in moral discourse, is nothing but a general and a calm passion, which takes a comprehensive and a distant view of its object."[43] The view that passion is something quite distinct from reason is the basis of those ethical theories which

42. *Origin and Development of the Moral Ideas*, Chap. II.
43. *Dissertation on the Passions*, Sec. V.

imply that passion is an element in human nature which must either be subordinated to another element—the views of, for example, Plato and Butler (so Butler says that "self-love is in human nature a principle superior to passion")—or altogether crushed—the view of the Stoics, Spinoza, and most Eastern philosophies. Such views imply that human nature is a loose composite of elements, passion being one, an inferior or altogether undesirable element. We find the same idea prevalent in popular and literary thought. Thus Bernard Shaw declares that to him "the tragedy and comedy of life lie in the consequences of our persistent attempts to found our institutions on the ideals suggested to our imaginations by our half-satisfied passions, instead of on a genuinely scientific natural history."[44] Here the term passion is used to stand for a certain kind of strong passion (much as "drink" is used in the sense of a certain kind of strong drink), with no clear perception of the universal element it contains.

The truth, whatever it is, underlying these views can be revealed only when we relate the emotional to the reflective consciousness and see that the latter is not independent of the former but rather a development of it. Our reason modifies, clarifies, unifies our emotions; it does not overthrow them. It strengthens one emotion at the cost of another; it weakens one for the sake of another. It is the emotional consciousness in which the significance of objects is primarily determined, and reflection always works in the interest of some realized significance.

The emotional consciousness is spontaneous. It takes the value of the end or object for granted. In loving or hating it raises no question as to whether the object is worth loving or hating. For passions there is no estimating, no problem of values. Hence when a single passion possesses the mind, there is a great felt unity of consciousness, which reflection is apt to weaken. Passion ensures concentration within the limits of its activity, not dissipation. Hence the evil effects on character when partial or nonessential passions determine the being, for all other ends are trampled upon or wrested to the service of the end that the passion determines. Passion is not blind but intensely keen-sighted—only it can see nothing but its own object. It rejects all ideas save those that are relevant to the service of its end. Passion knows only its own significance; hence its great value when its object is truly significant.

It is in the conflict of passions that the need of a further determining principle appears. When different passions arise with divergent claims to the engrossment of the nature, the being at the mercy of the mere emotional consciousness is distracted and torn. One passion is now predominant, now another; the former harmony is succeeded by an

44. Introduction to *Pleasant Plays.*

equally great disharmony. Each passion claims entire significance, and the mere emotional consciousness cannot settle the warring claims. In this mere conflict of passions either the unity of character is destroyed or else one is strong enough to overpower the others. If it is a new passion that destroys an older and in its turn engrosses the nature, there occurs a kind of "conversion" of the being, which feels thereby renewed or revolutionized.[45]

PRIMACY OF THE EMOTIONAL CONSCIOUSNESS

Reflection entering in puts an end to this conflict *à outrance*, as it does to other antagonisms. But reflection can only take us back to a further or more comprehensive significance. It cannot itself create significance. Hence it is concerned either, as we have already seen, with the choice of means to an end whose significance is undisputed or, as we now see, with the evaluation of ends in the light of a further equally undisputed end. The very motive to the activity of reason is itself, at the last, a passion. It is not, at the last, passions *per se* but contrary passion, that is opposed to reason.

This primacy of the emotional consciousness becomes clear if we reflect on the meaning of *duty*. The sense of duty arises either (1) when an end of action is imposed on the being from without and yet regarded as its proper end, or (2) when an end imposed from within has lost its original emotional significance. In the first case, action is determined by a negative realization of value—i.e., the significance of the nonfulfillment of the end is realized, and realized emotionally, and so motives conduct. In the second case, the realized significance has a more positive character, but there is now no longer the emotional spontaneity. In proportion to the prominence of the *ought*, the attractiveness of the end has diminished, both as a prospect of satisfaction and an actual satisfaction. Yet there is still an emotional realization of significance, though it is the significance of the rule, not of the act, that is realized, a less immediate realization, seeing it involves a sense of constraint in respect of the individual act. There is no emotional unity corresponding to the unity of conduct.

Our ordinary consciousness sets a higher value on the conduct which is freely or spontaneously determined. It dislikes the cold calculator who "rationalizes" every act of service to his fellows. He is disinterested, his will is good, his power of reasoning may be sure, but there is yet something lacking to full morality, a warmth in his interest,

45. Cf. James, *Varieties of Religious Experience.*

a spontaneity in the sentiment that moves him to act. Within certain spheres, those of the more primary affections, "dutiful" action does not carry full moral approval. Further, a man may come to be as much at the mercy of the immediate "reasonableness" of a proposed end as he was formerly at the mercy of impulse. This is well seen in the process of the education of "uncivilized" or "half-civilized" peoples. In a milder form, it is what we condemn as "sophistication."

The total absence of emotion would be the total negation of activity. There would be no spontaneity, no desire, no satisfaction, no sense of value. It is emotion which primarily determines significance; in its utter absence "nothing would matter."[46]

INADEQUACY OF THE EMOTIONAL CONSCIOUSNESS

Even though the emotional consciousness is thus both primary and necessary, it is essentially inadequate. In itself the emotional consciousness is either insecure or unprogressive. It is secure according to the strength of the emotions of approval and disapproval it contains; but these emotions generally work for conservation, not for progress. This is especially characteristic of religious approval and disapproval which tend to render the mind inaccessible to new thoughts. Further, morality based on the emotional consciousness, if once shaken or lost, can only with the greatest difficulty be restored. There is no true or enduring self-regard such as reflective morality ensures. Thus the more emotional virtue, once overthrown, is the more completely lost.

It is only, therefore, as the emotional consciousness becomes reflective that morality is rendered secure and perfect; and this is attained when emotion is attached to an object of the most comprehensive and enduring significance or when subordinate passions find their limits assigned within a central stable passion. We have indicated that this is achieved when the intrinsic significance of the self is realized both as distinguished from objects of secondary significance and as related to the world of other selves with their own intrinsic significances. By the first process the self-regard, the primary passion, is delivered from irrelevance; by the second it is widened to any degree of universality. But we must remember that, however far the individual self is thus carried to self-abnegation and self-forgetfulness in the recognition of a society of intrinsic selves of which he forms but a unit, such abnegation must arise out of the realization of his own self-significance. Without that

46. This fact is strikingly illustrated in an article on "Depersonalisation and Emotion" in the *Revue Philosophique*, November 1910.

self-regard the wider regard for others is meaningless. Reflection can reveal to us the meaning and relations of the self-significance, but that is itself determined by a primal passion, beyond reflection. Ultimately there is spontaneity of reaction, a primal passion beyond which we cannot pass—the end so given is beyond reflection, revealed in it but not determined by it. The self is rooted in its passion–nature, for apart from passion nothing has significance. Thence proceed our fundamental moral judgments. But as self-consciousness develops, the first unity of the being is lost in the competing claims of significant objects, and moral problems arise. Reflection may restore that unity so far as it can reveal one object whose significance readjusts these competing claims. The new unity is the unity of the realized character, with its corresponding comprehensive emotion. And this new unity, unlike the old, is progressive. It rests on a progressive realization of end, a progressive readjustment of the relation of one intrinsic self to others. The way in which, as morality becomes reflective, the significance of what is only partial, partially good, partially beautiful, fades as we dwell long in its presence, is the surest safeguard of our spiritual advance.

[Previously unpublished; written during Oxford University days]

Personality and the Suprapersonal

II ULTIMATE VALUES AS PERSONAL VALUES

All ethical philosophies—except one—have this point at least in common: they all agree that ultimate good or value is to be found only in states of conscious life, that nothing else than such states or such life can be conceived as good in itself, for its own sake. On this axiom the construction which follows is founded and if it is false the construction certainly fails. Yet to me the statement is self-evident, so self-evident that it seems impossible to disprove any contradictory view, for there is no more ultimate premise by which to test its truth or falsehood. If anyone maintains that there are other ultimate values than those of conscious life, I cannot argue against him; for I do not understand him. I know of no other ends-in-themselves than these. If anyone maintains that there may conceivably be other ultimate values or ends in themselves than conscious beings, this remains for me as blank a possibility as any other toward which our experience lends no support. For me, the terms "ultimate value" and "good-in-itself" are bereft of meaning when they are applied to any object which is not conscious life, to anything impersonal. Nothing which does not live and strive can seek for good, and no state of that which does not live and strive for good can be called good-in-itself.

It is impossible to prove what is axiomatic, but by the aid of some preliminary distinctions we may bring out more fully its significance. In the first place, we do not say that all states of conscious beings are good in themselves, but that *only* states of conscious being can be good in themselves. Obviously not all such states are good, for we seek to alter them in our very search for good, and may even, in extreme cases, regard the cessation of conscious being as better than its continuance. If only states of conscious being can be good in themselves, then only states of conscious being can be evil in themselves. To say "good in itself" is to claim that something ought to exist, to say "evil in itself" is to claim that something ought not to exist. But neither claim is made of the impersonal. Its existence is regarded neither as good in itself nor as evil in itself, but only in relation to conscious life, as furthering or retarding *its* good, as fulfilling or diminishing *its* value.

Here a second distinction emerges. The conscious being *seeks* after his good (and that of others as well as his own), always seeks though he does not always find. His good is realized, therefore, not in his mere existence as conscious subject, but in or by relation to what is objective. A difference of relation, a difference of object, certainly does not leave unaffected the value or good of the subject. In a word, the intrinsic value or value-in-itself which we express by the term "person" is somehow dependent on extrinsic values, on what is not value-in-itself. In so far, for instance, as any environment, social or material, of a conscious being evokes his faculties, satisfies his needs, arouses any emotion or activity in him which can be regarded as good—stimulates, for instance, his sense of the beauty or nobility of living—in so far that environment is an extrinsic value. Whatever fulfills or makes possible intrinsic value, while itself not also intrinsic value, may be named extrinsic value, being good or worth not in its own right but as accomplishing this service.

Further, it may accomplish this service either immediately or mediately, either by its very existence or as the condition of the existence of some other object sought. Contrast, say, a work of art and a machine in this respect. The former satisfies the subject directly, by its presence; it is an object which the subject seeks to have or to create, finding worth in the mere having or creating. At the other extreme stands the mere machine which subserves intrinsic value indirectly, not in its existence as object but in its products alone. It is noteworthy that the person can be regarded by his fellows as coming under any of these categories, either as intrinsic value in respect of personality or as immediate extrinsic value in respect of the stimulus of his presence or society or as mediate extrinsic value as serving, like a machine, the ends of these others. In effect persons are so interdependent that they naturally fall in respect of one another under not one but all three of these categories at the same time. The real ethical and social question is one of priority as between these. Is the person regarded by others as primarily an intrinsic value, such as they regard themselves, or is he primarily an extrinsic value; is he to them finally perhaps a mere machine, his value as person counting least, his value as means being the first or only consideration?

To this point we must return later. Meanwhile I have tried to insist on the distinction of mediate from immediate extrinsic value, because we sometimes tend to confuse one of these, immediate extrinsic value, with intrinsic value. There are outer objects which we seek, as we say, "for themselves," which we see to be good as the God of Genesis saw the whole world to be good. We seek nothing further from them than to know or perceive or experience them, to be in their presence. But this, we must clearly remember, is not to say that these are values-in-themselves or intrinsic values. It is for us that they are values, and what is not value-to-itself cannot be value-in-itself. It is the seeing and the knowing which is good in itself, not the seen and the known. If we say we want those outer objects for themselves we really mean that we want to see and know them. It is we who taste and see that they are good, we in whose experience of them their goodness, though not their existence, lies. As value the person stands utterly by himself, for it is the person which alone realizes values; but as subject of value he is necessarily dependent upon object of value.

But what, it may be said, of those "objects" which are not "outer," what of "thoughts" or "ideas" which also, no less than outer or material beings, we can distinguish from the minds which have or think them? Are these extrinsic or intrinsic values? But the very question involves, I believe, a confusion. Unless we are illegitimately using the term "idea" for that of which we "have" an idea, the distinction of mind and its ideas is not at all like the distinction of mind and outer objects. The idea can have no existence whatever except for the mind, and if we speak of conscious life as value-in-itself we are including ideas in the sphere of value-in-itself, though not as something in any way apart from mind. We cannot attribute value to ideas except as attributing value to minds. That the Idea or Notion, however interpreted, should be the goal of conscious life, that this so-called content of personality should endure, like the kernel extracted from a nut, while personality itself passes away, is a doctrine to which I can attach no meaning. The succession of persons on this view resembles, if it resemble anything at all, some monstrous cosmic torch race in which the torch is everything and the bearers of it nothing, in which victory belongs to the torch alone, not to those who sweat and run to win.

THE WORLD OF PERSONS AS A UNITY

Starting from our axiom that ultimate value can attach to persons alone
—"persons" being here employed as inclusive of all conscious beings
that in any degree at all can strive toward what they conceive as good
and so become ends to themselves—we have next to enquire as to the
nature of that whole of values, if there be such, into which persons enter
or which together they constitute. We conceive the physical world
as one coherent system in spite of all the spatial separations of its parts,
in spite of the various and the seeming contrary manifestations of its
forces. Can we likewise conceive the world of persons, regarded as
ultimate values, as also a coherent system, in spite of the distinctness,
difference, and only too real oppositions involved in their pursuit of
their ends? The question thus raised concerns not merely the coherence
or unity of particular groups, communities, and associations of persons,
but the necessary basis of all such unities, the ground of interpersonal
coherence revealed in the very nature of the distinct persons so uniting,
so cohering.

I propose first to criticize certain conceptions of that unity which
seem to me to rest on fallacy, next to review the actual facts on which,
as I believe, any true conception must be based, and finally to show that
these facts do reveal the reality and the nature of a coherent spiritual
world, regarded as a whole of values.

FALSE CONCEPTIONS OF THAT UNITY

There is one fundamental fallacy to which almost all false constructions
of this whole of values may be traced, *the fallacy that a whole inclusive of
units can be represented as a macrocosm of microcosms of the same order.* We
seek a unity inclusive of many like elements or individuals, and we often
obstinately refuse to think this more comprehensive unity, to name
this new synthesis, except in terms of the like elements which are unified
or synthesized. We think of a system of persons as a person, a system
of organisms as an organism, a system of minds as a mind; but the identification is in every case fallacious. It is just as if we were, for instance, to
think of an army as itself a soldier, or a constellation as itself a star. It is
in fact a logical impossibility that the unity attained through the coordination of like objects of any kind should itself be of the same character
as the unity of each of the like objects so coordinated. If any microcosms
were just miniatures of any macrocosm, then that macrocosm would

not bind together, could not be the unity of these microcosms. A system of persons can no more be a person than a system of planets can be a planet, or a system of triangles a triangle.[1] If we mean by the suprapersonal the whole in which persons are united, then the suprapersonal cannot be a supra- or super-person.

This fallacy is such an obstacle to the true understanding of the ethical unity of persons that it may be worth while to examine it in some detail. It has two chief forms, one the conception of the whole of persons as an organism or superorganism, the other the conception of the whole of persons as itself a mind or spirit. In reality the microcosm in this instance is an organico-psychical unity, neither organism (as usually understood) alone nor mind (as usually understood) alone; but the difficulty of comprehending the macrocosm as also such an organico-psychical unity leads to the emphasis of either aspect in the attempt to construct the whole in terms of the unit.

a. The Whole of Persons as Organism. The conception of the whole of persons as forming one organism or body may be traced back to the very beginnings of social reflection. It is natural to explain the greater or remoter in terms of the smaller or nearer unity, and there are always sufficient points of resemblance to make the identification of nature plausible. Our first question, when we turn to consider any kind of object hitherto unconsidered, is rather: What is it like? than, What is it? For we cannot say what it is until its nature is fully explored, but we can at once say what it is like in terms of what we know already. So it was natural to compare the unity of communities to the unity of the body, and we still speak of a "body of men," "the body politic," "the mystical body of the church," and so on. But we must remember that it is one thing to find resemblances, another to find identity, one thing to find analogy between organism and community, another thing to say that community *is* organism or organic. It would be an interesting study to trace how, for instance, during the Middle Ages, men began by finding points of resemblance between communities and bodies and ended by finding identity of nature. The grotesque conclusions to which the thoroughgoing identification of these two unities must lead are revealed with medieval candor in such writers as John of Salisbury or Nicolaus of Cues, a study of whose works would, I submit, form in this respect a most useful introduction to the study of Spencer and of Schäffle.

Here we are concerned with only one aspect of this identification.

---

1.   It may be objected that, for example, a system of armies may itself be an army; but in this and all similar cases the unit turns out to be not a true unit, but itself a system of units. So an army is finally a system of soldiers and a society a system of persons.

If the whole of persons is conceived of as possessing the kind of unity which an organism possesses, persons being related to one another as either the cells or the organs of organism are related to one another, then the whole of values which we are seeking becomes itself a value of the whole distinct from any values of the parts. Strictly speaking, I think it is illegitimate to attach teleological attributes to organism at all. When we speak of organism we speak of an abstraction, though the abstraction is perfectly legitimate when what we are investigating is itself the organic or physiological *aspect* of living things. But it is different when we are investigating the conscious or psychical aspect, and we cannot talk of value or end except in terms of consciousness. Since then it is just this aspect which is left out in the abstraction "organism," it is inappropriate to talk at all of organism as end to itself or of its parts as means to that end. We may speak, a little loosely, of the cells and organs of organism as serving the end of the whole, though the whole then becomes not the organism but the organico-psychical being. Thus we get, by a somewhat dubious process of construction, the conception of a structure with a single intrinsic end to which all its parts are interdependent means; and it is after this fashion that we are sometimes asked to construe the end of society. Society is then to be regarded as having an end in itself which is other than and beyond the ends of its members, an end to which they are in so far merely contributory means. Humanity, for instance, is thus conceived of as an end to which all men are but ministers, nationality as an end to which all the members of a nation are mere instruments, and so forth.

It is easy to show that this mode of conception is really a disguised form of an absolute-idea theory which, when plainly expressed, we agree in rejecting, since it regards as transcendent that which is in reality immanent. It regards humanity as something more than men, nationality as something more than the members of a nation. It suggests that it is possible to work for humanity otherwise than by working for men, to serve nationality otherwise than by serving the members of a nation. In so far as the end and value of society are regarded as other than the ends and values of its members taken as a whole, the latter count for less than before, becoming in so far mere means to an end which is beyond, not merely each as individual, but all as collective. Not only can we not give meaning and concreteness to such a value, but the postulation of it deprives of actuality the values we actually know. If the whole be such as to have an end which is realized otherwise than as the fulfillment of the ends of its parts or persons, then personality is in so far an illusion; for it rests on the being of each as an end in itself, and all its striving is understandable only on the supposition that each person and the other persons for whom also he strives are ends in themselves.

It is doubtless a permissible *hypothesis* that personality is an illusion, it is possible that we are in this sense, to use Browning's words, "God's puppets." But it is well to realize that this is the implication of the doctrine we are criticizing. If it were true, it would mean that we are working for an end we do not know, as the puppet serves an end it does not know. It is well also to realize that *ex hypothesi* we can never give significance to this conception, which must remain a blank possibility. It raises an insurmountable wall in face of which our philosophy can never even begin to advance. Finally, it is also well to realize that we must always philosophize on the ground of what we actually know and feel, for that at least must be part of reality, however great the portion which remains unknown, undreamed of in our philosophies.

In passing we may note that, if we cannot conceive the whole of values in terms of organism, we can still less conceive it in terms of mechanism. This is contradictory from the outset; for the parts which are related into mechanism are doubly not for themselves, since the whole is by definition not for itself. Dr. Bosanquet, for instance, suggests more than once that "If minds were visible as bodies are, . . . they would not look like similar repeated units, but rather each would appear as a member of a mechanism pointing beyond itself and unintelligible apart from others —one like a wheel, another like a piston, and a third, perhaps, like steam."[2] This mechanistic view I believe to be the most fundamental and vicious of all social fallacies. So interpreted, both the likeness, here unduly minimized, and the difference of persons have their *raison d'être* wholly outside themselves, wholly extrinsic. So personality becomes meaningless.

b. The Whole of Persons as a Mind or Spirit. The form of fallacy we have been considering does not stand by itself, but owes what plausibility it possesses to its association with a second form of fallacy which we must now examine, that according to which the whole of persons is conceived as constituting a mind or spirit, a "collective" or "super-individual" mind, which in turn may itself appear as an element in an "absolute" or universal mind. This fallacy we have already refuted in showing that no whole can have to its units or parts the relation of macrocosm to microcosms; but its prevalence justifies a fuller consideration of it.

Here I am not at all concerned with the question whether there be some "oversoul" in the sense of a greater mind or spirit into communion with which any or all individuals of a lower order may enter. Were that contention established it would leave this argument unaffected. What I am concerned to deny is that the actual unity constituted

2.   *The Value and Destiny of the Individual*, p. 50.

by any whole system of minds can be represented as itself a mind. It was so conceived, though I think with unhappy results, by Plato in the fourth book of the *Republic*, and it is still so conceived by influential psychologists and philosophers today.

Dr. McDougall, for instance, writes as follows: "We may fairly define a mind as an organized system of mental or purposive forces; and in the sense so defined, every highly organized human society may properly be said to possess a collective mind."[3] But this is to repeat the "macrocosm–microcosm" fallacy. A mind is no more definable as an organized system of mental forces than a planet is definable as an organized system of planetary forces. If when many minds enter within a system of mental relations they thereby constitute or "possess" a collective mind, why, for instance, when many soldiers enter within a system of military relations should they not constitute or "possess" a "collective soldier"? There is in truth common or social mind in the sense of the common or typical mental characteristics involved and developed in all society, and we may *in this sense* speak of the "mind of a race," the "soul of a people" and so forth. But the term "collective mind" is mere confusion.

I have tried to show elsewhere[4] that this doctrine of the "super-individual mind" is finally due to our taking "the individual" in an abstract sense, as if society were something set over against its members instead of being realized in them. If we understand that "the individual" is always also the social individual, the abstractness disappears, and with it the need for a transcendental "social mind" as the unity of society. Another form of the same illicit abstraction is found in the use often made of the term "self" in this connection. We are told, for instance, that in society the self "transcends itself" by entering into the larger unity of mind. But what is this "self-transcendence," and which item in this double and contradictory selfhood is the real self, that which transcends itself or that which is by itself transcended? We wander here in a region of contradictions. What poor selfhood is it that in all experiences of any depth must be "transcended"? Do you mean by self-transcendence only that in certain experiences the self enters into relation with something other than or beyond itself? But is not that true of *all* experience? The conscious being, the subject of experience, cannot act at all, cannot reveal itself, except in relation to objects, to a world. But why call that activity and revelation "self-transcendence"? To enter into relation with a world beyond oneself, whether material or psychical, is not to cease to be oneself. To be shut off from these relations is not to remain oneself.

---

3. *Psychology* (Home University Library), p. 229.
4. *Sociological Review*, April, 1913, and January, 1914.

To be wholly so shut off would be in fact to cease to be a self at all, to become nothing.[5]

It is true we speak of being taken "out of ourselves" when we become absorbed in some deep experience, even of being "beside our-selves" when, if ever, we feel inspired. But obviously we mean by that simply that we are taken out of the ordinary circle of our experiences, out of the thoughts and emotions which are the atmosphere of our everyday life, into new and greater experiences. In such experiences we may be more, not less, ourselves. To call such experience "self-transcendence," in order to find the reality of selfhood outside the selves for whom they are experiences, is to trade solemnly on the literal accep-tation of a metaphor. When, in particular, our experience is widened or deepened by communion with our fellow men, we are neither "absorbed" in them nor they in us nor are all together "absorbed" into one greater mind. The common experience of many minds does not become the single experience of one greater mind, nor the common will of many the greater will of one. It is still individual minds which enjoy the experience they recognize as common.

Those who cling to the contrary view speak of the distinction of self from self as merely "formal." But why formal? Can we conceive of minds as "forms," mere vessels, indifferently filled with "contents"? When a self grows, does it merely become filled with "contents," "notions," "thoughts"? It is implied that by the removal of the "formal distinctness" the selves would coalesce. Again the spatial metaphor, and this time not true even of spatial things. When you can bring two peas together and make them coalesce into a greater pea—or even conceive them as coalescing—then we may perhaps talk of the coalescence of selves.

The same fallacy takes a wider range when we conceive the whole of values not as a social mind but as an *absolute* mind. It too falls under the general condemnation that we are then conceiving the unity or syn-thesis of the whole as either an enlargement or an apotheosis of the nature of the several units of the whole. If we so conceive it, we are inevitably

5.   This is well illustrated by Ibsen in the 4th act of *Peer Gynt*. The irresponsible hero imagines he has found himself when he has merely become self-centered. His self, he boasts, is

"All that, in short, makes my breast heave,
And whereby I, as I, exist."

But the poet brings him after many disquieting experiences to visit a madhouse of which, in virtue of his theory of self, he is proclaimed King; and he learns that the logical fulfill-ment of that unreal selfhood is merely madness, for it is among the mad that

"No one has tears for the others' woes,
No one has mind for the others' ideas."

compelled to deny the reality of the units. You cannot make a greater circle the synthesis of an array of smaller circles without in fact denying that the smaller circles are really circles at all—otherwise the greater circle would merely enclose, not unify them. Likewise you cannot conceive a greater mind as the unity of a vast array of lesser minds unless you deny the reality of the lesser minds—otherwise the greater would merely enclose or control, and not be the synthesis of the whole. It is possible that a greater spirit may so enclose or control the minds or spirits which alone we know; it is not possible that it should be the synthesis of these unless in fact their meaning, their individuality, their distinct existence, is denied. That is why the Hegelians must "transmute" or "merge" the self in the absolute. They are really seeking to conceive the life of the whole as at once the macrocosm and yet the mere enlargement or apotheosis or "sublimation" of the microcosm. They want to make the totality or universality or synthesis of mind or spirit at the same time *an* absolute mind or spirit, *the* absolute mind or spirit.

The real impossibility of this project was realized by Fichte, who saw that the expression "the absolute Ego" was a contradiction in terms and, dropping the "Ego," spoke simply of "the Absolute."[6] But his successors, while retaining his term "the Absolute," seem to have lost sight of the contradiction discovered by its author, and have come to speak as if the term still meant *an* or *the* absolute Ego or subject or mind. Hegel was himself on the whole willing to sacrifice personality to his Absolute, but *his* successors have latterly been evincing the desire both to have and eat their cake. The world is spoken of as a place where personality manifests itself, where souls are made, but the making is unreal after all; for nothing remains in the Absolute save that mysteriously detached "content" with which the self was filled, the "content" of a timeless being, and therefore nothing is gained, nothing is new. The sacrifice and the struggle avail nothing, for what exists in the end existed even so in the beginning. The making of souls proves as valuable as the making of ropes of sand. I believe, indeed, that here we are brought face to face with the final problem, if not of metaphysics, at least of ethics—the problem of reconciling the undoubted fact that the world we know is a world in which personality is achieved through time and struggle with the necessity of thought which leads us on the other hand to seek after a permanent reality which always was and is and shall be, changeless and without shadow of turning. It may be that the problem is insoluble; it is certain to my mind that the neo-Hegelian solution is no solution. For, whatever happens, we must make our account with

---

6.   For the significance of this transition it is sufficient to refer to Professor Pringle-Pattison's exposition of it in *Hegelianism and Personality*.

our experience, and this Absolutism can never do, since it is bound to a conclusion which involves the denial of the reality of experience, of change, struggle, and time, of the process without which personality is not achieved, and thus of personality itself. The new philosophy of Bergson, which boldly denies the aforementioned necessity of thought, may be equally one-sided in an opposite direction, but at any rate, in insisting on the reality of change and time and becoming, it in so far rests on the foundation of what we know, it makes its account with experience. It is the strength of philosophic faith to believe in that which is invisible, but it is only the weakness of faith to deny the visible on that account. And possibly it may be the final act of philosophic faith to believe that there is no appearance which is not also an element of reality, nor any necessity of thought which can contradict, however it may reinterpret, the experience of life itself.

The same fallacy meets us again in certain theological doctrines of the immanence of deity. Here again the suprapersonal becomes the macrocosmic person, now conceived not as above the personal microcosm but as revealed within it. Like the absolutist, the immanence-theologian wants to have and eat his cake. We may regard deity as immanent and revealed in every manifestation of life and spirit, and in so doing we may do well; or we may regard deity as the highest manifestation of spirit, the highest toward which even the lowest feebly reaches and looks, and again in doing so we may do well. But we cannot regard deity as at once both the whole and the highest, as both the unity in which all life is one and some ideal personality toward which all life perhaps tends in its degree. If God is really the whole there is no need for us to seek Him in one direction rather than another. For we are already in God, and in every activity we are equally finding Him. "Not I but the God in me" will be true of every action, and will serve for neither approbation nor condonation, for neither is now needed. The distinction of higher and lower disappears, or at any rate becomes merely one of more and less.

It is most certainly true that we can seek nothing which we do not already in part possess, that we can worship nothing whose nature we do not adumbrate in ourselves.

> Wär' nicht das Auge sonnenhaft
> Die Sonne könnt' es nie erblicken;
> Lag' nicht in uns des Gottes eigne Kraft
> Wie könnt' uns Göttliches entzücken?

It is also true—and more relevant to the mood of the seeker and worshipper—that we worship what is *beyond* ourselves, seeking not meaningless identity but effectual communion. It is not that the part seeks the whole —how can it?—nor that the part worships the whole—again how can it? It is needless and illogical to assume that a being absolutely wise and good need be comprehensive of all personality, still less of all reality. I can see no philosophical reason to suppose that if there be one all wise and all good spirit there should not be any number of beings beside Him and not merely absorbed within Him. Nay, I see no contradiction in supposing that if there be one spirit all wise and good there might be others likewise all wise and good. The contrary view rests on an unfounded analogy between physical completeness and psychical perfection. If we create God after our own image, if we regard Him as *a* mind or spirit, possessing in perfection the attributes we ourselves possess in part, it is not the unity or whole of spirit we so conceive. If on the other hand we prefer to give the name of God to this great cosmos of life within which all particular things live and move and have their being, possessing not only the perfected nature of any one part or kind of being, of man, humanity, or soul, but the unity and nature that no part can ever possess, since it is that which binds it to the whole—then we renounce the conception of a God after our own image and should honestly accept all the consequences which flow from the renunciation.

It may be objected that in speaking of God as perfect Spirit you have left out the third of the necessary trinity of attributes involved in perfection. You have regarded Him as all wise and all good, but to be perfect involves being all powerful as well. Complete the trinity and it appears that what is perfect must also be all comprehensive, for what is all powerful must be universal, in and through every activity of the cosmos. It must be answered that the attribution of omnipotence to any existence is contradictory if that existence be only a part, and meaningless, if it be the whole of reality. If it is the whole to which you attribute omnipotence, over what is it omnipotent? If only a part, the part again becomes the whole, for the attribution to it of omnipotence deprives the rest of character, of existence. If one person be literally all powerful, all other persons are phantoms. If, however, I really have power so much as to move a finger at my will, so much as to conceive a thought, that power destroys the present claim to omnipotence of any other power in the universe. To be all wise does not, any more than to be all good, involve such all comprehensiveness of the being so endowed. One aspect of omniscience may, indeed, be the knowledge of the power, which is the knowledge of the nature, of all other beings. It is therefore a possible attribute of a personality, as all goodness is, but omnipotence is an impossible, because finally an unmeaning, attribute of any personality. The understanding of this truth would, among other things, set the whole problem of evil in a new light.

Enough has perhaps now been said by way of showing the directions in which we must not look for the understanding of that whole of values or persons to which each particular person is bound. We may now turn to the positive aspect, and consider the actual facts relative to this whole of persons, seeking finally for an interpretation or synthesis of these facts.

WHAT WE REALLY KNOW OF
SUPRAPERSONAL UNITY

The facts in whose interpretation we must find our whole of values, our suprapersonal unity, are pre-eminently those relative to the *interdependence* of persons. The mere fact of *likeness* of nature or *identity* of type is wholly inadequate as a clue. This type-identity compels us, indeed, to think of some common origin of life, or, as it were, some single mold whence living beings have issued; but it does not reveal the character of whatever present and continuous unity holds all the representations of any type, the realities which manifest the type. To find this unity we must enquire into the relations between those representatives, and particularly the relations of interdependence.

These relations fall into two great orders. One is the *successive* dependence of the generations, of every life upon those which have preceded; the other is the *reciprocal* dependence of contemporaneous lives within the community. The one binds through time, the other in every present stage.

a. The former is revealed primarily as biological succession. Herein each life is utterly dependent, being derived from pre-existent lives. The person looks beyond himself to a future of other persons. Much of the life and activity of each individual is meaningless on the assumption that he lives merely for himself; and this applies to his psychical as well as to his organic nature. On the organic side, "so far as we can at present understand the matter, the physiology of death, and that of reproductive and social activity in all their wide manifestations, belong to the physiology of the species."[7] Likewise much of the psychical nature of every person, his desires and affections, lose meaning, until we realize that these are directed, not to the present life alone of himself and others, but to the future life of those who are to succeed. In this way each knows himself, body and spirit, to be part of, to belong to, a whole of persons continuous through time.

Besides this direct dependence, there is the wider dependence due to the social transmission of the gains of the past and present to the

---

7.   J.S. Haldane, *Mechanism, Life, and Personality.*

future. Whatever any generation has thought or wrought becomes a kind of capital, expressed in symbols or mechanisms of many kinds, and thus becomes, through the educability of all young life, the *means* to the increase of personal values in all succeeding generations. We are thus doubly the heirs of the past and confer a double legacy upon our heirs. (And of course the evil no less than the good is transmitted.) Now the higher the standard of life the greater is this legacy. For each individual life starts from a seeming-common basis of nescience and inexperience, and the higher it advances from this state the more educable must it have proved. Thus where society is most advanced it is most dependent on the past.

It should also be remembered that since each new life unites the inheritance of two parents, and each of these again of two others, and so on, every life within any area of effective community derives itself from an intermixture of stock so extensive that, if we go back far enough, it must make every person the direct descendant of a whole community. Nay, if we can think back still further and remember that communities themselves have not lived in isolation from the first but have arisen out of one another, it may appear that wherever we have community of type at all there we have also common origin, common biological dependence. Life, though it reveals itself in individuality, arises out of essential and ever-completer intermixture. Each new life owes itself, not to one linear series of past lives, but to a whole past race, finally, perhaps, to a whole past history of the universe.

This historic dependence must not be misunderstood. The successive children of the race owe their lives to their parents, and finally to the whole race, but they are not themselves mere reproductions of past lives, merely epitomes of the race. Life is always new. Intermixture is the universal way by which all higher life renews itself, but there is something more in this renewal of life than we can hope to understand. Intermixture alone makes nothing new. It is the process by means of which new life is created, it does not account for the newness of that life. Each new life is a new center of initiative, of individuality, which we can never explain wholly in terms of past lives. Again, though no life can be understood as existing for its own sake alone, it can still less be understood—as Mr. Benjamin Kidd, for instance, would have us think—as existing for the sake of the succession alone, for the sake of the future alone. So to think of it is to reduce the whole chain of values to universal unintelligibility. Each becomes then a means to future values which in turn prove to be themselves but means to a remoter future, and so *in infinitum*. Unless we understand that each life is also for its own sake, we cannot understand how it is for the sake of other lives.

b. Persons or selves are bound up in contemporaneous no less than in historic interdependence, and here we reach the facts which most of all reveal the nature of superindividual unity. For the relations we are now to consider, unlike those already considered, are *reciprocal* relations. Herein persons are united in common dependence upon one another. In heredity one being is dependent upon other beings who are not in turn similarly dependent upon the former, one generation is dependent upon previous generations which do not owe a similar debt to their descendants. Historic dependence is the dependence of a chain of values through time, but this reciprocal social dependence is the common dependence of a whole of values in the present, and it is this which finally affords us the clue to the nature of a *whole of values through time* as well.

To understand it we must, I believe, start from the basis that all interdependent selves are essentially alike, and that it is this likeness which alone makes all social relations between them possible. Some hold that in respect of social interdependence it is difference which is primary, and in proof of this they point to the complementary services social beings render to one another, services made possible by their differences. There are two great orders of such complementary service, one based on the organic differences of the sexes, the other based on the differences of aptitude, intelligence, occupational interest, and so on, which determine the great system of the division and cooperation of labor. But here too, we must note, the differences, though in one case the very precondition of life, and in the other a necessary means of its progress, are still subsidiary to a likeness of nature in those who present them. Made possible by the difference of the sexes, is there not a value which is a value alike for each, one end which each alike seeks and attains, is there not also a sentiment which has one name for each and one meaning for each? Just as physiologically even sex-differentiation is a differentiation of like structures, so psychologically and socially it is likeness which is still primary, which gives meaning to the difference, which makes the high harmony of the sexes possible. Similarly in the sphere of the division of labor; for that division is simply a means of cooperation, and men cooperate because they all alike find value, directly or indirectly, in or by means of the common product of their labor. The harmony of men in society is not the extrinsic harmony of the parts of a machine, but the intrinsic harmony of beings who are alike in being like ends to themselves. The only social relation where difference is really made the basis of the division of labor is the force-determined relation of master and slave, wherein the like nature of the slave is denied in making him simply a means to the ends of another; but that is also the denial of society.

We conclude that the interdependence of persons within society is essentially an interdependence of the like interests, and thus of the like values of persons; and we regard this as the final reason why the interpersonal harmony of persons, and the "suprapersonal" whole thus established, cannot be understood in terms either of mechanism or of organism (at any rate as we usually conceive organism), or again in terms of some personal or suprapersonal mind of which persons are constituent parts but whose meaning or value is in some way apart from or beyond these persons. The supreme fact that the individual seeks not his own personal welfare alone but something wider or greater, so far from invalidating, really establishes this conclusion. For whose is the wider, greater welfare that we seek, if not that of a whole of persons, and how can we seek their welfare unless we conceive it as of like nature to our own? How can we understand or seek a greater value except in terms of the value we find in ourselves? How can we even sacrifice ourselves to others, to our country it may be, unless we sacrifice the lesser for the greater of two values, comparable because like?

Further, this case of the sacrifice, *strictly so-called*, of the individual for his society, is an abnormal case, and, when it is rendered necessary, is so rendered by the imperfection of society, by its failure, by that disharmony which is the relative absence of society—not by its essential nature. The capacity for sacrifice, in the strict sense of that term, measures the socialization of the individual, but it measures also the disintegration of the social world to which he belongs. Normally the social being fulfills and does not sacrifice his value in his devotion to his society, in the service of the whole of which he is a member. Nearly all moralists have understood this truth, that the service of others is not sacrifice but fulfillment of oneself. One cannot freely seek any end, whatever it be, without both revealing and fulfilling one's nature in the search, and the greater the object of devotion the greater the fulfillment of the subject, since each fulfills his life in fulfilling the ends for which he lives. Conversely, if the end pursued has value at all, the attainment of it is necessarily a social service as well. He who seeks knowledge, wisdom, beauty, power over nature, or any universal end whatever, seeks a good which is meaningless unless it is a good not for the seeker alone but potentially for the world. He cannot really fulfill himself without serving others, nor can he really serve others without fulfilling himself. Yet this in no way detracts from the worth and nobility of the service, for he who seeks any universal end is in the best sense disinterested, devoted, that is, to the end he pursues, and attains success only in the measure of his devotion.

THE INTERPRETATION OF THE FOREGOING FACTS

In the light of the foregoing facts of interdependence we may finally seek to understand the nature of the whole of persons. We started from the axiom that all ultimate values are personal values, and we have seen further that these values are all interrelated, members of a system of values. It follows that the whole constitutes both a sum and a system of values, and we have now to show how it can at the same time be both.

The very expression "sum of" — whether it be "parts" or "pleasures" or "individuals" — has fallen under a perhaps justifiable philosophic ban. Yet it seems to me quite clear that the whole of persons is, whatever besides, a sum of values, in the sense that, if the whole of persons has intrinsic value, every person must as such have or be intrinsic value. If the general argument to this effect seem insufficient, the following considerations, based on our ordinary estimate of values, may be added:

1. We generally feel that, if any personality is lost, it is a loss of the whole, even though the loss seem infinitesimal in relation to the whole.

2. What affects many persons or lives, whether beneficially or disastrously, we regard, *ceteris paribus*, as intrinsically of greater significance than if it affected only one or a few of these; in other words, a greater value is concerned in the event.

3. We accept as right the sacrifice of the one or the few for the many. If then it is right, it is because the greater value is thereby conserved, but if it is also sacrifice, it is because some lesser value is thereby lost.

Many similar considerations might be adduced, but they all lead simply to the general position we have already adopted, *viz.*, that if values are ultimately personal and if the whole of persons is not itself a person and thus a value other than that which its units are or contribute to one another, then the whole is, whatever besides, a sum of values.

But persons, so far as society extends, are essentially interested and interdependent, and does not the expression "sum" connote mere aggregation without system, the very antithesis of society? The answer is simple. If I say that one value is dependent on another, I do not mean that, because existing in that dependence, it is any the less a value. On the contrary, I mean that if it were not for the other it would not be *what it is*, i.e., an existent value. Its value, in other words, is independent of its dependence as a value. Persons do form the completest system or whole of which we have knowledge, but that fact does not derogate at all from the claim of the least unit in that system to be a value in itself.

Further, the system which they form is not itself a further value *of the same order* as the persons who form it. It is necessary to be very clear on this point. For it is here that a system of intrinsic values differs from any system of extrinsic values. Take the illustration of a number of precious stones of various sizes, set and arranged to form an ornament. Here the constituent parts are themselves values, but the whole which they form is more valuable than the total of their separate values. But can we regard a system of values-in-themselves as similarly a greater value-in-itself? A value-in-itself is a value-to-itself. If the unity is then a value in itself, it is a value to itself; and this supposition leads us back to the view we have already found it necessary to reject, that the system is itself a person or subject of values. But a system of values-in-themselves is not necessarily a value-in-itself, any more than a system of minds is itself a mind. If we ask then for whom the system is a value, we must reply, for its constituent units who are values-in-themselves. Here is the clue to the solution of our problem. A society is an extrinsically valuable system of intrinsic values. To regard the value of the system as extrinsic is not to minimize its importance. That on which intrinsic values depend may possess, does possess, the very highest significance, so that the preservation of it may be well worth on any occasion the sacrifice of many intrinsic values. But it is worth that sacrifice, not for its own sake, but for the sake of the persons who depend upon it, who are fulfilled thereby.

It is in the light of the *dynamic* character of every social system that the conception we have already attained gains its full significance. We must seek thus to attain a synthesis of the two series of interpersonal relations, the contemporaneous interdependence of persons and their interdependence through time.

We say that society endures through time, though its members pass away. This does not mean that society endures apart from its members, but that society endures though its members are successive. How are we to understand this continuity? What do its members communicate to one another that there is this continuity maintained through their succession? In one word, they communicate society itself. As a flame is communicated from coal to coal, so is the life of society communicated, in conscious and unconscious ways, from person to person. It is communicated, not transferred. The inheritance of society, like that of life itself, is not a gift which one relinquishes when another receives it. And it is so communicated, so communicable, because it is in no sense outside its members, but lives only in them, is their nature or being in fact. Society is neither prior nor posterior to its members, for the term "person" and the term "social person" are at every stage of life identical in connotation. When persons enter into any social relation it is their respective attitudes toward one another which constitute the relation. The relation consists in their correspondent ways of being in respect of one another, in correspondent aspects of personality. If I love or envy or help another, it is I who feel or act so, and my conduct may raise a corresponding emotion or activity *of* that other; corresponding, in the sense of being a response to mine, not necessarily a response in the same kind—love may be answered by hate, envy by contempt. By every response a social relationship is created, being essentially an attitude of social beings toward or in respect of one another. My attitude toward another, his to me, would not be actual if either of us were for the other nonexistent—but it is still *my* attitude and *his*. The flame of society arises only when person and person meet, but it flames *in* each of them, in no way outside them.

All this may seem very obvious, as in fact it is, but it is often ignored when we think of society or any particular social organization as permanent or continuous. We seem often to think of society as a permanent background to the lives of men, something therefore apart, or as a permanent home in which they shelter, something therefore above and containing them all. If we analyze more carefully we see that this is to confuse society with the outer environment which it shapes. Consider, for instance, the character of permanence which social customs and institutions possess. A custom is a way of acting common to the members of a group; an institution is a definite form of relationship established by social beings in respect of one another. The custom endures only as it is impressed on and accepted by the like and plastic nature of the successive generations; the institution endures only as it is reaffirmed, re-established by the wills of the successive generations. Both are continuous just because they are thus renewed. They are forms of psychical activity, existent only as psychical fact. But like all psychical fact they determine outer environment. Men shape, accommodate the material world to the exigencies of customs and institutions, and the outer forms so created are also permanent, but permanent in a different way, from the inner or psychical forms. They are not rebuilt in the minds of the successive generations; they endure through generations as all outer objects endure, with a permanence correspondent to the degree of control man owns over outer nature. It is these that are the enduring house of the social spirit, built and improved, in the degree of his intelligence, by social man. All the equipment of life, the machinery by which man masters the world, the records of his achievements, the outer symbols by means of which knowledge is stored and the sense of beauty manifested—all these are the work and the treasure of society—but they are not society. To find the unity achieved by persons in community we must look for another kind of continuity and permanence than these possess. The unity we are seeking is the unity of a psychical system, which is continuous not as enduring apart from the minds which form it at any time but as communicated in the unique social mode of communication.

The full meaning of this unity is revealed only in the light of social evolution. In that process, so far as we know it, there can be traced a movement from a less to a greater coherence of society, such as at any rate to reveal the idea and the significance of a fully coherent world of persons. For instance, it would be easy to show, from a study of that process, that the greater the extrinsic value of the system grows, the more possible does it become for each to remain an intrinsic value both to himself and to others. But this is too vast a subject to be discussed within our limits here.

Finally, there is no whole of life achieved as it were an integer formed by the fractional lives of persons; there is a whole of life only in so far as the lives of any or all persons are themselves integral and complete in their kind, and this is made possible by the increasing dependence of all within a system which, as it grows completer, serves each the more in serving all.

[1915]

The Deep Beauty of
the Golden Rule

12

The subject that learned men call ethics is a wasteland on the philosophical map. Thousands of books have been written on this matter, learned books and popular books, books that argue and books that exhort. Most of them are empty and nearly all are vain. Some claim that pleasure is *the* good; some prefer the elusive and more enticing name of happiness; others reject such principles and speak of equally elusive goals such as self-fulfillment. Others claim that *the* good is to be found in looking away from the self, in devotion to the whole—which whole? in the service of God—whose God?—even in the service of the State — who prescribes the service? Here indeed, if anywhere, after listening to the many words of many apostles, one goes out by the same door as one went in.

The reason is simple. You say: "This is the way you should behave." But I say: "No, that is not the way." You say: "This is right." But I say: "No, that is wrong, and this is right." You appeal to experience. I appeal to experience against you. You appeal to authority: it is not mine. What is left? If you are strong, you can punish me for behaving my way. But does that prove anything except that you are stronger than I? Does it prove the absurd dogma that might makes right? Is the slavemaster right because he owns the whip, or Torquemada because he can send his heretics to the flames?

From this impasse no system of ethical rules has been able to deliver itself. How can ethics lay down final principles of behavior that are not your values against mine, your group's values against my group's?

Which, by the way, does not mean that your rules are any less valid for you because they are not valid for me. Only a person of shallow nature and autocratic leanings would draw that conclusion. For the sake of your integrity you must hold to your own values, no matter how much others reject them. Without *your* values you are nothing. True, you should search them and test them and learn by *your* experience and gain wisdom where you can. Your values are your guides through life but you need to use your own eyes. If I have different guides I shall go another way. So far as we diverge, values are relative as between you and me. But your values cannot be relative for you or mine for me.

That is not here the issue. It is that the relativity of values between you and me, between your group and my group, your sect and my sect, makes futile nearly all learned disquisitions about the first principles of ethics.

By ethics I mean the philosophy of how men should behave in their relations to one another. I am talking about philosophy, not about religion. When you have a creed, you can derive from it principles of ethics. Philosophy cannot begin with a creed, but only with reasoning about the nature of things. It cannot therefore presume that the values of other men are less to be regarded than the values of the proponent. If it does, it is not philosophy but dogma, dogma that is the enemy of philosophy, the kind of dogma that has been the source of endless tyranny and repression.

Can it be a philosophy worth the name that makes a universal of your values and thus rules mine out of existence, where they differ from yours?

How can reasoning decide between my values and yours? Values do not claim truth in any scientific sense; instead they claim validity, rightness. They do not declare what is so but what *should* be so. I cling to my values, you to yours. Your values, some of them, do not hold for me; some of them may be repulsive to me; some of them may threaten me. What then? To what court of reason shall we appeal? To what court that you and I both accept is there any appeal?

The lack of any court is the final *fact* about final values. It is a fundamental fact. It is a terrifying fact. It is also a strangely challenging fact. It gives man his lonely autonomy, his true responsibility. If he has anything that partakes of the quality of a God it comes from this fact. Man has more than the choice to obey or disobey. If he accepts authority he also chooses the authority he accepts. He is responsible not only to others but, more deeply, to himself.

Does all this mean that a universal ethical principle, applicable alike to me and you, even where our values diverge, is impossible? That there is no rule to go by, based on reason itself, in this world of irreconcilable valuations?

There is no rule that can prescribe both my values and yours or decide between them. There is one universal rule, and one only, that can be laid down, on ethical grounds—that is, apart from the creeds of particular religions and apart from the ways of the tribe that falsely and arrogantly universalize themselves.

Do to others as you would have others do to you. This is the only rule that stands by itself in the light of its own reason, the only rule that can stand by itself in the naked, warring universe, in the face of the contending values of men and groups.

What makes it so? Let us first observe that the universal herein laid down is one of procedure. It prescribes a mode of behaving, not a goal of action. On the level of goals, of *final* values, there is irreconcilable conflict. One rule prescribes humility, another pride; one prescribes abstinence, another commends the flesh-pots; and so forth through endless variations. All of us wish that *our* principle could be universal; most of us believe that it *should* be, that our *ought* ought to be all men's *ought*, but since we differ there can be, on this level, no possible agreement.

When we want to make our ethical principle prevail we try to persuade others, to "convert" them. Some may freely respond, if their deeper values are near enough to ours. Others will certainly resist and some will seek to persuade us in turn—why shouldn't they? Then we can go no further except by resort to force and fraud. We can, if we are strong, dominate some and we can bribe others. We compromise our own values in doing so and we do not in the end succeed; even if we were masters of the whole world we could never succeed in making our principle universal. We could only make it falsely tyrannous.

So if we look for a principle in the name of which we can appeal to all men, one to which their reason can respond in spite of their differences, we must follow another road. When we try to make our values prevail over those cherished by others, we attack their values, their dynamic of behavior, their living will. If we go far enough we assault their very being. For the will is simply valuation in action. Now the deep beauty of the golden rule is that instead of attacking the will that is in other men, it offers their will a new dimension. "Do as you *would* have others. . . ." As *you* would will others to do. It bids you expand your vision, see yourself in new relationships. It bids you transcend your insulation, see yourself in the place of others, see others in your place.

It bids you test your values or at least your way of pursuing them. If you would disapprove that another should treat you as you treat him, the situations being reversed, is not that a sign that, by the standard of your own values, you are mistreating him?

This principle obviously makes for a vastly greater harmony in the social scheme. At the same time it is the only universal of ethics that does not take sides with or contend with contending values. It contains no dogma. It bids everyone follow his own rule, as it would apply *apart* from the accident of his particular fortunes. It bids him enlarge his own rule, as it would apply whether he is up or whether he is down. It is an accident that you are up and I am down. In another situation you would be down and I would be up. That accident has nothing to do with my *final* values or with yours. You have numbers and force on your side. In another situation I would have the numbers and the force. All situations of power are temporary and precarious. Imagine then the situations reversed and that you had a more wonderful power than is at the command of the most powerful, the power to make the more powerful act toward you as you would want him to act. If power is your dream, then dream of a yet greater power—and act out the spirit of your dream.

But the conclusive argument is not in the terms of power. It goes far deeper, down to the great truth that power so often ignores and that so often in the end destroys it, the truth that when you maltreat others you detach yourself from them, from the understanding of them, from the understanding of yourself. You insulate yourself, you narrow your own values, you cut yourself off from that which you and they have in common. And this commonness is more enduring and more satisfying than what you possess in insulation. You separate yourself, and for all your power you weaken yourself. Which is why power and fear are such close companions.

This is the reason why the evil you do to another, you do also, in the end, to yourself. While if you and he refrain from doing evil, one to another—not to speak of the yet happier consequences of doing positive good—this reciprocity of restraint from evil will redound to the good of both.

That makes a much longer story and we shall not here enter upon it. Our sole concern is to show that the golden rule is the *only* ethical principle, as already defined, that can have clear right of way everywhere in the kind of world we have inherited. It is the only principle that allows every man to follow his own intrinsic values while nevertheless it transforms the chaos of warring codes into a reasonably well-ordered universe.

Let us explain the last statement. What are a man's intrinsic values? Beyond his mere self-seeking every human being needs, and must find, some attachment to a larger purpose. These attachments, in themselves and apart from the way he pursues them, are his intrinsic values. For some men they are centered in the family, the clan, the "class," the community, the nation, the "race." It is the warfare of their group-attachments that creates the deadliest disturbances of modern society. For some men the focus of attachment is found in the greater "cause," the faith, the creed, the way of life. The conflict of these attachments also unlooses many evils on society and at some historical stages has brought about great devastation.

The greatest evils inflicted by man on man over the face of the earth are wrought not by the self-seekers, the pleasure lovers, or the merely amoral, but by the fervent devotees of ethical principles, those who are bound body and soul to some larger purpose, the nation, the "race," the "masses," the "brethren" whoever they may be. The faith they invoke, whatever it may be, is not large enough when it sets a frontier between the members and the non-members, the believers and the non-believers. In the heat of devotion to that larger but exclusive purpose there is bred the fanaticism that corrodes and finally destroys all that links man to the common humanity. In the name of the cause, they will torture and starve and trample under foot millions on millions of their fellowmen. In its name they will cultivate the blackest treachery. And if their methods fail, as fail in the end they must, they will be ready, as was Hitler, to destroy their own cause or their own people, the chosen ones, rather than accept the reality their blinded purpose denied.

How then can we say that the golden rule does not disqualify the intrinsic values of such people—even of people like Hitler or, say, Torquemada? In the name of his values Torquemada burned at the stake many persons who differed from their fellows mainly by being more courageous, honest, and faithful to their faith. What then were Torquemada's values? He was a servant of the Church and the Church was presumptively a servant of Jesus Christ. It was not the intrinsic values of his creed that moved him and his masters to reject the Christian golden rule. Let us concede they had some kind of devotion to religion. It was the distorted, fanatical way in which they pursued the dimmed values they cherished, it was not the values themselves, to which their inhumanity can be charged.

Let us take the case of Hitler. Apart from his passion for Germany, or the German "folk," he would have been of no account, for evil or for good. That passion of itself, that in his view intrinsic value, might have inspired great constructive service instead of destruction. It was the method he used, and not the values he sought to promote thereby, that led to ruin, his blind trust in the efficacy of ruthless might. Belonging to a "folk" that had been reduced in defeat from strength to humiliation, fed on false notions of history and responsive to grotesque fallacies about a "master race," he conceived the resurgence of Germany in the distorted light of his vindictive imagination. Had Hitler been a member of some small "folk," no more numerous, say, than the population of his native Austria, he might have cherished the same values with no less passion, but his aspirations would have taken a different form and would never have expressed themselves in horror and tragedy.

The golden rule says nothing against Hitler's mystic adoration of the German "race," against any man's intrinsic values. By "intrinsic values" we signify the goals, beyond mere self-seeking, that animate a human being. If your group, your nation, your "race," your church, is for you a primary attachment, continue to cherish it—give it all you have, if you are so minded. But do not use means that are repugnant to the standards according to which you would have others conduct themselves to you and your values. If your nation were a small one, would you not seethe with indignation if some large neighbor destroyed its independence? Where, then, is your personal integrity if, belonging instead to the large nation, you act to destroy the independence of a small one? You falsify your own values, in the longer run you do them injury, when you pursue them in ways that cannot abide the test of the golden rule.

It follows that while this first principle attacks no intrinsic values, no primary attachments of men to goods that reach beyond themselves, it nevertheless purifies every attachment, every creed, of its accidents, its irrelevancies, its excesses, its false reliance on power. It saves every human value from the corruption that comes from the arrogance of detachment and exclusiveness, from the shell of that kind of absolutism that imprisons its vitality.

At this point a word of caution is in order. The golden rule does not solve for us our ethical problems but offers only a way of approach. It does not prescribe our treatment of others but only the spirit in which we should treat them. It has no simple mechanical application and often enough is hard to apply—what general principle is not? It certainly does not bid us treat others as others *want* us to treat them—that would be an absurdity. The convicted criminal wants the judge to set him free. If the judge acts in the spirit of the golden rule, within the limits of the discretion permitted him as judge, he might instead reason somewhat as follows: "How would I feel the judge ought to treat *me* were I in this man's place? What could I—the man I am and yet somehow standing where this criminal stands—properly ask the judge to do for me, to me? In this spirit I shall assess his guilt and his punishment. In this spirit I shall give full consideration to the conditions under which he acted. I shall try to understand *him*, to do what I properly can for him, while at the same time I fulfill my judicial duty in protecting society against the dangers that arise if criminals such as he go free."

"Do to others as you would have others do to you." The disease to which all values are subject is the growth of a hard insulation. "I am right: I have the truth. If you differ from me, you are a heretic, you are in error. *Therefore* while you must allow me every liberty when you are in power I need not, in truth I ought not to, show any similar consideration for you." The barb of falsehood has already begun to vitiate the cherished value. While *you* are in power I advocate the equal rights of all creeds: when *I* am in power, I reject any such claim as ridiculous. This is the position taken by various brands of totalitarianism, and the communists in particular have made it a favorite technique in the process of gaining power, clamoring for rights they will use to destroy the rights of those who grant them. Religious groups have followed the same line. Roman Catholics, Calvinists, Lutherans, Presbyterians, and others have on occasion vociferously advocated religious liberty where they were in the minority, often to curb it where in turn they became dominant.

This gross inconsistency on the part of religious groups was flagrantly displayed in earlier centuries, but examples are still not infrequent. Here is one. *La Civilita Catholicâ*, a Jesuit organ published in Rome, has come out as follows:

> The Roman Catholic Church, convinced, through its divine prerogatives, of being the only true Church, must demand the right to freedom for herself alone, because such a right can only be possessed by truth, never by error. As to other religions, the Church will certainly never draw the sword, but she will require that by legitimate means they shall not be allowed to propagate false doctrine. Consequently, in a state where the majority of the people are Catholic, the Church will require that legal existence be denied to error. . . . In some countries, Catholics will be obliged to ask full religious freedom for all, resigned at being forced to cohabitate where they alone should rightly be allowed to live. . . . The Church cannot blush for her own want of tolerance, as she asserts it in principle and applies it in practice.[1]

Since this statement has the merit of honesty it well illustrates the fundamental lack of rationality that lies behind all such violations of the golden rule. The argument runs: "Roman Catholics know they possess the truth; *therefore* they should not permit others to propagate

---

1.   Quoted in the *Christian Century* (June, 1948).

error." By parity of reasoning why should not Protestants say—and indeed they have often said it—"We know we possess the truth; therefore we should not tolerate the errors of Roman Catholics." Why then should not atheists say: "We know we possess the truth; therefore we should not tolerate the errors of dogmatic religion."

No matter what we believe, we are equally convinced the *we* are right. We have to be. That is what belief means, and we must all believe something. The Roman Catholic Church is entitled to declare that all other religious groups are sunk in error. But what follows? That other groups have not the right to believe they are right? That you have the right to repress them while they have no right to repress you? That they should concede to you what you should not concede to them? Such reasoning is mere childishness. Beyond it lies the greater foolishness that truth is advanced by the forceful suppression of those who believe differently from you. Beyond that lies the pernicious distortion of meanings which claims that liberty is only "the liberty to do right" —the "liberty" for me to do what *you* think is right. This perversion of the meaning of liberty has been the delight of all totalitarians. And it might be well to reflect that it was the radical Rousseau who first introduced the doctrine that men could be "forced to be free."

How much do they have truth who think they must guard it within the fortress of their own might? How little that guarding has availed in the past! How often it has kept truth outside while superstition grew moldy within! How often has the false alliance of belief and force led to civil dissension and the futile ruin of war! But if history means nothing to those who call themselves "Christian" and still claim exclusive civil rights for their particular faith, at least they might blush before this word of one they call their Master: "All things therefore whatsoever ye would that men should do unto you, even so do ye also unto them; for this is the law and the prophets."

[1952]

Unity and Difference: The Ordering of a Multigroup Society

13

[*In many of his writings MacIver has been concerned with what he holds to be the greatest peril of modern society:* "*the exclusiveness of group against group, by means of which the stronger groups prevent the weaker from sharing the benefits and the opportunities of the community, by reason of which the stronger grow proud and intolerant and prejudiced, denying their common humanity, while the less advantaged grow bitter and frustrated. Thus on all sides rancor and cleavage increase, and the energies of men are turned from creativeness to destructiveness, from cooperative gain to universal loss.*"[1]

In this essay, culled from four of his papers, he seeks both to define "the new and the most urgent challenge of a very old problem, . . . the problem of unity and difference," and to suggest how best we might attack it, "how we can in some degree remedy this situation, remove so far as we can this great and growing trouble."]

---

1. *Civilization and Group Relationships*, p. x.

THE POWER OF GROUP IMAGES

If the proper study of mankind is man he is a sadly retarded student. The last thing to which man applies his intelligence is himself, and particularly himself as related to other men. Science with all its triumphs has not triumphed here, and the present almost inconceivable mess of human affairs is the climactic result of the triumphs of science in other fields and its utter failure in this one. This statement is made deliberately, without qualification and with full recognition of the fact that science provides no dynamic for society and no final goals. Say what you will of man's inhumanity to man, go as far as you will in laying the blame on man's unruly passions and the swollen interests of individuals and groups and nations. But these passions would not have led man blindly into the mire except for his ignorance of where they led, and these swollen interests would not have conspired to their own destruction had they not grossly miscalculated the ulterior consequences of the behavior they prompted.

Thus the insight of Socrates is vindicated. Or let us take Shakespeare instead. Hamlet offers a recorder to the scheming politician Guildenstern and bids him play it. "I cannot," he replies, "I have not the skill." And Hamlet replies, "Why, look you now, how unworthy a thing you make of me! You would play upon me; you would seem to know my stops; you would pluck out the heart of my mystery; you would sound me from my lowest note to the top of my compass; and there is much music, excellent voice, in this little organ; yet you cannot make it speak. 'Sblood, do you think I am easier to be played on than a pipe?" Naively we think just that. Without knowing their "stops," in complete ignorance of their responses, we would play upon other groups and other peoples—and the discords that fill the whole earth are the result. There is surely no greater source of human misery and frustration than this.

In the universal business of human relations the simplest precepts of science, the mere commonplaces of the art of knowing, taken for granted in every research, in every engineering task, in every other enterprise, are rejected. We teach schoolboys the elements of science, but we do not teach them—or ourselves—the first rudiments of the science of human relations. Here we draw the most sweeping conclusions from the most inadequate premises, or from none at all. We generalize about other groups on the flimsiest misinformation, so long as we can give a moral color to the generalization. We would never dream, for example, of saying that all Basutos are six foot tall or that all male Zulus wear golden earrings. That would be grossly unscientific. But, like Tennyson's farmer who announced that "the poor in a lump is bad," we are ready to believe that certain nations are wholly evil-minded and their members monotonously uniform in their evil traits. If we do not like trade union policies, then the workers are a subversive and misguided lot; if we like these policies, then the workers are the saviors of the earth. If we like the Soviet ideology, then everything that proceeds from Russia is good, and we applaud actions we would most vehemently denounce if committed by others. If we dislike it, then everything Russia does is bad or at the least suspect. Without hesitation we attribute motives, good or bad according to our prior inclinations, to explain the behavior of groups other than our own. Of all judgments the attribution of motives hidden behind overt behavior is the most precarious and the most unverifiable, and our confidence in making them is equaled only by our irresponsibility.

We do not know how to comprehend groups. That is part of the trouble. We have no education for the understanding of groups. So we resort to the conception of them as bigger but grotesquely simplified persons. Our ignorance, played upon by our emotions and our interests, sets up wholly unwarranted *images* of collectivities of every kind. We do not need to know the other group or the other nation; we look on the image we have made, and that serves instead.

When we consider its results we must surely agree that this making of idols, cast in the shape of demons and very occasionally of saints, the images of evil and of good collectivities, is the most deadly of all intellectual sins. We slide into it so easily. It comes so naturally to the aid of our local egoisms, our group prides, our loyalties, our devotions. It besets us all—even scientists of high renown, who in their own fields would shrink with horror from so gross a betrayal of intellectual integrity. Among primitives the idol-making habit may be relatively harmless, perhaps even beneficial, as cementing the unitary and semi-isolated group. But in a modern civilization, where diverse groups must live together to make one community and where diverse nations must live together to make one world, this habit has become the most insidious enemy of the well-being of all. In the United States we have the most diversely patterned union of diverse groups to be found on earth, dedicated to the principle of their equal rights and opportunities—and nowhere does the business of idol-making flourish more, and nowhere does it portend greater perils.

Clearly the need is for social education. Clearly our hope lies there. It is not an unreasonable hope, since the particular images we make, the particular shapes they assume, are products of indoctrination and, moreover, are very malleable under certain conditions. One day we image the French as a nation of degenerates and another day they become again a puissant people marching with us in the van of civilization. There is a changeful relativity about most of our social images. Walter

Lippmann deserves credit for having called attention to these thought-forms, but the word he popularized to describe them, "stereotypes," conveys overmuch the notion of fixity, of indelibility. We prefer, for this and other reasons, to name them social images. Experiments in education already show that they are amenable to training. Happily, this educational process of training does not need to use the methods of counterpropaganda; for it is indubitable that in the light of knowledge the demon-images shrink into phantoms, the baseless fabric of a vision now opened to the truth.

But our methods of social education must be thoroughly revised, indeed revolutionized, if we want to pursue this end. They must be reoriented to the demands and conditions of our age. The task is vast and formidable, but not beyond our reach. The response to such experiments as the "Springfield Plan" is encouraging. The sense of the need is growing, though there are stubborn resistances to be overcome. Among other things we must remodel our teaching of "social studies," of civics, and of history. They must be made, in the best sense, more realistic, informed with new knowledge of social situations, brought to life by the translation of great but graying traditions into the actualities of man's hard struggle to new goals, and directed to the primary question of how men and groups of diverse opinions and faiths and origins and interests can live together and together make the one community. As nearly all students will tell us, most of our current instruction in "civics" and in "government" is dull and unresponsive. Social education is not much advanced by routine information about the machinery and the departmental structures of government, nor is it made appealing by sweet anecdotes about Washington and Lincoln or by noble platitudes about democracy—which shy away from the issues of democracy for the Negroes and for our Mexicans and for the Japanese-Americans and for the Jews. If we teach that way, then we shall find, as Marie Syrkin says in *Your School, Your Children*, that "the same boy who earnestly applauds the Gettysburg address in the school assembly will join the Silver Shirts or the Ku Klux Klan and be unaware of any conflict between the two acts."

We must teach the meaning of democracy, getting down to the earth of it. We must teach in new ways and we must provide the teachers, in school and in the community, with new knowledge. We extol democracy but we do not comprehend it. Even when we fight in its name or for its sake our faith is dim because its meaning is unclear. Unless we vitalize it, it will not animate our people or realize itself within our lives.

Democracy was born of the struggle of groups—religious groups, economic groups, ethnic groups—against the intolerance and abuse of power. The struggle of groups against domination and discrimination goes on endlessly. Democracy is always in process of becoming, never fulfilled. It makes new demands in the multigroup society we have inherited, and we are flagrantly failing to meet them. Everywhere in this country of ours the prejudicial images of other groups impair our strength and darken our future, the anti-images of Negro and of White, of Jew and of Christian, of Catholic and of Protestant, of employer and of worker, of all the warring sects and schools that are not content to pursue their ends by honorable means but, armed with all the devices of modern propagandism, becloud every issue and everywhere stir up tension and tumult.

What can the educator do about it? If he does his proper job he can do more about it than all the rest. His proper job, or no small part of it, is to educate the young for the society in which they live. This society is a multi-group society. In this country the average youth receives some ten years of schooling. During these years he can be taught saving knowledge, dynamic knowledge, about living in a multigroup society. He can be taught how we make false images of anti-groups. He can be taught the danger that lies in supporting our values, *whatever they be*, by falsehood and misrepresentation. He can be given a fair and unromanticized story of the groups who compose our people, depicting their struggles and their contributions to the life of man. He can be taught to meet persons as persons, and not as labeled specimens of types. He should be taught these things most explicitly, with special attention to the most menacing anti-images, according to time and place, whether the powers of darkness have chosen the Negro or the Jew or the Oriental or the Catholic or the Communist or the Capitalist or any other category as the front of their warfare against light. And the student should be taught these things in the living experience of new habituations that every community and nearly every classroom can provide.

It is no easy task for the teacher. Apart from his own prejudices he is subject to pressure from the prejudices around him and above him. He has another great danger to meet. Prejudices are the servants of values, of loyalties and of faiths, and he dare not and must not attack the values they falsely serve. His especial task is to uphold two values among the rest, the worth of truth itself and the worth of democracy. If he is a genuine teacher he can take satisfaction in the fact that these two values are conjoined. Only through the victory of truth over prejudice can diverse groups together sustain the democratic community.

The social scientist should provide the teacher with more adequate means for his continuous task. We need to explore the nature and functioning of social groups, the formation of their value-systems, the role of leadership in them, the conditions under which group images emerge, spread, and change. The social psychology of group images is an unexplored subject that should be full of interest to the sociologist. A number of years ago the author conducted a study of the attitudes of Canadians toward the people of the United States. Canada has a heterogeneity of population elements similar in many respects to that of the United States. At the same time it is constructed, along their continental belt, of five major sectors almost wholly islanded one from the other. Nevertheless, from coast to coast, across geographical barriers, across the "social distances" that separates Quebec from its neighbors of the west and of the east, regardless of all differences of social position, of ethnic derivation, of experience and other factors, there was a practically unanimous verdict delivered on the characteristics of the American people.

These were the opinions of Canadians about their "big neighbor," about the same kind of people, for the most part, that they are themselves. But from the different environment the neighbor people is treated as a collectivity, seen in relation to the respondents as another collectivity, and this act of "hypostasization," as the philosophers call it, helps to explain the remarkable unanimity.[2] It helps to explain why the Canadians with one voice credit Americans with certain quite specific shortcomings and with certain quite specific virtues. It is not the viewpoint the people of the United States take of themselves. If they blushingly accepted the virtues attributed to them, such as being "generous" and "practical," they would still repudiate the charge that they are, in any particular sense, "dollar-chasing" or "materialistic." These are attributes of a social anti-image—and indeed one far less obnoxious than most—and this image is not derived from experience. On the contrary, the social image becomes blurred as a result of closer and more understanding contact. Those who know their neighbor people least tend to have the most clear-cut images.

By an anti-image I mean the image a group projects of some antithetical or polar group, the representation of out-group by in-group and *vice versa*, of minority group by majority group and *vice versa*, of any group by any counter-interest group. The anti-image is the defensive-offensive response of the threatened interest, whether it be economic or political or cultural on any level. It is an ideological device to evoke in the group a fighting consciousness of its separateness and superiority. The group is extremely amenable to appropriate suggestion concerning the evil or malicious designs of the countergroup. It has no controls against these suggestions. Every collectivity is a question mark to every other, and any representation of a group that satisfies the egocentric emotions of another is easily accepted. In

2.   For an analysis of this study see the present writer's Introduction to H.F. Angus (ed.), *Canada and Her Great Neighbor* (New Haven, 1938).

this sense peoples as well as smaller groups are question marks. An irresponsible reporter tells the people of the United States how "England" feels about them and produces a pleasantly painful glow of resented injury, sharpening the anti-image of England. What the "United States" feels about England is reported back in the same spirit, and so misunderstandings grow and endanger the common interest. Everywhere, for all groups in all their relationships with others, this process is at work.

Many "movements" live by the fabrication of these anti-images. We have developed no educational safeguards against the credulous reception of them. They are the stock in trade of every unscrupulous propagandist. They will not suffer any issue to be fought out on its merits or any cause to be adjudged by its rightful claims. They rationalize every social injustice, every kind of exploitation. They give the joy of righteousness to every selfish and domineering interest. They are most powerful when they can do most harm, in the time of troubles. Hitler's success with the anti-image of the Jew is only a large-scale example of a method that many groups in this country, led by tricky propagandists, are pursuing all the time. Only a rare exception among these propagandists is so naive as to wear a particular color of shirt.

The exposure of our total civilization to this menace is primarily a failure of education, and beyond that a failure of science to provide the armory of education. We shall get further by regarding it as a failure on the front of knowledge, a failure of science and more particularly of social science, than as a failure of morals. No doubt in the last resort it is a moral goal that must animate our educational endeavors. Always there is a moral goal back of the behavior of men, including scientists, and the bland assumption by some scientists of intellectual indifference is itself often the disguise of moral valuations. But in the conflict of moralities we have no clear line of social solution unless we can call to our aid the light of truth. These anti-images work their evil first by distorting the truth. Only the forsaken lovers of darkness can resist us if we make our campaign in the name of truth.

In the name of morals alone we cannot fight this menace. The image makers are great moralists. They call for high and holy crusades. They are vindicating the honor of white womanhood, they are upholding the purity of their race, they are defending their gospel against the crucifiers of Christ. The more moralized they make their cause, the more dangerous it becomes. The historical record repeats this story endlessly. We need the aid of science to counteract the poisons that fester in moral enthusiasms. On this ground these images can easily be attacked. There is nothing vague or obscure about them. They are as clear-cut as they are false. Their falseness can be exposed, and the mind of youth will take the lesson.

We lose so much by refusing to seek, for ourselves and for others, the truth the anti-images betray. We cut ourselves off from the enriching experience of our multi-group society. We raise walls to narrow our horizons. We cannot reach out to the understanding of those who differ from our own type. We become caged within the sterile consciousness of our own kind. But beyond these losses to personality there loom the social costs. Can we perhaps learn the deeper lesson of the disaster the Nazi creed has brought upon the world? Can we learn to distinguish between the creative sturggle that brings strength and the wrathful blind division that first corrupts the heart and in the end tears down all that we have built?

[1945]

OUR STRENGTH AND OUR WEAKNESS

"The basis of our strength in the United States is spiritual." So did the President speak in his annual message to Congress in the year 1948. The statement can be a platitude or it can be filled with deep meaning. The President went on to say that our spiritual strength is gravely impaired by our denial of the substance of civil rights to large sections of our people.

Many years before, another President of the United States, in a very crucial period of our history, also spoke about the denial of civil rights. He spoke then of the mission of the United States. Here is what he said: "It was to lift artificial weights from all shoulders; to clear the paths of laudable pursuit for all; to afford all an unfettered start and a fair chance in the race of life."

That was in the year 1861. The ideal thus expressed became the American dream; it became the American hope, and, a little optimistically, the fulfillment of it came to be thought of as the "American way of life." It is a dream and it is a hope that is very far yet from being attained. Since that time there has been some retrogression from the ideal.

However, more recently the forces that seek to realize it have been gaining new impetus. We are at present in a period in which the reassertion of that American faith is again becoming stronger. There never has been a time in which we needed it more, in which we needed more to rally and consolidate whatever spiritual strength we have. For now we need it not only for the sake of our own well-being but also because we have become, without wishing to be, almost without knowing it, the great guardian of the peace and prosperity of all mankind.

If we have any spiritual strength as a people it must lie in something we have in common, not in the creeds that divide us. It must lie in what solidarity we possess as a people; even if in nothing else than in our vision of belonging together. It means that beyond our differences there must be the fiber of solidarity. We do not want to abandon differences. That would be sterility. We do not want uniformity. That would be spiritual death. But we must know how to meet anew the first and most eternal problem of social man—to take these differences of ours and harmonize them into a people's unity. That is eminently our problem today.

In our time there are two spiritual faiths that are contending for the mastery of our world. The one faith rejects and would destroy difference. It would require that all men share the same ideal, speak the same opinions, and utter the same creed. The other faith is that which would reconcile differences in unity. It would not suppress them, it would transcend them, so that differences can live in peace together.

These two faiths are today contending for mankind. The one faith is totalitarian, the other is democratic; we claim to stand for the latter faith. We claim to do so, but we put ourselves at a disadvantage compared with those who stand for the opposite faith. Our faith is harder to follow—that is its challenge and its greatness. We betray that faith by the practice of discrimination. We thereby confound our purposes and darken our future. We are in danger of rejecting our position as a guardian of the prosperity of man.

"All men are created equal." Listen then to this story. One wintry morning in 1945, in the city of Washington, there was a colored woman who began to feel the signs of travail. With her sister she sought a maternity hospital. They could not get a cab and started walking, but they were too late and the labor pains came on after they had gone part of the way. As it happened, they were opposite another hospital, some distance from the one they were going to. They were going to a colored hospital.

At this point, the woman could go no further and the sister rushed up the steps of the hospital and asked them to take her in as an emergency case. The hospital said, "No, we are for Whites only." Incidentally, that hospital was church-supported, church-maintained.

The mother was delivered of the child on the sidewalk and the hospital very kindly provided a sheet! I say that happened in the city of the Lincoln Memorial.[3]

There are two kinds of division that are blocking our way, preventing the attainment of what we like to call the American way of life. There is first the division that arises between groups when they magnify their

3.   The story is vouched for by Joseph D. Lohman and Edwin R. Embree, *Survey Graphic*, January, 1947.

genuine differences and make them, shall I say, *absolute*. We have differences, say of faith, of social attitude, of cultural attachment. We make that difference a ground for cutting off any intercourse between us and those who have another faith. We make the difference total.

Difference that becomes division secretes a social poison, in the last resort the poison of war. This happens on every level, and not least on that of the great religions. If there is complete separation, if there is no sense of anything in common, so that the worshipers of different faiths have no chance of meeting on the same ground or under the same roof, then in religion as elsewhere we are making difference absolute and engendering the poison that absolute division contains.

Whereas, if you take difference properly—the honest differences of men who are honestly seeking the truth in their own ways—there can be no such segregation, because back of these differences there are certain fundamental agreements. Division rejects the saving, binding *common*. When religious difference becomes division you would think there were no such thing as common brotherhood and no belief in a common need, a common purpose, a common God.

But there is a second kind of division between groups that is just as deadly and that is more meaningless and more futile because it is related to nothing that has any intrinsic significance. I refer to the division that cuts off the intercourse between men, not because they differ in faith, not because they differ in opinion, but because they have a different birthplace, a different origin or a different speech or a different nationality or a different color of skin or some other irrelevant difference. It is very easy for men to turn this irrelevant difference into absolute division, because to do so nourishes our ego, our group ego. It is poisonous food but it feeds our pride.

So everywhere there has been a tendency to turn difference—irrelevant difference—into separation, with cumulatively evil consequences. It is manifest in the ethnic and racial discrimination that prevails in the United States. It has become for us the greatest evil in this country of many differences. So many of our people were born in a different place, brought up in a different way, learned to speak a different language, or have a different color of skin. On that basis we keep the other man down, we discriminate against him, we deny him opportunity. We do not know what we are doing; we do not realize what it costs.

In this country more than in any other there has been the constant proclamation of the equal rights of men and the demand for the equal opportunities of men. Nowhere else has there been so authoritative an expression of the principle that birth and class and creed and origin do not count compared with being a person. Nevertheless while this principle is enshrined in our Constitution and in our tradition it would hardly be an exaggeration to say that in no country today is it more violated than it is in this country. So much so that people in other countries often are surprised that we have to struggle so hard to bring this cause nearer to victory.

In this country some forty million people suffer from some kind of serious discrimination. That is how wide and threatening our divisions are. And this is the country that is, more than any other, composed of people of many origins. Surely in the light of its own origin it is the manifest destiny of this country to overcome the irrelevant divisions of birthplace or skin color. For us today it is, at the same time, a prime necessity, as well as the opportunity for our greatest truimph. The ideal has been visioned by all the leading thinkers and leading statesmen of the country from the time of the Constitution; from the time it was first proclaimed in the Declaration of Independence and given a charter in the Bill of Rights.

It was well in the nineteenth century before the principle of the equal rights of groups pervaded the national consciousness. Then it entered into popular thought, into everyday attitudes, and became the dynamic of the "American way of life." The great novelists, poets, statesmen, and thinkers were all giving it expression and finding in the United States the fulfillment of democracy.

It won, for example, robust and flamboyant expression in Walt Whitman:

I speak the password primeval—I give the sign of democracy;
By God! I will accept nothing which all cannot have their counter-
    part of on the same terms.

The same idea was expressed in more gentle and more familiar ways by many writers. Take, for example, the novels of Mark Twain—what lies underneath his picturization of boys and men? It is this same conception, this same idea, that we are all equally human across our differences. The same conception received a new impetus from the attitude of large groups of immigrants who came here in the latter part of the nineteenth century. What they wanted, what they hoped for, was to share in this democratic recognition, to be participants in as well as beneficiaries of the mission of America.

In the Middle West this attitude found its fullest expression. In a sense the United States became the spiritual product of its own Middle West. It was there that the growing tradition found its focus and thence it spread over the rest of the country and became the thing that we think about still, sometimes a little wistfully, perhaps, as the American way of life.

That tradition, thus developed in the nineteenth century, suffered a decline. After all, the mode of expression it found was a little optimistic, a little shallow, a little untested, undisciplined, and so when new temptations came the ideal suffered—when group after group came to attain some greater degree of prestige or domination than others, when groups once small became large and seemed to challenge, economically or otherwise, the old groups. The ideal waned and discrimination increased, nearly up to the time of the past war.

The situation was no better—in fact, it was even worse during the First World War. But with the coming of the Second World War there has been a very interesting change. There has been a resurgence of the old ideal and, above all, some mustering of forces to try and carry that ideal through to great success.

Perhaps it is because the United States of America, entering into its new world orbit, has become more conscious of the need for unity, but for whatever reason there has been in every area of our social life, economic, political, religious, educational, some change of spirit. There has been some recognition, though far from enough, of what deadly harm intergroup discrimination does this country and this age.

Of all the costs of discrimination, the most disastrous is not the economic but the spiritual. I am thinking of the loss it means to that sense of purpose and that solidarity wherein lies all the strength of a people. Intergroup discrimination has been destroying the spiritual heritage of America and if we lose that heritage we dissolve into scrambling, hustling, power seeking, profit seeking groups denuded of worth, without dignity among ourselves, and without respect from the rest of the world.

Whatever is distinctive about this country, its spiritual heritage comes from the recognition and the liberation of the universal in man, transcending division and harmonizing differences. It is this heritage, exalting the rights and the liberties of men, that more than anything else America must stand for if it stands for anything. It cannot stand on alien traditions but on this thing that is peculiar to its own being. Without that, we are spiritually impoverished, voiceless, and inarticulate before the world.

And it is this thing, this priceless heritage, that our narrow egotism, our shallow pride, our thoughtless discriminations, are threatening to destroy in us. If they destroy it, they destroy our national being. And if we are talking about costs, what are all other costs compared with this?

[1949]

THE NATURE OF THE CHALLENGE

I want to try to put before you a few quite elementary considerations about this problem, because it seems to me that the elementary considerations may here be the most essential.

In our world today multitudes are held by a philosophy, by a faith, which has given up this problem, a philosophy that demands unity without difference. This reversion to primitivism has come in the train of violence and fear of economic privations and instabilities, of intellectual credulity and of the shattering of older values.

Under these stresses there has risen this new-old faith. This faith has triumphed for the moment over large portions of the earth, this faith that gives up the problem altogether, that substitutes violence for reason and substitutes passion for comprehension.

But you cannot give up the problem. You cannot kill it. The problem endures. You can silence it, suppress it, but it is one thing that force cannot kill. It is always there. And the moment the force relaxes, it reappears. It asserts itself with a redoubled power, taking vengeance on its own suppression.

This problem the totalitarians have not faced and they have not killed. The problem lives. It lives and it rankles beneath all the loudness of force and falsehood. The problem of unity in difference, of difference in unity, may seem remote and abstract, but actually it is the problem of all living. It is the problem of the individual and the group, of the group and the nation, of the nation and the world.

It is only as we master that we understand. It is only as we face it that we truly live, and it is only in so far as we solve it that our science, our philosophy, even our faith, can be enduring and built on truth.

We have inherited a complex world. It is the world we must live in, willy-nilly. This is the price of past achievement and it is the condition of future advancement, this world teeming with difference. We can perhaps for a time ignore it or, like petulant children, we can deny it, but we can't escape it. We cannot defeat it. We only defeat ourselves. By defeating ourselves I mean defeating our ultimate values, however they are understood—the value of personality, on the one hand; the value of truth, on the other hand.

We cannot reject difference without rejecting also the common in the universe. We cannot reject it without in the last resort defeating our heritage of civilization. That I think is the final reason for believing in democracy, because for all its defects democracy does accept the fact that we live in a complex world that teems with difference. Whatever its advantages may be, totalitarianism denies that fact and would reduce the world to the proportions of its own violent and childish denial. It has to reduce and suppress everyone not in accord with that narrow vision, that egocentric interest.

It has to enslave all science, to reduce it to its own technology, its instrument of oppression, and the kinds of science that it cannot use it destroys. I refer particularly to the social sciences—to anthropology, to sociology, to the economics of welfare, to political science, to all the sciences of culture. In so far as it cannot use them, it destroys them. The philosophy it cannot use, which is all other philosophy than its own, it enslaves—the free play of mind to express the manifoldness, the meaning, the unity, of the world. And the religion it cannot enslave, which happily is most religion, it also seeks to destroy, setting up its own faith to destroy all other faiths.

Science, philosophy and religion have so far a common cause, a common cause that links them with democracy—but that is not enough. It is not enough to have a negative cause. We must seek for some deeper ground of unity, for some positive common cause.

We must turn again to the elementary and perennial problem of unity and difference. Let me first say one quite elementary thing about it. There are three ways in which we can treat differences: We can suppress them; that is if we have the power and the brutality. That is the way of violence. That is the way of modern dictatorship, making power the sole measure of the right to exist.

Secondly, we can ignore them. We can pretend that they do not matter. That is the way of tolerance, of superficial liberalism, as though the proper method of meeting the difference of our values, the difference of our needs, were a mixture of indifference and patronage. That anaemic method won't stand any strain. It devitalizes all values. It won't meet any crisis, and it is not the democratic way.

The third way to deal with differences is to admit them, to recognize differences that are not ours, ways that are not our ways; to recognize that they are real, that they matter, that they are important, and troublesome, but that they belong in the same world as ours and that they have the same right to the same world as have our own. The same right, but no greater right; if they claim a greater right they lose all right, for they rest their claim on force.

We can accept that position if we have a certain rather simple but rather deep faith, the faith that there is something bigger than our differences, that there is some greater unity, a unity that perhaps may even create our differences. That is one aspect of the democratic faith, or perhaps I should say the democratic faith is one aspect of that greater faith. To seek this ground of unity, to explore this faith, is in my view the ultimate purpose of our inquiry.

Let us not seek it where it cannot be found. For example, let us not imagine that we are going to find this ground of social unity, this more basic faith in a subscription to any platform, to any orthodoxy, to any set of principles whatever.

A platform, an orthodoxy, a set of principles, is the proper ground of unity for a school of thought, for a political party, for a church, but it is not the ground of unity for a community, for a country, for a people.

This complex world in which we live, which we are inheriting, has distinguished the two grounds of unity—not separated them but distinguished them. To confuse them again is simply one way of returning to primitivism.

There is ample room for both grounds. For example, the freedom of the church can exist within the larger freedom of the community; nevertheless, this has been a difficult lesson for us to learn. It is still a difficult lesson for some schools of thought. It is a difficult lesson for some churches. It is a difficult lesson for some philosophies. Sometimes it is a difficult lesson for science, or scientists, should I say?

Any absolute claim, such as the absolute claim that a church may make, is easily infected with totalitarianism, but if it becomes so infected, it surrenders its own profounder claim, its own peculiar claim, because it makes its appeal no longer to the heart of man.

I say it is easy to confound the two grounds, the unity of the school, of the party, of the church; and the unity of the community, of the nation, the country, the people.

The latter springs from the solidarity of sentiment that grows from the interdependence, from the constant interchange, from the habit of everyday, from the constant participation one with another in everyday life.

Take, for example, the family. A family doesn't rest on any platform, on any orthodoxy, as a family. It can reconcile or it can rise above difference because it can find another ground of unity. And in this respect a nation is more like the family than it is like the church. The common sentiment of the family may embrace a thousand differences. The common sentiment of a nation can embrace many more, because of the constant weaving of threads that link us together, provided the right conditions are given.

I have no time to dwell on that, but I simply would like in passing to stress that word "conditions," to mention two conditions for the constant weaving of that greater basis of unity. The two conditions are: (1) That men are free to follow their differences; (2) That they are not balked and embittered by economic frustrations.

I do not know which of these is more important than the other. I believe they are both essential. I believe that given those two conditions the natural processes of solidarity will give us that greater basis on which we can go forward.

But don't let us pretend that differences don't matter. It is enough if we believe in the brotherhood of man, in the worth-whileness of personality, in this unity that embraces us. In the quest for further unity let us not seek for any absolutism. To be absolute in any sphere, in the sense of trying to impose our orthodoxy on any other men, is to be ridiculous.

All systems are partial. None comprehends the whole. All are subject to change, revision, restatement, revaluation, endlessly. But the common sentiment and the common quest endures. It is not peculiarly possessed by the scientist or by the philosopher or by the theologian. It is the heritage of our civilization. We need it. We need the common and the different. It is not only the heritage of civilization; it is actually the world of nature, in so far as we comprehend it. It is the condition of all the fullness and richness that we can achieve in life.

We need science with its established and universally accepted knowledge, but we need more than science. We live by bread and we live by faith. That is the glory of it and, if you like, that is the devil of it, because it has always been hard for the believing human being to let other beliefs live.

But that demand is the inexorable demand of civilization. It is not as such the demand of philosophy or the demand of religion or the demand of science, but if in this world, this kind of world we now inherit, philosophy, religion and science are to save themselves, if they are to help save the world, then they must also follow this way and they must, for that is their especial task, help others to find this way.

[1941]

THE ORDERING OF A MULTIGROUP SOCIETY

We have viewed from many different angles what is a major source of discord and unease in the society in which we live. The unity of the nation, the strength and well-being of the community are being threatened by the maladjustments and the frustrations that arise in the relations of group to group, by the prejudices and suspicions and the hostilities and the fears and the discriminations that arise between group and group. It has become, I believe, perhaps the major problem of our particular society at this particular time.

The issue is not the difference between groups, but the way in which we react to these differences. The issue is not the conflict between groups. Everywhere men and groups are engaged in some kind of struggle.

Everywhere men and groups are, among other things, seeking to get ahead, and, while it has its harmful effects, it also has its beneficial effects. In any case, it is the condition of a dynamical society, and it is not here our concern.

We are concerned here with something different, with something more sinister. We are concerned with the disabilities, whether for cooperation or for competition, that exist between group and group, with the exclusions, with the denials, the rejections that keep groups apart, that shut groups up so that they do not share in the common fresh air of the world in which we live, with exclusions and denials that threaten their personalities, that obviously interfere with their life chances everywhere, that invade their integrity, that poison the springs of life and of faith.

Here has lain our concern, in those relations between group and group and in those denials and exclusions and discriminations that are contrary to the fundamental principles on which this country is presumed to have been founded. This source of discord and unease has not been growing less in our day; it has been growing greater.

We have seen that the threat to our society from this source is a real and a grave one. We have seen that it permeates every sector of our social life, that it enters into our economic relations, into our social intercourse, into labor organizations, into professional organizations, into every aspect of life. In every relation of life it tends to frustrate, to thwart the hopes and disturb the innermost thoughts of groups. That is why I dare claim that it is perhaps the major problem of this present society at this present time. . . .

In a peculiar sense, this issue of group relations is a problem of our own country. In this country we have reached the ground for a higher stage of civilization with respect to groups and their relations, because in this country we no longer identify the people or the state with any ethnic group, with any faith, with any section, and therefore for us in this country it is not a problem for political reform, as it may be in the first instance in many parts of Europe.

We have passed that stage on the whole. If we lived up to our Constitution and our codes, the difficulties we are suffering from would largely disappear. There may be some changes we should make in this respect but, on the whole, we have already conquered the political citadel. The trouble is that constitutions and codes do not control men's thoughts and actions and attitudes.

With us the trouble is not mainly one of political relations. It is not one, in the first instance, of the guarantee of civil liberties by constitutional law. It is a question of our social relations, it is a question of our social attitudes, and the reason why our codes and our Constitution in this respect are not too effective is that there is a discrepancy, a disharmony between the legal, the political side, which we have won, and the social side which we have certainly not yet won.

So the main issue is that of a better ordering of group relations. The question is for us one of our response to other groups, of our attitudes toward other men, and that should be the controlling fact in any program we offer, in any steps we take toward betterment. The controlling fact is the need for social education, for social re-education. What can we do about it? If I am right in saying that the essential trouble—while there may be things that can be corrected here and there by changes in provisions and regulations—lies in social attitudes, then there is no short or easy road to our goal.

In fact there is a danger in taking short cuts to this goal. We must not only have our hearts in the right place, we need wisdom as well as right emotion if we are going to face this question; and our emotion, unless it is guided by wisdom, will make things worse instead of better. Sometimes that has happened among us.

The trouble does not lie with any particular group. The trouble lies between groups. It is the question of the relations between them, and therefore, to remedy it, we cannot seek a specific for a particular group alone. We probably should not concentrate too exclusively on any one group when it comes to the matter of saying what should be done to improve things.

We cannot get ahead far by pressing the particular claims or the particular rights of any one group, because so long as you are doing that, first, you are not touching this matter of social attitudes, and, second, you are still putting the accent on difference, and that is where a large part of the trouble lies. Instead of finding remedies for this group, for the evils, the troubles, the discriminations that this group or that group suffers, our main task is to advance along the whole front. Otherwise, we may gain a little here, but we lose it because we do not hold the line. The line has not gone forward, and the line is the line of our social re-education.

This statement may be misunderstood. I do not mean to suggest that we should not take steps to expose the discriminations that particular groups suffer from. I do not mean to suggest that we should not be active in showing up the evils of discrimination in particular instances and its effects on particular groups. What I mean is that, having done so, we must proceed to apply a larger principle that is relevant to all groups. What we do for one, we are doing for all, we are doing for ourselves. The accent must not be on difference, because that is already our trouble.

The ailment does not depend on the existence of any particular group, no matter how manifest the trouble may be with respect to it.

The evil is a universal one. Sometimes it is one group, sometimes another. Sometimes it is, say, the radical; sometimes it is the liberal. Sometimes it is the Roman Catholic, sometimes it is the Jew, sometimes it is the Protestant. It depends on the conditions where the evil strikes. But its root is the same always, without reference to the particular people who may be the particular victims at any one time.

Therefore I do not believe we are going to get very far in solving this problem merely by strong advocacy of the claims of any one group, or by showing—good as the case may be—the contributions that any one group makes. That is all very well in its place, but it is not the solution to this problem. There was some difference of opinion on this point, as to whether it was a good thing or not to have, let us say, a Czech hour on the radio, a Greek hour, or an Italian hour, and so on. I tended to side with those who thought that it had little efficacy for this particular purpose.

It is like this: You have an hour on the radio, let us say, or a column in the paper. How does it look to the outsider? The rest of the time the radio is American, and this hour is Czech. That is what it looks like. In other words, you are separating the group from the totality of the community.

I suggested that we might even claim that to have a "woman's page" in a paper was itself an invidious and possibly odious affair, if you really saw it right, unless you had also a "man's page." All the rest of the paper is for the dominant majority, and we will give one page to the women! But that point raises a question I would rather not discuss!

What we have to advance toward is the common rights of all groups, and we can help by showing how some are denied these common rights, and proceeding to indicate these rights in the name of all rather than in the name of any group.

All groups everywhere are different. All men everywhere are different. So there is no question in any sane mind of an attempt to abolish differences. It is not even a question of the assimilation of differences, if you mean by that expression the reducing of them to one uniformity. Nor is it a question of the toleration of difference. To be tolerant is still like giving some group their hour on the radio. You give them a little space; after all, you allow them to exist. But tolerance in the long run, though there are times when it is a necessary first step, is really an insult. It is not tolerance that is the issue. It is the reception of the differences into the unity of the whole society. And that is quite a different thing.

These differences, I say, exist everywhere, and the trouble is that we misconceive them all the time, misconceive what they are and misconceive what they mean. We do so because it is around differences that our group egoisms and our group interests cluster, and so the assertion of difference is associated with claims of superiority, denials of equality;

and differences tend to be distorted into the caricatures that our prejudices and our ignorances create.

Such disorted ideas of other groups abound where, as peculiarly in these United States, we have a multigroup society. They do two things that are contrary to truth. First, they exaggerate the difference between the group that makes them and the group they are supposed to represent. They give the one group many virtues, and, of course, they give the other group many less favorable qualities. Thus they exaggerate the differences between groups, and, even more, they exaggerate the likenesses within the single group. They suggest quite fallaciously that those who belong to a particular group are extremely alike in certain important qualities.

All groups do this thing. Minority groups do it as much as majority groups. Subject groups do it as much as dominant groups. We all do it. We paint unflattering pictures of other groups, and we come to think that every group is a rather simple embodiment of a particular set of attributes. For example, you find the Gentile's conception of the Jew uniform, as if there were one kind of human being called a Jew and he was like that everywhere. Whereas actually, if any comparison is possible here, Jewish people are one of the most variant of peoples, not only if you think in terms of differences of origin, but if you think of differences of individuals, families, and subgroups. Nevertheless, the Gentile still cherishes the simple image of the Jew. Of course, if they knew how they quarreled among themselves, perhaps they would change their minds!

All groups are always doing that kind of thing, perverting our relations because we meet in terms of these pictures and not of realities. I suppose we do it partly because it is easier. It is a lazy substitute for understanding, but, even more, we do it because it is the best support for our group pride, our group interest, our group prejudices, whatever they may be. These emotions are sustained by nothing so much as by our carrying around in our heads these unfavorable images of groups that are not ours.

So it comes back to this: that the major task, if we are going to get ahead, is the task of social education. What do we mean by that? What can we do by that? There is a great fundamental premise that somehow we have to get across in education. The premise is that what we have in common is more fundamental than what we have separately, that that which unites us is deeper, more profound, more important, more real, than that which separates us.

It is very necessary that this fundamental premise should be stated and restated with all the ingenuity we can display, and it is particularly important in this day and age because we live in a time when every group is organized, when every group has its special voice, when we have new devices of propaganda for spreading these voices. Since everybody belongs to a group, these group voices fill the air. We hear these warring voices all the time, but we do not hear the voice of the whole, the voice of the community, and we have to find some way of bringing that common voice to the hearing of the people.

Education can be set going in many ways to this end. I am not suggesting that there are not other important steps. I am merely saying that the fundamental way to form a better-ordered society is the way of education, because the great trouble lies in our attitudes. Our first job is to show up the falsifications that come from the tensions between group and group. We have to show how these bring danger to the commonweal, to our own country, and beyond that to our common humanity.

We can start in the schools. At present we have practically no *social* education. We educate people in civics and so forth, but that is really secondary. If you educate people socially you educate them concerning the way in which they should be related to other men. That is primary. We can start with the schools, and if we get it in the schools, we shall get it in the families, we shall get at the springs of indoctrination.

We must enlist, also, the churches, the various faiths, and if we succeed here we can go further and have an impact on the more distant chambers of government.

I suggest that this is the order in which to proceed: to proceed from the family, the people, and the church to the state, and not the other way around, in this educational program.

It is a vast program, a very difficult program, you may think. True, but at the same time there are many agencies that can be enlisted if we set about it. It is a good sign that this need for social education is beginning to be realized. We are seeing signs that the churches are to a greater extent becoming aware of the need. But it is only a beginning—a much greater awareness is needed.

Before we go much further in that awareness, we have to set down certain lines upon which this teaching can develop. To begin with, there are two sides to the teaching itself. We have to expose false teaching, we have to show the consequences of that false teaching, because they mean a serious disruption of the whole basis of our common life. Then we have to help spread truer views about men and groups and the relations between them, truer views of the nature of society, truer views of what civilization means and how groups belong together within this civilization, truer views about this American society of ours, which peculiarly depends for its strength and stability on the spread of these truer views.

There are two media through which such instruction can be conveyed. One is the living word, the great medium of the word. The other is our way of life. One without the other may be vain. In other words, we have to give examples, we have to *live* relationships. Examples spread, both pernicious ones and the others, and if we combine the word with a way of life that represents a truer sense of relationship between groups, then we shall get ahead.

I believe the time has come for a really great social movement in this direction. Our generation has been going through a time of war and upheaval and crisis and tension. That period has been a bad one for the harmonious relations between men everywhere, not only between countries but within countries. All have been affected by this atmosphere. Even those who fight in the name of democracy against intolerance may become affected somewhat by the very thing they are fighting against. There is a danger because the evil is in the air, and it is congenial to a time of war and tension.

We need to bring that time to an end. There is great need of new goals and new standards. Of course, nothing would help it so much as if we had a peace of understanding between peoples and an end of the stimulation of hatreds between peoples, because that spirit penetrates down into the smallest group.

It is very largely a question of bringing men to see what perils our society is facing. In this day we have to get beyond the narrow group ethics that tend to dominate us, the narrow group ethics which, when we have no great binding faith, separate group from group. Each group has its own purposes, and it struggles for these purposes. So we have the ethics of the group but we haven't the ethics of the whole. We have to get beyond the fragmentation ethics of a divided society.

That is the trouble of our time. We have to appeal to the more universal, to the common. It is there if we take hold of it. The great faiths, although they speak with different voices, have all back of them a certain universality of ethics that is entirely opposed to this fragmentary ethics of the divided group. We have to appeal there, and in the last resort we have to appeal to the understanding and the hearts of men. We have to think in terms of new standards and new goals, and we should think of a charter, a sort of charter of human relations that needs to be set up. Our age needs a new, a somewhat different, charter—a charter that will think not of the relations of individuals but of the relations of groups, so that groups may be unified freely without loss, without prejudice, within the whole.

That unity is so much deeper than the differences that, once people see it, they cannot lose it any more. To teach this lesson is the great task of social education in the strictest sense of that word. Through social education alone can we attain this salvation of the society in which we live. To teach it we need new modes of expression, new forms, new words, new symbols.

As you have gone out of this building [the Jewish Theological Seminary of America], you have noticed that over the portal there is a symbol, the symbol of the burning bush, the bush that burned but was not consumed. I have more than once reflected on coming inside this door that I, too, in a far-off island, was brought up in a church which had that same symbol, a different church. It suggests something, that the symbol is greater than our differences, and we need symbols for this unity. That symbol of the bush that burned, the tree that was not consumed, suggests the kind of living spirit that animates, endures, lights, warms, but does not destroy. We can think of that as the spirit of man, the thing that has to be rescued from these differences. We can think of that tree as the symbol, and we may, perhaps, add to it another saying about a tree whose leaves were for the healing of the nations.

[1941]

STATE *and* SOCIETY III

Do Nations Grow Old?

14 Do nations grow old and die, even as men do? Is there set for the race, as for the single life, one immutable law of mortality? It is a commonplace of our thinking that they do. We discover in history the ruins of vanished states—"Assyria, Greece, Rome, Carthage, what are they?"—and the thought occurs that our time too is coming. As the Greek moralized over Persia, the Roman over Greece, as we today moralize over Rome, will not some new future people moralize over us? Are there not already gloomy prophets who foresee the end, and trace in our present life the symptoms of senility?

I hope to show in this paper that this common view is superficial and false, and that if ever a nation dies or is dissolved, such a disaster is no necessary fulfillment of the law of its existence. Because a society lives, it does not follow that it shall die.

The chief scientific support of the popular idea is found in the vicious "social organism" theory which Herbert Spencer did so much to perpetuate, the view that a society is a kind of organism, like the living body of a plant or animal or man, showing a similar relation of part to part and of part to whole, a similar unity and a similar course of life. If we regard a community as an organism, we are ready to attribute to the larger unity the qualities that distinguish the smaller.

An organism is born, develops, reaches maturity, declines, and dies. It comes into being and passes out of being. Within these limits of appearance and disappearance its life may be represented as a simple curve slowly mounting up and more suddenly declining. If the supposed analogy holds, a society, too, is born into being and passes out of being, a society, too, may be represented as following a gradual upward curve till, having reached a culminating point, it descends quickly through decline into extinction. Such an idea is undoubtedly at the back of our minds when we speak of the "decline and fall" of nations, or even of the "maturity" which preceded the decline, maturity being the culminating point of the simple curve of life. But all the time we are thinking on the lines of a most inapt analogy. A community is not born and a community does not necessarily die. A society has no maturity, no predestined culminating point. It does indeed exhibit growth and decline continually, but to understand that growth and decline, we must banish the idea that it is the growth of something which was born and the decline of something that must die. We must banish the idea that a society is always at some point in a simple curve of life.

It may seem a hard saying, this that a society is not born and does not die. Has every society existed before Time was? Does not history tell us of the beginning of some societies, even modern history? Did the communities of America have no beginning? Can we not name the very year of their birth? And if they have had a beginning, must they not, too, have an end? Can a society be an exception to the general law that Time devours all his children?

The answer is simple. In a society the generations of life are integrally bound together, young life with old life, parents with youth. Now life is a process of evolution, and evolution knows nothing of beginning or end. It knows nothing of a time when life sprang out of lifelessness, and nothing of a time when life shall be resolved in lifelessness. Evolutionary science cannot say whether there has been a beginning or whether there will be an end. It knows an intermediate space only. It has the vision of a traveler on a road who can trace backward the path he has trodden and foresee a very little of the path to come, but cannot even conceive a beginning to the road or to his traveling. A living thing by its very nature cannot conceive a beginning to life. But life is essentially and always social life. Every living thing is born into society and owes its life to society. Wherever there is life, there is a society however rudimentary. Science, knowing nothing of the birth of life, knows therefore nothing of the birth of society. And the same is true of its end. It is only that which is born that must die, and unless we show that a society has been born, we can never show that it must die. We can go further and say positively that any society which exists today must in fact be the evolution of a society that has existed from the unknown beginning. Individuals, generations, succeed each other in a chain of life. But society is always there, not successive like the generations, but continuous, changing incessantly but never dying. If the stream of life flows anywhere today, it is a stream that has flowed continuously from beyond the bourne of time. Every living thing is born into a society of which he in time becomes a member, and so the society itself, its spirit constantly renewed by its successive members, the inheritors of the traditions and thoughts and usages of their fathers, lives on. It is like a flame that never dies because it is constantly fed. So long as a single human being endures, a society has existed from the remotest past until now. Every living being is thus a member of a society which has endured through all time. The very existence of a single society today is the last proof that societies do not necessarily follow a simple curve of life, up to maturity and thence down to extinction. The law of evolution reveals direction alone, not beginning nor end, the pathway of life, and neither its entrance nor its goal. It reveals an up or a down, a progress or a retrogression, a sinking or a rising of life. It reveals no law of mortality. Therefore in order to understand the progress or the decline of a society, we must remember that we have no right to make it subject to that law of mortality which inexorably governs the living body, the organism.

Societies develop, they do not begin. The new life of America did not begin when English adventurers settled in Virginia, or English Puritans in New England. Alike they brought their social life into the new land. There are no new societies save in the division or extension or reformation of pre-existent societies.

It is needful to make a distinction at this point, for the term "society" may be used in two senses, only one of which is here intended. Thus, on the one hand, Scotland is a society, so is the United Kingdom, so is the city of Manchester. Here society means an integral (though not necessarily self-sufficient) community, including within itself all the essential social activities or functions, a common life, in short, of greater or lesser extent. On the other hand, a lodge of free masons is a society, a trade union is a society, a church and a university are societies. But these are not communities, they arise within the common life, and are means for its greater fulfillment. Notice the difference. The community, the integral society, is a life, an end in itself, a living whole. The association, the partial society, is usually a means to that life, and usually rests on a contract of its members. The association comes into being when the contract is made, and dies when the contract is cancelled. The society for the abolition of slavery came into being when men agreed to use their joint endeavor for the removal of a social disgrace: it ended when the object of its existence was fulfilled. Other associations are concerned not with the attainment merely but with the maintenance of some social end, and therefore are more enduring : supreme among these is the State. But the community is greater even than the State. It is not an institution, something set up, not an association, something agreed upon: it is that which establishes institutions and forms associations. When we speak of society in this sense we mean some area, greater or smaller, of communal life. It may mean village or parish or city or country, provided that within it all the essential activities of life are found. This proviso excludes those imperfect communities, such as monasteries and nunneries, which, though maintaining a common life, do not maintain all the essential functions of life. What I mean by society throughout this paper is any community which is a real focus of social life. It is the community and not the association with which we are here concerned.

Now every society so understood is a very complex thing, a web composed of many threads crossing and recrossing. Parts are closely united, parts remotely. Every large society contains numerous smaller ones, and every small society enters into the social life of wider groups; all common life is a question of degree. There are bonds uniting all mankind, there are bonds uniting two human beings and in so far separating them from all the rest of mankind. There are countless degrees of unity and difference within all society. The difference has been realized from the beginning, the unity is only being slowly realized today. But this mere fact of infinite grades of unity extending out from the innermost circle of the family to the uttermost bounds of humanity is already a sufficient disproof of the doctrine which makes of any social group, the nation, for instance, a self-subsistent organic whole, subject to the organic law.

I do not intend to follow out that argument, I wish rather to make appeal to history. Were the social-organism theory true, every community must have a time of birth, a time of growth, a culmination, a time of decline, and an hour of death. That is the process of the organic life. Every present society would then be at some stage in that process of growing old, whether young, adult, or senescent. And the last stage would mean an inevitable process toward dissolution, without hope of recovery, to be evaded by no effort its members could make. And there would be on record many instances of past societies which had run their course and disappeared out of life.

History shatters that illusion. History indeed shows that societies are not necessarily immortal. Peoples have perished of violence and of pestilence. There are today on the earth societies of human beings which are undoubtedly in process of extinction, where no new life in equal quality and vigor is united to the old to continue the society. There are today in Asia and in Africa and in America aboriginal peoples who are dying out under the conditions of life brought to them by superior races.

Therefore a society is certainly exposed to the danger of mortality: it may die, but yet it is not its nature to fulfill a cycle of life that ends in death. The wrecks of history are like the fossils of prehistoric animals, they tell us that some types of living creature have disappeared, leaving no successors. They do not tell us that all types must so disappear, for we know in fact that many types have survived, some with no change, others changing to meet changing conditions. We cannot predict the death of mankind of racial old age because we have discovered the bones of saurians.

We may now take some historical instances, those that most readily occur when we talk of the fall of nations, and show that, whatever their decline and fall may mean, it does not mean the passing out of existence of a society. Let us take first the community or communities that made ancient Greece, as we know it from the time depicted in the Homeric poems. W may say that Homeric Greece passed away, that the Greece of Herodotus and Thucydides passed away, that the Greece of the Macedonian supremacy passed away; we may take broader periods, and speak of ancient and medieval and modern Greece. But make the periods what we please: there is never a point at which the community dies, as there is an hour in which the organism dies. There has been a continuous Greek society from the beginning of history until today, a society whose level of civilization and vigor has risen and fallen and risen again. What we find is never the death of a body, but always the transformation of a spirit. The former is momentary, determinate, final; the latter is gradual, continuous, infinite. Here there is no body that as it ages at last subdues the spirit. For a society is neither old nor young, and need not grow older or younger. Hence its life is not subject to the rhythm of organic life or to the law of organic mortality. The organic life appears at a definite point out of the unknown and, fulfilling its simple curve, disappears at a definite point into the unknown. But for the curve of communal life there is no base line whence it arises and into which it falls. This is evident if we trace the course of the Greek communities, from the days of Homeric barbarism, barbarism half hidden by the splendor of the past, to the height of fifth-century achievement, down through Macedonian and Roman domination and lastly Turkish oppression, and up again after it all, not indeed to anything of its former height, but at least to the higher level revealed in new national unity and consciousness of liberty. Customs and manners and institutions and forms of civilization pass away, but the social life, of which these were merely expressions, may persist throughout it all. To that life we can assign neither beginning nor end.

We may take as a further illustration the case of that community whose downfall has more than any other impressed the historian with a sense of the mortality of all things human. It is an illustration which brings out clearly the need for distinguishing the passing institutions from the undying life of society. At a certain period of history, the social life centering round the city of Rome had extended so far as to make of Italy a social unity, an integral society. The decline of that society is the most momentous in history, but its life has survived every historical disaster. Through all the history of Rome there has lived a continuous society, sometimes threatened with destruction, at the hands of Gauls or Carthaginians or Goths, but never destroyed, rising and falling to social heights and depths alike almost unparalleled, sometimes torn and disunited, sometimes almost overwhelmed by the wave of barbaric immigration, but in the end revealing in rediscovered unity the immortal integrity of communal life. The Roman Empire passed away, but the social life of Rome and Italy never failed altogether. The life changed just as the language changed in which it found expression, but both life and language remained. States come into being and are dissolved, but society which creates them is greater than they. The Roman *empire* was not a society, not a living thing, but an imposed system, an institution. When the communal life of Italy slackened, it could no longer enforce that system over the communal life of its subject communities. The system collapsed, the life survived. It may even be that the growing life of these subject societies— "the bursting of the ripe seed," as one recent writer has expressed it—was as much responsible for the collapse of empire as the weakening life of Italy. As a community grows strong it refuses to accept institutions imposed from without, institutions it has not itself created for the furtherance of its own life. At any rate we must distinguish the fall of a State from the death of a community. The State, the institution, collapses, it may be in an hour, the society lives on and creates new institutions, a new State. The fall of a State is a commonplace of history, the death of a society is an event most rare and most abnormal. Most of the societies that have figured in history have indeed suffered eclipse, but none of these has perished, and some have risen again and are even now rising, a witness to the eternal possibility of social rejuvenescence.

When we understand that the terms "birth," "maturity," and "death" have no necessary connection with the life of a society, we have taken the first step toward the understanding of that incessant rise and fall, the increase and the decrease of social vigor and vitality. It is not something measurable, this spiritual activity (if it is not the life of a body, what can it be but the life of a spirit?). It has a thousand manifestations— political, religious, philanthropic, literary, artistic, intellectual—some of which may be in vigor while others are in decline. A people's religious or literary activity may be greatest when its political activity is least, though this is very far from being the rule. On the contrary, all those activities seem to be bound up together, being but different expressions of one common life. As that life stirs to new activity, not in one only, but in manifold forms does it reveal itself. The great reformation of religious thought and the great renaissance of science and art and literature almost together heralded the new world. On the whole, then, we can estimate in some rough fashion the relative intensity and advance of social life. We agree that Athenian society flourished most in the time of Pericles, that Roman society declined from vigor to complete decadence under the emperors, that England became great and strong in the days of Elizabeth. We judge, usually—and rightly—the social vigor of a people not by its artistic or intellectual eminence, but by the degree in which it cooperates in the maintenance and welfare of the state, the central institution of the national life and the first expression of its unity. But the social vigor shown in a strong and active state generally shows itself at the same time in every form of social activity, in the life of the thousand societies of commerce, science, art, and education.

How are we to understand this social life? What are the symptoms of its vigor and decline? A society is a common life, dependent for its vitality on the worth of its members and on the degree to which these members contribute that worth to the community. There are the elements of all social well-being, the worth of the individual, his personality, and the extent of his cooperation with his fellows, his sociality. These are the tests of all society, not one alone, but both together. The ant and the bee give themselves up to their society, but because they have little to give, all their social sacrifice avails them little. The hermit gives nothing to his society, and therefore a country of hermits, were they never so great and wise, would also attain to nothing. But in a true society the two factors, the strength of individuality and the strength of sociality, work together, and indeed they never can be really independent of one another. For as each of us makes his society, so does our society make each of us. Our individuality if it is strong goes out to strengthen—if it is weak to weaken—our society; to our society we owe in turn the measure of our individuality. The opposition of society and individuality is accidental, in essentials they develop out of one another, and as a true society seeks to develop individuality, so the most gifted individuality finds its expression and fulfillment in society. The more the members of a community enter into the life of that community, the richer by the amount of what they themselves have brought becomes that life. This ever renewed flame of social activity rises and falls continually. Its quality is the quality of the social units whose common life it is—if the fuel is poor, how can the flame be bright? Its intensity is the degree in which these members are united in that common life—scatter the coals and what once glowed in a radiant focus will flicker feebly in dispersed and meager fires. It is this spiritual activity we call society, this conscious cooperation in a great common life, that sustains within it the life of every contributor, as the energy of its ardent center keeps every coal in a fire aglow. To fall away from that fire is to pale and grow cold like a cinder, to lose the communion of society is to lose the community in which each life is quickened.

If that be so, we must interpret social progress and social decline in terms of spirit at the last. On whatever physical conditions a society depends, we must remember that these change but little while the society is passing on from phase to phase. The earth, the physical basis on which all life is forever dependent, alters scarcely at all in the memory of man: the productivity, agricultural and mineral, of the soil, the heat of the ·sun, the succession of the seasons, these vary to a scarcely appreciable degree from generation to generation. The physical changes that do occur are mostly those brought about by men's own ingenuity and invention, are social products. The endless activity of man is progressively making the physical conditions always more favorable, making nature always more subservient to his ends, to his length of life, to his security and comfort of life. Nature is passive to his hands. For our purpose, therefore, we can regard the physical basis of society as in itself stable and unchanging, and we must turn, if we are to inquire into the conditions of a society's decay, to its own inner spiritual nature.

Historians are fond of giving reasons for the decline of peoples and the fall of states. These reasons, if our account is true, are at best secondary conditions, results of a lowering of the spiritual activity rather than its causes. This and this alone is social decay, the slackening of the social will, the loosening of the bonds that unite men, not forcibly but freely, within their society, the progressive weakening in each of the social purpose which is the first principle of the social life of all. Mr. Balfour in his essay on "Decadence" is right in refusing to admit that mere historical circumstances, external events, the defeat of armies, the mistakes of statesmen, constitute the full explanation of the waning of social life, the social enfeeblement that is made catastrophic when it involves the dissolution of a State. "It is in vain that historians enumerate the public calamities which preceded and no doubt contributed to the final catastrophe. Civil dissensions, military disasters, famine, pestilences, tyrants, tax-gatherers, growing burdens, and waning wealth—the gloomy catalogue is unrolled before our eyes, yet somehow it does not in all cases fully satisfy us. We feel that some of these diseases are of a kind which a vigorous body politic should easily be able to survive, that others are secondary symptoms of some obscurer malady, and that in neither case, do they supply us with the full explanations of which we are in search." Defeat, pestilence, and famine may decimate a people and not crush its spirit or its vitality. It is the strength and character of its spiritual unity that makes or unmakes a people. Not decimation of numbers, a loss speedily reparable, but enfeeblement of spirit is the ultimate social misfortune, and the cause of social disaster. So Byron says of Greece:

> No foreign foe could quell
> Thy soul, till from itself it fell.

As with decadence, so with progress. We must interpret progress in terms of this spiritual activity alone. Herbert Spencer explained all progress as differentiation, the growth of heterogeneity, and undoubtedly the increasing complexity of social life, as of all life, is the surest and most striking sign of its development. But to call this the progress of society is to make structure prior to the life that animates and shapes structure. As a society advances, it grows in complexity, it requires more and more associations within it to express the fullness of its communal life. But it is that life which brings the new complexity of structure into being, and here we are concerned, not with the result, but with the nature of the cause. Progress has no meaning except in the light of purposes and needs. It is those purposes and needs, consciously realized, that are the driving force in the differentiation of society. The life and the needs of life are here at any rate before the structure. It is this life and the meaning of its progress that concern us here. And here there is but one form of explanation, that which looks at the spiritual activity whose two aspects are personality and sociality.

It is of course true that, without appropriate physical conditions, a community, like a plant in poor soil, will never develop. There will never arise the fine flower of civilization in the snows of northern Greenland or the parched wastes of Central Australia. The Eskimo and the Australian Blackfellow are as surely stunted by their physical surroundings as the actual lichen of the snows and the mulga scrub of the desert. And yet, we must repeat, the physical conditions remain almost constant,[1] and therefore do not explain the progress of the peoples who do progress. In explaining the rise of Greece, we may lay stress on the opportunity given by a mountainous country with a great seaboard and a Mediterranean climate. But these remained when the life of the Greek cities dwindled to insignificance. In explaining the rise of England we may lay stress on her island isolation and her mineral wealth—but no one believes that these will ever save England from decadence. Therefore they are not the sources of her greatness—though without them that greatness might never have been fulfilled. It is the heightening of the social spirit, the strengthening of the social will, which is the will to realize oneself in the greater realization of one's community as apart from the will to realize oneself at the expense

---

1. The exhaustion of the mineral resources of a country would be an exception. Such a change might involve a social decline, but there are no clear historical instances.

of that community, it is the growth of the sense of solidarity as each appreciates more and contributes more to the worth of the common life—there is the meaning of social progress.

But, it may be objected, have you not overlooked one physical factor which is no more constant than the social spirit itself, and the development or degeneration of which has tremendous importance for society? Granted that the world of outer nature does not change appreciably from age to age, save when it is changed by man, are not our human bodies themselves inconstant and variable? It is one of the chief arguments of the modern pessimist that the individual organism is growing finer as civilization advances, is threatened by all manner of new dangers. This is not the place to inquire whether here also the gain does not greatly exceed the loss, whether the history of human organic evolution, like the history of human social evolution, does not offer fair grounds of hope and reveal, in spite of perils and setbacks, a verifiable progress. All that is important for our argument is that this bodily change is in the end the result of the spiritual activity of man, is the readaptation of our bodies to new conditions of life, which we ourselves have willed. If then there is decadence here, the cause is the same as before, a spiritual failure in the members of the decadent society. *If* there is decadence—but all that is so-called does not deserve the name. We must begin by distinguishing the atrophy of no longer useful organs from the decay of the organism. A writer in the *Edinburgh Review* has expressed the difference admirably in the following passage:

> People cry out, in Chamberlainite phraseology, "eyes are going," "teeth are going," "hair has gone!" If it were true, it would only be a minor incident in human evolution. Mankind are a species of bald apes: if the hair of their heads degenerates, as that of their bodies has already done, it would seem a very natural progress of evolution. But teeth also are "going." Doubtless in evolving from the simian stage, there has been a great diminution of size or degeneration of the jaws. Men do not have the massive and protruding jaws that characterize gorillas, nor are their teeth of the same strength. The wisdom teeth in a considerable proportion of humanity never develop at all; and their degeneration is, in the opinion of many, a valuable and desirable eventuality. . . . It is no doubt pleasant to have eyes which can distinguish the satellites of Jupiter, but they would be of no great service in civilized life; far more valuable is the mental vision which gradually gives us the mastery of our fate. It would occasionally be serviceable to have jaws and teeth which could crack a cocoanut; certain pastimes would doubtless be facilitated if our sense of smell was as acute as that of a dog; and in listening to an indistinct speaker it would be of undeniable utility if our degenerate ear-muscles still

retained their former function, so that we could adjust our ears like a horse or a donkey. But the loss of these aptitudes has been attended by the gain of other more important aptitudes; so that their progressive degeneration has helped us to obtain the mastery over all animals in which they have retained full development. . . . It is scarely possible to examine any region of the body without finding evidence that along with evolution of new structures, there has gone a progressive degeneration of old structures.[2] "Claws are going," "hair is going," "tails have gone," such might have been the refrain of a pessimistic ape-man a hundred thousand years ago. And the complaint must have seemed well justified: for how was he to keep warm in winter without his furry coat? and how was he to climb about the trees if he had no tail wherewith to swing himself among the branches?

You see, tails were very useful in that primitive society. But when man had attained to cooperative housebuilding and the use of tools, they had willed away the use, and indirectly the possession, of tails.

There is no escape from the conclusion: it is in the spiritual activity of society that the nature of social progress and decadence is found, there and there alone. This inevitable conclusion is also one full of hope. It relieves the mind from the fatalistic doctrine, a necessary corollary of the social-organism theory, that societies grow old and decay inevitably by mere lapse of time, with no hope against an inexorable law. In truth, societies grow in experience, in knowledge, and in power, as each generation hands down its gains. They do not grow in age, for each generation is new, new as was the inconceivable beginning of life, indeed with an increased capacity of life in so far as past generations have striven to improve it. We can discover no law which burdens the new generations with an inherited weight of age. Society alone is granted that rare and inestimable possession, the advantage of experience without its penalty of powerlessness. To grow wiser without growing older is perhaps the highest boon a man could ask of the gods. That boon is granted to society.

We talk of young peoples, of new nations. Let us remember that no nation is younger than another, except in spirit, in the strength of the social will. The peoples of America are no younger than the peoples of Europe; the new nations of our colonies, of Canada, Australia, and New Zealand, are the children of an older England only in the same sense as we ourselves are its offspring. If their spirit is younger, it is because new conditions

---

2. Wiedersheim in his *Der Bau des Menschen* reckons in human beings 15 organs that are progressing, 17 that are decaying though still partly useful, and 107 that are rudimentary and altogether useless.

of life stimulate old energies, because new opportunities and new freedom renew the spirit. But let us not for one moment suppose that a new country is the only or the surest stimulus of the spirit of society. Far more potent forces exist stored within every community, the challenge of the ideal still so imperfectly realized, the vision of present attainment which past attainment has made possible. When that challenge and that vision enter the heart of the members of a society, uniting them more closely in common effort, in social solidarity, its life is already renewed. "Here or nowhere is our America." Thus and not otherwise does a society become young. While its ears are open to that challenge and its eyes to that vision, it will never know old age.

Even to the individual, bound as he is to the wheel of organic change, there comes at intervals, longer or shorter, a period of renewal, a sense of greater good, of greater worth in existence, as if fresh oil had been poured on the flame of life. To the unaging community that period may come at any time. Our organic bodies refuse at last to respond to the call of the spirit. They lose that power of response which is the very principle of life. But a society can always renew its body, its body is the shell of institutions and customs it has created for the protection of its spirit. If these grow old it can cast them off like an outworn garment, it can replace them, as it has done before, by new and better institutions and customs. Our will at last avails not, for all our vision of health and strength, to stay the oncoming of decay, but the will of a society avails; if only it sees the vision, if only it hears the challenge. It is therefore absurd to talk, as men have talked in every age, of the *inevitable* decadence which must sometime at the last befall our country. For indeed society is a spiritual thing to which there belongs no natural destiny of decay and death. Into that ever rejuvenated life each of us is taken up, in spite of our mere organic fate. If that life fail, it is a failure of the spirit, unpredictable as the coming and going of the wind. And if it fail, it may be renewed; for the failure is not the inexorable failure of old age preceding dissolution, but like the falling of the wind, the abating of a power which again springs into rediscovered life.

[1913]

The Foundations of Nationality

15 In the eyes of its early prophets nationality was a principle either too holy to be analyzed or too simple to require analysis. But that principle brought into the modern world new and insistent problems, and these cannot be understood, still less solved, without a scientific analysis of the meaning and character of nationality. The spirit of the scientist has become no less necessary than the spirit of the devotee—though, in this as in other things, that people is happiest which can best combine the two.

It is noteworthy that we often speak indifferently of "nationality" or of "consciousness of nationality." We speak of the "growth of nationality" when we mean that men become conscious (or more conscious) of some common quality or nature, and attain a conscious unity of life, a common inspiration and activity, on the basis of that recognition. Without this *recognition* of what is common, nationality cannot exist, or at any rate cannot work and live. It is therefore a first step in analysis to consider what those common factors are on the recognition of which nationality depends, to consider the *foundations* of nationality, as a precondition of any insight into its nature and working.

No quality or interest, however common, can be a basis of nationality unless it is regarded as common by those who possess it, and any quality or interest whatever, if so regarded, can be a basis of nationality. But we cannot therefore say simply that nationality depends on the recognition of common social qualities or interests. For we may not only fail to recognize factors of community which really exist, we may also "recognize" factors of community which have no reality beyond the recognition. Not all the foundations on which the structure of nationality rests are equally substantial. In particular the consciousness of race or ethnic origin, at one time regarded as the cornerstone of nationality, has proved to be in nearly every case a delusion. But it is important to remember that the opposite error, the failure to recognize existing community, is far more common, and that all actual consciousness of community has some true basis, though it may not be that which it seems to have. Thus the consciousness of race or ethnic origin is often a falsely simplified expression or reflection of the consciousness of nationality itself. Again, it is of the very essence of nationality that it rests on the consciousness of difference no less than on that of likeness. For each nationality is determined by contrast with others, and a nationality regards itself not only as distinct from others, but nearly always as possessing some *exclusive* common qualities, being thereby separated from others as well as united within itself. Now what holds in respect of the recognition of likeness holds even more of the recognition of difference—the recognition may not always correspond with the reality. This is especially true of difference because as a general principle men assume difference until they are driven to recognize likeness. The whole history of society bears this out. Differences lie on the surface; likenesses have to be sought deeper.

The significance of these facts will be perceived when we have (1) set out the chief qualities or interests in the recognition of which, either as common or as exclusively common, the foundations of exclusive nationality lie, and (2) drawn up a table showing how far these various factors are actually united in particular instances of nationality. The chief qualities or interests in the recognition of which, either as common or as exclusively common, the foundations of nationality must be sought are these :

(1) Ethnic Origin.
(2) Language.
(3) Territory, i.e., as occupied effectively, not as politically owned (7c).
(4) Economic Interests.
(5) Culture, i.e., characteristic standards and modes of life.
(6) Religion.
(7) Political Unity.
(7a) Political Tradition, outcome of (7) when long established.

(7b) Political Subjection.
(7c) Political Domination.

These factors are of course not wholly independent of one another, but they are all distinguishable, and are found variously combined and separated. Further, any or all of them may be common but not exclusive to a particular nationality or both common and exclusive. When a factor is both common and exclusive it may be regarded as a pure determinant of nationality and is then denoted by the symbol I in the chart on page 218. When common (to the whole or the vastly greater part of a nationality) but not exclusive, it is denoted by X. Thus the English language is common to the English people, but not exclusive, being shared by the American people. In the case of territory when a nationality occupies the whole of a definite area and is in no way territorially mingled with other nationalities we may likewise denote them by I; in all other cases we must denote them by X. Thus nearly all imperial nations must be marked X. Again, when nation and state exactly coincide, we may represent the coincidence by the figure I under the factor of political unity; but when either a nationality is divided over more than one State, or a State includes more than one nationality, we must write X under the same factor in respect of any such nationality. For instance we must set X against this factor in the case of the American nation, since they have admitted diverse ethnic and national groups to their political rights. In the case of some other factors, and particularly of economic and cultural interests, it is or should be obvious that, especially in the world of civilization, absolute objective demarcation as between nationalities is quite impossible. In the civilized world national differences, whatever they may amount to, are not differences in "culture-stage"—they are differences in the subtler group-qualities, differences of moods and manners and temperaments, not in the universal character of their standards and achievements. One nation excels in one art, another in another, one has a more favorable opportunity than another for some economic or scientific achievement, but no one possesses a unity of culture at once independent of and in every respect superior to that of others. But if a nationality is deeply conscious of its own culture as being unique, or if it is deeply conscious of the severance of its economic interests from those of its neighbors, we may, in terms of our previous definition, regard such cultural or economic interests as for it pure determinants. In the case of economic interests, this sense of absolute severance seems to occur in the modern world only under the coercive control of dominant over subject nationalities; and in fact it is clear in every case that political conditions, the establishment of tariff-walls, for example, largely determine both the unity and the separation of such interests.

Since we are concerned with the *consciousness* of common quality or interest, variety of opinion may exist in respect of particular items in the chart. I have taken various representative nationalities—the terms British, German, Russian, etc., referring to those and those only who are conscious of *being* British, German, Russian, etc., not to all comprised within, or possessing *legal* nationality (i.e., merely political rights) within, the British or German or Russian Empire—and sought to show the factors on which they depend for unity. Being subjectively limited, these may vary somewhat from time to time—a state of war, in particular, intensifies the consciousness of common national qualities and may turn a normally imperfect determinant into an abnormally pure determinant. I have tried to represent the various factors as they are determinant of the normal consciousness of the respective nationalities.

THE FOUNDATIONS OF NATIONALITY

	(1)	(2)	(3)	(4)	(5)	(6)	(7)	(7a)	(7b)	(7c)					
British	O	X	X	X	X	O	X	I	O	I	(7a)	(7c)			
Americans (USA)	O	X	X	X	X	O	X	O	O	O	None				
French	X	X	X+	X	X+	O	O	I	O	I	(7a)	(7c)			
Italians	X	X	X+	X	X	O	O	O	O	O	None certain				
Russians	X	I	X	X	X+	O	X	I	O	I	(2)	(7a)	(7c)		
Germans	X	X	X+	X	X+	O	X	O	O	I	(7c)				
Jews	I	O	O	O	X+	O	I	I?	I	O	(1)	(6)	(7b)		
Japanese	I	I	I	X	X	O	I	I	O	?	(1)	(2)	(3)	(7)	(7a)
Spaniards	I	X	I	X	X	X	I	I	O	O	(1)	(3)	(7)	(7a)	
Swiss	O	O	I	X	O	O	I	I	O	O	(3)	(7)	(7a)		
Poles	I	I	I	X	X	X	O	I	I	O	(1)	(2)	(3)	(7a)	(7b)
Czechs	I	I	I	I	X	O	O	O	I	O	(1)	(2)	(3)	(4)	(7b)
Magyars	I	I	I	X	X	O	X	I	O	I	(1)	(2)	(3)	(7a)	(7c)

I denotes a factor *recognized* as exclusively common; *X* a factor recognized as common but not exclusive; *O* denotes, in respect of any factor, that there is no community co-extensive with nationality; *X* + denotes a near approach to *I*. The last column shows the "pure determinants."

There is possible, we may repeat, a divergence of opinion in respect of particular items in the chart and there is sufficient heterogeneity within modern nations to make generalizations in respect of certain factors, e.g., religion, always precarious; but the general result remains unaffected. A number of very significant conclusions may be drawn from the chart. Here we must notice in particular that, for the various nationalities we have selected as representative, (1) there is no single factor present in *all* cases of the consciousness of nationality, (2) in no two cases are the factors on which this consciousness is based exactly the same, (3) it is not necessary for nationality that there should be any "pure determinant" whatever. It does not follow from the last-mentioned fact that nationalities need not represent distinct types. Thus there is undoubtedly an American nationality although there is no exclusive basis for it in the form of some *specific* common quality or interest. It does clearly follow, on the other hand, that nationality is not to be identified with any or all of its foundations, that it is something essentially psychical and necessarily indefinite, being a certain consciousness of likemindedness which may be developed in a great variety of ways and under a great variety of conditions. It is certain that in every case of the *formation* of nationality there must originally have been subjection to the two great formative influences of common social life and common environment. But there are all degrees of common life and there is generally continuity of environment, so that there are also all degrees of likemindedness. How then can we distinguish that degree which makes nationality? It can be only in terms of the desire of a group for political unity, for a common (not necessarily exclusive) political organization. The criterion is by its very nature imperfect, but no other seems available. If then any people who bear a common name do not, however scattered they may be, desire to share in a common political life, they may be conscious of common ethnic origin as perhaps Gypsies are, but they cannot be called conscious of common nationality. If it be true that the Jews (who are represented as an ethnic group in the chart) have lost the desire of political reunion, then it may be said of them that they have lost the national self-consciousness, retaining the ethnic factor alone. If again a self-governing colony lacks the desire to be at least federated to the mother-country, it must be said of it that it has lost its original nationality and become a new nation.

Why is it that a community may waken, as it seems in a moment, to the consciousness of nationality? Why is it that the most diverse or opposite influences, the glory no less than the misery of a people, the desire for deliverance or the lust of domination, the materialism of the exploiter or the idealism of the orator and poet, can evoke or direct that spirit? Why is it that the sense of nationality expands, diminishes, or is transformed from time to time, and that the members of a nation may, having changed their sky, change also in time their essential nationality, as the Americans have done? Why is it that the spirit of nationality may be hailed as the liberator of the world, and that yet some profound minds can look upon it as an evil thing, whose course "will be marked by material and moral ruin, in order that a new invention may prevail over the works of God and the interests of mankind"?[1] And how must so ambiguous a spirit

---

1. Acton, *History of Freedom:* Essay on Nationality.

develop if it is to resolve the troubles which it brings no less than maintain the benefits which it can bestow?

We may find some help toward the solution of these questions in the analysis we have already made. The sentiment of nationality depends for its character on the character of its many and various foundations; it is transformed with the transformation of any or all of these; and it finds its true fulfillment when men recognize the true nature, the interdependence and coordination, and the rightful claims of these. This may be shown if we trace, though here it can be done only in the most meager outline, the evolution of nationality. It is commonly said that the sentiment of nationality is a quite modern phenomenon; it would perhaps be more accurate to say that this sentiment has in modern days revealed itself in new and decisive forms. The process of its evolution, leading to these modern revelations of its power, is necessarily, in the universal interdependence of social factors, complex and hard to trace, but the main stages are sufficiently clear. They may be stated as follows:

1. There is a stage of society, before government has grown strong or any political fabric developed, when the group is held together by an intense and exclusive communal spirit, the spirit of the clan or, in a somewhat more developed society, the spirit of the tribe. A good instance of the working of the more primitive type may still be seen in the institutions of such simple peoples as the Veddah groups. Here the group-consciousness is wholly isolated. "Most clans [a clan consisting of merely two or three families sharing a single cave or meeting on one hunting ground] have only a dim idea of the bare existence of others, and in consequence there is no question of marriage outside the clan, which is so common a feature of the next higher stage of development." [2] To the clan-limited consciousness even the tribe, as a union of clans, is a circle too vast to be one inclusive community, and here, as always, the limit of community is the limit of the intelligence of its members. It is noteworthy that these wretched Veddahs, who cannot even count and have no names for days or months, yet regard themselves as vastly superior to all outside the group. [3]

It is rare to find a clan-limited consciousness of this type, but the tribe-limited consciousness is the commonest of phenomena in primitive life. Here again the consciousness of community rests upon a number of factors regarded as all common and all exclusive. It is not that kinship

2. Hobhouse, *Morals in Evolution*, on the Rock-Veddahs as described by the Herrn Sarasin.
3. Cf. Westermarck, *Origin and Development of the Moral Ideas*, II, 170ff., for other illustrations of this attitude among primitive peoples.

determines the tribe, *or religion, or tradition.*[4] Locality, kinship, religion, tradition, customary law, perhaps also communal ownership, together weave the magic circle which bounds protection, service, and fellowship. To belong to the tribe means to belong to the kin, to worship the tribal gods, to be initiated into the tribal institutions, to have the same friends and foes, the same interests, the same thoughts, as all the tribe. In the analysis of such a community it is necessary to set *I* under all the factors of community. The primitive tribe is a circle wherein universal uniformity is the absolute condition of exclusive devotion.

2. But all development is achieved at the cost of uniformity, at the cost of the simplicity of old allegiances. The development of society implied in the first place the growth of the institution of government and created a new devotion that at first may have seemed identical with, but in time revealed itself as distinct from and on occasion contradictory to, the old—the "loyalty" of the subject to the ruler, the chief, the government, the dynasty, as distinct from the devotion of the tribesman to his whole tribe, of the citizen to his country. "For chief and tribe," "for king and country," made an easy and inspiring phrase, but the identity of service implied in the phrase was by no means always a reality. The new sentiment was greatly fostered by militarism and by the alternative consequences of militarism, victory or defeat, domination or subjection. Victory enhanced the power and glory of the ruler, defeat revealed the more the necessity of his strength. The same influences developed the distinction of class within the community, and created conditions under which the opposition of classes—which came, and still comes, very near to being an opposition of subject classes and governing classes—broke finally the homogeneity of the tribal life. Thus was born in every developing community a long period of confused and crossing loyalties which men sought, often vainly, to harmonize or identify. It might be shown, were it not for the limits of an article, how the confusion became intensified when different associations began to appear in their distinctness from the State and, in the name of the specific interest for which each stood, to make claims contradictory to those of the State—or rather of the actual governments of existing states—on the common members of both. Thus in particular the conflict of religions which followed the Reformation created also the antithesis of Church and State, and so introduced a new and profound disturbance of the old unity of communal devotion, just as the trade-union is today creating a newer and, as it may prove in the end, no less profound a disturbance. It is not suggested that these great disturbing principles have come like serpents into the Eden of a primitive

4. The false simplification due to regarding any one factor, as, for instance, Maine and Bagehot regarded kinship, as the sole or even primary determinant of early communities is well pointed out by Westermarck, *op. cit.*, II, xxxiii and xxxiv.

life. Primitive Edens are really very wretched affairs, and the seeming serpent may reveal itself as the deliverer of social man, in showing him the fruit of the tree of the knowledge of good and evil. In the Western world the culmination of the confusion of loyalties was reached under Feudalism.

3. The sentiment of nationality proper emerged when men again sought, under the conditions just described, to realize and distinguish the claims of the complete community to which they felt themselves to belong, discerning this devotion from other conflicting loyalties. It is not to be supposed that this new development was in its turn due to simple or merely "ideal" motives, though we cannot here delay to consider this question. But the desire for the political freedom of the nation was the dominant motive which gave strength and direction to the sentiment of nationality, as could easily be demonstrated by an account of the historical circumstances under which that sentiment arose. The two great political developments of modern days, the growth of nationality and the growth of democracy, have thus a common principle, or rather they reveal the same principle working under different conditions. (a) On the one hand, when a community which feels itself one is either parceled out between several governments or is in whole or in part subject to what it regards as alien domination, there arises the nationalist claim proper, the demand of a nation not so much for self-government as for a government of its own. (b) On the other hand, when a nation already possesses, as a whole, a government of its own, just the same principle is now revealed in the completer demand of democracy. Nationalism is the spirit of protest against political domination, the impulse to that free national unity which itself is the foundation on which the common interests of the nation must be achieved. To attain the demand of nationalism is not to achieve these interests, it is to have built the foundation only of their achievement. Nationality is not the end but the beginning.

Hence we have to realize very carefully the limits of the ideal of nationality. It is the failure to realize these limits which perverts that ideal from a savor of life into a savor of death. *Nationality can be a true ideal only so long as and in so far as nationality itself is unrealized.* As soon as it is attained, as soon as a nation is a unity free from alien domination, a new ideal must take its place. The ideal must now be to realize, on the basis of nationality, the interests of the nation—and that ideal must be sought in other ways, for though nation is marked off from nation, the *interests* of one nation are not, as we have seen, similarly marked off from those of others. The preliminary idea of nationality, the establishment of the autonomous nation-state, is sought through difference; the ideals of the enfranchised nationality must, in view of the interdependence of the interests of nations, be sought through coordination and intercommunity.

Nationality provides an adequate ideal only while men are seeking liberty from alien political control. That ideal is, until that attainment, certainly of all ends the most imperative and most fundamental, for the attainment of a true basis of common action is the necessary precondition of the realization of common good. But when an ideal is achieved it is vain to regard it as any longer an ideal. When national liberty is achieved, the true inspiration of nationality is fulfilled, except in so far as it is necessary to maintain what has been attained—but no community can live merely to maintain its foundations, it necessarily builds upon these. If on the attainment of the claim of nationality no further ideal emerges, then nationalism moves rapidly to the corrupt extreme of chauvinism. It was so in the case of revolutionary France, it has obviously been so in the case of many present-day nations. But chauvinism is the spirit in which one nationality exalts itself at the cost of others—in the long run at the cost of itself. That it is at the cost of itself is clear enough when we remember how many interests of present-day nations have ceased to be exclusive to each. In so far as interests are exclusive, the interests of each are independent of those of others; in so far as they are nonexclusive, the interests of all are interdependent, and what injures those of one injures also those of others.

4. The slow recognition of interdependence and its consequences, slow especially as compared with that rapid growth of interdependence which the scientific development of the means of communication has ensured, has been leading toward a new stage in the evolution of nationality. It has been making modern nations, almost against their wills, or at any rate the wills of their governments, parts of a greater society, partners in a common interest. It has been breaking down the idea that nationality must be fostered in exclusiveness, an idea no less absurd than the supposition that the character of an individual must be fostered in isolation. Nationality is no more obliterated by international relations than personality is by interpersonal, i.e., social, relations. On the contrary, the current of social intercourse brings psychical stimulus to the nation no less than to the individual, as the whole history of civilization reveals. Again, the development of international interests has been making interstate coordination necessary and inevitable. But the two methods along which this has been pursued have proved hopelessly inadequate. The one method consists in special conventions and agreements in respect of particular questions, such as the international agreements in respect of passenger and freight transportation by land and sea, of post and telegraph, of patent and copyright, finally—and on these it is that governments have ironically lavished their greatest care!—on the rules of war itself. The other method consists in the system we call diplomacy, this fragile bond of connection, the breaking of which means so much, being

the only definitely constituted relation between modern States. Whatever views we may hold as to the relative services and disservices of secret diplomacy, it is surely difficult to maintain that any such system can be an adequate organ of the inter-community of States.

The future of the nations of Europe, for a long time to come, will be decided by their ability to see past the accumulated hatreds and losses, tragedies and terrors, of this almost universal war, to the necessity of establishing some saner system, some international organization as permanent and as extensive as the common interests of the nations. There are many and great difficulties to be overcome in the realization of such an end, but there is only one final difficulty, the refusal of men to will the end. Its realization is Utopian only so long as men think it so.

If men cannot or will not advance to intrinsic ends—to the deeper level of common interests where they face the same problems, the same needs, the same destinies—they must pursue extrinsic ends. If the nations are not joined by the deeper common interests, they are set against one another by their narrower differences; if they do not strive toward those common possessions that form abiding satisfactions, they must wrest miserably from one another those most partial goods which one or another can still exclusively enjoy.

Because all civilized peoples pursue ends which are essentially common no one can really love his own people who really hates another. If he seem to, unless his hate be mere ignorance, yet he loves in her only what is external, superficial, picturesque, only what serves his *amour propre*, immediate comfort, or personal interest, for he loves only that which separates her from others, disregarding the deeper good which unites. In the light of this truth we may surely say, modifying Browning's phrase, How little they love England who only England love! If only, when the time comes, the nations, standing among the ruins of war, could be made to understand the significance of this truth, it would mean the commencement of a happier civilization as well as of a new stage in the evolution of nationality.

[1915]

Society and State

16

It is a noteworthy fact that most of the serious attempts, during the last century and a half, to reach a comprehensive political principle have owed their inspiration to Hellenic ideas. This is as true for Rousseau, "citizen of Geneva," whose abstract love of "nature" transmuted itself into a very concrete affection for a city-state, as for certain writers of our own day, and especially Professor Bosanquet, with his ideal of "Christian Hellenism,"[1] itself inspired by the great Hellenic throught of Hegel. This Hellenism has indeed taught us so much that it may seem ungrateful to accuse it of misleading us. Yet the conditions of our modern life are in some respects very different from those of Hellenic society. In particular, within the small circles of the Greek world certain distinctions lay concealed which in the wider reach of the modern community are or should be manifest. An application to modern life of a purely Hellenic theory is on that account dangerous, and seems to the writer to have in fact misled many of those theorists who, from Rousseau onwards, have adopted it—who have found in Hellenism the key to the modern state.

1. *Essays and Addresses*, p. 48.

Within the small circle of the Greek city the distinction of state and society lay concealed. It might be interesting to trace the rise of this distinction in the political consciousness of later ages,[2] but here it must suffice to say that the distinction is an essential one and that its validity is shown by the incoherence of the logic which obscures or denies it. In particular, the theory of the general will is, in the hands of most of its interpreters, a virtual denial of this necessary distinction, and I propose before going further to examine briefly the forms of this doctrine held respectively by Rousseau, Hegel, and Professor Bosanquet, and to show that in every case they are vitiated by a too narrow Hellenism.

1. The General Will, said Rousseau, is the true sovereign and ultimate authority in a state, and, in its obvious sense, this is the accepted doctrine of all democratic states, whose machinery is so constructed that, in one way or another, the ultimate decision lies with the mass of voters, the "people." Politically, then, the "general will" is and must remain sovereign. So far Rousseau is justified. But Rousseau, not content with the necessary political sovereignty of the people, went on to show *not* that such a sovereignty was a moral thing, but that it was *identical* with a moral sovereignty. The general will, Rousseau explained, cannot err. The rightful sovereign *must* act rightfully. Now, that the sovereign "can do no wrong" is a logical and obvious legal position. Legality cannot transcend law; morality can, and it is just the necessary moral righteousness, not the legal rightness, of the sovereign that Rousseau was concerned to uphold. For him the political organization was in no way made distinct from the complex and indeterminate social structure and therefore the bonds of state were just the bonds that keep a society together, the moral sanctions of society. Thence arose the refinements of theory by which Rousseau vainly tries to maintain the identification. First, the general will is distinguished from the "will of all"—not in truth a distinction between two kinds of *political* willing—and then it is asserted that the former always wills the good, though it may be unenlightened. The legal formula asserts the legal rightness of the sovereign's action and leaves its moral rightness open, but the dictum of Rousseau asserts its moral rightness and thus makes the political sovereign an anomalous "person" liable, it may be, to intellectual error but in every other respect infallible—a "person" absolutely good but somewhat short-sighted. It is the danger of modern Hellenism to confound the actual with the ideal, and in this strange conception of inerrant will united to fallible judgment we have a good instance of that confusion. Here already we find Rousseau losing hold of the

---

2. Ritchie (*Priniciples of State-Interference*, p. 157) quotes an early instance, viz., St. Thomas Aquinas (*De regimine principum*) translates the πολιτικὸν ζῷον of Aristotle by *animal sociale et politicum*.

political principle, seeking a political sovereign which no state can ever recognize because no state can ever find it.

Rousseau identified the common will with the good will, but without going into the difficult places of psychology we may say that, although it may be to the general interest or good that the general will should be fulfilled, the general will is not therefore the will for the general good. And the practical difficulty is no less than the psychological. A will which cannot be determined by any positive standard can never be a legislative authority or source of positive law. Will is liable to persuasion, and the persuading will is therefore sovereign over the persuaded. So the will of the people may be the will of a single individual, does sometimes mean the will of two or three. To analyze the complex of influences moral and social determining a given act of will, a specific act of legislation, is difficult in the extreme; to isolate among these determinants an original or sovereign will is impossible. For all practical purposes we must find a definitive sovereign, a political sovereign; we must ask not whether it is Pericles persuading the demos or Aspasia persuading Pericles, but what will it is that wills the decree, that actually commands or consents.

The whole attempt to identify the principle of democracy—as any other political principle—with that of morality is foredoomed to failure, and ends in setting on the political throne a crowned abstraction. For a will that is not realized, that is no man's will, is meaningless. What profit is it that this "general will" does not err—if it does nothing at all? Even if on any occasion the "general will" as understood by Rousseau came into being, it would simply be an interesting social fact, a coincidence; for political purposes it would be identical with a *majority*-will. In every case, therefore, the majority-will—which extended far enough becomes the "will of all"—must be the political principle, and to determine political obligation in terms of any other is worse than useless.

It is his consistent attempt to identify the political with the social order that leads Rousseau into the vagaries of his political logic. Why cannot the people be represented or act through deputy? Logically there seems to be no reason why the general will should not will legislation by its representative. But Rousseau is thinking of the whole complex of ideals and interests and aims animating a society—and that cannot be represented. Why, again, does the *Contrat social*[3] afford us that strangest of all spectacles, the apostle of freedom prescribing "dogmas of civil religion," declaring that "if anyone, after publicly acknowledging those dogmas, acts like an unbeliever of them, he should be punished with death"? Again the answer is that Rousseau has utterly failed to distinguish the sanctions of all social order from the proper bonds of the political organization.

---

3. *Contrat social*, Bk. IV, Chap. 8.

2. Hegel[4] finds fault with Rousseau because, while rightly adhering to the principle of will, he "conceived of it only in the determinate form of the individual will and regarded the universal will not as the absolutely reasonable will (*an und für sich Vernünftige des Willens*) but only as the common will that proceeds out of the individual will as conscious." It is a little like accusing the author of a physiological treatise of not writing a work on psychology when the writer has in fact merely mixed up the two. After all, is there not a common will and is not this common will the basis of any state or institution? Behind the definite institution, the work of conscious will, the philosopher may look for a rationality or universality which that conscious will yet has not for itself. It is at least permissible to search. But no fact is explained away by the greater rationality of another fact, and for the state, for any *institution*, the fact of will is just the fact of "common will, proceeding out of the individual will as conscious." The will on which state institutions are based must be a conscious will, the will of the citizens, or they would never come to be. State institutions are not built like the hexagons of a beehive, by an instinct of unconscious cooperation. Society in the wider sense is not an "institution" and there it may be permissible to look for a will or a reason that is greater than the will or the reason of the constituents. But though, in the construction of any institution, we may build wiser than we know, the plan of the building and the cooperation of the builders must be consciously resolved upon.

To Hegel as to Rousseau there was ever present the tendency to interpret the State in terms of Hellenism, and that in spite of his being credited with discovering the distinction of state and society. In reality his account of that distinction is neither clear nor satisfactory. The society which he distinguishes from the state—what he calls *bürgerliche Gesellschaft* —seems to hang strangely between actuality and ideality. It is a community resting on the "particularity" of desires, on economic need, and yet in discussing this economic community which is "different" from the state Hegel treats of law and police, essentially state institutions. On the other hand, the economic system is not the only social grouping, though a primary one, which can be distinguished from the state organization; we might equally distinguish, e.g., the institutions through which arts and sciences develop, the educational system, the church, charitable institutions, *le haut monde*, and so on, names which cover a kaleidoscopic variety of constantly re-forming elements.[5] But the state cannot be

---

4.   *Grundlinien der Philosophie des Rechts*, § 258.
5.   Hegel's incidental treatment of these parts of the social system is bewildering. What is to be made of such a statement as the following: "Inasmuch as consciousness (*Wissen*) has its seat in the state, science (*Wissenschaft*) too has it there, and not in the church" (§ 270)?

regarded as absorbing within itself the free and living interplay of all these social forces; for one thing they are many of them not bounded by the limits of any state; and therefore it is absurd to say, *tout court*, that the State is "developed spirit," "the world the spirit has made for itself," and so forth.

3. The foregoing argument bears directly on the misconception of the "general will," and I propose next to consider the more or less Hegelian account of that doctrine set forth in Professor Bosanquet's book *The Philosophical Theory of the State*. In no modern work are the inconsistencies and contradictions of applied Hellenism more apparent.

Professor Bosanquet's general position is as follows: Liberty is the condition of our "being ourselves" or willing ourselves, and this liberty is identified with the life of the state. "It is such a 'real' or rational will that thinkers after Rousseau have identified with the state. In this theory they are following the principles of Plato and Aristotle, no less than the indications which Rousseau furnished by his theory of the general will in connection with the work of the legislator. The State, when thus regarded, is to the general life of the individual much as we saw the family to be with regard to certain of his impulses. The idea is that in it, or by its help, we find at once discipline and expansion, the transfiguration of partial impulses, and something to do and to care for, such as the nature of a human self demands." He adds two considerations "to make this conception less paradoxical to the English mind." "(*a*) The State, as thus conceived, is not merely the political fabric. The term state accents indeed the political aspect of the whole, and is opposed to the notion of an anarchical society. But it includes the entire hierarchy of institutions by which life is determined, from the family to the trade, and from the trade to the Church and the University. It includes all of them, not as the mere collection of the growths of the country, but as the structure which gives life and meaning to the political whole, while receiving from it mutual adjustment and therefore expansion and a more liberal air. The State, it might be said, is thus conceived as the operative criticism of all institutions —the modification and adjustment by which they are capable of playing a rational part in the object of human will. . . . (*b*) The State, as the operative criticism of all institutions, is necessarily force; and in the last resort, it is the only recognized and justified force." [6]

The first and greatest confusion into which Professor Bosanquet falls is that he uses the term "state" in two quite different senses. We find him, on the one hand, defining the state as a "working conception of life" (p. 151) or even, after Plato, as "the individual mind writ large" (p. 154)— and it is clear that here he means by state the unity of all the social forces

6. *The Philosophical Theory of the State*, pp. 149–152.

at work in a community of human beings; on the other hand, when he comes to talk of state-action, it is at once obvious that he is now using "state" in its proper signification of "*political* society," with its definite form, its definite and limited type of action. Hence we are told that the means of the state are not *in pari materia* with the end (p. 187) and are left with the anomalous conclusion that the "real will," the "rational will," "the will that wills itself," can never will any positive action whatever, much less "itself," can only "hinder hindrances" (p. 191). Hindrances to what?

The same confusion underlies Professor Bosanquet's distinction of "real" and "actual" will, by means of which he attempts to solve the problem of political obligation. The distinction intended is itself a true and suggestive one, though wrongly expressed. It rests on the primary distinction of "good" and "seeming good." People will what, if they knew the case fully and truly, they would no longer will. They will the seeming good because it seems the good. It is an obvious fact enough, but I may set down as an illustration an instance mentioned by Balzac in the novel *Cousin Pons*. "The mortality in French hospitals," he declares, "caused by women who take food privately to their husbands has been so great that physicians have now resolved to enforce a rigid personal search of the patients on the days when their relatives come to see them." Now Professor Bosanquet's distinction of "real" and "actual" rather obscures the psychological relations here involved, and suggests a false antithesis of "real" and "actual" will. The opposition is not between two wills, a "real" and an "actual," but within the single act of willing, between the motive and the intention, if we care to use such terms, or between the object intended, the giving of food, and the end it was meant to serve, the restoration to health of the husbands. There is but one object willed, the giving of food. We cannot say even that the health of the husbands was "willed," still less the death of those husbands. A motive or end is not an act of will, "real" or otherwise. Would Professor Bosanquet say that these women "really" willed the recovery of their husbands, but "actually" willed the giving of food? [7]

It has to be remembered that Professor Bosanquet introduces this distinction of "real" and "actual" will in order to answer the question of political obligation. "We have thus far been attempting to make clear what is meant by the identification of the state with the real will of the Individual in which he wills his own nature as a rational being; in which identification we find the only true account of political obligation"

---

7. It looks as if Professor Bosanquet's distinction rested on such an opposition as this: they "really" will the recovery of their husbands, they "actually" *cause* their death—not an opposition in terms of will at all.

(p. 154). But this in fact does not touch the real problem. It is only too obvious that an "actual" state is not the "real" state of Professor Bosanquet, and the question of political obligation is : "On what grounds and how far is a citizen bound to obey the actual laws of the state?" What might be the principle of political obligation in an ideal state—where the question would never arise—is very different from what must be the principle under actual political conditions. The will of an actual state, in respect of any definite act of legislation, is and must be based on a majority-will. It is not because he finds his "real" will embodied in legislation from which he actually dissents that the citizen is obedient to the law. A thoroughgoing identity of will is in the nature of the case impossible, and we must look instead for some persistent identity of interest, giving unity to the fundamental will on which the state, like any other institution, must rest, and consent—no longer unanimity—to the secondary acts of will through which the state fulfills its end. We ask too much if we expect an identity of will. In an actual state no individual can have this ideal, this harmony of his will and the state-will, realized all the time. Granting the first unity—the primary will for political life resting on the primary good of political life—we must thereafter be content to rest political obligation on common *good*, and at most only indirectly, through that notion, on common will.

Professor Bosanquet in fact refuses to recognize the necessities of the situation. To avoid Rousseau's difficulty that where a portion of the people must accept the will of another portion there is no freedom, Professor Bosanquet would declare that the general will is the rational will and thus true freedom—a double confusion for, first, the *political* principle must be the majority-will, and second, supposing *per impossibile* that the majority-will were purely rational, yet to identify freedom with enforced subjection to reason or good and to call such subjection self-government is indeed a "paradox." Doubtless a man may be forced to be free—Rousseau's own dangerous paradox contains a certain truth—but to identify such enforcement with "self-government" is to strain language and meaning to the breaking point. It involves an impossible identification of good and will.

On both sides Professor Bosanquet's account fails to answer the concrete question of political obligation. The conception of an abstract self willing an abstract good will never be an explanation of why and when the actual citizen should loyally identify himself with the positive commands of a very concrete government, enforcing measures whose ultimate conformity to his own "true" nature he may not unreasonably refuse to take for granted.

II

The basal fallacy of all such views lies, as I have pointed out, in the identification of state and society, in the refusal to draw a clear distinction here. "We have hitherto," says Professor Bosanquet, "spoken of the State and Society as almost convertible terms. And in fact it is part of our argument that the influences of Society differ only in degree from the powers of the State, and that the explanation of both is ultimately the same" (p. 184). This position vitiates the whole of Professor Bosanquet's account of the state, and it may be well, therefore, if we attempt positively to distinguish the meanings of the two terms "state" and "society," to point out so far as may be the relation of the political organization to the whole social order.[8] The difference involved is all-important, a difference of kind and not of degree, in fact almost the whole world of difference between an end and a means.

If the state does not absorb into its own life of organization the other forms of social life, the worlds of art, science, religion, and social intercourse, not to speak of the family life, in what relation does it stand to these? On the one hand, of course, the form of the state depends on the whole character of a society; it is just what it is because of the character and temperament of the people who make the state. But that is not the question. Relations of this character are not reciprocal. No doubt a hundred social forces have determined the present shape of an Englishman's hat, but that work of art does not equally determine those social forces. In fact, determination would lose all meaning if it worked equally in opposite directions. The state, however, does exercise a certain control over the individual and social centers of movement and influence. In the first place, because of what it stands for, because it preserves and upholds through its organization the very existence of society, that being its primary end, it has a certain superiority of control, not merely of influence, over alike the partial organizations and the free life of society—a control which in no way contradicts the essential claim to spontaneity made by that life. Suppose the state thought a certain religion undermined the security of society, it would interfere with that religion; suppose it thought a certain industrial concern deprived its workers of the opportunity to live as social beings, again it might interfere. It would here be protecting one social grouping against another.

But of course state action has a much wider area than that just indicated. Individualistic writers like Mill and Spencer limited the state

8. Logically the Hegelian argument involves a thorough-going socialism, and that is why some socialist writers have rightly claimed Hegel as one of themselves in spite of much in his teaching that seems directly opposed to their doctrine.

to that type of action, and so gave away their case. The state as the central organization can come forward to organize when such organization is clearly of advantage, and in this way exercise direct control over—though here it would be wrong to admit interference with—the various social activities. For one thing, the various and infinite societies which constantly arise within "society" develop secondary organizations, and these must be interorganized. For another, the central protective organization can greatly further the partial organizations and thus the life which these support. Take, e.g., the economic life of society. To a certain extent state organization can develop that life without destroying its spontaneity —and so we find the state regulating forms of contract, controlling coinage, determining the conditions of limited liability, establishing a bank, even assuming entire control of those industries which, so to speak, bind all other industries together and make their free development possible, the industries of intercommunication. Or again take family life. The family is not simply an element in the state but essentially something more. Yet the state does not merely recognize and protect the family. It claims a certain control. It regards marriage, e.g., as a political institution so far as to insist on certain regulations, registration and so forth, and it defines to some degree the rights and duties of relatives, making them legal and not merely social rights and duties. It might reasonably prohibit the marriage of persons suffering from certain forms of disease, though here, as always, the limit of state intervention becomes a difficult *practical* problem.

The state is thus determinate, a closed organization of social life; while society is indeterminate, an ever evolving system spreading beyond and only partially controlled by the definite network of the state. That network of organization, by enclosing within it a portion of society, gives that portion a certain unity and definition, but neither cuts it off from a wider society of which it is essentially part nor within that portion substitutes its own external mode of action, its necessity, for the spontaneity that is the mark of all life, social and other. Such a protective and controlling organization it would be better to think of as an enclosing and inter- penetrating network than as, say, a shell, even a living and growing shell—for it is essentially true that the whole social life of a community is not comprehended within the form of the state.

III

The question we are considering is in no sense "mere theory"—for political science there is no such thing—and we may finally turn briefly to consider certain important practical applications. I believe the answer to the socialist ideal must rest on the distinction just drawn, but into that larger question I shall not enter here.

1. Hellenistic writers such as Hobhouse[9] and Bosanquet often speak as if they were still living in the Aristotelian state four thousand citizens strong—as if a single center of interests were still possible and the station and duties of the individual could be determined simply in terms of citizenship in a state. Such a view is wholly inadequate, not only because the modern state is too vast to serve such an end, but also because it is too much differentiated. The view in question overlooks the whole development of the political consciousness since Aristotle wrote his *Politics*. The state stands for an area of common good, not for the whole of common good. The life of the individual citizen cannot therefore be lived wholly in the light of the ideal for which the state stands. In modern conditions the ordinary citizen simply cannot live all the time for the state, though he can still die for it on occasion. For certain classes, indeed, for the politician, the civil servant, the soldier, social ends seem more nearly to identify themselves with the political end, but even for these, and in the attempt to serve such an end, there will arise in the very state organization social groupings with narrower ideals, a political party, e.g., or a military order. For an adequate social life smaller and nearer centers are necessary— the district, the city, the village, and the numerous associations they include. Social life can no longer in practice and should no longer in theory be centralized into state life. The individual should not be summed up in his citizenship, otherwise the claim of citizenship will itself become a tyranny and its essential moral value be lost. "The modern wilderness of interests" will not be set in order by our pointing simply to the road of citizenship. For the main road of citizenship, which we must make straight as possible, though it intersects a thousand paths of social interest, cannot and should not absorb them.

2. These paths of social interest do not stop at the frontiers of states. The political interest is determinate and has limits, the social has none. Here, therefore, for the proper understanding of international relations, it is most necessary to distinguish state and society. On the assumption of identity we can have no unity of peoples until they are absorbed in some world-state. For each state by its very definition is a determinate and self-

---

9. For the Hellenism of Mr. Hobhouse, *cf.* the following passage from *Morals in Evolution:* "Untroubled by any conflict between the secular and the spiritual power the Greeks could readily conceive a political society as an association for all the principal purposes of life that are not covered by the smaller association of the household. On this side their ideal of the state has never since been equalled." On the contrary it has been the great beneficial result of the conflict between the secular and the spiritual power that more than anything else it has helped to make clear the essential distinction between state and society.

sufficient unit. A man can belong to one alone, can owe allegiance to one alone. Citizenship has hard and fast limits. In respect to the sphere of its sovereignty every state is demarcated absolutely from every other. Consequently if political will were identical with social will, the members of one state would remain totally alien from those of every other state. States would stand to one another as Spinoza and Hobbes imagined them to stand, isolated as the pre-civil individuals of their imagination, totally independent until some contract is agreed upon, even then totally independent because there is no higher will to make agreement binding. But of course it is in international relations that the distinction of state and society is most clearly revealed and that the common interests of universal society most manifestly weave new unities in spite of political separation. A man may perhaps "denationalize" himself (though that is hardly the proper word) by leaving his country, but he cannot "desocialize" himself without leaving the world of men, or at least of civilized men.

Society, therefore, and not the state, is the "world the spirit has made for itself." "The spirit" does not isolate itself in states, as Hegel's argument assumes.[10] On the contrary, the growth of civilization means the growth of ever widening community, the "realization" of social interest beyond the limits of politically independent groups. Society widens and the sense of community grows. In particular, the privileged classes of the different peoples, the authors of most past wars, become more and more allied by social intercourse, by common commercial and intellectual interests. M. Tarde has pointed out how classes of men whose occupation, even if in a competitive way, brings them into constant association with one another develop a friendlier spirit toward one another than classes not subject to this socializing influence. The same holds of peoples. It is not civilization but inter-civilization that develops mutual sympathy between states. The highly socialized Greek cities, because each held to an ideal of autonomy and self-sufficiency, the ideal of "completely independent totality," were not intersocialized, and accordingly displayed the intensest hostility to one another. But the aloofness of Greek states is impossible in the modern world, which is pervaded by intersocializing influences of literature and commerce. Common ideas and common trade[11] have

10. Hegel is rather confusing on this point. For instance he says (*Gr. der Phil. des Rechts*, § 330) that the state is "not a private person but a completely independent totality" and yet immediately adds that it is related to other states (§ 331) and instances the nations of Europe as "forming a family on account of the universal principles of their legislation, their ethical usages, and their civilisation" (§ 339). How can "completely independent totalities" form a family?

11. For this reason universal free trade would be preferable to universal protection. I may quote Hobhouse on this point: "The doctrine of natural liberty, particularly as

formed everywhere social bonds which cut across the line of states, and
have made Western Europe, looked on as a whole, an effective society.
Thus an educated Englishman comes to have more in common with an
educated Frenchman than he has, say, with an English agricultural laborer.
The alien, shut out from his state, has yet a closer social affinity to him
than his fellow citizen.

We should note here that it is just on the sense of community that
organization rests. Political organization, the completest and most
self-sufficient of all organizations and indeed the most necessary, ultimately
requires a definite kind and degree of felt community. But there are other
degrees and forms of community. At a certain stage every society, every
grouping founded on whatever sense of community, becoming conscious
of its unity, strengthens or confirms it by some form of organization,
makes for itself as it were an integument of organization, so there are
as many types of organization as there are of society. The political society
is based on the distinctive organization of law; other societies develop
quasi-legal or contract organizations which in turn the political society,
as possessing the supremest form of organization, tends to inter-organize.
But when the community extends beyond the limits of a state, the single
state can no longer of itself ratify the society. So international relations
arise, which are no longer strictly legal relations at all, but only approxi-
mations to these. There may be many degrees of approximation, representing many degrees of international social integration, from alliances and
federations down to the minimal organization represented by Berlin
treaties and Hague conventions, extradition laws, and so forth. A federation of Europe would therefore in no sense be a new thing. Europe is
already federated.

At the same time we should perhaps further note that those writers
are mistaken who assume as a logical development of this principle
an ultimate world empire.[12] The principle is that a felt community
between men in course of time produces a contract organization in respect
to all definitely recognized common elements, that every society, when
it becomes conscious of itself, develops an institutional aspect. But community can be felt only in so far as community exists; and the amount
of community necessary for a true political society, is, as experience
has shown, a very large one. Community must, perhaps should, always
be partial, is rendered partial at the outset by the ultimate fact that men
and peoples are marked off from one another not only by their own

---

preached by Cobden and the Free Traders, also told heavily on the side of peace, just as the
recrudescence of militarism in our own day has been associated, not in this country alone,
with economic protection." *Morals in Evolution*, Vol. I, p. 278.

12. *Cf.* Tarde, *Les lois de l'imitation*, 2nd ed., Chap. 8, p. 420.

necessary differences but also by their occupancy of different portions of the earth's soil. It is on this difference that the territorial state is immediately based, making certain boundaries, often not very obvious boundaries, the rigid dividing line where one sovereignty ends and another begins. In such territorial states it is at once obvious that the political line is not a social frontier as well. So far as the territorial principle goes, country is marked off from country just on the principle on which district is separated from district and parish from neighboring parish. Of course between districts, and even between parishes, further differences are found, and so between countries there are differences of national type, temperament, education, and language, sufficient to justify at once the community and the separation involved in political society, the determinations of government which constitute a state. A world-state would mean that the world had become in certain definite respects a homogeneous society. But as a general rule community and separation, centralization and decentralization, both within and beyond the limits of the state, and just because of the social forces that underlie the state, must go hand in hand, must develop *pari passu*, the two being not antagonistic but complementary principles. Most empires have been failures because they pursued the principles of centralization alone : the Roman empire in particular, when at the last it became a world-state and not simply an aggregation of states around one central state, showed how impossible it was for a completely centralized system to meet the needs of peoples of different temperaments and living under very different physical and social conditions. If centralization is necessary for peace and order, decentralization is equally necessary for development and life.

I have tried to point out one or two applications of this vital distinction of state and society. There are many others to be made, and of these the economic application is perhaps the most important. It is only by keeping this distinction in mind that we can hope to understand the difficult relations of political and economic forces. But to touch on this subject here would be unduly to extend the limits of this paper.

[1911]

On "Society and State": Bosanquet-
Hoernlé-MacIver Letters

17 BOSANQUET TO MacIVER

Jan. 31, 1911

My dear Sir:

I am very much pressed with work just now, and am unable to write at length about your interesting paper on my book, or rather about the remarks on my book in your paper.

Of course there is a very great deal that might be said, and if I seem curt, it is only that I may not be drawn too far.

Your distinction of Society and the State is, I agree, important. I have recurred to it, and made rather more of it, in the Introduction to the second edition, which I daresay had not reached you when you wrote your paper. But I do not agree that the book fails to put it in the proper light. I don't think you have sufficiently considered the account of the principle of delimitation of states, in connection with the discussion of the relation of state to humanity in the last chapter. And I think that the ultimate expression of the

In reproducing this correspondence here, I have changed abbreviations to full words—e.g., *wd* to *would*—but have left spelling and punctuation alone, except where these would have made for clumsy reading. In one or two instances I have inserted a word; this is indicated by brackets. —Ed.

social will must always be the political will. It must finally determine the rank and relations of *all* institutions. I stick to the phrase "operative criticism" which implies, of course, unity with the living principle of the whole, both social and political.

And I think you are plainly wrong about the real and actual will. You would have to say that there is no such thing as a conflict of the good will and bad will, which is in principle the same as that I speak of. You can't make the bad will merely an intention conceived in carrying out the good will—a mere mistake. Of course in ultimate theory something like this comes out; but that the wills are two as well as one seems to me beyond doubt. It is a queer illustration of this but I am sure your interpretation of Balzac's fact is wrong, for most cases at least. When a woman hides a red herring in her bonnet to take to her husband in hospital she has not in mind his restoration to health—though that end is implied in her main will—but to take him something tasty which he will like at the moment. It is *all but* a conflicting end, as her concealment shows. The fact is an everyday fact, and its nature quite familiar to all social workers.

The will of the state is always treated as positive, I think; it is the means that are negative. And one must remember that negation is never bare negation. But I am prepared to defend the indirect nature of political promotion of good life through thick and thin. I have given examples in the book, and indeed every case is an example. But I must not be led further. I hope you will develop the distinction between State and Society fruitfully.

Sincerely,
B. Bosanquet

BOSANQUET TO MacIVER

March 12, 1911

My dear Sir:

Many thanks for your letter and article.[1] I agree with you that one cannot treat these things properly in a letter. One makes it too long for a letter, and too short for complete explanation. If I am able to return to the subject, I will bear your argument in mind. At present I am rather pressed, having a new edition of my Logic on my hands, as well as a review of Professor Baillie's "Phenomenology" which in any case will be unduly delayed, and other serious work after that.

If I don't mean to start a correspondence, I have no right to raise any points. But it seems pointless with the pen in my hand not to try even to

---

1. "Society and State."

hint at any explanation. And I don't mean that I shouldn't be much interested to hear from you if you cared at any time to write; but only that I couldn't undertake to give a fitting answer.

I will just say then, that I define the state against society mainly by two things: (1) its end, which I take to be that of Ethics—the good for man; and (2) by its means, which I take to be in the main external, in the removal of hindrances to the fulfilment of capacity.

(1) 1 is not, in my view, the end of any (other?) social institution. (Whether you call the state one among other social institutions or not seems to me verbal. If it is an institution, it is the institution of institutions, so to speak.) A church, a dwelling's company, a public house, a temperance association, have each of them a limited aim making for good life; none has for its aim good life as such.

The State (2) differs therefore by being the common adjustment of all these, in virtue of the total idea of good life, and of the universal applicability of its means, viz. external regulation. Left alone, the social institutions are always at loggerheads with each other, and often with themselves. It is, in my view, the State and the State alone, which through its superior idea of good, conjoined with its universal practical controls, forces them to adjust themselves to the order and condition of good life. You may say, "but society as a whole, though no one institution, has this same aim." I reply, society as a whole does not exist, except in and through the state. It alone is conscious of the *whole* social end, surveys it all, and adjusts all details to it.

I don't see your difficulty with "the State." It is merely the subject of a generic judgment is it not? = Every state qua state? Now I have written what would justify you in continuing the argument. But I don't think we can really have it out in letters. I daresay you will write a book about it, and then I shall see your view more fully.

I am assuming you meant me to keep the article.

Sincerely,
B. Bosanquet

MacIVER TO BOSANQUET

April 24, 1911

My dear Sir:

I am much obliged for your letter of March 12th which enables me to see very clearly the position you hold regarding the relation of the state to society—so that if I still differ it can no longer be through misunderstanding of your view. Perhaps then you will let me answer your points briefly, not necessarily in view of a rejoinder, for I recognise sufficiently the difficulty of sparing any time for such correspondence and your kindness in replying to my previous criticism.

You "define the state against society mainly by two things" : (1) its end, the end of Ethics, the good for man; (2) its means, "in the main external." My position would be that the state has for its end the good for man *so far as* that can be furthered by the external means at its command, but that the limitation involved is so great that we can no longer say that the state secures or controls *the* ethical end. If there are societies which can use other than external means how can they *so far* be controlled by a society limited to such means? These other societies have qualities of operation beyond the political sphere. Further, since external means can never really secure any ethical end itself, but at most the conditions required for its fulfilment, we have the anomaly—which I think you admit—of means being totally inadequate to end. If the state cannot directly secure the ethical end how can it control *in every aspect* those societies which directly secure some part of that end, the family, for instance?

I am not for a moment denying that the state is the supreme society. I believe it is, but still I think "society" is greater than the state. You reply, "Society as a whole does not exist." But by society I do not mean any one society or even any union of societies. It is obvious that a great part of our social intercourse is conducted not on the basis of our membership of any particular society but in virtue of a social nature which is constantly creating and recreating social media. We may take, though it is an unnecessarily extreme case, the instance of an Englishman travelling on the continent. He is "in society" all the time but if you ask, what society?—it is difficult to answer. So far in fact as there is community of nature between fellow beings, so far there is continual social adaptation. If so, no one state can limit and completely determine the social conduct of any of its members. His membership of his state does not sum up his social individuality, either extensively or intensively—not extensively [because] he enters into social relations with nonmembers of his state; not intensively, because his intercourse with his fellow citizens cannot possibly be limited by merely external conditions such as alone a political institution can lay down. Certainly I would grant that the state is the "institution of institutions," but society is not an institution at all. It is a life continuous and progressive, the creator of institutions however supreme. Might we not say that just as Government rests on the political will, the will of citizens who recognise each other as such, so does the state rest on the social will, the will of individuals who recognise in each other a large community of interest, nature or ideal, in virtue of which they establish or maintain a society of which they are all members. Their membership binds them to one another in certain definite ways—an institution with supreme external control is absolutely necessary—but surely even here there is a "limited liability." It would be regarded as wrong, e.g., if a state were to attempt to force a religion on any minority of its members. But if so, how can you say that "the state is conscious of the *whole* social end, surveys it all, and adjusts all details to it"?

I feel that this statement is inadequate but perhaps it may help to make my views also clearer. If you have time to answer, I shall be grateful.

Yours sincerely,
R. M. MacIver

BOSANQUET TO MacIVER

June 19, 1911

Dear Mr. MacIver:

Just a line in answer to your very interesting letter of April 24. I think that what we are confronting is at bottom the relation of "outer" to "inner." In a great part of my book I consciously addressed myself to that problem, and I hold, on the whole, by my treatment. I will write down some propositions which seem to me to go to the heart of the matter. To take arguments to pieces, and work out each one, is such a very lengthy procedure, and I, like you no doubt, am full of business.

Every "inner" has an "outer" and there is no real existence which is wholly either the one or the other. Every "inner" is greatly affected by and affects its outer and through it all other "outers." The problem of the mode and degree of this influence is the most interesting, difficult, and dangerous, of human life. The entire "outer" of human life is institutional; birth, death, sickness, the mealtime, the family, the house and home, the place of business and conditions of the vocation, the church in all its forms, are institutional expressions of an inner life. The centrality and focus of all this outer world is naturally and necessarily the state, which is the result of the whole (not a prior cause which determined it) but also in reaction upon every part. For every individual there must be one such supreme focus of the outer life, and one only. The adjustment of outer and inner together, starting from the side of the outer, to the best life, is the problem of politics, which is the concentrated expression of the social "outer." It is an interesting paradox that the freedom of external sociality is greatest where the force and recognition of the state are greatest and deepest. This is really very natural and obvious. It is just as the best-built house gives you the great capacity of effective life. But in detail the reaction of outer upon inner is a very delicate problem— really, I think, *the* test of a statesman. It is enormously powerful, although, as I maintain, mainly indirect. Take the relation of the State to Art and

Religion—the things most out of its apparent sphere. How it ought to deal with them for the best at any given epoch is a fearful problem; but if it, *prima facie*, lets them alone it is none the less dealing with them. It only lets them alone in a certain way and on certain terms, conceived in the interest of the best life. I must stop now but I think the crux is here.

Yours very sincerely,

B. Bosanquet

BOSANQUET TO MacIVER

March 23, 1912

Dear Mr. MacIver :

You must have thought me very uncourteous to take no notice of your letter of Jan. 29 accompanying a number of the Int. J. of Ethics.[2] The fact is, your letter actually reached me in a nursing home; and I am only now making up the arrears of correspondence.

I am much interested by your paper, and feel, as one so often does, that the difference between us is one of proportion, and angle of vision, and that there is very much on which we are in substance agreed. But just because it is a difference of this kind, to go into it further would need a treatise of some length. For though I agree in much of the substance of your contention, I think there is no statement in the article which I should not from my point of view desire to criticise and rewrite. Much of my life has been passed in the exact study and teaching of ancient history, and I could not subscribe I think to any of your statements, e.g., about Greek civilisation. The Mediterranean and Black Sea coasts from Trebizond to Marseilles were in my view much more socially one in the 5th century B.C. than they ever have been since, though not of course over an area extending so far from the sea as the civilised area now extends. The inhabitants of the several hundred cities or cantons (not towns of course, they were large territories) met as the English speaking race meet today, as members of the same civilisation, and with some recognition of common institutions.

So with the 18th century compared with today. France and Germany, e.g., have grown and are growing apart. No French writer, it has been remarked, could possibly have the influence in Germany today which Rousseau had from 1760 to 1810.

There is heaps and heaps more of the same kind to say. I do not think there is anything in the theoretical contention which is not thoroughly answered in my introduction to ed. 2 of the [Philosophical] Theory of the State.

2.   Containing MacIver's article, "War and Civilization."

As to what you say about peace, of course I wish it might be so, and would do anything to promote it; and would not *in public* insist very much on the difficulties. But it worries me that you do not seem, to me, to appreciate the facts, and therefore do not really prepare yourself to deal with the problems which must arise. As to leaving national honour to honourable third parties—in private matters there are thousands of disinterested men of honour. In a dispute between England, say, and Germany, there is no disinterested party on the surface of this globe. Or substitute for "honour," what I see coming between us and Germany, an honest and fundamental difference of conviction as to the course of history in the future desirable in the interests of humanity, such as to produce collision. You may reconcile a difference like that by reason and discussion; but you can't arbitrate on it; it is too deep in men's hearts. You can't arbitrate on your religion, and these convictions *are* men's religions. One must go to work in a deeper way. At least that is my view.

Yours sincerely,
B. Bosanquet

HOERNLÉ[3] TO MacIVER

12 April 1912

Dear Mr. MacIver:

Many thanks for that offprint[4] and your long covering letter, which makes your point about the "real" and the "actual" will very clear. I think I agree with you that there is no getting away from the difficulty you urge against Bosanquet, however much one strains to squeeze the maximum meaning—even to an abuse of language—out of what he says. You may have noticed that Bosanquet has a peculiar trick or habit of mind which often leads him to treat as non-existent the very difficulties which puzzle other people most. I have just had a curious illustration of that, inasmuch as it so happened that I read Fred Henderson's "Socialism" and then immediately picked up Bosanquet's article on "Socialism and Individualism" in his "Civilisation of Christendom." It is not merely that B. treats Socialism as attacking private property as such and in all its forms (instead of its attacking merely private ownership of land, means of production, and means of communication), but that he does not meet a single one of the points which Socialists urge against the present economic constitution of society. There are many good things in B.'s article, but so far as meeting the central positions of actual Socialism is

---

3.   Then a prominent political philosopher at Oxford.
4.   "Society and State."

concerned, it is largely irrelevant. So—to return to the "real" and "actual" will—in his Philosophy of the State. I gave you in my last letter the line of argument along which I try to get the most out of the distinction, but I should fully endorse your statement of the difficulty when it comes to the actual clash of majority-will and minority-will. You say that the minority "ought" (within limits) to obey the majority-will, though "it is not and never can be" their will. Yes, but why *ought* they? And if there are limits, as I admit there are, though they are most troublesome to define (can you formulate a satisfactory principle?)—is it not after all a matter of *will* for them to obey or not? In short, can you say, in the end, "ought" to anyone except in the name of his own will? To base the ought on force is, you will admit, to abandon the idea of the state as a moral organism. But is there any alternative to force other than will? And, after all, voting implies the will of the minority to accept its beating and live according to the will of the majority *as if* it had been their own? Of course, again there is the limit; we may, e.g., conceivably have civil war in Ireland before the year is out; and again the submission may be merely temporary, a waiting for the first opportunity to reverse the obnoxious legislation. But most commonly even bitterly attacked legislation stands. Is it then true to say that "it never can be" the minority's will? Though there again is a puzzle, in that people will express disapproval with all degrees of conviction and severity and yet live in accordance with, and therefore de facto *will*, the very laws of which they disapprove. It is all a mighty tangle, and all ways of straightening it out seem high-handed.

Yours sincerely,

R. F. Alfred Hoernlé

MacIVER TO BOSANQUET

25th April 1912

Dear Mr. Bosanquet :

Your criticism always stimulates me into replying, though I have allowed an interval to elapse in order not to bore you with my correspondence. I should like now to defend two points which you attack in my article. First as to the general issue of war and peace. You say there are differences between nations too deep to suffer arbitration. "You can't arbitrate on your religion, and these convictions *are* men's religions. One must go to work in a deeper way." True, but there is never any need to arbitrate on these things, or at any rate there would not be were it not for the existence of armaments and the possibility of violence. You need only fight with arms for your religion if someone is foolish enough to attack your religion with arms. The actual causes of war today are not these inexpugnable convictions, but some incidental dispute over territory, some encroachment by a petty official (less often by a high official or statesman acting under his executive power, i.e., without special national authorisation for the offending act), at most some overt wrong done it may be under the stimulus of a strong conviction but itself, unlike the conviction, "justiciable." Can you give a single instance in modern history where the honour or convictions of a nation have been violated, except by armed aggression of some sort, in a way itself precluding by its very nature justiciable remedy?

I am quite conscious of the difficulties of arbitration, but I think you add unnecessarily to them. You say—"In a dispute between England, say, and Germany, there is no disinterested (third) party on the surface of the globe." But arbitration doesn't mean that when England and Germany dispute say about territorial rights in Morocco, Italy or Austria or U.S.A. will be called in to settle the case. It means an arbitral international court, composed not of nations but of representatives, representatives chosen for their high judicial capacity and sense of honour. It is surely possible to find in every civilised nation on earth representatives of this high character and integrity.

"One must go to work in a deeper way." But the whole issue hinges on the truth that war is not a deeper but a shallower way. Arbitration may go wrong, accidentally; but if war does decide right, it is *only* accidentally. And everyone who values his convictions hates the idea of trusting them to a kind of arbitration which is actually—since superior might can surely never be the test of conviction—as accidental as the turning of a coin.

The difficulties of arbitration are the difficulties of every development not yet matured. I honestly believe that the only ultimate difficulty is the slowness of the dispersal of certain prejudices as to the essential alienation of nations from one another, prejudices which the growing intercommunity of peoples has indeed begun to disperse, and notably among the labour classes of the Western world.

You deny this growth of intercommunity, at least in certain cases. To me it seems obvious. Even your extreme case—the case of France and Germany—supports that view. There was in the 18th century, to which you refer, no such intercommunication between the working classes of these two countries—the bulk of the peoples—as there is just now. There was in the 18th century no such financial and commercial interdependence between France and Germany as the recent threat of war proved clearly enough that there is just now. Nor do I even see any authority in the remark you quote that "no French writer could possibly have the influence in Germany today which Rousseau had from 1760-1810." Political alienation there may be, but since I base my argument on the distinction of society and state I can hardly admit, in view of the above and other connecting facts I could quote, that there is growing social alienation. And here is an extreme case.

Lastly, as to my Greek history, you take the case of the "Mediterranean and Black Sea coasts from Trebizond to Marseilles" in the 5th century B.C. and say the intercommunity then was greater than it has been ever since. Well, in the first place you had throughout Greek cities then, while now you have different *peoples* along these coasts, whose difference complicates the general comparison of past and present. But further the fact of common civilisation does not involve intercommunity in the series of colonies sprung from the source of the common civilisation. The wars of the Greek colonies prove this. So does the fact expressed in the words of Freeman that "in old Greece the amount of hatred between city and city seems to depend almost mathematically upon their distance from one another"! In any case I should think Thucydides III 82-3 a sufficient answer to your statement as to the 5th century B.C. I do not know what authority you have for affirming actual social intercourse of an intimate character between the Greek cities from Trebizond to Marseilles but I fancy that in an age when the rate of bottomry was something like $33\frac{1}{3}\%$ actual social intercourse was at a minimum!

I was very sorry to hear of your illness and earnestly hope you are quite recovered. I am looking forward to reading, after my work of the term is over, your published Hibbert lectures.

Yours very sincerely,
R. M. MacIver

Power and Human Rights

18 From the beginning of recorded time, where the tribes and kindreds of men won the first release from the pressure of subsistence and first began to strive for the "good life" and not for mere living, there appeared a threat against these emergent goals. It was the man of power, or rather the little inner group of apt and contriving men, who held the reins of power. Some kind of government was needed, but the power that went with governing divided the community, so that the interests of power began to prevail over the community. The conflict thus generated has gone on through all history. It has taken various forms but one form became expressed in the claim of the government for "human rights."

What are these "human rights"? What is meant by the denial or the suppression of them? We can answer by asking first: What are those strivings toward the "good life" that power—any control of man over man, through whatever means, institutions, or agencies—so often suppresses or distorts? There are two interdependent kinds of human values, and two alone, that have a universal and fundamental quality and that nevertheless have always been sacrificed to the wantonness of power. One is the creative culture of the group, the ever changing expression of its arts and creeds and tastes and modes of living. This culture is vital only when it is free. The other is the personality of the human individual, as he seeks the means and the opportunities to develop in his own way within the culture of his group.

Power, for its own ends, not because of the necessities of order, has frequently assailed alike the integrity of the culture and the integrity of the person. It has injured the former by imposing the rigidity of its own code and coercing all who deviate from it. It has done so equally under the aegis of the Church and under the aegis of the State. And it has thwarted and suppressed the free growth of personality, both by insisting on uniformity and by denying access to opportunity. And it has done so equally under the aegis of the Economic System and under the aegis of the State.

So, from the earliest times, the men of vision have raised their voices on behalf of human rights. They denounced oppression and sometimes they drew pictures of a golden age, in the future or in the past, in which men look on one another as brethren, in which every man sits under his own fig tree, "none daring to make him afraid." At first these utterances were mainly those of denunciation and of exhortation, in an age before constitutional means of curbing power had been devised. There was more fervent denunciation by the Hebrew prophets, more gentle exhortation by the Chinese sages. Thence we move on to a period, pioneered by Greece, when the citizens learned ways of exercising control over their rulers. But this great learning was attained uneasily and fitfully, and it died out of the world with the coming of the "divine" Augustus. As the Middle Age ripened, the concept of human rights was revised under the classical form of the "law of nature," the ideal pattern of equity that was but another expression of the law of God. This concept was given the greatest amplitude and dignity by St. Thomas Aquinas.

But no constitutional link was made, or indeed could have been made, between the law of nature and the ways of princes. So as we pass toward modern times we have a new beginning. The cry for human rights now becomes more than exhortation or protest. It becomes the precise demand for the legal and constitutional embodiment of specific claims to liberties, and then to opportunities. For now again, and under more favorable conditions than in the time of the ancient city-state, men have begun to tame Leviathan.

There were stirrings in the "free cities" of the Renaissance and earlier. But the true foundations of a new order were laid in the growth of parliamentarism in England. At first, and in intention, it was no more than the assertion of the liberties of groups and classes. But standards were thus established and precedents were set, and with the changes in the disposition of power more and more groups and ever larger classes won the extension of these liberties for themselves. In an earlier time a group of headstrong barons wrested certain rights for themselves from a shifty king, and the formula of their demands became, much later, the revered first charter of democratic liberties. Similarly, when oppressed religious sects grew in strength and demanded—for themselves—liberty of conscience and of faith, they set a precedent that broadened into the democratic liberty of thought and opinion.

But the major movement was carried by the middle classes, growing in strength and wealth as feudalism decayed. In England—saved from the devastation of continental wars—they successfully asserted a cumulative series of rights against a ruling class, until the ruling class ruled no more. They fought in the name of "the people." To make the rights they won properly and inherently "human rights," all that was needed was to give full and true significance to the concept of the people. This was the message of Rousseau and of Jefferson and of Lincoln. It was the explosive idea behind the French Revolution. It was the expansive idea that spread through Western Europe and for a time seemed likely to triumph throughout the world.

But the foes of human rights never surrender unconditionally. The curbing of power is never secure. In modern civilization power is protean and takes unexpected shapes. New forms of the organization of interests create new concentrations of power. New advances of science and technology make possible more formidable and far-reaching controls over the minds of men. The scale of government and the means at its command are magnified. Its ancient power to make war becomes overwhelmingly more destructive, and in the ruin that follows there are bred new doctrines of violence and fear and hate. New dogmas and new strategies insidiously undermine or boldly affront the democratic creed, becoming most dangerous when they assume the mask of the faith they seek to kill. So in the world of today the integrity of the group and the integrity of the individual are being invaded in ways alike more subtle and more deadly than any that ever were devised by the most ruthless of earlier tyrannies. Over a large part of the earth human rights are prostrate; elsewhere the threat of a similar subjection looms.

Nevertheless human rights are more widely discussed and more deeply yearned for than perhaps ever before. There is indeed much talk of a worldwide charter of human rights. A Commission of the United Nations has after much travail produced a Declaration of Human Rights. But a fatal difficulty stalls any measures for its implementation. The state, and particularly the most portentous modern embodiment of "the state," insists that every charter of human rights shall be subject to one proviso, *viz*., that these rights shall not limit *its* right to take any measures it deems necessary for its own security or for the "public welfare"—and that proviso nullifies the charter.

Before the rights of the collectivity the rights of the group and the rights of the person fade to nothingness. Irresponsible power, the power that tramples human rights, enthrones itself in the collectivity. The state, in its abstract immortality, becomes the justification for the death of the people.

It is well in such times that we should gain and steadfastly keep, against all the ideologists and sycophants of power, a clear understanding of the principle of human rights. To it testify the wisdom of the East and the age-long struggle of the West.

[1950]

Liberty and Authority

19 THE MEANING OF LIBERTY AND ITS PERVERSIONS

When we contemplate the mass of utterances devoted to the subject of liberty we find it hard to escape the conclusion that of all the arts the most backward is the art of thinking. I am referring not to any profound or highly technical art but to an intrinsically simple one. I do not mean the art of fathoming the secrets of nature or the art of calculation or the art of philosophical speculation. I do not mean an art that depends either on erudition or on the skills of the laboratory. On the contrary it is an art that the metaphysician is as apt to sin against as the common man. It is an art that the leaders of men betray at least as often as do those they lead. It is an art that is not taught in the schools, and rarely in the colleges. Instead, there are special crafts and professions the primary purpose of which is to confound this art altogether. It is an art that established authority always suspects and often represses. In some countries today the practice of it is forbidden under the severest penalties. And yet, in this age wherein the techniques of propagandism are so highly developed, there is perhaps no art that it is more imperative for men to learn.

These are bold statements, but anyone who will take the

trouble sincerely to contemplate the history of disputations concerning this word "liberty" and its meaning can be convinced, I believe, of their truth. Whatever liberty is, all men are agreed that its presence or absence is of vital importance to them. Whatever liberty is, they have always been ready to fight for it—or about it. But for all the fighting and all the disputing the same confusions and sophistications flourish today, flourish as persistently and as triumphantly as ever in the past. Here there is no record of progress. While we have conquered great kingdoms of knowledge, while we have been penetrating to the heart of the atom and to inconceivably far-off galaxies, we have attained no consensus concerning the condition of this liberty that touches all of us so nearly. Statemen and even scientists, men of letters and men of law, perpetuate the same misconceptions about it that we find at the very dawn of reflection. And if we have not attained any greater clarity or any greater understanding it is not because we are dealing with something in itself abstruse and baffling —it is rather because our interests, our prejudices, our warm immediate impulses will not let us approach it, examine it, and see it for what it is.

We will devote our attention to one thing only—the meaning of a word. How do we ascertain this meaning? There is no question of validity or invalidity in the mere assertion : "I attach this meaning to this symbol." It may be a kind of antisocial act to use a word in a very different sense from that of its common acceptance, but this is in itself no offense against the integrity of thought. In a specialized context it may be appropriate, or even necessary—since there are always more meanings than available words—to use a common word in a specialized sense. Where then does the offense come in? When can we justly speak of the perversion of meaning?

The word we are concerned with is one of universal use. The philosopher and the scientist have no technical term to substitute for it. It signifies an immediate datum, something that cannot be analyzed into components or reduced to simpler elements. It signifies the state of being free, and this being free is as ultimate as being warm or pleased or angry. One indication of the ultimate character of the concept is that while in the English language we have two words for it ("liberty" and "freedom") no perceptible nuance of difference has developed in the generic usage of them. How can we define a word of this sort? We cannot use other words that more clearly express its meaning. We can, of course, offer cases and illustrations. We can relate its meaning to other meanings. We can consider the conditions on which the state of being free depends. We can bring out its implications. We can specify particular modes of its manifestation, particular areas in which it is present or absent, as when we speak of religious liberty, economic liberty, political liberty, and so on. We can specify within any given situation who is free and in what respect. We can turn about and define it indirectly, as the absence of its negation, the absence of restraint. But in all this we are merely identifying a meaning, not defining it. It is a meaning we must simply recognize, simply accept. The universality of usage sets it for us. It is understood by the child and by the savage as well as by the civilized man. It is a meaning we cannot do without, and thus we find that when people offer us some alternative and different meaning they nonetheless imply that it is equivalent to the universally accepted meaning. Here, as we shall see, is the root of the worst perversions. On this account much that is written on the subject of liberty is worse than futile. It confuses the issues, obscures that which it pretends to clarify, even sophisticates liberty into its own contradiction. Hence the greatest sinners against reason have been the reasoners, the philosophers, and high priests.

The history of the more pretentious writings on liberty, from the time of Plato to the present day, amply substantiates this charge, but within our present limits all we can do is to point out the nature of the more persistent and frequent misconceptions.[1]

We begin with those who honestly accept the universal meaning but, being led to define it by the double negative, as the absence of restraint, are never able to see it positively again and fall in consequence into immediate error. Their argument runs as follows: liberty is the absence of restraint, therefore all restraint is a curtailment of liberty. They reason in the void of their negatives. Shall we, to bring them back to common sense, add yet another negative, and ask them, what then of the restraint of restraint? Is it not obvious that liberty— except on a desert island, where, alas, it is an unprized commodity —is subject to constant invasion and must be constantly safeguarded? Is it not obvious that the absence of restraint, whereby men in society enjoy any kind of liberty, is the presence of superior restraint on the forces that would suppress this liberty?

Here the commonest form of error is that which rests on the simple antithesis of the realm of liberty and the realm of law; one the "free" life of man in nature or in nonpolitical society and the other the coercive order of the State. Many writers on liberty have been content with this untenable antithesis. It was the view of Thomas Hobbes that liberty existed only in the interstices of law. And his contention has been upheld with undiminished vigor by many later schools, by the utilitarians such as Bentham and Mill, by the neo-Darwinians such as Herbert Spencer, by the robust individualists and nature worshipers after the manner of Thoreau, by the philosophical anarchists, and by the economic conservatives who at the

---

1. The best analysis of the subject within my knowledge is Dorothy Fosdick's book, *What Is Liberty?* (New York, 1939).

present day echo the sentiments of Herbert Hoover's trumpet blast, *The Challenge to Liberty*. Every law, they say, is an encroachment on liberty. Every new law reduces yet further the shrunken area of liberty.

Yet the argument is most patently fallacious. You cannot *think* about it without discovering its error. True, every law restrains *some* liberty for *some*. But in so doing it may well establish some other liberty for some others—or indeed for all. The law that forbids an employer to dismiss a worker because he joins a trade union gives the worker a liberty that, as worker, he lacked before. The law that forbids another to trespass on my property assures me the liberty to enjoy my property. Every law establishes an obligation, but the obligation is the reverse side of a right. The obligation may lie on the many and the right rest in the few, as for example under the law imposing a censorship of opinion. Or the right may be established for the many and the corresponding obligation be imposed on the few, as when a law compels factory-owners to introduce safety devices. Since liberty does not exist in the void but in the relations between men, all liberties depend on restraints just as all rights depend on obligations. The naïve Hobbesian stand ignores this simple truth.

In a deeper sense too it misapprehends alike the nature of liberty and the nature of law. Laws may be tyrannous, but tyranny is the quality of particular enactments and has nothing to do with the essential character of law. Law is not command, though many jurists have mistakenly defined it so. A legal code is a system regulating human relationships within the frontiers of a State and applying to all who live within it. It is a necessary basis of social order, a guaranty that men will act on certain principles in their intercourse with one another, that, for example, they will fulfill their contracts and will not use violence to gain their ends. Remove this system, and every complex society would be reduced to chaos. Men could not foresee the consequences of their actions, could not undertake any enterprise that looked beyond the moment, could not possess any security of mind or body. The liberties we possess are relative to the social order in which we live and in large measure are created as well as sustained by that order. When our rights perish our liberties perish too. How vain then is the saying that liberty exists only "in the interstices of law"!

When men define liberty as the absence of restraint, the trouble frequently is that they at once think of some kinds of restraint and forget others altogether. They do not realize that in every society all kinds of restraints and liberties—legal, constitutional, economic, social, moral, religious—inevitably coexist in endless combinations for the different groups who live in the same community. There is no simple totality that may be named *the* liberty of the individual or *the* liberty of the people. When Herbert Hoover, in the book already referred to, speaks of "the American system of liberty," he finds it realized in the particular range of economic liberties that depend on equal *legal* rights, with practically no reference to the opportunities and conditions on which the exercise of these rights depends. He opposes economic controls by government, not on the ground that they are misguided but on the ground that they cause "myriad wounds to liberty." He decries "regimented agriculture" as a blow to liberty, without inquiring whether the farmers, wisely or unwisely, want the "regimentation." He decries "regimented currency," without considering that currency is always "regimented"—by someone. The controls he disapproves, wisely or unwisely, he regards as inconsistent with liberty or even as part of "the American system of liberty." He seems scarcely conscious of the fact that if two thousand individuals are in a position to control or direct half the industry of the country, therein also lies an important aspect of the problem of liberty.

Every law restrains some liberty, but before we can condemn it on that account we must put to ourselves two vital questions. First, *whose* liberty? For every law gives some men something that they will to have or to do, while restraining them, and all other men, in the contrary direction. Second, *what* liberty? For there are many kinds of liberty, and they conflict one with another, and some can be attained only by the restriction of others, and the advancement of one man's liberty generally means the setting of a limit to the similar liberty of another man. In the simplest terms, when one man or one group dominates another, they arrogate to themselves precisely the kind of liberty over others that they deny the others over themselves. Certain liberties are incompatible with one another, certain liberties are again incompatible with the possession by others of the like liberty. Therefore the answer to the question, *What liberty?* involves always a comparison of liberties and an assessment of their relative values. Here, incidentally, is where the negative definition of liberty as the absence of restraint proves quite unhelpful. For instance, I regard the liberty of men to think as they please as more important, more valuable, than the liberty of other men to control their thinking. The absence of one kind of restraint means far more to me than the absence of another kind of restraint. So I am driven back to the ultimate, the positive, and yet not further definable meaning of liberty. Then the problem of liberty becomes a far more complex one than it seemed at first, when we were content with the negative definition. For now we have to ask : What combination of liberties and restraints is most serviceable for the existence of what men seek when they place a high value on liberty?

Of such a nature are the more significant and searching questions that emerge when we pass beyond the elementary confusions that beset our thinking on the subject. But our immediate concern is with these confusions, and so we proceed to a second group of them. Here we meet the people who start from the universal meaning of liberty but, finding that the state of being free is realized for themselves under certain conditions, forthwith postulate that liberty itself, liberty for all men, is attained under the same conditions. They confound their personal liberty, or the liberty of some group to which they belong, with universal liberty. There are certain things they want to do, certain goals they want to achieve. If there is no restraint on this doing or achieving, that is liberty enough for all men. If all men are free to worship *their* God, that is religious liberty. If all men are free to express the opinions *they* cherish, that is intellectual liberty. Since their God is the true God and their opinions the right opinions, it must be so. They bid us, for example, distinguish liberty from license, license being the liberty to do the things they disapprove. They believe in economic liberty, meaning thereby, if they are employers, the right to run their business as they please, to hire and fire as they please. They believe in "liberty of contract," and maintain, with the Supreme Court in the case of *Adair* vs. *the United States*, that "the right of the employee to quit the service of the employer, for whatever reason, is the same as the right of the employer, for whatever reason, to dispense with the services of such employee." They think it is no interference with the liberty of opinion to restrain the opinion of radicals, if they themselves are conservative, or the opinion of conservatives, if they themselves are radical. They universalize as liberty for all men what is liberty only for the particular group, persuasion, or class to which they adhere.

This interest-limited conception of liberty explains the defeats that the principle of liberty has suffered in many of the battles won in its name. The demand for liberty is a most powerful incentive when it is directed against a particular oppressor or a particular oppression. But those who win liberty for their own cause often refuse it to others. Sects that resist to the death the intolerance of established faiths may become no less intolerant when they in turn are established. Nations that have won political liberties have often used their newfound strength to dominate other nations. The principle of liberty is most apt to be defeated by its own triumphs.

From the interest-limited conception of liberty it is only one step to the final perversion. We have thus far confined ourselves to such views as profess to mean by liberty that which is its universal meaning. About this universal meaning there can be no doubt. The child knows it who is forced to work when he wants to play. The savage knows it who is prevented from following his tribal customs. The criminal knows it who is put behind prison bars. The property-owner knows it who is not allowed to use his property as he pleases. Everywhere in human society, for better or worse, there are hindrances and prohibitions set by the will of others to that which we want to do, and everywhere the condition of which we are thus deprived is called liberty. The meaning of the term may be extended to include the absence of other obstacles to action than those that depend on the will of men to prevent our acting, though then the word "opportunity" is more appropriate than the word "liberty." Or again it may be extended to include the absence of hindrances in ourselves to the fulfillment of the things our hearts desire. Thus we speak of men as being "slaves to their habits." But this is clearly an analogical variant of the universal meaning, not to be pressed too far, certainly not to be made the ground for a redefinition of a term so necessary, so widely used, so unmistakable in its primary applications. The partisans of every cause have redefined the term "liberty" as something else than that which men everywhere mean by it, as something identifying it with their particular cause, thereby creating the worst confusions. They redefine it, and still they appeal to the emotions generated by the universal meaning. They redefine it, and transfer to this new meaning the values that properly attach to the original meaning. This is a far worse offense than those we have already indicated. This offense is "the lie in the soul."

Yet a long line of philosophers have followed this fashion. In the modern world it was set by Rousseau and it attained its philosophical culmination in Hegel. Today it is exploited most notably, though far from exclusively, by the apologists of antilibertarian forms of government. For the curious thing about these final perversions is that they enable men to justify in the name of liberty the most extreme suppressions of liberty. Our modern sophists draw a distinction between real liberty and apparent liberty. They proclaim that we are free only when we do what we *ought* to do — or rather what they think we ought to do; only when we desire what we *ought* to desire — what they think we ought to desire. They say that liberty is self-realization, the realization of the true self. They say that we find liberty in surrender to the "law" of our being, to the law of God, to the law of the State as the organic whole in which we are fulfilled. They do not say that self-realization is good and liberty is good, and seek for some relation between them. They say the one *is* the other. If they make any distinction at all, it is between a superficial and spurious liberty on the one hand and true liberty on the other. So Bernard Bosanquet, for example, contrasted our "actual" will and our "real" will. With sublime Hegelian arrogance they confer reality on what they think ought to be, and degrade to unreality that which they think ought not to be.

So it is not surprising that they often end by merging liberty in its own contradiction. It is the supreme example of having one's cake and eating it too. Rousseau again led the way when he spoke of men being "forced to be free." He was not content with saying "forced to be good," "forced to be rational." He gloried in what seemed to him only a paradox — instead of a perversion. In this he has had a multitude of followers. They transmuted liberty into self-surrender, self-abnegation, obedience, subjection. Hegel reconciled the opposites by announcing that they were one. The individual who is "forced to be free" might protest, but of course it is not his true self that protests. Hegel knows better. In the same spirit Treitschke explained that Germany would restore the people of Alsace "against their will to their true selves." In the same spirit Gentile explains that the absolute corporate State confers more liberty than the democratic State. In the same spirit Spengler and Spann and Freyer and the whole host of Nazi apologists explain that dominance, mastery, totalitarian authority, assure to those subjected to them the blessings of "true liberty."

These apologists will not face the issue that they value other things more highly than liberty and that they reject liberty for the sake of those other things. That position would at least be honest. Instead, they pervert the universal meaning of liberty in order to deny the most obvious of facts. They would destroy the meaning of liberty because they are afraid to admit its meaning. They call it something else, hoping that thus no one will claim it for what it is.

So after the many centuries in which men have talked and written of liberty we find proclaimed from the high places doctrines more perverse and fallacious than ever were uttered at the beginning of reflective thought. I have tried to show that each of these doctrines rests on a quite elementary error, on the most simple inability—or unwillingness—to apply the art of thinking. Liberty cannot be identified with any cause—except the cause of liberty—for its whole challenge is for the right to choose between causes. The analysis of the meaning of liberty, in its application to social realities, opens up the most fruitful questions. They remain mostly unexplored. We cannot advance to the more meaningful problems because they lie beyond this ever renewed fog of intellectual confusion.

[1940]

AUTHORITY AND FREEDOM IN
THE MODERN WORLD

Everything a man does, everything he thinks, everything he believes, expresses some accommodation between authority and freedom. No matter who we are or what we are, wherever we live, we find ourselves within a structure of authority that limits, sustains, and incorporates whatever freedom we may own.

Everywhere man sets up authority or at least is subject to it; everywhere he wants some freedom. Nearly all men want more freedom than they are given. The greater freedom some men want would curb the lesser freedom of others. Many men want to escape from some authority. Some men want to escape from the freedom they have. Romantic philosophers were once inclined to cast their fancy back to an idyllic age when men lived the simple life of nature, unbounded by artificial rules,

> Ere the base laws of servitude began,
> When wild in woods the noble savage ran.

But the so-called savage, noble or otherwise, was as law-bound as his most modern successor, for "custom was the king of men." Without authority man is lost, his powers dissipated. And without freedom his powers are frustrated or perverted.

But enough of this eternal antithesis. It merely sets the stage for the real issue. There is no over-all conflict between freedom and authority, but there are incessant conflicts between authorities and freedoms. No one, outside of a madhouse, was ever an anarchist in the full sense of the term. And the most absolute authoritarian wants all the freedom in the world for himself. Laws may be tyrannous, but only under laws are we free.

It is here that the real questions begin. How should authority be constituted and within what limits? What authority should control what? Is there any area of human life that should be left entirely free, without rules laid down by any authority? Is there, should there be, any final authority to which all others are, or should be, subordinated? A political authority, or a divine authority, or a pure authority such as some have sought in reason or the law of nature? Is there, should there be, a final court of appeal for every activity of man? Men move forever from old to new authority, from new to old, and new hopes of freedom are forever burning. Can we learn anything from history, from the endless struggles, triumphs, and defeats of the past?

My subject is "Authority and Freedom in the Modern World," and in modern times the fronts of change along which authorities and freedoms clash are vastly extended. To deal with the subject at all, I must bypass a thousand problems and seek instead to offer a perspective against which we may view them.

A cardinal fact about the modern world is the multiplication of authorities. That goes with the diversity and complexity of interests, with specialization, with the proliferation of sects and creeds. In this process it appeared that there were many kinds of authority, as well as many areas of authority. Let us broadly distinguish three kinds. First, there is the comprehensive authority that lays down rules and is backed by the power to enforce them. This is, *par excellence*, political authority. Next, there is the authority that lays down rules the violation of which may involve some penalty, the loss of privilege or status or opportunity or economic position. This is the kind of authority possessed by many voluntary organizations, such as the business firm, the trade union, the university, the social club, the church. Finally, there is the authority that makes no formal rules and is buttressed by no specific sanctions of any kind, but where it—or he—makes pronouncements within the appropriate area they carry weight. This is the sense in which we attribute authority to the expert, the sage, the celebrity, the social leader.

As authorities multiplied, authority itself changed. For we must observe that authority does not exist except as it is recognized, except as it is respected. Which means that, in the last analysis, those who accept authority also make it. That is not true of power, and therein lies the vital difference between mere power and authority. As attitudes change, authority must change too. And in modern times it has been responsive to broad changes in the way men have come to think about authority. But, before we proceed to this aspect, let us look back for a moment.

When human society began to take shape and become organized in local tribes or small communities, the notion prevailed in each of them that one authority, one only, had all the answers to all problems. This was the way of the fathers, the hallowed custom of the tribe. It assigned functions and services and decided disputes. The chief, the headman with his council of elders, was the agent, the vindicator, of the law of the tribe. By his side, however, there appeared another exponent of authority, the sage, the man especially learned in the tribal lore, the medicine man, or the priest. Each was presumed to apply or to expound the one primal authority, the law of the tribe. Each, in his different place, held thus a kind of derivative authority.

But when the small community became merged in the greater one, these two derivative authorities in turn developed into two separate systems of authority. One became the state, the other the church. They became the two great engines of social control. Possessing authority, each possessed also power. Thus arose trouble, for who was to assign the place of each? The concord of these two authorities was never easy, and an important part of history is the record of their conflicts and changing relationships. There was no possibility of agreement concerning the application of the formula, "Render unto Caesar the things that are Caesar's and unto God the things that are God's."

In some civilizations, notably the Greco-Roman, the secular authority established a complete dominance over the religious one which, apart from some special cults, became little more than a ceremonial system of soothsaying and magic sacrifice. In others, notably the Egyptian, the authority of the priests was nearly always potent, and under some dynasties it took complete control. In the civilization of the medieval world, the controversy over the claims of the two authorities was never-ending and full of confusions, until at length the rise of great territorial sovereignties and the schisms that broke the unity of the ecclesiastical power brought into being the new problems of authority and freedom that belong to the modern world.

The medieval drive toward a single system of authority, with the papal authority its apex, yielded before the Renaissance drive toward the alternative single system of which the sovereign was the apex. Neither system allowed much room for freedom as we understand it today. Freedom was regarded either as belonging to the spaces where authority did not intervene or else was presumed to lie simply in the ready assent men may give to rules which are laid down by the rightful authority and are befitting to their place and grade in society. Here we find the sharpest contrast between earlier doctrines of freedom and those that have revolutionized the modern world. It is important to understand the significance of this change.

No single lore holds within the modern community. No one system of beliefs, of usages, of ways of living. That is why authority is so different now, both in its meaning and its range. In the simpler community the ruler was the accepted guardian of the common ways. The hierarchy of authority expanded as the community grew. The community became a graded structure. Men were of high or low degree according to the law of life, the law of nature, and the law of God. There was a graded upper class, and there was a lower class with its inferior degrees. The lines of order were set, and the bonds of authority held them fast. The name of freedom could not be invoked to challenge that divinely appointed order.

> Take but degree away, untune that string,
> And hark, what discord follows!

All this the modern age has changed. Authority is not accepted in its own right. Neither the appeal to nature nor to God justifies any more the subordination of man to man. The modern community divides into various groups with diverse beliefs, diverse interests, and to a considerable extent diverse customs. Authority has now to vindicate itself. It is no longer predetermined. The distribution of power is complex. It is no more a class monopoly. Those of low estate have been exalted. Power everywhere competes with power. Organization is everywhere; where there is organization, there is power; and where power is *organized* power, there is authority. Thus there are many foci of authority. And with this development the meaning as well as the nature of authority has changed.

So far as political government is concerned, the major trend was from a class-determined authority to a folk-determined authority. In earlier times there had been important movements in the same direction, particularly in the culminating period of the civilization of Greece and later in the days of the Roman Republic. But in these earlier civilizations the process was arrested—there were adverse conditions, not least of which was the institution of slavery. The modern state has carried the process through.

But, in doing so, it has dispossessed the old residences of authority. The class hierarchy rules no more. Class right is as dead as divine right. The man who can win the popular vote, the labor leader, the strong man of affairs, the effective propagandist wields more power than once accorded to rank and station. What then of authority? Does it belong to the people? The people speak with many voices. In earlier times authority was *over* the people, above them. Is it a condition of authority that it be looked up to? But can the people look up to itself? Can it, should it, look up to those it makes its agents or its servants? When officials are agents, there is some assurance of freedom. But what then assures authority, without which also freedom cannot survive?

This is no idle or merely theoretical question. There is no freedom without order. There is no order without unity. There is no unity without authority. Given the sense of unity, authority is safe. If the people speak with many voices and there is no stronger consensus beneath the contending voices, unity is dissipated, and freedom commits suicide. But the sense of unity must not degenerate into the demand for conformity, or freedom is again lost.

In every society there are forces that would destroy essential freedoms. These forces are very active in our own society today. In every society there are forces that would dethrone and dissipate authority. Democracy in being is the reconciliation of authority and freedom. One of the serious troubles of our democracy is that our understanding of it is so superficial. It is a finer and deeper thing than most of us realize. It is not to be summed up in such simple phrases as "the rule of the people." One of its greatest virtues is that under it alone can authority and freedom live together. But, to achieve this goal, it is needful that the people understand the obligation of their freedom.

In older times the people did not create authority. They certainly did not control it. For the main basis of authority was social status, the status of a ruling class that monopolized power and land ownership and fostered the traditions and the doctrines congenial to this monopoly. This ancient basis of authority has crumbled, and with it the traditions and the sanctities that attached to it. Wealth and power take many forms and have many different locations throughout society, regardless of old class distinctions. But, with all this spread and redistribution of what once was a class monopoly, unity is as necessary as before. And over this unity authority must preside, while nevertheless the diverse free associations of democracy retain their necessary autonomy. But now the authority must be created and sustained by the good sense of the people themselves. While they are subject to it, it must still be in this sense *their* authority.

Two major devices were developed to assure that authority over the people would still be *their* authority. One of these was designed to make authority responsible. This was the system of periodic popular elections, which made authority responsive to the movements of public opinion. The other device, no less necessary than the first, was to limit the area within which government could operate. The law of the constitution determined these limits. The electoral system was a guarantee against the tyranny of government, the constitutional system a guarantee against the tyranny of any majority. The second assured to the people the fundamental freedoms. These belonged, and must always belong, to the realm of the mind : the freedom of speech, the freedom of assembly, the freedom of doctrine. Only by safeguarding this area against the intrusions of power can the creative forces of humanity be liberated.

We are speaking, of course, of the modern democratic state. In lands where the old class oligarchy has suddenly been destroyed, in lands where the conditions of democracy had not been prepared, the downfall of the old order brought a mere reversal of it, dictatorship, setting up under the hollow name of the "people's state" a monopoly of power and authority more exacting and more tyrannous than the old. For when authority has no roots, naked power must take control.

All this has a great lesson to teach the democracies. The union of authority and freedom requires that we respect authority no less than we love freedom. We have been whittling away the sense of authority. We have been making government too much the mere battleground where narrow interests contend for mastery. We have exalted our divisions at the expense of our unity. We have been willing to sacrifice the greater values of the whole for the sake of the immediate advantage, the specious temporary gain, of a group. Too frequently we elect to office noisy little visionless men. If these are the agents of the people, how can they win respect? Do we take ourselves so lightly? How can authority be strong when we respect it so little? How can freedom be secure?

Only if we realize the vast responsibility that must attach to government, only if we cultivate the sense of the whole, only if it overrides our divisions and the economic interests of particular groups, only so can authority dwell at peace with freedom. Government must be a partner with freedom, not merely an umpire called in to see that every group plays according to the rules. Otherwise authority is too weak to sustain unity, and the power of dominant groups will erode our fundamental freedoms.

We have spoken of the devices by which the democratic peoples have broken the arrogance of class domination and the tyranny of irresponsible power. But no devices automatically save us. No elections and no constitutions can be of any effect except as they are the instruments of a people nurtured in the traditions and the doctrines of freedom and justice. The people must possess the integrity alike to respect themselves and to respect authority. Their respect for themselves must protect the realm of the free mind, the realm that power shall not invade. Their respect for authority will assure that they elect men to office who will measure up to the responsibility entrusted to them.

Let us be clear about this—there is no authority inherent in forms or in constitutions. The greatest political, the greatest spiritual inheritance is dead unless it lives in us. We sometimes speak of the authority of the law. But law of itself has no intrinsic authority and no power. There are dead laws as well as living ones; both kinds are in the statute books. The law lives in the respect for the law, far more than in the sanction it contains. But the authority behind the law is, in the first instance, the lawmaker and, beyond him, the whole system of government and all it means for the people whose government it is. If government means little, authority is weak. If it stoops to petty devices, authority is humbled. If it is corrupt, authority is betrayed. In a democracy, authority is a trust, a trust bestowed by the people; and if they are careless of that trust or of how it is bestowed, they squander their freedom as well. The final reconciliation of authority and freedom lies in the conscience of the people.

[1954]

Interests and Social Pressures

20 INTERESTS

When a number of men unite for the defense, maintenance, or enhancement of any more or less enduring position or advantage which they possess alike or in common, the term "interest" is applied both to the group so united and to the cause which unites them. In this sense the term is most frequently used in the plural, implying either that various similar groups or advantages combine to form a coherent complex, as in the terms vested interests, moneyed interests, and labor interests, or that the uniting interest is maintained against an opposing one, as in the expressions conflict of interests and balance of interests. Interests so understood usually have an economico-political character.

The importance of compact interest groups in the development and the vicissitudes of states was recognized by the great historians of antiquity in the struggles leading to the legislation of Solon and of Cleisthenes, in the tenacious system of the Spartan oligarchy and later in the struggle of the orders at Rome, in the agrarian reforms of the Gracchi and in the conflicts which led to the establishment of the principate and the empire. Modern historians have seen in the clash of interests, as the conjuncture of conditions and events favored one side or another, one of the universal factors in social and political change. In one of its broadest forms it appears in the conflict of older agrarian interests with the aggressive interests associated with commerce, finance and industry. To the Marxians all history is a record of a series of clashes between various changing class interests; in the modern economic order the important conflict of interests is that between capitalist interests and those uniting the wage-earning classes. These economic interest complexes, however, are limited by competitive differences within themselves and are crossed by interests of varying potency derived from other than purely economic considerations, such as those of status, race, nation, region, and religion.

The historical dominance of interest groups has at various times been challenged by conceptions of society based on individualistic doctrines, such as those of the social contract and of natural rights. In the formation of modern democratic institutions there are discernible two very different attitudes of revolt from the feudal system of established class interests; in the earlier stages the two work together, but later their latent contradiction appears. One is the democratic idea, the other the opposition of the growing interests which industrial development has stimulated, the interest of manufacturing and trading groups seizing their opportunity to dethrone the interests of the landed class. The feudal system of estates was a system of interests adjusted to the domination of property in land. The growth of other forms of property required a modification of the system but not necessarily of the principle. The "divine right of kings" was with relative ease transformed into the "divine right of freeholders." The English Revolution of 1688 was simple because it merely extended to a slowly increasing class and a slowly changing situation the old principle that the property of the country should govern it. Writers like Locke and Harrington were not revolutionary prophets but new interpreters of the old doctrine of the political role of property interests. Their social contract individualism was sharply limited by their theory that the state exists for the preservation of property. With the industrial changes of the later eighteenth century the concept of interests ceased to be formulated in the simpler terms of homogeneous "property." The new economic interests evoked by the Industrial Revolution revealed a different kind of struggle, which has continued with additional complications up to the present.

On the other hand, the democratic idea in its pure form was essentially opposed to the interest principle. It translated the doctrine of natural rights into the "self-evident" maxim that "all men are created equal" and drew from it the conclusions which Locke and others who had used the same language had conveniently refused to draw. This was the principle the uncompromising logic of which was enunciated by Rousseau. It was the principle which inspired the Declaration of the Rights of Man and which in revolutionary France abolished all corporate interests within the state. It was the principle of the Declaration of Independence. It was in a later form the Benthamite principle that every man is to count as one and that the greatest happiness of the greatest number is the goal of the state.

The conflict of these two doctrines received much illumination in the course of the eighteenth and nineteenth centuries. The groups which were seeking political power were ready for the time being to enlist under the democratic banner, but when the battle was won the victory proved generally to belong to the interests represented by these groups rather than to the people as a whole. One of the most significant illustrations of the initial convergence and later divergence of the two doctrines is afforded by the events following the American Revolution. It is seen in the transition from the language of the Declaration to that of the Constitution. Historians of the school of Beard have stressed the part played by economic interests in the framing of the Constitution and in the struggle between the Federal and the Republican, or Jeffersonian, party. They have maintained that if Thomas Jefferson still employed the language of the Declaration after the development of the Federalist-Republican schism, it had become the language of agrarian protest against capitalist control. It need not be assumed that the ideal of democracy as enunciated by John Adams or by Jefferson had no vitality in its own right; but certainly the evidence is good that it was serviceable also, because of its vitality, to the protagonists of struggling interests. So far as the framers of the Constitution are concerned, they have left no doubt as to their conception of the role of interests. They recognized that "a landed interest, a manufacturing interest, a mercantile interest, a moneyed interest with many lesser interests, grow up of necessity in civilized nations, and divide them into different classes, actuated by different sentiments and views."[1] They recognized that this conflict of interests creates the problem of government and is the origin of factions or parties. But they thought that this conflict must be held in check and some balance of interests must be established in the very framework of government.

The question as to how far the state is based on group interests, whether thought of in terms of class or of economic function or of territory, and how far on the general interest of a whole community has been a prominent issue in modern political theory. The followers of Rousseau, the school of Fichte and Hegel, have insisted on the subordination of group interests to universal state purposes. Some present-day writers, such as M.P. Follett, take the same point of view.[2] Others maintain

1. Madison in *The Federalist*, No. 10.
2. For example, in *The New State* (New York, 1918).

that the state while deriving cohesion from interest groups is in principle above them and is ideally the impartial arbiter of their claims.[3] The opposite point of view is represented by such writers as Bentley, who in his *The Process of Government* claims that political issues are inevitably determined by the strength of group pressures. The adherents of the Marxian school go even further and assert that the state is essentially for the domination of one class over another; they lay stress on the solidarity of the controlling capitalist interest in the modern state. The Marxist ideal, however, points to a coming socialist state which will be essentially classless and in which the interest principle will be overthrown. The Soviet experiment has tended to give a new emphasis but also a redirection to this ideal. A somewhat different conception is held by such writers as Duguit, Benoist and Cole, who have maintained that the reorganization of the state through the representation of purely functional groups would restore to the machinery of government a reality which the "democratic" system of territorial representation lacks and would also make possible a more effective coordination of these interests within the whole. Since, however, interest groups find an important means of expression and influence through political parties and since political parties seem an inevitable condition of any democratic system, the efficacy of these proposals remains doubtful. Both the fascist and the socialist conceptions of the state assume the coercive abolition of political parties.

In economic theory the concept of interests has not been so prominent. In earlier stages this was perhaps due to the identification of economics with "political economy." The cameralists and the mercantilists took their stand on the solidarity of national economic interests. The physiocrats did work out a system of economics based on an assumption of the relative social utility of interest groups. Although Adam Smith had on occasion referred to group interests, to the classical economists they were unimportant for the explanation of economic phenomena as compared with competitive individual interests. The historical school of economists, however, stressed the role of the group rather than that of the individual and in studying the rise and fall of institutions necessarily paid considerable attention to the conflict of interests. Socialist economists tended to stress interests even more strongly but for the most part limited their attention to the interest complexes of broadly defined social classes. The possibility of a more thoroughgoing study of the economic role of interest groups as such is suggested by the work of economists like Sombart and Veblen. Furthermore, alongside the more formal studies of economic theory there have always been studies of practical economic

3.   W.E. Hocking, *Man and the State* (New Haven, 1926).

problems and of economic institutions, in which the question of group interests has generally been accorded considerable attention.

In the theory of law interests have generally been considered as sources of conflict requiring readjustment through social agencies. From this point of view judicial decisions and the law behind them constitute a specially sanctioned process for the peaceful settlement of conflicts of interests. Law is on this ground contrasted with customary and other nonlegal modes of determination of the range of interests, and the development of law is attributed to the inadequacy of these modes as interests have grown in variety and in complexity. Under such conditions custom develops too slowly to keep pace with social changes and leaves too many "areas of discretion" which are productive of social disturbance. Voluntary agencies of adjustment, although they play an important part, are also quite inadequate, often lacking sufficient authority to compose the issue and often, when effective, tending to disregard the interests of members of society other than those who are directly involved in the dispute. John Dickinson has said: "No fact is more important for an understanding of social processes or of the development of agencies of social control than that a conscious adjustment of interests between numerous parties cannot shape itself initially through the spontaneous action of all the interested parties, but must ordinarily result from the special efforts of some external agency . . . charged with the task of surveying the situation as a whole and devising a plan." [4] Such an agency not only is authoritative but also can adapt its determinations to the requirements of each changing situation.

Some writers on the theory of law have given a greater reality and concreteness to the old conception of legal rights by translating them, in the language of Ihering, into "legally protected interests." Rights, in other words, become a particular species of social interests, selected for recognition and confirmation by legislation and judicial decision. This idea has in turn led to the concept of the state as essentially an organization for the determination and adjustment of the interests operative within a society. By Krabbe, [5] for example, the state is conceived as a regulatory power over interests, in consideration of the necessity for the continuous adjustment of these interests for the sake of practical harmony. The state, in his view, should be regarded not as the "possessor of public interests" but as a complex of agencies which administer a series of public services and of organs which generally bring into a workable system the various

---

4. J. Dickinson, "Social Order and Political Authority," *American Political Science Review*, XXIII (1929), 293–328, 593–632.

5. Hugo Krabbe, *De moderne staatsidee* (The Hague, 1915), tr. by G.H. Sabine and W. J. Shepard as *The Modern Idea of the State* (New York, 1922).

conflicting interests of the community. This process Krabbe speaks of as "an evaluation of interests," although in interpreting this statement the saying of Korkunov should be borne in mind that "law is the determination, morality the evaluation of interests."

In the field of sociology and social psychology the term interests has also had considerable vogue. From the beginnings of modern systematic sociology, writers have sought to distinguish and classify the various aims or strivings of human beings which give rise to the varieties of social phenomena and especially of group behavior. Herbert Spencer dealt with what he called the "internal factors of social phenomena," and Lester Ward sought to classify "social forces." Ratzenhofer employed instead the term interests, being chiefly concerned to show how variant or antagonistic interests of individuals and groups explain or illustrate his theory of social conflict. This usage was adopted by Albion Small although for a different purpose and was popularized by him among American sociologists. Small offered his own classification of interests; and various other writers, such as Ross, Ellwood, and Hayes, engaged in the same task. Their definitions of the term were essentially psychological. Thus Small said that "an interest is an unsatisfied capacity corresponding to an unrealized condition, and it is predisposition to such rearrangement as would tend to realize the indicated condition."[6] His own list reduced itself to the following : health, wealth, sociability, knowledge, beauty, rightness. The crudity of this list is obvious; and, while it was improved upon by the other writers referred to, the difficulty of finding a basis for classification remained. Nor was the attempt to explain social phenomena as expressions or embodiments of specific interests particularly successful. Moreover a fundamental difficulty lay in the confused application of the term at once to the subjective phenomena of motivations or desires and to objective phenomena, such as wealth. For this reason MacIver has proposed that a clear distinction should be drawn between attitudes or states of consciousness, on the one hand, and interests, or the objects toward which these states are directed, on the other.[7] The confusions and difficulties of the interest concept have led various sociological writers to reject the term altogether and to substitute such terms as values and wishes.

If the term "interests" is used with this objective significance as the correlative of attitudes, the concept becomes particularly useful in the explanation of the growth and change of social organization. Under more simple conditions of society the social expression of interests was mainly through caste or class groups, age groups, kin groups, neighborhood

---

6. A.W. Small, *General Sociology* (Chicago, 1905), p. 433.
7. R. M. MacIver, *Society: Its Structure and Changes* (New York, 1931), Chaps. III, VIII-IX.

groups, and other unorganized or loosely organized solidarities. The coherence of these groups was fostered by appropriate traditions—established interpretations, as it were, of the interests or values which the groups embodied. A social class, for example, sustained its relative dominance not simply by insistence on the merits of the interests which were peculiar to its members but indirectly by the translation of these presumed merits into an ideology of prestige and social function. The attitudes thus engendered in dominant and inferior groups alike both masked the group interest and helped to perpetuate it. With the advance of civilization interests are organized in particular associations and in this way become more specialized, defined, and limited. In an industrialized society with its division of labor and its opportunity for widened contacts every interest of any proportions establishes an organization for its promotion. Many quite limited and selective interests are enabled to draw their scattered adherents into personal or impersonal relations over greater areas, while the more universal interests extend correspondingly the range and the size of their organization. Thus the most marked structural distinction between a primitive and a civilized society is the paucity of specific associations in the one and their multiplicity in the other.

This definite organization of interests reacts upon the character of the interests as well as on the modes in which they are pursued. A broad distinction may be drawn here between like and common interests. Persons have like interests in so far, for example, as each seeks a livelihood for himself. They have common interests in the degree in which they participate in a cause, as the welfare of a city or country, which indivisibly embraces them all. The two types of interest are inextricably combined in their attachment to associations. Thus the like interests which lead to economic association are reinforced by the sense of membership in a corporate unity on the success of which the attainment of these like or distributive interests depends. Moreover the association gives a greater stability to the interests which it promotes. An organized interest, especially if it assumes the form of incorporation, achieves a certain continuity in spite of the fluctuating devotion and the changing composition of the membership.

With the increase of organization the conflict of interests takes new forms, and the problem of establishing some harmony between them thrusts new tasks upon the state. There are some interests which remain localized and others which have special local aspects. But on the whole the attribution of interests to localities, the principle on which the system of representative government has been built, has diminishing significance. Moreover, inasmuch as with the development of communications many of these interests, both economic and cultural, are organized on lines that transcend the boundaries of individual states, the regulation or protection not only of such interests as may be deemed more specifically national but also of those which have inevitably a wider range introduces considerations at variance with traditional ideas of the sovereign independence of states.

International conferences reveal on a larger scale that essential problem of the reconciliation of interests which every social organization, temporary or permanent, has to face. Every organization presupposes an interest which its members all share, and its task is to find a way of reconciling with or adjusting to this wider interest the conflicting interests of its component groups or individual members. While some attention has been given to this subject, for example, by the school of M.P. Follett, much remains to be done to clarify the nature of the problem, to analyze the varying forms which it assumes and to discover methods by which the larger interest of the whole group can be most effectively maintained against the particular interests which divide it.

[1932]

SOCIAL PRESSURES

The term social pressure, in the singular, is sometimes applied to the constraint of the social order on the organic or native impulses of man, which are variously represented as being inhibited or balked or "sublimated" or at least diverted, by the compulsion of the mores and the necessities of social organization, into new channels dissociated from the biological drives. This general point of view is common to various psychiatric schools and has inspired certain theories of the nature of society.[8] Such modern theories are logically the successors of the social philosophies which opposed society to nature, prevalent from the time of the sophists and running through the social contract doctrine and other forms of individualism down to the current protests against the standardization of behavior and of individuality attributed to the machine age.

When used in the plural, however, the term has acquired a more specific sense. Beyond the range of direct authoritarian controls, effected through officials or other accredited social agents and expressive of established codes, there exist socially created constraints which emanate from less sanctioned or less responsible sources; informal and opportunistic in their operation, they fluctuate incessantly in intensity and direction. These constraints may be called social pressures.

---

8. See, for example, Trigant Burrow, *The Social Basis of Consciousness* (New York, 1927); and "Social Images versus Reality," *Journal of Abnormal Psychology*, XIX (1924–25), 230–235.

A distinction may be drawn here between mass social pressures directed against minorities which do not conform to the demands of a dominating and emotionally charged popular movement and group social pressures emanating from particularist groups which seek to advance their interests through activities intended to restrain or divert the behavior of resistant elements. The former type would be exemplified by the unofficial coercions characteristic of the earlier stages of the Nazi campaign or by the ostracism of those who trade, intermarry, or otherwise enter into relations with members of a group exposed to the hostile attitude of a dominant religious, racial, nationalist movement; the latter by the attempts of blocs or of business interests to induce favorable conditions by tactics which bring to bear at individual points the power of wealth, organization, power, or position.

The distinguishing fact about social pressures is that they depend generally upon informal even if concerted tactics and that they operate directly against nonconforming individuals. One aspect of this fact is brought out in R. E. Park's comment: "The pressure group is not an army which seeks to win battles by frontal attacks on hostile positions; it is, rather, a body of sharp-shooters which picks off its enemies one by one." This statement, however, is more applicable to the second type of pressure group referred to above. Mass pressures do indeed operate at individual points but they also exercise a broad restraining influence on the opposing front. What characterizes both types is the informal, opportunistic, extralegal nature of the coercive tactics they employ. Social pressures are thus to be distinguished not only from authoritative controls but also from the regular processes of indoctrination and habituation to which the established mores of every group subject its members. They belong to an unstable condition of movement and of strife.

The relation of social pressures to authoritarian controls, on the one hand, and to the established mores of the society within which they are exercised, on the other, may assume a considerable variety of forms. Because of the element of coercion inherent in these pressures, the former relation is of primary importance in determining both the varieties and the techniques of pressure tactics. Social pressures may be exerted by means which are legally permitted or by methods which the law forbids, or again not only the methods but also the objectives may be opposed by the law. There is a distinction, for example, between the pressures which employ certain techniques of "unfair" competition banned by the law and the pressures directed against the law itself or its administration, such as the relatively successful attempts to defeat or nullify the Volstead Act. For all types of pressure it is obvious that the attitude of governmental agencies is of vast significance. Even for the large category of social pressures which do not directly clash with the laws a generally favorable or unfavorable attitude on the part of authority is an important limiting or releasing factor. This is true not only because social pressures, being usually expansive, tend to reach or pass the margin where they may be interpreted as contravening the law but also because the activity of law-making may be turned, as in the case of the boycott, against the exercise of the social pressure.

The significance of governmental attitudes toward social pressures becomes more apparent when it is realized that the administration of legal justice is itself subject to the constant impact of social pressures. These may seek to extend or limit the interpretation or application of the law, as in the Scopes trial; they may demand severity or lenience outside of judicial or equitable considerations, as in indictments for certain types of sexual offense or in the trial of certain types of offenders, from Negroes to business magnates; they may even obstruct the regular machinery of jurisdiction, as evidenced by the popular antagonism which made German lawyers reluctant to defend the Communists accused of the burning of the Reichstag building or as expressed in the boycott of the lawyer who defended Sacco and Vanzetti. On a smaller scale social pressures operate to limit arrests or convictions for petty violations of the law or for infringements of outmoded laws, which thus fall into desuetude.

At one end of the scale of relations between social pressures and authoritarian controls is the situation in which the extralegal pressures proceed from the authorities themselves. This situation is frequent under so-called dictatorial governments, where the executive dominates the legislative and judicial powers. Under democratic conditions is found the intermediate situation, in which governments or officials cooperate actively with particular pressure groups; in adding, for example, extralegal to legal trade restrictions or in supporting campaigns to give preference to domestic products. Another aspect of this situation is illustrated by the alliance of political authorities with militant religious groups, so evident throughout the history of religious persecution and still occurring in minor forms, as in the treatment meted out by the New York City officials to Mrs. Margaret Sanger in her campaign for birth control. At the other end of the scale belong those cases where the authorities actively resist the social pressures or where the pressures are directed against the authorities themselves. This can occur on a small scale, as in movements against individual officials, such as magistrates or judges, or on a large scale, as when mass pressure is directed against the prevailing system of authority. The latter is illustrated by nationalistic movements, such as that represented by the Indian swaraj or by the Irish "home rule" agitation; but it appears also in nonrevolutionary forms, as when an unpopular tax proposal is withdrawn by a government under indications of public resentment or when an unpopular government, under the parliamentary system, resigns from office apart from any constitutional necessity.

The foregoing cases reveal more particularly a quality inherent in some degree in all social pressures—their dynamic relation to the existing social structure. Like Hobbes' liberty they appear in the "interstices of law." They impinge restlessly upon the law-established order, sometimes supplementing it, sometimes limiting it, and occasionally undermining it or even seeking to overthrow it. The conservative function is seen in the drives made against the disturbers of tradition or the prophets of a new order. Social pressures are directed against them, whether they occupy pulpits or university chairs or, more rarely, seats on the judicial bench or whether they merely stand on soap boxes in the public parks. The limiting function is seen in the way in which legal liberties are curtailed by economic impacts, as when advertising interests intervene to effect the inclusion or exclusion of news in the press. The revolutionary function appears particularly in those social pressures which are generated or accentuated by wars and economic crises, ranging from concerted resistance to the payment of taxes or the collection of debts to the great historical upheavals which overturn states.

For the same reason social pressures are specially brought to bear wherever a social order is in the making or when, for whatever reason, it is not adequately protected by law. This situation occurs, for example, where an alien group, with prestige but without legal authority, exploits a "backward people." Again, in the absence of an authoritative international code pressure methods are resorted to in order to render effective the existing international mechanism of the League of Nations.[9] These may operate as disguised or overt economic inducements or through the stimulation of public opinion in other countries, and if possible in the recalcitrant country, against the governmental policy detrimental to the functioning of the League. The barriers which political boundaries present to the permeation of opinion making influences set rather definite limits to the use of the latter method.

The relation of social pressures to the mores, the social as distinct from the legal codes, is also highly significant. Some of the cases cited above belong to situations where there is a clash between mores and laws. In such situations the mores, restrained in their operation, generate social pressures which bear on the authorities whose duty it is to administer or execute the laws. Normally, because of the diverse mores of groups bound within the same legal system, there is an unstable play of pressures and counterpressures. An illustration is offered by the history of the administration of the Volstead Act. More permanently the condition

9.   This was written in 1934—Ed.

occurs in the struggle of economic groups which employ their various extralegal weapons for pressure purposes. In general it may be said that wherever groups are pitted against one another in any kind of struggle, whether they be class groups, race groups, religious or other cultural groups, there is resort to the techniques of social pressure.

When the mores rally strongly to the side of a pressure group and when at the same time the latter is able to control the governmental system, the tactics of pressure become irresistible. Such situations occur on a large scale when a people's sense of its own solidarity, thwarted or dammed up by historical vicissitudes and thus supercharged with emotion, breaks violently through the resistances to its expression. The mass social pressures thus generated are peculiarly domineering and oppressive with regard to nonconformities. There are then neither effective legal restraints upon them nor overt counterpressures which are found in more complicated situations. The Nazi outburst offers the most striking illustration of this type of pressure, although it is a distinctive feature of all "fascist" movements.

The term pressure group has recently come into use to signify any aggregate, organized or unorganized, which applies pressure tactics. This usage is serviceable if at the same time a distinction is drawn between an interest group and a pressure group. Even if it were true that all interest groups seek in some way or at some time to exercise social pressures, the distinction would be relevant. For the exercise of social pressure is not inherent in the concept of an interest group, say of a musical organization or a philatelic society, whereas it is the defining function of a pressure group. Social pressures, in a word, constitute a particular method of achieving results—one of the many methods which interest groups may adopt.

The tactics which are the essence of social pressures are intended not directly to change attitudes but to control the behavior of recalcitrant or nonconforming individuals. Thus, although propagandism may involve an element of social pressure, it is not necessarily a form of it. The attempt to convert another to one's faith by expounding its values may come within the order of propaganda but not of social pressure. Pressure involves more than persuasion : it implies some kind of external inducement to change or limit the activity of others, ranging from direct or indirect economic inducement to ostracism, intimidation, and violence. In other words, it always acts by creating some tension in the individuals to whom it is addressed. If, as is frequently the case, it makes use of the symbols—the flag or the hearth or even the cross—dear to those whom it assaults, it does so in order to constrain or divert their actions, not to liberate them. It promises or threatens with a view to making others conform. This is true whatever the scale of the pressure, which may be as localized as the refusal of villagers to buy from a heterodox storekeeper or as far reaching as the march of the bonus army on Washington, of the unemployed on London, or of the Fascists on Rome.

A pressure group is defined by its techniques, an interest group by its objectives. A pressure group as such has no internal function but is directed outward, to the overcoming of resistances. The concept of pressures is therefore of more limited significance for the interpretation of social systems than for that of interests. Interests may be opposed, but the relation of conflict is only one of the manifold relations they exhibit. Broader uniting interests may underlie narrower dividing ones. The theory of interests can therefore be applied to explain alike the solidarity and the equilibrium of a social system as well as the conflicts that exist within it; whereas the theory of pressures can be made an explanation only of the divisions, the dominances and the resistances within a society.

The limitations of the pressure theory are manifest in the work which more than any other attempts to interpret social arrangements as merely the adjustment of unstable pressures: Bentley's *Process of Government*. It is true that this study is ostensibly confined to the field of politics, which might seem specially favorable for the exposition of pressure operations, but the result is nevertheless unconvincing. In the first place, Bentley does not effectively distinguish pressures from interests, although he denies implicitly the operation of a general interest which modifies and limits the techniques of pressure. Consequently, in the second place, he assumes too readily that the agreements arrived at in the political arena represent the sheer diagonal of particularistic opposing pressures, a view which seems hardly compatible with the relative stability of the political system and the orderly development which it exhibits over long periods. The manner in which cooperative factors are linked with competitive and conflicting ones is lost sight of, so that pressure processes are assigned a larger and more constructive role than they can maintain.

In general the theory of the function of pressures in society still awaits development. The number of descriptive studies of particular types of pressure has increased in recent years. In the political field there are various works on lobbies and blocs; in other works the intensive employment of social pressures in times of war is documented; in the economic field studies have been made of the pressure tactics of public utility and other corporations, including the investigations by the Federal Trade Commission; much of the literature on strikes, lockouts, and boycotts likewise illustrates the phenomena of economic pressures. Particular pressure groups in other fields, for example, the Ku Klux Klan, have also been described in some detail. It is incidently significant that while American writers have notoriously neglected the study of social classes, they have added considerably to the specific literature of social pressures. But there is lacking on the whole any effective analysis of the relation of social pressures to social conflicts; of their role in the building up and breaking down of social structures; of the conditions under which they are most effective and of the various types of pressure which develop in different cultural situations; of their manipulation of the symbols and their attachment to the thought forms in or through which the mores of the various groups find expression.

The fact that the literature of social pressures is at once so descriptive and so recent is noteworthy, as is the fact that so large a portion of it is American. Pressure groups, as distinct from class groups, are characteristic of a heterogeneous and changeful society, offering special opportunities for the economic exploitation of new conditions and for the formation of unstable expansive groups not integrally related to the established order. Pressure techniques are facilitated also by the elaborate interdependence of a highly industrialized society and by the new means of communication and contact which modern invention has devised. When such conditions develop rapidly, foci of economic power emerge without pre-established status and outside of the authoritarian controls. Therefore, once the fact of their power comes to be realized and resisted, they inevitably resort to pressure tactics. The unorganized juxtaposition of diverse racial and national groups struggling for position and prestige dependent largely on their different facilities for the acquisition of wealth has been an additional factor. The extreme case of the dissociation of power from status is to be found in the organized "rackets" also characteristic of such a society, which are able to maintain themselves by pressures acting not merely on the groups they exploit but even, directly or indirectly, on the authorities whose duty it is to suppress their criminal activities.

The earlier, mostly European, writers on class conflict and the other more ancient forms of social struggle, such as those of racial or religious groups, did not envisage a situation of this kind. Hence the literature of social conflict throws little light on the actual operation of social pressures. It deals rather with the nature and development of opposing interests, the necessity and rationale of social struggle and the functions and results of conflict in general. It considers social conflict as analogous to military conflict, particularly as the broad clash of great organized collectivities on an economic or racial front. It treats rather sparingly the tactics of these struggles, much more their general strategy. But social pressures are concerned mainly with tactics. The pluralist as distinct from the Marxist point of view conceives of society as diversified into manifold and relatively autonomous organized groups. It offers therefore a more likely approach to the study of social pressures. But most of the writers of this school have so far been more interested in the larger questions of the trend toward a pluralistic social structure, of the relation of voluntary associations to the state and of the reconstruction of society based on the explicit recognition of group autonomies.

[1934]

Sovereignty and Political Obligation

21 ANTIGONE: AN ANCIENT TALE RETOLD

Ever since human beings set up organizations they have been beset by the problem of clashing loyalties. In early times the conflict arose chiefly between the demand of the state and the contrary demand of the faith or of the kin. Already there were two or more loyalties, and sometimes they could not be reconciled. Aristotle, who probed into so many things, remarked that it was perhaps not the same thing to be a good *man* and to be a good *citizen*. But long before Aristotle the conflict had stimulated the poet philosophers of Greece. It was a favorite theme of Greek tragedy—indeed it is the chief theme of all the great tragedies of all peoples. The Greeks took the theme from the heroic legends in which it first found expression. In the starkest form it animates the tragedy of Orestes and the tragedy of Oedipus. But it was the burden of many another tale, and one of these is the subject of our discussion here.

Think over the great dramas of all times, and you will find that they concentrate on the issue of clashing loyalties. Begin with what is perhaps the greatest of all plays, Hamlet, and the same theme provokes the poet to his profoundest reflections. The hero, the vacillating prince, is bidden by the insistent and horror-fed demands of a prime loyalty to do an act that violates his whole attachment to the ordered ways of life. He shrinks but cannot evade the choice, and his shrinking only brings in the end a greater cumulation of tragedy.

From these old themes I choose the story of Antigone, because it has been discussed by various philosophers some of whom have declared that Antigone chose aright, and others of whom have said she made the wrong choice, while one philosopher, with his usual Olympic indifference to the conditions under which men must live and act, proclaimed that she was both wrong and right![1] But the reader must decide for himself after he has heard the story.

Antigone is the daughter of Oedipus, King of Thebes, most renowned of all tragic figures. When Oedipus is gone, his two sons take over Thebes as rulers, but one of them drives out the other and becomes the sole ruler of the city. One was named Eteocles, and the other Polynices. Eteocles drove out his brother from greed of power.

Polynices, now exiled, gets together an alien army at the city of Argos. This army invades the home city of Thebes. The enemy is outside the walls. There is much hand-to-hand conflict, as was common in the old Greek warfare, and in this conflict the two brothers meet and kill one another. Thereupon another member of the family, whose name is Creon, takes command. The besiegers are defeated; the city is again safe and free.

The first thing that Creon, the new king, does is to issue an edict. This edict provides for an honorable burial for the hero, Eteocles, and it brings down denunciation and disgrace upon the other brother, the traitor. The body of the invader lies outside the walls of the city and the king proclaims that it must not be given the customary burial rites. It must lie outside the walls for the birds and beasts. The traitor must be dishonored in every way possible and Creon vows dire punishment on anyone who disobeys his edict.

Here is where Antigone enters. Antigone not only is the sister of the "traitor" who lies outside the walls, she is also the niece of King Creon. She feels the strong pull of the kin-bond because, according to the rites of their religion, the nearest of kin must pay burial dues to the dead. It is a most sacred obligation. It is sacred in two senses—first, because it is the law of the kin, and, second, because it is for her the law of God.

Antigone is forbidden by her king to perform this sacred function, these last rites. What shall she do? Shall she obey her king or shall she obey her religion and be true to her kin? She decides that the sacred obligation to the kin comes first. She goes outside the walls and sprinkles a handful

---

1.   Hegel, in his *Philosophy of Religion.*

of dust on the body. That is all that is necessary. It is a symbolic thing. The sprinkling of dust suffices.

She is discovered. She is brought before the king. The king is incensed. In his fury he condemns her to a terrible death. She pleads with him, but he declares that to show any sympathy, any mercy, any consideration for a traitor, is to destroy the very foundations of all law and order. It is to destroy the state. The first duty of every citizen is to insure that law abides.

If one in any way condones treason, then he is shaking the very edifice on which everything is built. Such is the argument of the king. Antigone is led away. Presently the lover of Antigone appears. To make things still more perplexed in this tangle of clashing loyalties, he is the son of King Creon. He, very soberly, very quietly, and very earnestly, pleads again with the king. He puts before the king what his duty is to religion, to his gods, and what will happen if he flouts the divine command.

However, the king again asserts his position. He, above all, must uphold the law. He will never permit anyone who has been a traitor to escape the penalty. So, the lover, the son of the king and the lover of Antigone, at last yields, goes out with the intent that he will not survive his beloved one. But he does not move the king.

Antigone is condemned to be immured in a rocky prison to die a slow, lingering death there. She is led away. The chorus of the play, composed of Theban elders, now sings a song of the triumph of love. It begins:

O Love, unconquered in battle, you make havoc of possessions, you keep your vigil on the soft cheek of a maiden; none can escape you, neither the immortal gods nor man whose life is for a day. And he whom you visit is beside himself.

Then, in the play, at the last moment, the ancient prophet of the people comes before the king. He is terribly concerned. Dreadful signs are happening. The omens are threatening. All things portend catastrophes for Thebes, and it is because the king has flouted the will of the gods.

To this last argument the king very reluctantly and finally yields. He decides that perhaps he went too far. So, to avert this doom, he will go and see that the slain traitor is given at least some kind of burial. He dare not disobey the manifested will of the gods; he will go and liberate Antigone, to avoid the wrath of Heaven.

He arrives at the rocky tomb where Antigone is imprisoned. Antigone, faced with the prospect of this long, lingering death, sealed up in these walls, has taken her veil and hanged herself. The king and his company come and witness the scene. In the company is Antigone's lover and the young man in madness rushes at the king, threatening him. The king escapes and then the lover kills himself with the sword with which he threatened the king.

There the play ends. But the last word, spoken as usual by the chorus, is as follows: "Wisdom is the greatest of things and reverence to the gods should be inviolate."

The story of Antigone is one that philosophers have discussed right through from the time of Plato to the present. They have taken different positions concerning whether Antigone did right or wrong. Should she have chosen that way? Should she not?

Antigone, as everybody admits, was faced with a terrible decision whichever way she chose. Some read one lesson in the play as presented by Sophocles; some another. The king, some say, was wrong because he overstepped the divine law. In his desire for revenge, he proceeded too far and paid no attention to the sanctities or the obligations of kinship. Antigone, some say, was wrong because she was not in the position of king and she as a citizen was bound to obey. Others point out that the whole tenor of the play is to arouse our feelings in favor of Antigone. And the words with which it closed, "reverence to the gods should be inviolate," some understand to mean that the playwright accepted the argument of Antigone.

Finally, there is the position of Hegel that "In the light of eternal justice, Antigone was both right and wrong." And so was Creon.

May I be excused if I find this ineffable impartiality very unpleasant—and not least when the philosopher in question professes to speak "in the light of eternal justice."

Commentators are still arguing the ancient question. The *Political Science Quarterly* some time back contained two articles by John Dickinson on the theory of sovereignty, in one of which the author condemned Antigone for making the wrong decision. He contrasted what he called the "primitive attitude" of Antigone with the "mature comprehension" of Socrates.[2]

Socrates had been in what looked like a somewhat similar position. But it really was different. Socrates was condemned to death, unjustly as he believed, and as everybody who knew him believed. When at the last moment some of his friends contrived to visit him in prison and provide him with means of escape, so that the way was open for him to escape from Athens, Socrates refused to move. He said, "No. How can I? Here I am now an old man. I have lived in this city all my life, and the laws of this city have established all my ways. Without them none of us could live. These laws, these codes under which we live, I have accepted them

2. John Dickinson, "A Working Theory of Sovereignty," *Political Science Quarterly*, XLII (1927), 424–548; XLIII (1928), 32–63.

throughout my life. They brought me into the world. They educated me. I owe everything to them. We cannot say in turn, if they dishonor us, if they even at times treat us as we know we should not be treated, even if they condemn us to death, we have no right to turn back and say, 'In return we will violate you.' They have a greater claim on us than we have on them."

So Plato put the case in the name of Socrates. I am not at all sure that Socrates himself had these ideas, but Plato wrote the dialogue called *Crito* in which he represented Socrates as arguing thus against his friends. John Dickinson, accordingly, contrasts the behavior of Socrates who refused to disobey the law even to save his life, even though he was falsely condemned, with the attitude of Antigone who felt that she could take it to her own conscience to say whether or not she should obey.

Dickinson used the same argument that King Creon used—the law is first and paramount. If we break the law deliberately, if we deliberately defy it, then we are voting for the dissolution of society, as it were. We are then denying the foundations on which all our order, all our stability, all our peace, all the conditions under which we live, everything we have, depend.

There is, however, some confusion in this argument. More than one kind of law is necessary to hold a society together. Custom, too, is a bond of society, and surely the moral law is also, and the faith by which men live, and the conscience that animates all loyalties. What we call "the law of the land" would not be very strong if it were not also for custom, and custom would not be strong unless there was also a thing called conscience. There are many ties that bind men, not one alone. The legal code is a very essential, a primary one, but it is not the only one. It is not the only foundation of social order. As Dickinson himself put it elsewhere, there is a "law behind law." The problem of Antigone is one we all have, in our own way, to meet. We are not in the position of a king or a princess, or somebody else who has to make this decision in high places, but every one of us sometime or other must choose between conflicting values and conflicting codes.

For example, if you are a doctor, you have sometimes to decide which of two loyalties you should obey. If you are a lawyer, it comes to you in another form; if you are a clergyman it comes in yet another form. Everyone, according to his responsibilities and his relationships, must at some moment choose which code to obey and which to violate.

I remember I was once discussing the political doctrine of Machiavelli with a class of students. Machiavelli, as you know, shocked the world, because he said that rulers should not try to be ethical if it did not pay them; their first duty was to keep things secure and if they had to go against humanity and cheat and deceive and break their promises, if that were the only way they could make the state secure, then they should do just that.

So I asked first what was to be said in favor of Machiavelli. To bring home the point I raised the question about what they, the members of this group, would do under certain conditions. Would they be willing to tell a lie deliberately, and justify it? Was it ever *right* to tell a lie? That was the issue — whether it was right.

I took various hypothetical cases, after which the minority who had said "no," yielded — all but one member. I was not trying to convert them to anything. I was trying to find out what they really thought and I took certain cases, including one that concerned a doctor and his patient.

When I finished, one student alone took the complete negative — "No, it is never right." I did not seek to discredit the viewpoint anyone really had. I was about to leave the matter there when one of my students said, "May I tell a personal story?" This was his story. "I was born in Vienna. When I was thirteen years old, my father was very ill and the doctor was called in. I saw the doctor as he left my father's room and I said to him, 'How is he?' He answered, 'Your father does not have long to live.' I said, 'Doctor, please do not tell that to my mother, I beg you!' The doctor replied: 'We had better prepare her for it. I shall tell her the truth.'

"That was seventeen years ago," the student said, "and my mother died in a week of the shock. My father is still alive." I did not draw any moral. I do not know what the moral is, but you see now the kind of problems we are bound to face, problems where the codes clash, problems where we have to choose between loyalties, problems where we have to get beyond the rules to our final values.

[1952]

SOVEREIGNTY AND MORALITY

[*In April*, 1917, *the* New Republic *carried an article by Walter Lippmann in which, among other things, he attacked the notion of a political monism that equates citizenship in a democratic state with a single undivided allegiance.*[3] *This elicited a letter from Alfred E. Zimmern condemning* "*the insidious syndicalism to which Mr. Lippmann seems in danger of falling a victim*" *and reaffirming the age-old doctrine that* "*political allegiance takes precedence* [over] *all others because it embraces the common concerns of the whole community.*" *The state, Mr. Zimmern argued, must insist upon* "*the undivided loyalty of its citizens*"; *otherwise,* "*the sense of civic obligation and responsibility*" *is certain to be*

3. Walter Lippmann, "A Clue," *New Republic*, X (April 14, 1917), 316–317.

weakened and social stability impaired.[4] *To this the editors of the* New Republic *replied that Mr. Zimmern had confused the "simple fact that the state had ceased to enjoy possession of the exclusive loyalties of men" with his normative judgment that this ought not to be so, and went on to itemize seven points that, in their judgment, destroyed Mr. Zimmern's argument.*[5] *MacIver's contribution to this controversy follows.*]

No question of principle has more vital consequences than that on which Mr. Zimmern and Mr. Lippmann have joined issue in your pages. It is therefore of the utmost importance that confusion in the formulation of this issue should be avoided. This, I think, Mr. Zimmern fails to do, and your otherwise conclusive note on his letter seems to me not to penetrate the heart of his failure. Mr. Zimmern quotes with approval, as "sound" thought, this passage from Dr. Troeltsch: "Now, therefore, there abide these three, individual morality, state morality, and cosmopolitan morality, *but the greatest and most important of these at the present time is state morality.*" So far from being sound, this statement involves the elementary confusion of morality with allegiance. The distinction is clear if we remember that scarcely a law passes of which some minority does not disapprove. Sometimes, not infrequently, the disapproval takes on a consciously ethical character, *i.e.,* the objectors feel that the welfare of the whole is hindered and not furthered by the law. Yet rarely do they refuse obedience, and one motive to their obedience is the conviction, which all good citizens share, that it is right, save under rare conditions, to obey laws of which they disapprove. In a word, the state in passing the law does not express their morality, but it retains their allegiance. They think it for the welfare of the whole that they should so obey. If at the same time they strive for the repeal of the law they exhibit very simply morality and allegiance. On the other hand there are cases where men think it wrong to obey, where allegiance is for them immoral. Is this the condition where the two kinds of morality, individual morality and state morality, stand opposed? How can it be, when the law is the expression, or at least the revelation, of the morality of those, whether majority or merely politically dominant part, of the members of the state who made it? In other words, the ethical opposition is at most between the morality of the many (or, it may be, the politically superior) and the morality of the few (or the politically inferior)? I say "at most," because the difference may arise merely from the ignorance on either

4. Alfred E. Zimmern, "Supremacy of the State," *New Republic,* XII (September 15, 1917), 191–192.

5. *Ibid.,* pp. 192–193. See also the comments of Herbert Croly in that same issue, pp. 179–183.

side of the conditions under which the other is acting. Always there is only one kind of morality, and always it is individual morality. This Mr. Zimmern admits, inconsequently, when he says, "The claim of the individual conscience is, of course, indefeasible."

If so, what is the meaning of this much asserted claim of the supremacy of state morality over individual morality? It might mean that men *ought* always to regard the will of the state (which in fact becomes the will of the government) as expressing or coinciding with the moral law. This was in fact the morality of primitive men and peoples, and it is still accepted by those who, consciously or not, find a divine sanction behind the political fiat. Now, for those who accept it, this attitude is itself the expression of an elementary form of individual morality. It is the answer of men's consciences at a particular stage of social evolution. But very few men today would subscribe to such a view. For the civilized peoples it belongs to a world they have outgrown. This cannot be what Dr. Troeltsch and Mr. Zimmern mean by the supremacy of state morality. What then can they mean by it? What alternative remains except the loose meaning that the will of the state, however determined, *ought* always to be obeyed, or that individual morality is identified with obedience to law, which in turn is understood as "state morality"? There is certainly a morality which opposes this doctrine, and if history can vindicate anything, it must surely have vindicated, perhaps even now is vindicating, this opposing morality.

The historical question is far too great to be opened here, but one comment may be permissible. The claim of state supremacy, understood as above, has often been successfully opposed. But it is never defeated by the opposition of unorganized individuals, only by individuals organized into another association alongside or within the state—until the present age usually a church. But this in turn should not be interpreted as revealing an opposition between group or associational morality and state morality. It never was a clear conflict of church and state—any more than it has become, for example, a clear conflict between trade union and state—as two distinct ethical unities with opposing moralities. The churchman was also a citizen of the state. Thus the division was always a division *within* the state, and generally at the same time a division within the church. This, I think, is generally overlooked, for example by Mr. Laski in his admirable *Studies in the Problem of Sovereignty*. There is no plurality of ethical Leviathans, as he seems to imply. Take for example the conflict "between church and state" which he first examines, that which issued in the disruption of the Free Church of Scotland. Why *disruption?* Because the conflict of principles involved was one which struck home to the consciences of men who were both citizens and churchmen, and to some the one claim was paramount, to some the other. When the decision was taken, they still remained both citizens and churchmen, but a particular church was disrupted in the process.

If it were once clear that morality is always an individual thing (however shaped by social influences) we would be rid of many confusions. We could no longer set up as distinct and opposing ultimate moral types the "moralities" of states, of economic and other groupings within and across states, of churches, and of that greater international unity which is in process of birth as the reaction of men's consciences everywhere to the utterly intolerable evils of our age of absolute states.

[1917]

The Social and Political Ideas
of Bertrand Russell

22   I shall not attempt to discuss all the ideas of Bertrand Russell. He has fetched too wide a compass, as man and as author. What shall we make of a man who has been a don of Trinity College, Cambridge, and also professor of philosophy in the Government University of Peking, who is the son of a viscount and grandson of an earl and is also a socialist and a pacifist, who is a Fellow of the Royal Society and has been an inmate of an English jail? What shall we make of an author who combines the higher mathematics with modernist ethics and realistic metaphysics with economic and social theorems, who has written works on China and Russia and the industrial civilization of Europe and America, and who has thrown in for good measure certain disquisitions on religion and psychology? We cannot serve him up whole at a single critical banquet—at any rate the present writer is unequal to that Aristotelian task. So we will leave aside all of the mathematics and most of the metaphysics, and bestow attention on the social ideas of our author. We will descend with our author into the cave where the prisoners of time fight about the shadows of the eternal. For Russell has followed the prescription of that ancient philosopher who was also a socialist, and who declared that in the ideal state the philosophers must leave the upper realm of ideas, and must descend "to the general underground abode and get the habit of seeing in the dark." Plato maintained that they would understand things down below far better than the native inhabitants, but there are others who doubt this reasoning and declare that the philosophers stumble helplessly in the world of common affairs, whether it is that their eyes are unaccustomed to the gloom or perhaps for other reasons of a less flattering kind.

But I am not so much concerned with the question whether our philosopher is right or wrong. I shall endeavor to resist the strong temptation to evaluate his social theories, to criticize some and vindicate others. What I regard as more appropriate to this occasion is the study of a remarkable personality, as it has responded to the conditions of the strange age in which we live, as it has revealed itself in a series of most unusual literary works. I shall seek to show the relation between the mind of a man and his message. Whether the message comes winged to us or unwinged, we may at least understand the manner of mind whence it proceeds.

Russell's first pronouncement on a social question occurred in 1896, when at the age of twenty-four he delivered and published a series of lectures on German social democracy. He was then a Fellow of Trinity College, Cambridge, devoted mainly to mathematical studies. The excursus was symptomatic of the deep and sympathetic interest in new social movements which Russell has always combined with a love for abstract thought. The book does not reveal the position which Russell was later to reach. It treats the social democrats of Germany objectively and critically, without taking their side of the struggle, except in so far as he pleads that friendliness to the working classes on the part of the rulers of Germany is the "great and pressing necessity for Germany's welfare." But he deprecates the class-consciousness of the socialists no less than the class-consciousness of their rulers. His hope is for the mitigation of both extremes and a peaceful development toward moderate democracy. No doubt Russell's acquaintance with the struggles of the social democrats made a deep impression upon his mind, but it was only in later years that he found his own characteristic attitude toward these social problems.

From Marx and Bebel our author returned to the higher mathematics, and for many years made no further descents into the cave. Mathematics was for him a refuge from the disillusionment which the experience of life produced on a mind acutely responsive to the idea of perfection, and acutely sensitive to the sufferings of mankind. In an essay on "The Study of Mathematics," written in 1902, the author appears as the passionate spectator, *sub specia aeternilitis*, of this underworld of life. In it we read:

Mathematics, rightly viewed, possesses not only truth, but supreme beauty—a beauty cold and austere, like that of sculpture, without appeal to any part of our weaker nature, without the gorgeous trappings of painting or music, yet sublimely pure, and capable of a stern perfection such as only the greatest art can show. The true spirit of delight, the exaltation, the sense of being more than man, which is the touchstone of the highest excellence, is to be found in mathematics as surely as in poetry. What is best in mathematics deserves not merely to be learnt as a task, but to be assimilated as a part of daily thought, and brought again and again before the mind with ever-renewed encouragement. Real life is, to most men, a long second-best, a perpetual compromise between the ideal and the possible; but the world of pure reason knows no compromise, no practical limitations, no barrier to the creative activity embodying in splendid edifices the passionate aspiration after the perfect from which all great work springs. Remote from human passions, remote even from the pitiful facts of nature, the generations have gradually created an ordered cosmos, where pure thought can dwell as in its natural home, and where one, at least, of our nobler impulses can escape from the dreary exile of the actual world.

Another essay of the same year, entitled *A Free Man's Worship*, attains the very peak of this austere philosophy. Russell has written nothing that vibrates so tensely with the poignant contrast between human aspiration and human fate. It is Stoic in its attitude, with the resolution but not the calmness of the Stoic, with the resignation but not the consolation that the Stoic found. For nature itself is hostile to man, hostile to his dreams and to his hopes, and all that man prizes he barely holds through a brief hour of struggle until the unresting forces that lie without snatch it again from his hands. The free man is he who scorns the comfort of false beliefs, who faces without entreaty or submission a ruthless universe, who neither erects a vain God in the image of his ideals nor surrenders these ideals because the cosmos refuses to enshrine them.

Amid such a world [he says], if anywhere, our ideals henceforward must find a home. That Man is the product of causes which had no prevision of the end they were achieving; that his origin, his growth, his hopes and fears, his loves and his beliefs, are but the outcome of accidental collocations of atoms; that no fire, no heroism, no intensity of thought and feeling, can preserve an individual life beyond the grave; that all the labors of the ages, all the devotion, all the inspiration, all the noonday brightness of human genius, are destined to extinction in the vast death of the solar system, and that the whole temple of Man's achievement must inevitably be buried beneath the debris of a universe in ruins—all these things, if not quite beyond dispute, are yet so nearly certain, that no philosophy which rejects them can hope to stand. Only within the scaffolding of these truths, only on the firm foundation of unyielding despair, can the soul's habitation henceforth be safely built.

In such a world man is tempted to worship Power, to placate it, to name it good. Such was the creed of Carlyle and of Nietzsche, and of the comforters of Job. But power is largely evil, and no true object of worship. Yet it is vain to rebel against it, like Prometheus. The Christian attitude of resignation is the wiser. Freedom lies in the submission of our desires, but never of our thoughts. Through this gate of renunciation we pass to "the daylight of wisdom, by whose radiance a new insight, a new joy, a new tenderness, shine forth to gladden the pilgrim's heart."

When [he continues], without the bitterness of impotent rebellion, we have learnt both to resign ourselves to the outward rule of Fate and to recognize that the non-human world is unworthy of our worship, it becomes possible at last so to transform and refashion the unconscious universe, so to transmute it in the crucible of imagination, that a new image of shining gold replaces the old idol of clay. In all the multiform facts of the world—in the visual shapes of trees and mountains and clouds, in the events of the life of man, even in the very omnipotence of Death—the insight of creative idealism can find the reflection of a beauty which its own thoughts first made. In this way mind asserts its subtle mastery over the thoughtless forces of Nature. The more evil the material with which it deals, the more thwarting to untrained desire, the greater is its achievement in inducing the reluctant rock to yield up its hidden treasures, the prouder its victory in compelling the opposing forces to swell the pageant of its triumph. Of all the arts, Tragedy is the proudest, the most triumphant; for it builds its shining citadel in the very center of the enemy's country, on the very summit of his highest mountain; from its impregnable watchtowers, his camps and arsenals, his columns and forts, are all revealed; within its walls the free life continues, while the legions of Death and Pain and Despair, and all the servile captains of tyrant Fate, afford the burghers of that dauntless city new spectacles of beauty. Happy those sacred ramparts, thrice happy the dwellers on that all-seeing eminence. Honor to those brave warriors who, through countless ages of warfare, have preserved for us the priceless heritage of liberty, and have kept undefiled by sacrilegious invaders the home of the unsubdued.

So we are led to a conclusion somber but not unrelieved. In fact there is in it a note of that Promethean defiance which the author has just deprecated.

> Brief and powerless is Man's life; on him and all his race the slow, sure doom falls pitiless and dark. Blind to good and evil, reckless of destruction, omnipotent matter rolls on its relentless way; for Man, condemned today to lose his dearest, tomorrow himself to pass through the gate of darkness, it remains only to cherish, ere yet the blow falls, the lofty thoughts that ennoble his little day; disdaining the coward terrors of the slave of Fate, to worship at the shrine that his own hands have built; undismayed by the empire of chance, to preserve a mind free from the wanton tyranny that rules his outward life; proudly defiant of the irresistible forces that tolerate, for a moment, his knowledge and his condemnation, to sustain alone, a weary but unyielding Atlas, the world that his own ideals have fashioned despite the trampling march of unconscious power.

I have quoted these extracts from this remarkable essay, partly because it expresses most adequately that passionate and sensitive spirit, always critical and always searching, in which Russell confronts the facts of existence, partly also because it represents a milestone in the progress of his thought. For in certain respects Russell is an elusive and unstable thinker. His constructive vision is always dissolving into new forms. What holds fast is his sense of ultimate good and evil. What is good is the free creative spirit. Life is creation, and life is good, and its great enemy, the essential evil in the world, is the power that wars against creation, all that crushes and restricts, all that dominates and regiments, the blind unreasoning will that exults in Force. In the *Free Man's Worship*, Russell found that evil thing in the cosmos itself, whose might stood arrayed against the hopes and joys of men. It reminds one of the spirit which animates *Tess* and *Jude the Obscure*. But this evil power takes on a new character in the later writings of Russell. It is conceived as no longer without, but within, humanity. The cosmos is no longer the villain of the tragedy of which man is the suffering hero. Now the evil thing is made by man or, rather, by men. It is the institutional system within which society is bound, and especially the forms of militarism and capitalism. And behind the forms there lurks the evil in the nature of man. The fatalism goes, though the conviction of good and evil abides. Man comes to play a double part, at once the hero and the villain of a tragedy that is peculiarly his own.

The precipitate which effected this change of disposition was the

First World War. In the years between the *Free Man's Worship* and the outbreak of the war Russell was devoted mainly to philosophy. He became a leader of the so-called neo-realists. He was engaged in elaborating theories of perception, enquiries into the nature of our knowledge of the external world, and in such congenial tasks as the refutation of the flimsy anthropomorphism of the pragmatists. These happier activities were rudely broken by the war. Russell was no Hegel who could calmly pursue his disquisition on the Absolute while the guns were thundering outside his city. The war not only changed the current of his life, it changed his faith and his hope. "To me," he says, "the chief thing to be learnt through the war has been a certain view of the springs of human action, what they are, and what we may legitimately hope that they may become." His conclusions appeared in the volume *Principles of Social Reconstruction*, published in America under the title *Why Men Fight*. It is the most stimulating and optimistic of Russell's works. What is evil in the world, what causes war and hatred and the waste of power, is not human nature itself; it is the suppression and distortion of human nature through cramping necessities and social oppressions. It is the frustration of the entire principle of growth, which, being liberated, leads mankind to fulfillment with the same urgency as trees seek the light. "In the modern world, the principle of growth in most men and women is hampered by institutions inherited from an earlier age." Our impulses are not harmonized with our desires. The primitive hunter, for example, had an impulse to hunt, which was in harmony with his desire for food. The modern artisan has the same desire, but he has no impulse toward the work whose wages provide him with food. Russell, who must always have his Devil because he is so impressed with the evil and the frustration of the world, now discovers him in outgrown institutions. But this devil, unlike the cosmos, can be overthrown, and Russell, against the cruel background of the war, advances with burning hope to the assault.

Power, the constant enemy, now takes the embodiment of Authority and Tradition. "All institutions," he declares, "if they are not to hamper individual growth, must be based as far as possible upon voluntary combination, rather than the force of the law or the traditional authority of the holders of power. None of our institutions can survive the application of this principle without great and fundamental changes; but these changes are imperatively necessary if the world is to be withheld from dissolving into hard separate units each at war with all the others." The fortress of authority is the state, and Russell proceeds to show "how great, how unnecessary, how harmful, many of its powers are, and how enormously they might be diminished without loss of that which is useful in its activity." He admits that the state is indeed necessary, and that it renders an essential service by substituting law for force and order for chaos. But it is obsessed by the ideals of power, and because it nourishes war and the fear of war it causes a vast amount of misery. The world is controlled by this false spirit, but it can be exorcised, and the task of all true thinkers is to reveal its falsehood, believing that truth, if joined to courage, will at length prevail. We must teach men that the fulfillment of their desires, and of those unguided impulses whose roots are deeper than desire, depends on the control of power. We must teach them that in order to live well they must have good relations with their fellowmen, and that the enemy of good relations is repressive or coercive power.

All our present institutions, Russell maintains, are infected with the same disease. Our property institutions encourage the acquisitive desires, and cramp the constructive and artistic impulses. They stimulate the love of money, and that love kills the springs of the more sensitive love of a hundred finer things. The fruits of the spirit are blasted by the winds of power. Take education. We want to control the young minds entrusted to our care, we want to produce belief rather than thought, and uniformity rather than free enquiry, so that on the subjects that really count the child is met "with dogma or stony silence." We are afraid of thought, for fear always rides with power. On this subject Russell writes with glowing fervor which illuminates the protestant depths of his heart.

> Men fear thought as they fear nothing else on earth—more than ruin, more even than death. Thought is subservient and revolutionary, destructive and terrible; thought is merciless to privilege, established institutions, and comfortable habits; thought is anarchic and lawless, indifferent to authority, careless of the well-tried wisdom of the ages. Thought looks into the pit of hell and is not afraid. It sees man, a feeble speck, surrounded by unfathomable depths of silence; yet it bears itself proudly, as unmoved as if it were lord of the universe. Thought is great and swift and free, the light of the world, and the chief glory of man.
>
> But if thought is to become the possession of many, not the privilege of the few, we must have done with fear. It is fear that holds men back—fear lest their cherished beliefs should prove delusions, fear lest the institutions by which they live should prove harmful, fear lest they themselves should prove less worthy of respect than they have supposed themselves to be. "Should the workingman think freely about property? Then what will become of us, the rich? Should young men and young women think freely about sex? Then what will become of morality? Should soldiers think freely about war? Then what will become of military discipline? Away with thought! Back into the shades of prejudice, lest property, morals,

and war should be endangered! Better men should be stupid, slothful, and oppressive than that their thoughts should be free. For if their thoughts were free they might not think as we do. And at all costs this disaster must be averted." So the opponents of thought argue in the unconscious depths of their souls. And so they act in their churches, their schools, and their universities.

All these fears are foolish or worse. Beyond our fears lie the truths which alone can save us. If we can learn to substitute trust for fear, trust in life, trust in humanity, a new age will be born, a truer religion, a finer morality, a better society. Before our eyes will dawn the shining vision of the future, and with the triumph of thought the springs of peace and joy will be unsealed.

So the brief sun of hope shone in our author's sky before the clouds of new disillusionment darkened it again. We must remember that the work from which we have quoted was written in the earlier days of the war, when the sudden tragedy of civilization made new hope a necessity of life. But in Russell the vision of the future was not the projection of a faith which has first come to terms with the realities of the present. With his strong ethical preoccupation Russell had now found the source of evil in outworn institutions, which stood in strange contrast with the innate spirit of man. So long as he was merely critical of an existing order he was able to maintain this contrast. But when he turned to consider alternative institutions, the uncertainty of his position revealed itself. If the main fault lay with our institutions, then a new set of institutions would deliver mankind. But would it happen so? A doubt falls across the page whenever Russell raises this question.

We observe this doubt in our author's treatment of socialism. Russell calls himself a socialist, but he has always been a most uncomfortable one for all true believers. To begin with, he deprecates any elaborate system of organization, and regards the existing power of the state as vastly excessive. And every now and again he makes some disconcerting utterance, disconcerting to any believer in his own theory of institutions, as when he says, for example, that "in a socialist community it is to be feared that instead of an increase of self-direction there would only be an increase of mutual interference." (*Principles of Social Reconstruction*, Chap. IV.) And he makes incidental remarks concerning human motives and desires which suggest that pride and envy and malice and the love of power and a whole array of vices are inbred in humanity. But he cannot run with the theological hare of original sin and hunt with the socialist hound of economic determinism. If the blame lies so entirely with institutions, he must exonerate human nature, and if he deplores the vices of men he must at least in large part acquit institutions of the responsibility for the evils of the world. There is a hidden uncertainty in Russell's ethical thought which disturbs the discerning and sympathetic reader.

The uncertainty comes to light in the works which followed the *Principles*, especially in *Roads to Freedom* and *Prospects of Industrial Civilization*. In these works Russell sets out to examine the alternative institutions which might liberate humanity from the prison of the past. *Roads to Freedom* was written in the latter days of the war, when the sense of its wastefulness had become, to a mind like Russell's, a nightmare, when the first revulsive hopes of a new world had grown weary in the long days of attrition, and when the author himself had the peculiarly bitter experience of a complete alienation from the prevailing spirit of his countrymen, culminating soon after the book was written, in a period of imprisonment. In this time of almost unendurable stress Russell turned to the systems which promised a way out from the evils and sufferings that men brought upon each other. The roads that promised freedom were socialism, anarchism (in its proper philosophical sense), and syndicalism. One may observe in passing that the American publishers, with that intellectual timidity which characterizes this continent, changed the title to *Proposed Roads to Freedom*. This is in fact all that these roads are to Russell, but in America even a title is sufficient *epater les bourgeois*.

The first part of the book consists in a descriptive account of the systems in question. It is in the second part that the particular attitude of the author is revealed, and in it we find in a marked degree that uncertainty which is only suggested in the *Principles of Social Reconstruction*. For while Russell roundly declares that the abolition of private ownership of land and capital is a necessary step toward peace among men and between nations, the net effect of his criticism is to weaken the belief which his earlier work instilled, that men can by institutional change achieve salvation. There are in fact two unreconciled strains in Russell's thought. He would reorganize the whole social structure, and yet he feels that all organization is restrictive and dangerous to the spirit of man. "All law and government is in itself to some degree an evil," he declares. Some law and government is a necessary evil, and therefore he cannot accept anarchism. But much government is an unnecessary evil, and so he is at odds with socialism. "State socialists argue as if there would be no danger to liberty in a state not based on capitalism. This seems to me an entire delusion. Given an official caste, however selected, there are bound to be a sect of men whose instincts will drive them towards tyranny." And even of guild socialism, to which he is more attracted, he expresses the fear that if the Guild Congress were all-powerful over the questions of economic production, "the evils now connected with the omnipotence of the state would soon reappear." Moreover, the evils of which he is so conscious now present themselves to him as lying deeper than institutions, as rooted in human nature itself. In speaking of the socialist view that capitalism is the source of war, he remarks: "The outlook of both socialists and anarchists seems to me, in this respect as in some others, to be unduly divorced from the fundamental instincts of human nature. . . . Man is naturally competitive, acquisitive, and, in a greater or less degree, pugnacious." So the roads to freedom may lead instead, directly or indirectly, to tyranny. In his constant search for the devil, Russell turned from the cosmos to outworn institutions, and from institutions he now seems to be turning to the heart of man, to something that looks very like what the theologians call "original sin." For the attainment of a world full of happiness, he now tells us "the obstacles imposed by inanimate nature are not insuperable. The real obstacles lie in the heart of man." And yet, so perplexing is our author, he remarks in this same volume, speaking of the proper social attitude toward crime, that "the first thing to recognize is that the whole conception of guilt or sin should be utterly swept away." But the spirit of *Erewhon* scarcely befits a world so full of the vision of evil.

The fact is that Russell is far more at home in the realm of ideals than on the difficult and doubtful roads whose signposts proclaim that they lead thither. On the roads he stumbles and gropes, and he is safe only when he takes the wings of thought and returns to his heights. There alone is he happy, and there his utterance is clear and strong. No one can resist the attraction of his picture of the world that might be, no matter how he doubts his companion picture of the world that is or his route map of the *terra incognita* that lies between. "The world that we must seek is a world in which the creative spirit is alive, in which life is an adventure full of joy and hope, based rather upon the impulse to construct than upon the desire to retain what we possess or to seize what is possessed by others. It must be a world in which affection has free play, in which love is purged of the instinct for domination, in which cruelty and envy have been dispelled by happiness and the unfettered development of all the instincts that build up life and fill it with mental delights."

"Such a world," he adds, "is possible; it waits only for men to wish to create it." Yes, that's the rub. Not the cosmos now, not principalities and powers, not authority and tradition, but just the will of men. The goal is clear in his sight, and the starting-point is clear. But the building of the road between them—there is the age-long task. He who thinks it possible is brave, but he who thinks it simple is doomed to disillusionment and final despair.

The roadway from the world that is to the world that might be is the perpetual problem of the ethical mind, and from now on it obsessed the mind of Russell. In his discontentment with the results of Western civilization he made eager pilgrimage to Russia. There too disappointment awaited him. The new order was founded, even more than the old one, on authority and usurpation. Its idealism was consumed from within by the fierce necessities of power. Perhaps, thought Russell, it is the whole industrial world that is on a wrong foundation. The Bolshevik commissary is but the revolutionary model of the American trust magnate. So the pilgrim pursued his quest to China. Here was a land of ancient civilization, almost untouched by the mechanizing process of industrialism, a land where contentment walked hand in hand with frugality, a land of quiet dignity and serener dreams. But though Russell found much to admire in Chinese life, he also found much to question. In China he had sought a solution and, as everywhere else, he found a problem instead. Perhaps he was seeking too much. Perhaps he did not sufficiently realize that ideals too are on the move, and must always far outstrip the heavy march of actualities. Perhaps he was asking for "better bread than can be made from wheat," which is indeed permissible if one is patiently cultivating wheat, but foolish if one thereby despises bread.

As by-products of these investigations there appeared two volumes, *The Practice and Theory of Bolshevism* and *The Problem of China*. They prepared the way for the latest of Russell's attempts at a social synthesis, *The Prospects of Industrial Civilization*. Before we turn to the latter, we shall briefly characterize the by-products.

Russell went to Russia a theoretical believer in communism. He returned with a profound distrust of the practice of it, though still rather as one who regarded the practitioners as having betrayed the faith. This attitude produces here the same curious feeling of uncertainty in the reader which we discovered in some of Russell's earlier work. The author seems somehow to be living and moving "in worlds not realized." Is the faith sound and only the practice wrong? Is the system good while the authors of it are evil? At any rate, Russell admitted, it has failed, and he asks in some perplexity, why? His answer is as follows. The principle of comunism is good, but the world was not ready for it. The new world cannot be created until the opinions and feelings of ordinary people are prepared to receive it. The principle is good, but the men who realized it are fanatics who sought to impose it on the world, reckless of what they destroyed in the process, other good things, better things.

We are not here concerned with the critique of communism, but with our author's response to it. From this standpoint the most interesting thing is that Russell's faith in the efficacy of institutions as prime movers in human deliverance had again received a shock. If communism as well as capitalism was capable of holding men in bondage, if in fact it added material squalor to spiritual subjection, how can we look for deliverance through any institutions? After all, if we have living ideals, will they not evoke the institutions that are best adapted to them, and if we have false gods, will not our best institutions be turned to their service? "The ultimate source," says Russell, "of the whole train of evils lies in the Bolshevik outlook on life; in its dogmatism of hatred and its belief that human nature can be completely transformed by force." But still our author has not come to a final reckoning with institutions. He feels, I think rightly, that the doctrine of reaction which tempts the disheartened believer in institutions is also false; that it is too cheap a conclusion which tells us, for example, to preach brotherhood and pay no heed to the unemployed, or peace and never mind about the League of Nations; that the glib poet was wrong who said

> "For forms of government let fools contest,
> Whate'er is best administered is best."

There is a curious passage in the book before us which throws light on the author's baffled but unended search.

I confess [he says], that when the spectacle of present-day Russia forced me to disbelieve in Bolshevik methods, I was at first unable to see any way of curing the essential evils of capitalism. My first impulse was to abandon political thinking as a bad job, and to conclude that the strong and ruthless must always exploit the weaker and kindlier sections of the population. But this is not an attitude that can be long maintained by any vigorous and temperamentally hopeful person. Of course, if it were the truth, one would have to acquiesce. Some people believe that by living on sour milk one can achieve immortality. Such optimists are answered by a mere refutation; it is not necessary to go on and point out some other way of escaping death. Similarly an argument that Bolshevism will not lead to the millennium would remain valid even if it could be shown that the millennium cannot be reached by any other road. But the truth in social questions is not quite like truth in physiology or physics, since it depends upon men's beliefs. Optimism tends to verify itself by making people impatient of avoidable evils; while despair, on the other hand, makes the world as bad as it believes it to be. It is therefore imperative for those who do not believe in Bolshevism to put some other hope in its place.

The chapter from which this quotation comes is entitled "Mechanism and the Individual." The title suggests the new direction in which the thought of Russell turned from the *cul de sac* of the Russian Revolution. Might not the enemy—that evil thing which is the source of evils—be the control of organization over the human spirit, the subjection of the creative mind to its own creations? It is then no longer a simple question of capitalism versus communism. It is not a new evil, but an ancient one which takes Protean forms, and which must be fought anew in every age and under every system. It is not institutions themselves but the bondage of institutions. Institutions are necessary; the mechanism of life is necessary, but it is also perilous. Our civilization has conquered us, enslaved our minds. We must look, thought Russell, to the Far East, where mechanism does not reign, where institutions are more simple and more in harmony with the inner life, where the restless organizing spirit of the West no longer frets away the native joy of things.

So Russell turned his face to China. One feels, however, by this time that our author somewhat resembles the wanderer in Schubert's famous song, "Dort, wo du nicht bist, dort ist das Glück." [1]

In China he found indeed a less acquisitive society, more tolerant, more urbane, more sensitive to the natural beauty of the unhurried hours, but he found also vast poverty and vast ignorance. And he found also the cramping influence of family claims and of the excessive reverence for old age. Had Russell been a native of China instead of a visitor, one is tempted to think that, with his temperament, he would have been as much a rebel against these things as he is against the conditions of Western life. Moreover, he found that China was looking eagerly toward that very West for deliverance and new birth, and that it needed badly some things which the West could bestow, above all, science and technical skill. He feared that in gaining these things it would also succumb to what he calls the mechanistic outlook. He explains in *The Problem of China* just what he means by this expression. "I mean," he says, "something which exists equally in Imperialism, Bolshevism and the Y.M.C.A.; something which distinguishes all these from the Chinese outlook, and which I, for my part, consider very evil. What I mean is the habit of regarding mankind as raw material, to be molded by our scientific manipulation into whatever form may happen to suit our fancy. The essence of the matter, from the point of view of the individual who has this point of view, is the cultivation of will at the expense of perception, the fervent moral belief that it is our duty to force other people to realize our conception of the world. The Chinese intellectual is not much troubled by Imperialism as a creed, but is vigorously assailed by Bolshevism and the Y.M.C.A., to one or other of which he is too apt to fall a victim, learning a belief from the one in the class-war and the dictatorship of the communists, from the other in the mystic efficacy of cold baths and dumb-bells. Both these creeds, in their Western adepts, involve a contempt for the rest of mankind

---

1. "Where you are not, there is your bliss!" From *Der Wanderer*, by Georg Philipp Schmidt (1766-1849).

except as potential converts, and the belief that progress consists in the spread of a doctrine. They both involve a belief in government and a life against Nature." The Chinese, he tells us, are free at present from this disease. "Unlike the Y.M.C.A., they have no wish to alter the habits of the foreigners, any more than we wish to put the monkeys at the zoo into trousers and stiff shirts. And their attitude toward each other is, as a rule, equally tolerant." But he has grave forebodings. Russell is very apt, in his later writings, to utter forebodings. China is in the throes of transition. She must seek material advance, but there is danger that in the process she will lose her soul. In the East as in the West the way of civilization is beset by perils.

All the peculiar qualities of Russell's mind appear in an intensified form in the latest of his social studies, *The Prospects of Industrial Civilization*, which he wrote in collaboration with his second wife, Dora Russell. It has the same perplexing habit of inciting contrary hopes and fears. At one moment it offers the prospect of a better world under a new system, at another it shows human motives in so dark a picture that one wonders whether a new system would matter much. At one moment it points to science as the deliverer, at another to socialism, at still another it suggests that the important issue is not that between socialism and individualism, communism and capitalism, but that between mechanism and life. At one moment it tells us that an optimistic view of the present discontents is justified, and almost on the same page we read that "our own civilization appears to be growing decrepit and ready to fall." The inconsistencies and perplexities which we discover cannot be attributed to the joint authorship of the volume, for we have already seen their source in the mind of its main author. There is, moreover, a certain bitterness of comment, a readiness to impute motives of a sinister character, which checks that confidence in basic human nature on which alone our hopes can be built. The social synthesis which Russell here achieves is not so much a synthesis of the objective facts as a blending of his own hopes and fears, of his likes and dislikes, within which we vainly seek for either assurance or direction.

We conclude once more that our philosopher is not at home in the cave of the everyday world. He begins by expecting too much of the inhabitants of the cave, those creations of habit and instinct, and in revulsion he is apt to misconceive the motives that prompt their short-sighted actions, their struggles and their follies. In another book Russell declares that "men's morals in the mass are the same everywhere: they do as much harm as they can, and as much good as they must." Often Russell seems to see humanity in an unreal light. He tends to view everything in the sharpest contrasts of good and evil. He is an ethical impressionist.

He cannot paint the vivid greys of life—for him it is all sun or blackness. And where he cannot find the narrow gateway to heaven, he must find the broad road to hell.

In nearly all his social writings Russell has a way of enumerating the constituents of well-being or happiness, the things that make life good. The enumeration varies somewhat from book to book, but always it rings clear and true. Then he proceeds to show how in the business of living men treat those things that are desirable and lovely, and we no longer feel the same sureness of touch. It is true that in this business of living men stumble and miss the way. It is true that their passions drive them into the thorns and thistles and that they take selfish short-cuts that end in the morass. But all is not said when these tales are told. There is endeavor as well as folly, there is triumph as well as disaster. And always, always the army is on the move. The too impatient critic, his eyes set on far-off goals, loses sight of the endless marvel of what humanity is and does.

These comments are particularly evoked by *The Prospects of Industrial Civilization*. Following his wont Russell enumerates four ingredients which are requisite in the good community, these being instinctive happiness, friendly feeling, enjoyment of beauty, and knowledge. We wish he would stop to show us the place of these desirable things in the life of the individual and in the relations of men. We wish he would illustrate their effects and examine their operation, with the same impartiality with which one examines a mathematical principle. We wish he would convey to the reader that sense of their abiding values which is present in the author's mind. We wish he would even appeal to the reader and exhort him so that he can more fully relate the appreciation of these values to his own way of life. But Russell does none of these things. He limns the ideal in a few lines and then, turning passionately to the inhabitants of the cave, cries out, Look on this picture—and on that! And the second picture is so utterly unlike the first that the contrast either arouses protest because most men do not believe it, or generates despair in those who do.

Let us, to illustrate, consider his treatment of the four ingredients of the good community. The first is instinctive happiness. "I mean by this," says our author, "the sort of thing that is diminished by ill health and destroyed by a bad liver, the kind of delight in life which one finds always more strongly developed in the young of any mammalian species than in the old." This delight in life is the greatest of all personal goods. It cannot be attained if the natural needs are thwarted. For example, "very few adults, whether men or women, can preserve instinctive happiness in a state of celibacy." Russell proceeds to point out that under modern conditions of industry our instincts are in many directions thwarted, our need of spontaneous and variable activities, our need of occasional quiet and solitude, our need of contact with the earth. There is truth in this indictment, as other writers have shown. But it is only one side of the truth. The more we learn of actual conditions of life in other ages, the less sure are we of that idyllic correspondence between needs and opportunities which is presented as the happier contrast to our present age. Men do not sow and reap to garner such dead-sea fruits. They are the by-products of a civilization, not what it seeks nor yet what it achieves. The true picture must include the gain as well as the loss, but Russell has eyes for the latter alone. He is apt, in consequence, to misjudge the motives of men, as when he tells us that, in consequence of their thwarted instincts, middle-class men, when they are no longer young, "rejoice in war because it gives them a chance to thwart the young who have to do the fighting." But surely the motives of men cannot, even with the vaunted aid of psychoanalysis, be reduced to terms such as these.

The second of the ingredients which made the good community is friendly feeling. This also belongs to the instinctive side of our nature. It is no use, for example, to preach it as a duty, for that leads only to hyprocrisy. "There are two methods," Russell tells us, "of increasing the amount of this kind of feeling. One is physiological, by regulating the action of the glands and the liver; everyone knows that regular exercise makes one think better of other people. The other is economic and political, by producing a community in which the interests of different people harmonize as much as possible and as obviously as possible." These are sound and shrewd observations, but notice how Russell develops them. He proceeds to point out that under capitalism there is a certain degree of opportunity for a man to rise or sink in the social scale, and therefore no acceptance of inequality as inevitable or divinely ordained. "In medieval society the inequalities were as great as they are now, but they were stereotyped, and accepted by almost everybody as ordained by God." Hence there was far less envy or social conflict, far more friendly feeling. The only cure for the unfriendliness which he attributes to our age is the abolition of inequality altogether. To secure this we must abolish the competitive system. "Getting and spending, we lay waste our powers." If only we could substitute laziness for the fierce energy that consumes our lives. "If we were all lazy, and only worked under the spur of hunger, our whole society would be much happier. Think of a man like the late Lord Northcliffe, working like a galley-slave to produce bloodshed and misery on a scale hitherto unknown in human history. How admirable it would have been if he could have been persuaded to lie in the sun, or play bridge, or study chess-problems, or even take to drink. But, alas, such men have no vices." I have great sympathy with our author's remarks on the late Lord Northcliffe, but a like statement, in still stronger terms, could be made concerning Cesare Borgia or a multitude of other historical notables who did not belong to the industrial age. Nor is it a cogent argument in favor of laziness which points to the results of mischievous energy. Besides, many people would assuredly not be happy if they were compelled to be lazy—their instinct of activity, to use the psychological jargon, would be balked, and on the other hand we fear that many people who might be encouraged to develop their laziness would develop also certain other characteristics which are not conducive to friendly feeling. The prescription is too simple, and human nature is too complex.

The third in the list of desirable things is enjoyment of beauty. This is a pervasive and subtle good which takes new forms in every age, and which in any age is fully possessed only by the few, who are not dulled by habit or engrossed by the cares of life. It is no easy task to decide whether it is present in greater degree in one age or in another. But Russell impatiently and with little argument condemns our own as peculiarly antagonistic to it. He declares that industrialism creates an atmosphere which is poisonous to the growth of art. "When the whole world has adopted commercial industrialism, the artistic habit of mind will everywhere be stamped out in youth by people who cannot see any value in it unless its possessor is already labeled as a celebrity."

Last of the great excellences comes knowledge. Here surely one would expect our somber prophet to find something of our own day deserving a little meed of recognition. But no, he will not leave us this shred of pride. Ignoring the splendid advances in physics and chemistry, in astronomy and biology, which crown our age, ignoring the marvelous applications of science to life which are transforming our civilization, and among which we need merely instance the progressive conquest of disease, Russell maintains, first, that commercial industry is antagonistic to pure science, and second, that applied science has done far more harm than good. "Science," he says, "hitherto has been used for three purposes; to increase the total production of commodities; to make wars more destructive; and to substitute trivial amusements for those that had some artistic or hygienic value." Russell is here offering us a half-truth as if it were the whole, and half-truths are the enemy of understanding. We expect something more from our philosophers who claim to have descended from the mountains of the sun.

In fact, we cannot help feeling, as we read these later writings of Bertrand Russell, that his temperament, always peculiarly sensitive to the spectacle of the evil in the world, and profoundly affected by the gigantic ravage of our times, has gained the ascendency over his science. He is disillusioned with life, and though he holds as firmly as ever to his first ideals he sees the world more and more through the distorting mirror of his disappointment. For it is the last, and perhaps the worst, illusion of the disillusioned man that he sees life steadily and sees it whole. He does not perceive that his very disillusionment is a temperamental screen between him and the truth.

Russell sees things in clear-cut antitheses. Man must be either hero or villain of the play. The alternatives are always salvation or damnation. He is an evangelist with a gospel—not always the same gospel. But he offers on each occasion the same dramatic choice. If society rejects this message, he says in effect, its doom is sealed. The time of acceptance is brief, and the engine of destruction is at the door. But society moves too slowly and too confusedly for his impatient zeal. So his thought tends to grow more catastrophic. In all his later books he conjures up visions of menacing disaster. His forebodings outrun his hopes. This is curiously illustrated by his recent little book named *Icarus*. The title is indicative— Icarus, given "wings" of wax by his father Daedalus, who flew too near the sun and dropped into the sea. The subject is the future of science, and Russell, who once hailed science as the deliverer of men, now pictures strange and sinister possibilities. Here is one of them. "It will be possible," he suggests, "to make people choleric or timid, strongly or weakly sexed, and so on, as may be desired. Differences of emotional disposition seem to be chiefly due to secretions of the ductless glands, and therefore controllable by injections or by increasing or diminishing the secretions. Assuming an oligarchic organization of society, the State could give to the children of holders of power the disposition required for command, and to the children of the proletariat the disposition required for obedience. Against the injections of the State physicians the most eloquent Socialist oratory would be powerless. The only difficulty would be to combine this submissiveness with the necessary ferocity against external enemies; but I do not doubt that official science would be equal to the task." Such fancies would be excellent material for an up-to-date *Gulliver's Travels*, but they sound too grotesque in the earnest discourse of a philosopher.

For Russell, let us repeat in conclusion, has at least kept faith with his ideals. The earth may dissolve, but he will still proclaim them. The heavens may fall, but he will still, in the language of his famous essay, "defy with Promethean constancy a hostile universe." We may feel that he is needlessly concerned over the dissolution of the earth and the falling of the heavens. We may feel that civilization is not so brittle as he fears. The events of our little day, the follies of an hour, will not overwhelm it. It is not so tender a plant, liable to be blighted by every cold wind, for its roots are deep in the buried ages of the earth and its life is hidden in the abiding mystery of all that lives. The decision of an hour, no matter how momentous it seems to us, will neither destroy our civilization nor bring a new era to birth. Beyond us as well as before us stretch the unknown horizons. What we see is a brief span and what we foresee is nothing.

True ideals shine in their own light, but our cave of time and space remains dark. The ideals, if they are true, abide, though all our prophecies pass with the prophets.

[Previously unpublished; written *c.* 1924]

The Political Roots
of Totalitarianism

23 The roots of totalitarianism are in human nature itself. It is an ancient system of thought, a very ancient system of life. It is in truth the oldest of all systems, for its essential character is the denial of differences, even more of the right of differences, within the membership of the chosen group, the ingroup, the folk to which we belong. And with that simple denial goes the simple affirmation of total difference between our folk and all other folks.

Totalitarianism denies that differences can live together, differences of faith, differences of opinion, differences of thought. It conceives the whole as the enlarged ego. There is one blood, one heritage, one standard, one destiny for all the folk. These things are peculiar to the folk, its jealous and exclusive possession.

All that is new in the totalitarian spirit is the more intense revival of the old. For these conceptions dominate every primitive people and are recessive but still active in every civilized people. To become dominant again, all that is needed is the subjection of the people to sufficient pressure, to frustration, disillusionment, and economic misery. Some yield more readily, others after greater resistance, but it is only a question of degree.

I

These general statements can be supported by an enormous mass of historical evidences, but obviously I cannot cite them here. Should anyone doubt them, let me refer to a crucial test of their truth. Have we not all observed that at the very touch of war every people forsakes its freer principles and moves rapidly toward totalitarianism? Peace-time liberties are abrogated and all civil rights gravely diminished. The censor is enthroned, and every utterance that is not in accord with the prevailing mood becomes "subversive" and is forcibly suppressed.

Even a war against totalitarianism must be conducted on totalitarian lines. People with a strong tradition of liberty regard this surrender of principle as a temporary sacrifice to the necessities of war. But should the war bring with it defeat, humiliation, the crash of all securities, social and economic, then liberties and civil rights may not revive, then the system of totalitarianism, instead of passing away, may be established and cherished as the only road to salvation. For a torn, distracted people demands its Fuehrer, its Messiah, and spreads its liberties under his feet as he promises to lead them to the promised land.

These are the most auspicious conditions for modern totalitarianism. Special circumstances produce its special forms, such as the very characteristic system that flourished in Germany. I am not going to consider what particular combination of traditions, prejudices, of tensions and pressures, of privations, trials, and sufferings led to the erection of this particular system.

We know that when people pass through great trials or tribulations, when they are subjected to heavy tensions and pressures, particularly when their sense of security is shattered, perhaps above all when their self-esteem is profoundly shaken, then something that we can always discern in men becomes loosed—a fierce, blind, primitive urge. That fierce, blind, primitive urge, under these pressures, under these economic and spiritual tensions, begot modern totalitarianism.

II

What is modern is not its spirit, its creed, its world outlook. In this sense democracy is far more modern than totalitarianism. What is modern in totalitarianism is simply the manner in which it applies the most ancient of social principles to the conditions of a complex modern civilization.

All the power and exactitude of technological advance are devoted to the main end of centralized control. But there is nothing new in the doctrine of the all-competent, all-embracing state. It is merely that under totalitarianism the practice has come nearer to the principle, because of the new mechanisms of control.

The doctrine itself, and the partial application of it, is as old as human history. It recurs endlessly in the history of human thought, from the time of Plato to that of the present apologists for dictatorship. Even the greatest radical of the eighteenth century, Jean-Jacques Rousseau, could not conceive the state except in terms of totalitarianism, of the "total surrender." Even in the most democratic countries people spoke, and sometimes still speak, of the state and of sovereignty as though they constituted the corporate whole of life. The tradition is indeed ancient, even if the ideology is new.

We needed this word "ideology" to express the difference between the creed that is actually operative and the elaborate rationalization and explanation that is offered in its name as a fighting front. The ideologies are themselves the greatest instruments of indoctrination and of control. I do not suggest that ideologies are peculiar to the totalitarian state, but only that they are peculiarly necessary to it, so as to persuade the people to give up their liberties, their very personalities, at the demand of the all-claiming state.

The ideologies may be utterly different, uterly opposed, as have been those of Nazi Germany and of Russia, but they are enlisted in the service of the same totalitarian creed. Since they are built on the same foundations the differences between them, no matter how noisy they sound, are in the last resort only superficial.

The ideologies are new, but they are new only as the modern reconstruction of old ideas, often of old prejudices. They set forth, in the service of totalitarianism, certain ideas concerning the relation of man to the state and consequently of man to man. Sociologically, these ideas are all inadequate or false.

III

A famous orator, or if you please, a political philosopher, once said, "The people is never corrupted but it is often deceived." Whether we accept that in full or otherwise, at least it seems to me to be often true concerning certain things, concerning the larger ends that we pursue as members of a state or community.

Everwhere men seek certain things and among other things a kind of unity with their fellow-men. We seek somehow to get absorbed into a larger whole. In fact, our instincts, if you will permit me to use that old-fashioned word, seem to drive us into some form of community and we are always trying to find the form, vaguely conscious that somehow we are moving from one form or another. That is always the way it has been with mankind.

The philosophy of totalitarianism, nourishing ancient prejudices, distorts this essential quest of man for unity. Let me try to justify this statement by some considerations on the social and political nature of totalitarianism. First, it denies that which is common to humanity. In its conception you are given the isolated, insulated nation. The inevitable conception of totalitarianism is nation against nation; nations separate in all respects that matter, its own a proud nation, exclusive, complete, self-sufficient, and self-righteous.

One Nazi writer, who happened also to be a Protestant theologian, said: "The constitution of a nation means the wrathful separation of one from the rest." One of the forerunners of the totalitarian idea said: "Mankind is nothing but a sociological expression," and I think that very well sums up the attitude. But the fact happens to be otherwise. Every nation is sharing in very important influences that come from others and this idea of separation—cultural, spiritual, and economic, as well as political—is a myth and a very dangerous myth.

In the second place, it denies what is common to the nation, as well as to humanity. There is something very significant in the conception of a nation, of nationality. It has a very remarkable saving grace. Everyone in the nation, every citizen, is *equally* a member of it. Every American is equally an American despite what a few "hundred percenters" say. Every Frenchman is equally a Frenchman.

The idea of nationality does not allow for grade or distinction. It includes the rich and the poor, the educated and the uneducated, the conservative and the radical, people of all schools and creeds. If they are citizens, they are equally incorporated in this very pervasive and remarkably useful and important conception of the nation. And that is a conception that totalitarianism destroys. It has mutilated the nation. It says: "You are a German only if you accept this faith, if you belong to this cult, otherwise you are outside the pale." This proclamation strikes at the very foundation of community.

One could go on to explain in some degree why these ideas have grown powerful again, but I have to limit myself to a few points. A third aspect of the distorted image of unity arising under the pressures and necessities of totalitarianism is that it cuts the community to the measure of the state. That seems to me to be one of the most fatal of all mistakes, of all untruths, because the community is never the same as the state.

In the community we live and move and have our being. In it the creative principle of life has endless play. It is spontaneous, it is free-moving, it is the free weaving of relationships between man and man.

It didn't matter so much in the olden days whether you made the state the measure of the community. It doesn't matter so much if you go to relatively primitive areas and say that the state and the community are identical. Where it matters and where it is essentially false is in the great modern community, with its differentiation and with its enormous new controls over the private lives of man. Under these conditions, to make the state the measure of the community is to strike at the roots of the essential freedoms of society. What it means is that you are using coercion in the wrong place.

I am not suggesting what the right place is, but I am quite sure this is the wrong place. For you must treat, for example, a body of scholars or a body of artists in the way you treat a body of soldiers. If you have a squad of soldiers and order them about, that is what a squad of soldiers is for, although even there sometimes a little initiative may help. Nevertheless the function of the squad is to obey, and the better it obeys the better squad it is.

If a group of artists or even a group of professors is made into a squad and ordered about, they are not only awkward and out of place, but the better they obey the worse artists they become and even the worse professors. If you make them toe the line, whether it is the line of chalk or the party line, you are taking away their character, their truth.

It is all right for the soldier, as a soldier, to be ordered about, but ordering destroys the meaning of the whole area of expressive culture. This ordering goes so far that even the comedian can no longer crack his jokes without being told what to crack them about. He too must show a proper spirit, which means that jesting also becomes a bootleg occupation. Because it cannot flourish otherwise, it too goes underground.

IV

Thus in their blind desire for strength, for unity, for group assertion, or for dominion, men under totalitarianism have followed the trail leading back to the most primitive indifferentiation. Perhaps I can sum it up by saying that totalitarianism falsely identifies the two ultimate bases of human loyalty.

When men unite themselves with others, they are seeking, among other things, that which is common, inclusive, not divided up among them, not distributed like portions or dividends. We seek something not mine nor yours, but ours, and from that sense of *ours* springs the abiding loyalties of men.

But there are two kinds of loyalties, two kinds of common attachment. We belong, for example, to families, to communities, and that type of belonging, the unity of the group, is one of the two great forms of human loyalty. But there is another kind of common bond that is not personal in this sense and that is no less important an attachment. We pursue causes, we accept faiths, we seek cultural and scientific ends; we have values, we have philosophies, we have some view of life or some sense of a goal.

All these things are causes that bind us, just as do families, groups, communities, and nations. They constitute another great basis of human loyalty. But what totalitarianism does is to identify the two, although in fact they are not identifiable, since when we attempt to do so we mutilate the faith.

Totalitarianism will not allow differences to be different. Here at least is the great advantage that a democracy enjoys, in so far as it is true to itself. It allows men to pursue these two different kinds of loyalties together along the lines that properly belong to each. We can still have our own faith, and we can still belong to the one community, but we do not force the one into the framework of the other. Faith stands in its own right and the community lives in its own right.

That, I think, is perhaps the greatest liberation that men can have, and its denial is possibly the greatest tyranny.

[1940]

Mein Kampf *and the Truth*

24 Truth does not depend on power, whether the power is with us or against us. It does not obey our will or bend to our passions. The fact that Hitler was supreme over Germany and mustered all the instruments of power to compel acceptance does not make what he wrote and said any more true—or any less true—than it was when he was a prisoner at Landsberg on the Lech. The fact that he and all his works have fallen does not make what he wrote in *Mein Kampf* any less true, or any more true, than it was before. Truth remains unchanging and it can be found only if we seek it with open minds, with devotion to it, with willingness to find and follow the evidences, wherever they may lead.

Therefore the greatest enemy of truth is he who denies others the right to seek it, he who abuses his power over men to silence them and to punish them unless they accept as truth what he proclaims to be truth. This supreme offense against the light has often been committed in past times by

In this essay, prepared for the Office of War Information in the Fall of 1945 and previously unpublished, MacIver examines the main arguments and evidences used by Hitler in the first volume of *Mein Kampf*. Quotations are from the English translation published by Reynal & Hitchcock (New York, 1939).

men in power, but never with greater intolerance than by Hitler and his party. In *Mein Kampf* Hitler dealt with many subjects of the greatest importance, not only to Germans but to all peoples. He made sweeping pronouncements on nearly all human affairs. He discoursed on German history and world history, on war and peace, on the nature of government, on race and nation, on the psychology of the masses, on religion, on good and evil, on human destiny, on the whole nature of things. It was not permissible within the limits of his power to inquire whether these doctrines were based on the facts of history, the facts about race and nation, and the facts about human nature. It was not permissible to draw different conclusions or to entertain different beliefs.

That ban is no more. We can now approach *Mein Kampf* with open minds. It is said that truth makes us free. We can now cherish that great liberty. All the advances human beings have made have come with the pursuit of truth, with a patient search for the relations that exist between things, for the knowledge of the nature that lies outside us and the nature that lives within us. There was a time when the German people, led by its schools and universities, were eminent in this pursuit. Now they are again free to add to their great contribution of the past, to pursue their role in the cooperative advance of civilization.

It cannot of course be said that all our beliefs depend on knowledge, that all our convictions can or should be verified by the evidences. We must make a distinction between our beliefs concerning human values and our beliefs concerning the reality of things. The difference is a simple one. Our beliefs concerning values do not say that something is true but that something is good, or at least good for us. Such beliefs are dynamic and seek fulfillment through action. Our beliefs concerning the reality of things postulate not what is good but what is true and it is these that we can bring to the arbitrament of science. Science does not in the last resort tell us what goals we should pursue, what purposes we should cherish, what things are good or bad, lovely or ugly, but we betray our beliefs about values if we try to support them by false evidences or distort reality to make it conform with our beliefs. The danger is that our values may lead us to destroy or to deny the evidences, to fight against the truth. There should never be any conflict between our values and the truth we can discover. We should never support our values on falsehood. If our vision is beclouded by prejudice we follow false trails, we fight against our own well-being. Thus we are traitors both to our values and to the truth. Thus we suffer and cause others to suffer. Thus we make great efforts that end in frustration, disillusionment, and defeat.

Even more harmful than the false conception of specific facts is the false conception of relationships. In a modern society many diverse groups, differing in interest, in situation, in experience, in faith, live together. The welfare of society depends on the relations between them. But if one group is indoctrinated with false opinions about other groups it will treat these other groups in a way that is harmful to them all. The same thing applies in the relations between peoples or nations. Misunderstanding, the false conception of interests and relations, may do enormous damage that could be avoided by better knowledge. In *Mein Kampf* a great deal is said about the relations between nations, about what a nation is and about the part certain nations play in the history of mankind. It is very important to examine these views, to test them by relevant knowledge.

In times of trouble men and peoples are particularly tempted to embrace false notions about themselves and about others. In such times they care less to seek the truth. They listen the more readily to those who appeal to their emotions, who arouse their passions, who offer them quick salvation. In times of trouble wisdom is even more necessary than at other times, but it is also harder to attain. Men are then less tolerant, less regardful of consequences. Thus in the end they add new evils to their old ones. Only by the discipline of the mind and of the heart can men find a way to overcome the evils that have befallen them. It was said by a Greek poet that through suffering men learn wisdom. Perhaps we should say instead that suffering is the road to new wisdom or to new folly, according as we meet it with open minds or with darkened hearts.

Adolf Hitler wrote *Mein Kampf* in a time of trouble. He wrote it in a fever of conviction. He set down his opinions with a certainty that could tolerate no alternative views. He made many accusations against other groups and other peoples. He violently denounced all men whose opinions differed from his own. Was he justified in his accusations and his denunciations? Was what he wrote essentially true or was it in the main misguided? Did his program rest on understanding or on prejudice? We should not judge it either by its temporary triumph or by its final collapse. We should try instead to discuss it as any man's opinions, be he great or small, powerful or powerless, should be discussed. Let us interpret its meaning, let us go to the evidences to find the truth or the falsehood of its statements. Let us examine the relation between its policies and the grounds on which they are advanced.

There is indeed another judgment, the long-run judgment of history. The generations to come will more accurately decide what the teachings of this book have done to the people of Germany. But meanwhile, for this generation, it is of importance to form a just opinion of *Mein Kampf*, without prejudice and without favor. It should throw a needed light on the road they should now follow. It may help them to prepare a better path to a better future.

The spirit of *Mein Kampf* was the spirit of division, the spirit of war. This spirit had the power first to change the life of a people and then to turn the course of history, but it moved inevitably to destruction and dissolution. Every age must find its faith anew. Again from our suffering will come either the folly that sows new seeds of destruction or wisdom that recreates the world.

HITLER'S YOUTH AND EARLY IMPRESSIONS

We shall not dwell much on the autobiographical chapters (1 and 2) of *Mein Kampf*. They are not strictly autobiographical since they do not give any intimate or realistic account of Hitler's youth, of his family life, or of his home environment. Their chief interest for us is the light they throw on the conditions under which the young Adolf developed his passionate German nationalism. His father was a petty Austrian official who retired at an early age, strongly Austrian in his sympathies, devoted to routine, and proud of his position as an ex-functionary of the Austro-Hungarian empire. The father was masterful, the son headstrong. There were endless clashes between them. The son wanted to be an artist. The father bitterly opposed it. The father was greatly disappointed in his sons, none of whom was turning out as he had hoped. He died suddenly of a lung infection, and Adolf under his mother's guardianship went on with his schooling, not, however, with much success. However, in the Realschule at Linz there was a history teacher to whose fervent lessons Adolf was responsive. They stimulated the Pan-Germanism he had already displayed in the conflicts with his father. When he says this teaching made him a young revolutionary, he meant this of course in a nationalistic and not in a socialistic sense. He was also a revolutionary at home in a sense that he reacted as sons often do against the ways of the father. Later conditions conspired to turn his Pan-Germanism into a devouring flame and to give to one who otherwise did not seem to have much likelihood of success a unique and fateful opportunity.

When Hitler left his home for Vienna he faced the usual struggle of youths who have no credentials and no previous attainments. He gives a vivid picture of the sufferings and humiliations of the poor in Vienna, and above all, of the consequences of the uncertainty of the daily bread. He sees the need for a better economic system, but primarily as a necessary basis for the development of a strong nationalism. Through nationalistic pride he sustains his strong egoism during a period of poverty and privation. He belongs to the superior people which he thinks of as the superior race. He shows contempt for other peoples. Though he is outcast he belongs to the great race. In the revolts of his childhood he had learned to hate Austria and the Austro-Hungarian empire. Now he begins to dream of a dominating Pan-German empire.

His dreams are already extreme. He wrongly thinks of the Germans as a race. He claims that even the last German must be included in a single Reich. Such a Reich would surely have to be world-embracing, since the Germans, like other peoples, have migrated in considerable numbers to many parts of the earth. He claims that when *all* Germans are thus united, Germany would have the moral right to fight for foreign territory if necessary to assure its economic sustenance. What he means by this we shall see more clearly later on.

REACTION TO SOCIAL DEMOCRACY

Though Hitler admitted that "What I knew of Social Democracy during my youth was precious little and mostly wrong" (p. 50), he did not hesitate to characterize and denounce it. In his account (Chap. 2), we see the tendency of violent devotees to lump together all the parties and groups that oppose their programs and to brand them all alike with the grossest charges. All who take a different view from themselves are traitors or fools or cowards or weaklings. According to Hitler, Social Democracy was a terrorist party, and its heart was a Jewish conspiracy. Behind it "rises the grinning, ugly face of Marxism" (p. 66).

It should be pointed out, first, that Social Democracy in Austria and in Germany was not mainly Jewish. It had some Jewish leaders and a Jewish following, more particularly in Vienna. But the majority of the leaders were non-Jewish and the bulk of the members were drawn generally from the working classes. In the second place, Social Democracy was not inherently Marxist but on the contrary was often engaged in struggles against the Marxists. Its political philosophy was a different one. In the post-war Reichstag the Social Democratic coalition did not include the communists who bitterly and continuously attacked it. In fact, it may well be that if the German communists had made common cause with the socialists Hitler would never have come into power. In the third place, Social Democracy was not in Germany a revolutionary doctrine and in this respect it differed fundamentally from Marxism.

Hitler here, as elsewhere, refuses to concede that his opponents could possibly be decent people. So he denounces in the most intemperate terms men who, whether or not we agree with their particular policies, were animated by a genuine desire for a reconstructed Germany. The Social Democratic party in the Reichstag had a progressive, not a revolutionary, policy, and in the light of later history it seems clear that

Germany would have been saved from its later disasters had this party been allowed to continue its direction of the state.

In Hitler's statements there is an extremely revealing comment on the political use of terrorism. He had suffered from what he calls the brutality and mental terrorism of his fellow workers on some construction job. He shows in *Mein Kampf* that he felt no sense of fellowship with the working class into which his lot had thrown him. He refused to have anything to do with their unions and vehemently denounced these organizations. In return his fellow workers threatened him with violence and compelled him to quit the job. Hitler's reflection is that the way to deal with the Social Democrats is to apply to them the same brutality. Nothing, he observes, will be so impressive or so effective. He hugs the idea of breaking down the opposition of other groups by the method of terrorism. The masses need to be dominated. It is the only treatment they understand. His favorite way of saying this is to assert that they have a "feminine mentality." The masses, he explains, love the ruler who terrorizes over them. It is true that there are many who are responsive to dictation, but there are many also who abhor it. The number of those who are responsive is greatly augmented in times of grave trouble or crisis when people feel distracted and helpless. Of this fact Hitler and his party later took full advantage.

FIRST INVECTIVE AGAINST THE JEWS

The opening attack on the Jews in *Mein Kampf* (Chap. 2) exhibits Hitler's violent intolerance of all who do not conform to his own pattern. He has already indicated this intolerance in his references to the non-German nationalities in Austria. He felt no sympathy with the struggle of nationality groups for rights within the Austro-Hungarian empire. The idea of live and let live was alien to him. He expressed disgust at the fact that the Germans of the Viennese working classes fraternized with Slavs and other non-German workers. Everything good in Austria-Hungary was German. The German, among other things, "was the sole owner and propagator of a truly artistic mind" (p. 90). This intolerance now found its full outlet against the Jewish minority. In Vienna Hitler came under the influence of the anti-Semitic *Volksblatt*, owned by Karl Lueger, who was for a time Mayor of Vienna. Lueger became one of his heroes, "the greatest German mayor of all times" (p. 72).

Hitler tells us he studied carefully the Jewish question before arriving at his conclusions. But the violent accusations he makes were not based on actual observations but on the anti-Semitic pamphlets which he eagerly read. For example, he is quite unwilling to admit the simplest distinctions between the attitudes of different Jewish groups. To him they are all engaged in a universal conspiracy against the rest of the world. Very little inquiry would have been necessary to show that the Jewish people are deeply divided among themselves and follow the most diverse philosophies. Some are orthodox, some are reformist, some have entirely abandoned the Jewish religion. Some are conservative, some are reactionary, some are socialist but not Marxist, others are Marxist. Undoubtedly many intellectuals of Jewish origin have been followers of Marx, but this can be explained by the fact that the Marxist has a natural appeal to people who are treated as social inferiors or are subject to intolerance or persecution. Of course, on the other hand, many Marxists are not Jewish. The outstanding leader of Russian Marxism, Lenin, was not Jewish, nor were the great majority of his colleagues. Trotsky was an exception. It was not "Jewish blood" but the sense of oppression and of exploitation under the czarist regime that stimulated the leaders of the Russian revolution and led them to embrace the communistic philosophy.

Such simple facts and simple distinctions are unheeded by Hitler in his sweeping invective. He ends it with words that reveal an inordinate presumption. He is under commission from on high. In persecuting the Jews he is doing the work of the Lord. This idea became an obsession with him, a kind of mania. We shall see new expressions of it as we proceed.

REFLECTIONS ON DEMOCRACY

Hitler at the outset professes a "certain admiration" (*eine gewisse Bewunderung*) for English democracy and the British parliament but soon acknowledges his profound distaste for the principle of democratic government in any form (Chap. 3). Apart from a characteristic attack on the good faith and morals of the representatives of the people—he accuses them particularly of cowardice and futility—his argument follows two lines. First, democracy is an offense against nature. Nature, he says, operates through the aristocratic principle, whereas democracy gives power and position to inferiors of low mentality instead of to the natural born leaders. Second, democracy opens the way for communism. The masses are susceptible to communistic propaganda, and democracy is the rule of the masses.

The first argument assumes that in a non-democratic order, where not the will of the people but the strong arm of possession controls, the natural-born leaders come into their own. There is indeed no system of government which assures that the best or most capable men will become the rulers. The history of government shows that oligarchies of every kind have had foolish and weak and cruel rulers, as well as sometimes good or statesmanlike ones. At the same time it is historically unsound to claim that the leaders of democracy have shown themselves more incapable than leaders under other systems. The history of England, for example, and of the United States, gives ample evidence against this thesis. It is curious, by the way, that Hitler speaks of the democratic system as preferring "a simpleton, to a statesman like Pericles" (p. 104). Pericles was the chosen leader of Athenian democracy at the time of its fullest development. The people may certainly choose poor leaders, may be misled by mere demagogues, but democracy has at least the advantage that it can freely change its leaders when they prove incapable. In times of crisis democracies have often had the good sense to choose highly capable leaders. It is enough here to point out that Churchill and Roosevelt proved to be such in the crisis of the war.

As for the representatives under a democracy, Hitler has nothing but contempt for them. Yet if he had known something of the history of the English parliament he might have learned that the representative body has fought many a brave fight for human liberties. For that matter it is utterly unfair to charge the Reichstag under the Weimar Constitution with cowardice. It made valiant efforts for reconstruction in the face of the most formidable difficulties.

Hitler makes no reference whatever to the main arguments on the side of democracy. In particular he has nothing to say on the danger of uncontrolled power, power that is not subject to recall and not responsible to the people. Much of the record of government consists of the exploitation of men by men, of group by group, of class by class. Much of it is consequently a record of spoliation and destruction. Democracy arose as the resistance of the peoples to the exploitations of irresponsible power. Moreover, it did not arise among weak or backward peoples. It arose in the higher levels of civilization, among the peoples who were more advanced in culture and in all the arts. It developed first among the Greeks, in the flower of their civilization. In the modern world it first arose in England, as England grew in power, and thence it spread to France, to the United States, to the British dominions, to the more prosperous and advanced nations of the Western world, including Sweden, Belgium, Holland, Switzerland, Norway, and Denmark. It is obvious that Hitler's violent words about cowardice and futility are utterly improper in their broad application to these countries.

The second charge against democracy, that it is the breeder of communism, was employed with much greater effect. Mussolini used this argument in the early days of the fascist movement and there is no doubt that it considerably helped his cause. Large industrialists and many people of the middle classes, having a dread of communism, espoused fascism as a shield against it. The Nazi Party took the line that democracy was powerless against communist inroads, and from 1931 onward there was a strong sentiment among many groups in Germany, as the German press of that period witnesses, that Nazism was becoming the only alternative to communism.

The idea that communism is the offspring and inheritor of democracy needs correction. Certainly no one could justly claim that democracy was the breeder of communism in Russia. There the communistic movement was the reaction of working-class groups and some intellectuals to the autocracy, oppression, and mismanagement of czarism. Generally, communist movements have been strongest in situations where an oligarchical order is decaying from within and subject to domestic revolt on the part of oppressed classes. Sometimes a democracy of the Western type, set up after the collapse of such an oligarchy, has been unable to maintain itself, the ground for it being unprepared. An immature democracy, born under these conditions, has sometimes been overthrown by a communist revolution, though more often it has been defeated by conservative reaction, as happened in China immediately after its first proclamation of democracy, in Spain, and in various Eastern European countries. Italy may be included in the same category, since democracy, though existing there for some length of time, was still weakly supported by the people. On the other hand, countries where democracy has fully established itself have been disinclined to revolutionary activities of either the communist or the fascist type. Examples are the United States of America, England, the British Dominions, Switzerland, and the Scandinavian countries.

The broad conclusion is that where democracy is weak or insecure the tendency in times of crisis is either a reversion to fascism or a revolution to communism, but where democracy has entrenched itself it is unlikely to be overturned either by a reaction from the right or a revolution from the left.

We may note in passing that Hitler wrongly identifies democracy with majority rule. Any system of government—oligarchy, dictatorship, or democracy—may be supported by a majority of the people. The difference is that in a democracy majority rule is combined with minority rights, and not least with the right of minorities to advance their opinions and their policies and to seek under a system of free discussion and of free voting to make their views prevail.

CONCERNING PUBLIC OPINION AND THE PRESS

In several passages on public opinion and the press (Chap. 3), Hitler expresses his intense hatred of liberalism and, more generally, of the liberty of discussion. He develops the same ideas in a still more extreme way in Chapter 10, where he brands the democratic press as one of the major causes of the collapse of Germany. He declares that the press betrayed the people and fed them on poisonous propaganda. In the realm of politics, so long as men are free, there are bound to be strong differences of opinion. Each side claims to know the truth and carries on continuous propaganda against all other parties. So long as all parties can be heard, then the reader can use his own judgment and can discount the extreme claims of one side by listening to the counterclaims of the other side. Only by hearing both sides can men form an intelligent opinion of their own. The peculiar danger of men like Hitler is not that they denounce the opinions of others but that they seek to suppress these opinions altogether. In retrospect, Germany and the whole world has cause to mourn that the Nazis destroyed the freedom of the press and monopolized the expression of opinion. When the right freely to discuss public affairs is abolished, men are subject to the most deadly form of enslavement, the enslavement of the mind.

Characteristically Hitler calls the democratic press the Jewish press. It is true that the great liberal organs of Berlin and Frankfurt, the *Berliner Tageblatt* and the *Frankfurter Zeitung*, were edited by Jews. But outside of these two cities the democratic press of Germany was not Jewish, and Hitler, as so often, seeks to excite prejudice by applying the term "Jewish" to the whole anti-Nazi press.

The charge Hitler brings against the free press, that it calumniates and slanders innocent opponents of its views, could not justly be maintained against the two important organs he singles out for abuse. These were conspicuously free from such malicious methods. On the other hand the defamation of opponents was the consistent policy of the *Völkischer Beobachter*, the special organ of the NSDAP, and the lowest depths of foul calumny were sounded in *Der Stürmer*, where persons of Jewish origin or with any Jewish connections were regularly pictured as indulging in the wildest and most debasing orgies.

THE MYTH OF THE FREELY CHOSEN LEADER

After his fashion Hitler claims there are two kinds of democracy: the ordinary kind, which with complete disregard of the historical facts he calls Jewish, and the true kind, which he calls German democracy (Chap. 3). In the latter system, he tells us, there is the free choice of the leader. This leadership principle was greatly extolled in later Nazi literature. In what manner, however, the leader is freely chosen remains very obscure. Sometimes it is said he is chosen by destiny, sometimes by providence. He is assumed to be the choice of the folk, and the state he rules over is called the folkish state. The folk acclaim him but no majority ever elects him—that method is ruled out. Majority election means for Hitler the rule of the masses, and he constantly expresses his distrust of the masses. We have then to resort to the conception that the folk, not by election but by some spontaneous, almost unanimous action acclaims the true leader and sets him in power. We have to suppose that the folk is united in sentiment, one in mind as well as in heart. The folk in this sense is of course a myth, but for Hitler those who did not agree with his ideas did not really belong to the folk. The denial of the right to differ is inherent in his whole philosophy. On that basis the use of such words as "free" and "democratic" is utterly out of place, for the primary fact about democracy is that it not only admits but also establishes the right to differ, and without this right the word "freedom" becomes a mockery.

The exponents of Nazi philosophy sought to support by examples the myth of the freely chosen leader. But to find them they had to go back to very early German history, in the obscurity of which they could assert that Arminius and others were thus chosen. Possibly a very simple and small folk, where everyone personally knew the members of the group, might appoint a leader by acclamation, but obviously this method has no relevance to a modern state with its many groups and its divergences of viewpoint and of interest. Where, however, a dictatorship of the Nazi type has once been established and where its monopolistic propaganda and its terrorism have been continuously at work, it is easy to claim that any decision taken by the leader is the expression of the true sentiment of the folk. This was the purpose of the occasional plebiscites organized by the Nazi dictatorship. It could then point to a nearly 100 per cent approval, conveniently ignoring the compulsions which underlay its controlled plebiscite.

Possibly the nearest genuine approach in a developed state to the leadership principle enunciated by the Nazis was the Roman dictatorship in the early days of the Republic. But even so it was an entirely different thing. In times of grave crisis the Romans suspended the regular form of government, entrusting to a single leader the guardianship of the state until the crisis was ended, when he again yielded up his authority. It should be noted, however, first, that this was a rare procedure adopted in moments of great peril; second, that under the Republic it never lasted longer than six months; and, third, that the leader was chosen not by the people but by the Senate, even though he was likely to be a man in whom the people had peculiar confidence.

CONCEPTION OF THE MASSES

When Hitler speaks of the people (as in Chap. 3) he thinks of them either as the masses or as the folk. The masses he despises. The folk he extols. The difference is that for him the folk are not the actual human beings who live their everyday lives. The folk is an idealized conception. They are the true Germans, and the true Germans are those who applaud his leadership, who conform to a type he approves, who as men enlist on his side and die for him, and as women breed soldiers for him, who are not corrupted by following other doctrines than his own, and who of course never intermarry with inferior, that is, any other, peoples.

But for practical purposes Hitler has to deal with the people as they are, not with the folk as he pictured they should be. Then he thinks of them as the masses. And the problem is to control them and make them the instruments of his will. The people, he says in a later passage, "in an overwhelming majority are so feminine in their nature and attitude that their activities and thoughts are motivated less by sober consideration than by feeling and sentiment" (p. 237). What then is necessary is to use without scruple the appeals to which their feelings and prejudices are responsive and to combine these appeals with a masterful and ruthless domination. The masses have been seduced by false doctrines, such as socialism, pacifism and internationalism. They have to be converted. They should not be instructed or told the truth; instead they should be stirred to fury by passionate oratory. In short, they are to be deindividualized, to be consolidated into a multitudinous mob which like a raging torrent will sweep away opposition.

Hitler had himself in the highest degree the arts of the demagogue. He had an instinctive perception of mass psychology. Emotionally he could easily identify himself not with the people but with the mass spirit in the people, that is, the spirit of the people when their feelings have been so worked upon that they disregard their differences and restraints and inhibitions and the acceptances and decencies of ordinary life. The masses are the people when they are infected with a homogeneous unthinking mentality. This mass spirit was congenial to Hitler's own. By stimulating it he could turn it into a great volcanic force at the service of the leader. A view of life, he tells us here, "may in general only hope for victory if the broad masses, as the bearers of the new doctrine, declare themselves ready to take upon themselves the necessary fight" (p. 127).

The anti-intellectual character of the Nazi philosophy is here exhibited. The education of the people, in order to keep them transformed into the masses, should pay less attention to knowledge than to indoctrination combined with physical training. This program was later carried through in the schools, the universities, and the various youth training organizations. For the nation as a whole the principle was carried out in the most intensive way through the Ministry for Popular Enlightenment and Propaganda and through the *Reichskulturkammer.*

THE JEWS AS A RACIAL DANGER

Obsessed by the idea of race and racial purity Hitler gave a new direction and purpose to anti-Semitism. The anti-Semitic position had hitherto been based, at least ostensibly, on religious tradition—the Jews had (it was said) crucified Christ and rejected Christianity. On this ground they were from time to time subjected to persecution. Suffering from social and political discrimination and confined to ghettos, they had to take up occupations that were regarded as ignoble or unworthy of a Christian, and hence in the Middle Ages, when "usury" was forbidden by the church, they became the chief money lenders. Thus was created an additional ground for prejudice against them. But racialism was alien to the Middle Ages and became significant only in quite modern times. Hitherto, when it suited the interest of those in power to attack the Jews, the name of religion was invoked. It was so done by Lueger and the Austrian Christian Socialists.

Hitler discovered that the sentiment against the Jews could be effectively turned in another direction. It could be used to foment racial prejudice* and so to strengthen his Pan-Germanist appeal. It is clear from many passages in Chapter 3 that Hitler thought not only the Jews but all other peoples were inferior to the Germans. His attack on the Jews was a device to show up by contrast the great superiority of the Germans. Hence he bases his anti-Semitism not on religion but on race. The German was the complete antithesis of the Jew. The more he covered the Jew with obloquy and disgrace, the more he showed up the racial superiority of the German.

Anti-Semitism thus became for Hitler a political device. By increasing (to the limit) the prejudice against the Jews, he sought to unify all Germans in a common hate and in a common pride. He counted also on the fact that prejudice against the Jews prevailed in other countries and that thus he might win sympathizers to his cause in those countries. Later on when he came to power his action in forcing considerable numbers of Jews to flee as refugees to other countries was a means of increasing prejudice among various groups in those countries, especially at a time of severe economic depression.

It is a common tendency of groups everywhere to sustain their own self-esteem by asserting their superiority to other groups and by excluding those groups from the privileges and rights they themselves enjoy. This common tendency, this natural human weakness, is usually held in some restraint by a system of public rights. The Nazi philosophy, rejecting such restraints, stimulated this tendency to the full. Hitler, however, was himself more fanatic on the subject of the Jews than most Nazi leaders, and it was his personal influence that directed the policy of extermination later carried out in the concentration camps.

THE POPULATION QUESTION

When considering clearly the suppositions for German statesmanship's activity in foreign politics, one necessarily came to the following conclusion:

Germany has an annual increase in population of almost 900,000 souls. The difficulty of feeding this army of new citizens would become greater with every year, and was bound some day to end in a catastrophe, provided ways and means were not found to avert this impending danger of hunger-pauperization in time.

There were four ways in which to avoid such a terrible future (pp. 168–169).

The passage here quoted is the introduction to an elaborate discussion of German foreign policy based on a Darwinian theory concerning the survival of the fittest. The starting point is the annual increase of the population. There are four ways, Hitler claims, of meeting this problem. One is a restriction of the birth rate. A second is the increase of the productivity of the domestic soil. A third is the acquisition of new territory for the surplus people. The fourth is the development of trade and industry so that the additional food supply needed can be obtained through the exchange of manufactured goods.

Of these four ways, the first, he tells us, is contrary to the law of nature. The second is quite inadequate. The fourth is briefly dismissed as less "healthy." So there remains the only healthful and natural way, the third, which Hitler claims to have "no end of advantages" (p. 178). It is essential for Germany to acquire fresh territory. Moreover, this territory cannot be in the main colonial because colonies are unsuitable for European settlement. Therefore the necessary accession of new German territory must be found in Europe.

We shall presently consider what is implied in this policy, but first let us look at the grounds on which it is advocated in *Mein Kampf* (Chap. 4). If Hitler was right in his ideas about population, then the policy he advocates here, however cruel its consequences, would be vindicated. He appeals to the laws of nature and he states them with complete assurance. We do not learn the laws of nature by intuition but through scientific inquiry. Hitler dogmatically claims authority for a doctrine of perpetual warfare. Is it not reasonable to ask whether science gives him any such authority? Is it not imperative to do so before committing ourselves to such tremendous consequences?

When we do so we soon discover that the question of population and the notion of the survival of the fit are not so simple as the author of *Mein Kampf* believed. There are some problems here on which we need more light than we yet possess, but we do know enough of the ways of nature to draw certain conclusions. The following points, for example, are clearly established and they suffice to refute the doctrine of Hitler.

In the first place, there are a great many ways of surviving in accordance with nature's laws. Some animals survive by their cunning, some by their speed, some by their protection against those that prey on them, some by breeding large numbers. Those that produce a very numerous offspring of which only a small number survive show no evidence of greater fitness than those that have a relatively small natural increase. On the contrary, the general rule is that the higher animals breed far fewer offspring than the lower ones. Man himself is one of the least prolific of all animals, and the civilized peoples are generally less prolific than the primitive.

In the second place, among human groups there is no evidence to support the claim that the most warlike are also the most fit. The savage groups that engage in constant raids and tribal wars have not bred a stronger or healthier kind of human being than those that live in comparative peace. In the third place, there is a different fitness for every different environment. Every kind of animal finds or makes an environment congenial to itself. Civilized man has enormously modified the environment in which he lives. This new environment requires different standards and makes different demands than the environment of the primitive. Just as some types of animal survive only in cold climates, others in hot climates, some in dry climates, and some in moist climates, some in mountains and others in the plains, some in deserts, and some in the forests, so the different stages of human society depend on different kinds of environment. Nature lays down no single law of fitness. Nature sets up no absolute standard of values. Hence fitness is always changing and is always relative to the changing environment. When man modifies his environment he modifies also the conditions of fitness.

When, therefore, Hitler says that the severe pressure of natural selection is nature's way of seeing to it that only the fit survive, we should ask: What kind of fitness survives under what kind of conditions? The people of India have a far higher death rate than the people of Germany.

Does that mean that the Indian as more subject to natural selection is a more fit being than the German? Where the pressure of natural selection is heavy we find a high death rate accompanied by a high birth rate. It has, however, been the achievement of civilization to replace that order of things by a low death rate accompanied by a low birth rate. It is of course possible for the birth rate to fall below the limit necessary to insure the maintenance of a strong and healthy people, but that is another issue which must be met in a different way. The point here is that a surplus of population over what the country sustains is not a condition of fitness or a sign of progress, nor is there any evidence given by nature that the way of fitness is through the internecine struggle of different groups of the same species. This kind of struggle is rare in lower nature.

The considerations set out above are far from being a complete account of a complex subject. They correspond, however, to the evidences of modern science and they should be enough to show the unwisdom of such dogmatic statements about the laws of nature as are made by Hitler in *Mein Kampf*.

VIEWS ON WAR AND FOREIGN POLICY

In accordance with the viewpoint developed by Hitler in the previous section, Nazi policy was war-oriented from the first. It was only a question of time and opportunity. While Hitler was making public profession of his desire for a peaceful settlement with other countries, he not only prepared intensively for war but was animated by the spirit of war. This underlying policy is clearly indicated throughout *Mein Kampf*. In Chapter 5, where he is dealing with the First World War, he reveals his opinion that war is both a necessary and a desirable condition of human society. He rejoiced in the coming of the war of 1914. The period of peace in which his boyhood was passed he thought of as a "foul and lingering illness." He disparages peaceful relations between nations. For him the alternative to the heroic reign of force is the decadent reign of fraud. He has no respect for the achievements of peace or for the great advances in human well-being registered in the remarkable peaceful era that came to an end with the First World War. Since he believes in the inevitability of war he pleads that his country should seize the first favorable occasion and strike the first blow. If by doing so it is blamed for the resulting war, he can always answer that it is a war of self-defense, a war for the sacred right of self-preservation.

In his discussion of the population problem Hitler repudiated the idea that Germany should seek to sustain a growing population through peaceful advances in industry and trade. For him that would mean degeneration. For him war is the highest and greatest purpose of the nation. He can see nations only as utterly separate and in the last resort hostile entities. He applies to nations, entirely without scientific warrant, the principle of natural selection. War determines which shall survive. War is the means by which the final supremacy of the Germans over all other nations must be demonstrated. Internationalism is the resort of weaklings and cowards. "What has been denied to kindness will have to be taken with the fist" (p. 180). Any other views are pacifistic nonsense.

For Hitler, with his intense nationalism, the object of war is solely national dominance. He is not concerned with its effects on the welfare of the people. He is not at all deterred by the frightful costs of modern warfare. He is perfectly ready to see the people—the masses—suffer and be destroyed. He is devoted not really to Germany but to an abstract conception of Germanism. So long as the cause triumphs, what matters to the people is of small account. If indeed he seeks to have the people healthy and vigorous, if he wants them to produce healthy and vigorous children, it is in order to make them a more effective instrument for waging war. For the normal values of human beings, for the things that make life enjoyable and desirable to them, he has no regard.

Consequently the first question of foreign policy is the choice of allies for a program of war. He had from the first regarded the alliance of Germany with Austria-Hungary as a menace. He calls it an absurdity. It was "disastrous from the point of view of a racial policy" (p. 191). For him the main question then became whether Germany should seek some rapprochement with England and look for conquest to the east or should seek an alliance with Russia so as to be free from a war on two fronts when attacking England. In the Nazi Party there were conflicting views on this subject between those who saw England as the main enemy and sought a war of revenge, believing at the same time that with the defeat of England it would be easy to dominate the rest of the world, and those who saw in Russia the great opportunity for German expansion, especially in the grain-bearing Ukraine. The latter view was dominant in Hitler and it was strongly supported by the ex-Russian Rosenberg. The question was fundamentally one of the method to be followed under a program of domination that would finally deal with both Russia and Great Britain. So it turned out in the course of events that when during the Second World War Hitler regarded Great Britain as already defeated he proceeded forthwith to the war against Russia.

HITLER'S THEORY OF GOVERNMENT

The State is not an assembly of commercial parties in a certain prescribed space for the fulfillment of economic tasks, but the organization of a community of physically and mentally equal human beings for the better possibility of the furtherance of their species as well as for the fulfillment of the goal of their existence assigned to them by Providence. This, and nothing else, is the purpose and the meaning of a State. Economy is, therefore, only one of the many auxiliary means necessary for reaching this goal. But it is never the cause or the purpose of a State, provided the latter is not based from the start on a foundation that is wrong because it is unnatural. Only thus can it be explained that the State, as such, need not even have a territorial limitation as its assumption (pp. 195-196).

The instinct of preserving the species is the first cause of the formation of human communities. But the State is a folk organism and not an economic organization. A difference that is as great as it remains incomprehensible to the so-called "statesmen," especially of today (p. 197).

The nature of the state is the subject of political science and of political philosophy. No one who is acquainted with the history of government and who is aware of the many forms and varieties of states could possibly be satisfied with Hitler's definition of the state and theory of government (Chap. 4). It is ridiculous to assume that different states enclose different species of human beings. As we have pointed out, there are no species of human beings in a scientific sense, but even if there were they could not be identified with the citizens of different states. An endless series of historical conditions have determined the changing boundaries of states. The sense of community felt by the members of a state is not derived from an original blood-bond but from the conspiring influences of common tradition, common experience, common environment, intermarriage, and association in common interests and enterprises, and so forth. What makes a state is the fact of inclusive government. If the people included under one government feel sufficiently united by ties of sentiment and tradition then they become a nation, and the state is a nation-state. But a nation is in no sense a species of the human race.

It is in the sense explained above that Germany, or Great Britain, or France, or Russia, or the United States, or China, or any other politically bounded community constitutes a state. That being so, it is surely unreasonable to deny that the state has anything to do with any definite program of economic development. The purposes of the state are the purposes to which the government of that state devotes itself, and in so far as the people have power they are the purposes that receive their support and authorization. Why then should anyone presume to say that the state has nothing to do with a subject of the greatest importance to men, viz., the nature and the development of the economic system? It in no way clarifies the question to declare that the state is a "folk organism" (*völkischer Organismus*). We have seen that Hitler does not use the word "folk" in a realistic sense. We have seen that he held a low opinion of the masses and disapproved of majority decisions and of popular government. Yet here he claims that the state is a community of physically and mentally equal (*physisch und seelisch gleicher*) human beings. Again we move in the realm of perilous abstraction, utterly regardless of the real beings who are citizens of the real state. Of course no community consists of *equal* human beings, whether physically or mentally. But for Hitler the community is a mysterious blood community, and in some mysterious way the blood speaks through the leader, and what it says is the voice of the folk. In more prosaic language what the leader says—*provided the leader is Hitler*—is always right. But no intelligible theory of the nature of the state and of the purposes of government can be built on this kind of primitive dogmatism.

THE PURPOSES AND METHODS OF PROPAGANDA

Hitler's views on the methods of propaganda (Chap. 6) are very instructive. They have to be considered in the light of his conception of the masses, already discussed. Hitler's own steep rise from complete obscurity was due to his mastery of the art of propaganda, and the history of the Nazi Party is the story of the success with which he developed and employed this weapon. In the part of *Mein Kampf* before us Hitler explains some of the devices that make propaganda most effective. He explains, for example, that it must be simple, without too much argument, that it must appeal to the prevailing emotions and sentiment of the people, and that it must constantly reiterate the same points.

Hitler himself made most effective use of these devices. His speeches rang endless changes on a few themes. He employed always the same gestures and the same attitudes, the same mannerisms, the same invocations, the same denunciations. He did not always say the same things. What he said he adapted to the situation. This also is the way of the skilled propagandist. When it suits his purpose he declares himself the lover and bringer of peace, and at another time he extols the virtue and necessity of war. He calls Russia the enemy of mankind and expresses his admiration for England. Or he calls England the mortal enemy and Russia becomes the kindly neutral. But the mode of appeal, the incitation of the mob spirit, the catch phrases about the "international Jewish conspiracy," and so forth, are always the same.

He explains moreover that the propagandist must not be concerned about any truth that is inconvenient for his purposes. What, he asks, would we think of the advertiser of some brand of soap who at the same time admitted that other brands were also good? So it is with the political propagandist. He must not allow that there is any truth or right on the side of his opponent.

That this is the regular way of propaganda is perfectly clear. But Hitler was not content to stop at this point. So long as the public can hear different advertisers of soap parade their respective wares, nobody can complain if each assigns exclusive merit to his own. And so long as the advocates of different political prescriptions are allowed alike to appeal on behalf of their respective programs, the opportunity to hear both sides of a case leaves the final decision to the judgment of the public. Propaganda, however, becomes something quite different and the dangers arising from its distortion of the truth are enormously intensified when it becomes a monopoly or when those who support one policy are able to impose serious difficulties and grievous penalties on those who support any other. As the Nazi Party grew in strength they followed these methods of suppression until at last they had completely monopolized the whole business of propaganda.

The monopoly of propaganda means also that it is supported by various extreme compulsions. The owners of power can now distort the truth without fear that their falsehoods will be exposed or even discovered. Since the other side is unheard, the mind of the listener is unduly impressed by the weight of one-sided evidence. He can no longer correct the effects of misrepresentation by learning the contrary evidences. After a while the incessant inculcation of a single doctrine has an hypnotic effect. Only the very strong can resist it. The minds of the multitude, and above all the minds of the young, are first taken captive, then enslaved.

The consequences of monopolistic propaganda are most serious when it is employed to inculcate hatred and division. Unfortunately this is also, as Hitler knew, one of the most effective methods of propaganda. There is always some prejudice between group and group. It is easy to work on this prejudice. It is easy to appeal to the fears and the passions of men on the ground that some insidious enemy is attacking them. As Hitler says, people are motivated less by sober consideration than by feeling and sentiment, and this is peculiarly so when because of the monopoly of propaganda they are denied the means of sober consideration. Then their passions, instead of being restrained by reflection, are the more stimulated by the specious arguments of the group in power, who find that by exciting hatred against other groups they can most easily hold the multitude on their side. Debarred from expression in other directions, the multitude vents its feelings in violent outbursts of stimulated hatred. The attack on the Jews was an example of this technique.

When propaganda is monopolized there are other pernicious consequences. There is nowhere one can go to learn the truth, no authority to whom one can appeal, no court that will honestly decide the issues of fact. The reason that is in men and that has always to struggle against their prejudices and blind passions is disarmed, for reason guides us by demanding that we give due weight to different evidences, to the evidences both for and against a course of action or a way of thinking. Reason asks us to count the costs, bids us view the alternatives and assess the probable consequences of choosing one or the other. All these activities are balked where the evidences are officially distorted, where the costs are officially concealed, and where the alternatives are officially misrepresented — without our being given any chance to learn otherwise. Monopolized propaganda can no longer distinguish between its own truth and its own falsehood. It is not content to say: Believe this, for here is the evidence (however distorted); it also says: Believe this, for if you don't you will be punished. It makes force always the final argument. You cannot have monopolistic propaganda without also the concentration camp. However persuasive Goebbels might be, he required the cooperation of Himmler.

Under such circumstances men live in a twilight of uncertainty where nothing is secure, nothing sacred, nothing private. The art of propaganda is one thing when it is a method of persuading against the persuasions of the other side. It is an entirely different thing when it is associated with compulsion or terror, so that there is no other side.

THE NOVEMBER REVOLUTION

In Chapter 7 Hitler gives his view of the causes that led to the capitulation of Germany in the First World War, and of his own reactions at that time. Since these views became an extremely important basis of the whole National Socialist position and of the powerful propaganda the Party developed in the years immediately following the war, it is necessary to examine them in some detail.

Hitler's main contention is that the German army was not defeated in war but was betrayed, stabbed in the back, by treachery at home. The traitors were the Social Democrats and of course the Jews. The Jews, Hitler claimed, were the subtle enemies who "organized the revolution and smashed Prussia as well as Bavaria" (p. 252). They sowed dissension and instigated subversive propaganda. They fomented strikes and social discord. The aspirants to leadership over a republican Germany abetted them. The government had neither the intelligence nor the courage to crush these domestic enemies. The government did not even have the sense to meet with effective propaganda the cunning enemy propaganda directed to the army as well as to the home front. Even the army was infected by this poison and by the defeatist attitude engendered in the general population. The objective of the Social Democrats and of the Jews was to sabotage Germany. "A handful of miserable criminals" (p. 268) took over the fatherland and were responsible for the debacle. These were the "November criminals."

It is easy to see how persuasive such a story might sound when elaborated by unscrupulous propagandists. It was highly gratifying to nationalist feeling to be told that the army was never defeated, that its glory was undiminished, and that its heroic efforts would have been crowned with success but for the vile treachery of civilian criminals. It is of course true that the German army fought with great valor throughout the war. It did not need to be defended on that score. But was it true that its final capitulation was caused by the subversive propaganda of a group of defeatists?

The subject has been carefully investigated by the historians of various countries, and there is also much evidence in the reports of the Committee of Inquiry appointed by the Reichstag. It is quite clear from these investigations that Hitler's charge is untrue and utterly unjust to the men who became the leaders of Germany at the end of the war. In brief, the following points are established:

1. The German army had an ample supply of all the requirements of war at the start of the 1918 offensive. There was no shortage of munitions due to a failure of the home front. Nor was there at that time any breakdown of army morale. There was war weariness in all the belligerent countries. That was not peculiarly a German phenomenon. The element of truth in Hitler's account is that in Bavaria there was great dissatisfaction with the conduct of the war, increasing irritation against Prussia showing in a separatist movement, and a great demand for peace.

2. There is no reason to doubt that the strength of the armies opposing Germany, vastly augmented by the fresh forces the United States was pouring into the front, the inability of Germany to match the ever increasing manpower and armaments of her opponents, the effects of the blockade and the failure of the submarine war, the breakdown of Austro-Hungarian resistance and the crumbling of Bulgaria, combined with the disaster that ended the German offensive in the West, gave an overwhelming military advantage to the other side. This was the decisive fact. There was no military ignominy in defeat under these circumstances and it would have been only folly to have continued the war. Germany had

miscalculated the strength of her enemies, especially when the United States was brought into the war by the policy of unlimited U-boat warfare. It is possible that the strategy of Hindenburg and Ludendorff hastened the denouement. They hoped by the vast offenses of the spring and summer of 1918 decisively to defeat the opposing allies, before American reinforcements could arrive in large numbers. With the failure of the summer offensive the German cause was lost. When the prospect of German victory vanished it was both good military policy and intelligent statesmanship to give up the struggle. The terrible consequences of fighting on against all military calculations was amply revealed when the Hitler government itself carried on an irredeemably lost war after the end of 1944. This policy brought upon Germany a vast additional amount of utterly needless destruction.

3. The end-the-war movement on the home front had very little importance before September 1918. The Spartacist movement, the refusal of the Minority Socialists to vote war credits, and the appearance of a Communist Party led by Karl Liebknecht represented the attitude of only a small portion of the population. It was not until after the defeat of August 8th that the people generally began to feel that the war was lost. By that time the Kaiser himself declared to his generals that the war must be stopped. A month later, with the collapse of the Macedonian front, and the determination of Austria to get out of the war, the situation had become hopeless. This was in effect admitted by Ludendorff, who on September 28th pronounced the German situation desperate and said an immediate peace was essential. Ludendorff conveniently changed his position later, and after the war he joined those who fostered the theory of conspiracy.

4. The Social Democrats did not sabotage the war. Their main organ, The *Vorwaerts*, did stand for a peace based on negotiation and conciliation instead of a dictated peace. So did similar groups in France and England. It was entirely possible for intelligent and patriotic citizens to believe in such a policy, and in retrospect who can deny that it might have been a wise one. In October 1918, *Vorwaerts* did say that "victory was not to entwine itself with the German flags" (p. 254). But this was when already the same conclusion had been forced upon the leading generals. Hitler entirely misrepresents the position taken by *Vorwaerts*. It was pleading for the kind of peace that would bring not a new war but a reign of peace, for the benefit alike of the vanquished and the victors.

We have already pointed out that Hitler was quite mistaken in identifying the Social Democrats with the Marxists. The difference appeared in many ways and not least in their respective attitudes toward the prosecution of the war.

5. German official statistics of the war disprove Hitler's claim that

the Jewish people shirked war service and filled all the clerical offices. Although before the war Jews were excluded from the Prussian military caste, two thousand of them received commissions during the war. Jews were called to the army just like all other German citizens. They could not have stayed out of uniform even if they had wanted to. That they played their part with the rest is shown by the fact that 35,000 Jews received decorations for war heroism and that some 80,000 were front-line fighters. The total number of Jewish citizens in the Reich was around 550,000. When the war situation was desperate at the end of September 1918, it was Walter Rathenau, a Jew, who advocated a last line of resistance through a universal call to arms. He was the man who afterwards was calumniated and finally murdered by Nazi sympathizers.

With these facts before us—and they could be greatly multiplied— we may surely ask whether a program that resorted to such gross misrepresentation, that so passionately inculcated hatred and disseminated prejudice, was not destined, if it succeeded, to have evil consequences for Germany and for the world. In particular, the following comments seem in order.

Hitler lays great stress on physical courage and frequently denounced his political opponents, quite falsely, as cowards. It cannot be denied that many of his followers possessed physical courage and were ready to sacrifice their lives for his cause. But there is another kind of courage that perhaps is more rare and that is more constructive and in the longer run even more valuable. This is moral courage, which includes the courage honestly to face the truth, the courage that refuses to distort or conceal the evidences, the courage that does not resort to falsehood and slander in order to support its cause. We have seen that there is strong evidence to show that the First World War was lost by Germany through military defeat, not through the treason of its people or the treachery of their leaders. Hitler refused to face this truth. His emotions were repelled by it and so he flatly denied it. He used all his powers of oratory, he aroused every prejudice and passion, he traduced thousands of patriotic and innocent people, rather than face the truth. Unfortunately for the world, he succeeded too well. Did he not thereby destroy the saving power that comes from facing reality? There were many in Germany who had the constructive courage to recognize the facts and on that basis to seek to rebuild their country on stronger foundations. They conquered many difficulties in order to lay these foundations. Hitler crushed them all when he came to power. The spirit that refuses to admit the truth is the same spirit that denies to men of different minds the right to hold their own opinions, even the right to exist.

We should observe also that Hitler in these pages does not direct his main invective against the Treaty of Versailles but against his own countrymen. It was never his interest to achieve merely a revision of the Treaty, with respect to those clauses that were particularly onerous for Germany. Such revisions as were achieved later under the Weimar Republic were of small moment to him. He does attack the war guilt clause, but only on propagandistic grounds; he stated himself that he was ready similarly to attribute the whole blame to the other side (p. 236). He himself would certainly have imposed an even more harsh treaty if victorious, and he found no fault in this regard with the Treaty of Brest Litovsk. Believing in war as the arbitrament of fitness he was willing to go to all lengths in crushing a defeated foe. To do so was for him, as he tells us in passages already referred to, to follow the law of nature. He could see the world only in terms of conqueror and conquered, the dominating and the dominated. He was sure that Germany was appointed by destiny to dominate the world. Therefore he refused to accept the truth about the defeat of Germany in the First World War.

THE BEGINNINGS OF THE
NATIONAL SOCIALIST MOVEMENT

At the end of the war Hitler, discharged from the hospital, continued his connection with the army, though now in a nominally civilian capacity. He found some kind of occupation with a battalion of his regiment that presently was transferred to Munich. What happened there, though nobody could have dreamed it at that time, was to become of terrible significance for Germany.

Bavaria had been going through a series of political upheavals. As so often happens, when conditions are bad and discontent runs high, the progressive groups were deeply divided and were fighting bitterly against one another. Kurt Eisner, a moderate and rather dreamy socialist of Jewish origin, had led a revolution that threw out the Wittelsbachs, and became Premier. He was assassinated by a group of reactionaries, led by Count Arco-Valley, and the socialist government that tried to carry on was overthrown by a communist uprising, supported by some communist soldiers. An army composed of government forces and free corps troops marched against Munich and seized control, taking heavy vengeance and punishing by death one out of every ten of the communist soldiers.

This period of violence and unrest had already begun when Hitler arrived in Munich. He was there during the communist regime and became an informer on communist activities. The fact that the socialist Eisner had been a Jew and that there were Jewish members active in the communist groups intensified his anti-Semitism. He was assigned to a military course on political action. One of the groups on which he was instructed to report was a handful of obscure men calling themselves the German Workers' Party. He went and was impressed by the doctrine of one Georg Feder, an engineer who had certain economic ideas. These ideas were quite immature. Feder made a distinction between financial capital and material capital. The latter was good, the former an invention of the devil—or rather of the Jew. This doctrine mightily appealed to Hitler. He saw a new light. He knew nothing about economics but here was a new slogan, a new weapon against the Jews, and ever afterward he was obsessed by the notion that most of the evil in the world, and particularly in Germany, was due to "the Jewish international stock exchange." Curiously enough, Karl Marx—who of course was opposed to all forms of private capital—became for him the great instigator of this "Jewish financial conspiracy." We shall leave this point for later comment.

Hitler found another advantage in Feder's ideas. He saw in them a strong ground of appeal to small bourgeois elements, which he hoped to attract to his party. At this time the rate of interest was very high, largely owing to the prevailing confusion and uncertainty. Small traders were suffering heavily on this account. So the cry of relief from interest slavery was welcome to many in the middle classes. Here was a way to undermine the socialist movement, by offering a new brand of socialism. Thus the program of Pan-Germanism could gain many recruits from the classes to whom it had hitherto made relatively little appeal. It would now become "National Socialist," but this part of the National Socialist platform was later minimized, and Feder, at first a leading member of the party, sank into obscurity.

What made these days in Munich (Chaps. 8 and 9) so tragically historic was that Hitler now joined this obscure group and by his ceaseless energy and propagandistic skill built it into a national party. These qualities of his, together with the capacity for oratory that he now discovered, soon made him the leader. The original leaders of the group, Harrer and Drexler, became secondary. Hitler was the man whose ringing and violent words attracted ever larger audiences. Hitler became the Führer.

HITLER'S REFLECTIONS ON
"THE CAUSES OF THE COLLAPSE"

In a long chapter on the collapse of Germany at the end of the First World War (Chap. 10), Hitler proceeds to attach responsibility to all groups that were out of accord with his own ideas. It is not always clear whether by the collapse he means the military collapse or the revolutionary change from the Reich to the Weimar Republic. Anyhow he lumps the two together and claims that both were due to the same causes.

There are flagrant contradictions in his account. He makes the admission here that the German army was greatly outnumbered, that the enemy also knew how to fight, and that the armaments on the other side were far greater than those disposed of by Germany. Yet he obstinately refuses to admit that these factors could explain the defeat. Again, while he rightly extols the heroic courage with which the Germans fought, he paints in lurid colors the terrible decay of the German people. But obviously a decadent people, a people that had lost its vigor and morale, could not have carried on so enormous a struggle and could not have displayed so effectively in war the military virtues that for Hitler are the highest of all. In this kind of warfare the army is the people in arms. Yet to Hitler, while the army was magnificent, the people were largely fools or cowards. They were suffering, he says, "a truly evil degeneration." They were poisoned through and through by subversive ideas. Education was all wrong, morals were corrupted by money, art was diseased, culture was effete, treason was rife, health was undermined, religion was spineless, and the younger generation was tainted by "the sins against blood and race." As for the upper classes, they too, Hitler explains, had lost all sense of leadership. The monarchy was seduced by flatterers, the nobility had become ignoble, were demeaning themselves by entering the world of finance, and were even marrying Jews. In short, everything was rotting —except the army.

This comprehensive diatribe exhibits strongly the influence on Hitler of Oswald Spengler, who was profoundly reactionary and hated modern civilization, but who, unlike Hitler, thought the "decay" inevitable. It also follows the line of Houston Stewart Chamberlain, who, like Hitler, became German by naturalization. It is an interesting fact that the most extreme nationalists are often men who have abandoned their original nationality. Rosenberg is another example.

Hitler's Pan-Germanism was particularly offended by everything that made for cooperation and free dealings between nations. The idea that nations could prosper together through the arts of peace was rejected as an insidious Jewish doctrine. The devotion of a country to economic prosperity he regarded as cowardly pacifism. The way to true prosperity was by the sword. He saw no alternatives except greed and materialism on the one hand and military domination on the other. The splendid achievements of Germany in industrial development he scorned, although even success in warfare was dependent on industrial advance. The remarkable contributions of Germany to science and technology he disregards. Her cultural attainments he vaguely praised so long as they belong to a more heroic past. But he despises the freedom of spirit, the intellectual integrity, the disinterested exploration of nature, without which the greater cultural advances are never achieved. While, for example, he praises Goethe, it is clear he had no sympathy with the universalism that made Goethe great. All his ideas are limited by his narrow nationalistic horizon, and for the sake of this unbounded nationalism he would crush the free spirit of men in all its pursuits, as indeed he and his party did when they came into power. In short, while he exults in Germanism he has no understanding of Germany. But unfortunately he did understand very well how to make tempting promises to the people and how to excite their prejudices in a time of national abasement and economic distress.

Of genuine reforms making for the welfare of the people almost the only one Hitler cared for was the improvement of physical fitness, since he saw here a condition of greater military strength. In the course of this chapter he has a long and somewhat curious excursus on the terrible evils of syphilis. He is of course entirely justified in deploring this grave disease, with its disastrous consequences to the health of the stock. What makes his account curious is that he associates this disease with all the social and cultural tendencies he dislikes. Syphilis poisons the body and they poison the mind. For him syphilis and the marriage of Germans with non-Aryans are in the same category. Furthermore, in giving syphilis a prominent place in the collapse of Germany he does not reflect that the prevalence of syphilis was as great in many other countries. As a remedy he prescribed early marriage. Whether or not the prescription would be effective, he gives no indication of how it could be put into practice. But the early marriage presumably would mean a higher birth rate, to furnish greater armies for the dominant state. More power is the goal, not more health or more welfare. Hitler speaks about the profanation of love, but love seems to mean for him merely the mating of healthy bodies, without reference to the blossoming of new, finer, and deeper relations between man and woman.

It would take too much space to dwell on the many charges brought in this chapter against the people and the leaders of Germany, both before the war and in the troubles that followed, but we may note again his extreme detestation of all democratic methods and principles. Thus he makes the Reichstag a main cause of the weakness of Germany. It was a "grave digger of the German nation and the German Reich" (p. 369). He calls its members knaves and cowards. It was no mere coincidence that as soon as the Nazis came into power the Reichstag building was burned down in a mysterious fire. The Reichstag inherited the legacy of the war and it was composed of members, many of whom showed the highest courage and integrity in seeking to find a way out of a disastrous condition for which they certainly could not be held as primarily responsible. Branded as traitors by the conservatives and under attack from the extreme left wing, the government probably did as well as any government could have done in the chaos and tumult of the times. It had to suppress armed assaults like those of Kapp and the later Munich *Putsch* organized by Hitler and Ludendorff, Its president was attacked by assassins and some of its prominent leaders were murdered. Hitler was foremost among those who quite falsely claimed it had betrayed the country.

In times of grave national dissension the wise policy, the truly courageous policy, is hard to find and hard to follow. Men are embittered and desperate, susceptible to the counsels of rashness and the appeals of fanaticism. Extremity breeds extreme doctrines. At no time is there so great a need for the qualities that make a people great. The struggle for a new and better society is not so spectacular as the death struggle of war. But it is under these conditions an even more heroic fight, for it is beset with greater temptation as well as with greater difficulties. Under the Weimar Republic Germany was making a first advance along this new hard road, in spite of obstructions and setbacks. But the headstrong policies of men like Hitler at length prevailed. In consequence, a new and worse disaster befell the whole world and Germany ended in deeper ruin. For our whole civilization there is no way out so long as the people of any great country respond to the siren voices of such leaders. There is no way out so long as the ideals they proclaim are powerful. Only when people everywhere respond to ideals and aspirations congenial to the civilization we have built, ideals that at length unite nations under a greater law instead of dividing them sharply into antagonistic camps, can we hope for a more enduring peace, a reign of justice, and the liberation of the minds and the hearts of men.

Having enumerated his long list of "causes" for the collapse of Germany, Hitler ends up by returning to his major theme, the uniqueness of race, the primacy of the German race, the difference between the German race and all other races. "In the non-recognition of the race problem" he discovers "the deepest and the ultimate cause for the ruin of the old Reich" (p. 388). The German race had refused to recognize nature's primal law. Let us now examine the law as enunciated by this student of the lessons of nature.

NATION AND RACE

All that is not race in this world is trash (p. 406).

In Chapter 11 Hitler expounds his primary thesis, the doctrine of race. It contains an amazing number of misconceptions and erroneous statements. Hitler knew nothing of biology or of anthropology, of the principles of eugenics or of the laws of nature. He accepted without the least investigation the false premises of Houston Stewart Chamberlain and Alfred Rosenberg. These premises were derived from some French chauvinists who put forward certain racial theories in the nineteenth century, particularly Count Gobineau, Lapouge, and Ammon. No anthropologist or biologist of any standing subscribes to these theories and many writers in this field have exposed their falsehood. The main arguments put forward by Hitler sum up into three main contentions, and we shall consider them in turn.

1. Hitler speaks of the "inner seclusion of species," terming this "one of the most outstanding principles of Nature's working" (p. 389). It is roughly correct that species breed within their own specific kind, though there are numerous instances of hybridization. However, the essential falsehood implied here is that nations or even what we call races are different species. There are, as every biologist will testify, no species of *Homo sapiens* but at the most only variations of one species—and in nature such varieties interbreed very frequently. Neither the German nor the Aryan (if there is an Aryan) is a distinct *species* of man. Therefore whatever law may apply to species has no application whatever to the intermarriage of Germans with other peoples.

The differences between groups and nations are certainly not differences of species. Wherever a number of people together occupy the same territory, the conjunction of cultural and environmental conditions, together with the effects of interbreeding, tend to confer on that group certain prevailing characteristics. It is impossible fully to distinguish characteristics that are culturally acquired and those that are responsive to environmental conditions. The various factors work together. The culture influences the environment and the environment the culture. Throughout human history there has been endless cultural borrowing, so complex in its ramifications that while the source of certain traits can sometimes be distinguished, the relation of the culturally borrowed to the indigenously developed is on the whole unfathomable.

Every group and every nation is itself the result of a process of interbreeding that goes back far beyond the limits of human knowledge. Invasion and migration have gone on through countless generations. Conquering peoples made slaves of their female captives and bred offspring from them. The intermixture of different peoples has proceeded wherever they came into contact. In this sense all peoples are hybrids, the hybrids of hybrids. For limited periods some groups have been kept apart from others by geography or by their own cultural exclusiveness. But the cultural inheritance they thus maintain was itself the result of prior intermixture. This has been the case, for example, with the Japanese and with the Jews. Over a period of history they maintained a nearly complete exclusiveness, but neither was a separate or pure stock, unmixed with the blood of other peoples. Both were already, in the sense referred to, hybrids.

2. Hitler contends that hybridization always means an offspring not only inferior to that of the higher group or "race" but also subject to progressive degeneration (p. 392). Here again we have a statement that not only is too sweeping but also has an entirely fallacious application. When mating does occur between different species it is rarely a clear issue of the mating of higher and lower, and nearly always an instance of the mating of types each of which has its own particular qualities. When interbreeding occurs in nature the crosses are often as vigorous as either one of their respective parents. Nature of course sets limits to inter-mating and there are special cases where though intermating is possible the hybrids are sterile—the mule is an example. But normally where nature permits intermating the offspring tend to have different but not necessarily lower qualities from those of either of their progenitors. The cattle breeder and the horticulturist make great use of this fact.

Hitler assumes not only that various human groups are different species of man but also that these are clearly differentiated as higher and lower species. The question of higher and lower arises in the relation of the advanced peoples to the backward peoples, but even here anthropologists are usually unwilling to assume any intrinsic or biological difference. How far the backward peoples are intrinsically inferior in human qualities, if at all, is an unsolved question. The effects of culture, economic opportunity, and differential environment as these operate over hundreds of generations cannot be assessed. It is much more clear that different families have differential qualities than that different peoples have them. This is heredity, not race. Even so, sometimes the stocks that display poorer qualities show a surprising development under changed conditions. While there are here some questions on which scientific opinion differs, the conclusion of Hitler that interbreeding between individuals of different nations or "races" results in a deterioration of the stock is entirely unscientific. Where, however, there is social disgrace in intermating, the product of such intermarriages, such as the mulatto of the Southern United States, lives under particularly disadvantageous conditions which often have a prejudicial effect on his morale. On the other hand most of the greater civilizations have arisen at the meeting point of peoples where interbreeding was prevalent and where different traditions met. This applies to the people who made the greatest advance ever achieved in human culture, the Ancient Greeks. It was at the points where they came particularly in contact with other cultures, such as Athens and Argos and Corinth, that they attained their highest level. If we were to follow the records of the past we should find the same story over and over again, down to the French and the English and the Americans, and, for that matter, the Germans of the modern world.

3. Hitler's third contention is as false as the other two. In his national

pride he claims that the Aryan race is not only superior to all others but that it alone is the authentic and essential bearer of human culture (pp. 397-398, 405). Curiously enough, this position was derived from a Frenchman, Count Gobineau. It was exploited by some German enthusiasts, including Richard Wagner, who for all his musical genius was less than knowledgeable in this field. His son-in-law, the ex-Englishman Chamberlain, did most to elaborate it. According to this view the Aryan was essentially German. Of the Aryan race the most important branch was supposed to be the blond and blue-eyed Nordic. The Nordic race was identified with the German. It was superior to all the other Aryan groups, much superior to the Mediterranean or Latin race, and of course vastly superior to all beyond.

The whole conception is a myth without foundation. There is in the first place no Aryan race. The term "Aryan" is Sanskrit. It was originally used by an English scholar to refer not to a people or a race but to a group of languages. This usage was extended by Max Müller to signify a larger series of languages, the Indo-Germanic, regarded as stemming from Central Asia. All scholars in this field now recognize that there is no implication of racial unity or even affinity in the fact that various people use the same language or have different languages with identical roots. No anthropologist of any competence accepts the theory of an Aryan race. The myth is the pure product of nationalistic egoism.

Suppose, however, we apply the term "Aryan" to the Teutonic peoples or even more largely to the peoples who speak the various Indo-Germanic languages. Suppose also we ignore the fact that they are all a mixture of many elements. Can we still claim that the so-called Aryan peoples are the bearers of human culture, that "everything we admire on this earth" is the product of these peoples? Nothing could be more false. Many peoples outside of these have made primary contributions to the sum of human culture. The first great civilizations developed while the so-called Aryans were for the most part still primitives. In China, for example, there arose a splendid civilization, rich in the plastic and the graphic arts. In the valleys of the Euphrates and the Tigris and the Nile great advances in civilization were made to which the peoples we call Semitic made important contributions. Many of the most historical discoveries in the arts of writing, engraving, sculpting and building, in astronomy and in geometry, come from these non-Aryan peoples. All the great religions were born in the East and it was Palestine that gave a religion to the whole Western world.

It is also a foolish and empty boast to claim that of the peoples who inhabit Europe the Nordic or Germanic ones have any exclusive birthright of culture. The culture of the Western world has been largely derived from the peoples of the Eastern Mediterranean. The legacy of Egypt and

Crete to Greece, of Greece to Rome, and of Greece and Rome together to the Western world can hardly be overestimated. In the Middle Ages it was again Italy that made the most outstanding contributions to cultural advance. The pretensions of Chamberlain and his school are utterly biased and unscholarly, and when to support their cause they even claim that Jesus and Columbus and Dante were in some unexplained way Aryans they become merely ridiculous.

There is a pride that pardonably, if not always justly, exalts the virtues and achievements of one's own people, one's own nation, one's own family, one's own group. This pride sustains the spirit of fellowship and often evokes devoted service. But there is another pride, the product of meanness, envy, and abasement, the blind egoism of the petty spirit that reviles all that is great and worthy in others in order to sustain its own self-esteem, the arrogance that excludes all others from the rights and privileges it claims for itself. This is the kind of false and ignorant pride Hitler and his fellows display in their assertions about race and nation. This is the kind of pride that, according to the ancient proverb, goes before a fall.

THE ARYAN AND THE JEW

Hitler concludes his assertions concerning race and nation with a new and even more venomous diatribe against the Jews (Chap. 11). His primary thesis is that the Aryan, the German, is in every respect the complete opposite of the Jew. He needs a devil to set off his god. The Jew becomes that devil. In his misguided zeal he imagined that the blacker he painted the Jews the brighter in contrast would shine the German *race*— not the German people.

It would require a whole volume to examine in particular all the charges Hitler here makes against the Jews, for a slander can be conveyed by a single word whereas it may need the long and careful marshaling of much evidence to show its falsehood. We shall limit ourselves to a brief discussion.

First there is the charge that his religion is for the Jew merely a device for secular conquest. The Jew sees in religion "only a means for his business existence" (p. 423). It is not religion that unites the Jews but a set of racial qualities. The Jew has no religion in any true sense, no faith that has a moral or spiritual basis.

We have already pointed out that the historical persecution of the Jews was directed against them on the ground of religion. They had crucified Christ, they obstinately rejected Christianity and clung the more tenaciously to their ancestral faith. Under the influence of the

Church the Jew who renounced his religion and accepted Christianity found protection against persecution and was admitted to membership in the community. Nevertheless, the Jew generally refused to abandon his faith and preferred to suffer grievous evils and to be confined in wretched ghettos. His faith was so closely bound in with his whole way of life that even apart from religious convictions he loathed to abandon it. The religious practices of Judaism dominated his social life and his habits to an extent that is not characteristic of a Christian community. The consequent exclusiveness of the Jew, which was met by the counter-exclusiveness of the Christian, was undoubtedly rooted in this fact. To say then that his religion was only a Machiavellian mask for purely secular aims is to contradict all the evidences of Jewish life. On specific points respecting Jewish religion Hitler is also wrong. He says, for example, that the Jew does not recognize any belief in a hereafter and therefore has no religion. But some of the religious creeds of the East, such as the Confucian and the Buddhist, do not affirm the concept of personal immortality. And in the later development of Jewish religion, the belief in immortality was upheld. The idea of rising from the dead, which was at length given so great a role in Christianity, was suggested in some of the later prophets and passed into the tradition of the Medieval Jews.

Second, there is the charge that the Jews are united in one world-wide conspiracy to undermine and to destroy Christian society. It seems incredible that a wholesale accusation of this kind should have been widely believed and that in the twentieth century it should have become the official doctrine of a country so advanced in cultural attainment as Germany.

There is of course no genuine evidence to support the charge. Hitler adduces the notorious "Protocols of the Wise Men of Zion." The history of this work is a curious one. It purports to be the record of a meeting of a group of Jewish leaders who in the year 1897, the year when the first convention of the Zionist Congress assembled in Basel, held a secret session of their own in that city. Actually the record was concocted in Russia under the auspices of the czarist secret police. The plot it reveals was taken from a satiric work published in 1864 by an ingenious French author, Maurice Joly. Joly was an ardent monarchist of the old school who hated Napoleon III as a usurper and dictator. He called his book *Dialogue aux enfers entre Machiavel et Montesquieu*. It explained in the style of Machiavelli how the modern dictator plays on the feelings of the masses in order to become their tyrant. The technique, the author cleverly explains, could be applied on a larger scale as a way to dominate not one country only but the whole world. Joly had a remarkable insight into the relation between the dictator and the masses but his book, published anonymously, went into oblivion, though not before the secret of its authorship was discovered by the French police, who put the author in prison.

Some ingenious anti-Semite unearthed this book and saw the possibility of using it against the Jew by substituting the Jews for Joly's dictator. In this form it was put at the service of the Russian secret police with the addition of anti-Semitic materials from other works. Thus was born the Protocols. It was used by the Russian police as a weapon against important political personages, and Rosenberg, when he fled from Russia, brought a copy with him to Berlin. Thereafter it was exploited on a large scale. By a strange irony of history, a work originally written to expose the world-wide peril of dictatorial domination was taken up in a spurious form by a dictator who himself sought world domination, and was used by him as authentic evidence of a Jewish plot against the world.

Hitler proceeds to connect the Marxists with this satanic plot. Here he stretches his ingenuity to the limit. If all Jews are capitalistically minded, how do Marx and his followers fit in? Are they not engaged in the most thoroughgoing assault on capitalism and its works? Ah, here we have "the most villainous betrayal of all times" (*den imfamsten Betrug aller Zeiten*). Marxism is the bait with which the Jew lures the workers. The Marxist exasperates their evil lot, takes advantage of the stupidity of employers who refuse to meet their reasonable needs, pretends the greatest sympathy for the exploited, and offers them a land of promise beyond the horizon. But it is all done in order to get the workers under his control and then to enslave them. From above, the big Jewish capitalists through their financial machinations are engaged in the enslavement of the upper classes, while down below their colleagues are busy enslaving the masses. Then when the job is complete they throw off the mask. Having destroyed the integrity of the whole people and having woven their web of financial domination, they come into their own and rule the world.

Since there is no scintilla of evidence for this profoundly improbable plot, and since the only purported evidence has been proved to be a forgery, we might dismiss the whole matter as the nightmare of an anti-Semitic imagination. But where prejudice is rife even the most absurd accusation leaves its imprint on the mind. We shall therefore take it a little more seriously than it deserves.

No student of Marxism, however adverse to the tenets of Marx, no reputable economist, has ever countenanced any such theory. It is in flagrant contradiction of all we know concerning the objectives of the followers of Marx. Many non-Jews are Marxists and a great many Jews are utterly opposed to Marxism. Those Jews who favor it do indeed yearn for a social revolution but this attitude is to be interpreted in an entirely different way. They are Jews who take this form of revolt against the discrimination, social and economic, to which they are often subjected. They think that if what they call capitalistic society were transformed they would be liberated from this discrimination. It is a natural and easily understandable reaction.

In one country alone has a revolution motivated by the spirit of Marx been successful in creating a well-established regime. In this country, Soviet Russia, the Jews do not dominate. The only important Jewish leader, Trotsky, was exiled from it. Furthermore, the regime did not set up the kind of financial capitalist domination dreamed of by Hitler but something utterly alien to it. These facts are exceedingly obvious, but a man who labors under a violent prejudice is not interested in obvious facts.

Finally there is the charge that the Jewish people are out to "bastardize" (*bastardieren*) the other peoples, and notably the Germans, to destroy the purity of the blood, the integrity of the race. With diabolic joy the young Jew waylays the innocent German maiden. Nevertheless, while he destroys the racial purity of other peoples by corrupting their women, the Jew guards the more the exclusiveness of his own race. "The Jew does not marry a Christian woman, but always the Christian a Jewess" (p. 434).

These statements are quite erroneous, even apart from the false premise about races and racial purity. Statistics on intermarriage are very inadequate but such researches as have been made tend to show that rather more Jewish men than Jewish women intermarry with non-Jews. But even were it the other way around it is difficult to see how that kind of disparity could be interpreted as evidence for Hitler's conclusion. In most communities intermarriage of either kind is relatively infrequent. In this sense the Jew, partly because of his own tradition, partly because of the social discrimination to which he is so often subjected, does on the whole maintain the exclusiveness of his group. The orthodox Jew has strong taboos against intermarriage. As the result of the social processes to which they have been responsive the Jews generally have come nearer than other peoples to the "inner exclusiveness" that Hitler preaches. Hitler ought logically to have praised the Jews as the great example for the Germans to emulate!

THE MOVEMENT IN BEING

In the last chapter of the first volume (Chap. 12) Hitler expounds more fully the principles and procedures on which the success of a movement like his own depends.

In the first place there must be, as he points out, a deep discontent pervading the people. The objective of the movement is to capture this discontent and harness it to the purpose of the leader. The movement must adopt every device to win the adherence of the masses. It must make any promises, particularly of an economic nature, that will entice them away from opposing camps. Hitler admits here very clearly the purely propagandistic nature of the economic program the Nazis profess to combine with their nationalism. The workers had to be enlisted, and they could be enlisted only by offering them economic betterment and especially economic security. To Hitler these offers are "concessions" and "sacrifices" for the sake of the greater cause. "No social sacrifice," he says frankly in speaking of his economic program, "is too great" if it will advance the cause (p. 465). The masses were inclined to radicalism. He too would offer them radicalism, so long as it was necessary in order to gain their support.

He goes on to explain that for the coming struggle, which from the first he sees as warfare, the immediate requisite is not the provision of arms but the inculcation of a martial spirit. First the people must be inspired with a burning zeal. There must be the concentrated dynamism of devotion to a cause, and then the means of action will be found. As the movement grows it must find appropriate embodiment in an authoritative organization within which it will be shaped and dedicated to the final struggle.

Hitler had a sure instinct concerning the path to his goal. He had a clear perception of the kind of organization that alone could carry it into effect and of the way in which that organization had to be built. There is indeed an interesting connection between his complete failure to understand the motives and ideals of other men and of different causes, on the one hand, and on the other his keen appreciation of the methods necessary to make his own cause prevail.

The connection is well exhibited in this chapter. Hitler totally misrepresents the objectives of all other parties in the state. Could anything have been more grossly unjust than to charge with treason those men and groups who were honestly seeking to rescue Germany from the plight into which she had fallen at the end of the First World War? Could misrepresentation go further than in the assertion that those citizens who were internationally minded—by which he meant those who sought a peaceful settlement between Germany and other countries—were those who believed in force and brutality? But misrepresentation is itself one of the methods not only appropriate but also necessary for the kind of authoritarian domination Hitler had in view. Only if large masses were indoctrinated with a passionate and truth-destroying conviction that they had been betrayed, that all other parties were in league with their enemies, could they become the fit instrument for Hitler's purposes. Only by falsifying the record could they be brought to this conviction.

Only with the aid of falsehood and calumny could Hitler come to power and only by that aid could he remain in power.

This much he himself knew. He tells us in this chapter that objectivity is weakness and that fanaticism is strength. But what does objectivity mean? It means simply the regard for truth, the clear appraisal of the facts, the balanced judgment of alternatives. These things Hitler rejects.

Next Hitler proceeds to describe the methods by which the movement was to be organized. As it grew beyond the first nucleus it had to build everywhere local cells, unit groups of devotees who were converts to the cause. These cells were to function in complete subservience to the sole leader. "All committees are subjected to him and not he to the committees" (p. 478). It is interesting to note that the authoritarianism of the movement grew more complete in the course of time. In the early editions of *Mein Kampf* the approved procedure is that the chairman of each local group is elected by that group. In the later editions the procedure was changed to appointment by the next highest leader and so through the various levels up to the top of the hierarchy. Only the top leader is supposed to be elected, but since he had the movement entirely in his hands such election was of course purely nominal. Yet Hitler without any consciousness of irony calls this system "the principle of Germanic democracy."

It was indeed a strange democracy that tolerated no differences of opinion anywhere along the line. At first there were diversities of viewpoint in the inner circle. Men like Drexler, Feder, and Julius Streicher had notions of their own. Hitler found ways of dominating these men as well as later dissentients. The last way was the famous purge of 1934, when Röhm, von Schleicher, and many others were put to death without trial. Hitler's nature could not tolerate any difference of opinion whether inside or outside his own party. In this chapter he makes it perfectly clear that the only way he knows to deal with those who differ from him is to annihilate them. He alone is judge of right and wrong. God is with him, and all who dispute his judgment are on the side of the devil.

The civilization of the modern world is endangered whenever this spirit of primitive intolerance comes into power. This civilization is built on the complex interdependence of nations and of groups. It is one in which differences must cooperate with and supplement one other. But the primitive spirit that lived in Hitler abhors cooperation and for interdependence substitutes sharp division, thus tearing asunder the great fabric man has built. There were many men who encouraged Hitler without reckoning the consequences; there were those who supplied him with funds and thought they still could control him. There were many who rejoiced with him when his movement began to grow. They thought he would save them from some danger they feared. But they did not fear the more terrible danger that lay ahead. "A fire had been lighted," said Hitler in his pride, "and out of its flames there was bound some day to come the sword." The fire had indeed been lighted and the sword was indeed forged in that fire. But the sword was double edged and slew also those who forged it, and the fire could not be stayed until it had brought destruction to the ends of the earth.

THE CENTRAL ERROR

With one further comment we conclude our review of the first volume of *Mein Kampf*. We have sought to bring out the violent bias, the contemptuous intolerance that pervades it. We have given reasons to show that the spirit that animated it is deadly to the creative culture that ennobles and enriches the life of modern men and to the complex civilization that sustains this life. In closing, let us venture to ask this question. Wherein lies the central error of the philosophy that lay back of Hitler and his movement?

We find it in his primitive conception of the nature of social unity, of the bond that unites men whether as families or as groups or as nations. For Hitler this bond is sheer uniformity, compulsive uniformity, uniformity of belief, uniformity of goal. Difference is for him poison. He would remake the whole world in his own likeness. He would make his own country a simulacrum of his own narrow personality. He would impose that narrow personality on the world. To this end he was ready to destroy all its free creativeness, all the spontaneous forces of that moving life and that broadening spirit that is infinitely greater than not only the personality of any mortal man but also the imagination of even the greatest of men.

In this spirit of pitiless conformism Hitler conceives the state. He abhors what he cannot comprehend—the democratic state where the differences of men are allowed free play within the bounds of the common law, where unity is not based on conformity but on the larger sense of the whole that binds men the more fully, the more deeply, because it permits their differences, their individualities, to find expression. Since for Hitler unity is compulsive and undifferentiated he must conceive the state as all-embracing. He demands that the people surrender themselves wholly to its service, to the fulfillment of its demands upon them. He wants the state to absorb their entire being, to leave them nothing of their own selfhood. This is what he means by the "nationalization" of the masses. They must become "nationalistic with the entire vehemence which is harbored in the extreme" (p. 467).

Here, in a more vulgar way, Hitler is following the philosophy that so many German philosophers, from the time of Fichte and Hegel, have espoused, the philosophy of the absolute state. The "unconditional principle of authority" rules it. There is one authority, one will, one aim. When Hitler speaks of the nationalization of the masses he makes it clear that this implies their complete subjection to himself and to his party. It is the enslavement of the people. They can have no free organizations, no free opinions. The community is in chains, bound fast by the steel of government. It does not matter that this philosophy is devoted to the glory of the nation. It is not the fettered nation that is thus glorified, but the abstraction of the nation in the mind of the tyrant. So Hitler glorifies Germany. But Germany has become for him a false abstraction, a false concept of a race that mirrors his own ideal of himself. No matter what this philosophy offers, no matter what glowing pictures it presents of greatness and dominion, it is still the philosophy of the master who demands the soul as well as the body of the slave, the philosophy of the tyrant who knows no arbiter but force.

In its vast arrogance this philosophy even dares to give to that enslavement the name of freedom. It is true freedom, says Hitler, this service of the state in which he alone is free. The old autocracy did not deny its true nature. The new and greater absolutism went further and identified itself with freedom. It compelled the slave to say that he was free. This last observation was made by a French lover of liberty in his attack on the first of our modern Caesars, Bonaparte. It is even truer of the man who, let us fervently hope, may prove to have been the last.

GOVERNMENT *and* SOCIAL CHANGE IV

The Philosophical Background
of the Constitution

25 Whatever may be the eruptive forces that precipitate the grand events of history, it can scarcely be denied that the particular contours of these events are molded by the thoughts of dominant minds. Underneath may lie the tensions and strains of the mass, but on every peak and crag are inscribed the insignia of the architect, the creative thinker. This holds as true of the American Revolution as of the French or of the Russian. It is as manifest in the more sober outlines of the Constitution as in the flaring upthrust of the Declaration of Independence.

In the political agitations that preceded the establishment of the Constitution the architectonic ideas were not indigenous but were derived from European, and above all from English, speculative thought. The thinkers who heralded the Revolution went back in particular to seventeenth-century England for the form and the idiom of their political philosophy. In America itself the speculative ground for this utterly unexpected event was unprepared. Neither the earlier theological preoccupations of the Puritan aristocracy nor such democratic revolts from them as were represented by Roger Williams had any relevance to the emergent issues. The older American tradition was decaying. The back country, to which the new immigrants, the ex-indentured men from Scotland, Ireland, and Germany were penetrating, was as yet politically mute. Among the leaders, in Charleston as in Boston, the Tory style was in the ascendant. There was nothing here from which to fashion the philosophy appropriate, indeed necessary, for the making of the new republic. Never in the history of the United States were the minds of men so exercised by argument over doctrines and theories of government as in the three decades of debate and contention that began about 1761. But the principles they proclaimed, the broad inevitable principles by which men justify alike their aspirations and their ambitions, were formulated in the England of a century before. For in that England, in the sequence of crises ending in the "Glorious Revolution," out of all the heresies and schisms of that time, there had emerged one distinctive mode of thinking, one "ideology" if you will, that proved notably congenial to the spirit of the new America. Of that mode of thinking the most adequate exponent was John Locke, and, curiously enough, Locke spoke in terms that were far more applicable to the American than to the English scene.

The seminal works of the age were English and French, those of Montesquieu, the physiocrats, and Rousseau on the one hand, and those of Locke, Harrington, Blackstone, Hume, Adam Smith, Algernon Sidney, and Tom Paine on the other. But Locke came nearest to the heart of the case. If an occasional criticism was passed on his plan of legislation for Carolina, as was done by John Adams—who did not accurately report it—it was only to show how "the most resplendent genius" may fail in practice.[1] *The Second Treatise on Government* was almost beyond criticism. How satisfying was Locke's persistent association of the ideas of liberty and property, with the unqualified corollary that no man could rightly be taxed without his own consent! How convenient for this undeveloped continent was his view of property, itself probably derived from his own acquaintance with American conditions, as that which a man appropriated by his labor from out the vast storehouse of nature! How well his simple concept of the "state of nature" served to turn men's thoughts from traditional notions of sovereignty, and how easy it was to see, with Benjamin Franklin, the same "state of nature" in the life of the American Indians! How comfortably did Locke's "law of nature," breathing quiet optimism and what Samuel Johnson of King's College spoke of as the "milder deism," fit in with the temper of an age that was retreating from a Calvinistic God to the God of nature, the invisible hand, the "legislator of the universe"! It is no wonder that Jefferson spoke of Locke as one of the three greatest men of all time, linking him with Newton and Bacon.

1. *Works of John Adams*, ed. by C. F. Adams, IV, 463–64.

The *ispsissima verba* of the *Second Treatise on Government* fell naturally from the lips of the fathers of the Constitution. These words seemed to express the very nature of things. "Do not every man's feelings," asked Franklin, "declare that his property is not to be taken from him without his own consent?" [2] Add to Locke's teaching Montesquieu's more explicit docrine of division of powers, inject into it some republican fervor, and you have the whole substance of the Virginia Bill of Rights, and indeed of all the preambles, manifestoes, and declarations of principle that followed.

I am not implying that the thinkers, publicists, and debaters of the constitution-making age merely echoed the doctrines of seventeenth-century England. They were theorists for a purpose and they took from these doctrines what was congenial to that purpose. English philosophy of the seventeenth century was the arsenal from which they drew the intellectual weapons they needed. Even Locke was treated in this way. Locke had made the legislature supreme over the executive and over the courts. But this aspect of Locke's theory the Americans finally rejected and in the rejection lay one essential difference between the emergent political system of America and that of England.

The pragmatic adaptation of European political ideas throughout the political developments converging on the Constitution is best revealed if we distinguish three stages of that process. In the first stage, beginning perhaps with the agitation over the Stamp Act, the main protest is in the name of fundamental law within the existing order, established by charter, by precedent, by the common law, by the series of acts beginning with Magna Carta which defined the principles of the British constitution. These principles, as the resolution of the Massachusetts house of representatives, inspired by Samuel Adams, stated in 1765, were "founded in the Law of God and of Nature" and were "the common rights of mankind."[3] But the appeal was for the vindication of rights regarded as already established within the Constitution. The nature of these rights had been set forth once for all by "the great Mr. Locke." They were summed up in his words that the legislature "cannot take from any man any part of his property without his own consent." "The position," declared Samuel Adams, "that taxation and representation are inseparable, is founded on the immutable laws of nature."[4]

The ingeniously simple formulations of Locke were, however, two-edged. In his political philosophy, as in his epistemology, Locke always refrained from drawing the more radical conclusions implicit

2. B. Franklin's marginal note on Ramsey, *Thoughts on the Origin and Nature of Government*, p. 27.

3. Samuel Adams, *Writings*, I, 23–24.

4. *Ibid.*, I, 175.

in his premises. He went so far and no further, never inquiring whether the road he followed did not lead far beyond his acceptable goals, beyond the doctrine of toleration and beyond the rights of freeholders. It was the spirit of Locke's political philosophy, and not its radical implications, that was so congenial to the thinkers and statesmen of America. A minority of radicals, like Samuel Adams, might draw the democratic conclusion that the ultimate sovereign is the people and that men owe no allegiance to laws they have not approved or to princes they have not set up. He interprets Locke in the terms of democratic individualism. "Mr. Locke, in his treatise on government...shows that express consent alone makes any one a member of any commonwealth." [5] But for the vast majority there was as yet no denial of a common allegiance nor on the other hand any readiness to accept the more radical implications of the "consent of the people." A few, like Patrick Henry and James Warren, were beginning to speak the complete language of the "rights of man," so much less circumspect than the Lockean language of "natural rights." The English republicans, particularly Algernon Sidney and Milton, were being read with new interest, but more for their views on liberty than for their republican sentiments. Benjamin Franklin had commended both for the education of the youth of Pennsylvania [6] and had given a special tribute to the "immortal *Discourses on Government* of Sidney, the British Brutus, the warm, the steady friend of liberty." [7] Harrington, who in his *Oceana* combined a republican philosophy with an aristocratic respect for landed property, was beginning to influence such men as John Adams and James Otis. [8] It is significant that Harrington ranks next to Locke among the English writers who had vogue in America. For Harrington political power went with land, and political leadership reposed with the landed proprietors. For Locke the preservation of property was the chief end of government. In its formative stage the movement that culminated in revolution was not a mass movement. Its philosophy was not by intention democratic. It had no thought to subvert the economico-political *status quo*. The foundation of order was already set. The basis of protest was established rights, and with John Adams and later with Alexander Hamilton the appeal was from the acts of a parliament that overstepped its bounds to the monarchy from which the original colonial charters emanated. [9]

---

5. *Ibid.*, II, 257–58.

6. *Works*, II, 386–96.

7. *Ibid.*, II, 295.

8. Cf. T. Dwight, "Harrington and His Influence upon American Political Institutions," *Political Science Quarterly*, II (1887), 1–44.

9. Cf. *Novanglus* (Works of John Adams, IV, 99ff.) and *The Farmer Refuted* (Works of Alexander Hamilton, ed. J. C. Hamilton, II, 43–55).

This inherent conservatism of the first stage may be illustrated by the attitude of the most cosmopolitan of American thinkers, Benjamin Franklin. Although later in attacking the order of the Cincinnati, he declared that he saw "more propriety, because less hazard of mischief, in having hereditary professors of mathematics" than in having hereditary legislators,[10] he nevertheless clung to the principle of a hereditary, though constitutional, monarchy until the tide of revolution rendered it untenable. And although in the revolutionary period he proclaimed that "the franchise is the common right of freemen" his earlier view was that those who had no landed property should have no vote in the affairs of government.[11]

As the rift with Great Britain widened into a chasm we enter upon the second stage, which may be roughly identified as the decade from 1772 to 1782. Now the doctrine of "natural rights" becomes the indubitable ground of revolution and the necessary foundation of a new order. The social contract doctrine takes on a new amplitude. The consent of the people must mean that of the people as a whole. The more radical note dominates. The Massachusetts delegates to the first Congress of 1774 are warned in New York not to be too extreme for the milder temper of the Southern delegates, and find that the South is prepared to go further than themselves. A year later it is the young Southerner Jefferson who is entrusted to state the American case, and in the most eloquent language he proclaimed the rights of a people born free and equal. Presently that language passed into the Virginia Bill of Rights and into the Declaration of Independence. The principle of liberty was released from the bracket of property. All power abides in and derives from the people. Governments are not merely their trustees, they are also their servants.

Two contemporary books written by Englishmen had their effect at this juncture. It may seem curious that Blackstone's *Commentaries* was one of them. But Blackstone, jurist as he was, stated in the simplest and indeed the most naïve form the Lockean principle of inherent and indefeasible rights. Blackstone, whose work was very popular in England, was already being taught at William and Mary College. Burke in his Conciliation Speech of 1775 called attention to Blackstone's vogue in America. "I hear," he said, "that they have sold nearly as many of Blackstone's *Commentaries* in America as in England. General Gage marks out this disposition very particularly in a letter on your table." The other work was Tom Paine's *Common Sense*, published in America a few months before the Declaration of Independence. It is hardly con-

---

10. *Works*, VI, 371. Cf. R. Eiselin, *Franklin's Political Theories*, pp. 79–80.
11. Cf. Eiselin, *loc. cit.*

ceivable that the iconoclastic passion of this manifesto would at any other time have deeply stirred the country. The time was exactly ripe. The old Whig appeals, from the parliament of England to the realm, from laws to royal charters, from executive encroachment to the constitutional monarchy, were ended with the fight at Lexington. And now came a pamphlet which branded monarchy as an abomination and inveighed against kings as the worst tyrants of the people. America was not only to be free, it was to be the one free land on earth, liberated from the oppressive traditions of the lands beyond the sea. This was the significance of Paine, that he proclaimed the end of the colonial attitude, and that he supplied the prophetic vision of a new Jerusalem on American soil, not the old Puritan vision but the dynamic myth of the one emancipated people, so that America might become the great "asylum for mankind."

As we pass into the third stage, wherein the issue was no longer the vindication of rights but the sure establishment of a greater state, there is again a very significant process of change in the atmosphere of thought. The change may be regarded as a mode of compromise between the dominant spirit of the first stage and that of the second, though there is a strong deflation of the more idealistic conception of democracy. Pragmatic aims are now more compelling than ultimate ideals. Nevertheless, theories of the state still play an important role. While it was the exigencies of the immediate situation, such as the need for compromise between the demands of the great states and those of the small states, that controlled the specific terms of the final covenant, yet men do not derive their practical expedients from sheer experience or from the mere light of nature. John Dickinson was demanding the impossible when he said at the Federal Convention: "Experience must be our only guide. Reason may mislead us."[12] Just as the Articles of Confederation and the state constitutions were heavily drawn upon to provide the formulas of the new document, so were the political theories of the time. Whether they are framing constitutions or pursuing their daily business, whether they are deemed to be demigods or to be more common clay, the thoughts of men run on the rails laid down in advance of action by their intellectual habits.

On the surface there was a greater doctrinal consensus in the second stage than in the third. The pragmatic test brought out the underlying differences. But the tide of effective opinion moved away from Paine and Jefferson in the direction represented by John Adams, who later wrote to none other than Jefferson that he had "never read reasoning more absurd, sophistry more gross...than the subtle labors of Helvetius

12. James Madison, *Writings*, IV, 186.

and Rousseau to demonstrate the natural equality of mankind." It moved in the direction of Sherman and the Pinckneys and John Dickinson and Madison and Hamilton, who tempered Locke with the pessimism of Hobbes or with the skepticism of Hume. The doctrine that all men were "created equal" was no longer a self-evident truth, when the question had become one of its application, not to a whole people as a unity but to the social order and to individual men. It is a necessary *datum* of the nascent constitution, that "the people are the only legitimate fountain of power"[13] and that "federal and state governments are in fact but different agents and trustees of the people."[14] But the people are not to be construed as Rousseau's "people," the totality of component human beings expressing their sovereign will. There was besides the nice question whether the slaves should be counted as persons, or as three-fifths of persons, or as not persons at all. Liberty must reign, but but it is Locke's "liberty," the liberty that is conjoined with property. The people must be sovereign, but in effect it is Locke's "people," the people with the stake of possessions, or even Burke's "people," the men of substance, discretion, and experience. The franchise must be universal, but the noxious growth of parties, otherwise "factions," must be avoided. The whole body of citizens must be the final arbiter of government, but under such conditions as to check what Alexander Hamilton called "the imprudence of democracy."

So in the constitution-framing stage the great problem of statesmanship is conceived as being the creation of such a balance between opposing interests or powers as will sustain the unity of the whole, protect each against all, and safeguard the established scheme of rights.[15] This was the problem to which the Constitution was the answer. There were statesmen of that age, some of its greatest figures, who thought—as Jefferson did on one count and Franklin on another—that the final problem of statesmanship was not properly set in these terms.[16] There are also worthy critics of our own day who agree with them. History does not decide between ideals. What history has decided is that, given the problem as the founders of the Constitution saw it, they solved it with eminent, and indeed unparalleled, success.

When the stream of history has once carved its channel we assume that it could have followed along no other path. But we can still raise

---

13. *The Federalist*, No. 49.
14. *Ibid.*, No. 46.
15. See, for example, *The Federalist*, No. 10 (Madison).
16. Franklin likened the system of checks and balances to the putting of one horse before the cart and another behind—and whipping them both, the result being an arrest of motion or the dissolution of the cart. Cf. *Works of Thomas Paine*, Conway ed., IV, 465.

at least this speculative question: What might have happened had such and such influences not been present? That there were other ways of stating and of solving the problem of the Constitution the debates of the time amply reveal. That the finally accepted way alike of stating and of solving it was influenced by the prevalent philosophies of government is equally clear. Even when we concede that these particular philosophies prevailed because they were in harmony with the attitudes or the interests of those who espoused them, their influence remains no less real.

Never before had the world seen an example of a balance of powers so elaborate and so consciously contrived as that provided in the Constitution. But the doctrine of balance had been proclaimed by various political thinkers, and particularly by those thinkers who, not only in the culminating stage but throughout the whole period of political ferment, were of most account in America. It was implicit in Locke, restraining the logic of his democratic ideas. A full generation before Locke it had been explicitly announced by Harrington as a primary condition of a stable state and embodied in his plan of an "equal commonwealth," his "empire of laws and not of men." Harrington was one of those detached and original thinkers who miss the tide of influence in their own time and place, to strike it again with greater effect in a later age. His ingenious and foresighted interest in the mechanism of representative government, his sense of the importance of land, and his combination of an aristocratic outlook with a zeal for republican institutions, made "the incomparable Harrington," as Otis called him, one of the most reputed authors of the constitution-making period. [17]

During this period the thinkers who had most effect were those who were at the same time liberalistic in policy and fundamentally conservative in outlook. It was precisely these thinkers who inclined to the principle of a balanced government. An example is Blackstone, who did not let his doctrine of indefeasible rights prevent him from finding an admirable proportion and balance in the British Constitution. Another work that was drawn on to the same effect was the *Essays* of David Hume. The studied moderation and the tempered skepticism of Hume were particularly attractive to Hamilton. It is significant that in the concluding paragraph of *The Federalist*, when Hamilton is seeking to sum up the whole matter, he has recourse to the "solid and ingenious Hume." "To balance a large state or society," he quotes from the *Essays*, "whether monarchical or republican, is a work of so great difficulty, that no human genius however comprehensive, is able, by the mere dint of reason

17. Cf. H. F. Russell Smith, *Harrington and His Oceana.*

and reflection, to effect it. The judgments of many must unite in the work; experience must guide their labor; time must bring it to perfection." This was also the spirit of Hume's great friend, Adam Smith, himself an advocate of a federal system of government for the British Empire. His economic doctrine was *par excellence* a doctrine of the balance of interests, the counterpart and indeed the logical foundation of the principle of the balance of powers. As such it appealed to Hamilton, who is recorded to have read the *Wealth of Nations* as soon as the first copies crossed the Atlantic. [18]

But none of these advocates of balance attained the authority of Montesquieu, "the oracle," says Madison, "who is always consulted and cited on this subject." [19] That the influence of Montesquieu was effective is evident not only from the definite embodiment in the Constitution, no less than in the earlier Bills of Rights, of his doctrine of the division of powers, but also from the frequent appeals made to his authority on other grounds. The ninth number of *The Federalist* is entirely devoted to meeting an attack on the republican principle, which professed to base itself on certain observations of Montesquieu, circulated "with great assiduity" by the opponents of the Constitution. Both Madison and Hamilton turn the tables on their critics by citing from that author a passage in which he dwells on the merits of a "confederate republic," a passage that Hamilton proclaims to be "a luminous abridgement of the principal arguments in favor of the Union." [20]

Nevertheless, the balanced state which Madison did so much to construct and Hamilton so much to defend had a character entirely different from that of the exemplars and models to which they pointed. The functional division of powers does not imply the constituent division of sovereignty itself. The latter had no real precedents. [21] It flouted an agelong tradition. It owed nothing to Locke or Harrington or even Montesquieu. Greatly influenced by European political philosophies as were the builders of the Republic, the fabric they constructed was in essentials, almost without their knowing it, profoundly new. That part of the ancient tradition of government that might have stood in the way they rejected almost without discussion. One of the ablest of the representatives at the Federal Convention, Rufus King of Massachusetts, expressed on one occasion his amazement that men were ready to sacrifice their substantial good to the "phantom of sovereignty." But it was only a phantom, vanishing before the face of necessity. They

18. Cf. C. G. Bowers, *Jefferson and Hamilton.*
19. *The Federalist*, No. 47.
20. *Ibid.*, No. 9. See also No. 43.
21. Cf. S. Mogi, *The Problem of Federalism*, I, Chap. 1.

did not reason with it, they merely ignored it. Therefore the political philosophy of the Constitution is a different thing from the political philosophies that moved its creators. In this respect they builded better than they knew, indeed better than the world yet knows.

[1938]

Two Centuries of
Political Change

26

I

Two centuries are only three times the lifespan of a man,
but in them the world has changed beyond the wildest
dreams of the wildest prophet. Nowhere has the metamor-
phosis been so incredibly vast and decisive as in the United
States. Two centuries ago the union had not even been
conceived. It was a period when rival imperial nations were
fighting for the spoils of America. That strife was nearing
its end. While the British and the French were at war in
Europe they were also fighting, in the more spasmodic
manner of those days, in the Ohio country, at Crown Point,
around Niagara and Lake Erie, and in Quebec. After some
minor victories and defeats the British won the Battle of
the Plains of Abraham and the whole of Canada, then mostly
an unknown wilderness, passed into their hands. With the
Treaty of Paris, ceding Canada and eastern Louisiana to
the British, control of the continent from the Arctic to the
then borders of Mexico passed into British hands. All that
remained was the resistance of Indian tribes on the fringes
of colonial habitation and some outlying French posts in
the West.

The military settlement was scarcely achieved when

new troubles arose. In those days the imperial powers of Western Europe were in the grip of the vicious and shortsighted theory of mercantilism, which held that the benefit of trading was one-sided, that it was desirable to export as much and import as little as you could, taking the balance in bullion or precious metals. Britain acted on this theory toward her American colonies, imposing a series of grievous restrictions on their trading and on their economic development. It looked on British America as imperial booty, a one-way market for British goods, and a source of profit for British governors and British adventurers. The whole story of the dispute between Great Britain and her American colonies illustrates the fatal miscalculations that come from shortsighted self-interest. As so often has happened in politics high and low, narrow self-interest divides and loses where enlightened self-interest would have united and won. The routine acceptance of outworn traditions is never a substitute for political intelligence. In this respect, though not in some others, the French in America had been wiser than the British. The French treated their American colonies as an integral part of France, bound to it by unity of interest. The British opposed their economic interest to that of their American colonies. The French lost America because the British had better resources and sometimes better generals. The British lost America because they had antiquated ideas of how these colonies should be treated. They undermined and finally destroyed loyalties they were not wise enough to cultivate.

We need not recount the story. One unwise intervention followed another. The protests of the colonists were mostly disregarded. Disaffection grew. Attempts at enforcement hardened the thoughts of the resistance. Blundering governors, particularly Hutchinson of Massachusetts, made matters worse, and blundering ministers in London, particularly Lord North, fanned the flame of revolt. Bold new voices were heard in America, those of men like Patrick Henry and Samuel Adams and John Adams. The final outcome was the War for Independence.

The thirteen colonies were separate entities, with local assemblies. The war brought them into a loose union through the Continental Congress. The British, who had enough European troubles anyway, gave up at length a struggle they could not hope to win.

It is significant that the colonists opposed England in the name of doctrines derived from England. They appealed to the British Constitution, to long-established English traditions, stretching back to Magna Carta. They appealed to English doctrines, to her great political philosophers. Practically every American statesman of that day was well versed in political theory. Not only in their representations to the British

Parliament but in their appeals to their own people they quoted Hume and Montesquieu and Sidney and Milton and Blackstone and above all John Locke, the philosopher who had most clearly formulated the principle of no taxation without representation. In the Declaration of Independence Jefferson used the very language of Locke, but with a boldness that went beyond the temper of that restrained philosopher. In passing we may note that in the early controversy over the new taxes the most effective argument was made by a boy of eighteen, a college undergraduate named Alexander Hamilton, who dealt incisively with the nature and limits of parliamentary jurisdiction.

Here we find a remarkable contrast with our own days. In this respect at least a change has taken place in the American political scene that cannot be reckoned as progress. Madison and Hamilton could pen a series of newspaper columns, under the guise of letters addressed to the people of New York State, in which they dwelt on precedents going back to ancient times and referred to sayings of Plato and Socrates and Polybius. Who of our statesmen would address the public in such terms today? Who of our statesmen would do it if he could? The level of political communication was higher in those days, and it never descended to the depths that some of our senators and congressmen are willing to exhibit. True, the reading public of these days was more of an elite, but it is equally true that the character of public debate, as it found expression in Madison and Jefferson and Franklin and not a few besides of the leading figures of that age, was far superior to that which has prevailed in our own times. Why this should have been so I do not ask at this point. I record the fact.

They say it is times of crisis that drive men to do some fundamental political thinking, which may be true, although the product of that thinking is by no means always so happy as it was in the founding period of the Republic. The interval of confederation that followed the end of the revolutionary war was a crucial one. There were strong forces that opposed any genuine union. The Declaration of Independence, for all its nobility, gave no lead in this direction. The idea of the supremacy of the individual state had a powerful hold. The issue was in the balance, a genuine union or a congeries of states that would harden into petty separate sovereignties. That is why it was supremely important that the founding fathers had a grasp alike of present realities and of future needs. Conscious of the present realities, they knew how to compromise and adjust differences. Conscious of future needs, they knew how to build a more perfect union.

The necessity for something better than a mere confederation soon became obvious. The Congress, beset by the jealous sovereignties of the states, was refused the power to levy taxes. Confusion, gross inflation, and practical bankruptcy ensued. It was time for the statesmen of that day to devise something far better. The call for a constitutional convention was too urgent to be denied.

The Constitution emerged out of incessant controversy and endless differences of opinion and of interest. Not a clause, hardly a line, but was fought over, and after debate and often amendment passed by a majority, sometimes a majority of one in the Constitutional Convention. But the foundations were laid and enduring stability established.

The Constitution that emerged was not the final embodiment of eternal wisdom that reverential but uncritical posterity has believed. It has undergone considerable change, partly through amendment but even more through the process of interpretation and the growth of constitutional customs. In some respects it was not, in its original import, a particularly democratic structure. The majority of the founding fathers were rather afraid of the voice of the people, and the system of checks and balance, as well as the complexity of the amending process, was designed as a restraint on full democracy. The spirit of the Constitution was not the spirit of the Declaration of Independence. The Jefferson group had little to do with the making of it. Nevertheless, the foundations of a great state were well and truly laid, and the concept of a true federation was for the first time fully realized. The Constitution could withstand all storms and needed only the processes of adaptation through the generations to changing conditions and needs to become the full and true embodiment of the spirit of a great people. The beginnings of that process came with the Judiciary Act of 1789, which prepared the way for judicial review, and of course with the Bill of Rights, which followed in 1791.

The Bill of Rights, or the first ten amendments, constituted the second great landmark in the creation of the American system. Already the constitutions and laws of various states, notably Virginia and Massachusetts, contained similar provisions. It is significant that the Bill of Rights was wholly directed against governmental encroachments on liberty. The civil rights of the citizen were thought of as threatened almost exclusively from that source. Thus, though the Bill of Rights was of primary importance, it introduced no safeguards against the exploitation of group by group, and above all it said nothing about slavery. Slavery was gradually disappearing in the North. Massachusetts, through its Supreme Judicial Court, had abolished it in 1783. Thus, in spite of the standards of the Bill of Rights, a rift was already being prepared between North and South that in the course of time would ripen into nearly fatal division.

So, by 1791 the form of the new state was established and its direction set. Thirteen colonies along the eastern seaboard, with a total population of 2½ million, became a state and the beginning of a nation. The form and the direction have endured throughout vast processes of cumulating change, during which these scattered communities of cultivators and merchants became the inheritors of a continent whose resources were beyond the wildest prophetic dream, and whose power, greater than any history had known and more beneficent in its greatness, was to reach to the world's end.

Man has never been able to predict what even the near future will hold. The builders of the Union knew almost nothing of the continent that fell to them. It is only a hundred fifty years since the new state bought for $15 million the vast domain of French Louisiana. It is only a hundred fifty years, a little less, since Lewis and Clark made their perilous way across the plains and the mountains to the mouth of the Columbia River. Tremendous tasks and incessant hardships were faced by the generations that opened up the land. And as it was being developed and more and more of its resources explored and harnessed, as the population grew and wave after wave of immigration came to share in its labors and in its fruits, as industry spread and cities grew great, inevitably political changes of great moment also occurred.

We shall review these under four heads:
1. Changes in the constitutional framework.
2. Changes in the functions and processes of government.
3. Changes in the nature and direction of public opinion.
4. Changes in international policies.

II

The full bearing and meaning of a constitution, no matter how well and wisely planned, can never be known to the planners. It has to meet the test of experience and the test of changing conditions. The processes of interpretation and adaptation are never ending. The Constitution of the United States provided a mechanism for its own amendment and an organ for its own interpretation. The organ, the Supreme Court, soon assumed a more important role than the founding fathers had contemplated. Its functions had been defined and broadened by the Judiciary Act of 1789, which prepared the way for the practice of judicial review. Its first great task was to vindicate the fully national authority of the federal government against encroaching claims of state sovereignty. This was primarily the work of Chief Justice Marshall and his colleagues. In 1803, under Marshall, the famous case of *Marbury* v. *Madison* decided that the court was competent to pass on federal no less than on state laws and to rule unconstitutional any of the former that in its opinion contravened the Constitution. Twelve years later *McCulloch* v. *Maryland* asserted the supremacy of the federal government over the range of the powers assigned to it and determined that the states could not tax federal instrumentalities. And again, in 1824, still under the leadership of Marshall, the court ruled that interstate commerce was a national concern and thus subject to the regulation of the national government.

The importance of these decisions can scarcely be overestimated. It is hard for us now to realize the strength of the centrifugal forces that threatened the integrity of the Union in its formative years. The confederate idea was still very much alive and as the contention between the North and the South became more serious, that doctrine received a new impetus throughout the South. There was still in many quarters a fear of the power of the federal government. To many the Union itself was simply and solely a union of states; state sovereignty was to them still the only true sovereignty. The Union was only the creature of the states, not really a state itself. This was in effect the concept of John C. Calhoun, who gave it a sharper edge when around 1850 he developed the doctrine of "nullification," as the legitimate resort of a state that held its rights to be seriously infringed by the action of the federal government. The rulings of the Supreme Court could not halt the growing cleavage between North and South, but they enunciated a principle of federal authority that has endured ever since. Without it the vast network of organization that in modern times sustains the complex business of the nation would have been impossible. Take, for example, the Interstate Commerce Act of 1887 or the much later decision that restored ratemaking rights to the Interstate Commerce Commission. Or take the National Labor Relations Act and subsequent decisions validating its powers. Or take the Tennessee Valley Authority. Whatever we may think of any particular exercice of federal jurisdiction, the upbuilding of the nation would have been frustrated in every direction had it not been for the constitutional defeat of the disintegrating doctrines that rejected the federal jurisdiction needed to meet state-transcending necessities.

The situation that accentuated the more extreme claims of state rights, the tension between North and South over the slavery question, proved unhappily to be one that no judicial decisions could resolve. The Supreme Court and the federal government tried various devices in their respective spheres. There was the Missouri Compromise of 1820 and, when relations were already much more strained, there was the Compromise of 1850. But no attempt to keep a balance between slave states and free states could succeed, since the growth of the nation gave an increasing preponderance of influence to the new nonslave states of the North and West. A nation could doubtfully remain half slave and half free, if the states on both sides of the line were nearly equal, but even this kind of precarious balance could not possibly continue to exist when the free states grew yearly more powerful and more prosperous as compared with the slave states. The Supreme Court handed down in 1857 the ominous Dred Scott decision, which denied any right of citizenship to the Negro and rejected the power of the national government to regulate slavery in the territories. But the decision further stimulated the antislavery agitation of the North, and when three years later Lincoln was elected President the die was cast. The greatest tragedy in the history of the United States was now staged, and the trauma it created was rendered so much the worse and the more lasting by the gross blunders of the "Reconstruction" period.

The abolition of slavery opened the way for new conceptions of civil rights and their embodiment in the legal and constitutional order. The Bill of Rights was mainly concerned with protecting fundamental liberties against encroachment by the state. They were not so much liberties assured by the state as liberties assured against the state. The fact of slavery was itself an insuperable barrier to the establishment of any system of human rights in a wider sense. The state set up in 1789 was, moreover, still a class-bound state. The suffrage was severely limited by property qualifications. A first impact of the growing West, of the new states added to the Union as the process of settlement advanced, was to foster a movement for the abolition of such qualifications. These new states rejected them, and already by 1820 five of the original thirteen had followed their example. It was, however, a full century later before the Nineteenth Amendment completed the operation by extending the vote to women. The Fourteenth and Fifteenth Amendments vindicated the civil and political rights of the Negro, although the Southern states contrived a series of devices to nullify these rights and it is only in the past few years, thanks to court decisions and to a general improvement in the position, that a considerable change has taken place in this situation.

The Declaration of Independence had boldly asserted that governments are instituted among men to secure for all certain fundamental rights. During the nineteenth century it was generally assumed that these rights were sufficiently secured if every citizen was equally free to vote and to speak his mind and to join all legal associations and to worship according to the dictates of his own conscience and to enjoy the equal protection of the laws. But during that century the growth of the country brought two major changes that at length provoked a broader conception of human rights and of the function of government in securing them.

One was the accelerating industrial development that brought with it giant corporations, combines and cartels, financial syndicates, mobile masses of workers congregated in great plants. These conditions created various new problems for government, and among them that of the protection of the economically weak against exploitation by the economically powerful. The other major change was in part the consequence of the new waves of immigration that brought millions from Eastern Europe, from Latin America, and other parts of the world to meet the growing demand for labor as the members of the older immigration from Western Europe were rising in the economic hierarchy. The end of slavery turned the Negroes into a lower caste, formally free but for the most part essentially disprivileged. The new immigrants tended to form a stratum above the Negro but below the "Nordic" older settlement from the British Isles, from Germany, and from Scandinavia. This new class structure was strongly buttressed by economic, educational, and social discrimination.

It is only in our own days that the concept of civil rights has at length been extended, through constitutional interpretation and legal enactment, to provide protection against the hazards and disabilities of unregulated employment and still later to mitigate the disparities of opportunity between group and group.

In 1905 the New York State Supreme Court invalidated a law to regulate the hours of labor in bakeries, on the grounds that such a law impaired "freedom of contract," which, the argument ran, was guaranteed by the Fourteenth Amendment. The stand taken by the courts, under the form of constitutional interpretation, continued through the first quarter of the twentieth century to block social legislation of this kind. It is true that in 1908 an Oregon law setting maximum hours of employment for women was upheld, the court admitting the claim that the physical and social needs of women might make this legislation necessary or desirable. But as late as 1923, in *Adkins v. Children's Hospital*, a federal law establishing minimum wages for women and children in the district of Washington was ruled unconstitutional.

The change of direction came about this time. New conditions and new needs were becoming manifest. New trends of public opinion were developing. In accord with these changes came a change in the interpretation of the Constitution. The most striking aspect of the change was the new significance the courts attached to the Fourteenth Amendment. It was registered in a famous case of 1925, *Gitlow v. New York*, in which the Supreme Court applied the "due process" clause to the protection of personal rights and fundamental liberties as against encroachment by state action. The court handed down a series of decisions outlawing various devices, such as "grandfather clauses" and "white primaries," designed to deprive the Negro of the vote. Later the Supreme Court gave the sanction of the Constitution to many acts of economic regulation passed by states for the purpose of promoting social welfare. With this sanction, and with the changes in public sentiment we shall be discussing in another section, there has been a considerable development of welfare legislation of various kinds. In effect the Bill of Rights has been enlarged to include the principle that every citizen, of every degree, of any race or creed, is entitled to reasonable safeguards and opportunities in the development of his capacities under the equal protection of the laws.

III

If one compares the tenor and scope of the legislation passed in the early days of the Republic with that which crowds the statute books of our own times a remarkable difference becomes evident. In the earlier period the attention of the legislators was directed mainly to the regulation of commerce, to tariff making, banking, land settlement, and so forth. Social legislation as we understand it today was completely absent. Labor legislation was practically unknown, and even the existence of the rudimentary labor unions was legally precarious. There was little enough in those days of the special organization of special interests that has led to so vast an amount of modern lawmaking.

With the growth of industry, the development of the West, and the advance of technology new problems one after another evoked new laws. The railway-building period enlisted the support of government, and most of the western lines involved deals for governmental subsidies and land grants. Thereafter farmer groups began to form in order to bring pressure on the railroads for more favorable rates, and in the seventies the Grange was organized to secure legislation for the control of the rate making of the railroads, which they succeed in obtaining in most of the grain-growing states. This was followed by the passage of the Interstate Commerce Act of 1887.

The next important trend of lawmaking began in 1890 with the passage of the Sherman Antitrust Act. It was a sympton of a growing distrust and fear of big business. With the rise of great corporations a good case could be made in favor of effective regulation for the protection of smaller units and the maintenance of competition. But public sentiment looked on trust busting as the answer. In any event the Sherman Act was too vaguely worded to attain its objective, and the courts interpreted it in a way that deprived it of much of its sting. Its most notable achievement came with the Standard Oil case of 1911. In 1914 two acts were passed that gave a new character to antitrust activities. One was the Federal Trade Commission Act that established the commission as an agency of investigation and enforcement. The other was the Clayton Act that attacked price discriminations, exclusive selling contracts, interlocking directorates of large-scale competing companies, and other devices tending to lessen competition or to create a monopoly. It also provided for "cease and desist" orders. At the same time it removed labor from the terms of the Sherman Act and protected it from injunctions in most cases.

Lawmaking was given a new and constructive turn under Theodore Roosevelt. The need for the conservation and intelligent development of natural resources was highlighted by the exposure of the ruthless and utterly wasteful deforestation brought about by industrial exploitation. The exposure came none too soon, since already much forest land had been irretrievably despoiled, with deplorable consequences to soil fertility and to the water supply of the affected areas. Now came the building of dams and irrigation systems, the creation of national parks, and in particular the initiation, directed by Gifford Pinchot, of a scientific approach to forest conservation. Since then, conservation measures have been further developed in various directions and applied to other waning natural assets, notably oil. The second Roosevelt in this respect at least followed in the footsteps of the first. The most distinctive achievement in his time was the Tennessee Valley Authority, a public corporation created by act of Congress in 1933. Centered in Tennessee and covering sections of six other Southern states it has undertaken the conservation and development of the natural resources of a total region, on a scale and with a coordination of local and state activities never approached before.

Franklin D. Roosevelt entered on his first term as President during the Great Depression. President Hoover, his predecessor, had sought to alleviate it by setting up the Reconstruction Finance Corporation as a money-lending aid to flagging business enterprise. When Roosevelt entered office the effects of the depression were reaching their maximum and the President, with his great popular support, was in the mood for more heroic experiments. The first device was an attempt to stop cutthroat competition through the code making of the National Recovery Act. It was accompanied by the Agricultural Adjustment Act, with its bounties to farmers for the limitation of their cultivated acreage. While the act was invalidated by the Supreme Court, most of its provisions were re-enacted a few years later. The major idea of the New Deal legislation was an elaborate system of governmental spending, operated through a series of special agencies, for the relief of unemployment, for rehabilitation, and for economic pump priming. While some parts of it were of a patched-up or emergency character, some others have certainly come to stay, and not least the type of legislation that was introduced by the Social Security Act of 1935.

We end this brief review by referring to a series of laws, wholly new in character, that indicate a reach toward a greater national integration. These are the laws that in the past few years have been passed by a number of states to combat occupational and other forms of anti-group discrimination. Congress itself may perhaps be said to have led the way, by outlawing such discrimination on public works and civil service appointments. There was also the experiment of the Fair Employment Practices Committee, set up in 1941 by executive order, "to take appropriate steps" to eliminate discriminatory employment policies in "defense industries" and later in "war industries." This new direction of public policy has been substantially supported by a series of Supreme Court decisions in favor of racial and intergroup equality, including a ruling against racial segregation on interstate buses and an opinion to the effect that "restrictive covenants" cannot be enforced through the courts. But a further definitive step was taken when New York State in 1945 set the example, quickly followed by a series of other states, of prohibiting discrimination in employment "because of race, creed, color, or national origin," and entrusting the administration of the law to a standing commission. It is most likely that this new trend will spread over a large portion of the country, since it is in line with other movements of which we shall later have occasion to speak.

Our survey of the changing or developing functions of government is inadequate to reveal the extraordinary growth, in scale and in complexity, of the business of lawmaking, with its attendant services of administration. One major consequence has been the swelling of governmental budgets, and especially of the budget of the national government. In 1930 the federal government spent $10 billion; the amount rose to $20 billion in 1940, and for the year 1952 the President submitted a budget of $85 billion. It is true that the national productivity has also risen considerably. It is also true that the more recent increases are attributable to unprecedented defense expenditures. But the total governmental expenditure for all purposes has reached a total beyond all previous conception. By way of comparison we may note that for the four years of heavy New Deal expenditures, between 1933 and 1936, the grand total appropriated for all measures of relief and public works was $8.75 billion.

Obviously so great an expansion of governmental business has led to many administrative changes as well as to many problems concerned with the relation and coordination of functions. The Civil Service System was not initiated in this country until 1883 and with its development there has been a considerable increase in the proportion of governmental employees appointed on some kind of competitive basis. The practice of departmentalization has inevitably been extended, raising in turn some serious questions of bureaucratic coordination. Numerous commissions and boards and bureaus have been set up to administer special wide-ranging legislative acts. Such agencies carry on not only executive functions but issue orders and regulations that are in effect legislative. The problem of efficiency in governmental operations is one that has been the subject of a series of investigations in our own days, leading to some institutional changes since the Reorganization Act of 1946. But, while the way to far-reaching reforms has thus been opened up, the objective is still a long way from being attained.

In another direction, however, an important advance has been made. Inevitably the trend has given an increasing fiscal predominance to the federal government over the state government, especially since the tax demands of the former have limited the ability of the latter to increase their revenues in response to new needs. The happier aspect of this situation is that the states have learned to enter into closer cooperation with the national government in several directions. In the first place, their citizens have benefited by federal grants-in-aid for the maintenance of welfare legislation, such as social security, unemployment insurance, public health services, conservation measures, and educational programs. In the second place, local administrations have come to make common cause with various federal activities, such as Selective Service, the Office of Price Administration, the FBI, and so forth. In the third place, a great many federal activities are conducted through local offices with localized personnel. Besides, a number of special interstate organizations have been created to carry out administrative activities transcending the boundaries of any one state, such as the Port of New York Authority. As a result of these developments most of the earlier antagonisms between the national government and the states have disappeared and the success of this "cooperative federalism" has vindicated anew the enduring federal principle.

IV

The people who constituted the United States in 1789 could not yet be called a nation. It was more political necessity than common sentiment that united them. The regional settlements strung along the Atlantic coast had different ways of life, different environments, different interests, and to some extent different origins. Intercommunication was slow and limited. There was in particular the growing cleavage between the plantation states and the antislavery states. On one political principle there was general agreement, and that was on the need for limiting the power of the central government. To that end the system of checks and balances had been devised. A farseeing statesman, like Alexander Hamilton, might stress the importance of a strong national government, but the prevailing opinion tended in the opposite direction.

The framers of the Constitution made no allowance for the operation of public opinion through political parties. The *Federalist* still spoke of parties as dangerous things, as "factions" tending to create troubles in the body politic. The idea that parties would determine elections, that without a party system no democracy could work, was not considered—partly because democracy itself, in our modern sense, was generally under suspicion. The device of an Electoral College for the choice of the President ignored the role that political parties inevitably came to play. The election of senators by the state legislatures was another device that showed the limited respect held for the popular vote. Yet from the beginning of the Republic public opinion began to express itself through the operation of parties. The Federalist Party supported the administration; the Democratic Republicans, led by Jefferson and Madison, opposed it. The election of Jefferson in 1800 was particularly significant in this respect, since that leader had a fine sensitivity to the movements of public opinion and a high ability to harness them to his cause.

The next important movement of public opinion came as the result of two increasingly potent forces. One was the voice of the growing cities, the working population of which began to demand recognition. The other was the voice of the westward expansion, from which a new conception of democracy was being bred in opposition to the older aristocratic regime. These forces carried Jackson to office in 1828. After he had been in office a number of years the various groups opposed to him joined together as the Whig Party. But in spite of vicissitudes Jacksonian democracy won its way.

As the slavery issue grew more acute, it became the determinant of a new party division. The Republican Party was organized, drawing to itself elements of the various rather fluid party groups of the time, and took its stand against slavery or for the maintenance of the Union. The old Jeffersonian Democratic Party was split by the slavery question, but its major strength was in the South. The victory of Lincoln turned the new Republican Party into one of the two major parties and it became the dominant one for a long period thereafter.

Sectional differences centering around questions of currency and credit, the Grange movement, and the tariff occupied the party stage after the "Reconstruction" period. Toward the close of the nineteenth century the United States, with its growing strength and its expansive economic interests, began to assume a more imperialist character and under popular impulsion embarked on the war with Spain over the Cuban situation. With the annexation of the Philippines it became, for a time, an imperial power.

The center of public interest soon turned homeward again. The major issue now became the exercise of some control over the excesses of the industrial and financial giants that had made such tremendous strides. There was a crusading spirit abroad, fomented by the revelations of the "muckrakers," and a series of reforms were brought about, laws against adulteration of foods and drugs, laws against unfair competition and against monopolistic tendencies, laws against railroad rebates and for the regulation of ratemaking, laws for the conservation of natural resources against wasteful exploitation, and so forth. There was also the first important movement to "clean up" local politics, a task that has no end.

So we come to our own period, the tumultuous age of world wars and their tremendous unanticipated aftermaths. The sway of public opinion between self-containedness and world involvement moved back and forth from the time of Wilson until the hour of Pearl Harbor. The emergence of the United States from the vast embroilment as the only great power of the Western world has ended that issue, so that new debate rages over the merits of alternative policies of positive action, not over the question whether we should have a positive policy at all. The bipolarization of power between Communist Russia and socio-capitalist America has definitely created a new era.

Public opinion has not caught up with the significance of the change, except in one respect. The Korean War has taught it the paramount necessity for the conversion of potential into actual military strength and for the upbuilding and reinforcement of the economic and military strength of war-wasted Europe. The Point Four Program constitutes a further recognition of the advantage to the United States of fostering, wherever possible, the healthly economic development of backward areas. But in other respects public opinion has not learned so far to appreciate the role of world leadership for which the country has been cast. The problem here is how to counter the efficacious propagandistic appeal that the Soviet Union, in the quest for dominance, is making to the proverty-sunken and land-hungry peoples of the Orient and other parts of the earth. This appeal is based on a positive, highly dogmatic philosophy, a creed offered in the name of deliverance. Our role of world leadership calls for the strong and clear assertion of our countercreed, one that has meaning for the peoples to whom it is addressed, one that is understandable by them and applicable to the socioeconomic conditions as well as to the psychology of these peoples. This is where we have been less successful.

Two developments of public opinion during this period of troubles have some bearing on this matter. One of these was precipitated by the Great Depression. The new sense of a need for social security, for protection from unemployment and from the grave hazards created by economic crises, gave Franklin D. Roosevelt an overwhelming majority in 1932. The laissez-faire individualism that had dominated public opinion received a severe shock from which it has never recovered. The concept of the welfare state, which sometimes is quite erroneously conjoined with that of the socialist state, gained an important following. The other development was the recognition, in degree at least, of the costs and other evils of the various forms of economic discrimination, of the undemocratic denial of equal opportunities to Negroes, Orientals, Latin Americans, Jews, and to some extent to the peoples of the later immigration from Eastern Europe. With the restriction of this immigration under the immigration laws of 1921 and 1924 a period of relative stabilization began. But apart from this there were new influences at work that have led, as we have already pointed out, to a marked change of attitude and of policy. Especially in the past ten years an important advance has been made in this respect. This advance, if it continues, can be of high significance for the success of the United States in its international policies.

V

To make the Republic a going concern, to establish its integrity, to give it a direction and a policy, to create the foundations of a new tradition, to make its Constitution come alive, to restore its ruined finances and to settle the myriad problems that were the offspring of a war for independence—that was the Herculean task the country, still hardly a country, faced in 1789. Never in its history, not even in our own most troubled times, was strong and wise leadership more essential.

Not least was leadership needed for the guidance of the international relations of the new sovereign state. Happily it was forthcoming. The first statesmen of the Republic understood one thing that so many statesmen of so many countries have in later days failed, with disastrous consequences, to grasp. They knew that when you liquidate a war the next great achievement is to liquidate its animosities. When, four years after the founding of the Republic, Britain became again engaged in the conflict with France, George Washington issued a proclamation of neutrality. The resentment against Britain was still exceedingly strong. Washington was violently denounced as a tool of Britain and an enemy of republicanism, but he and his advisers stood firm, in spite of the grievances the new state had against Great Britain and in spite of the additional grievances that arose through Britain's treatment of American shipping during the war.

The policy of the early Republic was directed to establishing its own borders and in the process settling its differences with the powers that had once owned some part of its territory. The Jay Treaty guaranteed its neutrality in the war between Britain and France. The Pinckney Treaty settled territorial issues with Spain, followed by the Adams-Onis Treaty that brought in all of Florida. Fortunately for the Republic, no one on either side of the Atlantic dreamed of the potential value of the territory that was becoming the United States of America. So France parted cheaply with Louisiana and Spain conceded Florida.

The process was interrupted by the sheer stupidity of the War of 1812, one of those wars that result from misunderstandings based on old resentments aggravated by bungling diplomacy. The war itself was a series of costly miscalculations on both sides. It ended in 1815, the year of Napoleon's final defeat; and there followed the greatest age of constructive peace that Europe has known, and in America the tremendous process of expansion, consolidation, and development that, apart from the disastrous interrruption of the War Between the States, filled the nineteenth century.

In the period after 1815 international relations fell into the background. There were no troubles of the peace, and America's eyes were turned almost wholly to the domestic scene. The new spirit was signalized by the Rush-Bagot Treaty that provided for mutual disarmament on the Great Lakes. This was the beginning of an arrangement between two states that is unique in the history of nations, a frontier permanently disarmed, a great token of amity that at the same time has been a potent influence for abiding peace. It was thus inevitable that when future difficulties arose between England or Canada on the one side and the United States on the other, as they did, for example, in the matter of the Alabama claims, the mutual desire for a peaceful process of settlement has overcome all dangers until the very notion of an appeal to war has become in effect unthinkable.

During this earlier period the major positive development of international policy in the United States was the Monroe Doctrine of 1823. It proclaimed the end of European imperialistic ventures in the American hemisphere and it was directed particularly against Spain, at a time when the Latin-American states one after another had won their independence. It expressed a new consciousness of America. It was a form of protective nationalism that viewed any offensive action by a European power anywhere on the continent as a danger to the United States. At the same time it contained the first hint of a concept of Pan-Americanism that, however, did not take definite form until a much later date. The more modern association of the Monroe Doctrine with a philosophy of isolationism is, however, a complete misapprehension of its original purport.

No European power challenged the Monroe Doctrine, and with this matter settled a long period went by before the international relations of the United States entered on any distinctively new phase. There were of course, from time to time, issues over tariffs or fisheries or trading rights; they all seem of minor significance, even though they may have been quite troublesome at the time. The period of civil war and of what passed for reconstruction turned attention away from international developments, save for the international problems that the war itself provoked.

In fact it was not until the eighties of the nineteenth century that the United States began to emerge as a world power, as a state whose interests extended well beyond the American continent, a state which therefore had a stake in the settlement of international problems. There was, for example, the incident in Samoa, and when Germany began to take offensive measures against that island, the United States intervened and participated, along with Great Britain, in bringing about an adjustment of the interests of the three powers. Then there was the trouble in Hawaii, which ended in its annexation. The new position of the United States was symbolized under Harrison's administration by a law that authorized the appointment of ambassadors to countries that reciprocated.

Another aspect of the changing situation was the new interest taken in the affairs of Latin America. Secretary Blaine unsuccessfully planned in 1881 for a Pan-American conference, and did achieve one in 1889. It was the first of a series and, although its immediate results were slight, it led to a permanent inter-American organization. In two important cases the United States came forward as a champion of Latin-American states. One was the matter of the Venezuelan dispute with Britain. The other, which brought about the Spanish-American War, was the trouble between Cuba and Spain. This war led to a further extension of American interests over the world, through the annexation of the Philippines. There were, however, other activities of the United States on the Latin-American scene that were much less auspicious for Pan-American harmony. And it was not until the policy of military intervention and dollar diplomacy was transformed into the "good neighbor" policy that any approach to real inter-American unity was opened up. This is a subject on which we shall have something to say in another connection.

In the period that ended with the outbreak of World War I the United States was a world influence rather than a world power. It had expanded its range of interests over the earth, but its interests were on the whole interpreted as economic interests rather than the intrinsically political concern with the balance and distribution of power. Thus American diplomacy in respect of China, as exemplified by Hay's "open door" policy, was directed not to assure the sovereignty or territorial integrity of China but rather to gain a share in the commercial advantages of trade with China. The change came when the United States, by entering the war, and still more by its primary role in the winning of the war, was in effect forced to assume the place of a major power, participant and influential in all world affairs. Wilson's "fourteen points" was a bid for world leadership that nearly succeeded, but in the end was frustrated partly by the bitter and shortsightedly vindictive policies of our European allies and still more by the recrudescence of political partisanship and isolationism in the United States. The withdrawal of the United States from the League of Nations marked a retreat to an old and, as was soon to be proved, an outmoded tradition.

The period between the two world wars gave one of the most dismal exhibitions in history of the miscalculations of little-minded statesmen. The legacy of a bad peace, which Wilson did his utmost to prevent, was a heavy handicap to start with. The blunders and failures of the international policies of our former allies accentuated the American desire to return to a normalcy that was beyond recall. Even as late as 1937, when the storm clouds were rapidly gathering over Europe, our statesmanship still thought that we could safely withdraw from the consequences by the passing of a Neutrality Act. But the United States had already become too great and important, had made too many commitments, had too many world-embracing interests, to be able ever again to retreat into hemispheric seclusion. Such power and influence must assume corresponding responsibilities, and if these responsibilities are ignored in the first instance they are forced upon us later, with far more pain and cost.

After the experiences of the past dozen years it is hard to think back to the attitudes that prevailed before them. Let me quote from a book that had quite a vogue in some circles in those earlier days. The author besought Americans to keep out of it all, to look at home and forget what was brewing in the rest of the world. "Fortunately," he said, "we need no friends; fortunately we need fear no enemies." We should not even trade abroad. We don't need their goods, he said, let us keep ours to ourselves. "The choice is between abolishing the poverty that is in America and the mingling of it with the poverty of other nations." The book was *America Self-Contained* by Samuel Crowther. How strange now to recall the words: "we need no friends . . . we need fear no enemies."

We refused to join the League of Nations, for which our temporary leadership was responsible, and that inadequate device crumbled away before the breath of war. Now we are the main sustaining force of the United Nations, and are chiefly concerned to prevent another and more formidable world war. To prevent it we are devoting now a substantial fraction of a vast national budget to military defense. For the first time in history our mission has become to achieve such strength and to devise such international policies as will ensure peace over all the earth. We are not only bound up in world affairs, we have been called upon to be the supreme sustaining force of a whole world order. With the impoverishment of Europe and above all with the decline of the power of Great Britain, with the tremendous growth of a counterpower driven by ambitions and animated by a spirit that, unless contained and finally mitigated, would imperil all our hopes and crush all that America has meant, we have no alternative but to accept the call of destiny. It is the most magnificent task this country has ever undertaken. Whether we can achieve the necessary statesmanship is the question of the age. New movements are stirring throughout the East, new conditions are pressing hard upon the West. We are called on first to comprehend the situation, the whole situation, and then to meet it. International policy must now be paramount. On its success our future, our role in history, depends.

VI

Can contemplation of the manner of past changes give us any guidance on the changes that lie ahead, even a little ahead? Let us limit the question by observing that no one can predict future *events*, if we mean by events something more than recurrences in a strongly patterned sequence. We cannot predict novel discoveries or the conjunctures of diverse forces that precipitate new situations and new problems. We can, however, with somewhat greater hope of success, attempt to assess the near future of those *processes* of change that are responsive to certain irreversible developments in the human environment.

The most indubitable of these irreversible developments is technological advance. This advance means, among many other things, an ever-greater potentiality of production at a decreasing cost in labor power. It means a greater utilization of all kinds of natural resources, including many whose significance is still unknown. It means even swifter communication and travel and transportation. It means even more devastating agencies of destruction. It means even more intricate interorganization and even more intensive and massive forms of organization.

These ungainsayable processes will have their continuing impact on government. They assure that the functions of government will tend to increase rather than to diminish. Leviathan may be tamed but he cannot be slenderized. The problem of effective democratic control over government will grow greater rather than less.

The imposition of new functions on government can be directly and indirectly traced to the problems created by technological advance and the elaborate organizational structures created by it. Wherever a new technique is devised, whether it be a new way of organizing men or a new way of manipulating natural phenomena, it thrusts a new job on government. Witness the radio, television, the airplane, the harnessing of atomic energy. So the problem of democracy becomes an increasing one to keep the vast apparatus of government under control and under vigilant supervision.

The developments of technology have among other consequences made people more mobile and more insecure. They have increased alike the leisure and the restlessness of men. Consequently, the need for economic security has been more strongly felt. The welfare state has come to stay and is certain to develop further. The increasing productivity of labor is also a consequence of technology that is bound to continue with no assignable upper limit, especially as the practice of birth control is most likely to spread to the populous countries of the East as they become industrialized.

Technology, for all its gifts, increases the hazards of life. The demand for insurance against hazards of all kinds, economic disabilities, economic liabilities, accidents, health risks, family risks, and various other contingencies will surely increase. The field of insurance will be patterned between voluntary agencies and state agencies. Certain minima will be guaranteed by the state, but beyond that there will be numerous new opportunities for assurance through nonstate organizations to provide for all kinds of supraminimal guarantees.

The greatest of all hazards, one that has become vastly more formidable than ever before, is the hazard of large-scale war. The immediate outlook, though darkened by the attitude of the Soviet Union, is by no means wholly unfavorable. With the balance of power moving in our favor, a period of stalemate is a reasonable prospect, given unremitting effort on our side. In that case the future will depend on the wisdom of our policies and on the fulfillment of our trust. With sympathetic and forethoughted statesmanship in our relations with the Orient, our situation can be greatly improved. If we can avoid any serious economic depression, or at the least if we can avoid through social insurance the worst consequences of any economic crisis, then our position is far better than that of any dictatorial system. For democracy is not subject to the secret strains and tensions that continued dictatorship generates. Democracy grows from within and becomes the stronger the more fully its creed is accepted, whereas dictatorship decays from within so that its creed loses vitality and is in time transformed into the mere terrorism of power.

[1953]

The Papal Encyclical on Labor

27 In 1891 Pope Leo XIII issued a pronouncement on the rights and duties of the workingman, which has since that date been the standard of Catholic doctrine on the subject. In the encyclical of Pope Pius XI, issued on May 25, 1931, it is claimed that its predecessor "completely overthrew those tottering tenets of liberalism [i.e., *laissez-faire*] which had long hampered effective interference by the government," and that it made the leaders of the nations "at last more fully conscious of their obligations." These claims will seem excessive to the economic historian who traces the gradual awakening, particularly from the '30s of the nineteenth century, of that social consciousness which in the light of the human costs of an uncontrolled factory system evoked a cumulative series of protective acts. The principle of legislative protection for the worker was fully inaugurated long before the encyclical of Leo XIII, and was first established in non-Catholic countries, beginning with England and finding its fullest nineteenth-century development in the legislation of Australia and New Zealand.

The encyclical of Leo XIII, the *Rerum Novarum*, was significant, but it could scarcely be called epoch-making. It proclaimed that wage-earners should be specially cared for by governments and that wage rates should be adequate for decent subsistence. Its most decisive demand was that which called for the establishment of associations of workingmen and of employers, separately or jointly, according to the conditions. The voice of the Church thereby blessed the trade union, but emphasized the need for special Catholic organizations. Many commentators found in this recommendation of Catholic unions the main objective of the encyclical. It was intended to combat the secession of workers to Socialist unions, which were dominantly anti-Catholic, by proclaiming the interest of the Church in the welfare of workingmen and providing a type of organization which would be consistent with Catholic aims and would be under Catholic leadership. As a consequence such unions were in fact established in various European countries, especially in Germany, Italy, Belgium, and Holland. They attained a considerable membership—in Germany at the end of the First World War the members of the "Christian unions" numbered 1,000,000—though far below that of the other unions. The latter were fighting organizations, while the "Christian unions" followed Catholic doctrine in believing in the harmonious adjustment of the claims of labor and capital.

And now, after forty years, comes another official proclamation by the Church. It cannot be thought that it was merely to celebrate this anniversary that the present Pope issued *Quadragesimo Anno*, one of the most elaborate and lengthy of all papal pronouncements. Nor can its object be merely to reiterate and amplify the doctrine of his predecessor. The times have changed, and the most conservative and long-lived of all institutions is confronted with new problems of policy. Within the framework of the age-old traditions of pontifical authority, once more asserted in this document, there are interesting indications of a new situation and of a policy designed to meet it.

To understand this aspect of the encyclical we must consider some recent developments not only in the labor situation but also in the status of the Catholic Church. Pope Pius himself recognizes the relative lack of success of the Catholic unions to increase or even to retain their membership. He also recognizes the growth of communism as opposed to socialism, and though maintaining with Leo XIII that socialism and Catholicism are incompatible, he tempers his criticism of the former with some words that approach commendation. For he remarks that "its programs often strikingly approach the just demands of Christian social reformers." It is the growth of left-wing socialism and, above all, of communism which the Vatican has in mind, and in view of which it formulates its program.

But other changes complicate the issue. The Fascist State, while repressing Socialist unions, has established a new system of syndicates rather on the lines of trade guilds than of trade unions, but definitely incorporated within the Fascist system and controlled by Fascist leaders. This is part of Mussolini's program to tie the whole socioeconomic life of Italy to the Fascist chariot. It substituted the Fascist party for all other political parties, including the Catholic Partito Popolare, organized to great strength after the war by the brilliant Catholic priest Don Sturzo, now living in practical exile in London. Above all, it endeavored through the Fascist youth associations to indoctrinate the rising generation thoroughly in Fascist principles, while the Church has always claimed and has recently reiterated (in the encyclical of January 11, 1930) a prior right over the mind of youth. Under the concordat the Catholic Youth movement and the organization known as the Catholic Action which promotes it were allowed to exist, but on condition they refrained from political activities. The organization of workers presented another field in which the State encroached on the former activities of the Church, for it substituted the Fascist syndicates for the old unions, including the "white unions," as the church-controlled labor organizations of Italy were sometimes called.

Here, then, is one of the foci for that eternal struggle of powers which is part of the historical legacy of Italy and which many believed was at length ended by the concordat of February 11, 1929. Important as that concordat and the treaty which accompanied it were, it by no means ushered in a final harmony of relationship between the Italian State and the new sovereign State of Vatican City. For the premises on which each rests are hard to reconcile. Both, it is true, are anti-Socialist and anti-liberal in the sense that they are fundamentally opposed to economic *laissez-faire*. But both make comprehensive, in fact absolute, claims on the allegiance of their members, and it is profoundly difficult for two absolutes to live together. One absolute is based on a principle of corporate nationalism; the other, by its very nature, cannot accept that principle. On the whole, it is the Fascist State, rather than the Church, which has hitherto made concessions, particularly in re-establishing religious instruction in schools under the control of the Catholic hierarchy. But the equilibrium of the two powers remains an uneasy one, and deep-lying differences of attitude come sporadically to the surface, as in the very recent clashes between Catholics and Fascists in Rome itself. At the time of writing [1931] news comes that the friction of the two powers has reached a crisis of great moment, for Mussolini has taken the radical step of banning the activities of the Catholic Action itself.

To this developing situation we may perhaps attribute the renewed emphasis on the necessity of Catholic unions both of workers and of employers. When, for example, Pope Pius deplores that associations of employers and of captains of industry are "still few in number," he must surely be thinking of specifically Catholic organizations. And his reference to the Fascist syndicates contains a definite note of criticism. "It is to be feared," he says, "that the new syndical and corporative institution possesses excessive bureaucratic and political character, and that, notwithstanding the general advantages referred to above, it risks serving particular political aims rather than contributing to the initiation of a better social order." Several other references in the encyclical, though it is addressed "to all the faithful of the Catholic world," can apply only to the Italian situation. Where else, except, perhaps in Russia, is the statement applicable that "the destruction of a variety of prosperous institutions that were organically linked with one another has caused society to consist virtually of only individuals and the State"?

In addressing himself to this situation Pope Pius goes somewhat further than Pope Leo, though never out of line with the traditional economic teaching of the Catholic Church. He is fully as outspoken as Leo regarding the evils attendant on unchecked capitalism, declaring roundly that "the whole economic life has become hard, cruel, and relentless in a ghastly measure." Pope Leo had declared that "a small number of very rich men have been able to lay upon the teeming masses of the laboring poor a yoke that is little better than slavery." Pope Pius is more specific regarding the minimum of a "just" wage, declaring that it should be adequate to maintain the wage-earner and his family. The other members of the family may contribute to its maintenance— "but it is wrong to abuse the tender years of children or the weakness of woman" or to force mothers to engage from economic necessity in gainful occupations to the detriment of their family duties. The goal should be the adequacy of the wage of the paterfamilias for ordinary domestic needs. His prescription for the cleavage of labor and capital is the gradual attainment of some property by the wage-earner, and while he does not disapprove the wage contract as such he holds that it should be modified in the direction of partnership, so that "wage-earners are made sharers in some sort in the ownership or the management or the profits."

These latter pronouncements are in accord with the views of many thoughtful observers of present economic conditions who are alive to the evils of industrial insecurity and exploitation but reject the collectivist remedy for these evils. As such they will undoubtedly encourage in Catholic circles the trend toward social control of industry. But the demands of the encyclical, it should be noted, are made in the name of abstract justice. "Reason itself clearly deduces," says the Pope, "from the nature of things and from the individual and social character of man, what is the end and object of the whole economic order assigned by God the Creator." This may fairly be said to be the standpoint not of the Catholic Church alone but of all ecclesiastical bodies. When it is directed to practical problems of the day, when prescriptions for social-economic troubles are thus "deduced," some interesting questions are involved. One concerns the practicability of solutions ostensibly based on religious grounds. Another concerns the competence of religious authority to prescribe measures within an order such as the economic, where the relation of cause and effect, of prescription and application, depends on the operation of economic law or economic necessity. If, for example, "justice" should ordain that every family own an acre of land or possess an income of $10,000 a year, such an edict would at the present hour be rendered nugatory by the economic facts. And if it were set merely as a goal, its attainment might still involve conditions (such as birth control) which the same "justice" or the "law of God" might, by the same authority, be proclaimed as opposing.

It cannot in the present case be said that the Pope's program is impracticable. The demands for a living wage, for the restriction of economic exploitation, for the prevention of unemployment, and for the apportionment to the wage-earner of a "just" share of the fruits of industry are in broad harmony with the social consciousness of our age, and no economist would deny that in so far as they are not yet attained they could in very large measure be achieved. Their fuller achievement is partly a question of attitude. If the leaders of industry and of government, and if the members of the comfortable classes in general, were all as alive to the evils of the hazards of industry as some of them actually are, there seems no reason to doubt that these evils would mightily decrease. To inculcate these attitudes toward definite evils is a function which any Church is surely entitled to undertake. It is partly a question of means, and here the competence of an ecclesiastical organization is not admissible. This limitation is formally acknowledged by Pope Pius, when he says: "The so-called laws of economics, derived from the nature of earthly goods and from the qualities of the human body and soul, determine what aims are unattainable or attainable in economic matters, and what means are thereby necessary." But, also, it is in part a question of interpretation, for ethical terms such as "justice," "fairness," "sound and true order," "common good," are not self-explanatory and they are interpreted in very different ways by different men. It is easy to get men to agree that justice should be done, but ask them what justice means, and they speak with very different voices.

So when the Pope voices an appeal for economic justice he takes a stand which no man would deny. But when he proceeds to define justice, men ask, unless they are prepared to accept it all on faith, Whence is this notion of what is just derived? Now the official answer of the Church is that it is based on eternal "Christian truth," applied to the changing circumstances and needs of the day. This is in the religious sphere the correlate of the old juristic doctrine, that there is a "law of nature," eternal and perfect, discoverable by reason so that the laws of men may be framed in conformity with it. In the legal sphere this doctrine has gone out of fashion—the dictates of reason seemed too uncertain and variant. Waiving altogether the question of authority, we may ask in conclusion whether the economic teaching of the Catholic Church through the centuries has shown a consistent trend with which the pronouncements of the present encyclical are in harmony.

The ideal of poverty, especially as accepted by the monastic orders, made a strong impression on Catholic doctrine. Some of the Church fathers went so far as to condemn wealth altogether and to decry profit-taking. At best property was a trust, a stewardship, and acquisition for its own sake or for the private advantage of the individual beyond the decent needs of his station was disapproved. This is the view which was developed by the "Angelic Doctor," as Aquinas is named in the present encyclical. The leading idea was that there is a just price for everything, determined essentially by its cost to the producer. And the taking of interest or "usury" was forbidden on Scriptural grounds, though exception was made in so far as the interest was equivalent to a loss which the lender would otherwise suffer. This was the doctrine embodied in the canon law, and it was maintained without essential change till as late as 1830. In this respect, as has been pointed out by many commentators, the spirit of the Catholic Church diverged from that of various Protestant bodies. And it is not without significance that in its earlier development, particularly, there was a far closer relation between capitalism and Catholicism.

But the problem of economic justice proved insoluble in these terms when capitalism itself became an established system. For now it became meaningless to define a "just" price in terms of cost—there is no one cost where men work for a market. And it became impossible on any abstract grounds to determine what any man's labor was economically worth apart from the price he received for it. Whether that question could be answered or not in the simpler days of handicraft production, it was assuredly insoluble in the days of industrial specialization. And the development of a credit system made money so obviously a productive good that the old doctrine of usury ceased to have validity.

There remained, then, of the old ideal of economic justice only certain elements. Property is a stewardship, God-given, and therefore socialism is anathema. (But there have been and there are "Christian Socialists," too, who can make a good religious argument for their creed.) "The laborer is worthy of his hire," in the sense that he should

receive enough to sustain him decently and his family with him, and
if profits are made he should receive a "fair" share as one who is a partner
in their making. (The question as to what is "fair" still remains open,
since obviously the old formulae do not suffice.) And where these conditions are not assured, the State should take special guardianship of
the worker, and the Church should encourage him to form organizations
which under its direction and in a spirit of moderation can help him
to these goals. It is these surviving elements of Catholic doctrine which
are with unusual elaboration maintained in this encyclical. In so far
it is continous with Catholic teaching from time past. But the emphasis
is altered in certain directions, particularly in respect of the need for Catholic economic associations as already advocated by Leo, and again in
respect of the danger lest the political organization of labor prove ty-
rannical. And when we seek the reason for this emphasis, we are likely
to find it, as has been pointed out, in the present problems of the Catholic Church rather than in the eternal verities themselves. But this is
a dilemma which the interpretation of "eternal verities" has always
had to face.

[1931]

Government and the Goals
of Economic Activity

28   INDIVIDUAL ACTIVITIES AND SOCIAL GOALS

If we want to learn what ends men seek, what values they cherish, we run into a swarm of difficulties. For men vary one from another and every man is changeable and sometimes inconsistent. Each acts under the impulsion of immediate conditions, immediate wants, and immediate opportunities. Thus in times of crisis their behavior may be unlike the responses they give to ordinary situations. Two men may have broadly the same values and yet act differently, because one is more farsighted than the other. All men seek many different things and in the turmoil of their tangled activities the scale of their values may be hard to discern. Men do some things not because they want to do them but because they are in the net of circumstance. The act of a competitor, for example, may impel them reluctantly to take similar action. Or on the other hand, they do things because it is socially expected of them, though they would themselves have chosen a different course.

These remarks, which could be greatly extended, are made as a preliminary caution against the simplifications that so glibly sum up the values or goals of the "economic man," or of the "capitalist" or the "worker," or of capitalistic society or socialistic society.

More particularly, they are intended to suggest that we cannot adequately assess the values or goals of a group or a whole society by focusing attention solely on the activities of its individual members. There may indeed be an inconsistency between the values genuinely accepted by a group and a considerable part of the behavior of the members of that group. Each man may tend, under the incentive of private advantage, to ignore considerations of public good to which he fully subscribes. He may not realize that his individual deviation matters much. He perceives readily his own private gain, but the hurt to the public welfare is nebulous and seems so small. In these everyday affairs how little, he may feel, he can do for the advancement of the social good, and how much he can do to better his own chances. Consequently his average behavior may not adequately express his sense of values.

This kind of discrepancy between values and behavior is not the only one, but it has a relevance for our theme. It occurs in every type of society and is in no way peculiar to what is described as capitalist society. In the capitalistic type, however, there was developed a pleasant formula of reconciliation. The laissez-faire doctrine maintained that the private interest of individuals, in their economic pursuits, worked out for the economic good of all. The doctrine lingers on, but the experience of the early days of industrialism destroyed its potency. It could not overcome the evidence that the uncontrolled pursuit of private advantage meant the exploitation of the weak and the aggrandizement of the strong, with serious consequences for social well-being.

The discrepancy between the larger values and the momentum of the everyday pursuit of private gain persists now and always, no matter what form the economy takes. In the mitigation of this discrepancy government has always a role to play. Our task here is broadly to assess that role. We shall not be concerned with the disparity between men's *ideals* in a larger sense and men's behavior. The values we are concerned with are accepted values, values that men do not merely pay lip service to but which they on the whole recognize as their own, values they regard as capable of realization in our present society. Some of these values cannot be attained without concerted action, without institutional controls, without an established code—in short, without government.

THE ROLE OF THE CITIZEN
IN POLITICOECONOMIC ISSUES

We are concerned in this statement with the formidable and far-ramifying question of the role government can or should play in forwarding the goals of economic life or, somewhat more explicitly, in advancing that whole area of human welfare that depends on economic activity and on the manner in which this activity is organized. Around this question major political conflicts have raged throughout modern history, and now the issue in its most aggravated form resounds in the international arena, where a system of government that abrogates all forms of private economic activity militantly opposes all other systems as outworn and inherently exploitative.

We could not pretend to deal here with the whole range of so vast a theme. Our interest will be focused on the question: What are the primary objectives in the light of which the policies of government will be determined if, in its exercise of controls over economic activities, it is animated by the desire to make these activities as serviceable as possible to the goal of human well-being?

We shall seek to set out these objectives without the qualifications that are involved in various situations within which governments must operate. For example, we pass by the conflict between the requirements for national security and the requirements for greater social advancement, or again the conflict between the conditions making for the greater prosperity of one's country and those making for the general economic well-being of other countries. The second of these conflicts may be on the whole and most of the time an illusory one, because most of the time what we do to restore the economic well-being of other countries redounds in the longer run favorably to our own prosperity. The first is inherent in the present state of world order or disorder, but theoretically it raises no problem of practical alternatives, since if national security is really imperiled the diversion of resources to the economically unproductive costs of defense must be regarded as an elementary form of insurance.

We shall limit in another respect the treatment of our theme. Government must act in situations involving many complexities, in situations in which, aside from other complications, the direct and indirect advantages of a given program must, at least roughly, be weighed against the direct and indirect repercussions of its implementation; not only so, but government is subject, in all its economic operations, to the pressures and counterpressures of various interest groups. It is therefore out of the question to affirm that the functions of government in the furtherance of economic well-being are such and such; or even that, no matter what the situation, they should be such. The functions of government, under a democratic constitution, are those that the people sufficiently approve by voting for their representatives. We shall therefore put our question in the form: What values broadly accepted in the community are specially relevant for the guidance of the citizen on politicoeconomic issues? Can we set down any simple propositions expressive of these values as general criteria that he should seek to apply, with due regard for qualifying conditions, when particular measures involving governmental action in the economic field are under consideration?

Problems of economic policy, as they actually present themselves in the political arena, are complex and tangled. They rarely appear as *purely* economic problems. They are bound up with questions of group liberties and group controls, of group advantage and group disadvantage, and beyond these lie the larger questions of the impact on national solidarity and on the creative cultural life of a people. Even the economic gain or loss can rarely be calculated, since there are so many intangibles that may make the longer-run results different from those of the partly calculable shorter run. No important problem of economic policy would ever be solved if we had to wait for a conclusive scientific demonstration that this or that solution would have precisely these results.

In a democratic society most governmental policies contain some measure of compromise. What is significant is the trend. The trend reveals the deeper tides of public opinion, responsive not merely to the changing situation but also to the changing ethic of socioeconomic life. The spirit of the times is more important in determining economic policies than is the prevalent doctrine of the economists, and not infrequently has been at odds with it. The role of the citizen is decisive. He is not likely, by and large, to be concerned seriously with economic analysis (though possibly giving attention to polemic presentations of "economics in one lesson" or oversimplified analyses in a one-page advertisement or a fifteen-minute broadcast or a basic-English editorial or a cartoon). But he can be influenced by leaders who assess the trends and give more conscious direction to the underlying ethic and show its relevance to particular problems where it is obscured by group interests. It is therefore in this area that the churches can play a significant part, given enlightened leadership. It is not easy for them, and may indeed be unwise, to take sides directly on the economic issues that continuously agitate the political arena. But they can align themselves with the economic ethic that lives and moves in the community and help so to express it that it is disembarrassed from the specious pleading of private interests.

TWO PRIMARY PRINCIPLES

If we ask what principles we can derive from broadly accepted values to guide the economic activity of government we must be content, unless we are rash enough to turn our particular predilections into universal premises, with certain simple propositions. There is, however, a wide consensus, in effect an agreement, among men of good will, no matter what their differences on questions of policy, on certain fundamental desiderata. They agree in thinking that a well-ordered economic system should serve certain broad ends and should be so constructed that it will not sustain, for the mere production of wealth, a system of economic relationships that grossly subordinates the interests of some to the interests of others. For our present purpose it will suffice to adduce two broad propositions that are in accord not only with Christian ethic but also with the judgment of equity accepted by the great majority of men and increasingly revealed in the trends of legislation.

1. *All men should enjoy the minimum economic conditions and opportunities requisite for a decent and healthy life.*

It is only in recent times that this principle has received general recognition. In earlier times two factors stood in the way. One was the class-bound character of society, where a demarcated upper class exclusively controlled the means of production. The other was the relative poverty of all societies that depended, as nearly all did in the main, on a simple agricultural economy. It was only with industrial advance that the principle of the minimum standard became practically realizable. And, while on the one hand the resources to maintain it were now becoming available, on the other hand the need of it was made more urgent by the precarious dependence of the wage earner, who could no longer in times of distress find refuge in the patriarchal shelter of the agricultural kin-group.

Today the principle is accepted generally in all industrialized countries, and it is the basis of the various forms of socioeconomic legislation that have increasingly become a charter of security against the hazards of capitalistic society. When we say the principle is now accepted we must add that without the organized political power of the classes that need it most, the mere recognition of the equity of the principle would not have sufficed to bring it into operation. The extent to which it is made effective varies considerably in different countries. Our own has been one of the slower to recognize the need for it. And there are still important limitations and qualifications against its full implementation.

The principle is obviously one that depends on governmental action for its adequate application. Voluntary schemes for the protection of its members are partial, insufficient, serviceable only for the more privileged groups, and least likely to be available where the need is greatest. Only government can establish an all-inclusive and impregnable system.

The principle covers the physical well-being of the individual, so far as it depends on protection from the hazards of modern social life. It includes, therefore, besides proper nourishment and decent housing, medical care, insurance against accident and unemployment. It includes access to educational opportunity and broadly to a kind of work for which a man's capacities fit him. It includes protection against economic privation in old age.

On some aspects of this program Americans have still to make up their minds. Acute controversy rages around any extension of it. It is important that the citizen should learn to distinguish between the self-interested pleas of special groups and the genuine advantages, the real costs, and the proper limits of socioeconomic security. In some quarters the cry of "socialism" and "communism" is raised whenever it is proposed that disadvantaged groups be given elementary protection not only for their own sake but for the sake of all. Those who raise this cry are blind to the fact that the chief danger to the system they uphold comes from the haunting fears and corrosive insecurities in which multitudes still live. If they could imagine themselves in the place of the unprotected, if they could envisage what life means within the shadow of this fear, they would be wiser as well as better citizens—and they would falsify their own fears as well.

The principle can be defended on several grounds. The ethical ground is intrinsic and prior. A community, a state, may be thought of, in Aristotle's terms, as a partnership in the good life. In order that citizens may live that life they need this elementary protection. The modern state provides general education for its citizens, for all of them whether they can pay for it or not. It is precisely the same ground that justifies the provision of general protection against the hazards that otherwise would defeat and frustrate the fulfillment of life. All men owe everything they become to the heritage of their community. The individualistic spirit that assumes its own capacity to succeed, its self-made superiority, is mere arrogant blindness. Men differ endlessly in qualities, but all men, whatever their potentialities, are utterly dependent on the nurture they receive. Only where all men are given the opportunity to achieve can difference of achievement be assessed in terms of merit. But achievement is not all that counts. And the basic argument for our first principle is that it vindicates alike the primary brotherhood of man in community and the potential worth and dignity of man himself. It is thus a primary expression of the essential Christian ethic—and indeed of the ethic of all the great religions. The principle can be defended also on narrower grounds. As has often been pointed out, the price of incapacity, like the price of disease or the price of discrimination, is paid by the community. The wastage of human resources is a community loss—just as much as the wastage of manpower in warfare.

In a country with ample and still-developing resources, such as the United States, the argument is trivial that the cost of protection by social insurance would be an undue burden on the taxpayer or on the economy. We do not grudge the cost of new highways, because we know that in one way or another they yield more than compensating returns. Even less should we grudge the cost of this protection, nor would we if we had the imagination to see the far greater returns, returns not merely in an enlarged economic prosperity but even more in the advancement of the solidarity of our democracy and in the evocation of the human qualities of those who still live within the shadow of a great fear.

One of the primary distinctions we need to make today is that between the so-called welfare state and the socialistic state. The confusion, often deliberately fostered, is most prejudicial. Whether we approve or disapprove of thoroughgoing socialism is here irrelevant. Socialism as a doctrine advocates the nationalization of the means of production. This is a different proposition from the advocacy of an inclusive system of social insurance. Its objectives are different and its methods are different.

Our first principle has a wider range than we have so far indicated. It includes the opportunity to develop and utilize capacity as well as the mere protection against economic hazards to life and health. It implies therefore the establishment of certain fundamental freedoms. It implies, for example, that no irrelevant barriers be allowed to close the avenues to achievement against any class or group within the community, against any ethical or racial or religious or economic or ideological group—an implication limited only at the point where any such group in turn seeks to deprive other men of the same right and opportunity.

Here our principle appears as a simple principle of equity. Government alone cannot guarantee its implementation, but government alone can establish and sustain the universal standard, provided the goal is given reasonable recognition within the society.

It is not—or at least it should not be, as we shall seek to show—the function of government directly to define or to pursue the goals of living, but only to establish the conditions under which men can more fully and more freely seek their goals. Our first principle is concerned with one great system of requisite conditions. Our second points to another such system, one that is complementary to the first. The first depends on the exclusive prerogative of government, that it alone can establish standards that apply alike to all the members of a community. The second depends on another exclusive prerogative of government, that it alone is invested with the final right of coercive power.

2. *Economic power must be held continuously in check, so that it does not exploit individuals or groups, exalt private interest against public advan-*

tage, restrict access to opportunity, suppress the liberty of opinion, or other-wise dominate the creative life of the community.

This broad function of government views economic resources and economic relations in their second aspect. Economic means are at once equipment for living and power to command service, which in effect is power over other men. When economic means are highly concentrated in private hands the aspect of power becomes of major importance, and those who exercise this economic power, while they seek to control government itself, can in turn be controlled only by government. Such political control in turn requires, under democratic conditions, the constant alertness of public opinion. Under modern conditions economic power, concentrated in great corporations, in cartels, in financial syndicates, in trade associations, in political lobbies, and so forth, is elusive and works quietly in many directions with the great resources at its command. Another form of economic power, that of the great trade unions and trade union federations, has developed, possessing the formidable weapon of the strike, a weapon which can bring the whole economy to a standstill when employed without restriction. This latter form of economic power is at times opposed to the older forms, but at times it in effect makes an accommodation with them, as when price increases follow wage increases in the spiral of inflation.

On every side, then, there is need for control over the encroachments of economic power. It is primarily the task of government to prevent these encroachments, by setting limits to price agreements, by curbing tendencies to monopoly, by broad regulation over credit and banking, by preventing the destructive waste of natural resources through competitive exploitation, by intervening when the strife of worker and employer threatens the public welfare, by setting up standards and limits of various kinds in the public interest, and so forth. There is always the danger that economic power will in one way or another, directly or indirectly, hold up the public. There is always the need for political power to counteract this danger. In brief, given a sufficiently enlightened public opinion, the function of government will be properly exercised in harnessing economic power to the conditions that make for the general weal. It is an endless and endlessly difficult function.

Our second principle has a further implication. If we call on government to curb the use of economic power by private organizations, to control tendencies to monopoly, and to regulate or even, it may be, to take over those areas of economic activity the nature of which makes competition impossible, extremely wasteful, or socially undesirable, it is because economic power, thus concentrated, is a dangerous thing and the only resources to control it is the overruling authority of government. In a so-called capitalistic system, which is of course in fact always a sociocapitalistic system, economic power and political power remain distinct at important points—they are not merged into a single type of centrally operated power, which is the political form. But in a totally socialized order they are wholly fused. One of the final questions of social organization is whether, under such conditions or any near approach to them, our fundamental liberties could survive the pressures and persuasions that so complete a monopoly of control might entail. If economic power must be vigilantly held in check when it is in private hands, the need for the curbing of that pervading and secretly moving power does not cease when it is exercised by government instead, even though the power may now be formally responsible and ostensibly no longer secret.

Our two principles, taken together, conceive government as providing a framework of ordered liberty and opportunity within which men can more fully and more freely make the economic means serve the goals of living. The goals themselves are not, under these two principles, determined at all by government. It is highly important that primary goals should not be determined by the fiat of government. To see why, and to conceive more adequately the relation of government to the economic life, we must restate some elementary propositions regarding the nature of government, the nature of the economic system, the relation between them, and the relation of each and of both together to the goals they serve or can serve.

THE POLITICAL METHOD
AND THE ECONOMIC METHOD

Government is a way of regulating the affairs of a community through the laws and administrative rulings of an authority exclusively invested with final coercive power. This power may or may not be limited by a constitution. It is a system for the ordering of the relationships between men, as a condition of the satisfaction of the great variety of human needs or objectives. It is, thus viewed, apparatus for the provision of conditions required for the pursuit of human goals. Whatever the ends men seek, whether private ends or common ends, they need an established order within which to seek them, and in any complex society this order is assured and developed by government.

The primary function of government is regulation—regulation not as a goal in itself but as a condition of the pursuit of goals. We do not want regulation for the sake of regulation, as something to enjoy, as something to live for. Take any governmental operation, the work of any office, department, bureau, board, commission. What is its product? Not something men live for, but something utilitarian in the proper sense. Take, say, the work of the Interstate Commerce Commission or the Federal Reserve Board. What it provides is a way of ordering the relations of men in a particular area of activity. It does not prescribe the goals of action—it merely defines the conditions under which people engaged in that area of activity may do what they want to do. It is of primary importance that government regulation follow this principle. As soon as it goes farther it employs the alien means of coercion to determine what goals men seek. This is the road that leads to totalitarianism.

The only position consistent with man's fundamental liberties is that which was well expressed by T. H. Green when he declared, in his *Lectures on Political Obligation*, that the state should not prescribe any actions the value of which depends not on the external doing but on the spirit, the attitude, of the doer. If government imposes a way of thinking, a way of believing, a way of writing, a way of feeling, it is destroying the very meaning of what is thought or believed or felt or written. This is the final tyranny that invades the very citadel of personality. Sometimes well-meaning religious people move down this dangerous road when they ask government to support their moral code. Government should never legislate morals as such. It should limit itself to prohibiting actions that do overt and ascertainable harm to others.

That is what we imply by speaking of government as a system for the provision of means to human ends. Every form of government, it is also true, is the expression of values either of the ruling party or of the community as a whole. Democracy is based on a sense of human values, but democracy in particular rests on the realization that it cannot, without betraying itself, impose by coercion the endorsement of its values by any minority—or majority.

If one great utilitarian apparatus is the political, the other is the economic. Both orders provide or ensure the *conditions* under which men are enabled or equipped to pursue their ends, as individuals or as groups. Some of these conditions only the political means can assure, such as the establishment of a guaranteed contractual basis for the dealings of men with one another, the enunciation of standards universally binding over the community, and so forth. Some of these conditions the economic means can assure much more flexibly than can the political, such as the exchange of goods and services on the basis of accepted medium of exchange, the adjustment of supply to demand within a market structure, and so forth. But the conditions under which a considerable number of man's wants are met may be determined alternately through the political mechanism or through the economic mechanism. Thus wages or prices or the conditions of work or the rates of interest or the rewards of enterprise may be settled by the "higgling of the market"—by some combination of competing and bargaining between individuals or between groups—or by political regulation. Indeed, a major issue of our times is precisely how far the one way should be employed and how far the other. For while the economic way has limits to its potential application, there is no limit to the range of the potential application of the political way.

Before we go further we must, however, define what we mean here by the economic way. Let us suppose a total communism were set up. Let us imagine that everyone gave according to his capacity and received according to his needs—raising no questions about how capacities are adjudged and how needs are assessed. In this utopian world the economic way of settling things, as described here, would have ceased to exist. In the actual "communistic" states we know the political way has over great areas superseded the economic way, but the economic way is for certain purposes still found quite necessary. One can within limits rent a better apartment if one can afford to pay for it. One receives higher wages if one works more efficiently—and so forth.

In a more capitalistic society there is of course a much greater area over which the play of economic forces, apart from any centrally regulative machinery, is determinant. This play of economic forces, as they mesh and clash and adjust themselves without over-all regulation, constitutes the economic way. Wherever it operates there is, so far, a self-regulating system, in the sense that the results of its operation are responsive to the interrelations of the economic forces themselves and not directly to the ever-ruling will of any planning agency or authority. Prices move according to the changing demand and supply. Unemployment increases when inventories mount up, and so on. The results of the system can in degree be controlled by various kinds of manipulation exercised by powerful economic groups. But that is because they are in a position to increase or diminish one or other factor in the price equilibrium, not because their word is law. This kind of "self-regulating" system is the antithesis to a politically regulated one.

One difficulty in understanding the role and the relation of the two systems arises from a certain confusion that tends to haunt the term "economic." If we understand by economic activity all such activity as is concerned with the acquisition or the manipulation of the means of production, distribution, or exchange of marketable goods and services—any roughly corresponding definition will equally serve here— then there is much economic activity that falls within the political sphere. All governments inevitably carry on numerous economic activities. They buy and sell, they employ labor and pay wages, they compete in the market for goods and services—aside altogether from the particular forms of production that they operate themselves. Some governmental operations take goods out of the market area altogether, as when they convert private land into a public park. But not even nationalization of property puts an end to economic activity, as above defined, in the management of that property. Every organization, whether political, educational, religious, or anything else, carries on economic activities. In short, economic activity is not exclusive to what we think of as economic organizations.

And there is no demarcation to be drawn between political activity and economic activity. The line is between two *methods* of doing things: one the political method, which directly regulates, through laws, decrees, administrative orders, and so forth; and the other the economic method, which employs the specific economic means of competing, bargaining, trading, performing all kinds of market operations. The political method, in its full scope, is exclusively carried on by public organizations, in the sense that only such bodies possess the right to make rules coercively binding on all men within their ambit. The economic method is predominantly or characteristically carried on by private organizations or private individuals, for the sake of the private acquisition of economic means.

As has already been pointed out, the political and the economic methods offer themselves as alternative ways of conducting any and every kind of economic activity. The question, however, is not which of the two should be employed but how much, how far, of this method and of that. Our two principles are in effect statements of broad considerations that on any particular issue might give us reason to choose one or the other.

Another confusion, closely related to the first, besets the use of the term "economic." It occurs when we draw a hard-and-fast distinction between the areas of economic and of noneconomic activity. The greater part of human labor is occupied with the making of a living or the acquisition of wealth in some degree. In a capitalistic order the means thus provided accrue in the purely neutral form of money—wages, salaries, interest, rent, profits—purely neutral in the sense that a dollar is a unit of a medium of exchange that can be converted at will into an equivalent amount of goods and services of any available kind. Obviously, however, not all goods and services are money-commanded, nor again can money command the spirit in which services are rendered. Money commands the means prerequisite to our satisfactions, not the satisfactions themselves. In its developed form the economic system is a means apparatus, a means of providing the means to satisfactions.

The only direct qualification on this statement is the inverted economic activity that finds its satisfaction in the acquisition of means *as such*, divorced from the satisfaction arising from the prospective utility of the means thus acquired. The classical example of this inversion is the case of the miser, who has completed the process in which the intensive pursuit of means tends to blur and then obliterate the perception of the goal to which it was primarily directed. This is a situation entirely different from the common one in which the pursuit of the means to a satisfaction is itself satisfying as a process of accomplishment in the skillful or successful adaptation of means to ends. One charge not infrequently brought against the industrial system is that it so often fails to provide this kind of satisfaction.

Our main point here, however, is a different one. All our goals require some means, some equipment, for their pursuit. To carry on that pursuit, no matter what it be, we must at the same time receive an economic return for so doing or else we must depend on the means that have been already provided for us by other or previous activity of ours or of others. That is equally true whether our activity is preaching the gospel or writing poetry or making shoes or bringing up a family or running an empire. What then shall we call economic activity—how shall one limit its range? One man makes a living by preaching, another by driving a taxicab. Is the latter to be called economic activity and the former not? One man earns money by doing scientific research and uses it to support a family; another earns money by digging ditches and also thereby supports a family. Is the latter economic activity and the former not? Carry the argument further and it appears there are no such things as *economic* wants and economic needs or desires. Any kind of activity can have an economic aspect and most kinds do have one.

If there are then no economic wants there are, properly speaking, no economic goals, but only economic means to any goals. Indeed, the economic means as such are means to the means to goals. We make no genuine distinction when we call food and protection and apparatus and books and a home or any other thing we need for our goals, no matter what they be, economic goods. Why should butter and eggs be economic goods and museums and, say, codes of law, noneconomic? To obtain any of these an economic cost has to be met, a price has to be paid—as one aspect of the process of getting them. In a modern society we cannot obtain even fresh air or sunshine without some economic provision of some kind.

Our analysis here must be left incomplete, but we may have gone far enough to make our initial distinction clear. We started from the point that the economic system and the political system constitute two great means-structures or agencies through which the conditions or means required for the goals of living may be secured, and that to an important extent they offer alternative ways of doing so. The economic

way uses the mechanisms of our economic system, the political way
the mechanisms of government. Economic activity is, properly considered, a means-seeking operation, and so also, properly considered,
is political activity.

One last point must be made on this topic, since our conclusion
that economic activity is properly and strictly a quest of means may
seem at variance with the position taken by others. Economic activity
is, as we understand it, merely an aspect of a totality of behaving. An
author writes novels; he is interested in marketing them and takes steps
accordingly. In his actual writing the marketing aspect may be more
or less influential or even determinative. But no novelist worthy of
the name thinks of that alone. He makes use of the economic way and
so far is thinking of the means he can acquire for further ends.

But what, it may be said, of the man who spends his whole working
time in market activities? It is of course a matter of degree. Market activity as such remains a means to means. But human beings do not live
in separate compartments of their personality. Their other interests
are not excluded when they work in or for a market. Other attitudes
enter into their activity. There is companionship, there is some consideration for the needs of others in the process, there is the sense of work-
manship or the quality of achievement where opportunity is offered
to it, and so forth. Utilitarian interests are in this respect like utilitarian
goods. An automobile is designedly a means of transportation, but the
people who make and use automobiles want them to be something
more as well. The utilitarian requirement is made the opportunity for
the fulfillment of requirements of a different kind.

Economic activity involves at the same time economic relationships, but again when a man enters into economic relationships he acts
as a social being, not merely an economic one, so that certain satisfactions
of day-by-day living arise in the process of maintaining relationships
that were primarily entered into for economic reasons. One of the major
problems of a modern society is the establishment of an effective rapport between the economic aspect of a man's work and its other aspects.

THE ECONOMIC AND THE
POLITICAL WAYS AS ALTERNATIVES

The means to many of the goals of living may be sought by enlisting
for the purpose in hand either the mechanism of government or the
mechanism of the market. One or the other way or some combination
of both may be chosen, and the particular choice is nearly always a matter of controversy. Take, for example, the provision of medical care

within a community as a whole. In any modern society that provision is not left solely to the free play of the market. There are rules determining who shall be permitted to be medical practitioners and under what controls. These rules are in the last resort dependent on the sanction of government. The profession thus officially sanctioned in turn makes rules concerning the practice of medicine. It has, for example, rules prohibiting advertising and other competitive practices on the part of the doctors. In the last resort the sanction of these rules depends on government. There are again a great many provisions concerned with public health that are prescribed by government and carried out with the aid of the medical profession.

At present in this country there is a lively controversy over the question whether a further great expansion of the political method is or is not here desirable. Should medical service be provided for the people as a whole by state action or should we rely in general on private practice together with such devices as group health insurance, voluntary arrangements for hospitalization needs, and so forth?

Here is one of the multitude of issues that arise concerning the desirable range and limits of the political way as against the economic way. The controversy over each of them is continuously confused by irrelevant arguments. Special interests on one side or the other dress their appeals in the garb of sacred principles. In weighing these arguments our own biases and our lack of knowledge of the processes of implementation often prevent us from being logically determined by a sincere consideration of the merits of the case.

We have set out two broad principles that, if we could sincerely and knowledgeably apply them, would at least orient us properly in coming to a decision. But the application is never simple. Any change from the economic way to the political way or vice versa is likely to involve both a gain and a loss. If you choose one alternative you are likely to incur the loss of some value associated with the rejected alternative. Which way lies the net gain to the community at large? Exaggerated statements of the gain on the one hand and of the loss on the other are likely to be made respectively by the proponents and by the opponents of change.

To take our example, the establishment of a socialized or national medical service limits the freedom of doctors to practice as they please and it confers on government a new responsibility and with it a new power. On the other hand it brings medical service more adequately to those sections of the population who are least able to pay for it, and by giving them greater protection may help to raise the health standards of the whole people. There are also of course other considerations to be adduced on both sides. Which then is more significant, the gain or the loss? How great is the loss? How important is the gain? We can never fully reckon the alternatives. We must use the best judgment at our command.

In doing so, there are certain types of argument we should discount. So far as may be, we should attach more weight to the arguments of those who have, to the best of our knowledge, no special or private interest whichever way the decision goes. Special-interest groups may honestly feel that they are pleading not their own benefit but the general benefit, yet we all know how exceedingly hard it is to be unbiased when our own advantage or our own prestige is, or is thought to be, involved.

Again, we should beware of arguments that sweepingly prognosticate the direct consequences from any new intervention by government in economic affairs and denounce any change, no matter what its manifest benefit, as heralding "socialism," "communism," the "servile society," the "road to serfdom," or what not. Every modern society, at least outside of the Soviet bloc, is sociocapitalistic, some kind of combination of the economic way and the political way. It is inevitable that it should be so. There is no reason to suppose that measures of social insurance and other forms of welfare services are significant of a trend to communism. There is good reason to believe that the provision of such services, removing as they do the primary defect of a capitalistic society, the economic insecurity, the sense of unprotected detachment that undermines the foundations of social solidarity, is a safeguard against and not an invitation to communism. Communism has never succeeded in winning freely to its cause any society that was not shaken to the depths by economic and social despair. Even in those cases it has succeeded only during war-generated crises, when it could seize on government by the violence and cunning of its trained revolutionaries.

With such cautions and distinctions in mind we can weigh more adequately the alternatives when we are presented with one of the ever-arising problems regarding the choice between the economic way and the political way. Sometimes the assessment may be difficult; often, if we keep our primary principles clear, it should not be hard, at least where our particular interests are not involved. To take a simple case, there is, say, a program of forest conservation that requires governmental control over the wasteful activities of lumbermen that are out for short-run profits. The cry is raised that such control would be undue interference with private enterprise or with the rights of property. Any such objection is obviously using as a screen against the public interest a laissez-faire doctrine that has no relevance to the real issue.

We *must* use the political way as well as the economic way, and the problem for the good citizen is to try to assure, so far as his vote or his judgment counts, the best services of both. It is interesting in this connection that the economic way, the way of private enterprise, the way of the free market, if unchecked by government, degenerates through the operation of its own forces into an array of greater and lesser power systems that within their limits stifle the very freedom of enterprise whose banner they fly and become pseudopolitical entities of aggrandizement and exploitation. In short, the free market is not self-maintaining. It needs government to keep it so. Like all other free things its freedom requires the restraint of the forces that would control it, from within or from without. One of the hardest tasks of modern government is to keep within proper bounds the various monopolistic forces, the expansive organizations that subdue competition and can thus dictate their terms unless they are held in check by a vigilant political authority. In the elaborate interdependence of a modern economy any inclusive organization, or even informal combination, that has control over the supply of any one of a hundred commodities or any one of a vast number of services can, if not subjected to the over-all regulation of the state, hold up the community until its demands are met.

Every industrial society is all the time a kind of great laboratory engaged in experimenting in everchanging combinations of the political way and the economic way. So long as a society is free it is bound to experiment, in response to changing conditions and growing experience. And here we come to the final challenge of alternatives, that between communism, a system that on the ground of an inherited dogma rules out the economic way altogether, and the mixed economy of all other systems. The challenge, incidentally, is never one between communism and capitalism, since pure capitalism does not exist and never has existed, but between a rigid system that closes down one of the alternatives and a flexible system, sociocapitalism, that operates with both.

There is often, however, a misunderstanding as to the nature of this final challenge. We must not confuse the threat of communism, as a power system animated by a dogma concerning the inevitable processes of history and having aggressive designs to make the dogma come true, with the challenge of communism as a creed, as a system of values. Communism has won its major victories only under the former aspect. Under the latter it has never won the allegiance of a people that was free to choose. It has never won the verdict of a democratically governed people. It has never yet been chosen freely on its merits.

The reason is not far to seek. Soviet communism cannot offer itself as an alternative in a democratic fashion. Its proposition is always "all or nothing." It rejects with scorn any proposition except its total fulfillment, brought about in a single cataclysm that "destroys the machinery of the bourgeois state." It can proceed only by the road of revolution, with the violent suppression of the whole pre-existing order of things. Even if its party were greatly in the majority it could not suffer any minority that dissented from its creed. It is thus through and through antidemocratic and it is animated by a virulent hatred of those who resist its tenets. The proponents of other forms of socialism are ready to advance by degrees to their goal, and those who believe in private capitalism accept varying mixtures of socialism. Communism ridicules all such doctrines and has no mercy for their advocates.

Now in a democratic society there is always a choosing between alternatives, but the alternatives are always some change in the established ways or no change in that particular respect, always more of this or more of that, always a shift toward the left or toward the right. Public opinion moves in this direction or in that. There are trends of change and thus some preparedness for the next move, whatever the direction may be and whatever controversies may rage over it. The all-or-nothing alternatives that alone are congenial to the rigid Marxist mind are thus wholly alien to the spirit of democracy.

A free society is a flexible society, always experimenting, always, so far as it is also intelligent, seeking to adjust its conditions to its changing needs. It enthrones no dogma, it surrenders to no power system. Whatever mistakes it makes it never binds its own future. It uses the economic way but with some recognition of the need for limits and safeguards. These limits and safeguards are provided by the political way, but in turn a democratic society recognizes that limits and safeguards must be vigilantly assured against government also. For the danger is always the unguarded power of men over men, whether the power be economic or political. Some kind of equilibrium must always be sought.

The citizen cannot leave the decision to the experts or to the authorities. The choice of alternatives is always presented afresh. Being neither an expert nor an authority, he must bring to bear instead the principles of equity, the spirit of the good citizen, with whatever enlightenment he possesses. And in the longer run, whatever mistakes he may make in the process, it is only so far as such principles prevail that any society can advance toward the goals of living.

The alternatives continually present themselves and the citizen cannot evade the choice. He does not make the alternatives; he has only to choose between them. Nor can he take the line: "There is something I approve and something I disapprove in both the alternatives presented; I shall accept the best compromise or balance between them." This principle is good and applicable when a question is up for discussion, when we are in a position to formulate a policy or to offer amendments to a program, when we are seeking to educate ourselves—or others—

respecting the merits of a case. But in the political arena the choice is between alternative candidates, or sometimes between the acceptance or the rejection of a particular measure or policy. These are the alternatives out of which action results. These are the decisions that make history. These are the vital choices we have to make in the practical business of living. In these conjunctures we are not faced with opposing principles that are *equally* valid—for us. In the light of our judgment we have to choose between the better and the worse. The choice of the second best, when the best is not the other alternative, is the choice of the best. If we stand aside and refuse to choose, we are either indifferent to the issues or by our inertness are aiding the worse to win. In every important choice there is assuredly the need for balance, but it is the balance that weighs the gain against the loss.

[1953]

Government and Social Welfare

29 AN ANCIENT CONTROVERSY

Over the role of government in the promotion of social welfare controversy has always raged and will always continue to rage. Should government feed the hungry, or protect the debtor, or find work for the unemployed or land for the landless man, or provide medical care for the poor or security against the various hazards of life? Why or why not? How much or how little? Under what conditions? With what effects on personal responsibility, on individual initiative, on essential freedoms, on the spirit of progress? Where do we need more government, and where less?

This has always been a major question, wherever men have been free enough to ask it. Today it rises again, as it rose in the Jerusalem of the days when the Jews wanted to exchange their judges for kings, or in the Athens of the great legislator Solon, or in the Rome of Caius Gracchus, or in the guild cities of medieval times, or in the transition from the feudal to the territorial state, or in the great ferment of seventeenth-century England, or in the rise of modern nationalism, or in the nineteenth-century conflicts over the factory acts, or in the United States since the foundations of the Republic to the present hour. It is the problem of thus far and no further, the problem of the proper limits to governmental powers and to their exercise.

It is an eternal question eternally restated in every time of change, which means in *every* time. Is it then merely or purely controversial, holding no solution, because it is simply a matter of opinion inspired by interest, and opinions must always clash so long as interests do? I shall put to you the thesis it is not, need not, should not, be so; that while opinion alone will determine the precise limits of governmental action and still more the question of particular ways and means, increasing knowledge offers adequate guidance concerning the major direction of policy. Some of this knowledge is already at hand, and much more can be learned from experience and from the endless experiments conducted by many different governments under many different conditions.

A FALSE ANTITHESIS

In the first place, it is clear to every student of the subject that the issue is falsely stated by those who confront us with stark alternatives. We must choose order or freedom, said Thomas Hobbes, you can't mix them; they are like oil and water. We must choose between social security or individual liberty, they still tell us today. Or at least between more social security and less individual liberty. If we want security, we must invoke government with its intrusive compulsive power, and every intrusion of government narrows the realm of freedom.

Either—or? Liberty *or* government intervention? Liberty *or* servitude? Liberty without governmental interference, *or* loss of liberty when government in any way enters into our economic affairs, into our health programs, into our philanthropic activities. The intransigence of this *either/or* bedevils the solution of many problems. It is so unrealistic, so wholly unrelated to the evidence.

Law increases or diminishes the realm of liberty according to its kind. Government must lay down the rules of the game or it cannot be played at all. Who would dream of a game without any rules or without an umpire? A game in which every player made and interpreted the rules for himself? Who would dream up such a nightmare game and reach the extraordinary conclusion that it was the only kind to assure freedom and fair play for all?

Too often in the arena of action the banners of *either/or* are held aloft by the opposing sides. Too often it is still freedom *or* social security, more freedom *or* more social services, group welfare *or* individual welfare. The assumptions of the stark alternatives are not analyzed. The lessons to be derived from experience, from the available evidences, are not sought. It should be otherwise. The appeal must be not to slogans, but to evidences. The criterion must be not the assumption, but the result. Knowledge must be invoked as the ground of conclusions. Knowledge must come first and judgment after, though with clear recognition that the knowledge alone is insufficient and also that, however sufficient it might be or become, judgment is still necessary and never final.

The trouble is that our doctrines and our policies are seldom in accord. We do not read into our doctrines the lessons of experience. Our policies at length reflect the urgency of conditions and the pressure of needs, but our doctrines long remain undisciplined. So the adaptations we make to our needs are grudging and inadequately enlightened. The world of power loves to flaunt the banner of the unyielding absolute, and even when it yields to conditions the outmoded banner still flies. Recent history offers most flagrant illustrations. Look, for example, at how most peace treaties are made.

Sometimes, indeed, one is tempted to conclude that the men of action are less realistic than the men who are reputed to live in the ivory tower—but then one thinks of some academicians who have migrated to the political arena, and the generalization loses some of its glitter.

Let us compromise and call it a temptation of human nature, this setting up of false alternatives, opposing absolutes. In our own day it besets us again in an aggravated form. The world is divided into two, and there is great danger that the absolutism that grips one half of it will generate a counter-absolutism in the other. Half the world is pinned down to a dogma that misnames itself communism; but what of the other half, our half? Against the irrationality of an absolute that suppresses and imprisons human nature, our democracy has a wonderful opportunity to stand for a flexible working liberalism that adjusts itself to the needs of men. The counter-appeal of such a doctrine, clearly delivered, could be immense.

But in what mode do we, the inheritors of democracy and now its prime defenders, combat the doctrinal march of the communist absolute? Some of the powerful among us present us as the exponents of the opposite and equally unrealistic absolute, the absolute of *laissez-faire*. So we lose allies, and we exchange real wounds in a fight over phantom causes,

> Swept with confused alarms of struggle and flight
> Where ignorant armies clash by night.

These preliminary reflections have to do with the broad theme of the role of government in the advancement of social well-being.

And I say here with strong emphasis that our national interest and the causes we stand for would be greatly advanced if only we could carry into our public controversies the true spirit of inquiry, the concern to see the facts as they are, to examine problems in the light of conditions, and to test programs by resort to the evidence.

In dealing with highly controversial themes, we must deal with them not with the partisan drive to win a verdict, but in the spirit of open-minded inquiry, seeking a happy balance of diverse elements. There is at present no hope that this spirit, as it applies to the role of government, can come to life in the world behind the Iron Curtain. But can we not cherish the hope that it may prevail in the half that prides itself on its freedom—and not least among ourselves?

VALUES AND MEANS

Let us get closer to the actual topic. We have proper fears lest the increase of governmental controls should be hurtful to values we uphold, to freedoms we enjoy. The danger will differ according to the area of control. Any governmental control whatever over intellectual freedom is perilous. But some governmental controls over some economic conditions may be salutary or even necessary. Social security measures do not interfere with any major business activities or with the exercise of business initiative in its more important respects; but people express concern over the effect on the attitude of the worker. Governmental subventions to higher education do not interfere in any sense with the conduct of business; but we may be concerned that they will undermine the autonomy of the educational authorities, by the giving or the withholding of funds according as the programs conform or do not conform to governmental ideas. And we always have reason to fear the common disease of organizations that grow very big and powerful, the hardening of the arteries called bureaucracy.

We are all pretty well agreed on the values we want to defend. Who doubts that initiative is a good thing? Who does not believe in the spirit of enterprise? The vast majority of us agree also that education should be available in the widest range to all who are capable of profiting by it, for the enrichment of their own lives and for the service of society. We are mostly agreed that more needs to be done to safeguard and advance the health of the people, to make available, particularly to the less well-to-do, the benefits of advancing medical knowledge. But we are in doubt about the means for achieving these desirable things. We fear, or profess to fear, their effect on other things we value.

The trouble so often is that we lay down as postulates not only our values but also the means to our values. But the means should always be open to inquiry, experiment, and constant testing. As the conditions change, the means must be subject to reconsideration and revision. To assume unchanging means for the attainment of our values in a changing world is the essence of all reactionary movements. Individual initiative and freedom of enterprise are eminently desirable things; but for centuries certain groups and interests have handcuffed these values to an adamant negative. "Want is its own best cure," "Economic depressions are self-correcting," and so forth. Their only prescription has been, "Keep government out." Keep factory acts out, they used to say; keep workmen's compensation out, keep social security out, keep out federal aid to higher education, keep international organizations out—and keep out or throw out of the colleges and universities the people who favor any such things.

By locking the value, enterprise, to the means, *laissez-faire*, they had deliberately to reject another value, the value of social security. They knew this, but they did not know that they were endangering also the value they sought. They could not in the longer run prevent the coming of factory acts and workmen's compensation and social security measures; but by their opposition to such measures they alienated a large part of the working classes and thus made them more responsive to doctrines that sought to destroy free enterprise altogether.

The way of reason is the way of victory. This is the lesson of our industrial history, and in a time when anti-intellectual forces have become again peculiarly threatening, it is well that this position should be stoutly maintained.

The intelligent way is to take our accepted values and relate them pragmatically to the conditions and to the available means. Free enterprise is a value, but the maintenance of our values has also its necessary costs. Free enterprise is a virtue; very well, let us inquire honestly whether social security diminishes or extends its range. Initiative is a virtue; very well, let us inquire how we can preserve it. Let us ask, to begin with, whether there is less scope for initiative because we have public tax-supported education. Education is also a high value; let us consider how its development can best be made compatible with any needful governmental aid. The presence of incentives to every form of worth-while endeavor is eminently to be desired. Very well, let us examine realistically what forces balk the liberation of incentive and what forces advance it. Do lack of protection against a destitute old age and the fear of it increase initiative or have the opposite effect? Are people beset by anxiety more likely to be enterprising than are people buoyed by hope?

In passing, it may be suggested that these are questions of the kind to which our social sciences might well address themselves more seriously and on a greater scale if they want to vindicate their place in the sun. They are controversial questions, but the controversy is intensified by our prejudice and by our ignorance. They are challenging questions because there is much to be found out, and advancing knowledge can contribute much-needed guidance.

There is much experience to be tapped. We learn, for example, why our industrial civilization has, in spite of the rise in the standards of living, engendered among large numbers an increasing sense of economic insecurity. We learn how modern conditions enhance feelings of hazard and dependence. We learn how, when men have once attained some degree of political security, they inevitably aspire to economic security. We learn why the detached modern man cannot rely on self-help of patriarchal support for that security, amid the chances and changes of a mobile society. As we learn more of these things we realize the false simplicity of nineteenth-century individualism. When the devil can take the hindmost, we hand over too much of the free enterprise to the devil.

FREEDOM AND SECURITY

May not confidence, rather than rankling fear, be the spur to enterprise? May not insecurity be the comrade of subjection and not of freedom? The great apostles of early nineteenth century *laissez-faire* preached free enterprise. But free enterprise for whom? Not for the men and women and children in the mines and the cotton mills, without education, without opportunity, without any recourse. But free enterprise can never be safe so long as it is the sole prerogative of the few. If free enterprise is to be safe, the range of opportunity has to be widened. Only with some opportunity for the many, only with some security for them, can the breath of free enterprise pervade the whole being of society.

Too often we assume contradiction where a more realistic investigation would find only the need for balance and adjustment. The first-sight view is often mistaken, especially when it is supported by our prejudices or interests. There are still survivors of the old school that roundly declares governmental aid to those in need of it will sap their initiative and create a spirit of dependence. This is a branch of the larger school that views all social welfare activities of government as interfering with the beneficent laws of nature. They say so with the same blithe assurance that has led the Marxist to discover his own immutable laws. They do not honestly inquire into the evidences for the laws they postulate. They make their own privilege or their status or their sense of power the premise of their laws, without knowing it, without reckoning the consequences, even the consequences to themselves. Take the simple fact stated by Barbara Wootton:

> The more prosperous sections of the community have always protected (and still do protect) themselves against the hazards of industrial life on a scale quite beyond the dreams of the ordinary wage earner; and many of those who have taken larger risks have done so against a background of security which guaranteed something to fall back on in the event of disaster.

The irony of history waits near by when the otherwise secure contend that the genuinely insecure must not, for their own sake, be aided by government in attaining a minimum of security.

The service the scholar can render to society is to inquire into these things, find and read the evidences, and discover the true relations, as far as it lies in his power, in the complex skein of changing conditions and changing needs. It is a task demanding both courage and discipline, and the scholar, like other men, has to struggle with his own biases and scarcely knows when he is yielding to them. Imperfect sympathies combine to skew our very imperfect knowledge. But all experience, as well as the history of past errors, warns us that we cannot discover the relations of liberty and security, of liberty and government, *in the abstract*, and that our comfortable assumptions of simple laws of cause and effect are invariably wrong. The more we learn of the living texture of society, the more we must pass from the sheer conflict of irreconcilable opposites to the realistic equilibrium of diverse elements—law *and* liberty, social security *and* free enterprise, self-aid *and* community aid *and* state aid, authority *and* responsibility—an equilibrium controlled by experience and realistically responsive to changing conditions. The eternal advantage of democracy over all other forms of government is that it makes possible, through endless trial and not infrequent error, the attainment of this flexible equilibrium; but democracy will bring this happy result only if the lessons of experience are not overridden by narrow dogmas and narrow interests.

By the constant test of experience we must discover the place of voluntary social service and state social service in a changeful economy, the roles that different kinds of organizations are best fitted to perform, the insufficiencies and the abuses to which each kind is subject, the limits that common sense aided by knowledge should assign to each. It is a process demanding patience and discipline, but the strength and health and unity of our democracy demand it.

GOVERNMENT AND EDUCATION

Another aspect of the same lesson is revealed by an examination of national policies for education. For reasons that are in our day completely obvious school education has nearly everywhere become a function of the state, though there are a few countries where the church still retains some element of its former dominance. The system of control varies very greatly, particularly as to the respective roles of local and central governments and as to the autonomy of the educational authorities under the general supervision of the state.

The limits of governmental control remains a question that still arouses continual controversy. But in every well-established democracy the tradition is strong that the political authorities shall not dictate the content and the actual processes of the educational curriculum. In our own country a large autonomy for local educational boards has become a guiding principle, but there have always been tendencies to encroachment on it, and in some parts of the country the principle has been less fully recognized than in others. The picture is a complicated one. Here too there is a proper place and function for each of a series of authorities, from the educators themselves up to the federal government, if the needful provision of educational opportunity is not to be achieved at the price of the quality, the freedom, and the flexibility of the vast and endless educational enterprise.

There is, for example, much controversy over the question whether the federal government should take on, or perhaps resume, more responsibility by way of sharing, with the states and localities, the costs of education. Now, the wrong way of dealing with this question is to say to the federal government, "Hands off! That way lies bureaucratic control over our educational freedom."

In the first place, the federal government has a distinctly better record, where it has supported educational projects and institutions, than have a number of state governments. In the second place, this kind of hard-and-fast demarcation, based not on constitutional limitations but only on broad assumptions about consequences, is rarely tenable and is frequently violated by other policies of its advocates. Some of the strongest supporters of this hands-off doctrine, indeed, have shown themselves enthusiastic supporters of another and a much more perilous intervention by federal agencies in the field of education, by the way they approve the present activities of certain congressional committees. (Just as some of the most ardent supporters of the cry, "Let government keep its hands off free enterprise," are at the same time advocates of high tariff barriers.)

In the third place, the primary consideration is: How and how far can we make use of a particular agency or instrument in the service of a worth-while objective without endangering the objective itself? Federal control of educational policies, we nearly all agree, is wholly undesirable, while federal aid without such control might now be very serviceable. Well then, if we really want the service without the control, should we not, can we not, see to it that our legislators pass the kinds of measures that will assure the aid without the control? Are we not enough of a democracy to keep vigilant watch against controls to which we are opposed? If we cannot trust government, can we not, must we not, trust ourselves?

ACADEMIC FREEDOM

Now let us turn to another side of the educational picture, the question of academic freedom. There is one kind of political control over education that does not sufficiently win the attention of the people and that has nothing to do with the support or the advancement of education. State legislatures and sometimes municipal governments are making a new kind of encroachment on the proper prerogatives of the educational authorities. It is no longer simply the exercise of power to withhold funds or reduce educational budgets where the policies of these authorities are not pleasing to the politicians. Now governments are legislating more direct controls extending beyond the schools and beyond the public institutions of higher learning, to private colleges and universities.

They do this by passing certain types of loyalty acts that make conditions concerning the qualifications of educators. They do it by conducting investigations of schools and colleges, ostensibly checking on subversive tendencies, but actually creating an atmosphere of constraint and apprehension. And sometimes they sponsor legislative proposals that would put the stamp of law on the spirit of conformism. One could very well illustrate this last point by reference to the ten bills sponsored by the Illinois Seditious Activities Investigation Commission, eight of which failed to receive sufficient support in the Illinois legislature, while another, the major Senate bill of the Commission, was vetoed by Governor Stevenson.

No more splendid watchword could be proclaimed by any institution of learning than our own: *Man's right to knowledge and the free use thereof.*

As we explore the subject, however, we find there are also other obstacles than those set up when interest and prejudice and bias and passion are armed with power to prevent the free expansion of knowledge. We find, along with these, two obstacles of another kind. One is the inertia, the disregard, the positive dislike and fear of inquiry and the inquiring mind, the deliberate know-nothingism that for some unexplained reason has manifested itself again and again in our country. This anti-intellectualism, this obscurantist suspicion of the scholar, the egghead, has, in spite of all our educating, a considerable appeal to certain groups at the present time—even, we must admit, to some academic groups. The other obstacle, which indeed may be only a variety of the first, is the strong conviction of many that they already know the truth, that it is conveyed to them by their intuitions or their indoctrinations, and that, especially in matters that concern the ordering of society or even the ordering of the universe, any attempt of scholars to use their intelligence in the search for evidences, or to go to the sources from which these people claim to derive their convictions, is a vexatious activity of mischief-making minds.

These attitudes breed a shallowness of viewpoint, a readiness to accept first-view solutions of great and challenging issues, a superficial acceptance of noble traditions without any perception of their power or their depth, so that the generous impulses that move our people find no worthy expression, and so that in times like ours we are too susceptible to the fatally simple panaceas of those who seek to win their way thereby to greater power.

WHAT IS IT TO BE PRACTICAL?

These tendencies are indirectly aided by the remarkable expansion of American technology, since it has engendered a too exclusive devotion of our energies to the immediately utilitarian aspects of knowledge, the knowledge of mechanism. Other forms of knowledge, the knowledge of the ends of living as against the knowledge of the means, the knowledge of the enduring cultural legacy of the ages, are too often regarded as impractical, merely academic. We do not commonly recognize that this other knowledge, extending through literature and the fine arts to philosophical and religious contemplation, not only is distinguished by being good in itself, good for its own sake, but also prepares us the better to meet the greatest and most important of all practical questions, the questions that concern our relations to one another, in our own country, and our relations to other peoples. For here we are least adept. We are more skilled in dealing with machines than in dealing with social and political situations. Our failure to enlist the peoples of the East in our struggle against communist aggression is one of the most unhappy revelations of this weakness.

Americans pride themselves on being practical. Let us urge then that Americans become *more* practical, more practical in those areas where it matters most. Let us encourage reflective thought and discussion, so that the relations of government to social welfare will not be decided by slogans and preconceived notions and ancient shibboleths; so that we get down instead to the evidence, the needs and the reactions of human beings; so that we seek to understand their situations and their problems and discover by experience what the consequences may be if we pursue this course or pursue that other; so that we find by wise experiment what differences it makes if people are treated this way or that; so that we seek to understand the ways of people, at least as forethoughtfully as we try to understand the ways of the machine. Then our national policies in the fields of education and health and social service will approach a decent balance of the values at stake, preserving freedom without sacrificing welfare. Then the controversies that will still arise will be more constructive, for they will be more concerned with the limits and the quality of service. In the moving balance of realistic well-planned experimentation lies the only solution.

I venture to go one step further. It is only by following the same realistic approach in our relations with other peoples that we can recover that place of leadership in the world for which fate has marked us out and which may otherwise slip from our grasp beyond recall.

[1955]

WAR *and* INTERNATIONAL ORDER

V

War and Civilization

3O Does an institution die when it has lost its meaning, when
the conditions that made it intelligible or necessary have
given place to conditions in which it is no longer intelligible? If it did, then today the institution of war would
indeed be dead, the corpse of an institution with no animating breath. The process of the world has brought an
age in which it is strictly and simply without meaning.
The social conditions out of which war arose have been
transformed into social conditions which leave no place
for war. It were well if we could understand this transformation and so rid ourselves of the body of this dead thing.

To understand it we must understand how the significance of the "state" has been gradually, almost imper-
ceptibly, changing since first modern states arose on the
ruins of medieval empire. A process of social differentiation
has been going on, the details of which have often been
pointed out but the full meaning of which is almost wholly
ignored. The result is that our political thinking is at many
points archaic, and far behind our actual progress. Questions
of great moment are coming up for settlement, arising naturally out of the new conditions, and we are discussing
them in terms of the old. Our notions about the state are
derived from a world where quite different conditions

held, a world where the new questions could never have arisen because then a state was something quite different from what a state is now. We cannot answer the new questions until we understand the new conditions.

If we ask the average man who thinks or writes or talks about the state, "what then is the state?" he would be put to no little perplexity. "War," say the publicists, "is a relation between state and state." True, and there was a time when war had a very clear meaning as the hostile relation of states. At that time states were not only independent but separate, and separation makes hostility possible. At that time it was not merely states but communities that were separate and independent; and state and community were one. The state *was* the community. When the state went to war the community went to war. It was the people, the tribe, the city, the nation, and not merely the state that entered into war. But can we say today that the state is the people or the nation? Are the United Kingdom, Germany, France, and the rest, states and nothing more? We speak as if they were and thereby show our blindness to one of the most remarkable and far-reaching movements of modern civilization. While we are thinking in terms of the old world, we have all the while been unwittingly building up a new world and a new civilization. And the new civilization is in one respect totally unlike any the world has seen before. It is so new that we do not yet understand it. When we do we shall see that the new civilization has made war unintelligible—except as a survival.

I hope to show from two sides that today the state is not the same as the community or the society over which its legislation extends. On the one hand, the life of the community is far too wide, complex, and spontaneous to be wholly included within the sphere of state-action; on the other, the life of any community is part of the life of a far greater community. These are the two sides of a single development of civilization, which is transforming the character of the state, and in doing so is destroying the meaning of war.

Today it is the state and not the community that goes to war, for there is no community which is separate and independent today. A war today between civilized peoples is essentially "civil war," because the peoples are all today *inter*-civilized. It is the breakdown of existing community and not the assumption of hostility *between* communities. That war should have meaning at all it is essential that the state should be co-extensive with the community, that a people should be as independent of any other people as a state is of any other state.

In the true military age this was the fact—it was the fact for every civilization of the past. In the early civilization of the earth men generally lived in tribes, often on a very communistic plan, and the tribes lived in isolation from one another. The tribal system alone bound the members of the tribe together and in turn a man's place in the tribe determined his whole life. Within the tribe one essential sentiment of unity prevailed, the sense of tribal kinship, strictly confined to the circle of the tribe. Society was bounded by that narrow circumference for each. No community and no moral relation bound tribe and tribe. "The only place where the peoples could become acquainted with one another was the battlefield." (Eötvös.) That age of isolation was the heyday of war.

Even when the peoples grew civilized and the limits of community became larger, there was yet little intersocialization. Society and the political organization of society were not yet distinguished. When the state arose and took a definite name it claimed to sum up the whole of the social life within its borders. The state specially granted the right of intermarriage or commerce with members of other states, when such rights were not denied altogether. There was a religion prescribed by the state and a state-god, the God of the race, who was often also the God of War. The king or chief was the defender, with the political sword, of *the* faith, the faith of the people. On every side the state included the whole life of the people and thereby isolated it from every other people. For a state must be independent and separate. It must have definite frontiers to which its law extends and no further. Its members must obey no other law than its own. Therefore when society and state are one, each community stands in isolation. The Jew has no dealings with the Samaritan. The stranger is the enemy—the same word generally denoted both. In the Roman phrase, a man is a wolf to a man he does not know. Each tribe or race felt that community was possible only when the member of another was adopted into its own, and took on its race and, often, religion. The unity of the tribe meant its severance from other tribes, because it depended on those things which separated it from other tribes, its race and its race-religion.

One form of early community deserves special notice in this respect, because it was the most advanced in civilization, and because its legacy of thought determines our thought today. Many of our political thinkers of today derive their doctrine not from the actual conditions of our civilization, but from the political theory of Athens. Yet in this matter the city-community of Greece belonged to the ancient world, belonged to a past civilization and not at all to ours. In the city-community of Greece men have indeed become citizens instead of tribesmen. The bond of community is widened—it is now not common kin or common religion, it is common life, the life of the city, or rather of the citizen, for by no means all within the walls are distinguished as citizens. But citizenship here claims the whole life of man, as kinship did elsewhere.

The limit of the city is still the limit of community. Socrates was accused of "introducing" other Gods. "The city," said Aristotle, "decides what sciences are to have place within the community, and what kind the individual citizen is to study, and to what extent." In a word, state and society are one. Accordingly the life of the city, as of the tribe, is exclusive. The alien is either refused entrance altogether or is admitted on sufferance, without legal standing, often only on payment of a special fee. He is admitted at most within the walls of the city, not within the circle of citizenship. The life of the city, as of the tribe, is exclusive. The sentiment of race or religion vainly stimulates occasional movements toward inter-community of city and city. No real unity is achieved, except for a moment in face of the barbarian. For the city was the state, so far as a state existed, *and where the political society is co-extensive with and equal to the whole social life of the community, that community is thereby essentially cut off from all others.* The result is the same in ancient Greece and in medieval Germany and Italy—the incessant warfare of independent city with independent city, only ending in their being all alike submerged in absolutism. The cities of Greece and Germany and Italy were like quarrelsome children, shut up at last, as they deserved to be, in the school of despotism.

By almost insensible steps men learn to pass from old into new worlds. The new civilization, our civilization, did not appear when the modern territorial states came into being. Each considerable country was still a separate society no less than an independent state. To be an Englishman was practically to be the enemy of the Frenchman. Nor was true distinction drawn between political and other social forces. The state still claimed the whole control of society, not recognizing that it rests on and is itself an expression of the will of society. In France Louis XIV ordained that every Protestant must change his religion. In England the monarch or parliament once and again imposed political disabilities on those who did not believe the faith for the time-being established.

Yet slowly within the limits of each state a significant difference was revealed between the old and the new. The country state of modern Europe was the first large free state in the history of the world, the first large state whose political order was not imposed upon it. This characteristic, itself due to the widening of the circle of realized community, made a new distinction inevitable: the distinction between society and state, between the whole complex of social forces working in a community and that definite organized political order we call the state. The modern state has during these centuries been slowly realizing its nature. It is only after centuries of strife and bloodshed that, for instance, states have ceased to impose upon their members a state-religion, and have come to admit in practice if not in principle that some aspects of social life are beyond their control. [1] Slowly the place and meaning of the state is becoming clear. The process is yet incomplete, nor can we prophesy the form of its consummation, though the ideal is that every social attribute, however extensive or however limited—common race, common temperament, common speech, common culture, common religion, common humanity—should find a society adequate to the degree and kind of community it involves. This is yet far distant, but meantime two lines of the social evolution, interdependent and very significant, have been revealed. For (1) within the state, with the growth of "freedom" it has become manifest that society is more than the state and expresses itself in many forms and has a multitudinous spontaneous activity which is largely undetermined by the political order. It has become manifest that the state, the political organization, is created by a social will which manifests itself in other ways as well. Modern representative democracy is a recognition of the basis of the state on a social will that is more ultimate than and prior to the political will, to the "sovereign" that it creates. (2) This social will is not only more ultimate, it extends further than the political will. It is not bounded by the frontiers of states. It extends as far as felt community extends, and need only cease where community ceases. Therefore it crosses the boundaries of states and unites the members of independent states in a single society. Let us remember that war is the breaking down of all community, and ask what right the state has to carry on warfare, *when, as is now the case, the state is not co-extensive with society.*

Men are beginning to see that there is something more ultimate even than the state, that the state is not the whole expression, or the widest expression, of the common will of man, that it is one fundamental institution created by society, in a word, that society is greater than the state.

What then is society, and for what end does it maintain the state? Society exists wherever and in so far as human beings recognize any sort of community with one another and in any way organize themselves for the sake of common life or the furtherance of common ends. It includes an infinite variety of forms and infinite degrees of community. *No one form is all inclusive*, because none is sufficient for man's sociability. To meet one social need the church arises, to meet another the family, to meet another the city. Civilized life vibrates with social instinct. Beside the greater societies a myriad lesser ones are everywhere forming and reforming, dissolving and being created. Wherever men

---

1. In England up till 1829 a whole church—the Roman Catholic—was disqualified from political service.

recognize a common interest, great or small, in religion or in the study of earthworms, wherever they realize a common possession—be it a land or an idea—there a society springs into being. First the common interest, then the common will which it engenders, the will of the society whatever it be, directed to the maintaining and furthering of the common end. The greater our individuality, the more societies does it demand for its satisfaction.

The greater permanent societies stand for the great permanent ends, the societies of the state, the church, the family, the societies of production and exchange, the societies of learning and art. The state is *one among other societies*, fundamental, necessary, and the most authoritative, but neither alone fundamental nor alone necessary. The unity of the social world is not to be found in the state, but in the social will on which the state rests and which does indeed lend the state a certain authority over the other societies.

It is on this matter that the current ways of thinking are misleading and confused. The source of this perplexity is easily pointed out. For, on the one hand, the state does by its law control other societies to a certain extent, does, and with justification, legislate for other societies, including even family and church; and on the other hand, we feel dimly that there are limits to this control, that these societies have a life of their own, spontaneous and free, not merely a part of the state life. We feel that when extreme socialists claim that these should be simply state-institutions, they are devitalizing these societies. A man is more than a citizen. Men do not worship God because they are citizens of England— the God-of-the-nation day is past—nor do they bring up families and earn their livelihoods for the sake of the state. The welfare of the state, for all its fundamental importance, is a totally inadequate ideal. The tribe was the small and single society of the tribesman, the city was the almost all-comprehensive social center of the Hellene, but for us the state is neither tribe nor city—it has grown and differentiated in growing. For us history has been defining the place and the purpose of the state, and the process of its definition has been the record of our freedom. We have learned through centuries of strife that neither common race nor common faith nor common life is a necessary requisite of citizenship. A state, a political order, stands not for the whole of human life within its borders, but for a definite end or rather for all those ends which can be secured by established law and the central controlling organization that is primarily the executive of law. Here the state stands supreme. Whatever good enacted law can secure, it is the purpose of a state to secure: whatever a central organization backed by law can do, without hurting the spontaneity of social life, to secure any common good of its members, that it is the duty of the state to undertake. Each state seeks these things within its borders, and with the means at its command; beyond these it cannot go; beyond these the other social forces work out their ends.

In doing so these social forces have outpassed the boundaries of states. Society gaining freedom within the territorial state of the modern world passes also beyond its borders. For society has no frontiers, no limitations. It has only one condition, the recognition of common interest. It rests on the common will engendered by the knowledge of common good. The greatest social phenomenon of the present age is the expansion of society beyond the limits of any one state. It is perhaps the greatest distinction between the modern and the ancient world, but we have as yet failed to bring our political thought into accord with this development. Some of our accredited thinkers even speak as if we were still living in the little Greek city, whose life was rounded by the circle of its walls. Some still call the state, after Aristotle, [2] the "ethical whole" and say it "includes the entire hierarchy of institutions by which life is determined, from the family to the trade, from the trade to the Church and the University." It is less wonder if our popular writers often fail to distinguish, say, between the German state and the social world of Germany. The German state is, as every state must be, independent and self-complete. Its law reaches to a frontier and no further. In conferring German citizenship it rightly denies to its members the citizenship of any other state. But the social life of Germany is bound to ours by a thousand ties of commerce and culture and ideal. Or rather there is a continuous social order in which German and Englishman meet, uncreated by government or political system, and eventually indissoluble by political power. Government can foster or retard it, but it is more ultimate than government, because society is greater than the state.

If we once realized how the civilized world is being transformed from separated, isolated, independent societies into a single continuous society, international questions would at once appear in a new light. We should see, e.g., that the cessation of war does not depend on federations or treaties arbitrarily entered upon by independent self-sufficient states, not on the mere fiat of high contracting parties, not simply on the convenience of governments or the intrigues of diplomacy or the relations of monarchs, but the silent widening social will that ultimately all governments must obey. The mass of society, the great working

2. There was a better justification for Aristotle, because he spoke not of the "state" at all, but of the "city." It was significant of Greek thought that the one word "politikos" stood for "civil," "political," and "social" all in one. Similarly is it not significant of the backwardness of *our* thinking that we have only the term "citizen" to express membership both of a state and of a city?

mass of every people, have an interest in peace and not in war. Their
interests are one in every state; they form a single common interest.
Common interest when recognized begets common will. It is on this
common will that the world's peace is based. In particular the united
peaceful industrial society of Europe, which has absolutely no desire
for war and no interest except in so far as it pays for and suffers by war,
is gradually feeling its unity and finding a voice. Some labor leaders
have already threatened that in the event of war between western states,
the labor parties would by striking so effectually intervene as to bring
the war to an end. Such an attitude may seem a menace to the state, but
we must meet the menace in the right way. Hitherto the state has protected, more or less, the societies within the area of its jurisdiction. It has
acted, however, as if there were no continuous society reaching beyond
its borders. This society the single state cannot of itself protect. What then
shall protect this more universal society even against the single state?

The members of western states are already and are becoming more
and more members also of this greater society. This greater society is
becoming conscious of its common interest and in turn will establish,
through the cooperation of states, the means for its security. It has already begun to do so by "international law" and by the recently established international courts. Many people regard "international law" as
law in name only, and international courts as courts in name only. What,
they ask, is law that has no force behind it, or a court that can neither
summon offenders nor execute its decrees? Is not law without power
a shadow or phantom, and the tribunal entrusted with administering
it but the vain pulpit of impotent idealists, pitting moral suasion against
armed force? Such an objection is ill-founded. "International law"
is not yet law in the full sense of the term, but it is mere ignorance to
say that therefore it is futile. You are perfectly at liberty to deny to it
the right to the term "law," but you must admit its efficacy nevertheless.
States do not sign Berlin treaties or agree to Hague or Geneva Conventions without meaning something by it. And there are many rules of
international law that no civilized state would dream of violating. Would
any civilized state today commence hostilities without declaration of
war, or shoot down in warfare the ascertained bearers of a flag of truce?
The "law of nations," which even Napoleon declared to be universally
observed by civilized states, has been hitherto concerned more with
regulating war than peace, but if it can regulate war, the denial of community, are there not a thousand reasons why it should be still more
authoritative to regulate peace? [3]

3.   Since the First World War remnants of what was optimistically called the
international law of war have gone into the scrapheap — R.M.M.

Force indeed of some kind the law must have. But whence in the first instance does the law acquire its force? From governments or judges or armies or policemen? Simply from the social will to uphold the law, the will to obey it. Without that will not a government or court of law could exist for an hour. It is that will that evokes the force that waits behind the law, to enforce the law on any reluctant minority. Government is simply a medium of the will of society.

The assumption that law is only possible within a state is an unnecessary one. There was a time in the history of civilization when there were laws and no states, effective social laws. No legislature had ever enacted them, no chief had ordained them, but they ruled the tribes, were recognized and obeyed, upheld only by public opinion and the power of social approbation and disapprobation. So far as we can discern the dim beginnings of civilized life, first in the history of peoples came the law, never enacted or proclaimed, next the court, the jurisdiction, the "doom," revealing but not making law, and last of all the legislature took law into its charge. *International law is following exactly the same course.* The law itself has been growing into being from remote antiquity, the famed "law of nations," the "law which all men everywhere obey," dimly realized in the troubled political consciousness of the Greeks, interpreted by the Romans for the peoples within the Empire and after the pitiless wars of the Middle Ages first formulated by Grotius as a rule for independent states.

Here is the first stage, the slow revealing of the law. The second stage has now arrived. Two permanent international courts have now been called into being, the Hague Permanent Court of Arbitration, founded 1899, and the Hague International Court of Appeal for naval prizes, recently established. This is the beginning of the jurisdiction that comes after the law. Lastly will come the international legislature, to take into its keeping, maintain, modify, and enlarge the international law. Why should not such a legislature be as authoritative as, say, a Federal Legislature? It is the fulfillment of the present process of the nations. It would leave the integrity of nations unimpaired, or rather ensure it, for it is war that has always threatened the independence of peoples. It is a means neither to imperialism nor to cosmopolitanism, two false extremes. It would maintain the autonomy of states, as law maintains the liberty of individuals. And it would protect society. For while state is totally independent of state, and race, sometimes, clearly defined and separate from race, society is one, and links the nearest to the most remote and makes the most remote indispensable to the nearest. "I say, there is not a red Indian hunting by Lake Winnipeg can quarrel with his squaw, but the whole world must smart for it; will not the price of beaver rise?" If not sympathy or understanding, then at least commerce forms its nexus.

Even were they bound by this strong band alone, it would be enough to make war, the breaking down of community, disastrous both to the warring nations and to the neutral peoples with whom they form one society. This economic interdependence has recently been very strikingly illustrated by Mr. Norman Angell in his book *The Great Illusion*. I do not think, however, that the new economic conditions alone are our greatest security against war. War has always been expensive and has rarely paid itself to the conquerors, but this has not prevented wars. The surer safeguard is the growing inter-community of the nations, of which the economic interdependence is rather a sequel than a cause. It is isolation that sets the peoples to war. "They isolate themselves, expecting war," wrote Bastiat, "but isolation is itself the commencement of war." When nations are isolated, the strength of one is the weakness of the other, the pride of one is the disgrace of the other. When nations are intersocialized, the weakness of one is the weakness of the other, but the wealth, culture, and progress of the one contribute to the wealth, culture, and progress of the other. For it is an elementary fact that within a society every gain of the part is a gain of the whole directly in proportion to the solidarity of the society.

The civilized world is becoming more and more rapidly an effective society. Each country is becoming more and more bound up in the welfare of each. Every recent advance of science has been a means for the widening of the area of community, uniting men in ways impossible before. Railway, telegraph, telephone, Marconi apparatus, even camera, cinematograph, and electric theater, are they not all bridging the gulfs of isolation, bringing the peoples nearer to one another, and enabling them to realize the common factors of all civilized life? The will for peace grows with the means of community.

It is solidarity that is making war unintelligible: the credit system merely makes it more disastrous. Isolation is the source of all hostility, the alleged causes are mainly pretexts. Nations have carried on schemes of mutual devastation in cases where no possible gain but only loss could accrue, in the interests of dynasties or in the name of religion or of honor. The first two causes, dynastic ambition and religion, need no longer be reckoned with. The world in which they operated, in which men fought and laid countries waste to raise a Hapsburg to a throne or "enforce" a dogma, is also of the unreturning past. Democracy has made the one and enlightenment the other impossible. There still remains "honor," and—if we rule out the idea that commercial supremacy follows military power—"honor" alone. "Honor" stands out as the ostensible exception in international agreements. "Honor" is the last stand of the argument for war. Nearly all the states of the civilized world have been in these days binding themselves by treaty to refer subjects of dispute to the Hague tribunal, but they have all added the words "Provided nevertheless that they do not affect the vital interests, the independence, or the honor of the high contracting parties." It is thought that the honor of a nation can be entrusted to no international tribunal. It was once thought that the honor of an individual could not be entrusted to the law of the land, and it has recently been pointed out, notably by Mr. Asquith and by President Taft, that the justification of war in the name of honor is the justification of the duel. The reasons which have led civilized men on the whole to reject the duel, the impossibility of vindicating honor by the accident of superior swordsmanship, the iniquity of a tribunal at which the innocent is as likely to suffer as the guilty, the wronged man as the wrong doer, apply equally to the international duel. They apply indeed with greater force. For indeed no civilized nation ever insults another. A statesman may, a newspaper editor may, an admiral may—but a whole people—never! And we are as grossly misled in identifying, say, the editor with "Germany" and the admiral, say, with "Russia" as ever Louis XIV was in identifying the state with himself. A people will readily be persuaded that it has suffered an insult, but it never regards itself as having first offered an insult. It never does. "I do not know the method," said Burke, "of drawing up an indictment against a whole people."

Is not to refuse to admit affairs of honor to tribunal the drawing up of an indictment against all other peoples? Would we not otherwise say with President Taft: "I do not see why questions of honor should not be submitted to tribunals composed of men of honor." Perhaps the forthcoming agreement between the United States and Great Britain will be the beginning of the process that shall one day end in the destruction of the last plea for war, when governments recognize at last (in the words of the Hague commissioners) "the solidarity which unites the members of the society of civilized nations," the solidarity which is the most striking contrast between our own and all previous civilizations.

There is another very significant aspect of the intersocialization of the nations. Society, we said, was a question of degree. Within it there are groups united by many social ties, others united by few only. The members of a family are bound by the most numerous and the closest social ties; the members of a city have more than the members of a state; the citizens who are also members of a church, of a social order, of a club, of a council, have more ties than those who are not. It is the very nature of society to involve social groups and even strata. This is generally recognized, but what is less observed is that the lines of social grouping and stratification tend less and less to conform to political and racial boundaries. There is the society of learning. Its members are of every race and tongue. There is "society" in the sense of *le haut monde*, again international. There is the organization of labor, threatening even to bring internationalism into politics. Its members have in different countries the same political faith, and a faith not shared in by their fellow-citizens. So the member of the English labor party has even a political community with a German socialist which he has not with his fellow English citizen. And so with a thousand other groupings, artistic, scientific, financial, religious, industrial—unions of men crossing the line of states. The educated Englishman has more in common with the educated Frenchman or German than he has with his uneducated fellow countrymen. He is more "at home," more in society with him; he prefers his company. Lastly, do not our royal families, the ostensible heads of our states, intermarry with one another alone?

And yet we still talk of "states" going to war. We talk of "England's" going to war with "Germany." What, in the light of these facts, is "England," and what is "Germany"? Is it the state, or the nation, or the part of society which happens to be divided from another part by the accident of geography, though united by the essentials of intercourse? Is not war between states intelligible only when state and society are one? Is not war unintelligible today? Is it not a survival from the time when state and society were one?

The new civilization has made war unintelligible—it will some day make war impossible. But the unintelligible often has a long life, in politics at any rate. Meanwhile the burden of an inferior civilization retards the steps of its successor. The countless millions devoted to armament, which are least wasted when they are most wasted, could be applied to solving the problems of our day, the incessant problems arising out of man's struggle to make nature serve his ends. So the question meets us—by what means, while the peoples are yet only learning their solidarity, is it possible to set limits to the pace of expenditure for war? It is clear that no matter how unintelligible war may have become, no one of the rival states dare disarm alone. But this fact does not justify a *laissez-faire* attitude as it is often held to do. There is much that might advantageously be done while the world is only learning the conditions of its new civilization.

For instance, the following immediate steps seem obvious:

1. It is highly important to give to the Court of Arbitration and the Peace Conference, the representatives of the "society of the nations," the highest possible dignity, to appoint as members only men of the utmost distinction, and to make such appointment one of the greatest honors a state can bestow. The prestige of the court and of the conference will be in the present transitional stage the measure of its power, and the answer to those who still look on such courts and conferences as utopian.

2. It is unlikely that the reduction of armaments can be effected by the resolutions of any court or conference. States cannot delegate such power even to their highest representatives. The immediate proper work of the court lies in a different direction. Why in especial should not the Hague Permanent Court take over the work of the Institute of International Law, and prepare an authoritative statement of the Law of Nations, such as all states might accept? This would be of the greatest possible service to the cause of peace. It would be the express declaration of the law of "the society of civilized nations." Once declared, the civilized states would in all probability bind themselves to observe it.

3. Armaments will be reduced not by universal peace conferences, at first, at any rate, but by agreements between individual states. In all probability we shall very shortly see a treaty of arbitration in which the contracting states agree to refer *all* subjects of dispute to an arbitral court. If two or more countries agree to submit all matters to arbitration, why should they not make practical use of their agreement? Does it not open the way to some such agreement as the following: "If either or any of the contracting states have a cause of dispute with some non-contracting state, and if, the former offering to refer the dispute to an international court, the non-contracting power reject the offer and have recourse to arms, then the other contracting state or states shall render armed assistance to the contracting state to which international justice has been refused, to the utmost of its power." Such an agreement would be the logical outcome of a thoroughgoing arbitration treaty, and it would for all defensive purposes put at the service of every state so contracting the armed force of all the states so contracting. It would thus render it possible for these states to reduce their individual armaments. It is very probable that were once such a treaty entered into by any two states, the advantages it brought would cause state after state to follow the example set. Some military powers might and probably would hold out, but the disadvantages of their position, however strong the states might be, are too obvious to need comment. They would be compelled to maintain enormous armies while every other state was reducing its military expenditure in some proportion to the effective united military strength of the contracting states.

4. Why should not the small states disarm even now? The security of Switzerland, for example, cannot depend upon its miniature army, which is necessarily inadequate for warfare with the large surrounding states. Are not the small states protected by intersocial interests and by the mutual unwillingness of the large states that any one of their number should encroach on the smaller, far more than by arms? Is it because of their armies and navies that the international credit and the

internal prosperity, measured in terms of wealth, of Holland, Belgium, and Denmark stand higher than that of big-armied Germany or big-navied England? It is significant that Denmark, which has been foremost of the European states in proposing thoroughgoing treaties of arbitration, has already actually considered the possibility of disarmament.

These suggestions, haphazard and merely outlined, are here brought forward to show that, apart from any immediate universal action of civilized states, it is possible for individual members of the "Society of Civilized Nations" to take action toward securing the reduction of armaments and that greater internal prosperity which such reductions must produce.

If the argument we have stated holds, the new civilization, bringing to civilized peoples an ever-increasing and altogether new solidarity, is thereby making war more and more a meaningless survival. It is not our doing, we cannot help ourselves. We must accept the happier age, for the forces that are bringing it toward us are stronger than ourselves, stronger than our prejudice, stronger than our Nietzschean atavisms. Some, with eyes sealed to the movement of the age, still declare that war is "God's test of Nations," that he still "purges His floor with fire." Doubtless the battle is always to the strong—to whom else should it be? But if to be most warlike is to be most tested, what people in Europe shall stand beside the Turk? And how shall the United States compare with Chile and Peru? Doubtless the strong nations will be victorious in war as in peace, but the strong nations have found other tests than war. Or, if you prefer it, God has found in place of war the tests of social and commercial progress. And for those who think it a bourgeois substitute—well, there are still parts of the earth, among Pathans and Dyaks, and Fuegians, and the like, where the "divine test" is even today in fullest operation, as it has been "since the making of the world." Meanwhile those who can read the signs of the times will rejoice that there is being prepared for the nations the healing way of peace, unmenaced by the blind catastrophe of war.

[1912]

The Interplay of Cultures

31 The events and portents of our age show plainly that men must be taught how to live in the civilization they inherit. Just as men are taught how to care for machinery so they need to be taught how to care for the organization of society; just as they learn the art of making a living so they must learn the art of being civilized. There is reason to believe that the latter art is teachable, since the difficulty lies not in our primitive emotions but in the attachment of our emotions to a primitive philosophy. Perhaps we cannot argue with our emotions—perhaps we need not try—but we can expose the false premises of our primitive social creeds. And if we begin to do so early enough and keep on doing so long enough, we may surely hope that the teaching will not be in vain.

In the last analysis what we have to combat is a primitive philosophy. (The attribution "primitive" here means nothing more than that the philosophy in question arises out of older conditions and is incongruous with the facts and the corresponding needs of our civilization.) From the beginning philosophy has been concerned with the relation of the one and the many, with the one in the many in the one. The primitive conception of unity is baffled by multiplicity and abhors it. The civilized conception of unity reconciles unity with multiplicity. The recognition of the many in the one is the first step in social intelligence.

Every civilized society embraces the many in the one; every community becomes a multigroup community. In the growth of civilization two antithetical but not inconsistent processes advance at the same time. The standardizing forces of technological development promote a vastly expanded external order that up to the present has been regulated by individual states, though the time has come when for its adequate control some kind of unified world order is necessary. But this expansion does not bring about any correlative standardization of the cultural life. Instead there has emerged the greater variety and diversity of intra-community cultural groups, not only because communities have grown in scale and in density but also because specialization of social function and enlargement of social contacts and opportunities have stimulated the inherent tendencies of human beings to assert through specific group formations their variant values and interests.

In anthropological reference we speak of "culture-borrowing," of the influence and impact of one culture upon another, of the adoption and incorporation of "culture-traits" originating in other "culture-areas." Such concepts may perhaps suffice when we are dealing with primitive society. But they imply separate and indigenous cultural totalities, self-subsistent entities. In the world of civilization this condition no longer holds. It is no longer a mere matter of "borrowing." A modern society is a distinctive complex woven of many different traditions derived from diverse sources, and the interweaving of the traditions is unceasing. The resulting cultural complex, while none the less distinctive, includes and in fact is dependent upon numerous divergent and ever-changing subcultures. It is neither homogeneous nor self-contained. Nor is it self-perpetuating. All higher life, whether biological or cultural, attains renewal and integration through intermixture. That is the law of its existence, of its continuing vitality. Those who explain civilized society in the language of primitive culture totally misapprehend this law. When, for example, Oswald Spengler applies the term "pseudomorphosis" to certain changes brought about in one area of civilization through the impact upon it of another he is passing a judgment that depends solely on his own primitivist philosophy. In a complex civilization there are no "false forms" and there is no true form. There is no criterion to determine what a true form might be. The kind of purism that selects one aspect as the true form, simplifies and idealizes it, branding all other cultural expressions as false and irrelevant, as perversions of the innate spirit of the culture, is sheer dogma and illusion.

This kind of purism becomes most dangerous when it reaffirms a primitive philosophy of the state. The expansion of civilization has profoundly altered the character of the state. On the one hand the technological conditions, promoting vast industrial development, enlarging the scale of organization on every economic front, generating new economic powers and clashes of powers, and spreading a net of interdependence everywhere, have imposed upon the state formidable new tasks of over-all economic regulation. On the other hand the concomitant growth of intra-state cultural diversity has disrupted the primitive schematism of state and culture. As usual, the idea of the state has changed more slowly than its actuality. After bitter conflict the diversity of religions broke the identification of the state with a religious creed. It was revealed that the unity of the state was not destroyed but instead was re-created when authority ceased to make acceptance of a particular theology a ground for citizenship. In the Western world this was the first institutional triumph of a new conception of the state, the first great advance toward modern democracy. It prepared the way for further advances.

The forces of reaction fought back and are still powerful. In the realm of values no triumph is final, no liberation is secure. The primitive conception of the state, when it yielded in the religious field, took another stand. The intensification of the sentiment of nationality, strongly separating nation from nation, gave it a new opportunity. Now it identified the nation-state with a dominant *ethnic* culture. Ethnic and other cultural minorities, except in a few of the most democratic countries, were subjected to severe repressions. Their cultural liberties were regarded as hostile to the unity of the state. Their customs, their special cults, their mores, their traditions, were in various degrees "coordinated." This return to primitivism reached its monstrous climax in the Nazi state.

The attempt to impose these primitive concepts upon a civilization with which they had grown increasingly incongruous had already wrought much confusion and disturbance before it issued in the final violence of world war. If the new world is to be built on reasonably sure foundations it is of the highest importance that men and the leaders of men should at length realize the imperatives of our civilization. We must understand that the requisite kind and degree of unification vary for different activities, for different realms of human behavior. The demands of social order permit some activities to remain wholly free, set limits to others, and subject others again to drastic regulation. Cultural expression does not require, for the purposes of an ordered society, any control whatever save a marginal control at the point where it occasions specific and determinable detriment to the well-being of individuals or groups. Here the line of control should be set as far back as the mores will allow, for the simple reason that opinions and creeds and arts and styles and recreations and all primary valuations cannot be coordinated without destruction of their very being and of their creative power. Cultural activity depends wholly on the freedom of diversity. Economic activity, on the other hand, falls within a system of interdependent functions that for the efficient satisfaction of community needs must be highly organized and therefore regulated. Political and economic institutions inevitably form an integrated complex. At the same time the technological factors, ruled by the external standard of efficiency, show a still greater trend toward coordination, a trend not at all interfered with by the barriers of political boundaries. The same technology conquers in Soviet Russia as in the United States, in Japan as in England.

If then we envisage the lines along which our civilization has been developing we must conceive of three orders or kinds of organization. First there is the technological order, which is gradually embracing the whole world. Next there is the politico-economic order, which attains its greatest cohesion within the limits of the individual state, according to the variant modes in which government either regulates or takes over economic functions. This type of national economy of course does not preclude an international economic system to regulate and to facilitate economic relationships on an international scale. Thirdly there is the cultural order, which finds its greatest cohesion and its primary focus of unity within each cultural group, while at the same time admitting the development of less selective cultural unities on the scale of the nation-state and of more selective cultural unities that in the name of religion or other *Weltanschauung* far transcend the limits of the state.

Intolerance and violence, animated by primitivist philosophies, are active in many places and at all times to resist these processes and above all to clamp an alien unity on the cultural life. The first demand of our civilization upon us is that we understand the nature of cultural unity and do not seek to straitjacket it within a system that is not its own. From that blind zeal for a false unity comes nothing but evil. Any new world we contemplate must permit the cultural strivings of men to find their congenial locus. To this end the function of the state with respect to the cultural life must be again revised, just as with respect to religious creeds it underwent revision in the eighteenth and nineteenth centuries.

The free interplay of cultures works two ways. Every culture scheme, every ideology, every system of values, is susceptible to the influence of others. The official upholders of every orthodoxy, though that orthodoxy is itself usually the formalized product of cultural interplay, fear the influence, the "contamination," coming from other systems. There can be no objection to their efforts to keep their orthodoxy strong and "pure," so long as they are content to rally only cultural forces to their aid, but too often they are ready to summon the alien element of coercion. In spite of these efforts the contagion of cultural influence spreads. Certain modes of thought and ways of living prevail over the whole area of great states, over whole continents, in some measure over the whole earth. This pervasive interculture is subtle, unformulated, ever-shifting, the "style" of the great community, of the age, of the civilization. It admits of endless diversity, for the interplay of cultures that created it stimulates at the same time the divergent specific value systems that everywhere express, according to temperament or conditioning, the creative impulse in man. Thus the picture of a liberated modern society is one in which broad cultural tendencies dominate while nevertheless separatist philosophies and faiths and ways of life everywhere occupy the foreground, grow and contend, gain and lose, proliferate and merge and divide again in the endless flux of cultural change.

To these conditions of modern civilization we have to adjust anew the conception of the state. We have to reconceive both its unity and its function. We have to realize that its function, the character and range of its controls, must differ widely according to the order of social reality to which it is directed. For omnicompetence we must substitute a competence to which entirely different limits are set by the different orders. Above all we must recognize that political competence has by far its least extensive function within the cultural order, and that the false unity of totalitarianism is here, far more profoundly than anywhere else, convicted of treason to modern society. In some areas coordination is necessary, in others it is expedient, in others it is debatable; in the cultural area it is the blindest and most ruinous of crimes.

The ideal toward which the newer world must therefore strive can be stated briefly as the free multiplicity of culture groups within the universality of a coordinated external order. In passing, we may observe that this ideal came nearer to fulfillment in the larger political organizations of the ancient world, before Western orthodox religions arose and before the Western sentiment of ethnic nationality reached fruition, than it has generally come in our world of today. In the empires of the Middle East and in the Roman Empire the inclusive state seldom suppressed or discriminated against particular culture groups. The modern state, because of technological and economic developments, possesses and inevitably exercises means and agencies of control undreamed of in the ancient world. It cannot be content with the superficial framework of military power that sufficed for the ancient empire. The complicated interdependence of modern society calls for a very different pattern of authority. But the momentum of this authority often carries

into an area where it is wholly irrelevant and where the new interdependence, so far from imposing any new positive obligation on government, actually sets new limits to its proper jurisdiction. The multigroup society is the correlative of the "great society."

The principle of the multigroup society is still far from being fully
accepted, even in our democracies. While the equality of the *person*
before the law is formally established and rules out the more gross forms
of oppression, the equality of the *culture group* before the law is often
in effect denied. Thus the cultural values of minority groups are invaded,
not in the name of religion any more but in the name of ethics. Such
invasion is more frequently the act of local authorities than of the central
government. Even the ethics of a majority may be invaded in this way.
An instance is the manner in which a compact minority by the use of
political pressure keeps on the statute books legislation directed against
the practice of birth control, even where it is fairly certain that a considerable majority approves this practice. The compact minority in
question is not content to use its proper methods of influence and persuasion but appeals also to Caesar. On the other hand there are various
disabilities and discriminations to which minority groups are subject,
of a kind that formal equality before the law cannot prevent. Ethnic
groups, for example, may enjoy equal civil rights and still suffer serious
economic and social disabilities. Here, as elsewhere, if democracy is
to prevail, its institutions must be supported by the affirming spirit of
the people.

When we turn from the democracies to other countries, we find
that over the greater part of the earth government is in one way or another
identified with a dominant culture group, thereby bringing serious
hurt and frustration to all other groups. In democratic countries the
free interplay of cultures is on the whole assured by the institutional
structure itself; no democracy can profess a specific cultural creed without
denying its own being. In countries without this safeguard ethnic and
ideological forces create a dominating enclave that imposes its own
values on the whole community, limiting or suppressing the cultural
liberties of all other groups.

The imposition of the dominant culture takes place in diverse ways
according to the conditions. Thus in some areas the power-bearing
culture owns also sufficient prestige to make the institutions and the
practices in which it is embodied prevail without resistance over the
whole country. This is typically the situation in most Latin American
countries, where Negroes, Indians, mestizos, and others are in the more
developed areas for the most part culturally indistinguishable within
the embracing Spanish American or Portuguese American system.
In some of these countries there are, of course, ethnic minorities main-

taining separatist cultures, especially German and Italian groups, and there are besides the relatively untouched aboriginal cultures of the various hinterlands. But the typical Latin American situation presents here marked differences from the North American. The over-all cultural pattern of the United States is more composite, less dominated by specific institutions derived from one European source, more freely responsive to the different contributions of the various elements of the population—but on the other hand it exhibits what is in effect a caste distinction between the white race and the others, particularly the Negro race. The color line is by far the most formidable and unyielding of all the barriers that challenge North American democracy.

Soviet Russia presents another and very different type of cultural dominance, politically imposed. The claim made by the Soviet state that its numerous ethnic minorities are all accorded equal treatment and suffer nowhere any discrimination is true in a particular sense. But here the interplay of cultures has become nothing more than the reciprocity of geographical areas in the common cause of a single authoritarian culture. The areas retain certain externals belonging to their respective traditions, but these externals are no longer the symbols of their differential cultures. They retain their own languages, but the languages all express the same ideas. They retain their own schools, but all the schools inculcate the same indoctrinations. In short, culture is coordinated. Although the creed is different, the primitive form of unity, the primitive concept of the state, has been restored.

With these various types of cultural dominance we may contrast the type that holds in the multicultured states of Eastern Europe, from Poland to the Balkans. Here there is dominance without fusion. Here cultural values are traditionally attached to the soil. The inclusive state embraces areas thus consecrated to different cultures, but the interplay of cultures is restricted and perturbed by the fact that one ethnic culture controls the state and tends to regard the others as alien and dangerous to its power. No principle of ethnic self-determination in the political sense can meet the difficulty, since the territorial demarcations of the various cultures, even where relatively clean-cut, are too tortuous, too complicated, and too inconsistent with the economic conditions of political viability to admit the erection of a separate state for every ethnic group. Nothing but the genuine acceptance of a different concept of the state, in which political unity is reconciled with cultural and ethnic difference, can save these peoples from the impoverishing and disabling strife that has become endemic in their lands.

This brief review may serve to show that in our modern civilization the cultural focus is the group and not the state and that the claims of the two are still grossly in conflict and can be reconciled only by the development of a political ideology congenial to the conditions of a multigroup society. Even in our democracies the full recognition of this truth is still far from being attained. It is of the greatest significance, for the making of the newer world, that a charter of cultural liberty be set up as an ideal to be striven toward., For a limited number of countries such a charter was proclaimed in the minorities treaties that followed the First World War—but these treaties were born under an evil star. Nevertheless they showed the way we need to follow. Cultural liberation is one of the primary conditions of a more peaceful world. But it is also something more. For through it there would be achieved the redemption of the diversity of human gifts revealed in the diversity of human values, and thus an ever wider range would be opened to the creative spirit of mankind.

[1943]

The Second World War
and the Peace

32   AFTER THE PRICE OF WAR, THE PRICE OF PEACE

Do we want an enduring peace? Then we must be willing to pay the price. The price of victory does not cover the price of peace. Peace too must be won, and it would indeed be strange if so precious an achievement, unlike any other human achievement, fell without price into our hands. The winning of peace makes certain clear demands upon us. Are we prepared to meet them? We pay millions of lives and billions of dollars and countless tears for the chance of victory. Shall we offer nothing for the one great good that this victory makes possible, an abiding peace?

There are those who are ignorant of the price and those who are unwilling to pay it. There are the selfish ones who peer at their own narrow interests and will not raise their eyes, no matter what portents are in the sky. There are intolerant ones who make their group or their nation the standard of humanity. There are the embittered ones who have suffered grievously in the war and cry for what they believe is justice. There are the stupid ones who cannot think beyond the old traditions, or the old catchwords. These reactionaries are unwittingly the greatest enemies of peace. For a genuine peace, so far from being passivity, is a revolutionary thing. A war like this latest war is a revelation of the need for a revolutionary change. Somewhere, in the ordering of human affairs, there was profound fault to cause so dreadful a catastrophe. The problem of peace is to discover where it lay and to remove it. Any other peace will be merely a longer armistice. But we cannot find and we cannot remove so profound a fault if we persist in certain old attitudes, in certain old notions and valuations that have hitherto governed a great sector of human relations.

Peace has, first and foremost, what for want of a better name we shall call a psychological price. Since peace means a reconstruction of the relations between men as organized in states, it means also a reformation of the attitudes of men. The mentality of war-making is a precise opposite of the mentality of peace-making. War is division, peace is the healing of division. War is reciprocal destruction, peace is reciprocal construction. War is nation against nation, peace is nation joined with nation. Peace is the opposite of these things *if* it is genuine peace, if it is peace just as truly as war is war.

If we want this peace we must heal division. If we want peace we must join with other nations in peace, *with enemies no less than with allies.* Here is where the psychological price is demanded. Already, if they read these words, there are those who are saying: "This man is tender to our enemies. He is on their side. He is dangerous." Those who say so show that they are unwilling to pay the psychological price of peace. When we plan for peace we must abandon sides. We must think of the whole. If we want an abiding peace we must think in the terms of peace, no longer nation against nation, but nation joined with nation.

It is, if you care to put it so, a scientific problem. Assuming that an abiding peace is our goal we ask, simply and squarely: Under what conditions can it be attained? Since such a peace requires the cooperative activity of states, whether they have been our friends or our enemies, we ask again: Under what conditions can we secure this cooperation? To answer this question we must consider, among other things, how the peoples of the defeated countries will react to the terms we impose. Now one of the commonest difficulties in the way of our ordinary human relations is our inability to put ourselves in the place of others, to understand how our behaving affects their behaving. We look mainly at one side of the relation, our own. This difficulty is intensified when the other party is regarded as alien to us, and is greatest of all when the other party is or has been our enemy.

So in making a peace with a defeated nation the victors are most apt to disregard its needs, to brand it with inferiority, to subjugate it, to humiliate it. They do not ask: What effect will this have on the peace we make? They do not seek to understand the feelings of the humiliated people. They do not realize that after all the humiliated people are men and women just like the rest of us, and that they will react to such humiliation as we too would react. It is the old lesson that Shakespeare put into the mouth of Shylock in *The Merchant of Venice* when Shylock turned the tables and said: "I am a Jew. Hath not a Jew eyes? Hath not a Jew hands, organs, dimensions, senses, affections, passions? Fed with the same food, hurt with the same weapons, subject to the same diseases, healed by the same means, warmed and cooled by the same winter and summer, as a Christian is? If you prick us, do we not bleed? If you tickle us, do we not laugh? If you poison us, do we not die? And if you wrong us, shall we not revenge? If we are like you in the rest, we will resemble you in that." In the affairs of nations there is also this vicious circle of injury and revenge that can be broken only when we have the intelligence to make a genuine peace.

To make it we must understand how the other parties to the peace will react to it, not immediately but in the longer future. The best way to do so is to ask how we ourselves would react to similar conditions. To many men the very idea of being treated as they would treat their defeated enemies is simply unthinkable. They evade the thinking of it by talk about treating the enemy as the enemy deserves. We may answer again in the words of the great writer who understood the hearts of men: "Use every man after his desert, and who should 'scape whipping." Who can judge what a *people* deserves? Such talk conceals our unwillingness to face the true problems of peace. It is the childishness of group egoism.

In saying so we are not minimizing or glossing over the intolerable wrongs that our main enemy in this war has committed. We have unutterable loathing for the barbarous doctrines he has proclaimed and for the brutal manner in which he has enforced them. We deal with that subject in its proper place. Here the point is that in the making of this peace we have to face tremendous alternatives, and we must choose between them. After two world wars, devastating beyond previous experience, the opportunity is approaching when we can build at last an enduring peace. Shall we or shall we not seize the opportunity?

First we must set our attitudes right. It is simply a question of common sense. It is not utopian; it is immensely practical. War has become too deadly and too disruptive to be borne. Most men fear it and hate it. But many have short-sighted thoughts about the thing they fear and hate. They think, for example, that if the enemy is properly punished, if he is disarmed and rendered powerless, then we shall be at last secure. They do not reckon with human nature—and the peace of 1919 has taught them nothing.

If you want an abiding peace you must be ready to curb revenge and hate. If you want an abiding peace, you must not set up conditions that the vanquished nations will bitterly resent for generations to come. If you want an abiding peace you must put the welfare of the whole above the immediate advantage of the part.

These conditions are surely obvious to any one who reflects on the subject. Unfortunately it is a subject on which people have not been taught to reflect. What stands in the way of reflection is the simple ethnocentric character of national sentiment. Men are suffered with the sense of the superiority and prestige of their own nation—which would be all very well were it not that it betrays them into foolish notions about other nations. We display too often the attitude of the small boy who believes that nobody else's father is so strong and brave as his. If we win, it is because we are finer fellows; if we lose it is because of the treachery of the enemy or because of his overpowering numbers or because our own leaders have betrayed us. If we win we thank God and exalt ourselves; if we lose we do not mention God but we put the blame on scapegoats. So Hitler did after the First World War. So after the victories of the Second he exclaimed: "The deeds of our soldiers will go down in history as the most glorious victory of all time. In humility we thank God for this blessing." Hitler has the small-boy attitude in its extremest measure. Most of us have it in some measure, if without the ruthless and consuming fury of the German dictator.

Now any statesman of intelligence, if he is negotiating a peace, must reckon with this ethnocentric emotion. He must ask how it will respond to this or that treatment. It is very powerful, endlessly persistent, rooted in the depths of human nature. This is because it conveys the sentiment of community, because it is an expression of the social instinct itself. So when we insult or humiliate or suppress it, there is a terrific reaction. In the making of peace we must beware of offending it. Treat as you will the misguided priests and the lying prophets of the tribal God, so long as you leave standing the ancient altars of the tribe.

And when it is our lot to make the peace we must not let *our* ethnocentrism blind us either to the needs or to the reactions of other peoples. The new peace must be built on the equality of all peoples before the new law, the law of nations. The pride and prejudice we have displayed toward peoples of other color, must be controlled, if we haven't the courage and the wisdom to abandon it altogether. We must realize, among other things, that the peoples of the Orient must become as free and undominated as the peoples of the West. For our own self-interest we must realize it, for they vastly outnumber us, and if we treat them otherwise they will soon learn, if they have not learned already, to "better the instruction."

In this connection it is well to remember two further points concerning the sense of community, especially as it finds expression in national sentiment. The first is that though men make great sacrifices for the sake of it the sense of community is no pure altruistic self-effacing emotion. It is still "human, all too human." Men are very ingenious in identifying their particular interests with the cause of their community. When their own interests change they are too apt to discover that the good of the nation has changed in the same direction. A tragic instance was the manner in which many of the politicians of France and many of its large industrialists changed their attitude after the debacle of 1940 and embraced a program of cooperation with the Nazis to save their patrimonies and their skins. This instance leads up to the second point. The face of national sentiment that is turned toward other nations is peculiarly changeful. It can change overnight from detestation to admiration, or vice versa. The appraisal is always relative, never intrinsic. Illustrations are hardly necessary—there have been so many in recent times. Witness the various reversals of sentiment that have occurred with respect to Russia or the various changes of popular French sentiment with respect to Great Britain.

The reason we have dwelt on these two points is to show that there is no insuperable difficulty in the adaptation of national sentiment to changing conditions and changing needs. Show people the necessity, bring home to them the fact that to win an enduring peace they must change certain attitudes and renounce others—then they will pay the psychological price.

Perhaps in the last resort the only price is the psychological one. The economic benefits of assured peace are so great and so universal, as against the staggering costs of war, that probably even the munition makers, turning to other products instead, would profit by it. And certainly if there are special interests that fatten on war, we cannot regard the ending of that state of things as a price of peace, but rather as in itself a most desirable goal. It would indeed be ridiculous to think that the people as a whole pay any economic price for peace. But there is another kind of price that remains to be considered. We may call it the political price, though as we investigate it we shall see that here too the exaction is solely psychological, that what is required of us is again a certain change of attitude, a correction of an illusory tradition, rather than any more tangible costs.

There is an old notion concerning the nature of sovereignty that stands in the way. If we are to have an enduring peace we cannot allow every state, or any state, to act as though it were independent and absolute in determining its relation to other states.

At a certain stage in the history of Western civilization, particularly in the sixteenth century, a group of legalist thinkers developed the notion of sovereignty, though its origins go further back. In the sixteenth century it was developed to serve a particular purpose. It was a way of asserting the need for centralized authority in the transition from feudalism to the national state. It served that purpose and that purpose is now spent, but as so often happens the notion survived its usefulness. It was a pragmatic concept parading as an exercise in pure reason. People came to believe that this notion of sovereignty expressed the very nature of things. So it has become a dangerous notion, one most ill-adapted to the needs of our age. We should apply common sense to it and strip it of its pretensions. Then we would soon discover that this legal concept of sovereignty, as applied to the relation of states, is a monstrosity. For sovereignty is a claim of right as well as of power, and it is a claim of the right to use power without regard for the rights of other states. This kind of "right" is sheer irrationality.

What must be done about sovereignty? We have to amend the notion and change certain practices of states that appeal to the notion but have no rightful ground, since they depend solely on power falsely claiming to be right. We must accommodate the sovereignty of the state to the needs of men. The prevailing notion of sovereignty spreads a smoke screen over the facts.

Sovereignty is simply the authority that is exercised by or in the name of the inclusive political organization, the authority that government commands. "There is no power on earth that can be compared with it," said the old absolutist, Hobbes. That is true if properly understood. For in the modern world this authority alone has the final right of enforcement. It is invested with this final right where it is, and because it is, the final coordinating power over the affairs of men. Somewhere, if we are to have a system of law and order, there must be a final authority, beyond which there is no appeal. But here there are two points to remember. In the first place this authority can be, and often is, assigned to it by the people, which can set it up and pull it down and therefore can make it in turn responsible. In the second place this final authority is organized differently under different conditions, and its location depends on the form of political union. In a unitary state it is uni-centered. In a federal state it is multi-centered. Where states are not completely separate and independent, the more inclusive union maintains a last court of appeal concerning those issues with respect to which this independence is limited. Sovereignty requires a last court of appeal.

This simple fact has been magnified into a tremendous myth. A vast amount of grandiose nonsense has been written about sovereignty. It is presented as a sacrosanct mysterious power somehow residing in a super-organism called the state. In earlier times we were content to say it was ordained of God; but modern philosophers of the Hegelian school took over the notion and inflated sovereignty into a kind of transcendent will and power. This expansion of the myth has taken its most gross form in the imagination of the philosophers of totalitarianism. To them the state is not an organization to carry on the business of the everyday humans who are its members. It has a will that is not the will of these members or of the mere flesh-and-blood politicians who make laws and decrees. Sovereignty is a being supreme and ineffable. Awesome and inscrutable forces hover about it. The mere individual, as one Nazi exponent puts it, is "a serving member of one great organic structure that encompasses his existence, his life and his action. He is a point of intersection for the motions of these powers, elemental, higher, historical, supermundane, that after their own will consume his self and his essence." The state is a high and holy thing, beyond the thoughts and purposes of common men. If it is thought of as an instrument at all it becomes, for the followers of *Mein Kampf*, the instrument of the blood and instinct of the race. To that function it is directed by the One, the Führer, who knows best, who is the divinely appointed agent for the fulfillment of that function.

All this is dogma in the service of power. Authority is what we make it, or what we suffer it to be. It is an institutional device. It has the prerogatives we assign to it, or accept under it. The dogma has no necessary relation to the fact. The theology of sovereignty contains a clause that sovereignty is unlimited. Every federal state refutes that clause. It contains another clause to the effect that sovereignty is omnicompetent, in other words that no human interests or activities are withdrawn from its range of control. Every written constitution refutes that clause. Sovereignty is what we make it, and it cannot be defined as though it were a phenomenon of nature, which we must take as we find it.

We are therefore perfectly justified in asking what kind, what range, and what organization of sovereignty is best adapted to the requirements of our civilization. As soon as we ask this question we must recognize that completely independent states, bound to no other states by no obligations other than those they care to accept and only for as long as they care to accept them, are alike perilous to and incongruous with our modern civilization. For we live in a age in which a vast number of our interests and our activities are deeply affected by the behavior of other states than our own. Our interests, spiritual and intellectual as well as economic, are for the most part not bounded within the frontiers of a state. The state we belong to is not, and can never again be— unless we revert to some degenerate barbarism—a self-contained unity, a closed system. The traditional doctrine of sovereignty is a presumptuous denial of this truth.

We must give up the proud stubborn prejudice of independence, the historic prejudice of the independent state. We resent any foreign interference in *our* affairs—that is all very well, but we must ask once more: what then are *our* affairs? Are they still our affairs alone if what we do about them directly and vitally affects the well-being of other peoples? No one proposes that an external power should have the right to interfere with our purely domestic policies or our particular way of life. But there is a sphere of interdependence of such great importance for all concerned that the only reasonable course is to assign it, with proper safeguards, to an international system of control. At present every state acts as though it had the right to determine its foreign policy solely in terms of its own presumptive interest.

It has neither the right nor the power. There is no right where there is no obligation, where there is no constituted society governed by inclusive law. Nor has the individual state really the power to settle such issues. If it exercises its power to this end it is most likely to incite opposing power, and there is no certainty whatever that it will then achieve its objective. What then is this absolute sovereignty that states still assert, without any ground of right and without any efficacy of enforcement?

It may hurt our pride to abjure this prejudice of the independent sovereign will—but what is that price compared with the gain? The hurt will not be to our unity or to our loyalty—and the greatest menace of our civilization will be removed. The dogma of absolute sovereignty is maintained at an incalculable cost to the well-being of us all. Is it not better to give it up, to pay the psychological price?

[1942]

THE DEVIL AND THE PEACE

Sometimes there is a tragic cussedness about human affairs, so that men fasten more tightly on themselves the noose they are trying to escape. It is common experience that the action of our fears often begets the thing we fear. There are vicious circles in which each evil creates its successive evil. There is an urgency of need that drives us into deeper need, as when a man borrows at usurious rates. Most of us could walk safely over a narrow plank where safety is not in question, as when it is stretched a foot above the ground. But set it over Niagara Falls and in trying to walk it most of us would plunge below. Our anxiety to escape the devil throws us right into his arms. There is a devil of this sort waiting to catch us when we, or our leaders, go about the business of making peace.

The longer a war continues the more do people *everywhere* long and pray for a peace that will last. But if we could make the peace at the beginning of a war instead of at the end we could make a better peace. It is part of the tragic cussedness of things that we must make the peace when we are least capable, in spite of our greater desire, to make a good one.

When war breaks out we have been habituated to peace. We have some sense of what has gone wrong. We have some sense of proportion, not yet distorted by the heats and fantasies of war. As the war lengthens we become habituated to the ways and thoughts of war, and this developing mentality unfits us for the making of a good peace. The change in our attitudes is determinate and predictable. Our enemies, as whole peoples, take on more and more, for the civilian population, the aspect of fiends. They are not only our enemies, they are enemies of the human race. A good peace seems one that keeps them forever crushed and powerless.

At least three-fourths of the citizens of this country may be regarded as being in a favor of an international authority to maintain peace, as public polls show. But an increasing number express the view that the war guilt rests squarely not only on the enemy leaders or on the Nazis but on the whole German people. This feeling, if carried into the peace settlement, may well defeat the desire both for an international authority and for a lasting peace.

A statistical investigation has shown that peace treaties in modern times have stayed intact for an average of two years. That is what comes of all the blood and sweat and tears; that is what history does to the solemn councils and conferences of the "high contracting parties," when they meet to remake the world. Perhaps there is some truth in the claim that the most deadly cause of war is the preceding peace.

The democratic peoples are in this regard no wiser than others. They may even be worse. The democratic peoples, in the consciousness that the war is the act of the aggressor enemy, are easily persuaded that if only the present enemy is reduced to impotence the danger of future wars will be removed.

At the end of the Napoleonic Wars the same idea prevailed among the peoples of Europe with respect to France. But Talleyrand and Alexander of Russia had more perspective. The "Christian kings," meeting at Vienna and at Paris, planned an unusually good and lasting peace. They were not particularly peace-loving, but they had suffered a mighty shock from the upstart Napoleon. They feared another war, led by another dictator, would be fatal to their thrones. They were above the propaganda of the wars they had waged and they had no illusion that by crushing and mutilating the aggressor country, France, they would put an end to dictators and to wars. They knew that the tendency to aggression exists everywhere among men and groups and that only a strong union could possibly ensure peace. Guided by the statesman-like Alexander they constructed on that basis a settlement that gave Europe her longest peace in modern history.

For the most part, however, rulers and statesmen have shown no such prescience in the making of peace. A thousand times the pride and vanity of power have misled them, a thousand times they have miscalculated, a thousand times the peoples have suffered again.

Now we live in an age when the democratic peoples can profoundly influence the peace to be. And here is where the devil lies in wait for the peace. For now, besides the danger from the shortsightedness of power, there is the newer danger from the war-fed illusions of the peace-loving peoples.

Their instinct for an international organization is sound. In this respect they may well be ahead of their rulers. But since at the same time they readily believe in the essential wickedness of the enemy people, they can be misled into accepting spurious proposals for a world organization, in accordance with which the victorious powers would do the regulating of world affairs. Such a system would of course not be a genuine world organization but only an old-style alliance with a new name. They do not realize the comprehensive strategy that is needed for the winning of the peace. They are ready enough to admit that the victorious allies lost the last peace but they do not seriously face the fact that the same thing is likely to happen again.

This attitude is strengthened by the public pronouncements issued in the name of the Big Three or the Big Four after each historic conference. The war chiefs sit apart, in the remoteness and the secrecy imposed by war, like the Gods on Olympus, dictating the fate of men. They solemnly affirm that the peace will be lasting and secure. And we too easily think, as we listen to these pronouncements, that the peace as well as the war can be won by power alone.

But peace is the opposite of war and if it is to endure it must be prepared in an opposite spirit. Peace cannot be won by power alone. Peace is never the ripe fruit of victory. Those who are most successful in war-making may be least successful in peace-making, and it is part of this tragic cussedness of things that because they succeed in war they are in a position to determine the peace. Those who meet to make a lasting peace must do a very difficult thing—they must forget about war-making when they go in for peace-making. Peace is the greatest single work of construction to which men can set their hands. War is the greatest work of destruction, and the spirit in which it must be waged is fatal to construction.

When we make peace we must think well ahead, we must think of the time when war emotions as well as war conditions have passed away and have given place to different conditions and emotions, when the nations again live together in unity. And we must not make such terms of peace as will prevent the nations, enemies as well as allies, vanquished as well as victors, from living together, from accepting the new unity instead of preparing, openly or in secret, for the next war.

We cannot make effective war with a peacetime mentality, and it is no less true that we cannot make effective peace with a wartime mentality.

Many things conspire against our learning this lesson, and even if we, the ordinary people, could learn it, many things stand in the way of our making it count in the world of action. Whenever war ends it nearly always ends abruptly and its end nearly always finds us unprepared. During war the realistic discussion of peace conditions is hampered by military considerations. It is feared that this kind of discussion may be bad for our morale, may interfere with war aims, may give comfort to the enemy, may be premature in view of the uncertainties of the changing situation.

Our leaders are inhibited from the discussion of peace terms by our relations to our allies. The United Nations are united for the duration, and they have common commitments for the conduct of the war—but they have separate interests in the peace, and conflicts would immediately arise if they publicly discussed the terms of settlement. Somehow or other, sooner or later, they must find formulas for reconciling their divergent claims—they must decide about Poland and the Baltic States and Austria and the Balkans and Libya and the islands of the Pacific and a hundred other plaguy questions; and the attention they must devote to settling these issues deflects their energies and their thoughts from the yet greater problem of rebuilding the world so that peace itself shall be indeed established among the nations. So when the Allied leaders meet they give us grandiose, vague statements like the Atlantic Charter and the Teheran declaration. But the peoples have grown skeptical of fine principles eloquently delivered from high places. They remember what happened to these in 1919.

At Casablanca the Allied leaders proclaimed the war policy of "unconditional surrender." In some quarters there is the fear that if any peace conditions are now set out, especially such conditions as might give enemy peoples reason to expect that as peoples they would be incorporated into a happier world order, these conditions would qualify and compromise that policy. Such reasoning is both puerile and pernicious. Do we wage this colossal war for the mere satisfaction of triumphing over our enemies—or to win through their defeat some great positive goal? If the latter, is it not incumbent on our leaders to proclaim it to the whole world? There is no goal in "unconditional surrender." That is merely the voice of power, and great power without great purpose can work only evil. Why should we aid Goebbels to strengthen the will of the German people to fight on? In this respect Wilson was wiser in his generation than our present leaders are in ours.

Here is something that would at the same time strengthen the morale of our people and weaken the morale of our enemies—the clear announcement of the framework of a lasting peace. But at every turn that policy is blocked by the emotions congenial to the war mentality. The claque of righteous haters have their heyday, the Vansittarts, the Foersters, and all their tribe. They talk only of destruction, they do not seem to understand that when the time comes for the peace only a great work of reconstruction can save our civilization from its most deadly menace, the recurrence of world wars. The thing they hate is loathsome; but by their policy they are helping to perpetuate it. If we carry our hatreds beyond the war into the peace we shall infallibly recreate the thing we hate.

The democratic peoples yearn for a lasting peace, but their yearning will avail them nothing unless they can exorcise the devil who plays on their most righteous emotions. There are two particular temptations they must, for their future well-being, learn to reject. One is the delusion that the sole cause of war is the wicked enemy, and that if he is disarmed and manacled there will be peace on earth. The temptation to think so is peculiarly strong in this war, because of the utterly detestable character of Nazi doctrine and behavior. We must nevertheless remember that in all wars the enemy becomes the very incarnation of evil. It is the nature of war, not of the enemy people, that confirms this attitude.

We never get to the root of war by condemning the enemy people, no matter how bestial the misdeeds that are committed in their name and by their leaders. The root of war does not lie *in* countries but *between* countries. It lies in the lack of a final means of peacefully settling disputes between countries. There are numberless causes of *wars*—any unsettled dispute between any two countries may end in warfare. The dispute may be trivial or major—it makes relatively little difference so long as there is no authoritative way of settling it. The Crimean War took place over an obscure dispute; the present war arose out of a grave dispute.

But the cause of *war* is the institutionalization of war, and the only way to end wars is the institutionalization of peace, in other words, some effective international organization invested with authority to settle the disputes between governments. The aggressor in war changes from time to time. According to an authority in this field, Quincy Wright, the country that has been most occupied in warfare is France, followed in turn by Austria-Hungary, Prussia, Great Britain, and Russia.

To think we can put an end to the calamity of modern war by subjugating the wicked other people is to ignore one of the simpler lessons that history can teach us. The psychologist William McDougall once said that this way of thinking reminded him of a middle-aged spinster who believed that all women were born good and all men were born bad.

Another attitude that is fostered by wartime thinking is the trust in an alliance of the victors as an adequate bulwark of the coming peace. The good peoples have defeated the wicked peoples. All they need to do is to keep together. The alliance established in war will control and protect the peace. This notion is very popular today. The first lesson taught and reiterated in the greatest work on political philosophy ever produced in America, *The Federalist*, is that an alliance of states is no security against war.

"Compacts of this kind," wrote Hamilton, "exist among all civilized nations, subject to the usual vicissitudes of peace and war, of observance and nonobservance, as the interests or passions of the contracting powers dictate. In the early part of the present century there was an epidemical rage in Europe for this species of compacts, from which the politicians of the times fondly hoped for benefits which were never realized. With a view to establishing the equilibrium of power and the peace of that part of the world, all the resources of negotiation were exhausted, and triple and quadruple alliances were formed; but they were scarcely formed before they were broken, giving an instructive but afflicting lesson to mankind, how little dependence is to be placed on treaties which have no other sanction than the obligations of good faith, and which oppose general considerations of peace and justice to the impulse of any immediate interest or passion" (No. 15).

This lesson is confirmed by history. When a group of states forms an alliance over against other states it is more likely to lead to war than to peace. For it means that the other states in turn will seek to form a countervailing alliance, and in the contest for power between the two sooner or later open conflict will arise. Thus the various European alliances and counter-alliances of the last sixty years have kept the world in continuous ferment. Their rivalries and competitive armaments could lead to nothing but war.

Alliances, moreover, are unstable. The Allies have divergent power interests. The other side will seek to detach one or more of them, offering a more enticing bargain. Wartime alliances seem to be peculiarly unstable. In the reaction after war the former Allies become easily disgruntled with one another. Grievances and jealousies are engendered through their divergent and conflicting policies for the settlement, and particularly over the division of the spoils of victory. This happened after the last war. The cement of a common cause no longer bound the victorious Allies, and they fell apart. It is a significant fact that of our three chief enemies in the Second World War two were our allies in the first.

The balance of power is no balance at all. In the nineteenth century the balance of power had a particular meaning when the great military powers were all European, and Great Britain, ruling the seas, stood ready to throw its weight against any combination that threatened to become dominant. But military power is no longer concentrated in Europe. It is largely a function of economic power. Wherever economic power is amassed, in America, in semi-Asiatic Russia, or anywhere else, military power is at its command. The balance of power, in the old sense, no longer exists. There is no longer any "balancer," such as Great Britain was in the nineteenth century. The advance of technology and the spread of modern industrial systems throughout the world have entirely changed the picture. Relative power is always shifting, and the possible combinations of power are numerous.

A dominating alliance depends on relative power, the temporary and quite abnormal disposition of power that exists at the end of a war. It is to this disposition of power that wartime mentality leads us to entrust our future peace and well-being. There is the shield of our republic. We do not look ahead to the inevitable changes in relative power, to the inevitable recombinations of power. The alliance will keep the peace. And the grand irony of it is that this alliance, if it endures at all, will keep the peace only for the time that the peace needs no keeper. It is possible, if not very likely, that the alliance may remain both intact and dominant for a generation, resisting tendencies to disunity and to realignment and suppressing encroachments on its dominance.

But it is most improbable that, no matter what kind of peace we set up, another great war will break out within that period. It takes time for men to forget the actual experience of war. It takes time to recuperate from the exhaustion of a great war. It takes time for the seeds of war to grow again to the harvest. In modern history the average interval between wars has been over twenty years, and between great wars it has been in the neighborhood of fifty years. Who is foolish enough to predict, in view of the endless changes of power and of the conditions of power, that the dominating alliance of tomorrow will still dominate twenty or thirty or fifty years from now?

In short, the trust in wartime military alliance is a most dangerous illusion. Even the imperative of war can scarcely conceal the differences of interest and of policy between allies. As soon as they discuss the peace the differences between them begin to emerge. When peace at length arrives they are openly exposed, and there is no longer any common cause to heal their disagreements. Everywhere, from the highest to the lowest level, the champions of particular interests become clamant again. Everywhere there is jockeying for relative advantage. Nationality groups, power groups, pressure groups, prestige groups, come out in front or work behind the scenes. The unity is broken, the great cause is dissipated: the tired peoples acclaim the end of war and think less and less about the necessities of the peace. Only the clear proclamation of a greater cause, the initiation of a new international order, can any longer hold differences and disputes within bounds. Only so can the peace be really won.

Those who bid us trust to a postwar alliance of the victors, even though they may think of it as only a temporary expedient, have nothing to offer that can arrest this debacle of the immediate postwar years. They are even more dangerous to the cause of a lasting peace than those who bid us to forget it all, to return to the old ways, to give up our crusades, our excursions into world history. They are more dangerous because they divert into blind alleys the deep desire of our citizens and of all men for a genuine and dynamic peace. Our people want a world order; only if they are misled will they accept a military alliance.

In this war-end situation there is the final revelation of the tragic cussedness of human affairs. We fight the war for the sake of a better peace, the peace we shall make, not the peace our enemies would impose. For this we endure all sacrifices, accept all costs. We go all-out for war. We know that in making war half-measures spell defeat. And then, when it comes to the peace we are content with half-measures—where we have been willing to sacrifice all we are now willing to sacrifice nothing.

We did not desire the war but we do not flinch from its ultimate demands. We deeply desire the peace but we think it makes no demands upon us. And the tragedy is that if we devoted to this end one half of the intelligence, one tithe of the devotion, and an infinitesimal portion of the wealth we have devoted to the means, by that latter devotion we could win the goal for which we have expended all the rest.

[1944]

The Fundamental Principles
of International Order

33 All things move in accordance with the law of cause and effect, which rules human affairs no less than the external world. If *this* is done *that* follows. If *this* happens *that* also happens. Whatever we do or try to do brings its own particular train of consequences. Nothing can evade this law, neither our prejudices nor our prayers. Often because things are so complexly tangled, we cannot calculate the results of what we do; never can we fully calculate them. But that the consequent in the field of action depends on the antecedent, takes this course or that course according as we do this or that, is the most elemental of all truths. It is childish petulance if we say "we want *this* and we will do *that*"—without considering whether the *this* and the *that* are compatible.

Whatever we do to others evokes a specific counter-doing on their part. What will their counterdoing do to the things *we* want? To ask this question is the precondition of all intelligent behaving, of all wise planning, of all statesmanship. When the objective is a long-term one, we must seek to estimate not only the immediate reaction but also the later repercussions. This consideration obviously applies to any settlement between nations. Nations are enduring realities, and though its expression is always changing the spirit of a nation is unquenchable. If you crush it it will rise again; if you wound it it will become inflamed, will gain new strength and finally wound back. No consideration is more obvious, or more understandable, and yet in the making of peace it is generally ignored or disregarded. For it is a phenomenon as curious as it is painful that in lesser matters, such as business deals, we show far more prescience, far more regard for the law of cause and effect, than we, or our leaders, display in the decision of the greater and most crucial affairs.

Whatever else the makers of the coming peace do, they will set up some plan to re-establish and maintain peaceful relationships between States, the intercourse and traffic of the peoples, some kind of working arrangement between States. Here the supreme issue is a political, not primarily an economic, one. What kind of international organization? What kind of international control? Under what auspices? Fortunately this is not a question to which socialism has one answer and capitalism an opposite answer and sociocapitalism one in between, to which labor responds one way and capital another. The dividing line lies elsewhere. It should be obvious by this time that on the final issue of control there are two positions to choose between, and two only. One is the domination of a power alliance, the other is a total international order.

In times past a working international organization has now and then been maintained under the dominance of a single power. Imperial Rome, with her *pax Romana*, offered the most impressive instance. Imperial Britain, in the nineteenth century, played a not dissimilar role, throwing her weight against any serious threat to the status quo and thus limiting, if not always preventing, military aggression. She did not enter into a "balance of power" but rather acted as a "balancer" of powers. When new configurations of power and new techniques of war brought this role to an end the need for a new international system became acute. It was not supplied by the toothless League of Nations. There are some who cherish the idea that the United States can and should succeed to the role vacated by Great Britain, but they do not reckon with the complexity of the distribution of power in the modern world. They still think in continental, not global terms. We must choose between power alliance and world organization. The former is the line of least resistance and all our conservatives and traditionalists are beginning to advocate it. It appears to be supported by Premier Churchill, it has recently been espoused by Governor Dewey; its most plausible exponent, Walter Lippmann, has the ear of a large public. But many leaders and thinkers have gone on record in favor of world organization, and the question remains whether, once the issues are clearly presented, the great majority of men everywhere would not rally to this side. In any event the choice is so momentous that we cannot scrutinize too carefully the nature of the alternatives, the political principles on which they rest, and the prospects they respectively offer.

THE CASE FOR POWER ALLIANCE

Those who favor alliance claim that it is the more practical alternative, that it involves only the simple agreement of a few great powers and is manifestly in the interest of these powers, that it is the projection into the time of peace of a union already established in war, and that the massed might of these victorious powers, with their enormous material resources, would deter any upthrust in the calculable future of insurgence or aggression on the part of the defeated warmakers. They regard any global organization as an idealistic dream. They believe the Great Powers would not tolerate it. They think any genuine international authority, such as might control an international police, would mean an abrogation of national sovereignty such as no great State would accept. Besides, there are too many differences of interest and outlook between States to make any world organization feasible. The world is not ripe for an experiment so novel and so revolutionary. Better to clinch the union we have than to embark on a precarious venture for a kind of union the world has never seen. They are realists, they are afraid of an untried internationalism.

The power alliance that is most frequently envisaged would comprise the United States, Great Britain, and Russia. There are many, however, who doubt or distrust the adhesion of Russia and who place their reliance mainly on a Anglo-American bond. Others are anxious to see China within the alliance, so as to have a stronger assurance against Japan. Some of the advocates of alliance are devoted to partial or limited federations, ranging from a Pan-American union to the Pan-Europe of Coudenhove-Kalergi. There are numerous variations on this theme.

The power-alliance theorists build on certain assumptions. In the first place they assume that it is easier to construct and maintain a partial union of States, limited to defensive ends, than a total or global union. This assumption must be challenged. If the three great allied powers desire to create a dominating alliance they can undoubtedly do so. But if these great powers decide to create a world organization, inviting all other States to join under reasonable conditions, hardly a single State, small or great, defeated or victorious, would remain outside. The advantage of membership would be obvious, and indeed imperative. Every State, apart from the United States of America, was willing and most were eager to join so lopsided an international structure as the old League of Nations. So far, then, as the first step, the formation of union, is concerned, the victorious powers have free choice, whichever way they decide.

Here, however, the similarity between the two types of union ends. In function, in structure, in expectation of life, they are poles apart. A partial organization, a mere alliance, is a partisan organization. It is based on relative power, to hold in check opposing power. It is subject to the incessant fluctuations of power. If it endures at all, it must exert its power. In so doing it provokes the mustering of opposition, the counteralliance. It cannot keep the opposition permanently disarmed, and the end of it all is a new battlefront. That is the end if the alliance lasts long enough.

But this kind of alliance is internally insecure. To begin with, it means a peace of subjugation, therefore a peace with spoils, giving to each of the partners its territorial gains, its spheres of influence, and its areas of dominance. The division of the spoils not only will inspire in the despoiled a deep-working will to accumulate opposing power; it will also induce tensions and jealousies among the victors. In the first flush of their triumph these emotions will not be restrained by the fear of any counteracting power. They will be unleashed and arrogant. Each of the "partners" will feel that the others underestimate its just claims, with respect to the winning of the war and to the "compensations" it seeks for its past sacrifices. Why should we expect the United States and Soviet Russia to exercise a more harmonious or lasting condominium than that exercised by England and France after the previous World War? The partition of power affords no ground for agreement or for security. Many of our leaders are afraid of Russia's intention to dominate Eastern Europe and China at the same time that they look forward to an Anglo-American domination over most of the earth. Is it not rather childish of them to look to Stalin for an exhibition of saintliness they repudiate for themselves? If we're going to have a power alliance, Comrade Stalin is not the man who'll make the concessions. If we're going to play the game of "realism," Comrade Stalin is a mighty good player.

No matter how disguised, the scheme of power alliance leads directly back to the old world of international insecurity. It is based on the concept of power against power. It is at best a precarious conjuncture of force in a world where there are numerous possibilities for the development of opposing conjunctures. Wherever there is modern industry there is a potential locus of power—and modern industry has spread over the earth. Power alliance retains the imperialist outlook. It retains the dependence on armed force. It retains the strongholds of militarism. It fosters reaction everywhere, the belief in the superior people, the tradition of caste. And in the name of security it destroys the hope of security.

The argument for power alliance is sometimes speciously presented as a step toward world unity. Under its shelter, it is asserted, the inclusive organization can gradually be built up, and this is a sounder, more auspicious process than some over-all construction made according to an artificial blueprint. The argument is entirely fallacious. The relation of power alliance to cooperative world system is not the relation of part to whole. The two differ not in degree but in kind. They rest on entirely different principles and the one principle excludes the other. The alliance is predicated on conflict and division of interest; under it dominance and the need of dominance prevail. World organization is predicated on the common interest of the nations; under it military domination becomes unneccessary and has no ground of existence.

Power alliance has no direct relation to the peoples. It is engineered, controlled, and at length disrupted by power interests following the traditional methods of *Machtpolitik*. It is inevitably undemocratic even when maintained by democratic states. World organization alone can undertake the task of securing and advancing the well-being of all peoples, so far as that well-being depends on the provident ordering of the relations between them. Power alliance does not prepare the road of world organization—it blocks that road.

THE PRINCIPLES OF INTERNATIONAL ORDER

We have drawn the contrast between power alliance and world organization in order to clarify consideration of the principles on which an international order must be based. The significance of these principles is not realized, the necessity of them is not readily admitted, so long as we think of the alliance of Great Powers as either a substitute for, or an approach to, world organization. It is not a substitute in the sense of being another way of attaining the objectives of world security and world order. Those statesmen who, driven at length from parochial politics or from isolationism by the cumulative menace and tragedy of world war, proclaim their new belief in internationalism by advocating a league with Britain or with Russia or with both, are deceiving both themselves and the people. There is only one alternative to international disunity and potential anarchy and the prospect of World War III. That alternative is world organization. If we conclude that world organization is a dream, let us be honest enough to face the fact that there is then no hope of security of deliverance from war.

If this truth were faithfully revealed there would be much less inclination to regard a world organization as something chimerical or "idealistic." The peoples want an end of wars. They want an international order. If their will prevails an international order will come into being. But they do not know how to articulate their want. They do not know how to implement their will. They cannot deal with the special pleas of those who are committed, by tradition or by interest, to the system of power politics. They cannot penetrate to the secret seats where cunning little men, clothed in old authority, weave their "realistic" calculations. They need leadership. Over the world multitudes of them look to America for leadership. The United States has never really learned to speak the Old World language of power politics, of diplomatic intrigue, of imperialist expansion, of the "balance of power." It is most fitting that the United States should therefore take the lead in teaching men to speak the language of the New World, the world of cooperative internationalism. Unhappily some of our publicists and statesmen are belatedly picking up the old language and parading their new fumbling acquisition, at the very time that the peoples of the whole world have grown infinitely weary of it.

Let it be clearly understood that the only kind of international organization offering any hope of lasting peace is a world organization, that the only kind of international organization holding any promise of permanence is a world organization. The interests that divide the nations are extremely unstable and inherently incapable of satisfaction, while the interests that unite them are all profound and enduring.

What, then, are the principles on which such a world organization can and should be constructed? We shall avoid prejudice and misconception at the outset if we do not apply to it terms that properly belong to other kinds of political structure. We are not talking of a world state, not even of a world federation, as these terms are commonly used. We might perhaps call it a world confederation, though even then we would be employing that expression in a new and distinctive sense. What we have in view is a new institutional structure, appropriate to new conditions, authoritative within its limits, but operating within limits such as are not imposed upon the government of any existing State, whether unitary or federal. The new authority would be limited to the regulation and settlement of issues arising between States and the promotion and furtherance of measures for the common advantage of all States, within a prescribed range of competence assigned it in the constitutive charter of the international organization.

The opponents of international order will immediately raise the question of national sovereignty. It serves their purpose well, for the ancient notion of sovereignty, a notion framed by sixteenth-century lawyers to support the monarchical power, stresses the obsolete conception of the isolated State, and the appeal to it arouses in men the fear not of international regulation but of foreign dictation. The *realistic*

basis of this notion was destroyed by the economic and cultural interdependence of modern States, brought into ever closer relations by
a series of technological revolutions. It is obvious to common sense,
when it is not obscured by tradition, that no single State can claim a
right to order at its sole pleasure those matters that vitally concern and
equally belong to other States as well. No similar right has ever been
admitted outside of bedlam. The *legalistic* basis of the notion was undermined by the triumphant realization of the federal principle in the
United States of America. Federalism is utterly incompatible with the
ancient notion, for federalism means that sovereignty, as actuality,
can be defined, limited, *and partitioned*, as predetermined under the constitution of the federal State. It is therefore perfectly reasonable, and
perfectly logical, to consign to an international authority those carefully prescribed interests that in all equity belong to the family of nations
and that no one State has any just claim to decide for other States as well
as for itself. The first of these concerns is the maintenance of peace, if
on no other ground than that modern war grotesquely interferes with
the vital concerns of all States, neutrals no less than belligerents. The
notion that any one State has a *right* to make war (the right of sovereignty) is as illogical as the notion that an individual in a crowded thorough-
fare has a right to start a shooting match to settle a quarrel with some
other individual. The individual needs no such right to be a free man
and go about his business, and the State needs no such right to be an
independent State and manage its domestic affairs. Within an international order every State will renounce the pseudo-right to settle by
itself certain interstate concerns that on no basis of reason or of logic
belong within its exclusive competence, but as every other State makes
the same renunciation its genuine rights are thereby safeguarded, not
infringed. If this is dubbed, in traditional terms, an interference with
national sovereignty, then the sooner that notion of sovereignty is dis-
credited the better it will be for all of us. The world will have gained
order and security, new prosperity and new horizons, by the "sacrifice"
of a monstrous illusion.

THE STRUCTURE OF INTERNATIONAL ORDER

Let us now consider the structure of this international order. It is more
than a "league of nations," for it involves specific authority over those
affairs that are designated international. It is based on a constitutional
charter, and assume that all States, given the lead of the great victorious
powers, would readily accede. A condition here is that all the participant
States shall enter the new union as equal members. This condition may

at first seem a stumbling block, in view of the gross disparity of States in size, resources, population, and economic power. But the objection is unrealistic, since the prestige and power of the great States will not be abated by their formal equality with others. Moreover, the executive of the international union will in the nature of things be predominantly composed of the representatives of the great States. Since this must be so, whatever the mode of appointment, it is all the more important that back of the executive there should be an international assembly representative alike of all States, as the basis of authority and as a check, at need, on the activities of the international executive. At the present stage of political development it would be a blunder to require that all the member States should themselves have a democratic constitution. What is necessary at this time is that the international order should have a democratic basis, and this can be secured by according every State an equal vote in the constituent assembly. At the same time the constitutional charter might very properly lay down certain minimal conditions of admission to membership, including the provision that no member State shall deny to any minority the civil rights and liberties enjoyed by the rest of its citizens. This would in effect amount to a repudiation of fascism or nazism within the international order.

With the machinery of the international union we are not here concerned. "There are nine-and-sixty ways of constructing tribal lays." There may be no fewer ways of constructing the institutional setup of an international order. If the two or three Great Powers are willing, it can be constructed, but the precise form or pattern can hardly be foreseen, dependent as it would be on the deliberations of partners subject to very diverse influences and conditions. It may suffice, then, to add that no international system can dispense with a court of last resort, to adjudicate on all matters in dispute between States and to be custodian and promoter of the new international law. It would also be most desirable that, either attached to the court or functioning as a separate body, there should be an international organ devoted not to legal interpretation and adjudication but to the free exploration and formulation of equitable proposals for the advancement of the international order and for the readjustment of its institutions to the incessant processes of social change.

Under some such system international law would come into being for the first time in the history of the modern world, strictly speaking for the first time in human history. Here is the essential difference between a genuine international order and all the futile substitutes for it that have been advocated. A series of conventions and agreements, dependent for their validity on the good will and good faith of the treaty-making powers, lacking effective sanction and subject to abrogation

by the withdrawal or "denunciation" of any one of them in the name
of its indefeasible "sovereignty," is not law at all. It is not law as law
runs within the State. No State could hold together for a day if domestic
law were no more binding than what has gone under the name of international law. Any State would become an object of contempt and
ridicule if it solemnly devoted itself to making a set of courtesy rules
for the guidance of the internecine battles of its free and independent
citizens—and this is precisely the kind of business to which "international law" has applied the larger portion of its assiduous toils. There
can be no international security until international law, regulative of
the disputes that arise between States and groups of States, is clothed
with the full meaning and sanction of law. "Collaboration for postwar
security" is not enough. Defeat and subjection of the aggressor countries
will not suffice. Economic cooperation and trade agreements will not
suffice. Pledges and good resolutions will not avail against the tides
of change and the ever-recurrent causes of dispute between States. Nothing
will serve, nothing will control the menace of ever more devastating
war, but an international order at last anchored by international law.

THE SANCTION OF INTERNATIONAL LAW

We have said that to be law in the proper sense of the term it must be
binding, sanctioned. Here we come to the final issue. What is, what
can be, the sanction of this law? Let us first observe that the sanction
of law does not mean that on account of which the law is obeyed. For
the most part people do not obey the law of the State because they are
afraid of being punished if they disobey. There are many conditions
determining the law-abidingness of people, such as their indoctrinated
respect for law, their belief in the law, their inertia, their convenience,
their regard for the good opinion of others, their desire not to set a bad
example, and so forth. The specific sanction of law is not the ground
of obedience but the test and guardian of legality. Without its specific
sanction the law dissolves. Unless the violation of law is met by the
defensive reaction of the law itself, through law-sustaining process,
the law is null. There is the condition of all final law, that is, of all law
that maintains a fundamental order. The fundamental order is one that
denies to the subject the resort to violence. This is the order of the State,
and the extension of that order is international order. It too must deny
the resort to violence. Just as there can be no law within the State unless
the resort to violence is prohibited by sanction, so there can be no international law without a similar sanction. When Mussolini resorted
to violence against Ethiopia the League of Nations vainly opposed its

pseudosanctions. But there is no sanction against violence except an authority that operates in the same order and can convoke lawful might against lawless aggression. This power must be vested in the central authority, and it must totally deny to all within its jurisdiction the resort to independent force.

It follows that if international law and order are to obtain, States can no longer command independent warlike armaments. This conclusion cannot be put too strongly. The abolition of national armaments is a primary requirement of any international order. The requirement runs against all kinds of prejudice and traditional resistance but it remains inexorable. No State can refuse to disarm, on the condition that all other States do so, without rejecting the rule of law, for it is then claiming the privilege to assert its will by violence. Since at the end of this war we shall demand the disarmament of our defeated enemies, we can no longer vindicate our own armaments as a necessary defense against their further aggression. In the longer run the disarmament of our enemies will avail us nothing, unless it is the first step toward universal disarmament. We cannot keep our former enemies permanently disarmed if we retain armaments ourselves. Mere reduction of armaments is no solution. It is the fact of armament, not the scale of it, that bars the coming of international law. There is no guarantee of law unless it is accompanied by the total abolition of armaments of war. This condition can be attained by a graduated process over a relatively short term of years. Numerous objections will be raised, most of them casuistical, from interested quarters. For example, countries owning colonies may claim that they need armed forces "to keep the peace." The answer here is that if a police force is not enough to keep the peace the holding of that colony is itself an act of unjustified domination and quite contrary to the democratic principles that the victorious powers, and their allies—which include the great colony-owning powers—so loudly proclaim.

The final stage in the abolition of armaments would be the substitution of an international police force. This stage has its own difficulties and problems, but none of them is insuperable. We should observe that a police force is an entirely different thing from a military establishment. Unlike a military establishment it is not meant to oppose another force of the same order. It can therefore be extremely small by comparison, and it does not require heavy and costly equipment. With modern means of transportation it can be exceedingly mobile. For most purposes its mere existence would suffice. Its functions would include the suppression of any attempt to resort to violence by some adventurer seeking to win power by a *coup d'état* and the inspection of any reports concerning clandestine caches of weapons of warfare, where the regular police force of the domestic government either did not suffice or failed to perform these duties. The danger that the international police force would become itself an agent of tyranny would be obviated by the fact that it was under the control of an international excutive, subject in turn to a democratic international assembly. Like the regular police force it would also be an agency for the mustering of quick and expert aid wherever a large-scale calamity, such as earthquake or flood or fire or plague, called for its services. As for its composition, it would be made up of small national contingents in such a way that no one State could supply more than an assigned quota or percentage of the total force. These contingents would be under the central authority of the international executive. But we need not here go into further detail. We shall merely add that the international police force would most of the time be more a symbol of the authority of the international order than an operative agency for its support.

THE OBSTACLES TO INTERNATIONAL ORDER

There is nothing in this whole system, vitally necessary as it is for the new world in which we live, that imposes any excessive burden on human ingenuity. The obstacles lie elsewhere. One we have already dwelt on, the stubborn traditional prejudice that at every turn of the road blocks the way of humanity's deliverance from the evils it has unwittingly created for itself. Of one thing we can be sure, that the only substitute that is offered, the system of alliance, will not serve in the future any more than it has served in the past. Those who advocate instead a genuine international unity will therefore be vindicated in the long run, though that will be to them a small consolation, should their advocacy fail, in the vision of the new ruin that the lack of an international order will again entail.

The other obstacle lies in the possible, indeed I fear probable, terms of peace. An international order can hardly come into existence, and certainly cannot endure, unless it wins at length the loyalty of all the great States. Some conditions of peace that are now being proposed in certain quarters would make such loyalty quite unattainable. We must reconcile our aspirations with reality. The principle of cause and effect cannot be flouted. We know that if our own country were dismembered in defeat or subjugated or deeply humiliated we would never cease to struggle, we would pass through fire and water, we would count no other goal worth reckoning, until we had again mustered the strength to vindicate our unity and our national integrity, until we had challenged and broken the power that had humbled us. Whatever else we may think of the character of our enemies, let us not think they are different from us in this particular regard. If we do, then we had better abandon all hope of any international order or of any kind of enduring peace.

At this hour, for example, there are voices proclaiming: "The Germans know that they are beaten this time, but they nearly succeeded. They believe they can do it the third time, and they have already begun to plan for it. We must suppress them permanently." This argument is childish nonsense. Who are now planning the Third World War? Those who are going to fight it? Even given the worst possible peace terms, a generation will pass before another world war can break out. Those who will fight it, those who will be conditioned like the Nazi youth who are fighting this war, are still babes in arms or are yet unborn. It is their future attitudes, their future conditions, their future indoctrinations that will be decisive, and what these attitudes and indoctrinations and conditions will be will depend, more than on anything else, on how we treat them. Whether their evil heritage of militarism becomes dominant or recessive will above all depend, when our victory is complete, on what we do to them at that time.

It is a common delusion that if we can hold the Germans in check we shall thereby prevent future great wars. Those who cherish this delusion can hardly know much history, but they might at least reflect that of our three enemies in this world war, two were our allies in the previous one. Facts of this sort, of which history is prolific, show that the menace of war is endemic in a world of States not organized within an international system, and that it cannot be dispelled unless an international order is set up.

The terms of peace, no matter how wise, cannot avoid inflicting some hurts and causing some resentments. Some of the demands and aspirations of our allies are not compatible one with another. There will be some territorial "rectifications" that will create friction. Such things, in some measure, are inevitable. But it is the higher realism to avoid those hurts that will cause irremediable damage to our future security, those hurts that breed irreconcilable hostility in the peoples on whom they are inflicted. We must not repeat the follies of Versailles. If we care for the future we must have no more Polish Corridors, no mutilations of great States, no economically impossible States such as post-Versailles Austria. Nor must the victors seize all the spoils and then expect the despoiled enemies to settle down under a reign of peace. That inveterate imperialist, Mr. Churchill, has proclaimed that the allies have taken away all Italy's colonies "for ever." If that spirit prevails at the peace table there will be no beginning of security, no salvation from world wars.

[1943]

Some Implications of a Democratic International Order

34

It is an ancient complaint against the man of law that he is so identified with the established order as to be incompetent, or even impotent, to meet the challenges of a changeful society. Social change, it is asserted, is conceived by him more as a subversive disturbance of the establishment than as a condition of a process of constant legal readjustment. The law-ways, on this view, crust over the social ferment, precariously holding it in restraint below. The training, the interest, and above all the professional habit of the lawyer are regarded as unpropitious for the task of remaking continuously the necessary firmament of order. The jurist, so runs the charge, is usually limited to local problems of equity, with the problem of modifying the specific rule to fit the specific case and of finding the appropriate rule for the specific case—whereas the greater problem is not that of fitting the new need to the old order but of envisaging and building the new order for the new need.

THE SOCIOLOGY OF INTERNATIONAL LAW

With this charge as such we are not here concerned. Certainly the condition of any society is more and more a condition of flux, and the impact on a multigroup social organization of the ever advancing front of science and technology promises, apart from the other sources of far-penetrating change, to make this flux the permanent major premise of social policy. The particular role of the lawyer and the jurist in the inclusive business of social readjustment to change is not the province of this article, if indeed any single article could compass it. The appearance of the *Journal of Legal and Political Sociology* is one of many recent signs that this comprehensive issue is not going by default. Here we are concerned with the role of legal creativeness in an area that historically has been its peculiar concern. International law, more than any other form of law, has been made by lawyers. We must, however, distinguish private international law, the kind of *jus gentium* that first took definite shape under the guardianship of the *praetor peregrinus* of Rome and now regulates with decent success interpersonal relations across the frontiers of states, from what goes under the name of public international law. This article is nothing more than a plea that the jurist set himself to build the latter and far greater realm of order, for which such foundations as already exist have been laid over the centuries almost exclusively by the men of law. Here law must finally attain its farthest reach and power, setting up at length an assured system of order to govern the public relations of states.

Let us begin with a few quite elementary considerations. Without law there is no order and without community there is no law. Law need not be written down or imposed or administered by any authority; it may remain in the realm of custom. This is the way of law in the simpler societies, where there has been a small compact community to guard it. But in the more complex forms of society there must be established law, ordained and administered by appropriate authority. In the international sphere no law, properly so called, has hitherto existed, whether ordained or merely customary. What has passed as international law has been a set of conventions and partial temporary agreements lacking the validity and strength of law. Such customary rules as have been invoked have not been guarded by any co-extensive community. Such agreements as have been made have not been administered and enforced by any authority. Consequently they have not been capable of performing the eminent function of law in its proper sense, that of settling disputes by taking the issue to some decisive arbitrament outside of the parties to the dispute.

Now and again certain "high contracting parties" called sovereign states have convened and agreed on rules to govern their mutual interests. Some of these rules have been of a temporary nature, subject to periodic reaffirmation; others have been made without limit. Some of them have been, as it were, international rules of the road, for the convenience

of traffic—but without a policeman at the intersections. Others have
been rules to settle controversial questions, but without any assurance
that the "high contracting parties" would continue to abide by the settlement. Most of the minor rules have been very convenient for all concerned
and have been rather faithfully observed. Most of the major rules have
been violated without scruple, though some states have been much
greater offenders than others.

The main point, however, is that these rules have had no effective
sanction. Moreover, the great powers have usually reserved certain
issues that most directly lead to war. Even when such powers have
resort to war for the settlement of any issues, as in the Pact of Paris,
their declarations have been detached from any realistic means of giving
them effect. If the League of Nations had been born under a more favorable star, it might perhaps have built in time an international order.
But for reasons we need not here discuss the League passed from modest
efficacy in relatively minor matters to complete impotence in the face
of crisis.

The fatal defect of the "international law" that has hitherto existed
is most fully revealed by the fact that a large part of the "code" is devoted
to the elaboration of the rules of warfare. What kind of a law is this
that solemnly sets out the etiquette of law breaking? No doubt even in
war there may be a remnant of civilized usage accepted by the belligerents.
But war, since its office is sheer destruction, must of its essential nature
deny to the enemy nearly everything that humanity prizes. What then
remains for the "international law" of war? It rests on the assumption
that there is a vestige of community still uniting the belligerents. It
rests on the further assumption that war can be limited by certain humanitarian considerations. As one international law authority puts it:
"unable to regulate the resort to war, international law did continue the
ancient process of regulating the manner in which it was to be conducted."

The whole business of attempting to "regulate" warfare might be
fundamentally challenged. If the objective in war is to destroy the enemy,
what logic is there in regulating the mode of destruction? Is a state at
war likely to submit to the disaster of defeat, with the concomitant
annhiliation of its own soldiers and devastation of its own territory
if it can prevent that catastrophe by resorting to a mode of warfare
prohibited by a toothless "law"? Even laws properly so called are, as
the Romans put it, "silent in the clash of arms." If we appeal instead
to humanitarian considerations, what fine distinctions between the cruelty
and pain of different kinds of violent death can be persuasive when the
final alternatives of destroying and of being destroyed are weighed?

There are of course certain usages of warfare that belligerents on the whole respect because, and in so far as, these usages do not seriously interfere with the primary objective of war, the annihilation of the armed forces of the enemy. There are rules regarding war prisoners, noncombatants, unfortified places, the white flag, and so forth—but the desperation of war unleashes forces that cannot be restrained within set limits. There are some practices that belligerents abjure, such as the use of poisoned weapons and of dum-dum bullets, but it would be rash to claim that they do so out of regard for "international law," since they have good reasons to fear that the effect on the morale of their own troops of reprisals in kind would not justify the relatively slight immediate advantage of such practices. The failure to use poison gas in the present war must be explained in a similar way, since "international law" was no barrier to its use in the previous conflict.

All the branches of the "international law" of war suffer from the same sickness. Take, for example, the articles adopted by the Second Hague Convention regarding the commencement of hostilities. These prescribe a formal declaration of war and a notification to neutral powers. But Japan fought China without any declaration of this sort and it attacked the United States before it announced a state of war. Or take the articles dealing with the rights of neutrals. The military imperative has overridden these rights, and the very concept of neutrality has been confounded.

The sickness of "international law" is not confined to its specific branches, it permeates to the roots of the system. So long as the only sovereign authority is the individual state, "international law" can be no more than a group of conventions exposed at every point to the law-ignoring necessities of the ultimate violence of war. *So long as "international law" is largely occupied with the "regulation" of war, there can be no international law deserving the name.*

Let us return to our starting point. The foundations of order are law and community. Without community no law is accepted and no code evolves. Without law there is no security, no established right or obligation, no refuge from the violence of overbearing force. So long as the recognition of community stops at the borders of states, so long must law be impotent to pass these borders.

The international law we are contemplating will contain no chapter on the "law" of war. If war occurs after the law is in being it will constitute, like civil war, a temporary collapse of the whole established scheme of things. A "law" of war will be as alien to the code of international law as a "law" of revolution is alien to the civil code. With this point clearly before us, we can now turn to the consideration of certain prerequisites of the reign of law over the nations.

CONSEQUENCES FOR POSTWAR ORGANIZATION

First let us postulate that we are not envisaging a world order of democratic states but—what is an entirely different and much less utopian conception—a democratically organized world order. It would be nothing short of absurd to base any international policy on the premise that after this war all states, or even all great states, will become democracies. Democracy, to be real, cannot be an overnight reversal of historical conditions, or a formula imposed by victorious on defeated nations. It may well be that some of the defeated nations will ripen toward democracy more quickly than some of the victorious nations. Democracy needs something more than an appropriate ideology, a fact well illustrated by such different cases as those of Russia and China. Probably nothing will do more to hasten the ripening process than the establishment of an international order such as renders the peril of war remote. But at the best the construction of an international order cannot and need not be predicated on the fulfillment of that process. On the other hand it would seem no less absurd to build an international order exclusively composed of democratic states; that could be no more than another world-dividing and world-engendering "balance" of power, as fragile and as unstable as any of its precursors.

What then is intended when we envisage a democratic international order? What will make it democratic? What will keep it democratic? We are assuming without further question that any possible world order must rest on the democratic assumption that any scheme of an imperialistic world order is outmoded and impracticable. If so, then the following simple requirements are fundamental.

1. The member states of the international law-making association, be they great or small, advanced or backward, enter into it, and remain within it, as equal and equally self-determining units or "persons," with an equal status in the making and amending of the international constitution and in the voting on the laws presented to the international assembly.

This prerequisite encounters a few genuine difficulties, and a number of imaginary ones. The genuine difficulties revolve around the practical limitation of national sovereignty in the sphere of interstate relations as well as the consequent *moral* obligation imposed on individual states to control the demands of economic-interest groups so that they do not succeed in passing such measures as would endanger the harmony of nations. A high tariff program, for example, could easily lead to such dissensions and countermeasures as might prejudice the nascent international order. An instance of the imaginary difficulties is the rule of equality itself, giving seemingly equal power to equals and unequals alike—which was one of the accusations that Plato brought against democracy. In actuality the voting parity of the small or the backward states with the large or the advanced states, while it would give the necessary security to the former, would not seriously prejudice the greater prestige and influence of the latter. The power of resources, of leadership, of creative function, and of technological advance would still exercise its sway—no longer as sheer coercion but as expressed in expediency, economic advantage, cultural dependence, and the various other social forces that radiate from the foci of civilization. For this reason the disparity of intrinsic power, as against the equality of voting power, need create considerably less difficulty than arises, for example, from the same phenomenon within the Senate of the United States. Equality of status avoids an endless array of organizational problems that on any, other basis would be insuperable. In this relationship, as in the democratic system generally, the ideal principle is the only practicable one.

2. The equality of membership rights assures in turn the democratic procedure of the international assembly composed of representatives of the component states. This assembly becomes the legislative body enacting rules to govern interrelations of states, in accordance with an international constitution determining the competence of the assembly, the range of issues that lie outside the domestic sphere of autonomous states. Various safeguards may be deemed necessary by the constituent states so that the international constitution may not be subject to amendment by a mere majority. But with this proviso the processes of democratic procedure would apply to the specific enactments of the inclusive assembly.

Without some organization of this sort—and the recognition of international community requisite for its maintenance—international law cannot aspire to become genuine law. Guarding the law there must be consensus and sanction, but consensus can create sanction whereas sanction cannot create consensus. Given the consensus and the appropriate organization the ground is laid for the development, for the first time in history, of a new kind of law, the veritable law of nations. This kind of law cannot emerge simply as customary law. Without the appropriate organization the thorny sovereignty of every separate state defies the juristic principle of the *persona* bearing rights and obligations, and precludes anything better than the maimed and halting substitute for international law that has hitherto vainly claimed the title.

But we cannot stop here without being utterly unrealistic. Before the jurist can advance to the conquest of his greatest kingdom he must find a way of embodying in the international structure the creative principle of equity that has hitherto hovered, like a disembodied spirit, over the slow transformations of legal systems. War, like revolution, has often been the violent vent of the pent-up forces of social change. If it is to be abolished these cumulative and in the end irresistible forces must find another outlet, an outlet determined by social intelligence instead of by blind impulse. No imposed or constructed order can bank these forces; no code of established law can of itself be adequate to their demands. The inclusive organization must somehow be made responsive to them, or the firmament of order will crack and finally break apart. Man, the inventor, the rebel, the self-seeker, the visionary, is the restless unit of ever changing group formations. Every group, from the family to the nation, is subject to processes of expansion and of contraction. The international law must not seek to thwart these processes. If we are to have a world system at all it must be flexible, able to cope with a cohort of changes, changes in the equilibrium of population, changes in the production and distribution of wealth, changes in the locus of cultural and social dominance. Here then we propose a final institution, dedicated, on the highest level, to the application of equity.

Let us call this projected institution of the international order the International Equity Commission. We conceive this body as composed of a small number of members, say nine or eleven, representing states and state-groups. There might, for example, be one member for the Latin-American states, according to some plan agreed upon between them, and one member for the United States. There might be one member for Great Britain and the Dominions (outside of India) and one member for the Central European states. And so forth. But we need not discuss here the possible modes of organization, except to say that the members should represent all the great divisions of mankind, should hold office for a considerable term of years, say ten years, and should not be eligible for re-election. What, however, concerns us most is the role some such organization should—and in the writer's opinion, must—play in any world organization that can hope to endure.

Let us consider, in the briefest space, the functions that would properly fall to this highest embodiment of the principle of equity. They would certainly include the following:

1. To make proposals for the equitable treatment of the peoples of non-self-governing areas, in so far as any issue arises between such peoples and the governments still retaining sovereignty over them.

2. To make proposals for the reception into the Assembly of the Nations, as self-governing units, of areas at present not self-governing, whether colonies or dependencies of any kind, when the cultural development of any such area shall be deemed to make its claim equitable.

3. To make proposals for the settlement of issues arising between states and state-groups, in so far as these issues are not adjudicated by

reference to the established code of international law or cannot be settled by agencies for the adjustment of differences directly set up by the states concerned.

4. To make proposals respecting the transfer from one state jurisdiction to another of areas or population groups requesting such transfer.

5. To make proposals for the protection of the full rights of minority groups, on appeal from any such groups.

6. To make proposals regarding any issues referred to the International Equity Commission by states or state groups, or by any of the agencies of the inclusive international organization.

7. In general, to make proposals for the integrity and advancement of the international order and for the adjustment of that order to changing conditions, such as industrial transformations, population changes, changes in the modes of communication and transportation, and so forth.

We may point out that our International Equity Commission would differ considerably from any kind of World Supreme Court. Its primary function is not to interpret and safeguard the established constitution or charter of the international order—a task that might actually be assigned to a separate commission of international experts —but to assure that the principle of equity shall not be defeated in the impact of change upon the established ways. The International Equity Commission hands down not opinions but proposals. On these proposals the Assembly of the Nations would pass, in so far as they needed full international authorization. The prestige of the Commission would obviously be of prime importance for its success. It should be composed of the very best men available, noted for their experience and vision. The appointment to membership should be regarded as the highest honor that can politically be conferred on a human being.

To many people any such proposal will seem utopian. Perhaps it is after all a matter of our time scale. Either after this war or else after who knows what centuries of devastating struggle there will be set up some sort of international order with its genuine sanctioned law. When we shall come to terms with the logic of our civilization no man yet knows. The end of this war—if it is the end we are irrevocably pledged to attain—is the only propitious time we can now foresee. To plan for it now, with the boldest fortitude, may well be not a utopian escape but the most practical and realistic job to which human beings can set their hands and minds.

[1942]

ENDS *and* MEANS VI

Educational Goals

35 *What is it important that a man should know?* What is it important that we teach, we who teach those who are going to be the men and women of tomorrow? What is it important that they should learn if they are going to enjoy, shall we say, the inalienable rights of life, liberty, and the pursuit of happiness? Or, to put it in other words, if they are going to live effective lives while at the same time they serve their fellow men, what is it important that men should know?

I am not asking what a businessman should know. Nor a working man, and not any other specialized kind of man. What is it important that *a man* should know? Not a churchman. Not a Roman Catholic, or a Protestant, or a Jew, or a Hindu, or Mohammedan, or anything else. A man. Not an engineer, or a physician, or a carpenter, or a lawyer, or a plumber—but a man. And when I say man, I include, needless to say, woman.

We have to face that kind of question, because we live in this multigroup order of life, this multigroup society, where in our system of public education you cannot, you dare not, and you should not teach men to be an X-ist or a Y-ist, a Methodist or a Roman Catholic or a Unitarian or an Orthodox Jew. We have to teach them something else. We have to seek something that we can hope to call the universality of man.

In simpler societies people did not need to face that problem, because they were all brought up in the same customs, and they all shared the same faith. So they could evade that half of the problem of education. They often evaded the other half by having no formal education at all.

However, we have to face the full brunt of the question and look at man in his full universality, because we cannot teach the mores of one group, or the religion of one group, or the values of one group, if we are going to be true to education for the democratic society in which we live.

It is said that we need more drive in our education. The suggestion has been made that the way to get it is to give a vocationalism to teaching, even in the liberal arts colleges. I completely reject that answer. I think it is one of the many sidetracks we take because we fail to find the main track.

After all, the problems we have to face, the problems of the kind of families we live in, and the kind of cities we live in, and the kind of world we live in, and the kind of half-peace we live in, and all the rest of it, are not going to be solved by teaching us to be more professional and more vocational. We are not so bad at that job, anyway. There is something else we are not so good at.

It is no answer to say we ought to teach this–ism or that. To say, for example, we ought to teach democracy. I do not want to say we should teach people "democracy." We should teach them so that they will be democratic, so that their way of living, their responsiveness to our teaching, will make them so.

What then is it important that a man should know and should be taught to know in his youth?

We can, of course, at once mention certain obvious things that are important. I am going to leave out these things. For example, it is important that all men and all women should know how to be healthy, physically healthy, and should know the conditions of living in a physically healthy way, should know that thoroughly, straightly, and honestly. It is important that people should know the various things that will save them from the many pitfalls of ignorance, as they go about their daily lives. But beyond that, beyond those things? We will accept all that but we know the main issue lies elsewhere. Beyond that.

To go beyond that, let us get back to the beginning. Educating means imparting the knowing of something, by those who already know, to those who do not yet know. In other words, the focus of education is the communication of knowing. You know. Somebody does not know. You pretend, at any rate, to know more, and the other knows less. The imparting of that more, the equalizing of knowledge, so to speak, is what educating means. You see, I lay the stress on knowing.

Next I would like to distinguish four kinds of knowing. I am not dividing knowing into four kinds. I am just saying I would like to distinguish four kinds of knowing.

1. There is knowing how to do.
2. There is knowing what to do.
3. There is knowing how to think.
4. There is knowing what to think.

Let us not ask for any more kinds of knowing, for the moment. These four satisfy my purpose. I want to suggest that for our problem here, we are merely concerned with the third and the fourth of those kinds of knowing—knowing how to think and knowing what to think.

I say this because knowing how to do, which is extremely important, at least as important as knowing what to do—at any rate, a fairly large part of knowing how to do—is a matter of learning techniques, and we are not too bad about that. We are reasonably good. There are some techniques we are not so good at, but most techniques we are pretty competent about. We stand up well in the history of time, and among the peoples of the world, in that area. So I shall leave out, roughly speaking knowing how to do.

Then, as for knowing what to do, I do not need to discuss that because if you know the answer to No. 4, knowing what to think, you know the answer to No. 2. What to *do*, obviously, depends on what to *think*. So we can leave out Nos. 1 and 2. That simplifies things, and we are down to Nos. 3 and 4—how to think and what to think.

By the way, you notice I defined education in terms of knowing. I said the crucial thing is the process of knowing, the relation between the more knowing and the less knowing, and the equalization of the two. That is education. I lay stress on knowing, anyway.

Hence I am not talking about things like remembering, which is often, unfortunately, used as if it were an equivalent of knowing. Remembering is a refuge often taken. If we do not know how to teach, we teach people to remember, or, at least, we drill them in remembering.

That recourse is to be found not only on the lower levels of what we call education, but right up on the highest levels. For example, I have a recollection of being at a Ph.D. examination, where questions like this were hurled at the candidate who was thereby qualifying to be called a doctor of philosophy: "Who was the postmaster general at the time of President Coolidge?"

That is remembering. The practice is common enough, and I ask you: Is it not a poor substitute for knowing? If there is something that you can find by looking it up in *The World Almanac*, why trouble anybody's brain by making the remembrance of it a condition of getting a Ph.D.?

These detachable items of remembrance you remember only to forget. A lot of education in the school, in the college and in the university, unfortunately, amounts to this business of remembering in order to forget. You have to forget because, otherwise, your brain gets clogged with formless matter.

You know the lines of Wordsworth:

> Getting and spending we lay waste our powers,
> Little we see in Nature that is ours.

In the academic circle we change it to:

> Getting and forgetting we lay waste our powers.

So we come to Nos. 3 and 4, where the crucial issues of the goals of education lie in these questions: What about teaching people how to think and what about teaching people what to think? The first of these two questions might rather be: *Can* we teach people how to think? If we can, we should do it. When we come to the second issue, the question is more likely to be: *Should* we teach people what to think?

Now as to teaching people how to think, I claim in all seriousness that this is one of the things we do least well. We do a lot of things quite decently; but one thing we badly neglect or ignore—and a very essential thing, too, a primary thing—is teaching people how to think to the limit of their capacity. As with every other capacity this one is limited, and the limit differs widely for different people. But we do not seek to teach people nearly as far as they could go.

For example, take such a thing as speech. Speech is the most wonderful, flexible, rich, variegated instrument in the world, and we do not teach our people to appreciate the significance of speech. If somebody played a fiddle badly, we would all know it is being played badly. However, when somebody speaks or writes books, or otherwise, badly, we do not even know that it is bad.

We do not read right. Many college graduates have never learned to do it. We do not know how to read the more rewarding, more difficult books, the greater books. We shirk the task: it does not challenge us. We use textbooks as substitutes for that reading. The meat of the great books is chewed into a sort of baby cud by pedagogues for students.

We do not know how to read because we are not taught how to think. When I say "how to think," I do not mean to think abstractly. I mean to *think*—a universal operation—what we do all the time in every area, but which we are not trained to do well in any area.

To think means to distinguish, and then to relate, then to comprehend, and then to appreciate. We are called to do so in every relation of life all the time. We are not trained to do it and it does not come to us by custom or by a kind of social instinct.

To think is to see things in their relationship, to see a meaning in its context, to see a star in its constellation, to see an event in its setting, to see an action in a complex of a personality, to see a person in the light of his group, and to see a group in the light of its community, and the community in the light of the world of men.

To distinguish and relate, and then comprehend, and by comprehending or understanding, to appreciate—that is thinking. If we could follow through on that, we would know it is the way to save ourselves from a lot of the propagandistic perils that beset us. After all, what is propaganda? In a sense, we resist it. Too often it is an attempt to befuddle our thinking. We are too easily befuddled. We are not trained to distinguish and to relate.

We can do better. Here is a test of what I mean. Ask anyone who is a teacher to try this out. Give some quite good students a few simple fallacies, not the abstract form, but give good examples of fallacious connections of meaning you can pick out in people's arguments, and ask them to point out the fallacies. You will be surprised how often they will fail to do it—people you think are good. They are not trained to think, in other words, to distinguish and then to relate, to see things properly in their setting, truly in their context.

We need to follow this line to avoid many of the perils of ignorance, of prejudice and of propagandistic persuasion, and even of the passions that beset our lives. To think, to see things in their relationship, to see the near and the far, to see the small and the great, to see the part and the whole, to see things steadily and in their relationship. It is hard, but surely there are ways of trying.

We can well begin the learning of how to think by learning to use more aptly the common instrument of speech. First, to distinguish; then to relate; and last, to appreciate; and thereby to avoid false unities and false separations; thereby to get to the appreciation of unity in diversity; never to see one as though detached from the other.

I set out from the question: Can we teach people *how* to think? I suggested we can do more, far more, than we do, and that in doing so we teach people not only to be better thinkers, but also better citizens. I come lastly to the question: Can we teach them or *should* we teach them what to think? In other words, should we indoctrinate our students? Actually, we need not worry about that question. The answer is so simple.

All education indoctrinates. I can conceive of no education that does not. But two kinds of indoctrinations must be ruled out. One is the indoctrination that denies or takes liberties with scientific truth. The other is the indoctrination that indoctrinates one group, either directly or indirectly, against another. The latter is particularly pernicious in a democracy. In our general education we must not teach the values of one group over against the values of other groups.

Of course, if we can teach people how to think as I have suggested, we need no better prophylactic. Indoctrinations beset us on every side. They are bred in the home, in the group, the street, the church, all the settings of life. However, if we teach people how to think, we are giving them the best safeguard against dangerous indoctrinations.

We can then go boldly on to educational indoctrination. In what ways? I shall mention very briefly four kinds of indoctrination that I think are eminently honorable and proper. First, we ought to indoctrinate people because we want them to have a sense of belonging, a sense of home, an equilibrium which too many lack in our world today. Therefore, we must begin by indoctrinating people in the sense of place, their homeland I mean; in the sense of their homeland, of its traditions, of its services, of its unity, of what binds them to it and what binds it to them, of what binds it to the past and the future—the sense of that continuity—to give them the wider home feeling that in our multigroup society tends to be so lacking.

We should therefore teach them history in a certain way, not the minutiae of history, but history in the sense of the living, continuing context of the community as it passes through time. They are at a particular point of time and they are part and parcel of that great movement. They belong there. That sense should come to them from history.

Second, they should also be indoctrinated in the relation of their homeland to other homelands; in other words, the relation between them, their people, and humanity. In this connection it is very important to teach what human beings are really like, so far as we know it ourselves. That is an open question. However, we know a good deal. They should be taught, and pretty thoroughly and freely, what we do know. Thus we learn that other people are not so different from ourselves. Thus we learn that it does not make so much difference as we thought, with respect to the human quality of people, whether they live in Peiping or in Boston, whether they live in Atlanta or in Timbuctoo. We have learned that people are human beings, and we have learned something about what human beings are, their faults and, I hope, their potentialities, too.

Third, it is important that we should be oriented to nature. The sense of the world around and outside us is what we are concerned about, not the dissection of it. So when I speak about orientation to nature, I do not mean necessarily that they must learn physics if they are not going to be physicists, or chemistry, or geology, or biology, and so forth. I mean that they ought to know about the nature of the growth of plants and animals, the smell of trees and the flight of birds, the taste of herbs, the motions of the weather, and the feel of the earth, the circling skies, and so forth. They should be at home in the world they live in.

Now my last orientation. They ought to be oriented in greater achievements, so far as they can understand them, of man. I do not refer merely to great books that have been written, and I certainly do not mean mainly the great philosophies that have been thought; I mean the great achievements of man, as they are incarnated in various ways, incarnated in thought, in stone, in vision and dream, the great constructs of civilization.

That is orientation. That is also indoctrination. We need that kind of orientation very badly. So I want two things, you see. I want to teach people how to think, and I want to give them orientation, if I know how, and so far as they can learn.

You might say, "How are these things to be done?"—even if you agreed with me. I do not answer this question. You might say, "Where are the teachers?" I cannot answer that question. Perhaps the most important thing in education is, if we know how to make it concrete, to teach people the conditions, the activities, the responsibilities, and the virtues of being citizens of their country and of their world.

[1950]

The Art of Contemplation

36 The world being too much with us, we are being robbed of the finer satisfactions that demand a more leisurely pace. Among such satisfactions there are, for example, the pleasures of the discriminating palate, savoring in good company the subtler tastes and flavors that make the meal an experience and not merely a ritual for the conveyance of nourishment; the pleasures of rural rambles, where we stroll to no destination to enjoy the scenes of the ever-changing countryside, the hues of leaves and twigs, the sculpture of tree forms, the songs of birds and the rustle of hidden scurrying creatures, the smells of the good earth; and not least the pleasures of the easeful but active mind, when it freely looks around, dips into its treasury of memories, or loses itself in its visions. It is one form of such activity that is our subject here, the neglected art of contemplation.

It is the least accoutred of the arts, this art of contemplation. It needs no equipment, no tools, no materials, no special techniques. It calls for nothing outside ourselves. It bids us return to ourselves, not to get busy but to be still. Perhaps that is why we are so averse from it.

We are such busy folk, we look on time spent in mere contemplation as empty time, as abhorrent to us as a vacuum is to nature. Whether our work be as exacting as that of a

President of the United States or as light as that of a night watchman, we are equally too busy to indulge in contemplation. We cannot abide being alone with our thoughts. Millions of people are occupied to keep us occupied. And when everything else fails, when we are not getting together to discuss our own affairs or those of our neighbors, when we are not arguing over politics or exchanging views about the state of the world or the stock market, when there is no committee to attend and no friends at hand with whom we can have a drink and chitchat, there is always television.

We learn about things, we read about them, we talk about them, we debate over them, but we rarely contemplate them. What is the difference? It is essentially one of attitude. When you contemplate a situation you hold it steadfastly before you. You ask no questions of it, you demand no answers. You let the feel of it sink deep within you. You are motionless in its presence, absorbed in the being of it. So it appears before you in new perspective, undisturbed by your passions, unchanged by your interests. The situation you genuinely contemplate is freed from the intrusions and the irrelevances of utility, so that in its contemplation you yourself gain a new freedom.

Presently we shall consider the worth of this freedom, but let us first explore the quality of contemplation. It must not be confused with introspection, that fumbling and dubious operation in which the mind is supposed to look inward on itself. In contemplation, the mind absorbs itself in the scene, the object, the situation, with no attempt at control or manipulation, with no ulterior end to serve. Contemplation is steady reflection, when the mind is at home with itself, moving among its wealth of memories or pondering the way of things. Most of the time we act, so to speak, with the top of our mind. In contemplation we pause from this activity and let the situation under review engross our subconscious no less than our conscious being. We let it sink in, as we sometimes put it. We retreat from the immediate world of action, liberating ourselves from necessity.

Therein lies the great virtue of contemplation. We detach ourselves not from reality but from the encumbrances that cloud our vision of reality. We ascend not to a windowless ivory tower but to a vantage point from which we view the wider horizons. We set our preoccupations aside. Contemplation is not brooding, the way we brood over our troubles or our problems, our plans or our prospects, our mistakes or our misunderstandings. Jangled emotions control that kind of brooding, whereas contemplation must be serene. "The sessions of silent thought" may not always be "sweet," but they are unclouded by our fears, uncolored by our hopes. A gentle melancholy sometimes pervades them, especially when "we summon up remembrance of things past." Most of the time, however, they have the overtones of that happy poise that lifts us, while it lasts, above the urgencies of everyday affairs.

Contemplation is the leisure time of the mind, when it is no longer the servant of its drives. In one respect it is close to the scientific attitude, since it equally seeks to view situations for themselves, as themselves, aside from their utility to us. But its approach is quite different from that of the scientific researcher. He seeks the answer to specific questions, employing certain established procedures in the quest. Contemplation is not directed to questions of this type and it has no procedures beyond its own free-ranging motions.

Yet it is contemplation that presides over the highest reaches of science. The intuitive mind of the greater scientist, going beyond laboratory techniques and mathematical constructs, ponders the vast belongingness of things, feeling for the principle that unifies major fields of phenomena or seeking to penetrate to the nature of the bond that as yet remains merely a descriptive bracket for the like behavior of some broad range of phenomena. No experiments, no tests, no computing procedures provide the answer. But it may come to the synthesizing vision of the contemplative scientist, revolving the potentialities of interpretation in the stillness of the study. So it was with Newton when the significance of gravitation in the orbiting of suns and planets came to him. So it was with Einstein when he fathomed the doctrine of relativity. So it will be with the future great scientist who will offer an explanation of the formation and unity of the many-particled atom. So it has been also with various other scientists who have in their time opened up new paths of scientific discovery. What each of these leaders has done was to propose and develop the conception of a scheme of relationships, a bond of connections, that had hitherto not been conceived at all or at least never effectively applied. Once the magistral hypothesis has been formulated, a corps of scientists can follow it up, a new impetus has been given for experimental work in various directions.

There is another mode of contemplation that has had a profound effect on human society, influencing from generation to generation the aspirations and the beliefs of the peoples. This is the mission of the great religious leaders. Their concern is the world of values. They contemplate the plight of men, their mean ambitions and their petty prides, their lack of standards, the failure of human brotherhood, and the sorry mess they make of the business of living. They perceive the need for a higher authority, a power above them they can reverence and that commands obedience, and their intuition provides the answer. Their appeal is addressed to the need of their time and to the receptivity of the folk. Thus the great religions are born.

Contemplation is somewhat akin to meditation. In both moods the mind is steadily engrossed with one theme so that, like a ship with a lashed rudder on a calm sea, it maintains itself with little wavering toward the mark. But meditation characteristically is occupied with a theme already exposed to its view, with a text or utterance or philosphical position or a condition of living, say. So the cleric meditates on a passage of scripture or the Buddhist on the doctrine of Nirvana. Its objective is the edification or fuller enlightenment of the thinker, whereas contemplation characteristically has a broader reach, seeking to comprehend a totality or at least to survey the various facets of a situation that calls for further explanation or interpretation.

When we really contemplate a situation, we hover in thought above it, we muse over it, we let it inform us. In this age of ours, when leisure is given over to distractions, lest we be at home with ourselves, the healing power of contemplation is little understood. In this age of ours, when men of affairs carry their preoccupations back to their homes, the habit of contemplation is sadly in need of cultivation. It is a habit that makes no great demands on our time, only a brief retreat now and again when we seriously endeavor to look in detachment on the true proportions, conditions, and background of whatever may be on our mind. In an age when we are subjected to an endless bombardment of propaganda, urging us to buy this or that, to do this or that, to take this side or that, to believe this or that, an age when specious appeals to prejudice and to interest evoke so raucous a response from multitudes all too willing "to take suggestion as a cat laps milk," in such an age the habit of contemplation could save us from numerous ills.

To contemplate one must learn to live with oneself, to think for oneself. The ways of modern living make the habit more difficult to acquire. And our engrossment with techniques, with manipulative devices, so inevitable in an era of complex machines, complex organizations, complex problems, and complex research, increases the difficulty. For we tend immediately to resort to manipulative devices when we ought to begin with contemplation. This tendency, and its upward consequences, can be illustrated from many fields. It affects the scholar in his inquiries, and it affects the statesman in, say, the making of foreign policy. But to this subject we shall return.

The habit of contemplation can be learned only in solitude — which does not here mean in loneliness but in withdrawal into the privacy of one's own thought. The privacy of thought is at a discount now, along with all other privacies. This retreat needs no cell, no soundproof study, no ivory tower, but instead the will to shut out for a time all influences and all pressures, to resist the quick persuasions of our wishes and our beliefs, and in the resultant tranquility to establish communication with the situation we seek to understand. Once the habit of contemplation is acquired, it can find a very happy expression in fit company, the members of which are all prepared for the interchange of untrammeled thought.

Contemplation, if first nursed in privacy, can gain a new dimension when it is thus shared. For this is the true camaraderie of minds, and this is the true community of scholars. In its less advanced form it is the free mutual communication of the thoughts that come to us in our moods of prior silent contemplation. In its more perfect form it is the mutual stimulation of further contemplation in each of the participant members. In this interchange of thought, unhurried, uninhibited, reasoning together, following the word, the *logos*, wherever it leads, so engrossed in it that rivalries are forgotten and the desire to dominate is stilled, there is the most fulfilling of all the modes of human communication. I have glimpsed it now and again in some casual meeting as we sat outdoors on a quiet evening, or in some seminar discussion, and sometimes, a few times, in one of the more intimate sessions of a group of friends.

They are indeed moments when, as an evening of talking wears on, we find ourselves falling into mutual contemplation with our fellows. We may fall into it but we leap out again. We do not let it absorb us. We want to get on with the business. We know our conclusions before we start. We argue and we dispute. We do not reason together, we reason around one another or against one another. We throw facts at one another, and our facts are for us more significant than theirs. The spirit of contemplation quickly evaporates.

The scholar may be as prone to this tendency as other men. His study should be a retreat as well as a workshop. Too often it is only the latter, where he organizes his data, consults his authorites, practices his techniques, and adds to his notebooks. So he contributes his quota to the compendium of learning, and when, perchance, he becomes an authority himself, he discourages those few more audacious disciples who have a yen for what he calls mere theorizing and advises them there is no road that way to the passport of a Ph.D.

The scholar's workshop is most necessary, but without the retreat as well the great foundations of science would never have been laid and the towering summits of scientific achievement would never have been erected. It is in thoughtful hours, the contemplative hours, that the great germinal ideas emerge and the clues to great discoveries are suggested. And if this is true of the sciences it is even more true of the humanities, since the spirit of contemplation broods over the great plays, the great poems, the great compositions, the great paintings of all the ages. Not only so, but we who read or behold or hear them can feel their power and understand their message only if we too put on the mantle of contemplation, and when that spirit passes out of them there is nothing left but the dry bones of a ritual now bereft of meaning, the prey of grammarians and critics.

There is one area of study I have left out of the reckoning, an area once regarded as the summit of human knowledge, but now sunk in general esteem, beneath the floor of learning. I am speaking of philosophy. More than any other subject it has suffered from the decline of the spirit of contemplation. For the essence of philosophy is contemplation, contemplation over the meaning and range of knowledge, contemplation over the experience of living, contemplation over man's lot and destiny. A very few brave practitioners still struggle to keep philosophy alive but most of the brotherhood have abandoned it for symbolics or semantics or historical critiques on pragmatic conversions of it into something else. The decline of philosophy is itself a criterion of the neglect of contemplation.

I have been referring to scholars, but the spirit of contemplation is no less important for other men, for other callings, and for the greater business of us all, the business of living. Its prerequisites are so simple, only an attitude and a modest perceptiveness. The attitude is one of open-minded circumspection, the willingness to look all round a situation, without haste, without urgency of desire, finding a certain satisfaction in the process. The perceptiveness is less easy to describe, but its quality is a liking to savor the slowly accumulated impressions that come when the mind waits patiently to receive them.

More people, I believe, possessed the latter attribute in less sophisticated times, when work was less specialized and society less highly organized. I have listened to a group of country folk, assembled on a porch on a peaceful summer night, when no radio blared and, instead of the common desultory gossip about the neighbors and their children, the talk turned to the unusual question: Which of all the things you have ever done would you most want not to have undone? That led to a spell of pondering and searching of experience that engrossed the company long after the sun went down. And in long-past years I have sat on a winter night with country folk, on a distant island where it was customary for neighbors to foregather in someone's cottage around a central peat fire, and in the dim light of a single kerosene lamp they would talk of the mysteries of the sea or the quirks of human destiny or the nearness of death to life, with the intervals of silence while each brooded within his own thoughts.

Two conditions in particular fostered the contemplative mood among that simple-living folk. One was their exposure to nature in the open, on the sea or on the lonely moors, where the unpredictable operation of natural forces meant abundance or penury, sometimes life or death. This experience permeated the traditions of the folk and engendered tales of wonder and of dread. The other condition was the total absence of all our modern distractions, so that there was little resort except to quiet pleasures of sociable discourse, where imagination had free range and thoughts nursed in solitude were embroidered in the interchange.

It was easier in those days and among people so situated to form the habit of contemplation. Like some other practices that yield abiding satisfactions once the habit is formed, this one has to overcome a certain initial resistance. An effort is required to keep a total situation steadily in view, waiting dispassionately so that it may appear in perspective—which is the essence of contemplation. This ability cannot be attained without patience, effort, and cultivation. Where distractions abound, the immediate demands of the working day or the numerous siren calls that invade our leisure time, they are the natural enemies of contemplation. The art is never acquired and the satisfactions it brings remain unreaped.

And not the satisfactions alone. Let us not think that contemplation offers no reward beyond the pleasure of contemplating, the fresher air of widened horizons, the sense of inward emancipation from overweighted cares. These are rewards enough, but there are rewards of another kind, rewards for the doer no less than for the thinker, for the man of affairs no less than for the searcher after wisdom.

In every line of life there are decisions to make, problems to face, difficulties to overcome. When we deliberate over these we are usually concerned with the question: What policy will best serve our ends? Frequently we are content to ask: What action will give us the immediate results we want? But when we look at things this way we often fail to realize there are results beyond results and the former may bring us more harm than the latter bring good. And when we ask only the question: What policy will do *us* more good, we are most unlikely to see all sides of a situation, and most likely to miss something that matters greatly to all of us as well. Our interest controls our vision, and our consequent action may in the end confound us.

Here is why the habit of contemplation is so valuable even when we are dealing with what we call practical problems. Just because contemplation sets aside the practical approach it is often a better guide to practice. Within its calm survey and because of its unembarrassed unhastening outlook it is apt to perceive aspects of the situation that escape the more partisan eye. It seeks no gain, it pursues no goal, it is not out to justify any position or to establish any theory. Would we not escape many pitfalls and save ourselves from many blunders if before committing ourselves to a line of action we possessed the freedom of mind to indulge in some prior contemplation, entirely disregarding the need for action for a time?

What a difference it might make can be amply illustrated from every area of human relationships. The history of dealings of group with group, people with people, nation with nation, is an interminable record of tragic errors and gross misunderstandings, essentially because there is no area in which men are less willing to deliberate before they act and to contemplate before they deliberate. Nowhere else do men, even intelligent men, rush so quickly to conclusions and most of the conclusions are the offspring of preconceptions and prejudices. The more prejudiced men are, the more cocksure they are. What a difference it would have made, at any time in the past, what a difference it would make today, if people were minded to say: Come, let us take counsel together. Let us consider what the result will be to *them* if we treat them thus or thus, and then what the results will be to *us* because of the results to them. Let us consider what the more lasting effects are likely to be, ten years from now, fifty years from now. Supposing we keep them poor, will we be better off, will our country be greater and stronger? Suppose we deny them opportunites, will we have more? And so on. Obvious enough questions, but so rarely asked.

But it is not only the rank and file of men, it is also the leaders, the strategists, and the executives who frequently fail to contemplate before they reach decisions of high moment. It is a very old saying that the affairs of men are determined by a minimum spark of intelligence. In the utopia of my dreams every minister of state would take a prior course in the art of contemplation, and the foreign minister would be required to pass a particularly rigorous test. Of course this utopia would have a kind of academy not yet existent, an academy dedicated to the art and practice of contemplation.

To return from these vain conceits, I would in conclusion extol, as the highest of all human freedoms, the freedom that the spirit of contemplation bestows. Our freedoms exist on many levels. The ground freedom keeps a man out of jail and saves him from being the mere instrument of another's will. Above that extends an area of freedoms concerning our relations to the external world, by their very nature limited and regulated freedoms, including rights to acquire, possess, and dispose of property. Above these come the greater civil freedoms, a man's freedom to think his own thoughts, to communicate them at will, and to worship his own God. This area extends into the more special freedoms guaranteed by any genuine democracy. But, priceless as these freedoms are, we may possess them all and still not be masters of our own soul, still be the slaves of circumstances. For all these freedoms only assure that no man and no government is permitted to invade the areas they occupy. Our rights are fences against instrusion from without, but they cannot give freedom within. The mind of man is a great troublemaker and very often an enemy of its own freedom.

The contemplative spirit is the expression and the guarantee of this inner freedom. For it means that we are not inexorably engrossed in ways and means, are not so entangled in our problems and our schemes that we have no horizons beyond them. It means that our outlook is no longer confined to the aspects of a situation that concern us personally, so that we miss its intrinsic attributes, its range and depth and quality and see in it only obstacles and opportunities and demands and frustrations. Contemplation liberates us from this self-imprisonment within the walls of our needs and our cares. The contemplative spirit is unbound.

The world is full of calls to contemplation, from the motions of the incredible atom through the endless ways of life up to the ways of man, that creature so fearfully and wonderfully made, and out to the motions of the inconceivable galaxies. What human being is so poor of heart that he cannot somewhere find the food for congenial contemplation, and thereby a freedom from his mere selfhood he did not know before?

This plea for the practice of contemplation advances a final consideration. Let me put to you, contrary to my wont, a theological question. How would an eternal mind occupy itself? It is not embarrassed by problems, for everything lies open to it. It is not engaged in the making of policies or the building of enterprises, for it knows the unfolding plan of all creation. It seeks nothing, it needs nothing, it hastens nowhere. The whole of time is behind it and before it, so that time itself, the primary condition of all the doings of mortals, has no existence for it. What could occupy such a mind? One activity alone would be possible, one only would be worthy—the contemplation of it all, the eternal thinking, fulfilling and forever fulfilled, of the endless procession of the universe. Perhaps this conception was adumbrated by that first prophet, who said: "And God saw everything that He had made, and, behold, it was very good." May we not then surmise that we in our own lives come nearest to the divine mind when we learn the joy of contemplation?

[1965]

The Right to Privacy

37 Sometimes we speak as though privacy were a boon of which this complex civilization of ours has been robbing us. We deplore the inroads on privacy, the intrusions into our personal affairs, the official registrar with his big filing cabinets, the questionnaire monger, the telephone tapper, the nosy reporter, the gossip-gathering columnist, the TV man with his "candid camera," "the chield among us taking notes," the Post Official who censors certain periodicals out of the mails and that other official who "scans" letters coming from certain countries. We add to the count the lengthy forms we must fill in before we can get a passport and the elaborate scrutiny of our past life we are subjected to when we are being considered for a government job. There is certainly some ground for the charge, but we must not assume that privacy was more respected in older, simpler times. The private life is always exposed to threats, whether from our official guardians or from our near relatives or the neighborhood folk. There is good reason to hold that in our great urban centers there is more protection for privacy than in the small town.

There is, however, one occupational group whose members are far more exposed to assaults on their private life than were their predecessors. They are the people who hold a public position in democratic societies, especially in societies adhering in any measure to the puritan tradition. For such, any breath of scandal, any suggestion of moral delinquency in the present or in the past, constitutes a serious threat. It is likely to be investigated by some member of the opposition party, and any confirmatory evidence is exploited for party advantage, while eager journalists go all-out to blazon the affair under loud headlines for a public eager to read all the details. This has happened time and again, but the most notorious of recent instances was the Profumo case. It had its bizarre and its deplorable aspects, but it aroused a commotion that was quite out of proportion to its significance, magnified as it was by the fierce light that beats on men holding political office. Such men cannot enjoy the relative indifference to their neighbor's doings that in general characterizes our mixed urbanized societies.

Human beings are gregarious as well as social. They have always lived in organized clusters, and that means under authority. It was a condition of security, convenience, and order. In quite simple societies the pervasive authority was custom, presided over and interpreted at need by a headman, a group of elders, and sometimes a priest, a holy man or "medicine man." Custom had its own sanctity. With little diversity of occupation or of interest, there was less call for privacy, except for furtive lovers or perhaps an occasional cabal. There was besides little opportunity for privacy, as everyone was a near and rather exposed neighbor of everyone else.

In view of these comments, let us first state what we mean by the private life. It means an area of protection from any intrusion, even from those near and dear to us when we so desire, a freedom from prying eyes and eavesdropping ears, an area of protection from unwanted outsiders or snooping authorities, and the right to enjoy such protection so long as there is no clear evidence that one is taking advantage of it for the purpose of contriving some injury to the person or property of others.

Privacy is not merely the privilege of being alone by oneself, when one wishes to escape the presence of others. It applies equally to the meetings of two or more people who want to discuss their common interests or transact their common affairs without any overhearing or observation by others. It applies to communications that are meant only for the ears or eyes of the parties involved. Children need their privacy at least as much as adults. They have their own usages, their own affairs, their own dream worlds. While their privacy has to be limited where there are indications of abuse or harmful directions, too many seniors fail to realize how important it is for the young to have their own area of seclusion for their own affairs. They meddle and fuss and probe in a spirit of mistrust, or because they think they have a right to know every-thing the children are doing or thinking—an attitude that is destructive of mutual confidence.

Privacy is not to be identified with secrecy. We often seek privacy not because we want to conceal what we are doing or planning, but because the freedom from outside observation or participation is a con-dition of our personal integrity. There are moods in which we think best when we are shut out from the world, when the presence of even the dearest friend would be disturbing. There are communications with one who is in rapport with us that would be blunted or even aborted if a third party joined in. Different persons are congenial to us in different contexts, in our brighter and in more troubled hours, in the discussion of different subjects, in consultations about this problem or that. Privacy means the vindication of the integrity of the near group as well as of the individual. There is an emotional tone that sustains the relations of those who are mutually congenial. We need hardly point out how essential it is in the more intimate relations of man and woman, where intrusion is treachery.

The enemies of privacy operate on various fronts. Beside the individual intruder there is the crusader for some negatively moralistic cause, the sort who wants a law against everything of which he dis-approves, the watch-and-ward man, the man who buttonholes you and asks are you for or against. There is the "friend" or the ex-secretary or the former valet of some person of high distinction who writes for profit his "reminiscences" of the great man. There is the public official, local, state, or federal, who uses his office for personal aggrandizement, to gain the headlines, or to give vent to his sadistic impulses, and finds a convenient device to gain these ends through inquisitional investigations into the behavior and beliefs of those who can be accused of some vaguely defined offense, such as being "immoral" or "un-American" or "sub-versive." It is a device that has been employed since ancient times. Was not Socrates brought to trial for "corrupting the youth"? There is the employer, not yet extinct, who wants to know how his employees spend their free time, what meetings they go to, what church they attend.

There are thus two requirements for privacy. One is the level of living. Obviously the well-to-do have opportunities denied to the very poor, to those who live in congested homes in congested quarters, as well as to those who are housed in barrack-like cubicles. The other is the freedom from intrusion, whether it be from inquisitive friends or relatives, who would make your business their business, or from the Big Brother whose agents' eyes are always prowling, from the vigilantes who shop around for nonconformists, from the local band of worthies who clamor against "pernicious" books in the school library and are never so happy as when they ferret out some little "scandal" they can gossip over.

The small town or compact village, especially if it is remote from any great center, is of all locations the most hostile to privacy. One reason why the young want to migrate from it is to escape its censorious attitude. The great city has many men of many minds, and diversities of customs and ways of life abound. It is easier to escape the neighbor's attention, while frequently enough neighbors are quite indifferent to the presence of one another.

The notion that in the great open spaces men could live their own lives without much regard for what their neighbors thought, that the spirit of the frontier was one of aggressive independence, that while the pioneer was generous in helping a neighbor in trouble he went his own way and thought his own thoughts—such a notion is remarkably far from the reality. Whatever may have been the case in the rough mining camps that attracted footloose fortune seekers, the settlers on the land, from the first colonies in New England to the covered-wagon pioneers were for the most part subject to a rigidly enforced discipline. The latter were often groups representing "dissenting" sects, Baptists and Presbyterians and Methodists who felt constrained under the establishment, but the religious freedom they sought was for their own brethren in the faith alone. In their new communities, having put down lawless alien elements, they established their own strict orthodoxies. Privacy was very much at a discount. Any presumptuous moral delinquency could bring the offender before the authoritarian tribunal of the church, and the distinction between private and public affairs was little observed. The records are full of such charges as "attending places of vain amusement," intemperance, refusal to pay respect to the church, Sabbath violation, dancing, betting, and so on. All the respectable people belonged to the church and feared its censure. The eyes of the neighbors were upon them, and tale-bearing was not discouraged.

The city has always been the nurse of the ampler freedoms. Democracy is a transplant from the city and, tender shoot that it is, it is harder to cultivate along the countryside. The city mitigates pretensions, claims of privilege that have no relation to capacity. The city with its ceaseless mobility diminishes the significance of neighborhood—for better and for worse. But one consequence is that neighbors take little concern for one another and are the less likely to pry into one another's affairs. Except in an occasional slum area they don't sit around of an evening and talk about the people down the street. People who live next door to one another in an apartment house often have no more acquaintance than an occasional "good morning." Nobody lies awake at night thinking of his neighbor's sins or sorrows.

Different peoples vary not only in their regard for privacy but also in their views on what they wish to keep private and what they are willing to let the outsider know, hear, or see. To take an elementary indication, different peoples vary widely in the amount of bodily covering they think to be proper. There is also great variation between the attitudes on this matter of the same people as the generations pass. In Victorian times, in most Anglo-Saxon communities, and possibly most of all in England, ladies went bathing dressed from neck to ankles. Today in some communities "bikinis" and "g-strings" are tolerated; in others they are taboo. No doubt these differences are symptomatic of other differences in moral conceptions. Another significant variant is the extent to which acquaintances or friends are invited to visit the home. The French on the whole have been reticent in this respect. "The Englishman's home is his castle," but the castle is open to members of the right class. The American again is typically outgoing in the range and readiness of his hospitality. He is also unusually ready to tell outsiders and even chance acquaintances about his doings and his problems—and to inquire, but in a quite friendly way, into theirs.

A broader and more pervasive moral change is expressed in attitudes toward sex, and more obviously in the willingness to talk somewhat openly about personal sex relationships. The change is by no means universal but it is noticeable in the younger generation and in the formerly very reserved and "prudish" middle class, at least in the more urbanized areas. It is part of the same revolution that has filled the bookstores with sexy novels and books about sexual adjustments and practices, volumes that not long ago were or would have been banned. Another indication is the openness of petting and the relative frequency of premarital affairs among teenagers, who often enough are ready to let their freinds know about it. There is no invasion of privacy indicated here, but only a change of viewpoint as to what should be kept private.

The real offense to human dignity and honor is the wanton intrusion of officialdom or of a prying public into the life of the individual over matters that have no necessary relation to the preservation of order and peace. Churches established in power have been among the worst offenders. They have harried and persecuted and tortured people who did not subscribe to their theology, violating the elementary liberty of men to think for themselves. Governments have lent their aid, and in many other ways have been hostile to the moral rights of those who refused to surrender their integrity. While the privacy of religious belief is reasonably well-established in various lands, there is still considerable harassment of those who espouse some other forms of belief, political or moral. Our own country has in recent times been unhappily prominent in such activities. People have been denounced and publicly branded as "subversive," people who in their youthful years believed in the gospel of deliverance preached by the Communists and later, no matter how much they have changed their viewpoint, have been grilled by some federal or state "Un-American Activities" Committee which has insisted they expose their associates of that earlier time, accusing them of "contempt of court" if they refuse to divulge the names. Some have been imprisoned on that account, others, because of the resulting publicity, have lost their jobs. This outrage on the private life reached its peak under the notorious Senator McCarthy. Some of our greatest men were accused of un-American behavior, men like General Marshall and even that most innocent gentleman, Eisenhower, at the time President of Columbia University (in a report by the fumbling committee of a Far Western state). The most famous comedian who ever resided in the United States was treated with obloquy because he had associated with a Communist or two. It was after he had been condemned on a moral charge against patent evidence, and as a consequence of these humiliations he left our shores. The heyday is past, the well-fanned panic has subsided, but some of these committees, including the bellwether of them all, the House Committee on Un-American Activities, still operates with scarcely clipped authority. People are still being sentenced under contempt-of-court charges, including, for example, a faithful clergyman who ran in all good will an organization devoted solely to the cause of peace.

Dictators have little regard for privacy, but it is pennanted on the masthead of democracy. Respect for the private life is of the very essence of democracy, though some of our loud defenders of the faith betray it. As Justice Brandeis put it, the makers of the Constitution conferred on people the right to be let alone, "the most comprehensive of rights and the right most valued by civilized men." Autocratic rulers, fussy jacks-in-office, narrow-minded moralists, and busybody "patriots" conspire in their various ways to sap privacy by edicts, legal interpretations, and social pressures. There are so many who believe that what they believe is right or proper must be right or proper for those who have different beliefs.

The degree to which we respect the private life is an index of civilization. It cannot be safeguarded by the Constitution alone, by an establishment of civil rights alone. Such respect must be rooted in the attitudes of the people, in mutual tolerance and trust. Privacy is in the first place an admirable social convention, based on a regard for personality. Personality, with all its endless variations in man and woman, is the source of everything that has significance in human society. Its expression is the object of every form of art. It is the prime interest of every novel and every play. It is expressed in every creative work of man, in his painting and sculpting and designing and building, as well as in the higher crafts. It makes the difference between one philosopher's thoughts and another's. It is the spice of life, the ground of every deep-reaching enjoyment. Those who would burke it, to enhance their power or to make their own beliefs, their own morals, compulsive for other men, are in that respect still barbarians, no matter what their rank or prowess or prestige.

[Previously unpublished]

The Lottery of Life

38 A man's life-chances are the plaything of a thousand forces. Here we shall limit our consideration to the lot he draws in the world of work. We speak of equal opportunity for all men, of the career open to talents. It is the ideal of democracy, it will never be the reality of democracy. Some simple souls who have done well by themselves believe that the "best" man will always come to the top. How little they comprehend the luck of the draw, the snags and pitfalls, the misadventures and accidents, the arbitrary preferments, the curryings for favor, the casual meetings and missings, the class and clique manipulations, the drag of poverty or crushing obligations, that conspire against the recognition of quality and the quest for excellence. Talent, once given the opportunity to develop, will usually make some headway; hardheaded enterprise will usually win some degree of success. But chance and circumstance combine with the folkways and the foibles of men to thrust the equation of merit and reward into the never-never land of pious dreams.

We can take some comfort in the thought that the relation of talent to opportunity is certainly more positive today than it was in the caste-bound ages mankind is passing beyond. There was little of a lottery about it in the good old days. During that broad span of human history a man's lot was in essentials determined before his birth. Anyone born in the lower class had only a minimal chance of rising to the higher, even to its lowest grade, when birth was identified with quality and the red blood of the noble was blue. The low-born remained illiterate, impoverished, dedicated to the soil. He was born to his station, that of his parents and forebears. If he had the capacity for enterprise it was aborted; if he had native talent it had scant opportunity to show itself.

The doors of opportunity have been opening more widely. In the more advanced countries the barriers have been lowered for the dispossessed and the victims of discrimination, so that the nimble climber may make his way upward. The two-thirds of the world's population that recently were the humble subjects of overlords or colonial powers, serfs and peons, hewers of wood and drawers of water for the privileged, are now in full insurgence, engaged with the clumsy business of establishing some degree of self-government, but anyhow becoming men in their own right. Educational advantages are being extended more widely and more amply, and education itself is being delivered from some of its obfuscations, formalities, and biases. The ramparts of privilege no longer exclude ability from attaining some of the positions of distinction or importance for which it is qualified.

Signal as these advances are, the ideal of equality of opportunity, as of any other significant kind of full equality, remains visionary. The most superficial survey suffices to show that the correspondence between fitness and function, capacity and office, merit and advancement, is sketchy and often glaringly out of joint. The disparity between ability and station is far greater than can be attributed simply to the operation of prejudice and self-interest. Many never enter the race who might become front runners. Many are left behind because through bad upbringing or poor schooling their incentive was narrowed or misdirected. Many are diverted from the way of achievement by one or another besetting temptation or tangle of circumstances or by some mental quirk, perhaps stemming back to the misadventures of childhood.

There is no measuring tape that could tell us what percentage of jobs calling for some particular type of skill is allocated to the best qualified available persons. No doubt it would vary greatly for different areas of service. Who are in the running? Who have had the chance to qualify? Who are near or dear to the choosers? Who has recommended whom, and why? So many considerations other than special fitness may enter into the decision. While in various areas, including professional and executive positions, some standard of competence is a necessary condition of appointment or promotion, there are other quite important areas in which the criterion of fitness is often enough a minor consideration. Politics is a happy hunting-ground for many whose qualifications for office are sadly inferior, unless we regard as qualifications the ability to appeal to mass prejudice or to follow the dictates of strong interest-groups. We can all cite cases in which the smooth-tongued demagogue, some plausible stand-patter, or some evangelistic ignoramus defeated far more capable candidates of office in local or state or federal elections. Let us avoid any invidious selection and choose an example from an earlier time. After the fall of the Whigs in 1852, at a time when the issue of the extension of slavery into the new territories was becoming inflamed, the curious party of the know-nothings was formed, members of a secret club whose existence they denied—hence their name. They sought to divert attention from the perilous realities the country was facing by raising the issue of "Un-Americanism," so unhappily revived in our own times. They had no policy that had any relevance to the then grave problems of government. But they secured 43 seats in the Congress, and within one year had elected the governors of seven states.

To the mythical visitor from Mars it would no doubt be an interesting piece of earthly folklore to report that modern man is so avid to devise and to install the most efficient machinery for the production of cans and cars and cocktail shakers, while he pays only the most perfunctory regard for the efficiency of the services that are entrusted with his social and political well-being. In these latter areas the requisite qualities of public interest and trained judgment are so often bypassed for consider-ations of expediency, of group advantage, of social connections or mere-tricious popularity, of favors rendered or anticipated, of nepotism, of irrelevant distinctions.

So we elect men as judges because they have been political hacks, although they may be lacking in discretion and ignorant of jurisprudence. And we send some men to Congress who are tub-thumpers, yeamen, interest-mongers, gospellers, men more greedy for power than competent to use it. By a happy accommodation to conditions there are good men and true who do win out, and it may be fortunate that this happens some-what more often on the higher levels of policy-making.

Here again the element of lottery comes in. Some men of ability do make the grade. The United States, for example, has had some out-standing Presidents, some of modest caliber, and some whose place in the great roll-call is a blur of ineptitude. Some natural leaders do rise to eminence in their respective fields. Young scholars of high promise have a good chance of maturing into distinguished contributors in their chosen areas—for here the tests for recognition are more equitable than in the arena of public life. Some men of high professional capacity do achieve the coveted honors of advancement and influence. But over the range of public or private service there are the others, equally well-endorsed, who falter and fail to reach their goal—for whatever reason, accident, nonrecognition at a crucial stage, temperamental maladjustment, misguidance, a slip of some kind, discrimination, some consequence of poor upbringing.

At every stage on the march to position, authority, and recognition, some of the talented are stopped in their tracks. Some are stopped by their vices, some by their virtues. In many situations subordinates can be too honest, too free-minded, too honorable, they will not fawn on their superiors or lend themselves to gross chicanery. Some bosses prefer blind obedience to intelligent initiative, some are jealous of strong subordinates, lest they turn into rivals. Power drives higher up the line may mean an adverse selection down the line. Personal squabbles among the directors can oust effective members and damage their careers. Institutional systems, from party machines to university boards of trustees, have some tendency to look for "safe and sound" men to entrust with the responsibility of administering their affairs, in preference to men fertile in ideas and critically discerning who might disturb the *status quo*.

So it often happens that "the race is not to the swift, nor the battle to the strong." There is no umpire to assure that the running is fair, no judge to rule that the best man wins. The ablest contender is like a man who in a sweepstake holds a ticket on an odds–on favorite, but the horse may be scratched before the race or an outsider may come in first.

If there is no assurance that proven merit may find its befitting role, the case is much more precarious for yet undeveloped talent. Many so endowed will be unable to "break their birth's invidious bar and grasp the skirts of happy chance." For multitudes sheer poverty and the pressure of circumstance will level out aspiration and prevent the emergence of native worth. For others, the irrational brand of skin color or disesteemed origin or minority faith will keep many doors closed and put concerted impediments before formally open doors. There are so many disadvantages in the environment of the disprivileged poor, so many cultural stigmata, that only the most valiant and lucky-starred among them can ever vindicate their quality.

Under any decently efficient social order all the young would have freely accessible to them the amount and kind of education requisite for the evocation and the development of their capacities. Wherever talented youth are denied the opportunity to fulfill their promise, the waste is unqualified and irredeemable. One indication of this wastage is presented in the following figures.

"If we take the youth of the country with an I.Q. of 110 and over, it appears that about 46 per cent complete high school but do not go on to college; another 11 per cent enter college, but do not complete a four-year program; about a third graduate from college, and 10 per cent do not even finish high school. Less than half of the youth capable of acquiring a college degree do not enter college, and two-fifths of those who enter do not graduate. For every youngster who graduates from high school with the ability to earn a Ph.D. degree, there are another 25 who do not. Only 1 out of every 300 women with intellectual ability to earn a doctoral degree actually does so."[1]

If this is the situation in a country more amply provided with colleges and universities than any other, how vast must be the gap between native potentiality and educational opportunity in those many lands where education on any level beyond the most elementary is still the prerogative of the few! The consequent wastage of human quality and of the advancement of living is beyond all reckoning.

We have been citing figures concerning the loss of educational opportunity as being the most obvious and most available criterion of this wastage. Incidentally, we are not assuming that formal education, of prime importance as it is, offers the only avenue to achievement. There are enough examples of men who have made names for themselves, not only in business but also in the creative arts, without having passed through the academic gates. Still less are we assuming that the attainment of an academic degree is necessarily a better or even as good a qualification for a business or a political career, as compared with the appropriate apprenticeship in those arenas themselves. The Ph.D. degree is the cachet of the professional educator, for whatever it may be worth, but some of the greatest contributors to learning have got on quite happily without undergoing the laborious process of satisfying a group of meticulous examiners that they have compiled a sum of information concerning some small nook in the vast world of knowledge.

But the broad conclusion is unassailable. Without adequate education the vast majority are condemned to lives of penury and hardship, resourceless and bereft of opportunity. Without proper education they lack the discipline of the mind, the training of the faculties, the leverage for advancement. Not less important is the role education plays, education in the home as well as education in the school, in the process of enlightenment, in broadening the range of awareness and interest, which means the enrichment of living. A further consideration is that modern technology and modern social organization call for more intensive training than was necessary for effective participation in the work-a-day-world in older times. All barriers to education are enemies of civilization itself.

The son of a day laborer has about one-fiftieth of the chance to be listed in *Who's Who* that holds for the son of a parson or a lawyer. It would take the blandest complacence to assume that so gross a dis-

---

1. Henry David, "Manpower Problems and Education," in H. David (ed.), *Education and Manpower* (New York, 1960).

parity is due to the inferior heredity of the former. The children of sheer poverty among ourselves have still probably a better chance of rising to a position of importance than have the great majority of those who are born in the more undeveloped countries throughout the world.

As a result of the upheavals and insurgences of our times the lot of the disprivileged is nearly everywhere beginning to improve. And the momentum of these changes may still have a long way to go.

There is one great area in which the process of emancipation has a special character. For a good half of the human race it was assumed, until relatively recently, even by the most advanced and cultured peoples, that their life-function was simply to rear children, run the household, nurse the sick, and satisfy the sexual demands of the male. They were not supposed to have the talents requisite for the rough and tumble of the outside world. There were indeed a few queens who demonstrated the ability to rule, but that was by the grace of God and royal blood. Aside from these there was the one woman out of the millions of her sex who through some remarkable encounter with destiny broke through the trammels to reach greatness, a few saints and prophetesses, a Sappho, a Boadicea, a Joan of Arc. Only in our own age have women gained access on a broad scale to many of the occupational echelons formerly monopolized by the male, and the invasion is still far from being ended.

Across the record of history one barrier after another to the evocation of human capacities has been reduced, through revolts, mass protests, secessions, and long struggles, the seizing of the new opportunities of the changing times, a process greatly stimulated by the growing command over resources and the development of new powers over nature that could not be monopolized, so that the career open to talent has been made available to far larger numbers. A social environment has thus been created that is more favorable to the liberation of quality. The range of prejudice and disprivilege, of oppression and spoliation, has been restricted and subjected to more controls. But the life-chances of multitudes still encounter grave obstacles, beset by the conceit of power, by poverty and wretched education, by bureaucratic rituals, by the high hand of wealth and station, by the sicknesses of body and of mind that squalor, ignorance, and social impotence bring in their trail.

We have been dwelling on the inferior life-chances of the disprivileged poor. The odds that a child of theirs will win one of the prizes in life's lottery are greatly inferior to those for a child born to well-to-do parents. This obvious fact suggests the inadequacy of the lottery metaphor. In any decently-run lottery the selection of the prize winners is left wholly to the luck of the draw. The management does nothing to manipulate the result. Luck, which is merely our name for the happy or unhappy result of conjunctures we cannot foresee or predict, does play a part, as it does for all mortals. But the life-chances of social beings are to a considerable extent dependent on the organization of society. In the competitive societies of industrial countries the chances for the poor are somewhat improved; no doubt in a utopian society the adverse effects of environment would be nearly eliminated. Unquestionably, the equalization of social opportunity would mean the fullest conservation of the greatest of all our assets, our human resources, for their own sake and for the contribution they could make to social well-being eliminating the wastage and friction of all kinds of discrimination.

There would still remain the inevitable play of circumstance, the hazards of fortune, the favorable or unfavorable tides of affairs, the casual conjunctures that determine human associations, the slips and misunderstandings that make plans go awry, the arbitrary misuses of delegated power, and the whirl of emotions and interests that eddies around all significant decisions.

[Previously unpublished]

The Assault on Poverty

39 "The poor ye have always with you." That saying expressed
what when it was uttered was an ineluctable fact, if by the
poor we mean the poverty-stricken, the destitute, people
who lived on the lowest subsistence level and often enough
sank below it into the pit of misery and starvation. Practically
all societies were composed of a smallish elite, enjoying or
abusing the good things of life, and a much greater mass of
the poor. The rapacity and the inhumanity of the rich elite
often meant the greater oppression of the poor but it was
not the main cause of poverty. That was due to the simple
fact that there were not enough developed resources to
provide a decent livelihood for the population. Malthus
correctly emphasized one aspect of this fact, when he pointed
out that because reproduction proceeded at a higher rate
than the supply of food could be increased, population
would always outrun subsistence—unless something happened. And what had hitherto happened was the ravage of
disease and malnutrition—and war. Malthus's doctrine still
holds in principle, but so many important changes have
occurred since he wrote at the end of the eighteenth century
that now for the first time in human history the abolition of
abject poverty is not only in sight but depends entirely on
the policies of nations and the intelligence of men. The

abolition of such poverty is now a primary responsibility that falls upon us Americans and the other industrially advanced peoples.

What has made possible this primary revolution in human society is the advance of science and technology, a process that has been gaining momentum since the end of the eighteenth century. Although the population of the earth has vastly increased during this period, most notably in recent decades, it is beyond any reasonable doubt that with the productivity now available, every human being on this earth today could be assured the most elementary of all opportunities for a decent life, the abolition of abject poverty, by the devotion of our present resources to the attainment of this goal. With proper direction, including imaginative planning by an international council, the age-old plague of utter poverty could at length be ended, and all men across the earth could enter into the heritage of freedom from want.

There is no question that the means are available. Present productivity is ample. The capacity of the industrial plant we possess and the resources available to build new plants in the less prosperous lands could provide the equipment, the schools, the houses, the accessories necessary for reasonable comfort, for all men. The United States is embarrassed by the surpluses of food supplies it stores or wastes, and agricultural productivity could be vastly stepped up in the backward countries. With the prospective development of atomic power, the desert could be made to blossom like the rose.

But there remain formidable obstacles in the way of so desirable a fulfillment, not material obstacles but social and cultural ones. The preliminary obstacle is the inertia, the lack of imagination, the lack of concern, on the part of the peoples who have the resources requisite for the accomplishment of the great liberation. In a word, there is lacking a concerted sense of responsibility. We do not really feel we are our brothers' keepers. Our imaginations are not aroused to the benefits it would bring. The well-being of others is not seriously our concern. We are not touched by the misery other men endure, the needless stunting and maiming of life, the denial of opportunities to develop capacities, the pitiless unavailing struggle in swarming squalor. It is true that as a nation we have taken the lead in providing technical and economic aid to undeveloped countries, and that is so far a signal advance. But our aid is spasmodic, not coordinated, and in considerable measure motivated and limited by strategic considerations, one aspect of a "cold war" competition for allies. We need a five-year or a ten-year or a fifty-year plan in consort with all nations willing to cooperate, no matter on what side they are, a foresighted plan geared to the world-wide abolition of destitution and starvation. And the responsibility of all of us is to answer this call and bring our influence to bear on our policy-makers to work and plan, to promote in the councils of the United Nations a sustained campaign for the establishment of a great design to end this abject poverty. To aid in this endeavor is a high responsibility of our spiritual leaders.

We have reached the stage where old concepts of charity and almsgiving no longer apply. In a world where poverty was endemic, rooted in the nature of things, all that good will could achieve was charitable aid to the immediate needy of their neighborhood, a mere alleviation of distress. Beneficence did not touch the multitudes who drew a meager pittance from the soil they cultivated with their simple implements and who were at the mercy of drought and hail and floods and the ravage of locusts and the blight that came upon their crops. But now that technological advance has made the most distant peoples our neighbors, in such wise that our own fate is linked to theirs, now that our affluence includes the potential to inaugurate a situation in which all peoples can enjoy the minimum condition of a life no longer oppressed by sheer want and the ceaseless fear of want, charity in the old sense is outmoded and the call is for systems of economic equipment that in the mutual give-and-take of a world economic order will enable the hitherto helpless peoples to attain and maintain their own economic security. There will always be the need for the spirit of generosity and neighborly benevolence, but it will act on a higher and happier level.

Such is the attainable prospect, but again we must turn to the serious obstacles that stand in the way. Let us assume that the affluent and relatively affluent countries are ready to undertake an inclusive program for the abolition of sheer poverty, there would remain a whole series of problems. Many of these are rooted in the social concomitants of age-long poverty, the attitudes it breeds, the reactions it stimulates, the accommodations of habits and social usages, the whole environment that has grown responsive to it. Let us begin with an illustration for our own society. We still tolerate clusters of poverty, the slums of our cities, decaying mining towns, the huddled Negro shack-towns of the South. So long as people live in such areas they will remain in poverty, no matter what else is done to aid them. If we are to abolish poverty in the United States, we must abolish the slums and we must assure that the slum mentality is not transferred to the housing developments with which we replace the slums. The habituation to slum conditions has a powerful influence on those who have been subjected to them, thwarting their ambitions, lowering their aspirations, dimming their expectations, for only thus can they find life tolerable. They take refuge in substitute makeshift satisfactions. The young, being more exposed to the values and aspirations of the more prosperous classes, being educated in the formulas of what is called the American way of life, learn soon enough that the road is barred by their background and their slum environment, and still too frequently by ethnic discrimination, and accordingly they become frustrated and rebellious, ready to assert their claims in illegitimate ways, for example, by joining in gangs whose honorific titles, Knights or Noble Englishmen or Dragons and so forth, reveal their yearning for the status that is denied them. The moral whereof is that material aid alone will not suffice to lift to higher standards groups which have learned the habituations of poverty. Above all, the young must be given training and guidance for new responsibilites, new tasks, and new opportunities.

Similar considerations apply when we bring aid to poverty-stricken peoples whose culture and ways of thought are quite unlike our own. But here the giving of aid is surrounded by embarrassing difficulties, so that to be effective it must be only an aspect of a larger policy that demands not only skillful strategy but also wisdom. The strategy is necessary because otherwise the material aid will not serve its purpose. It will be put to wrong uses, it will be diverted into wrong hands, it will give the elite new means to dominate. Nor is technical aid a sufficient concomitant. The aid must be administered by supervisors who know the conditions and who at the same time have a proper respect for the struggling humanity they deal with. Here, too, is where wisdom is necessary. For when you bestow funds you introduce changes, work changes, habit changes, changes in expectations that may have, unless wisely directed, a serious effect on morals. The values and standards of a people inevitably are related to the conditions they have experienced. We have had many instances in the past in which the introduction of new resources, in the wake of industrial exploitation, has wrought havoc in the morale and integrity of native peoples. Even missionaries, dedicated to the redemption of such peoples, have misguidedly had the effect of demoralizing them. We should never try to do anything for people unless we can do it with them, so as to preserve their dignity, their own sense of values, while contributing to a new prosperity.

Beyond all the other impediments to the abolition of poverty there looms what has now become the most formidable menace of our times. Everybody is now aware, however vaguely, of what is called the "population explosion," but relatively few seem to realize its significance. The facts, however, are plain and incontrovertible. Until recent decades the birth rate and the death rate were more or less in balance, with gradual increases in the population as countries became industrialized and thus more productive. Birth rates were high but so were death rates. All that has changed. At the present rate of increase the population of the earth will double in some thirty years, an utterly unprecedented thing. Project that increase over two centuries more, and the population of the earth, now somewhat over three billion, will become five hundred billion. You may say that such projections are visionary, but they will certainly not be, unless mankind learns to control the situation. Already the prospect of betterment that industrial development offers to the peoples of Asia and Africa and Latin America is being dissipated by increased multiplication. The increase is due to conditions that will not change in any calculable future. It is due to what science has achieved, especially medical science, the control of contagious and infectious disease, the vast reduction of infant mortality, the introduction of effective sanitation and hygiene. Over the whole earth the rate of mortality is being reduced, the span of life extended. Even in the past twenty years the death rate has in many countries been cut in two, from a range between seventeen and twenty-five to one between seven and twelve. No change has more potential significance for all around well-being, for the liberation of mankind from the age-old oppression of misery and wasting disease. But the benefit, the new amenity of life, the opportunity to realize capacities, the higher standard of living, will be negated by the ever tightening pressure of population. It is nonsense to speak as though new sources of an increasing food supply will solve the problem, and even if it could, the density of population, should the present rate continue, would in two centuries turn the earth into a continuous barracks, with no green countryside. But long before then dire disasters would befall the pent-up peoples.

In a word, if we are to abolish poverty, mankind must deal effectively with the problem of overpopulation. It is now a prime responsibility, and for all of us there is the responsibility to recognize the facts, to support the movement for its recognition and the consequent steps to protect our heritage and our future.

Thus far we have been sketching the background conditions under which we must work if the now attainable goal of the abolition of poverty is to be approached. It calls for action on many levels. On the international scale there must be sustained and concerted action to provide the apparatus and the capital that will enable the great poverty-stricken areas to reach economic self-sufficiency, in accordance with a plan that will assure the effective utilization of these new resources while still enabling them to retain their self-respect and their cultural integrity. On the national scale it calls for the assurance of social security to all who are unable to earn a livelihood and would suffer without it the miseries of destitution. But it calls for more than that. It calls for adequate early training and guidance, with proper regard for capacity, for neglected and retarded and culturally impoverished youth. It calls for special measures for unemployed youth, as well as for all ranks of the unemployed. And it calls for the abolition of the degrading discrimination that numbs the aspirations and stunts and distorts the native abilities of millions of colored persons. Let no one think that such measures are a mere cost, a burden on the taxpayer. Even if they were, they would be worth it. But in truth the net cost is nothing or negligible. For where there is destitution there is more disease, more wastage, more crime—and these are costly to the state. In our study of delinquency in New York City we found that the areas of high delinquency were the areas not only of the worst poverty but also those where tuberculosis and other diseases were most rife, where there were more admissions to mental clinics, and more of a whole array of other sociopathological conditions, all of which are a wasteful and heavy price for our lack of responsibility. What the city fails to do, what government fails to do, is what we fail to do.

[1965]

The Unbalance of Our Times

40 When the world is shaken by climactic events, social man reacts to the shock in devious ways, ways more responsive to his feelings than to his reasoning powers. The revolutions, world-embracing wars, genocides, international tension, menacing new disasters, that have affected our times routed the complacencies of the ongoing social life, struck at long-cherished beliefs, and gave a shriller note to the nimble-witted interpreters of the times. The new note accented the social distemper, the disruption of morale, the murky experience of the late business of killing, the blank meaninglessness of aspiration in a world where millions could be blotted out in holocausts that made no distinction of age or sex, of valor or cowardice, of good or evil.

The end of it all had not been peace but the threat of a yet more terrible sword. In the aftermath of confusion victors joined with losers whom they had recently regarded as demonic. A new line of sharply hostile division ran across the whole earth, both sides embattled under the false flags of irreconcilable ideologies. Science gave to the strife a peculiar new significance by arming the opposing forces with a weapon that destroyed all prospects of victory for either side. What kind of a world had we inherited when it could be turned into mere desolation because some superheated general had blundered and given the order to shoot or some nuclear-armed airman had misread his signals, a world in which the embattled powers were feverishly striving to have the edge in overkill and which had been brought to the very brink on that account, while the peoples waited in hushed suspense for the next bulletin concerning Cuba?

At the beginning of the twentieth century, after an unusually long period of relative peace, the minds of men were geared to the idea of progress, with increasing prosperity in a peaceful world. The industrialized peoples were wholly averse to great wars, though aristocratic power-holders clung to the old military doctrines. World War I came upon them with a profound shock, and they had scarcely recovered from it when the evil legacy of the "settlement" that ended it bred the nationalistic fanatic who set the world afire in an even more slaughterous blaze.

Were human beings fully rational, were a majority of them sufficiently awakened to the causes of the disasters that had befallen them, they would have resolved and cooperated to put an end to the system, or lack of system, that in the last resort was responsible for it all. For a brief spell at the end of the war there was a surge in this direction. But the planning of the United Nations was skewed and emasculated from the beginning. The victorious sovereignties would yield nothing of their putative sovereign power. Might was for them still the word that was in the beginning and would be to the end. So the major concern of the great states became again offensive-defensive armaments within opposing alliances.

The cumulative tensions of a world beset by old and new troubles had inevitable effects on the moods and responses of men, more directly on the more imaginative, the more creative, and the more neurotic. Characteristically they reacted far less to the constructive demands of a disrupted age than to their need to express the feelings its disruption aroused in them. The spirit of disillusionment, of negation, of discontent with the whole heritage of man, prevailed. The confidence of the faithful in a divine providence was discomfited—the rain of bombs had fallen implacably on the just and the unjust. If it could be claimed that the side of righteousness had won, it was only to give new impetus to even more deadly unrighteousness. Pent-up feelings found expression in iconoclasm. The time was out of joint and it was vanity to think it could be set right. So they adjusted themselves to a vastly disturbed world by cultivating disturbance over the whole range of cultural expression, in the arts of painting, music, sculpture, in drama and the novel, in philosophy and religion. We use the word "disturbance" in a descriptive and not a derogatory sense. They rejected tradition and history as "irrelevant" to the present. The sense of violence and discord was conveyed in the manner in which they forsook old conceptions of order and harmony and beauty and propriety. In the eternal struggle within the arts between conservative and innovating tendencies the latter were wholly triumphant. The pendulum that in other times moved gradually back and forth now swung sharply over to one extreme. The general malaise provided the opportunity for a complete breakaway from the past. We may perhaps regard this whole new movement as a protest, in symbolic form, against the complaisance and submissiveness with which the peoples had been herded by their leaders into the abyss.

In good times men cling to the established ways. The prosperous always do, and in good times they legislate from a position of strength. Reforms may take place, but gradually and modestly. But after earthshaking storms a correspondingly violent change of attitude occurs. This movement, however, may be oblique to the need for change the disaster of the storms revealed. In good times the ills many still endure tend to be minimized. In troubled times, when emotion runs high, there is a tendency to expose to the utmost the depths of misery that fester beneath the social veneer. Drama and novel revel in depicting the sordidness and abject squalor of the conditions under which human beings are reduced to a merely animal existence. But this spirit of protest is quite different from that of the reformer of more tranquil times. The latter is realistic in presenting the disgrace of the slums, the wretchedness and exploitation of the underpaid, undernourished, and miserably housed children of poverty, and the callousness of the well-to-do who suffer such conditions to exist—we refer, for example, to Booth's study of London and Rowntree's of York and the writings of Sidney and Beatrice Webb and the pamphlets of the Fabian Society. Now the indictment includes man as well as his evil environment, and delights in the portrayal of the lusts and greeds and cruelties, the rapings and promiscuities and dopings and wanton mayhem that may be found in the lives of the poor. And for a kind of companion picture we get the vice and arrogance, the machinations and the hypocrisies and self-indulgences of, say, the dwellers in some well-to-do suburb or New England town.

The cultural manifestations of the general unbalance necessarily take different forms according to the medium of communication. It is different in literature with a more or less popular appeal, the novel and the drama, from what it is in current philosophical approaches, different again in such creative arts as music, painting, and sculpture. In the literary area the target is human nature itself. A large number of the new writers might have been called "muckrakers" by a former generation. But the difference is more significant than the resemblance. The earlier writers were concerned with political and economic corruption and called loudly for reform. The new writers would probe to the quick of human nature itself. They revel in unmasking the naked ugliness of life, the earthiness of sex urges, the grubby eruptions of ambitions, reducing values to elementary lusts, exposing the bankruptcy of aspiration, the sensual activism of conduct, futile adventures that end in dust and ashes. In this frame of slick adulteries and drab and shabby greeds, death itself is nothing but the final ugliness.

Some authors who might be placed in this category plumb the social depths in order to expose the consequences of a particular social evil, as, for example, James Baldwin does in *Another Country*. So also, when William Faulkner depicts the slovenly neurotic decadence of his white folk in the Deep South he is in effect indicting a social order that will not brace itself to inevitable change. Some other authors have found a curious symbolic way to indicate the wrongheadedness of our pathetic hopes. They tantalize us with tales of vain yearning for release from some impending evil in a nightmarish society or of vain expectation of the approach of some rescuer or guiding spirit. In the latter case the forlorn numbly look for some Godot to appear. The former type found its first and most notable expression in the novels of Kafka, in *The Castle*, for example, and even more subtly in *The Trial*, where an innocent man is accused of an unrevealed crime in a crazily bureaucratic society of irrational frustrations, so that he suffers endless bafflements and is never allowed to answer to the unknown charge against him, until at length two top-hatted strangers take him away and stab him in the heart. The post-World War I intimations of the contemptuous irrationality of the power that rules the affairs of men had an even stronger appeal for the post-World War II generation.

The more characteristic literature of this later time is not concerned, however, with such subtle exposure of irrationality. Having known in the experience of wartime how human beings abandon the decencies of civilization, these authors tend to regard such decencies as no more that a veneer, and delight to portray the ugliness and nastiness inherent in human nature. Some, like Mailer, expose it in the soldiers seeking release from or compensation for the tensions and shocks of modern warfare. Others find it in the ordinary goings-on of people. It may be in a quiet New Hampshire town or in the exurbia of New York City. It may be among the expatriates in Paris or the heterogeneous assortment of folk voyaging on the Ship of Fools. They are without goals, without values, without traditions. The human animal thus pictured has few redeeming qualities, not even the nobler vices. The satisfactions men pursue are consumed in petty gratifications, leaving them a prey to tensions from which they find no release.

In the realm of the fine arts the aspect of imbalance is mitigated by the necessity of symbolic presentation. The authors we have alluded to are minded to reveal what they take to be the raw reality of human nature. The creative artist has gone to what may seem the opposite extreme, divorcing his work from any attempt to portray things as they appear to the normal eye, and either confining himself to purely abstract forms, sometimes even without benefit of color, or else taking complete liberty in conveying mere suggestions or glimpses of objects in nature or in presenting distorted faces and limbs in a pictorial tangle. After a time of social disruption, in the revulsion from the past, the young artist is moved to attempt bolder innovations, to experiment more freely and more widely, to let his imagination range, and thus, perhaps, to expose the mood or the spirit of the times. All creative art is always new, usually a new variation or fresh interpretation of an old theme, until the trend of variation develops into a new theme, a new style for a new age. When the new style is a sudden birth, preceded by the briefest of gestations, it is likely to be extreme or violent. It can give a remarkable opportunity to the great adventuring artist, but the rank and file who merely follow it exhibit the grotesqueries and crudities of aborted production. We can trace the manner in which the new style was born in the work of one of the great ones, Picasso, a painter of extraordinary resourcefulness, who after early experiments in cubism, found a temporary haven in the beautiful compositions of his "blue" and "rose" periods, until the spirit of a war-torn world seized him and he turned his genius to arrestingly distorted human forms and tangled artistic enigmas, never resting until he gave more direct expression to the significance of war in his well-known "Guernica." The vogue he thus helped to develop inspired some remarkable works, but many of its followers exhibited more license than art. Their lines are abrupt, angular, drastic; the colors are often patchy, blatant, eye-confounding unless they are capricious, monotone drab. If the picture is given a title it requires a strong imagination to see any connection between it and the composition. The work either shouts at you or whispers, but either way it makes sense only to the initiates. It symbolizes the clutching at the immediate, the denudation of values, the rejection of significance, that characterizes the unbalance of our times.

Nowhere is this spirit more remarkably displayed than in certain happenings in the area of music. The music of the western world has been based on the modulations of a particular scale, the octave with its series of eight notes—the eighth having double the frequency of the first and thus becoming the first note of the next higher octave. The magnificent music that developed through the seventeenth, eighteenth and nineteenth centuries maintained this system through all its experiments and styles. In the twentieth century the constant urge of the creative artist to pass beyond the established forms led various gifted composers to seek out new directions, and Schoenberg in particular rejected the seven-tone scale in favor of a twelve-tone one, making all the semitones within the octave equally participant in the scale itself. He had a significant success, composing new music with new harmonics that called for a different way of listening. But the revolutionary avant-garde of the times found an extreme exponent in John Cage, a brilliant mind caught up in the current. The center of a small group of kindred spirits, he came to discard everything we know as music, harmony, counterpoint, sequence, coherence, even the ordinary musical instruments, producing sounds on anything that could give a percussive effect, bits of metal or wood, brake drums, a pressure cooker emitting jets of steam, a screeching sound amplifier, marks on magnetic tape, odds and ends of the junkyard. Between the sounds might come longish intervals of silence, and the succession of sounds was sometimes determined by chance, perhaps the tossing of a coin. When he did use a regular instrument, it was specially "prepared" — the piano, for instance, had wooden pegs fixed between the wires, with pieces of wood or glass inserted here and there.

We cannot surmise whether this iconoclastic radicalism may prove to have some significance in the history of music; if it seems bizarre and brash and chaotic, some musical genius of the future may find in it suggestions for the expansion of the range of positive musical expression. In the present context we take it simply as another manifestation of the same sweeping repudiation of established forms and values that is so characteristic of our times.

In this respect the artistic testimony is in keeping with the trend in philosophy. In former times philosophers wrestled with the great problems of man's place in the cosmos, of the unity to which all things belong, embracing the material and the spiritual, of the knower's relation to the known, and so forth, wholly speculative questions that lie beyond the range of science and tease the ambitious mind. Our age has renounced such philosophizing as futile. A thinker like Bertrand Russell declared such questions have no relation to reality. For him "the universe is all spots and jumps—without continuity, without coherence, or orderliness." One school of philosophers has turned philosophy into a kind of abstract or symbolic logic. Such matters, however, are of interest only to a small esoteric group of professionals, itself a significant indication of the changing times. But every period has its characteristic thought-forms that are reflected in the tone of its distinctive novels and plays and are more explicitly formulated in relatively popular philosophic works. In earlier times popular philosophies were usually associated with or derived from religious or theological doctrines, but religion has lost much of its authority with the intellectuals who now formulate such philosophies.

The most characteristic philosophy of the passing times is existentialism. It represents more an attitude toward man's life than an articulated system of thought. What is common to the very diverse exponents of existentialism is a mood, a sense of the alienation and sterility that characterize life in our time, with its false conformities and ritual acceptances, with its inner loneliness and homelessness, beset by anxiety and guilt.

It is generally accepted that the existentialistic doctrine owed its origin to a somewhat perplexing and curiously brilliant nineteenth-century thinker, the religious-minded Dane, Sören Kierkegaard. Obsessed by his own sense of guilt he viewed human life as a terrifying mystery, a scene in which man swayed between the pulls of great oppositions, time and the eternal, the finite and the infinite, life and death, the individual and God. Existence then becomes a series of tensions as man is driven by attractions and repulsions, and the result is that its vital tone is anguish (*angst*).

Nearly a century later this doctrine was taken up by two formidable German philosophers, Heidegger and Jaspers. Ignoring its religious element, they translated it into the tragic drama of the breakthrough into fleeting conscious existence which becomes only a flight from death, a brittle uncertainty that has a most certain end, with a haunting fear of the only fulfillment that is possible, the liberty, the return to the whole, which is death.

Being unresponsive to this type of philosophical fancy, I shall not attempt to expound it. What alone concerns us is that a writer of remarkable ability, Jean-Paul Sartre, developed a form of existentialist doctrine that belonged peculiarly to a war-torn age and consequently attracted widespread sympathetic attention. Other writers of the same time, notably Albert Camus, had followed a rather similar line, just as Kafka had done during and after the First World War, but Sartre, though not a philosopher, could take ideas from them, and particularly from Heidegger, and present them with a new slant in his plays and his novels. He is concerned with the "tragic truth of life," with the hostile forces that oppress the individual struggling to be free, with the need to grasp the immediacy and fullness of the present in which alone we live, and with the theme of overshadowing death that ends it all. Life is tension and strife, and full of inanity. But Sartre, a notable figure of the French underground, did have a positive note as well, for he concluded that the man who in the name of justice gives himself to change the world may thus be finding his freedom.

The general tone of existentialism, however, abjures any forward-looking expectations. Instead, it gives a grimmer and more stressful interpretation of the old epicurean adage, seize the day while you have it (*carpe diem*). We move in an alien world of irrational powers. The life-force drives us on in the quest of "being," but the end is always "nothingness." We are thrown back on our own immediate individuality, and it behooves us to live in the day given to us, to absorb ourselves in what life can offer, in sheer experiencing, and thus find the only freedom man can achieve. It is an elusive philosophy, with many variations, if we can call it a philosophy at all. It is, so to speak, refugee thinking, the thinking of men who have been thrust out of the familiar world of their habits and expectations into a world of monstrous violence and irrational hates. It seems like a bad dream, and the writings of Sartre and Camus, and of Kafka before them, have a curious nightmare spell. In the retrospect, at least, we can see them as expressions of a world that had gone wholly out of joint, the best answer these thoughtful and troubled men could give to the agony of an age. They are manifestations of the unbalance of our times—perhaps we can already say: of times that are now passing away.

What is past or is passing has bitten into experience. It lives on in its own momentum, it reverberates in the disoriented lives and thoughts of those who have lived through it. Continuing tremors from the social earthquake may register in the statistics of crime and delinquency or in a succession of *coups d'états* in countries that have suffered disruption or dismemberment or again in the uprisings of subject peoples who find strategic opportunities in a period of general unrest. On the front of the creative arts the shock finds expression in the violence of artistic innovation, in the rejection of established modes and traditional evaluations of excellence, and in the literary depiction of social wastelands and moral morasses. The reflective thinker in his turn attunes his philosophizing to the spirit of the times and prescribes a way of life that might salvage some of the dignity and freedom of the individual in the bleakness of a world of irrationality and negation.

Tension and unbalance go hand in hand. The unbridled violence that commits multitudes to mutual slaughter perverts all moral codes. But the time comes when the violence is stilled and the time follows when the tensions abate. It is then in the retrospect we realize the degree to which catastrophic experience had thrown out of kilter the characteristic cultural exhibits and the social responses of the period. Men may feel that their thoughts are still free when dire compulsions determine their activities, but the freedom itself is distorted by the tensions they cannot escape, even though some of the products of it may be of the highest quality.

This is written when there is a revival of expectations and some relaxation of tension, when there are constructive movements for the emancipation of minorities still subject to repression, when there is more hope that sanity will prevail in the international arena whence alone ultimate violence is to be feared, when therefore new appraisals and new directions may bring again the loose and moving equilibrium that is the only alternative to the unbalance of the times we have been passing through.

[1964]

Bibliography

BOOKS

Community: A Sociological Study. London: Macmillan & Co., 1917. 5th edition, 1965.

Labor in the Changing World. New York: E. P. Dutton & Co., 1919.

The Elements of Social Science. London: Methuen & Co., 1921. 9th edition, 1949.

The Modern State. London: Oxford University Press, 1926. Paperback edition, 1964.

The Contribution of Sociology to Social Work. New York: Columbia University Press, 1931.

Society: Its Structure and Changes. New York: R. Long & R. R. Smith, Inc., 1931. Revised edition, *Society: A Textbook of Sociology.* New York: Farrar & Rinehart, 1937. Rewritten and enlarged edition, with Charles Page, *Society: An Introductory Analysis.* New York: Farrar & Rinehart, 1949.

Leviathan and the People. Baton Rouge, La.: Louisiana State University Press, 1939.

Social Causation. Boston: Ginn & Co., 1942. Revised paperback edition, New York: Harper Torchbooks, 1964.

Towards an Abiding Peace. New York: The Macmillan Co., 1943.

The Web of Government. New York: The Macmillan Co., 1947. Revised edition, 1965. Paperback edition, New York: The Free Press, 1965.

The More Perfect Union. New York: The Macmillan Co., 1948.

The Ramparts We Guard. New York: The Macmillan Co., 1950.

Democracy and the Economic Challenge. New York: Alfred A. Knopf, Inc., 1952.

Academic Freedom in Our Time. New York: Columbia University Press, 1955.
The Pursuit of Happiness. New York: Simon & Schuster, 1955.
The Nations and the United Nations. New York: Manhattan Publishing Co., 1959.
Life: Its Dimensions and Its Bounds. New York: Harper & Brothers, 1960.
The Challenge of the Passing Years. New York: Harper & Brothers, 1962.
    Paperback edition, New York: Pocket Books, Inc., 1963.
Power Transformed. New York: The Macmillan Co., 1964.
The Prevention and Control of Delinquency. New York: Atherton Press, 1966.
As a Tale That Is Told: The Autobiography of R. M. MacIver. Chicago:
    University of Chicago Press, 1968.
Politics and Society. Edited by David Spitz. New York: Atherton Press, 1968.

REPORTS

Economic Reconstruction: Report of the Columbia University Commission. New
    York: Columbia University Press, 1934.
Report on the Jewish Community Relations Agencies. New York: National
    Community Relations Advisory Council, November, 1951.
The Institutionalization of Young Delinquents. Interim Report No. XI, Juvenile
    Delinquency Evaluation Project of the City of New York, December,
    1958. (Nineteen separate reports evaluating various New York City
    agencies and programs were issued by the Juvenile Delinquency Evalu-
    ation Project, directed by MacIver. Except for the report cited here,
    these were composite works and are not, therefore, included in this
    bibliography.)

BOOKS EDITED

FOR THE INSTITUTE FOR RELIGIOUS AND SOCIAL STUDIES (WITH PREFATORY NOTES)

Group Relations and Group Antagonisms. New York: Harper & Brothers, 1944.
Civilization and Group Relationships. New York: Harper & Brothers, 1945.
Unity and Difference in American Life. New York: Harper & Brothers, 1947.
Discrimination and National Welfare. New York: Harper & Brothers, 1949.
Great Expressions of Human Rights. New York: Harper & Brothers, 1950.
Conflict of Loyalties. New York: Harper & Brothers, 1952.
Moments of Personal Discovery. New York: Harper & Brothers, 1952.
The Hour of Insight: A Sequel to Moments of Personal Discovery. New York:
    Harper & Brothers, 1954.
New Horizons in Creative Thinking: A Survey and Forecast. New York: Harper
    & Brothers, 1954.
Great Moral Dilemmas: In Literature, Past and Present. New York: Harper &
    Brothers, 1956.
Integrity and Compromise: Problems of Public and Private Conscience. New York:
    Harper & Brothers, 1957.
Dilemmas of Youth: In America Today. New York: Harper & Brothers, 1961.

The Assault on Poverty: And Individual Responsibility. New York: Harper & Row, 1965.

FOR THE CONFERENCE ON SCIENCE, PHILOSOPHY AND RELIGION IN THEIR RELATION TO THE DEMOCRATIC WAY OF LIFE

Approaches to World Peace. New York: Harper & Brothers, 1944.
Approaches to National Unity. New York: Harper & Brothers, 1945.
Approaches to Group Understanding. New York: Harper & Brothers, 1947.
Conflicts of Power in Modern Culture. New York: Harper & Brothers, 1947.
Learning and World Peace. New York: Harper & Brothers, 1948.
Goals for American Education. New York: Harper & Brothers, 1950.
Perspectives on a Troubled Decade: Science, Philosophy and Religion, 1939-1949. New York: Harper & Brothers, 1950.
Foundations of World Organization: A Political and Cultural Appraisal. New York: Harper & Brothers, 1952.
Freedom and Authority in Our Time. New York: Harper & Brothers, 1953.
Symbols and Values: An Initital Study. New York: Harper & Brothers, 1954.
Symbols and Society. New York: Harper & Brothers, 1955.
Aspects of Human Equality. New York: Harper & Brothers, 1956.

ARTICLES

"The Ethical Significance of the Idea Theory," *Mind*, XVIII (October 1909), 552-569; XXI (April 1912), 182-200.
"Ethics and Politics," *International Journal of Ethics*, XX (October 1909), 72-86.
"Society and State," *Philosophical Review*, XX (January 1911), 30-45.
"War and Civilization," *International Journal of Ethics*, XXII (January 1912), 127-145.
"Do Nations Grow Old?" *International Journal of Ethics*, XXIII (January 1913), 127-143.
"What is Social Psychology?" *Sociological Review*, VI (April 1913), 147-160.
"Society and 'the Individual,'" *Sociological Review*, VII (January 1914), 58-64.
"Institutions as Instruments of Social Control," *Political Quarterly*, No. 2 (May 1914), 105-116.
"The Foundations of Nationality," *Sociological Review*, VIII (July 1915), 157-166.
"Personality and the Suprapersonal," *Philosophical Review*, XXIV (September 1915), 501-525.
"Supremacy of the State," *New Republic*, XII (October 13, 1917), 304.
"The Social Significance of Professional Ethics," *Annals of the American Academy of Political and Social Science*, CI (May 1922), 5-11. Reprinted with some changes in *ibid.*, CCXCVII (January 1955), 118-124.
"Arbitration and Conciliation in Canada," *Annals of the American Academy of Political and Social Science*, CVII (May 1923), 294-298.

"Civilization and Population," *New Republic*, XLV (December 2, 1925), 37-39.
"Trend of Population with Respect to a Future Equilibrium," in Louis I. Dublin (ed.), *Population Problems in the United States and Canada* (Boston: Houghton Mifflin Co., 1926), pp. 287-310.
"The Trend to Internationalism," *Encyclopaedia of the Social Sciences* (New York: The Macmillan Co., 1930), I, 172-188.
"Jean Bodin," *Encyclopaedia of the Social Sciences*, II, 614-616.
"Is Sociology a Natural Science?" *Publications of the American Sociological Society*, XXV (1930), 25-35.
"Is Statistical Methodology Applicable to the Study of the 'Situation'?" *Social Forces*, IX, No. 4 (June 1931), 479.
"The Papal Encyclical on Labor: An Interpretation," *Current History*, XXXIV (July 1931), 481-485.
"Sociology," in D. R. Fox (ed.), *A Quarter Century of Learning 1904-1929* (New York: Columbia University Press, 1931), pp. 62-91.
"Interests," *Encyclopaedia of the Social Sciences* (1932), VIII, 144-148.
"Maladjustment," *Encyclopaedia of the Social Sciences* (1933), X, 60-63.
"Social Pressures," *Encyclopaedia of the Social Sciences* (1934), XII, 344-348.
"Sociology," *Encyclopaedia of the Social Sciences* (1934), XIV, 232-247.
"Social Philosophy," in William F. Ogburn (ed.), *Social Change and the New Deal* (Chicago: University of Chicago Press, 1934), pp. 107-113.
"Graham Wallas," *Encyclopaedia of the Social Sciences* (1935), XV, 326-327.
"The Historical Pattern of Social Change," *Journal of Social Philosophy*, II (October 1936), 35-54. Also in the Harvard Tercentenary Publication, *Authority and the Individual* (Cambridge: Harvard University Press, 1937), pp. 126-153.
"Sociology," *Educator's Encyclopaedia*, 1937.
"The Philosophical Background of the Constitution," *Journal of Social Philosophy*, III (April 1938), 201-209. Also published as "European Doctrines and the Constitution," in Conyers Read (ed.), *The Constitution Reconsidered* (New York: Columbia University Press, 1938), pp. 51-61.
"Survey of the Project," Introduction to H. F. Angus (ed.), *Canada and Her Great Neighbor* (New Haven: Yale University Press, 1938), pp. xi-xxvii.
"The Social Sciences," in *On Going to College* (New York: Oxford University Press, 1938), pp. 121-140.
Introduction to Frank Tannenbaum, *Crime and the Community* (Boston: Ginn & Co., 1938), pp. xi-xiv.
"The Genius of Democracy," *Southern Review*, V (October 1939), 22-41. Reprinted in MacIver, *Leviathan and the People*, Chap. III.
"Calling All Social Sciences," *Survey Graphic*, XXVIII (August 1939), 496-497.
"The Modes of the Question Why," *Journal of Social Philosophy*, V (April 1940), 197-205. Reprinted in MacIver, *Social Causation*, Chap. I.
"The Political Roots of Totalitarianism," in R. M. MacIver, M. J. Bonn, and R. B. Perry, *The Roots of Totalitarianism* (James-Patten-Rowe Pamphlet Series, No. 9. Philadelphia: American Academy of Political and Social Science, 1940), pp. 5-8.
"The Imputation of Motives," *American Journal of Sociology*, XLVI (July 1940),

1-12. Reprinted in MacIver, *Social Causation*, Chap. VII.

"The Meaning of Liberty and Its Perversions," in Ruth N. Anshen (ed.), *Freedom: Its Meaning* (New York: Harcourt, Brace & Co., 1940), pp. 278-287.

"The Nature of the Challenge," in *Science, Philosophy and Religion* (New York: Conference on Science, Philosophy and Religion in Their Relation to the Democratic Way of Life, Inc., 1941), pp. 84-89.

"Some Reflections on Sociology During a Crisis," *American Sociological Review*, VI (February 1941), 1-8.

"After the Price of War, the Price of Peace," *Vital Speeches*, VIII (October 1, 1942), 765-768.

"Some Implications of a Democratic International Order," *Journal of Legal and Political Sociology*, I (October, 1942), 5-13.

"Group Images and the Larger Community," mimeographed for the Council of Jewish Federations and Welfare Funds, February 1943.

"National Power and World Unity," *New Leader*, XXVI (April 10, 1943), 4.

"Social Causation: A Rejoinder," *American Journal of Sociology*, XLIX (July 1943), 56-58.

"The Interplay of Cultures," in Ruth N. Anshen (ed.), *Beyond Victory* (New York: Harcourt, Brace & Co., 1943), pp. 34-42.

"The Fundamental Principles of International Order," *International Postwar Problems*, I (1943-1944), 17-30.

"History and Social Causation," a supplemental issue of *Journal of Economic History*, III (December 1943), 135-145.

Foreword to Karl Polanyi, *The Great Transformation* (New York: Farrar & Rinehart, 1944), pp. ix-xii.

"Group Images and Group Realities," in MacIver (ed.), *Group Relations and Group Antagonisms*, pp. 3-9.

"Summation," in *ibid.*, pp. 215-229.

"The Political Basis of Reconstruction," in F. Ernest Johnson (ed.), *Religion and the World Order* (New York: Harper & Brothers, 1944), pp. 93-100.

Introduction to Ferdinand A. Hermens, *The Tyrants' War and the Peoples' Peace* (Chicago: University of Chicago Press, 1944), pp. v-viii.

"The Devil and the Peace," *New Leader*, XXVII (September 2, 1944), 7-8.

"The Power of Group Images," *American Scholar*, XIV (Spring 1945), 220-224.

"The Cooling-off Period," in Gardner Murphy (ed.), *Human Nature and Enduring Peace* (Boston: Houghton Mifflin Co., 1945), pp. 225-227.

"Wrong Step Toward World Security," *New Leader*, XXVIII (August 25, 1945), 8.

"Mein Kampf and the Truth," prepared for Office of War Information for German translation, Fall 1945.

"The Need for a Change of Attitude," in MacIver (ed.), *Civilization and Group Relationships*, pp. 3-10.

"The Ordering of a Multigroup Society," in *ibid.*, pp. 161-169.

"Government and Property," *Journal of Legal and Political Sociology*, IV (Winter 1945-46), 5-18. Reprinted in MacIver, *The Web of Government*, Chap. VI.

"Intellectual Cooperation in the Social Sciences," *Proceedings of the American Philosophical Society*, XC (September 1946), 309-313.

"The Obstacles to World Government," *New Leader*, XXX (January 4, 1947), 6.

"My Religion," American Weekly (March 9, 1947), p. 21. Reprinted in *The Faith of Great Scientists* (New York: Hearst Publishing Co., 1948), pp. 26-28.

"What We All Can Do," in MacIver (ed.), *Unity and Difference in American Life,* pp. 151-157.

"The New Social Stratification," in Ruth N. Anshen (ed.), *Our Emergent Civilization* (New York: Harper & Brothers, 1947), pp. 103-122.

Introduction to Feliks Gross (ed.), *European Ideologies* (New York: Philosophical Library, Inc., 1948), pp. xiii-xv.

"Sex and Social Attitudes," in Donald Porter Geddes and Enid Curie (eds.), *About the Kinsey Report* (New York: New American Library, Signet Books, 1948), pp. 85-95.

"Our Strength and Our Weakness," in MacIver (ed.), *Discrimination and National Welfare*, pp. 1-6.

"What Should Be the Goals for Education?" in Bryson, Finkelstein, & MacIver (eds.), *Goals for American Education*, pp. 492-499.

"An Ancient Tale Retold," introduction to MacIver (ed.), *Conflict of Loyalties*, pp. 1-7.

"The Deep Beauty of the Golden Rule," in Ruth N. Anshen (ed.), *Moral Principles of Action* (New York: Harper & Brothers, 1952), pp. 39-47.

Foreword to Morroe Berger, *Equality by Statute* (New York: Columbia University Press, 1952), pp. vii-ix.

"The Scholar Cannot Stand Aloof from the World," *Princeton Alumni Weekly*, LIII (January 30, 1953), 10.

"Government and the Goals of Economic Activity," in Dudley Ward (ed.), *Goals of Economic Life* (New York: Harper & Brothers, 1953), pp. 181-203.

"Two Centuries of Political Change," in Lyman Bryson (ed.), *Facing the Future's Risks* (New York: Harper & Brothers, 1953), pp. 226-247.

"The Freedom to Search for Knowledge," *New York Times Magazine* (April 12, 1953), pp. 12, 42, 44.

"Signs and Symbols," *Journal of Religious Thought*, X (Spring-Summer 1953), 101-104.

"Authority and Freedom in the Modern World," in *Man's Right to Knowledge* (New York: Columbia University Press, 1954), pp. 56-62.

"Government and Social Welfare," in James E. Russell (ed.), *National Policies for Education, Health and Social Services* (New York: Doubleday & Co., 1955), pp. 523-532.

Foreword to Boris Gourevitch, *The Road to Peace and to Moral Democracy* (New York: International Universities Press, 1955), I, xiii-xiv.

(With Charles Frankel and Lyman Bryson) "Plato: *Crito*," *Invitation to Learning Reader*, VI (1957), 297-304.

"The Rights and Obligations of the Scholar," *Proceedings of the American*

Philosophical Society, CI (October 1957), 455-458.

"Main Worry: 'Mixed Relations,'" *U.S. News & World Report*, XLV (September 19, 1958), 77-78.

"The Graduate Faculty: Retrospect and Prospect," *Social Research*, XXVI (Summer 1959), 195-206.

Foreword to William C. Lehmann, *John Millar of Glasgow* (Cambridge: Cambridge University Press, 1960), pp. xi-xii.

"Juvenile Delinquency," in *The Nation's Children* (New York: Columbia University Press, 1960), Vol. III: *Problems and Prospects*, pp. 103-123.

"The Backwardness of Social Theory," *Mémoire du XIX Congrès International de Sociologie*, III (Mexico: Comité Organisateur du XIX Congrès International de Sociologie, 1961), 241-248.

"Discussion of Timasheff's Paper ['Don Luigi Sturzo's Contribution to Sociological Theory']," *American Catholic Sociological Review*, XXII (Spring 1961), 32-34.

"Comment on Civil Disobedience and the Algerian War," *Yale Review*, L (March 1961), 465.

"Science as a Social Phenomenon," *Proceedings of the American Philosophical Society*, CV (October 1961), 500-505.

"Disturbed Youth and the Agencies," *Journal of Social Issues*, XVIII, No. 2 (1962), 88-96.

"The Unbalance of our Times," *Sociologia Internationalis*, IV, No. 2 (1964), 185-192.

"The Art of Contemplation," *Indian Sociological Bulletin*, II (April 1965), 105-113.

"The Responsibility is Ours," in MacIver (ed.), *The Assault on Poverty: And Individual Responsibility*, pp. 1-7.

Introduction to Raymond Polin, *Marxian Foundations of Communism* (Chicago: Henry Regnery Co., 1966), pp. xvii-xx.

SOME COMMENTS AND CRITICISMS

Adler, Mortimer J. *The Idea of Freedom*. Garden City, N.Y.: Doubleday & Co., 1961. Vol. II.

Alpert, Harry (ed.). *Robert M. MacIver: Teacher and Sociologist*. Northampton: Metcalf Printing & Publishing Co., 1953.

Barnes, Harry E. *Sociology and Political Theory*. New York: Alfred A. Knopf, 1924.

Barnes, Harry E., and Howard Becker. *Social Thought from Lore to Science*. Boston: D. C. Heath & Co., 1938. 2 vols.

Barth, James L. *The Understanding of the Problem of Political Obligation by the Social Studies Teacher*. Unpublished M.A. thesis, The Ohio State University, 1958.

Bay, Christian. *The Structure of Freedom*. Stanford: Stanford University Press, 1958.

Becker, Howard, and Alvin Boskoff (eds.). *Modern Sociological Theory in Continuity and Change*. New York: The Dryden Press, 1957. *Passim*, but see especially Alvin Boskoff, "Social Change: Major Problems in the Emergence of Theoretical and Research Foci."

Berger, Morroe. *Equality by Statute*. New York: Columbia University Press, 1952.

Berger, Morroe, Theodore Abel, and Charles H. Page (eds.). *Freedom and Control in Modern Society*. New York: D. Van Nostrand Co., 1954. *Passim*, but see especially Harry Alpert, "Robert M. MacIver's Contributions to Sociological Theory," and David Spitz, "Robert M. MacIver's Contributions to Political Theory."

Berry, Brewton. *Race and Ethnic Relations*. 3d ed. Boston: Houghton Mifflin Co., 1965.

Bierstedt, Robert. "The Sociology of Majorities," *American Sociological Review*, XIII (December 1948), 700-710.

Bossard, James H. S. "The Functions and Limits of Social Work as Viewed by a Sociologist," in L. L. Bernard (ed.), *The Fields and Methods of Sociology*, New York: Farrar & Rinehart, Inc., 1934. Chap. XV.

Bramson, Leon. *The Political Context of Sociology*. Princeton: Princeton University Press, 1961.

Brecht, Arnold. *Political Theory*. Princeton: Princeton University Press, 1959.

Burns, Edward M. *Ideas in Conflict*. New York: W. W. Norton & Co., 1960.

Cahnman, Werner J., and Alvin Boskoff (eds.). *Sociology and History: Theory and Research*. New York: The Free Press of Glencoe, 1964. Essays by Alvin Boskoff, "Recent Theories of Social Change," Adolph S. Tomars, "Class Systems and the Arts," and Werner J. Cahnman, "The Rise of Civilization as a Paradigm of Social Change."

Cairns, Huntington. *Law and the Social Sciences*. New York: Harcourt, Brace & Co., 1935.

Cassinelli, C. W. *The Politics of Freedom*. Seattle: University of Washington Press, 1961.

Catlin, George E. G. *A Study of the Principles of Politics*. London: George Allen & Unwin Ltd., 1930.

———. *Systematic Politics*. London: George Allen & Unwin Ltd., 1962.

Cook, Samuel D. *An Inquiry into the Ethical Foundations of Democracy*. Unpublished Ph.D. dissertation, The Ohio State University, 1954.

Couch, W. T. "Objectivity and Social Science," in Helmut Schoeck and James W. Wiggins (eds.), *Scientism and Values*. Princeton: D. Van Nostrand Co., 1960. Chap. II.

Cox, Oliver C. *Caste, Class, and Race*. New York: Monthly Review Press, 1959.

Dowd, Jerome. *Control in Human Societies*. New York: D. Appleton-Century Co., 1936.

Easton, David. *The Political System*. New York: Alfred A. Knopf, 1953.

———. *A Systems Analysis of Political Life*. New York: John Wiley & Sons, 1965.

Emmet, Dorothy. *Function, Purpose, and Powers*. London: Macmillan & Co., 1958.

Frank, Jerome. *Fate and Freedom*. New York: Simon & Schuster, 1945.

Friedrich, Carl J. "The Concept of Community in the History of Political and Legal Philosophy," in Friedrich (ed.), *Community*. New York: The Liberal Arts Press, 1959.

Ginsberg, Morris. *Reason and Unreason in Society*. London: Longmans, Green & Co., 1947.

Gourevitch, Boris. *The Road to Peace and to Moral Democracy*. New York: International Universities Press, 1955. Vol. II.

Gross, Llewellyn (ed.). *Symposium on Sociological Theory*. Evanston, Ill.: Row, Peterson & Co., 1959. Essays by Don Martindale, "Sociological Theory and the Ideal Type," and Abraham Edel, "The Concept of Levels in Social Theory."

Haworth, Lawrence. "The Standard View of the State: A Critique," *Ethics*, LXXIII (July 1963), 266-278.

Hertzler, Joyce O. *Society in Action*. New York: The Dryden Press, 1954.

Hillenbrand, Martin J. *Power and Morals*. New York: Columbia University Press, 1949.

Hinkle, Roscoe and Gisela. *The Development of Modern Sociology*. New York: Random House, 1954.

Hook, Sidney. *Political Power and Personal Freedom*. New York: Criterion Books, 1959.

———. "The Strategy of Truth," *New Leader*, XXXIX (February 13, 1956), 21-24.

Jewish Community Relations Work Today: The American Jewish Committee's Views on the MacIver Report. New York: The American Jewish Committee, March 1952.

Kateb, George. "R. M. MacIver," *New York Review of Books* (March 25, 1965), pp. 25-26.

Kendall, Willmoore, *John Locke and the Doctrine of Majority-Rule*. Urbana: University of Illinois Press, 1941.

Konvitz, Milton R. "Are Teachers Afraid?" *New Leader*, XXXIX (February 13, 1956), 17-21.

Krislov, Samuel. "What is an Interest? The Rival Answers of Bentley, Pound, and MacIver," *Western Political Quarterly*, XVI (December 1963), 830-843.

Kroeber, A. L. *The Nature of Culture*. Chicago: University of Chicago Press, 1952.

Landecker, Werner S. "The Social Aggregate," *Journal of Social Philosophy*, VI (January 1941), 151-171.

Lasswell, Harold D., and Abraham Kaplan. *Power and Society*. New Haven: Yale University Press, 1950.

Lazarsfeld, Paul F. "Problems in Methodology," in Robert K. Merton, Leonard Broom, and Leonard S. Cottrell, Jr. (eds.), *Sociology Today*. New York: Basic Books, 1959. Chap. II.

Lippincott, Benjamin E. *Democracy's Dilemma: The Totalitarian Party in a Free Society*. New York: The Ronald Press Co., 1965.

Lipset, Seymour M., and Neil Smelser. "Change and Controversy in Recent American Sociology," *British Journal of Sociology*, XII (March 1961), 41-51.

Loomis, Charles P. *Social Systems*. Princeton: D. Van Nostrand Co., 1960.

Lundberg, George A. *Foundations of Sociology*. New York: The Macmillan Co., 1939.

Mabbott, J. D. *The State and the Citizen*. London: Hutchinson's University Library, 1948.

Martindale, Don. *Community, Character and Civilization*. New York: The Free Press of Glencoe, 1963.

————. *The Nature and Types of Sociological Theory*. Boston: Houghton Mifflin Co., 1960.

McDougall, William. *The Group Mind*. New York: G. P. Putnam's Sons, 1920.

McEwen, William P. *The Problem of Social-Scientific Knowledge*. Totowa, N.J.: The Bedminster Press, 1963.

Merton, Robert K. *Social Theory and Social Structure*. Glencoe, Ill.: The Free Press, 1949.

Muirhead, J. H. "Professor MacIver's Criticism of the Idealistic Theory of the General Will," *Mind*, XXXVII (January 1928), 82–87.

Mukerjee, Radhakamal. *The Philosophy of Social Science*. London: Macmillan & Co., 1960.

Mukerji, Krishna P. *The State*. Adyar, Madras: The Theosophical Publishing House, 1952.

Nagel, Ernest. *Logic Without Metaphysics*. Glencoe, Ill.: The Free Press, 1956.

————. *The Structure of Science*. New York: Harcourt, Brace & World, 1961.

Natanson, Maurice (ed.). *Philosophy of the Social Sciences*. New York: Random House, 1963. Essays by George A. Lundberg, "The Postulates of Science and Their Implications for Sociology," and Ernest Nagel, "Problems of Concept and Theory Formation in the Social Sciences."

Odum, Howard W. *American Sociology*. New York: Longmans, Green & Co., 1951.

Phelps, Harold A. *Principles and Laws of Sociology*. New York: John Wiley & Sons, 1936.

Ranney, Austin, and Willmoore Kendall. *Democracy and the American Party System*. New York: Harcourt, Brace & Co., 1956.

Rogers, Dale. *R. M. MacIver: Political Theorist*. Unpublished honors thesis, Cornell University, 1959.

Ross, Ralph G. "Academic Freedom and Faculty Status," *Commentary*, XXII (August 1955), 131–139.

Roucek, Joseph S. (ed.). *Contemporary Sociology*. New York: Philosophical Library, 1958.

Sait, Edward M. *Democracy*. New York: The Century Co., 1959.

————. *Political Institutions: A Preface*. D. Appleton-Century Co., 1938.

Sartori, Giovanni. *Democratic Theory*. Detroit: Wayne State University Press, 1962.

Schapera, I. "Malinowski's Theories of Law," in Raymond Firth (ed.), *Man and Culture*. New York: The Humanities Press, 1957, pp. 139–155.

Scott, James B. *Law, the State, and the International Community*. New York: Columbia University Press, 1938. Vol. I.

Simpson, George. *Conflict and Community*. New York: T. S. Simpson, 1937.

"War and Civilization," *International Journal of Ethics*, 22 (January 1912), 127–45.

"The Interplay of Cultures," in Ruth Nanda Anshen, ed., *Beyond Victory*, pp. 34–42. Copyright, 1943, by Harcourt, Brace & World, Inc.

"After the Price of War, the Price of Peace," *Vital Speeches*, 8 (October 1, 1942), 765–68.

"The Devil and the Peace," *The New Leader*, 27 (September 2, 1944), 7–8.

"The Fundamental Principles of International Order," *International Postwar Problems*, 1 (1943), 17–30.

"Some Implications of a Democratic International Order," *Journal of Legal and Political Sociology*, 1 (October 1942), 5–13.

"What Should be the Goals for Education?" in L. Bryson, L. Finkelstein, and R. M. MacIver, eds., *Goals for American Education* (New York: Harper & Row, 1950), pp. 492–99.

"The Art of Contemplation," *Indian Sociological Bulletin*, 2 (April 1965), 105–13.

"The Responsibility is Ours," *The Assault on Poverty: and Individual Responsibility* (New York: Harper & Row, 1965), pp. 1–7. Copyright © by The Institute for Religious and Social Studies.

"The Unbalance of our Times," *Sociologica Internationalis*, 4 (1964), 185–92.

Index